SIXTH EDITION

building a dream

A Canadian Guide to Starting Your Own Business

Walter S. Good

University of Manitoba

Toronto Montréal Boston Burr Ridge, IL Dubuque, IA Madison, WI New York San Francisco
St. Louis Bangkok Bogotá Caracas Kuala Lumpur Lisbon London Madrid Mexico City Milan
New Delhi Santiago Seoul Singapore Sydney Taipei

BUILDING A DREAM
A Canadian Guide to Starting Your Own Business
Sixth Edition

ISBN: 0-07-088954-6

1 2 3 4 5 6 7 8 9 10 TRI 0 9 8 7 6 5

Printed and bound in Canada.

Executive Sponsoring Editor: Lynn Fisher
Sponsoring Editor: Kim Brewster
Developmental Editor: Lori McLellan
Sales Manager: Megan Farrell
Senior Marketing Manager: Kelly Smyth
Manager, Editorial Services: Kelly Dickson
Supervising Editor: Joanne Limebeer
Copy Editor: June Trusty
Senior Production Coordinator: Madeleine Harrington
Permissions Research: Lori McLellan
Composition: Anne MacInnis
Interior Design: Sharon Lucas
Cover Design: Dianna Little
Cover Image: © Bill Frymire/Masterfile
Printer: Tri-Graphic Printing

National Library of Canada Cataloguing in Publication Data

Good, Walter S.
    Building a dream: a Canadian guide to starting your own business/Walter S. Good

6th ed.

Includes bibliographical references and index.
ISBN: 0-07-088954-6

1. New business enterprises—Textbooks. 2. Entrepreneurship—Textbooks. I. Title.

HD62.5.G66 2005   658.1'1   C2004-905698-0

Brief Contents

Contents

Preface

This self-help guide and workbook is intended to provide a vehicle to lead prospective small-business owners and potential entrepreneurs through the conceptual stages involved in setting up a business of their own in a logical and sequential way.

Many people fantasize about being self-employed and having a business of their own at some stage in their lives. For most, this dream never becomes a reality. They don't really know the risks involved and feel very uncomfortable with the uncertainty associated with taking the initial step. In addition, they don't entirely understand the tasks required to get a new business venture off the ground successfully.

For the past decade or so, the number of people who have started their own business has increased dramatically across North America. People's level of interest in and awareness of the entrepreneurial option has virtually exploded. This has been fostered and reinforced by governments at all levels, who have come to recognize the positive impact small-business start-ups have on job creation and regional economic development. Business magazines, the popular press, and radio and television have also fuelled this interest with numerous items on the emotional and financial rewards of having a business of your own. They have glamourized the role of entrepreneurs in our society, and established many of them, such as Ted Rogers of Rogers Communications Inc.; Christine Magee, of Sleep Country Canada; Terry Matthews, the founder of Newbridge Networks Corp. and Celtic House International Corp.; the late Izzy Asper of CanWest Global Communications Corp.; Gerry Schwartz of Onex and Indigo Books; Peter Nygard of Nygard International Ltd.; Bobby Julien of Kolter Property Co.; and Ron Joyce of Tim Hortons as attractive role models. This has been accentuated over the past couple of years with the phenomenal success and, in some cases, subsequent failure of many Internet-based companies. However, some businesses like Yahoo! and eBay have made a number of young entrepreneurs such as Jerry Yang, Jeff Skoll, Dave Filo, and Pierre Omidyar as well as many of their employees multi-millionaires or even billionaires within a very short period of time.

Building a Dream has been written for individuals who wish to start a business of their own or want to assess their own potential for such an option. This includes all men and women who dream of some type of self-employment, on either a full-time or a part-time basis. This book contains a comprehensive overall framework outlining the entrepreneurial process, descriptive information, practical outlines, checklists, screening questionnaires, and various other tools that will enable you to evaluate your own potential for this type of career and guide you through the early stages of launching a successful business of your own.

This book covers a range of topics that will increase your understanding of what it takes to succeed in an entrepreneurial career. From an overview of entrepreneurship and the entrepreneurial process, the book spreads outward to consider the skills, personality, and character traits possessed by most successful entrepreneurs, how to find and evaluate a possible idea for a business, buy an existing firm, or acquire a franchise. It provides a comprehensive outline for conducting a feasibility study to evaluate the potential of your concept and discusses the ways you can carry on your business, protect your product or service concept or idea, and find the financing necessary to get your new business off the ground. It concludes with a comprehensive framework for preparing a detailed and professional business plan.

Building a Dream is divided into "Stages," each of which provides a descriptive overview of a topic, some conceptual material indicating the principal areas to be considered or evaluated, and a series of outlines, worksheets, checklists, and other forms that can be completed in conducting a comprehensive assessment of that stage in the new venture development process. In addition, each Stage within this sixth edition is highlighted by a number of boxes. The **"Key Points"** boxes emphasize material in that Stage that is of particular importance and should be emphasized.

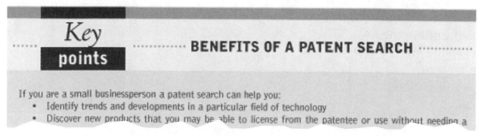

Key points ⋯⋯ BENEFITS OF A PATENT SEARCH ⋯⋯

If you are a small businessperson a patent search can help you:
- Identify trends and developments in a particular field of technology
- Discover new products that you may be able to license from the patentee or use without needing a

The "**FYI**" (For Your Information) boxes refer you to a number of Web sites that have supplementary material specifically related to the topics discussed in that Stage. This enables you to readily obtain further information on subjects that may be of particular interest.

BUSINESS PLAN OUTLINES AND TEMPLATES
Here are some examples of Web sites that have detailed instructions, outlines, or templates for developing a comprehensive business plan.

This sixth edition also contains an increased number of "**Entrepreneurs in Action**" examples illustrating how people are actually going about building their businesses and trying to make things work for them on a day-to-day basis.

Invention Sweet Music for Ex-City Rocker

When Hermann Fruhm played keyboards with local rock band Mood Jga Jga, its biggest hit was "Gimme My Money."

Now Fruhm is s'... 'ng that song ... real ... ross

shop, and started building the "retractable cartridge" for a multi-bit screwdriver. "After I built the prototype, I became absolutely passionate in believing this was a viable, commercial prod... "

Overall the book will provide a practical opportunity for you to realistically assess the potential opportunity for your concept or idea and enable you to develop a detailed program or plan for your own new venture.

STAGE ONE: WHAT IS ENTREPRENEURSHIP?

This Stage introduces you to the concept of entrepreneurship and provides an overview of the other elements that are required to launch a successful new business venture: a viable business idea or opportunity, an organization, resources, a strategy, and a business plan. It also discusses some of the myths and stereotypes that have evolved over time about entrepreneurs and entrepreneurship.

STAGE TWO: ASSESSING YOUR POTENTIAL FOR AN ENTREPRENEURIAL CAREER

This Stage provides you with an opportunity to assess your personal attitudes and attributes and to see how they compare with those of "practising" entrepreneurs. It will also enable you to evaluate your managerial and administrative skills and experience and determine your financial capacity for starting a business. The importance of conducting your business affairs in an ethical manner is also emphasized, and two examples of codes of ethics developed by small organizations are provided for your information and guidance.

STAGE THREE: EXPLORING NEW BUSINESS IDEAS AND OPPORTUNITIES

This Stage describes several sources from which you might obtain ideas for your prospective new venture and identifies a number of areas of opportunity for the future on the basis of dynamic changes now taking place within Canadian society. It also outlines a six-step opportunity selection process, describes the characteristics of an "ideal" or "model" business, and presents a framework for assessing the attributes of your product or service idea in comparison to this ideal. A number of entry strategies are outlined as well that can help you decide on the best way to proceed.

STAGE FOUR: BUYING A BUSINESS

The obvious route to self-employment is to start a business of your own based on a new or distinctive idea. Another route to explore is the possibility of buying an existing firm. This Stage deals with such issues as finding a business to buy and the factors to consider in making the acquisition. It also discusses a number of ways to determine an appropriate price to pay for a business and the pros and cons of buying versus starting one. A comprehensive checklist is provided for considering a number of potential business acquisitions.

We also discuss some of the issues involved in working in a family business—a situation that has some unique opportunities and risks, and can become very complicated. Planning for succession is typically the most important issue, so it is critical that the business have a viable succession plan in place.

STAGE FIVE: CONSIDERING A FRANCHISE

In recent years franchising has been one of the fastest-growing sectors of North American business. More and more people are considering the franchise alternative as a means of getting into business for themselves. This Stage explores the concept of franchising in some detail. It defines franchising so that you know exactly what the concept means. The broad range of types of franchises available is presented, along with an overview of the legal requirements associated with franchising and the terms and conditions contained in a typical franchise agreement. This Stage also discusses how to find and apply for a franchise, and presents an extensive checklist for evaluating potential franchise opportunities.

STAGES SIX AND SEVEN: CONDUCTING A FEASIBILITY STUDY — PARTS 1 AND 2

Stages Six and Seven provide a step-by step process for transforming your chosen new venture concept from the idea stage to the marketplace. This is accomplished by means of a feasibility study. A typical feasibility study considers the following areas:

- The concept of your proposed venture
- The technical feasibility of your idea
- A detailed assessment of your market potential and preparation of your marketing plan
- Managing the supply situation
- Conducting a cost and profitability assessment
- Indicating your plans for future action

Comprehensive outlines are provided to enable you to assess each of these areas in a preliminary way and to put your thoughts and ideas down on paper. Much of this material can be incorporated into your subsequent business plan.

STAGE EIGHT: ORGANIZING YOUR BUSINESS

One of the principal issues to be resolved when starting a new business is the legal form of organization the business should adopt. The most prevalent forms a business might assume include individual or sole proprietorship, general or limited partnership, and incorporation. This Stage reviews each of these forms and discusses the advantages and disadvantages of each from the standpoint of the prospective entrepreneur. It discusses how to select and register a name for your business and presents an overview of such issues as the types of licences and permits your business might require, your responsibilities for collecting and remitting a variety of employee contributions and taxes, the impact of provincial employment standards on your business, and protecting your investment.

STAGE NINE: PROTECTING YOUR IDEA

Many entrepreneurs are also innovators and inventors, and are faced with the problem of how to protect the idea, invention, concept, system, name, or design that they feel will be the key to their business success. This

Stage discusses the various forms of intellectual property such as patents, copyrights, trademarks, and industrial designs, and what is required to protect your interest in their development. It is also suggested that you be wary of organizations that offer to help you patent your idea and market it for you. Many of these offers are outright scams and should be avoided.

STAGE TEN: ARRANGING FINANCING

The principal question relating to any new venture is where the money is going to come from to get the new business off the ground. This Stage examines the major sources of funds for new business start-ups — personal funds, "love money," bank loans, government agencies and programs, and venture capital. It also discusses the main issues that need to be addressed when looking to raise capital from private sources. A framework for you to determine just how much money you think you will need to launch your business and where that financing might possibly come from is provided as well.

STAGE ELEVEN: PREPARING YOUR BUSINESS PLAN

This Stage, which serves as a capstone for the book, provides a framework for the development of a comprehensive business plan for your proposed new business venture, whether it is a retail or service business or a manufacturing company. It lays out the necessary steps in the business planning process such as:

- Developing a vision statement
- Formulating a mission statement
- Defining the fundamental values by which you will run your business
- Setting clear and specific objectives
- Developing a realistic business plan

It also explains what a business plan is, how long it should be, and why it is important that you develop such a plan for your proposed venture and actually write it yourself. It lays out the contents of a typical business plan and provides an outline to follow for developing a plan.

This Stage also contains two examples of completed business plans. Lite Bites Grill is an example of a relatively simple business plan for an exciting new restaurant concept to provide healthy and nutritional meals in a fast-food-type environment. The PlasiaTEK business plan, on the other hand, is for a new medical technology device that will require a number of months or years of testing and a significant initial investment to bring the concept successfully to market. These can serve as comprehensive and useful guides for you to follow in developing your business plan.

"FOR FURTHER INFORMATION"

The **"For Further Information"** section contains:

- a list of useful information you can obtain for little or no cost from banks, accounting firms, government departments, and other sources
- a number of useful contacts that can provide you with additional information on many of the topics discussed in the book

For Further Information

BANKS

ONLINE BUSINESS ASSISTANCE:
www.tdcanadatrust.com/smallbusiness/
resources.jsp

This section is followed by a glossary of financial terms.

Following the framework outlined in *Building a Dream* will give you hands-on, practical experience with the entire new venture development process and enable you to come up with a comprehensive plan for a proposed venture of your own selection. This plan will not only give you a better understanding of the potential opportunity and success requirements of your new venture idea, but also put you in a much stronger position to attract the necessary external resources and support to get your proposed business off the ground.

Good luck in successfully building your dream.

INTEGRATED LEARNING SYSTEM

Great care was used in the creation of the supplemental materials to accompany *Building a Dream*. Whether you are a seasoned faculty member or a newly minted instructor, we hope you will find our support materials to be among the most thorough and thoughtful available.

SUPERIOR SERVICE

Service takes on a whole new meaning with McGraw-Hill Ryerson and *Building a Dream*. More than just bringing you the textbook, we have consistently raised the bar in terms of innovation and educational research — both in management and entrepreneurship and in education in general. These investments in learning and the education community have helped us to understand the needs of students and educators across the country, and allowed us to foster the growth of truly innovative, integrated learning.

i-Learning
ADVANTAGE
McGraw-Hill Ryerson

INTEGRATED LEARNING

Your Integrated Learning Sales Specialist is a McGraw-Hill Ryerson representative who has the experience, product knowledge, training, and support to help you assess and integrate any of our products, technology, and services into your course for optimum teaching and learning performance. Whether it's using our test bank software, helping your students improve their grades, or putting your entire course online, your *i*Learning Sales Specialist is there to help you do it. Contact your local *i*Learning Sales Specialist today to learn how to maximize all of McGraw-Hill Ryerson's resources!

*i*LEARNING SERVICES PROGRAM

McGraw-Hill Ryerson offers a unique *i*Services package designed for Canadian faculty. Our mission is to equip providers of higher education with superior tools and resources required for excellence in teaching. For additional information, visit **www.mcgrawhill.ca/highereducation/iservices**.

TEACHING, TECHNOLOGY & LEARNING CONFERENCE SERIES

The educational environment has changed tremendously in recent years, and McGraw-Hill Ryerson continues to be committed to helping you acquire the skills you need to succeed in this new milieu. Our innovative Teaching, Technology & Learning Conference Series brings faculty together from across Canada with 3M Teaching Excellence award winners to share teaching and learning best practices in a collaborative and stimulating environment. Pre-conference workshops on general topics, such as teaching large classes and technology integration, will also be offered. We will also work with you at your own institution to customize workshops that best suit the needs of your faculty at your institution.

RESEARCH REPORTS INTO MOBILE LEARNING AND STUDENT SUCCESS

These landmark reports, undertaken in conjunction with academic and private sector advisory boards, are the result of research studies into the challenges professors face in helping students succeed and the opportunities that new technology presents to impact teaching and learning.

INSTRUCTOR'S SUPPLEMENTS

INSTRUCTOR ONLINE LEARNING CENTRE—
www.mcgrawhill.ca/college/good

Building a Dream includes a password-protected Web site for instructors. The site offers downloadable supplements including those found on the instructor's CD-ROM and a series of other resources.

INSTRUCTOR'S CD-ROM

Includes an electronic version of the Instructor's Manual and Microsoft® PowerPoint® Presentations.

Instructors can use this electronic resource to access the supplements listed below that are associated with the text and create custom presentations, exam questions, and Microsoft® PowerPoint® lecture slides.

> **Instructor's Manual** The Instructor's Manual, prepared by the author, includes a wealth of information to assist instructors in presenting this text and their course to its best advantage. It includes
>
> - Additional presentation that focuses on the preparation of a business plan
> - Typical outline for a course in New Venture Development
> - Venture Challenge Exercises that can be incorporated into a New Venture course
> - Discussion questions and corresponding answers for each of the video cases presented in the book
> - Details of publications and Web sites where further information can be obtained
>
> **Microsoft® PowerPoint® Presentations** A complete set of PowerPoint slides is provided for each chapter.

BUILDING A DREAM VIDEO PACKAGE

The video package contains carefully selected segments from CBC's Venture programs chosen by the author. It is an excellent supplement to lectures and useful for generating in-class discussions.

PAGEOUT

Create a custom course Website with **PageOut**, free with every McGraw-Hill Ryerson textbook.

To learn more, contact your McGraw-Hill Ryerson publisher's representative or visit www.mhhe.com/solutions

McGraw-Hill's unique point-and-click course Web site tool enables users to create a full-featured, professional-quality course Web site without knowing HTML coding. PageOut is free for instructors, and lets you post your syllabus online, assign McGraw-Hill OLC content, add Web links, and maintain an online grade book. (If you are short on time, we even have a team ready to help you create your site.)

WEBCT/BLACKBOARD

Content cartridges for this text are available in two of the most popular course-delivery platforms — WebCT and BlackBoard — for more user-friendly and enhanced features. Contact your McGraw-Hill *i*Learning Sales Specialist for more information.

STUDENT SUPPLEMENTS

STUDENT ONLINE LEARNING CENTRE — www.mcgrawhill.ca/college/good

The *Building a Dream* student Online Learning Centre (OLC) Web site provides a number of additional resources to enhance the textbook and the classroom experience for the student:

FINANCIAL TEMPLATES Students have access to Microsoft® Excel® financial templates to help them analyze the financial aspects of their new business ideas. These templates also facilitate preparation of the financial statements required for their feasibility study in Stage 7 and their overall business plan preparation in Stage 11. Accompanying the spreadsheets is a step-by-step guide to using the financial schedules.

ONLINE VERSION OF WORKSHEETS The OLC contains online versions of most of the worksheets found at the end of each Stage. The student can complete each of these worksheets on the computer rather than having to make copies and complete them by hand.

SAMPLE BUSINESS PLANS In addition to the two sample business plans provided in the textbook, the students will find examples of two other business plans on the OLC to further assist them in preparing a business plan for a venture.

VENTURE CHALLENGE EXERCISES The Student OLC also contains copies of the Venture Challenge Exercises found on the Instructor's OLC.

CBC VIDEOS The OLC allows students to view online the CBC videos corresponding to the video cases at the end of each Stage and to respond to the questions associated with each.

GUIDE TO EFFECTIVE BUSINESS PLAN PRESENTATIONS The OLC provides a guide on how to structure, prepare, and deliver effective business plan presentations.

Acknowledgements

Developing a workbook of this type can be accomplished only with the co-operation and support of a great many people. Much of the material would not have been developed without the dedicated effort of Steve Tax of the University of Victoria, who was largely responsible for many of the ideas that were incorporated into the first edition and have been carried forward to the current one. I am also indebted to David Milstein of David Milstein & Associates of Brisbane, Australia, for contributing the material on the "Big Picture" of strategic planning and to Vance Gough of Mount Royal College for the exercise on creative thinking. My appreciation also goes to Carole Babiak whose organizational and word processing skills enabled me to keep the material moving during the revision process.

Very comprehensive suggestions for changes and improvements based on the previous edition and drafts of this edition were received from:

- Sandra Malach, University of Calgary
- Rob Gawreluck, Grant MacEwan College
- Danielle Van Dreunen, St. Lawrence College
- Larry Drew, Conestoga College
- Teresa Menzies, Brock University
- Cheryl Pollmuller, Lethbridge Community College
- Samuel Boutilier, University College of Cape Breton

- Rob Salomons, Southern Alberta Institute of Technology
- Pam Welsh, Humber College
- Chris Bovaird, University of Toronto,
- Bob Walpole, Canadore College
- Alfie Morgan, University of Windsor
- Robert Dabous, Cambrian College

Their comments were very helpful in improving and refining the concept of the book to make it even more useful to students and prospective entrepreneurs.

My appreciation also goes to Kim Brewster and Rhondda McNabb, sponsoring editors; Joanne Limebeer, supervising editor; and Lori McLellan, developmental editor, all at McGraw-Hill Ryerson; and my copy editor, June Trusty, for keeping me on track, expediting the review and production of the material, and providing numerous useful comments and suggestions throughout the revision process.

I would also like to thank Moe Levy of the Asper Foundation and Shannon Coughlan of the Canada/ Manitoba Business Service Centre for their comments on several components of the book and their encouragement during the early stages of the development of the concept behind the workbook. Special thanks go to Dean Beleyowski for his assistance in compiling many of the Web sites and much of the other supplementary material included with the book. The belief of these individuals in entrepreneurship as a vehicle for successful economic development in Canada and their faith in the premise of the self-help concept may finally pay off.

Finally, I would like to thank the college and university students and others who have used the earlier editions of the book over the years and have gone on to start new business ventures of their own. Their insatiable desire to assess their personal capacity for a career in this area and their drive to explore the mysteries of franchising, venture capital, and similar topics associated with the formation of a successful new business has enabled many of them to build their dream. I hope all of us have been able to play a small part in that process.

What Is Entrepreneurship?

At 24 Jesse Rasch was the CEO of his own company, Webhosting.com, a company he grew from scratch into a multi-million dollar corporation with more than 150 employees. Despite his relatively young age, this was not Rasch's first entrepreneurial venture. He had owned and operated businesses since he was 17. He started Webhosting.com just as the Internet was beginning to take off in the mid-1990s and the business flourished practically overnight.

Jesse Rasch and other Canadians like him are starting businesses of their own more frequently than ever before. Of the more than 2.2 million businesses in Canada, over 99 per cent are small- and medium-sized. Every year more than 150,000 other Canadians join this number by initiating new start-ups, principally in the construction, retail, and business services sectors. This has led to a major entrepreneurial revolution across the country and caused the small business sector of the economy to become more widely acknowledged by all levels of government, the chartered banks and other financial institutions, and secondary and post-secondary educational institutions.

While the Canadian business start-up numbers are impressive, they do not put Canada at the top in terms of the most entrepreneurial countries in the world. A recent study entitled the *Global Entrepreneurship Monitor* (GEM) (conducted by the London Business School, Babson College, and others) ranked Canada twelfth in the world, behind such countries as Australia, New Zealand, India, China, and Mexico, but ahead of the United Kingdom and Singapore in terms of entrepreneurial activity.[1]

The overall economic impact of this revolution on Canada is difficult to determine precisely, but it is substantial and suspected to drive longer-term growth. It is being fuelled by such factors as:

- Structural changes in the economy, such as organizational downsizing or "rightsizing," with the subsequent loss of middle-management positions in many larger companies and government departments; this has led to considerable outsourcing of services previously performed in-house and the growth of self-employment to meet this need

- Younger Canadians wanting more independence and becoming increasingly interested in self-employment

- An increasing number of immigrants who often have difficulty with conventional employment because of their limited skills and/or language issues or whose academic credentials are often not recognized in Canada

- The aging population and a large number of baby boomers reaching their fifties, an age at which people often tend to look toward self-employment

- An increasing consumer demand for more personalized products and services that smaller companies are often better positioned to provide

The entrepreneurial revolution has also been propelled by the explosion in technology-based companies and the publicity surrounding the creation of many so-called "dot-com millionaires," although this bubble has burst for the moment at least. One thing that is clear, however, is that the proportion of total employment in the country accounted for by these smaller firms has increased dramatically. They have created the lion's share of new jobs, while employment levels in large businesses have remained constant or decreased.

This book has been developed for people who may be aspiring entrepreneurs and are giving some thought to the possibility of joining the many others who have started some kind of business of their own. Most of us

1. Paul D. Reynolds, W.D. Bygrave, and E. Autio, *Global Entrepreneurship Monitor 2003 Global Report*, Ewing Marion Kauffman Foundation, Kansas City, MO, 2004.

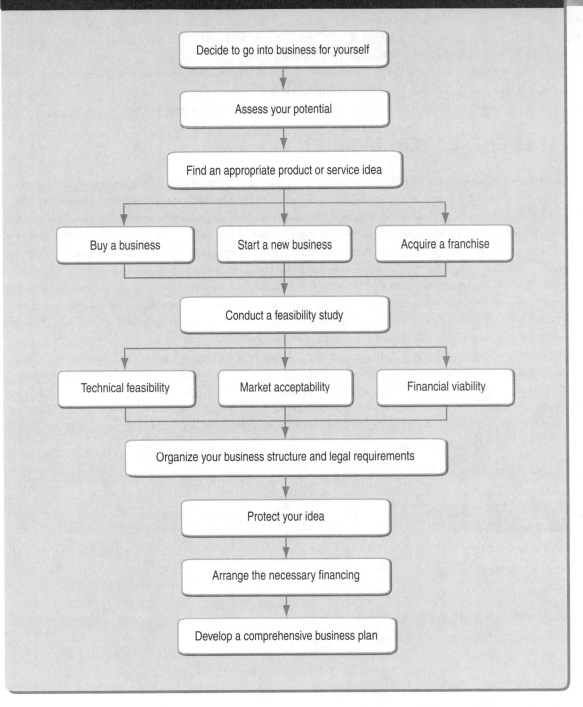

STAGES TO BUILDING YOUR DREAM

Decide to go into business for yourself

↓

Assess your potential

↓

Find an appropriate product or service idea

↓

Buy a business   Start a new business   Acquire a franchise

↓

Conduct a feasibility study

↓

Technical feasibility   Market acceptability   Financial viability

↓

Organize your business structure and legal requirements

↓

Protect your idea

↓

Arrange the necessary financing

↓

Develop a comprehensive business plan

have given some thought to owning and managing our own business at some point in our lives. Provided you know what it takes to be successful, it can be a very rewarding way of life. These rewards may be financial, in terms of providing you with a return for the time and money you and others may invest in the business and the risks you take in operating your own firm. Having an independent business also gives you the freedom to act independently, make your own decisions, and be your own boss. This can be a very important motivating factor for many people. It can also be a very satisfying way of life, full of the "fun" and personal satisfaction derived from doing something that you genuinely love to do.

Table 1.1 reflects the results of a survey of Canadian business owners, exploring the principal reasons they decided to go into business for themselves. The primary considerations were to seize what they felt was an attractive opportunity and to achieve a sense of personal accomplishment.

Starting a new business, however, can be very risky at the best of times. It typically demands long hours, hard work, a high level of emotional involvement and commitment, as well as significant financial risk and the possibility of failure. Your chances of succeeding, however, will be better if you spend some time carefully evaluating your personal situation and circumstances and trying to anticipate and work out as many potential problems as you can before you invest any money.

Stage One will introduce you to the concept of entrepreneurship and give you some idea of what is required to be successful. It will also discuss some of the folklore and stereotypes that exist around entrepreneurship and, hopefully, dispel a few of the myths that have come to surround entrepreneurs.

WHAT IS ENTREPRENEURSHIP?

Entrepreneurship is difficult to define precisely. Entrepreneurs tend to be identified, not by formal rank or title, but in retrospect — after the successful implementation of an innovation or idea. The example of Jesse Rasch in Entrepreneurs in Action #1 may help to illustrate this definition problem for you.

It is difficult to say the precise moment at which Jesse became an entrepreneur. At the age of 17 he started his first business, putting up real estate signs on street corners in Toronto for homebuilders and developers. He sold that company to his employees and moved on to set up another firm selling natural gas and other recently deregulated products to homeowners. It was clear that he had an entrepreneurial spirit from a very early age, as he was constantly dreaming up new ideas for businesses and looking for opportunities to be his own boss. When he started his Web-site development business, he dropped out of school as soon as the business started to take off, despite the apparent concern of his family.

For some people like Jesse Rasch, entrepreneurship is a conscious and deliberate career choice. For others, there may be some kind of significant *triggering* event. Perhaps these individuals had no better career prospects than starting businesses of their own. Sometimes the individual has received an inheritance or otherwise come into some money, moved to a new geographic location, been passed over for a promotion, taken an early retirement, or been laid off or fired from a regular job. Any of these factors can give birth to a new business.

TABLE 1.1 WHY CANADIANS START BUSINESSES	
To seize an opportunity	17%
To achieve a sense of personal accomplishment	13%
Dreamed of running their own business	9%
A chance to use their experience/skills	9%
To be their own boss	8%
Economic necessity; to make a living	7%
Had previous experience they wished to use	7%
To supplement their income from other employment	5%
To create a job for themselves	4%
Frustrated in their previous job	3%
To make lots of money	3%
Other reasons	15%

Source: Canada Business Service Centre (www.cbsc.org/alberta/tbl.cfm?fn=cutout&pf=1), accessed August 18, 2004.

1 Entrepreneurs in action

Conquering Cyberspace

At 24, Jesse Rasch was the CEO of Webhosting.com, a company he successfully grew from scratch into a multimillion dollar corporation with more than 150 employees. Don't let his age fool you, Rasch has owned and operated businesses since he was 17. He started Webhosting.com just as the Internet started to make its presence felt in the mid-1990s. His business flourished practically overnight as international commerce began using cyberspace.

While studying business at McGill University in Montreal, Rasch took notice of the growing number of companies joining the World Wide Web. He decided to continue studying business outside the classroom by starting a company in 1996 called DynamicWeb, which specialized in Web-site development and catered to Canadian Fortune 500 clients.

Rasch explains that the more the company developed sites, the more his clients began asking him to host these sites. After partnering with third-party companies in the United States that provided similar services, Rasch soon learned that there were not many companies that specialized in hosting services. So Rasch quickly assembled a party of computer science students to help build a platform that would allow DynamicWeb to host these Web sites and empower its customers to manage their sites through the DynamicWeb's Web browser.

His business really took off after this expansion, leaving less time to devote to business school. Rasch would drop out before graduating.

"We decided we should focus on the Web hosting exclusively and forgo the Web-site development because I didn't really see an opportunity for explosive revenue in that area," says Rasch. "And I needed to tell my mother that if I was going to drop out of school, I had something that had the potential of being very, very big."

But this was not the first time Rasch had demonstrated his talents as an entrepreneur. His first business venture was at age 17, when he started an A-frame real estate sign installation company called Signs Upright.

"To put it in simple terms, I had a truck and I drove around on the weekends and put up real estate signs on street corners for homebuilders and developers in the Greater Toronto Area."

He later sold the company to his six employees and moved on to start another organization that sold natural gas and other deregulated products in Canada. From an early age, Rasch had an entrepreneurial spirit that was constantly dreaming up new ideas for businesses, and he was always looking for opportunities to be his own boss.

After many entrepreneurial endeavours, it looked like his creativity and perseverance were starting to pay off. And it was only the beginning for DynamicWeb.

"When we started selling Web-hosting products on the Internet, it was retail, 100 per cent," says Rasch. "[We told the companies:] we will put up a Web site for your company and we will give you Web-based tools so you can manage your e-mail accounts, security, and storefront hosting online, any time of the day you want. You don't have to pick up the phone and call. That differentiated us from others who could not provide that level of automation to their customers."

Surfing the Web

Already Rasch had made a better mousetrap that he could offer to his clients. Yet his real success came when he changed the company's name and domain to Webhosting.com, after a domain name conflict with another company called DynamicWeb in the United States in October of 1998.

"We went looking for a brand new domain name and found Webhosting.com, which is a very powerful generic domain name, and powerful generics on

continued

Conquering Cyberspace — continued

the Internet are very attractive because they can yield a lot of what's called 'type-in-traffic.' People type in a domain name not knowing who will be there, but they are looking for the product based on a generic phrase that describes the product, which in our case was Web hosting."

When DynamicWeb became Webhosting.com, sales quadrupled. The company started attracting the attention of large telecommunication providers and communication-service companies such as Bell Canada and SBC Communications, who wanted to expand their services. Rasch then co-branded the technology he was using, InQuent.

"InQuent is our wholesale brand that sells to our channel partners," explains Rasch. "Webhosting.com was our retail brand.". . . .

Sitting on top of the company like a proud mountaineer on top of a large summit, Rasch says that being the president and CEO of a flourishing company consumes all of his time as well as his thoughts.

"You're always thinking about the company and it's always on your mind. When you have a vested interest financially, when you have given a commitment to your employees to keep them gainfully employed, and to your customers to always deliver the best product . . . it can consume you."

With so much time spent developing his company, at the age of 24, does Rasch feel he has missed out on anything?

"Academically, no," he says. "Socially, and from a personal human development perspective, I think so. [It's worthwhile] as long as you have your eyes wide open and you're conscious of the sacrifices you need to make to grow a company, knowing that one day, hopefully, it will all pay off."

And it does seem to be paying off. Rasch sold a 51 per cent stake in his company to SBC Communications (the second-largest local tele-phone provider in the United States) for a record U.S.$115 million.

While Rasch may now be on easy street, starting a company is full of challenges. He worked 18-hour days to keep a tightly held equity structure, and he originally found it very difficult to recruit the talented people he needed.

"The challenge of being able to hire smart people was very difficult, especially when you are small and your name is not in the news," says Rasch. "You have to convince people you are a stable company and that the paycheques will clear. As CEO, it really becomes a sales job and you have to spend a lot of time telling people that this is a really great place to work."

Looking back at the whole process, the upsides and the downfalls, would Rasch recommend the life of an entrepreneur to someone else?

"I don't think that everyone that goes to business school wants to be an entrepreneur," says Rasch. "I don't think that most people understand the sacrifices that entrepreneurs need to make to grow companies and I don't think that many people could deal with the uncertainties and the constant risks of that. There is great risk in having to make decisions knowing only 60 per cent of the facts but having to live with 100 per cent of the consequences. I was willing to do that.". . . .

As the boundaries of cyberspace continue to expand, Rasch will continue to find new ground to break and new frontiers to conquer. It may be a small world, but it keeps growing for this visionary entrepreneur. (www.webhosting.com; www.inquent.com)

Source: Tara Rose, "Conquering Cyberspace: Jesse Rasch Takes Web Hosting by Storm," *Business $ense*, Fall 2000. Used with permission.

The word "entrepreneur" is of French origin, derived from the term "entreprendre," literally translated as "between-taking." This term describes the activities by which an individual takes a position between available resources and perceived opportunities and, because of some unique behaviour, makes something positive happen. One of the first uses of the word was in the late 1700s by economist Jean-Baptiste Say, who is credited with developing the concept of "entrepreneurship."

Over time many other formal definitions of the term "entrepreneur" have emerged. Many of these modern definitions incorporate the notions of "risk taking" and "innovation" as well as the elements put forward by Say. For example, the *Fast Times Political Dictionary* defines an entrepreneur as *someone who sets up a new business undertaking, raises the money necessary, and organizes production and appoints the management. The entrepreneur bears the financial risk involved, in the hope that the business will succeed and make a profit.*[2]

Other definitions are quite simple, such as *an individual who starts his/her own business.*[3]

2. American Spirit (www.fast-times.com/political/dictionary.html), accessed August 18, 2004.
3. InvestorWords (investorwords.com/e2.htm#entrepreneur), accessed August 18, 2004.

Perhaps one of the most straightforward definitions is that an entrepreneur is *someone who perceives an opportunity and creates an organization to pursue it.*[4]

Many people have said that entrepreneurship is really a "state of mind." Though you may be extremely innovative and creative, prepared to work hard, and willing to rely on a great deal of luck, these qualities may still be insufficient to guarantee business success. The missing element may be a necessary entrepreneurial mindset: a single-mindedness and dedication to the achievement of a set of personal goals and objectives; confidence in your intuitive and rational capabilities; a capacity to think and plan in both tactical and strategic terms; and an attitude that reflects a penchant for action, frequently in situations in which information is inadequate.

Rasch, for example, feels that sitting on top of a company is like being a proud mountaineer on top of a large summit. "It consumes all of your time as well as your thoughts." Although he has since sold his interests in the Web-hosting market, Rasch continues to be an active investor and venture capitalist and gives back to the community through his Rasch Foundation and his involvement in a number of other charitable causes.

Entrepreneurship is not the same as management. The principal job of professional managers is to make a business perform well. They take a given set of resources — such as money, employees, machines, and materials — and orchestrate and organize them into an efficient and effective production operation. Managers tend to delegate much of their authority and to rely on the use of formal control systems, and are usually evaluated on the basis of organizationally determined objectives. In contrast, entrepreneurs typically rely more on an informal, hands-on management style and are driven by their personal goals. Their principal job is to bring about purposeful change within an organizational context. They break new ground and, in many cases, each step is guided by some larger plan.

As agents of change, entrepreneurs play, or can play, a number of roles or perform a variety of different functions in the economy. They can, for example:

1. Create new product and/or service businesses
2. Bring creative and innovative methods to developing or producing new products or services
3. Provide employment opportunities and create new jobs as a result of growing their business consistently and rapidly
4. Help contribute to regional and national economic growth
5. Encourage greater industrial efficiency/productivity to enhance our international competitiveness

You should keep in mind, however, that other people also play a significant role in determining who will succeed or fail in our society. For example, entrepreneurs will succeed only when there are customers for the goods and services they provide. But, in many circumstances, it is the entrepreneurs themselves who play the principal role in determining their success or failure. Many still manage to succeed in spite of poor timing, inferior marketing, or low-quality production by combining a variety of talents, skills, and energies with imagination, good planning, and common sense. The entrepreneurial or self-employed option has many attractions, but along with these come risks and challenges and the possibility of failure.

THE ENTREPRENEURIAL PROCESS

The successful launch of new business ventures requires a number of other components in addition to an entrepreneur. For example, while there may be any number of specific parts, virtually every new start-up also requires:

- Viable business idea or opportunity for which there is a receptive market
- Organizational structure for the business
- Access to financial and other resources
- Distinctive strategy that, if effectively implemented, will set the business apart from its competitors and enable it to become established

As illustrated in Figure 1.1, all of these elements are outlined and captured in the business plan.

---

4. William D. Bygrave, "The Entrepreneurial Process" in William D. Bygrave, Ed., *The Portable MBA in Entrepreneurship*, 2nd ed. (Hoboken, NJ: John Wiley & Sons, Inc., 1997), p. 2.

FIGURE 1.1   THE COMPONENTS OF SUCCESSFUL ENTREPRENEURIAL VENTURES

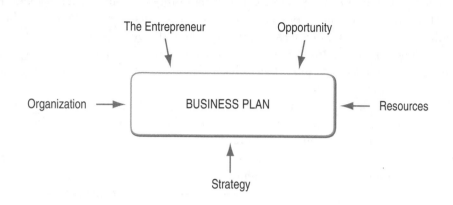

THE ENTREPRENEUR It all begins with the entrepreneur, the driving force behind the business and the co-ordinator of all the activities, resources, and people that are needed to get it off the ground. This individual will have conducted some assessment of his or her own resources and capabilities and made a conscious decision to launch the business.

THE OPPORTUNITY The entrepreneur must then find a concept or idea that he or she feels has the potential to develop into a successful enterprise. The concept behind the business must be carefully evaluated to determine whether there is likely to be a market, and if it might represent a viable opportunity. The object is to determine the magnitude of the returns that might be expected with successful implementation.

ORGANIZATION To capitalize on any business opportunity, an organizational structure must be established, with a manager or management team and a form of ownership.

RESOURCES Some essential financial and other resources must be obtained. The key usually is money. It is the "enabler" that makes everything else happen. Other key resources typically include physical plant and equipment, technical capability, and human resources.

STRATEGY Once a start-up appears likely, a specific strategy must be developed and a feasibility study conducted. The feasibility study is a way to test your business concept to see whether it actually does have market potential. It is a series of tests you should conduct to discover more and more about the nature and size of your business opportunity. After each test you should ask yourself whether the opportunity still appears to be attractive and if you still want to proceed. Has anything come up that would make the business unattractive or prevent you from going forward with its implementation? Throughout this process you probably will modify your concept and business strategy several times until you feel that you have it right.

THE BUSINESS PLAN The business plan not only describes your business concept, but outlines the structure that needs to be in place to successfully implement the concept. The plan can be used to assist in obtaining the additional resources that may be necessary to actually launch the business and guide the implementation of the strategy. It assumes you have a feasible business concept and have now included the operational components needed to execute the strategy. It describes in some detail the company you are going to create.

Figure 1.2 illustrates how these components interrelate, the action required at each phase of the implementation of the process, and where these issues are addressed in the book.

This process proceeds in one manner or another to a conclusion, resulting in the implementation of the business. While the model gives the appearance that this is a linear process and that the flow is sequential from one stage to another, this has been done to provide a logical structure for the book and is not necessarily the case. For example, the entrepreneur may pursue two or three different elements at the same time, such as finalizing an organizational structure while also trying to compile the resources necessary to get the business off the ground.

FIGURE 1.2 OUTLINE OF THE ENTREPRENEURIAL PROCESS

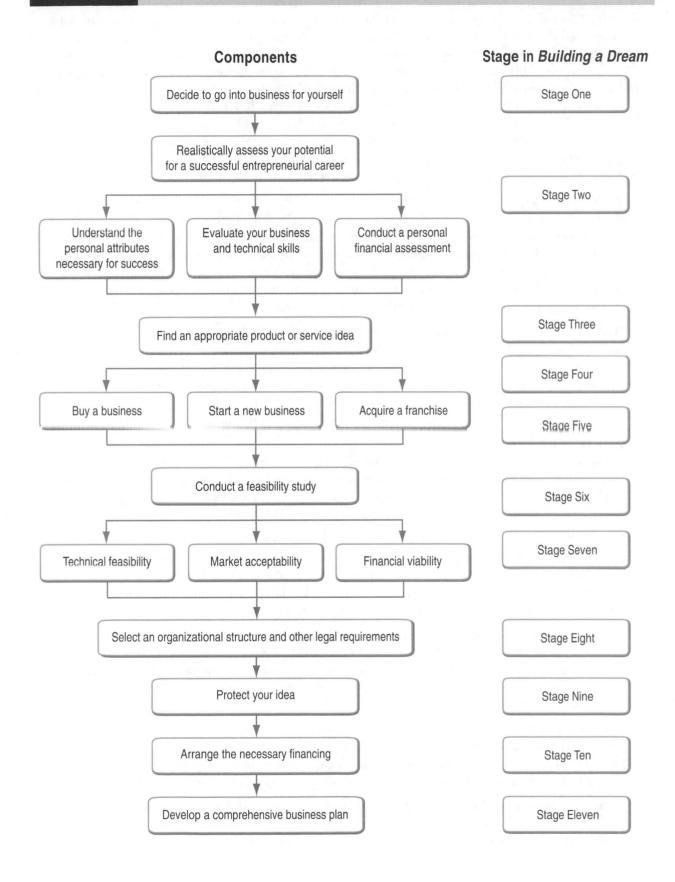

MYTHS AND REALITIES CONCERNING ENTREPRENEURSHIP

According to noted author-lecturer-consultant Peter Drucker, entrepreneurs defy stereotyping. He states, "I have seen people of the most diverse personalities and temperaments perform well in entrepreneurial challenges."[5] This suggests that some entrepreneurs may be true eccentrics while others are rigid conformists; some are short and fat while others are tall and thin; some are real worriers while others are very laid-back and relaxed; some drink and smoke very heavily while others abstain completely; some are people of great wit and charm while others have no more personality than a frozen fish.

Despite all that is known about entrepreneurs and entrepreneurship, a good deal of folklore and many stereotypes remain. Part of the problem is that while some generalities may apply to certain types of entrepreneurs and certain situations, most entrepreneurial types tend to defy generalization. The following are examples of long-standing myths about entrepreneurs and entrepreneurship:[6]

- **Myth 1** Entrepreneurs are born, not made.
  Reality While entrepreneurs may be born with a certain native intelligence, a flair for innovation, a high level of energy, and a core of other inborn attributes that you either have or you don't, it is apparent that merely possessing these characteristics does not necessarily make you an entrepreneur. The making of an entrepreneur occurs through a combination of work experience, know-how, personal contacts, and the development of business skills acquired over time. In fact, other attributes of equal importance can also be acquired through understanding, hard work, and patience.

- **Myth 2** Anyone can start a business. It's just a matter of luck and guts.
  Reality Entrepreneurs need to recognize the difference between an idea and a real opportunity to significantly improve their chances of success. If you want to launch and grow a high-potential new venture, you must understand the many things that you have to do to get the odds in your favour. You cannot think and act like a typical bureaucrat, or even a manager; you must think and act like an entrepreneur. That often means initiating action even if conditions are uncertain and existing rules have to be pushed to the limit.

- **Myth 3** Entrepreneurs are gamblers.
  Reality Successful entrepreneurs only take what they perceive to be very carefully calculated risks. They often try to influence the odds by getting others to share the risk with them or by avoiding or minimizing the risk if they have the choice. They do not deliberately seek to take more risk or to take unnecessary risks, but they will not shy away from taking the risks that may be necessary to succeed.

- **Myth 4** Entrepreneurs want to run the whole show themselves.
  Reality Owning and running the whole show effectively limits the potential for the business to grow. Single entrepreneurs can make a living, perhaps even a good one, but it is extremely difficult to grow a business by working single-handedly. Most successful ventures typically evolve to require a formal organization, a management team, and a corporate structure.

- **Myth 5** Entrepreneurs are their own bosses and completely independent.
  Reality Most entrepreneurs are far from independent and have to serve a number of constituencies and a variety of masters, including partners, investors, customers, employees, suppliers, creditors, their families, and pressures from social and community obligations. They do have the choice, however, to decide whether and when to respond to these pressures.

- **Myth 6** Entrepreneurs work longer and harder than corporate managers.
  Reality There is no evidence at all that entrepreneurs work harder than their corporate counterparts. Some do, some don't. Both are demanding situations that require long hours and hard work. However, as owners they are tied to the business and responsible in ways that are different from employees' roles.

- **Myth 7** Entrepreneurs face greater stress and more pressures, and thus pay a higher personal price in their jobs than do other managers.
  Reality Being an entrepreneur is undoubtedly stressful and demanding. But there is no evidence it is any more stressful than numerous other highly demanding professional roles, such as being the principal

---

5. Peter Drucker, *Innovation and Entrepreneurship: Practice and Principles* (New York: Harper and Row, 1985), p. 25.
6. Adapted from Jeffrey A. Timmons, *New Venture Creation: Entrepreneurship for the 21st Century*, 4th ed. (Homewood, IL: Richard D. Irwin, 1994), p. 23.

WHY SMALL BUSINESSES FAIL

1. Poor cash flow management
2. Absence of a reliable hiring system and a lack of understanding of how to hire, retain, and motivate the right people for the right job
3. Absence of performance monitoring and lack of understanding or use of performance monitoring information
4. Poor debt management: a combination of not paying their debts on time and not coordinating payments with incoming cash flows
5. Overborrowing; the company is excessively leveraged and debt is not being reduced
6. Excessive reliance on a few key customers
7. Poor market research leading to an inaccurate understanding of the market's wants and needs
8. Lack of financial and insufficient planning
9. Failure to innovate
10. Poor inventory management
11. Poor communications throughout the business
12. Failure to recognize their own strengths and weaknesses
13. Trying to go it alone; attempting to do everything themselves and not seek external help

Source: Deborah Barrie, MBA, Principle Profit Cranker Corp., deborah.barrie@profitcranker.com, *Failure Factors—Thirteen Common Causes of Business Failure* (www.cbsc.org/alberta/tbl.cfm?fn=tip4), accessed August 18, 2004.

partner in a legal or accounting practice or the head of a division of a major corporation or government agency. Most entrepreneurs enjoy what they do. They have a high sense of accomplishment. For them it is fun rather than drudgery. They thrive on the flexibility and innovative aspects of their job and are much less likely to retire than those who work for someone else.

- **Myth 8** Starting a business is risky and often ends in failure.
  Reality This statement is undoubtedly true in many instances. Some studies have indicated that upward of 80 per cent of new business start-ups fail within their first five years. However, success tends to be more common than failure for higher-potential ventures because they tend to be directed by talented and experienced people able to attract the right personnel and the necessary financial and other resources.

  Vince Lombardi, the well-known former coach of the Green Bay Packers, is famous for the quotation, "Winning isn't everything — It's the *only* thing." But a lesser-known quote of his is closer to the true

Used by permission of Johnny Hart and Creators Syndicate, Inc.

entrepreneur's personal philosophy. Looking back on a season, Lombardi was once heard to remark, "We didn't lose any games last season, we just ran out of time twice." Entrepreneurs learn from experience and are inclined to believe they have failed if they quit.

Owning your own business is a competitive game, and entrepreneurs have to be prepared to run out of time occasionally. Businesses fail but entrepreneurs do not. Many well-known entrepreneurs experience failure, sometimes several times, before achieving success.

- **Myth 9** Money is the most important ingredient for success.
  Reality If the other important elements and the people are there, the money tends to follow. But it is not true that entrepreneurs are assured of success if they have enough money. Money is one of the least important ingredients of new venture success.

- **Myth 10** New business start-ups are for the young and energetic.
  Reality While youth and energy may help, age is absolutely no barrier to starting a business of your own. However, many people feel there is some threshold for an individual's perceived capacity for starting a new venture. Over time you gain experience, competence, and self-confidence: These factors increase your capacity and readiness to embark on an entrepreneurial career. At the same time, constraints such as increases in your financial and other obligations grow and negatively affect your freedom to choose. The trade-offs between individual readiness and these restraints typically result in most high-potential new businesses being started by entrepreneurs between the ages of 25 and 40.

- **Myth 11** Entrepreneurs are motivated solely by their quest for the almighty dollar.
  Reality Growth-minded entrepreneurs are more driven by the challenge of building their enterprise and long-term capital appreciation than by the instant gratification of a high salary and other rewards. Having a sense of personal accomplishment and achievement, feeling in control of their own destiny, and realizing their vision and dreams are also powerful motivators. Money is viewed principally as a tool and a way of "keeping score."

- **Myth 12** Entrepreneurs seek power and control over other people so that they can feel "in charge."
  Reality Successful entrepreneurs are driven by the quest for responsibility, achievement, and results rather than for power for its own sake. They thrive on a sense of accomplishment and of outperforming the competition, rather than a personal need for power expressed by dominating and controlling other people. They gain control by the results they achieve.

FYI FOR YOUR INFORMATION

About Guide to Small Business: Canada An extensive source of information and links for Canadians running their own small business or thinking of starting one. This site will give you all the business resources, contacts, financial sources, and tools that you need to be a successful entrepreneur. (sbinfocanada.about.com)

Canada Business Service Centres A key network of business information and services and your link to the particular Canada Business Service Centre in your province or territory. (www.cbsc.org)

Industry Canada Canada's principal business and consumer site, containing a wealth of information useful to small business and access to the range of services provided by Industry Canada. (strategis.ic.gc.ca)

CanadaOne An online publication for Canadian businesses with articles, resources, promotional tools, a free directory for Canadian companies, and more. (www.canadaone.ca)

PROFITguide A site with articles, links, and quizzes of interest to Canadian entrepreneurs. (www.profitguide.com)

Small Business Canada Magazine This Web site includes selected articles from the magazine of the same name. Some additional features are available online. (www.sbcmag.com)

Video Case #1

Envirobond

Summary

A crash course on how not to run your own business. Mike Reid, an inexperienced small-businessman, started a company to produce a material made from small stones and organic glue for use in pathways and driveways. He reached out to his family and local bank for financing to help keep his dream alive, but the business did not get off to an easy start due to supplier problems and other issues. After a full season of activity and an investment of over $30,000, Envirobond is in the same situation in which it started — with no sales prospects and no cash flow. Reid now only hopes that he can survive until next year and begin again.

Questions for Discussion

1. What initial challenges did Reid face on starting Envirobond?

2. Would having a partner have helped Reid?

3. How important is outside help from family and friends when deciding to venture into a business of your own?

Assessing Your Potential for an Entrepreneurial Career

The discussion in Stage One should have served to dispel many of the popular myths concerning entrepreneurship. This section will expand on the theme of entrepreneurial characteristics by proposing and discussing two important questions that are vital to you if you are interested in an entrepreneurial career:

1. Are there certain common attributes, attitudes, and experiences among entrepreneurs that appear to lead to success?

2. If such attributes, attitudes, and experiences exist, can they be learned or are they inborn and thus available only to those with a "fortunate" heritage?

Research into these questions suggests that the answer to question 1 is yes, while the answer to question 2 is both yes and no. These answers, of course, are of little value to you on their own without some further explanation.

ENTREPRENEURS ARE BORN AND MADE BETTER

In 1980, Tom Wolfe wrote a perceptive bestseller that examined the lives of America's leading test pilots and astronauts. According to Wolfe, becoming a member of this select club meant possessing "The Right Stuff" — i.e., the proper mix of courage, coolness under stressful conditions, a strong need for achievement, technical expertise, creativity, etc. While Wolfe was not talking about entrepreneurs, his viewpoint is similar to the basic thesis held by many members of the "people school" of entrepreneurship: A person has to have the "right stuff" to become a successful entrepreneur.

There is considerable evidence, however, that a great deal of the ability and "right stuff" needed to become a successful entrepreneur can be learned (though probably not by everyone).

ENTREPRENEURIAL QUIZ

While most writers in the field of entrepreneurship agree that there is no single profile, no specific set of characteristics, that defines a successful entrepreneur, there do appear to be some common attributes, abilities, and attitudes. Prior to proceeding any further with our discussion of these entrepreneurial characteristics, it is suggested that you take the Entrepreneurial Quiz that appears as Figure 2.1, starting on page 34. This will enable you to compare your personal attitudes and attributes with those of "practising" entrepreneurs.

WHAT ATTRIBUTES ARE DESIRABLE AND ACQUIRABLE?

In a study of the 21 inductees into the Babson University Academy of Distinguished Entrepreneurs, only three attributes and behaviours were mentioned by all 21 as the principal reasons for their success, and they were all learnable:

1. Responding positively to all challenges and learning from mistakes

2. Taking personal initiative

3. Having great perseverance

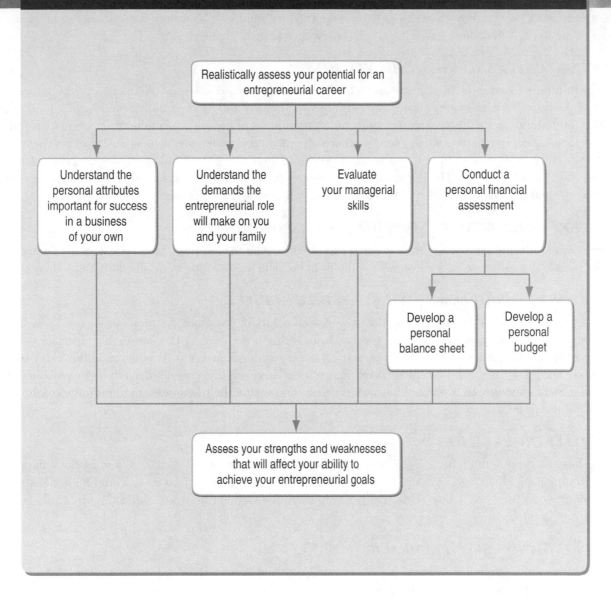

WHAT IS YOUR ENTREPRENEURIAL POTENTIAL?

Realistically assess your potential for an entrepreneurial career

Understand the personal attributes important for success in a business of your own

Understand the demands the entrepreneurial role will make on you and your family

Evaluate your managerial skills

Conduct a personal financial assessment

Develop a personal balance sheet

Develop a personal budget

Assess your strengths and weaknesses that will affect your ability to achieve your entrepreneurial goals

Other research has uncovered different lists of common learnable attributes. These qualities are also very desirable in the people with whom entrepreneurs want to surround themselves in building a high-potential business.

Following is a summary of the attitudes and behaviours that can be valuable in turning a business dream into reality. The proposed characteristics represent the conclusions of over 50 separate research studies into the essential nature of the entrepreneur.

COMMITMENT, DETERMINATION, AND PERSEVERANCE

More than any other single factor, a combination of perseverance and total dedication is critical. In many cases these qualities have won out against odds considered impossible to overcome.

Determination and commitment can compensate for other weaknesses you may have. It requires substantial commitment to give up a well-paying job, with its regular paycheques, medical insurance, and pension and profit-sharing plans, and start out on your own.

SUCCESS ORIENTATION

Entrepreneurs are driven by an immense desire to achieve the goals they initially set for themselves and then to aim for even more challenging standards. The competitive needs of growth-minded entrepreneurs are to outperform their own previous best results, rather than just to outperform another person. Unlike most people, entrepreneurs do not allow themselves to be concerned with failure. What they think about is not what they are going to do if they don't make it, but what they have to do to succeed.

OPPORTUNITY AND GOAL ORIENTATION

Growth-minded entrepreneurs are more focused on the nature and extent of their opportunity rather than resources, structure, or strategy. They start with the opportunity and let their understanding of it guide these other important issues. Entrepreneurs are able to sense areas of unmet needs and their potential for filling these gaps. Effective entrepreneurs set goals consistent with their interests, values, and talents. These goals are generally challenging but still attainable. Their belief in the "reality" of their goals is a primary factor in their fulfillment of them. Having goals and a clear sense of direction also helps these persons define priorities and provides them with a measure of how well they are performing.

ACTION ORIENTATION AND PERSONAL RESPONSIBILITY

Successful entrepreneurs are action-oriented people; they want to start producing results immediately. They like to take the initiative and get on with doing it, today. The true entrepreneur is a doer, not a dreamer.

PERSISTENT PROBLEM-SOLVING, NEED TO ACHIEVE

Entrepreneurs are not intimidated by the number or severity of the problems they encounter. In fact, their self-confidence and general optimism seem to translate into a view that the impossible just takes a little longer. They will work with a stubborn tenacity to solve a difficult problem. This is based on their desire to achieve the goals they have established for themselves. However, they are neither aimless nor foolhardy in their relentless attack on a problem or obstacle that can impede their business, but tend to get right to the heart of the issue.

REALITY ORIENTATION

The best entrepreneurs have a keen sense of their own strengths and weaknesses and of the competitive environment in which they operate. In addition, they know when they are in trouble and have the strength to admit when they are wrong. This reality orientation allows them to avoid continuing on an ill-advised course of action.

SEEKING AND USING FEEDBACK

Entrepreneurs have a burning desire to know how they are performing. They understand that to keep score and improve their performance they must get feedback, digest the results, and use the information they receive to do a better job. In that way they can learn from their mistakes and setbacks and respond quickly to unexpected events. For the same reason, most entrepreneurs are found to be good listeners and quick learners.

SELF-RELIANCE

Successful entrepreneurs trust the fate of their ventures to their own abilities. They do not believe that external forces or plain luck determine their success or failure. This attribute is consistent with their achievement and motivational drive and desire to achieve established goals.

In a similar vein, entrepreneurs are not joiners. Studies have shown that the need for affiliation, or a high need for friendship, often acts as a deterrent to entrepreneurial behaviour.

SELF-CONFIDENCE

The self-confidence displayed by entrepreneurs is based on their feeling that they can overcome all the necessary challenges and attain their desired goal. They almost never consider failure a real possibility. While this self-confidence implies a strong ego, it is a different kind of ego — an "I know I'm going to do well" type of attitude.

TOLERANCE OF AMBIGUITY AND UNCERTAINTY

Entrepreneurs tolerate ambiguous situations well and make effective decisions under conditions of uncertainty. They are able to work well despite constant changes in their business that produce considerable ambiguity in every part of their operation.

Entrepreneurs take change and challenge in stride and actually seem to thrive on the fluidity and excitement of such undefined situations. Job security and retirement are generally not of great concern to them.

MODERATE RISK-TAKING AND RISK-SHARING

Despite the myth that suggests entrepreneurs are gamblers, quite the opposite is true. Effective entrepreneurs have been found, in general, to prefer taking moderate, calculated risks, where the chances of losing are neither so small as to be a sure thing nor so large as to be a considerable gamble. Like a parachutist, they are willing to take some measurable and predetermined risk.

The strategy of most entrepreneurs also includes involving other parties in their venture to share the burden of risk: Partners put money and reputations on the line; investors do likewise; and creditors and customers who advance payments, and suppliers who advance credit all share in the financial risk of the business.

RESPONSE TO FAILURE

Another important attribute of high-performance entrepreneurs is their ability to treat mistakes and failures as temporary setbacks on the way to accomplishing their goals. Unlike most people, the bruises of their defeats heal quickly. This allows them to return to the business world again soon after their failure.

Rather than hide from or dismiss their mistakes, entrepreneurs concede their errors and analyze the causes. They have the ability to come to terms with their mistakes, learn from them, correct them, and use them to prevent their recurrence. Successful entrepreneurs know that they have to take personal responsibility for either the success or the failure of their venture and not look for scapegoats when things do not work out. They know how to build on their successes and learn from their failures.

LOW NEED FOR STATUS AND POWER

Entrepreneurs derive great personal satisfaction from the challenge and excitement of creating and building their own business. They are driven by a high need for achievement rather than a desire for status and power. It is important, therefore, to recognize that power and status are a result of their activities and not the need that propels them.

In addition, when a strong need to control, influence, and gain power over other people characterizes the lead entrepreneur, more often than not the venture gets into trouble. A dictatorial and domineering management style makes it very difficult to attract and keep people in the business who are oriented toward achievement, responsibility, and results. Conflicts often erupt over who has the final say, and whose prerogatives are being infringed upon. Reserved parking spaces, the big corner office, and fancy automobiles become symbols of power and status that foster a value system and an organizational culture not usually conducive to growth. In such cases, the business's orientation toward its customers, its market, or its competitors is typically lost.

Successful entrepreneurs appear to have a capacity to exert influence on other people without formal power. They are skilled at "conflict resolution." They know when to use logic and when to persuade, when to make a concession and when to win one. In order to run a successful venture, entrepreneurs must learn to get along with many different constituencies, who often have conflicting aims — customers, suppliers, financial backers, and creditors, as well as partners and others inside the company.

INTEGRITY AND RELIABILITY

Long-term personal and business relationships are built on honesty and reliability. To survive in the long run, an approach of "Do what you say you are going to do!" is essential. With it the possibilities are unlimited. Investors, partners, customers, suppliers, and creditors all place a high value on these attributes. "Success" resulting from dishonest practices is really long-term failure. After all, anyone can lie, cheat, or steal and maybe get away with it once, but that is no way to build a successful entrepreneurial career.

TOP 10 CHARACTERISTICS OF SUCCESSFUL ENTREPRENEURS

1. **Creativity** — have the ability to look at problems and needs from different angles and "think outside the box"
2. **Goal-orientated** — constantly set goals for themselves that challenge their creativity and strengths
3. **Hard-working** — willing to work long hours to complete tasks, go the extra mile
4. **Commitment** — remain focused on an idea or task
5. **Willing to take the initiative** — always want to be first, do not sit back and wait for others to take the initiative
6. **Spirit of adventure** — willing to try something new and different, pioneer
7. **Positive attitude** — do not let minor setbacks hinder their progress toward their overall goal
8. **Self-confident** — believe in themselves and their idea
9. **Persistence** — keep working at a problem until they solve it or find an alternative
10. **Need to achieve** — strong desire to accomplish something in life and leave a legacy

TEAM BUILDER

Entrepreneurs who create and build successful businesses are not isolated, super-independent types of individuals. They do not feel they have to receive all of the credit for their success, nor do they feel they have to prove they did it all by themselves. Just the opposite situation actually tends to be true. Not only do they recognize that it is virtually impossible to build a substantial business by working alone, but they also actively build a team. They have an ability to inspire the people they attract to their venture by giving them responsibility and by sharing the credit for their accomplishments. This hero-making ability has been identified as a key attribute of many successful corporate managers as well.

In addition to these characteristics, other attributes that have been associated with successful entrepreneurs are the following:

1. They are determined to finish a project once it has been undertaken, even under difficult conditions.
2. They are dynamic individuals who do not accept the status quo and refuse to be restricted by habit and environment.
3. They are able to examine themselves and their ideas impartially.
4. They are not self-satisfied or complacent.
5. They are independent in making decisions while willing to listen to suggestions and advice from others.
6. They do not blame others or make excuses for their own errors or failures.
7. They have a rising level of aspirations and expectations.
8. They have a good grasp of general economic concepts.
9. They are mature, self-assured individuals who are able to interact well with people of varying personalities and values.
10. They are able to exercise control over their impulses and feelings.
11. They have the ability to make the very best of the resources at hand.

The consensus among most experts is that all of these personal characteristics can be worked on and improved through concerted practice and refinement. Some require greater effort than others, and much depends on an individual's strength of motivation and commitment to grow. Developing these attributes should not be very different from personal growth and learning in many other areas of your life.

THE NOT-SO-LEARNABLE CHARACTERISTICS

The attributes listed next are those that many experts consider to be innate, and thus not acquirable to any great degree. Fortunately the list is quite short. It is from these not-so-learnable characteristics that the conclusion that entrepreneurs are "born, not made" is principally derived. However, while possessing all these attributes would be beneficial, there are many examples of successful business pioneers who lacked some of these characteristics or who possessed them to only a modest degree:

1. High energy, good health, and emotional stability
2. Creativity and an innovative nature
3. High intelligence and conceptual ability
4. The ability to see a better future and a capacity to inspire others to see it

It is apparent from this discussion that entrepreneurs work from a different set of assumptions than most "ordinary" people. They also tend to rely more on mental attitudes and philosophies based on these entrepreneurial attributes than on specific skills or organizational concepts.

Many of these points are summed up in "An Entrepreneur's Creed" in the Key Points feature below, a general philosophy outlining the entrepreneurial approach to doing business.

PERSONAL SELF-ASSESSMENT

The purpose of this discussion has been to have you evaluate your personal attitudes, behaviour tendencies, and views to determine the extent to which you seem to fit the typical entrepreneurial profile. Now you should complete Figure 2.2 on page 38, the Personal Self-Assessment Questionnaire, which will help you summarize your feelings regarding your potential for self-employment.

Many of these attitudes are illustrated by the comments made by Tom Poole in Entrepreneurs in Action #2 and Elizabeth Scott in Entrepreneurs in Action #3. Poole, for example, feels the principal character trait common to himself and other entrepreneurs is the "act of faith" — their strong belief that their concept or idea is "fantastic," and their readiness to jump in with both feet. Is this approach always successful? Of course not. But by being flexible and driven by a strong desire to "make it," he feels these individuals succeed more often than they should.

Key points ·········· **AN ENTREPRENEUR'S CREED** ··········

1. Do what gives you energy—have fun.
2. Figure out how to make it work.
3. Anything is possible if you believe you can do it.
4. If you don't know it can't be done, then you'll go ahead and do it.
5. Be dissatisfied with the way things are—and look for ways to improve them.
6. Do things differently.
7. Businesses can fail. Successful entrepreneurs learn from failure—but keep the tuition low.
8. It's easier to beg for forgiveness than to ask for permission in the first place.
9. Make opportunity and results your obsession—not money.
10. Making money is even more fun than spending it.
11. Take pride in your accomplishments—it's contagious.
12. Sweat the details that are critical to success.
13. Make the pie bigger—don't waste time trying to cut smaller pieces.
14. Play for the long haul. It's rarely possible to get rich quickly.
15. Remember: Only the lead dog gets a change in scenery.

For Scott, business is a "gritty reality" involving constant responsibility and considerable stress rather than the glamorous lifestyle commonly perceived by the general public. Yet she and others like her are continually prepared to undertake such burdens. Why? Perhaps, she comments, it's the need to challenge themselves, to test their potential, to push the boundaries, reach goals, fulfill a mission, and make this wonderful world better. After all, she reflects, is this not the essence of an unbridled human spirit?

2 Entrepreneurs in action

The Entrepreneur Exposed

Over the years, people have asked me many questions about my business. But there are two questions I have found myself answering most often: "Why did you give up a promising career to leap into the world of the entrepreneur?" (which my father-in-law continues to ask me weekly) and, "Would you do it again?" For the longest time I was unable to provide good answers, and quite frankly, I never gave them much thought. However, as I grow older and perhaps more philosophical, I have pondered these questions. The answers are slowly beginning to take shape, and I believe my conclusions might shed some light on entrepreneurs in general.

I think the answers lie in a character trait common to most, if not all, entrepreneurs. By "entrepreneur," I do not mean the corporate executive who takes an early retirement package to start a home-based consulting business (not that there's anything wrong with that). I am talking about that crazy s.o.b. who quits his job as a C.A. and sells his mother to secure the capital needed to start a rubbish-collection company. Take a look around you at the entrepreneurs that you know. What do these people have in common? Are they all a little wacky? Eccentric? Unorthodox? Most likely; it goes with the territory.

If the prospective entrepreneur were reasonable and orthodox, he or she would use conventional methods of measuring the risk associated with giving up everything for a leap into the unknown. The consequence of conducting a proper "decision-tree" analysis would be that no one would ever take the step.

So how does an entrepreneur approach the "go/no-go" decision-making process? Well (at the risk of revealing that I never really had a master plan), I think the typical entrepreneur does some initial research, becomes absolutely convinced that his or her idea is fantastic, and jumps. This act of faith is the litmus test for entrepreneurs. Some people may decide that an idea is great but requires more research, and some spend years explaining to their friends how they had developed the concept long before Ms. X (who went on to make a fortune with the idea). But true entrepreneurs leap in with both feet.

I decided to jump in February 1989. I quit my high-paying, secure job with a multinational company, moved my wife and two and one-half children into a camper van, and set out to find a business to run. My gamble paid off — the company I eventually bought has grown from three employees, a 1,800 square-foot "factory" and $350,000 in annual sales to the current 800 employees, five production facilities and $80 million-plus in revenue.

Do entrepreneurs always succeed? Of course not. We simply don't hear as much about the failures. But entrepreneurs do succeed more often than circumstances suggest they should. Why? Often for what business schools call the "wrong" reasons: the speed of their decision-making, the dearth of analysis and the fact that they hold nothing back, financially, physically or emotionally. How do these seemingly irrational actions improve the chances of success? By acting quickly, the entrepreneur reduces the likelihood of having the idea "stolen"; the cursory analysis allows the entrepreneur to avoid an analysis-paralysis affliction; and by investing everything, the consequences of failure are so dire that . . . well, they just cannot afford to fail! . . . .

Now back to the questions that I have been asked so many times over the years. First, why did I do it? Well, it was a "mix" of about one part crazy and two parts ignorance. And once I had taken the plunge, it was about 100 per cent fear. Most entrepreneurs, if pressed for an honest response, would likely acknowledge that their early days were not unlike mine.

Would I do it again? The answer is complicated. In this hypothetical situation, assuming I had the knowledge I have now, the answer is a categorical "No." Of course not. I would know that what I was undertaking was probably close to impossible. Equipped with this information, my analysis would result in a "no-go" decision. I may be crazy, but I'm not stupid!

But if you re-phrase the question and ask whether I would take another entrepreneurial plunge, the answer is "Yes, of course." Why? I think the Steve Martin film *Parenthood* contains the best answer to that question. Toward the end of the movie, a mother explains life to her risk-averse son (Martin). She tells of being young and going to the fair with his father. He always wanted to ride on the merry-go-round, while she preferred the roller coaster. On the merry-go-round, she explained,

you saw the same things go by again and again. It became rather boring. The roller coaster, on the other hand, was exhilarating, sometimes even frightening. But once she had ridden the roller coaster, she could never go back to the merry-go-round.

So, having taken the plunge and ridden the roller coaster, I can never return to the merry-go-round. And to those of you who are riding the merry-go-round, mix yourself a cocktail consisting of one part crazy and two parts ignorance. Drink it in one gulp and go for the ride of your life. (www.seppsfoods.com)

Source: Tom Poole, "The Entrepreneur Exposed," *PROFIT* (PROFITguide.com), July 12, 2001. Used with permission.

3 Entrepreneurs in action

Planet Entrepreneur

What galaxy was I visiting when I decided to become an entrepreneur!?

I ask this question every once in a while to relieve stress. For all the hype associated with entrepreneurship, the reality is anything but glamorous. The idea that entrepreneurs have plenty of time to enjoy foamy lattes, schmooze and parlay acquaintanceships into cash is largely fiction. Managing my business more often involves lunches at Taco Bell or Wrap-n-Go, with the odd flourish of warmth from a Second Cup coffee.

For an entrepreneur, responsibility, as Cervantes' Don Quixote says of death, perches forever upon the shoulder. It is a constant companion, an ever-present reminder of the impact decisions and actions can have on the business and on others.

Running a company is much like caring for a family — I have one of those too. Mornings begin with getting everyone organized and making sure my two sons get to school with full knapsacks and lunchbags. I then step delicately through the blanket of paper that is my office floor and begin the day. My relationship with WOMAN newsmagazine is my third 24-hour-a-day commitment. Since each was born, Ben and Byron have rested on one shoulder, WOMAN on the other.

Why do entrepreneurs undertake such burdens? Why are we compelled to initiate action, solve problems, produce results? I suspect every entrepreneur has a unique response. Perhaps it's the need to challenge ourselves, to test our potential, to push the boundaries, reach goals, fulfill a mission, make this wonderful world better. Is this not, after all, the essence of an unbridled human spirit?

In 1996 I launched WOMAN as a home-based business; I wanted to be in my own environment, accessible to my kids, do what I love and solve childcare dilemmas all at once. (Writing off the rent was also appealing.) But working from home is not for everyone. I sometimes long for a quiet place to go. But I've learned to work in close quarters with Super Nintendo. I've perfected focus, which has helped me manage the workload.

And there are small rewards. Ben and Byron sometimes join me at work-related events. Earlier this year, they came to a conference in Ottawa to listen to world-renowned women leaders. They found some speakers less than relevant, but not U.S. comedian Kathy Buckley. As she told of facing such monumental challenges as deafness, abuse and a tragic accident, her strength of spirit made a distinct impression, and may have instilled in them a

continued

Entrepreneurs in Action #3 — continued

new understanding of how I was able to launch WOMAN in the face of daunting odds.

Sharing the entrepreneurial experience with "the guys" somehow makes the responsibilities feel less onerous. Maybe the load seems lighter because I'm sharing it with people I care about. Which is why I've started to think maybe there is some truth in the perceptions that non-business owners have of entrepreneurs. For all the time we spend schmoozing

and talking, negotiating and forming strategic alliances, underneath it all perhaps we're really reaching out to connect with someone to whom we think we may relate, to share our experiences, thoughts and self with another human being.

Source: Elizabeth Scott, "Planet Entrepreneur," *PROFIT*, November 1999. Used with permission.

WHAT KIND OF ENTREPRENEUR ARE YOU LIKELY TO BE?

As you can see from the Entrepreneurs in Action examples, not all entrepreneurs are the same. John Warrillow, a Toronto-based marketing consultant, spent three years interviewing more than 500 small-business owners. He used that research to develop attitudinal profiles for three entrepreneurial archetypes:

CRAFTSPEOPLE Comprise 60 per cent of small business owners and derive their sense of self-worth from their mastery of a craft or trade. While they don't think of themselves as entrepreneurs, they still have the resources and confidence to operate independently. They are more interested in developing their skills than growing their revenue and generally work alone or employ one other person, often a spouse.

FREEDOM FIGHTERS They work hard to control their own destiny. That's because their prime motivator isn't growth, but simply being in business for themselves. They comprise 30 per cent of all small businesses and typically employ 3 to 50 staff and grow less than 30 per cent a year. More than half the freedom fighters are college educated, and 30 per cent are women. They are more likely to hire family and tend to treat their staff as family members.

MOUNTAIN CLIMBERS They are the 10 per cent of growth-oriented business owners who are motivated almost solely by achievement, usually measured in terms of company growth. You can usually identify mountain climbers by the fact that their companies grow by more than 30 per cent annually. As a result, they are the most high-profile and high-profit group. More than 75 per cent have college or university degrees. These go-getters work long hours, and expect a lot from themselves and their staff. Eighty-three per cent claim to be married.[1]

If you are planning to go into a business of your own, into which of these three groups do you think you would fall? Mountain climbers are the people we tend to read about in the newspapers and financial magazines and are likely to be the kind of individuals profiled throughout this book. It is important to recognize, however, that not everyone can or wants to be a mountain climber and there are many other opportunities for you to start a business and still be quite happy and do very well.

EVALUATING YOUR BUSINESS SKILLS

There is a lot more to succeeding as an entrepreneur than just having the proper background, attitudes, and lifestyle. This next section discusses another factor you should consider in assessing your potential for becoming a successful entrepreneur: Do you have the requisite managerial and administrative skills needed to manage and operate a business?

Possessing the necessary managerial skills is an essential ingredient to succeeding in any small venture. It is estimated that the principal reason for the failure of small firms is poor management. Witness the experience of restaurateurs Richard Jaffray and Scott Morison (Entrepreneurs in Action #4). They

1. Kara Kuryllowicz, "What Kind of Entrepreneur are You?," *PROFIT* (2000).

thought they had learned a lot in building up their chain of Cactus Club Cafes in the lower mainland of British Columbia. They figured they "could do no wrong," decided to branch out, and opened four additional Clubs, two each in Calgary and Edmonton. Within six months, they knew they had a problem, and six months later it all fell apart.

What could have gone wrong for these relatively seasoned entrepreneurs? "Everything," says Jaffray. Restaurant locations were selected by price rather than by location as they had been in British Columbia. They changed the original concept of the restaurants and abandoned their long-time practice of grooming existing employees to take over the management of new restaurants. They neglected to take local culture into account and charged British Columbia prices, which were 10 per cent to 20 per cent higher than comparable price levels in Alberta. In the end, three of the four Alberta locations were closed and the whole experience ended up costing them about $3 million.

Having learned their lesson and rebuilt the business in British Columbia, the pair are now looking to take their concept back into Alberta and also to the United States. This time they are not too worried. They feel they have been through it before and can be successful now. "Had we not gone right to the very bottom, I don't think we'd be as successful as we are today," says Jaffray.

4   Entrepreneurs in action

Rock Bottom and Back

It's 4:00 p.m. on a Monday, and business is booming in the newest uptown Vancouver location of Cactus Club Cafe. Hip young 20-somethings lounge in leather armchairs at tables surrounding a massive centrepiece mahogany bar, drinking Cactus Bellinis, a peach/rum/champagne/sangria slurpie billed as "better than sex." Others relax in plush leather booths next to massive windows framed with crushed velvet drapes. Still others gather around glowing-eyed gargoyle fountains, kibitzing with service staff as they sample diverse cuisine, ranging from jerk chicken and sea-salted fries to the Millionaire's Cut filet mignon.

It's an opulent yet informal, eclectic atmosphere that's become the tongue-in-cheek trademark of restaurateurs Richard Jaffray and Scott Morison. From the bawdy paintings in heavy gilt frames to the glass-enclosed courtyard, river-rock fireplaces and signature moose heads, the new $1.8-million restaurant is fanciful and fun. And that's a key component in Cactus Club's recipe for success, says Jaffray. The other ingredients? Innovative, high-quality food at a reasonable price, he says, and a service culture bent on entertaining customers. It's a formula that's proving popular with West Coast consumers, fuelling Cactus Club's growth into a 10-chain restaurant with 1998 sales of $20 million — up from $17 million in 1997.

But that success hasn't come without challenges. In 1996 an overzealous expansion into Alberta brought the company to the brink of ruin. Opening four restaurants in less than 15 months without adequate research and preparation proved nearly fatal, says Jaffray. Undaunted by the near-disaster, the

PERRY ZAVITZ

ambitious partners rolled up their sleeves to retrench and reorganize. . . . Their long-term goal? No less than 200 restaurants across Western Canada and

continued

Entrepreneurs in Action #4 — continued

the U.S. in the next 20 years. "Our objective," says Jaffray, "is to be the best upscale, casual, fun restaurant in North America." A lofty ambition, perhaps, but one the partners are confident they can meet by learning from their past mistakes and adhering to the first rule of business: know thy customers.

In fact, that axiom was instrumental in Jaffray's decision to abandon his initial idea of launching a company that would offer party cruises upon arriving in Vancouver from Calgary in 1984. After living in his '74 Dodge Dart at a local beach for a month, he discovered that Vancouver's often inclement weather isn't well suited to cruising.

Instead Jaffray began waiting tables for Earl's Restaurants Ltd., a popular family-restaurant chain. It was there he met Morison, a fellow waiter and would-be entrepreneur. Eager to strike out on their own, two years later the then 21-year-olds hatched a plan to capitalize on the popularity of Expo 86, launching an ice cream and cappuccino bar called Café Cucamongas.

Revenues reached $250,000 in the first year, enough to attract the attention of the pair's former boss at Earl's, Stan Fuller. Impressed with the duo's enthusiasm and commitment, Fuller approached them in 1987 about a potential partnership in a new restaurant geared to a younger clientele. His timing was perfect, since Jaffray and Morison were already looking beyond Cucamongas. It was win-win, explains Jaffray. The partnership provided them with the capital they needed to develop a full-scale restaurant chain, plus access to Fuller's expertise and experience. In return, Earl's got an investment in a new market without having to manage it. . . .

Morison and Jaffray sold Cucamongas and wrangled a $225,000 bank loan, giving them enough cash to finance their half-share in the new venture. In March 1988, the first Cactus Club Cafe opened in club-starved North Vancouver. The concept was simple: to combine the best attributes of a pub, restaurant and nightclub in a single nightspot. The vision, says Jaffray, was to establish a restaurant that would become a local neighborhood hangout, with its own character and vitality. A place where the food and atmosphere would entice customers into making a full night of it — not merely stop in for a drink or dinner.

Cactus Club seemed to fit the bill. Its quirky decor, music, party atmosphere and progressive menu proved popular with hip consumers. The menu featured Vancouver firsts such as tortilla wraps and microbrewed beer on tap. Staff, hired as much for their outgoing personalities as their waiting skills, were encouraged to engage and entertain customers. . . . By 1995 Cactus Club had grown to include five restaurants in the lower mainland. "We could do no wrong," says Jaffray.

Emboldened, in 1996 Jaffray and Morison decided to branch out, opening four Cactus Clubs, two each in Calgary and Edmonton. "Within six months, we knew we were headed for trouble big time," says Jaffray. "Six months later, it all fell apart."

What went wrong? "Everything," says Jaffray. For starters, restaurant locations were chosen not by market research as they were in B.C., says Jaffray, but by price. They tweaked their original concept and ended up with more of a bar than a fun eatery. A longtime practice of grooming existing staff to take over the management of new restaurants was abandoned; they neglected to take into account local cultures such as Edmonton's tradition of "happy hour" discount drinks. Plus, they charged B.C. prices — 10% to 20% above local price point — despite the fact that Alberta costs were lower. Unimpressed by the West Coast whiz kids, customers stayed away.

Staunching mounting losses in Alberta consumed the pair's attention. The inevitable result — sales flatlined and even dropped for their B.C. locations. . . . Within a year of opening in Alberta, they realized they would have to cut their losses or lose everything.

In the end, three of the four Alberta locations were closed. "The whole exercise cost about $3 million," says Jaffray. "We've been paying it off for four years."

Fuller is impressed with the pair's courage. "To their credit, they rolled up their sleeves and changed direction," he says. "They went back to what they knew and then made it better, and worked themselves out of the hole." Indeed, getting back on track meant building change into the company's overall management philosophy. The menu for example, which had remained the same for two years, is now changed twice a year. Menu covers are updated every six weeks. . . . Staff are encouraged to use their own creativity when it comes to service, and managers are responsible for establishing and regularly updating goals. These initiatives seem to be working. Today Cactus Club's nine restaurants are all profitable, and posting annual sales increases of 5% to 22% for the past three years.

While Jaffray and Morison remain cautious about again expanding into a new market, they aren't overly worried. They've been through this before. "Had we not gone right to the very bottom, I don't think we'd be as successful as we are today," says Jaffray. "We now know all the things that can go wrong." (www.cactusclubcafe.com)

Source: Diane Luckow, "Rockbottomandback," *PROFIT*, April 1999, pp. 53–55. Reprinted with permission.

WHAT SKILLS ARE NEEDED BY SMALL-BUSINESS OWNERS?

Businesses, whether large or small, have to perform a number of diverse functions to operate successfully. An entrepreneur, because of the limited amount of resources (human and financial) at his or her disposal, faces a particularly difficult time.

The business skills required by an entrepreneur (or some other member of the organization) can be broken down by function, as shown in Table 2.1.

INVENTORY OF YOUR MANAGERIAL AND ADMINISTRATIVE SKILLS

Now that you understand the range of skills necessary to enable your new business to succeed, the Managerial Skills Inventory in Figure 2.3 on page 39 can be used to develop an inventory of your skills and capabilities in several aspects of management. Your present level of expertise may be anything from minimal to having a great deal of skill. The goal of the inventory is to assess your present skills, with the purpose of identifying areas that may need improvement. Since each of these management skills is not required at an equivalent level in all new business situations, completing this inventory might also provide you with some insight into the type of business opportunities for which you are best suited.

WHERE CAN YOU ACQUIRE THE NECESSARY SKILLS?

It should be apparent from the lengthy list in Table 2.1 that few people can expect to have a strong grasp of all of these skills prior to considering an entrepreneurial career. The key question then becomes where and how you can acquire these skills. The available means for developing these business skills are outlined below.

JOB EXPERIENCE

Every job you have had should have contributed to the development of some business skills. For example, working as an accountant might teach you:

1. How to prepare financial statements
2. How to make financial projections and manage money
3. How to determine the business's cash requirements, among other things

---

TABLE 2.1   BREAKDOWN OF ENTREPRENEURIAL BUSINESS SKILLS

1. **Managing money**
   a. Borrowing money and arranging financing
   b. Keeping financial records
   c. Managing cash flow
   d. Handling credit
   e. Buying insurance
   f. Reporting and paying taxes
   g. Budgeting

2. **Managing people**
   a. Hiring employees
   b. Supervising employees
   c. Training employees
   d. Evaluating employees
   e. Motivating people
   f. Scheduling workers

3. **Directing business operations**
   a. Purchasing supplies and raw materials
   b. Purchasing machinery and equipment
   c. Managing inventory
   d. Filling orders
   e. Managing facilities

4. **Directing sales and marketing operations**
   a. Identifying different customer needs
   b. Developing new product and service ideas
   c. Deciding appropriate prices
   d. Developing promotional strategies
   e. Contacting customers and making sales
   f. Developing promotional material and media programs

5. **Setting up a business**
   a. Choosing a location
   b. Obtaining licences and permits
   c. Choosing a form of organization and type of ownership
   d. Arranging initial financing
   e. Determining initial inventory requirements

Working as a sales clerk might teach you:

1. How to sell

2. How to deal with the public

3. How to operate a cash register

Perhaps the best experience, however, is working for another entrepreneur. In that case you will learn to understand the overall process and skills required to operate your own business.

CLUB ACTIVITIES

Many of the functions that service clubs and similar organizations perform in planning and developing programs are similar to those performed by small businesses. Some examples of what can be learned from volunteer activities are:

1. How to organize and conduct fund-raising activities

2. How to promote the organization through public service announcements and free advertising

3. How to manage and coordinate the activities of other members of the organization

EDUCATION

Universities, community colleges, high schools, and government agencies such as local business development organizations and the Business Development Bank of Canada provide many programs and individual courses in which essential business-related skills can be acquired. Some examples of applicable skills that can be learned from these programs include:

1. Business skills (from particular business classes)

2. Socialization and communication skills (from all school activities)

3. Bookkeeping and record-keeping skills (from accounting classes)

YOUR FRIENDS

Most of us have friends who through their job experience and education can teach us valuable business skills. Some examples of useful information we may acquire from this source are:

1. Possible sources of financing

2. Assistance in selecting an appropriate distribution channel for your products

3. Information on the availability of appropriate sites or locations for your business

4. Sources for finding suitable employees

YOUR FAMILY

Growing up with an entrepreneur in the family is perhaps the best learning experience of all, even though you may not be aware of the value of this experience at the time. Some examples of what you might learn from other members of your family are:

1. How to deal with challenges and problems

2. How to make personal sacrifices and why

3. How to keep your personal life and business life separate

4. How to be responsible with money

HOME EXPERIENCES

Our everyday home experiences help us develop many business skills. Some examples of such skills are:

1. Budgeting income

2. Planning finances

3. Organizing activities and events

4. Buying wisely

5. Managing and dealing with people

6. Selling an idea

It can be hard for a single individual to wear all these "hats" at once. Partnerships or the use of outside technical or general business assistance can be an excellent supplement for any deficiencies in characteristics and skills a small-business owner may have. Thus, it often becomes essential to identify an individual, or individuals, who can help you when needed. This outside assistance might come from one of the following sources:

1. A spouse or family member

2. A formal partnership arrangement

3. Hired staff and employees

4. External professional consultants

5. A formal course or training program

6. Regular idea exchange meetings or networking with other entrepreneurs

ASSESSING YOUR PERSONAL FINANCIAL SITUATION

In addition to your managerial capabilities, your financial capacity will be a very important consideration in your decision as to whether an entrepreneurial career is right for you. It will certainly be a critical factor to those you may approach for a loan to provide investment capital for your venture.

YOUR PERSONAL BALANCE SHEET

Your personal balance sheet provides potential lenders with a view of your overall financial situation so they can assess the risk they will be assuming. Generally, if you are in a strong financial position, as indicated by a considerable net worth, you will be considered a desirable prospect. On the other hand, an entrepreneur with a weak financial position and a large number of outstanding debts may not meet the standards of most lenders.

From a personal standpoint, you might also want to reconsider becoming a small-business owner if you cannot afford a temporary or perhaps even a prolonged reduction in your personal income.

Your personal balance sheet includes a summary of all your assets — what you own that has some cash value — and your liabilities or debts. Preparing a personal balance sheet is a relatively simple process:

- **Step 1** Estimate the current market value of all your "assets" — the items you own that have cash value — and list them.
- **Step 2** Add up the value of these assets.
- **Step 3** List all your debts, also known as "liabilities."
- **Step 4** Add up your liabilities.
- **Step 5** Deduct your total liabilities from your total assets to find your "net worth."

Figure 2.4 on page 41 shows a Sample Balance Sheet Form that you can use to help organize your assets and liabilities. The items listed are not exhaustive; the form is provided only as a guide for thinking about your present position. Since every business opportunity has its own unique capital (money) requirements, there is no specific dollar value for the personal net worth necessary to start a business. However, you should keep in mind that most private lenders or lending institutions typically expect a new small-business owner to provide at least 40 to 50 per cent of the capital required for start-up. In addition, lenders consider the net worth position of prospective borrowers to determine their ability to repay the loan should the new business fail.

DEVELOPING A PERSONAL BUDGET

As well as determining your present net worth, you must also consider your personal living expenses when assessing your ability to provide the total financing needed to start a new business. In fact, you should evaluate your personal financial needs while in the process of determining whether an entrepreneurial career is right for you.

In some situations you will need to take money from the business each month to pay part or all of your personal living expenses. If such is the case, it is crucial that this amount be known and that at least that much be set aside to be paid out to you each month as a salary.

If your new business is starting off on a limited scale, you might wish to continue holding a regular job to cover your basic living expenses and provide some additional capital to your fledgling operation. In some cases, your spouse's income may be sufficient to cover the family's basic living expenses and it may not be necessary to consider your personal financial needs in making a go/no-go decision.

The Personal Living Expenses Worksheet shown in Figure 2.5 on page 43 is an effective means of estimating your present cost of living. From the totals on the worksheet, you can calculate the minimum amount of money you and your family will require on a regular monthly basis and determine from what sources this regular income will be obtained.

ARE YOU READY FOR AN ENTREPRENEURIAL CAREER?

EXTERNAL ROLE DEMANDS

It is not enough simply to possess a large number and high level of the characteristics previously discussed as prerequisites for a successful entrepreneurial career. There are also certain external conditions, pressures, and demands inherent in the small-business ownership role itself.

While successful entrepreneurs may share several characteristics with successful people in other careers, entrepreneurs' preference for and tolerance of the combination of requirements unique to their role is a major distinguishing feature.

Many of these requirements were mentioned earlier. What follows is a discussion of a few of the most relevant issues you should consider concerning your degree of readiness and preparedness for such a career.

NEED FOR TOTAL COMMITMENT

As an entrepreneur you must live with the challenge of trying first to survive in the business world, then to stay alive, and always to grow and withstand the competitive pressures of the marketplace. Almost any venture worth considering requires top priority on your time, emotions, and loyalty. As an entrepreneur you must be prepared to give "all you've got" to the building of your business, particularly during the initial stages of its development. Anything less than total commitment will likely result in failure.

MANAGEMENT OF STRESS

Stress, the emotional and physiological reaction to external events or circumstances, is an inevitable result of pursuing an entrepreneurial career option. Depending on how it is handled, stress can be either good or bad for an entrepreneur. The better you understand how you react to stressful situations, the better you will be able to maximize the positive aspects of these situations and minimize the negative aspects, such as exhaustion and frustration, before they lead to a serious problem.

Stress, in the short term, can produce excellent results, because of its relationship to the type of behaviour associated with entrepreneurial activities, especially during the start-up stage of a new business. There is some evidence that once individuals become accustomed to producing under stressful conditions, they seem to continue to respond in a positive manner; entrepreneurs tend to create new challenges to replace the ones they have already met, and to continue to respond to those challenges with a high level of effectiveness.

ECONOMIC AND PERSONAL VALUES

Entrepreneurs engaged in "for-profit" as opposed to social or "not-for-profit" organizations must share the basic values of the free enterprise system: private ownership, profits, capital gains, and growth. These dominant economic values need not exclude social or other values. However, the nature of the competitive market economy requires belief in, or at least respect for, these values.

DEALING WITH THE ETHICAL CHALLENGE

With the collapse of Enron and WorldCom and other incidents of a similar nature in the world of big business in recent years, a dramatic increase in the ethical expectations of all businesses and professionals has occurred. Increasingly, consumers, clients, employees, and others are seeking out those who define the basic ground rules of their businesses on a day-to-day basis.

Entrepreneurs are typically faced with many ethical decisions. These may relate to such issues as potential conflicts of interest between your personal situation and the interests of your business; temptations to provide gifts, expensive entertainment, or even bribes or kickbacks to certain people or organizations in order to attract or influence their business activity; or the use of proprietary or confidential information in order to influence the outcome of a deal or a sale. To be successful as an entrepreneur, it is important that you act and conduct your business in an ethical manner, and the significance of ethics when initiating a new venture must be emphasized.

What specifically do we mean by "ethics"? One dictionary defines it as *the moral quality of a course of action; fitness; propriety.*[2] One could think of ethics as a set of principles outlining a behavioural code that lays out what is good and right or bad and wrong. Ethics may also outline obligations and appropriate moral actions for both the individual and the organization.[3] The problem with these kinds of definitions, however, is that they think of ethics as a static description, implying that society universally agrees on certain fundamental principles that everyone regards as being "ethical." With society being a dynamic and rapidly changing environment, however, such a consensus clearly does not exist. In fact, considerable conflict and general disagreement over what would be considered "ethical" in most decision situations is probably more typical.

Another dilemma for the entrepreneur is the issue of legal versus ethical considerations. Survival of their business is a strong motivating factor for most entrepreneurs and the question arises as to how far they can go in order to help their business become established and successful. The law provides the boundaries defining just what activities are illegal (although they are often subject to some interpretation) but it does not provide any specific guidance for ethical considerations. So what is legal and illegal is usually very clear but what is ethical and unethical is frequently not obvious. Rather, situations involving ethical issues are often very ambiguous.

Because the system is so unclear and filled with situations involving potential conflicts, entrepreneurs need to commit to a general strategy for ethical responsibility. Many professional organizations and business associations have a code of ethics that members are expected to follow. Failure to do so can result in expulsion from the organizations. Definity Global Solutions, an employee-recruiting agency in Toronto, for example, is a member of the Association of Canadian Search, Employment and Staffing Services (ACSESS) and prominently displays the association's code of ethics on its Web site (definityglobal.ca/news.htm). This code is reproduced in the Key Points feature on the next page.

Many organizations, on the other hand, prefer to develop their own codes of ethics or conduct. These documents often lay out in considerable detail just how the company's management and employees are expected to behave in particular situations and what the company feels is the right thing to do. Home Security Metal Products, a supplier of security systems and alarms in the Ottawa area, has developed a very specific code of conduct that spells out how its customers are to be treated and how particular situations are to be handled by its managers and employees (www3.simpatico.ca/rh.campbell/codeof.htm). The company would like to see its code accepted by others in the industry as well. This code is reproduced in the Key Points feature on page 31.

Having a code of ethics can be a great start but it may not be sufficient to take the greyness out of an ethical situation and help you to determine a solution. It is easy to charge ahead without thinking and then rationalize your decision after the fact. Kenneth Blanchard and Norman Vincent Peale suggest using an *Ethics Check* that helps you to sort out dilemmas by examining the situation at several different levels. Their Ethics Check is intended to help you clarify issues by addressing three questions when confronted with an ethical problem:

1. *Is it legal?*

   Will you be violating either civil law or your organization's code of ethics?

---

2. *The American Heritage Dictionary of the English Language*, 4th ed., William Morris, Ed.
   (Boston: Houghton Mifflin Company, 2000).

3. V.E. Henderson, "The Ethical Side of Enterprise," *Sloan Management Review*, Spring 1982, p. 38.

Key points

DEFINITY GLOBAL SOLUTIONS INC. CODE OF ETHICS

1. We will serve our clients, candidates and employees faithfully, with integrity and professionally.
2. We will observe the highest principles of honesty and fair practice in dealing with clients, candidates, employees and all regulatory authorities, and will respect the confidentiality of records in accordance with law and good business practices.
3. We will provide leadership in the adherence to both the spirit and letter of all applicable human rights, employment laws and regulations. We will treat all candidates and employees without prejudice and will not accept an order from any client that is discriminatory in any way.
4. We will take all reasonable steps to provide clients with accurate information on each candidate's employment qualifications and experience, and will only present those candidates who have given us authorization to represent their application for employment.
5. We will supply candidates and employees with complete and accurate information as provided by the client, regarding terms of employment, job descriptions and workplace conditions.
6. We will not recruit, encourage or entice a candidate whom we have previously placed to leave the employ of clients, nor will we encourage or coerce an individual to leave any assignment before completion.
7. We will not restrict the right of a candidate or employee to accept employment of their choice.
8. We will maintain the highest standards of integrity in all forms of advertising, communications and solicitations, and will conduct our business in a manner designed to enhance the operation, image and reputation of the employment, recruitment and staffing services industry.
9. We will recognize and respect the rights and privileges of competitors in the true fashion of individual initiative and free enterprise and refrain from engaging in acts of unfair competition.
10. We will continually work toward strengthening our business relationships and continually improve our services.

Source: Definity Global Solutions Inc. (definityglobal.ca/news.htm), accessed December 11, 2003.

2. *Is it balanced?*

Is it fair to all concerned in the short term as well as the long term? Does it promote win–win relationships?

3. *How will it make you feel about yourself?*

Will it make you proud?
Would you feel good if your decision was published in the newspaper?
Would you feel good if your family knew about it?[4]

Regardless of the approach, having a code of ethics can be the foundation for the success of your business. By being honest and truthful and adhering to a clearly defined set of principles, not only will you feel good about yourself but you will also gain the respect of your customers, suppliers, bankers, and other business associates.

Consider the views of Elias Vamvakas of TLC Laser Eye Centres described in Entrepreneurs in Action #5. TLC clinics became the largest provider of laser eye surgery in the world, and Vamvakas attributes much of this success to the "goodwill cycle" the company created for the business and to a very conscious effort on its part to follow a specific set of ethical business practices. It is clear that integrity and ethical conduct can have a powerful impact on your success in creating a successful and growing business.

4. K. Blanchard and N.V. Peale, *The Power of Ethical Management* (New York: William Morrow and Co. Inc., 1988), p. 27.

HOME SECURITY METAL PRODUCTS
CODE OF ETHICS

1. An outright sale of an alarm panel should be accompanied by an explanation of the purpose of the installer's code and the capability of the lockout feature. The installer's code will be changed only for both parties' protection during that time when the panel is being monitored by the alarm company. Should the customer decide to obtain his monitoring services elsewhere, the original company will always change the code back to factory default at no cost to the customer.

2. Panels purchased outright by a customer will never be locked by the alarm company providing the monitoring services.

3. All panels will be tested to the Central Station, and as much as is possible or practical, will have all programming checked via upload/download software at some time following the end of the installation to assure that the system will function properly in an emergency and is programmed properly.

4. All alarm panels will have an autotest programmed in for the protection of the client.

5. Customers will not be sold "proprietary" equipment that cannot be monitored elsewhere other than the original installing company's Central Station.

6. Customers will be fully trained by the alarm company in the use of the system, including ways to prevent common user-caused false alarms. Panels will be programmed as much as possible with false-alarm prevention codes designed to assist in preventing false dispatches by authorities.

7. Companies will not knowingly solicit other company's monitored accounts. Customers wishing to leave will be treated with the same respect due when they were paying customers. If approached by a client coming from another firm, a courtesy call to the other company is in order, letting the company know what the client is planning to do, and giving the company a chance to save the account.

8. Customers will not be marketed to in such a way as to deceptively lead them to believe they are being given a "free" alarm system, and will be told clearly up front that this is simply another way to "finance" their purchase of an alarm system.

9. Companies should use care and good taste in advertising, such that fear tactics are never employed to sell services.

10. Older customers should have special attention and training paid to them, to ensure that they are actually capable of using the alarm system properly, before they commit to purchase.

11. Companies should at all times make it a high priority to install systems using only the best of components highly rated to prevent false alarms.

12. Salesmen selling alarm systems will not knowingly sell system designs that their company's installers cannot actually provide, leaving frustrated and unhappy customers. Sales staff will not engage in selling practices that emphasize "mini-systems" solely for the purposes of obtaining more monitoring contracts with less installation time and work for installation staff. All options including full perimeter system protection will be outlined to the customer.

13. All commitment terms of any long-term contracts for monitoring services will be clearly explained to the buying customer. Customers should be given a copy of any agreement and encouraged to read it through and clarify points they don't understand.

14. Companies removing leased systems will make every effort to remove all accompanying decals from the premises when they remove the equipment.

Source: Home Security Metal Products (www3.sympatico.ca/rh.campbell/codeof.htm), accessed December 11, 2003.

5   Entrepreneurs in action

Goodwill Hunting

Right from the beginning, we knew we had found a great business idea that we truly believed in, but the challenges of tackling a new, emerging industry were daunting. Looking back, we have learned that our success began with a "goodwill cycle" that started with ethical business practices. Doing the right thing, along with hard work, has sustained us through startup through the challenge of presenting public offerings, and still forms the basis of each decision to this day. It all started on the day I received a call from my best friend, Dr. Nick Nianiaris. He was completely exasperated with his friend and colleague, Dr. Jeff Machat, who was about to "throw away" his career. Dr. Machat, an award-winning ophthalmology graduate, had a potentially incredible future ahead of him, but he wanted to risk it all to perform a revolutionary new procedure called PRK (a procedure using a highly accurate laser to reshape the front part of a person's eye, eliminating the need for contacts or glasses).

My job, as the only senior business person that these young doctors knew, was to convince the wayward Dr. Machat that he should get back to practicing medicine as a "real" doctor. But I couldn't do it. He had traveled the world to study this new laser, and was extremely excited about the results. I was so impressed with his personality and drive that I became hooked on the same dream — we believed PRK would change the world as we knew it. TLC Laser Eye Centres was born.

We spent two years doing research on the procedure, the outcomes and other surgical business models throughout the world before raising the initial funds ($1.5 million from three investors and mortgages on both Dr. Machat's house and my own). Our time was filled with opportunities, decisions, and many hours of phone calls per week. It was difficult to decide upon an approach to entering this emerging industry. We considered setting up hospital associates, stand-alone clinics, and private clinics that simply rented equipment to doctors. We considered direct consumer marketing models as well as mobile systems. We even considered just being a financial company, providing consulting services and money to emerging practices. But as new partners, we made one key agreement: I would not be involved in clinical decisions and he would not be involved in business decisions.

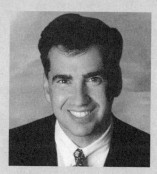

We felt that the ultimate winner in this emerging industry would be the organization that provided the highest level of clinical care while maintaining a business environment founded on integrity and the desire to always do the right thing. We decided to never take short cuts or jeopardize clinical care to satisfy business or financial needs.

Following these principles set in motion what I call a "goodwill cycle." Our company, with only one clinic in Windsor, Ontario, started to get a reputation for providing incredible results. It soon became one of the busiest clinics in the world, attracting worldwide attention. Dr. Machat was open to sharing his knowledge and experience. Doctors came from all over the world to talk with him, and manufacturers of lasers came with their blueprints and asked him to help with their designs. This openness and focus on positive clinical results attracted excellent doctors to TLC. Having the best doctors provided more referrals, leading to the opening of more clinics, which attracted more of the best doctors, and so on.

This goodwill cycle also extended to the staff, whose work involved helping people to see better. Positive affirmation (including hugs, chocolates, flowers and thank-yous) from delighted patients became a tremendous motivator. The staff loved their jobs and it began to show. Over the last five years, we have grown to employ close to 1,000 people. We currently hire more than two new employees every day. . . .

I have learned one very important lesson in business: Ethical business practices always work out for the best and unethical practices always result in disaster. Decisions about right and wrong need to be made every day. Will you strive to honor the intent of an agreement rather than the words that may be translated in your favor? Pay individuals what they deserve, not just what they will accept? Promote based on merit, not friendship? Try to preserve the reputation of competitors? We try to do the right thing, because although it may take a while before actions produce the appropriate reaction, they always do.

In the early '90s, the thought of laser vision correction was preposterous. But the industry has outperformed everyone's expectations, growing close to 100% per year since U.S. FDA approval. And TLC is the largest provider of this service in the world. I believe that if you know what you are doing is right and you really want to do it, you can achieve what others consider impossible.

Source: By Elias Vamvakas, Chairman and CEO, TLC Vision Corporation, "Goodwill Hunting," *PROFITguide.com* (www.profitguide.com/shared/print.jsp?content=1035), accessed December 9, 2003.

A FINAL ANALYSIS

The Entrepreneurial Assessment Questionnaire in Figure 2.6 on page 44 is designed to help you recap your thinking concerning what you need to become a successful entrepreneur. The questions involve considerations at various stages of a business's development, and some may not be applicable to the stage you have currently reached in your business planning. However, you should answer all applicable questions.

If you have answered all the questions carefully, you've done some hard work and serious thinking. That's a positive step. If your answer to most of the questions was yes, you are on the right track. If you answered no to some questions, you have more work to do; these questions indicate areas where you need to know more or that you need to do something about. Do what you can for yourself, but don't hesitate to ask for help from other sources.

This assessment of your entrepreneurial potential is based on a series of self-evaluations, and for it to reveal anything meaningful, an absolute requirement is for you to be completely honest with yourself. This, however, is only the first step. The road to entrepreneurship is strewn with hazards and pitfalls and many who start on it fall by the wayside for one reason or another. However, those who persevere and reach the end by building a successful venture may realize considerable financial and psychological rewards as well as a lot of personal satisfaction.

The remainder of this book can help you evaluate other important parts of this process and improve your chances for success. It will help you decide what else you need to consider and enable you to go after it. Good luck!

Video Case #2

Reaching for the Heights

Summary

Contractor Steve Smith came up with an idea to make extension ladders safer. He thought he had a "can't miss" product, one that retailers would be begging for, so he created a company called Strong Arms to make and market his ladder accessories. But getting his product into hardware stores across Canada has been a tougher task than even he imagined.

Questions for Discussion

1. What benefits might Smith have derived if he had initially sought help from outside sources, such as the manager of his local Home Hardware store?

2. According to retailers, what elements are essential for the successful launch of a tangible product such as the Strong Arm?

3. Why aren't retailers more willing to be of assistance to a budding entrepreneur?

4. What are the benefits of licensing your product to a national company like Caradon versus simply marketing the product yourself?

FIGURE 2.1 ENTREPRENEURIAL QUIZ

Below are a number of questions dealing with your personal background, behavioural characteristics, and lifestyle patterns. Psychologists, venture capitalists, and others believe these to be related to entrepreneurial success. Answer each question by placing an "X" in the space that best reflects your personal views and attitudes. The most important result of this exercise will be an honest, accurate self-assessment of how you relate to each of these dimensions.

	Rarely or no	Mostly or yes
1. Are you prepared to make sacrifices in your family life and take a cut in pay to succeed in business?	____	____
2. Are you the kind of individual that once you decide to do something you'll do it and nothing can stop you?	____	____
3. When you begin a task, do you set clear goals and objectives for yourself?	____	____
4. When faced with a stalemated situation in a group setting, are you usually the one who breaks the logjam and gets the ball rolling again?	____	____
5. Do you commonly seek the advice of people who are older and more experienced than you are?	____	____
6. Even though people tell you "It can't be done" do you still have to find out for yourself?	____	____
7. When you do a good job, are you satisfied in knowing personally that the job has been well done?	____	____
8. Do you often feel, "That's just the way things are and there's nothing I can do about it"?	____	____
9. Do you need to know that something has been done successfully before, prior to trying it yourself?	____	____
10. Do you intentionally try to avoid situations where you have to converse with strangers?	____	____
11. Do you need a clear explanation of a task before proceeding with it?	____	____
12. Are you a good loser in competitive activities?	____	____
13. After a severe setback in a project, are you able to pick up the pieces and start over again?	____	____
14. Do you like the feeling of being in charge of other people?	____	____
15. Do you enjoy working on projects that you know will take a long time to complete successfully?	____	____
16. Do you consider ethics and honesty to be important ingredients for a successful career in business?	____	____
17. Have you previously been involved in starting things like service clubs, community organizations, charitable fund-raising projects, etc.?	____	____
18. Did your parents or grandparents ever own their own business?	____	____
19. When you think of your future do you ever envision yourself running your own business?	____	____

	Rarely or no	Mostly or yes
20. Do you try to do a job better than is expected of you?	_____	_____
21. Do you make suggestions about how things might be improved on your job?	_____	_____
22. Are you usually able to come up with more than one way to solve a problem?	_____	_____
23. Are you between 25 and 40 years of age?	_____	_____
24. Do you worry about what others think of you?	_____	_____
25. Do you read a lot of books, particularly fiction?	_____	_____
26. Do you take risks for the thrill of it?	_____	_____
27. Do you find it easy to get others to do something for you?	_____	_____
28. Has someone in your family shared with you his or her experience in starting a business?	_____	_____
29. Do you believe in organizing your tasks before getting started?	_____	_____
30. Do you get sick often?	_____	_____
31. Do you enjoy doing something just to prove you can?	_____	_____
32. Have you ever been fired from a job?	_____	_____
33. Do you find yourself constantly thinking up new ideas?	_____	_____
34. Do you prefer to let a friend decide on your social activities?	_____	_____
35. Did you like school?	_____	_____
36. Were you a very good student?	_____	_____
37. Did you "hang out" with a group in high school?	_____	_____
38. Did you actively participate in school activities or sports?	_____	_____
39. Do you like to take care of details?	_____	_____
40. Do you believe there should be security in a job?	_____	_____
41. Will you deliberately seek a direct confrontation to get needed results?	_____	_____
42. Were you the firstborn child?	_____	_____
43. Was your father or another older male generally present during your early life at home?	_____	_____
44. Were you expected to do odd jobs at home before 10 years of age?	_____	_____
45. Do you get bored easily?	_____	_____
46. Are you sometimes boastful about your accomplishments?	_____	_____
47. Can you concentrate on one subject for extended periods of time?	_____	_____
48. Do you, on occasion, need pep talks from others to keep you going?	_____	_____
49. Do you find unexpected energy resources as you tackle things you like?	_____	_____
50. Does personal satisfaction mean more to you than having money to spend on yourself?	_____	_____

continued

Entrepreneurial Quiz — continued

		Rarely or no	Mostly or yes
51.	Do you enjoy socializing regularly?	___	___
52.	Have you ever deliberately exceeded your authority at work?	___	___
53.	Do you try to find the benefits in a bad situation?	___	___
54.	Do you blame others when something goes wrong?	___	___
55.	Do you enjoy tackling a task without knowing all the potential problems?	___	___
56.	Do you persist when others tell you it can't be done?	___	___
57.	Do you take rejection personally?	___	___
58.	Do you believe you generally have a lot of good luck that explains your successes?	___	___
59.	Are you likely to work long hours to accomplish a goal?	___	___
60.	Do you enjoy being able to make your own decisions on the job?	___	___
61.	Do you wake up happy most of the time?	___	___
62.	Can you accept failure without admitting defeat?	___	___
63.	Do you have a savings account and other personal investments?	___	___
64.	Do you believe that entrepreneurs take a huge risk?	___	___
65.	Do you feel that successful entrepreneurs must have advanced college degrees?	___	___
66.	Do you strive to use past mistakes as a learning process?	___	___
67.	Are you more people-oriented than goal-oriented?	___	___
68.	Do you find that answers to problems come to you out of nowhere?	___	___
69.	Do you enjoy finding an answer to a frustrating problem?	___	___
70.	Do you prefer to be a loner when making a final decision?	___	___
71.	Do your conversations discuss people more than events or ideas?	___	___
72.	Do you feel good about yourself in spite of criticism by others?	___	___
73.	Do you sleep as little as possible?	___	___
74.	Did you ever have a small business of your own while in school?	___	___

Adapted from Judy Balogh et al., *Beyond a Dream: An Instructor's Guide for Small Business Explorations* (Columbus: Ohio State University, 1985), pp. 26–28.

ANSWERS TO THE ENTREPRENEURIAL QUIZ

The answers provided in Table 2.2 for the Entrepreneurial Quiz represent the responses that best exemplify the spirit, attitudes, and personal views of proven, successful entrepreneurs. Here they are *not* arranged in numerical order (1–74) but by the characteristic that they are measuring (personal background, behaviour patterns, and lifestyle factors).

TABLE 2.2	ANSWERS TO ENTREPRENEURIAL QUIZ

Personal Background

Most Desirable Response	Question Number
Rarely or No	30, 36, 37, 43
Mostly or Yes	17, 18, 23, 28, 32, 35, 28, 42, 44, 74

Behaviour Patterns

Most Desirable Response	Question Number
Rarely or No	8, 9, 10, 11, 12, 14, 24, 39, 40, 48, 54, 57, 64, 65
Mostly or Yes	2, 4, 5, 6, 7, 13, 16, 20, 21, 22, 26, 27, 29, 31, 33, 41, 45, 46, 47, 49, 50, 52, 53, 55, 56, 58, 60, 61, 62, 66, 68, 69

Lifestyle Factors

Most Desirable Response	Question Number
Rarely or No	25, 34, 51, 67, 71
Mostly or Yes	1, 3, 15, 19, 59, 63, 70, 72, 73

WHAT IS YOUR SCORE?

Answering this questionnaire will let you determine the extent to which your responses match those that best exemplify the spirit, attitudes, and personal views of proven, successful entrepreneurs. To determine your score, count the number of your responses that appear to be correct in Table 2.2 and mark it in Table 2.3. Your responses in Table 2.3 have also been arranged by the characteristic they are measuring (your personal background, behaviour patterns, and lifestyle factors).

TABLE 2.3	SELF-ASSESSMENT: RESULTS

	Number of Most Desirable Responses
Your Personal Background	/14
Your Behaviour Patterns	/46
Your Lifestyle Factors	/14
Total Number of Most Desirable Responses	/74

WHAT DOES YOUR SCORE MEAN?

The Entrepreneurial Quiz is *not* intended to predict or determine your likely success or failure. However, if you answer and score the questionnaire honestly, it will provide considerable insight into whether you have the attitudes, lifestyle, and behavioural patterns consistent with successful entrepreneurship.

The higher your number of most desirable responses, the more your responses agree with those of successful entrepreneurs. High levels of agreement indicate that you *may* have the "right stuff" to succeed in an entrepreneurial career. You should make certain, however, that your responses reflect your real opinions and attitudes.

The word *may* is highlighted above because of the overwhelming importance of one particular set of attributes/characteristics: commitment, determination, and perseverance. Scoring well on the test is not necessarily a guarantee of entrepreneurial success. Anything less than total commitment to your venture, and considerable determination and perseverance, will likely result in failure, regardless of the degree to which you may possess other important attributes. Your total commitment and determination to succeed helps convince others to "come along for the ride." If you are not totally committed, both financially and philosophically, to the venture, it is unlikely that potential partners, your employees, bankers, suppliers, and other creditors will have the confidence in you to provide the level of support your business will require.

FYI FOR YOUR INFORMATION

Several other instruments are available that will also enable you to assess your potential for an entrepreneurial career. You might check out:

"Am I an Entrepreneur?" Self-Assessment Quiz This quiz will allow you to compare yourself with successful self-made businesspeople on some key traits and characteristics. It provides a comprehensive individual assessment and will give you some insight into your own distinctive style. (www.wd.gc.ca/apps/amianent.nsf)

National Entrepreneurship Test A light-hearted test from *PROFIT* magazine that enables you to rate your business potential. (www.profitguide.com/quizzes/entre.asp)

Entrepreneurial Self-Assessment A questionnaire from the Business Development Bank of Canada on attitude and lifestyle that will enable you to assess how consistent your character is with that of proven successful entrepreneurs. (www.bdc.ca/en/business_tools/entrepreneurial_self-Assessment/Entrepreneurial_self_assessment.htm)

The Entrepreneur Test Do you have what it takes to succeed as an entrepreneur? This interactive quiz will help you assess your entrepreneurial skills and indicate to what extent you have the personal traits important to a business owner. (www.bizmove.com/other/quiz.htm)

FIGURE 2.2   PERSONAL SELF-ASSESSMENT QUESTIONNAIRE

1. What personal weaknesses did you discover from analyzing your responses to the questionnaire?

_____

_____

_____

_____

2. Do you feel you can be an entrepreneur in spite of these weaknesses?

_____

_____

_____

_____

3. What can you do to improve your areas of weakness?

_____

_____

_____

_____

4. What did the questionnaire indicate as your strengths?

_____

_____

_____

_____

5. Do your strengths compensate for your weaknesses?

_____

_____

_____

_____

6. Does your lifestyle appear to be compatible with the demands of an entrepreneurial career?

_____

_____

_____

_____

FIGURE 2.3   MANAGERIAL SKILLS INVENTORY

The following questionnaire can be used to develop an inventory of your skills and capabilities in each of the five areas of management outlined in this Stage. For each management area, the questionnaire lists some corresponding skills. Rate your present level of expertise for each skill listed by placing an "X" under the appropriate number in the charts below (1 indicates minimal skill, while 5 indicates a great deal of skill). Beneath each section, in the space provided, briefly describe where and when you obtained this experience.

The goal of this inventory is to assess the level of your present skills, with the purpose of identifying areas that may need improvement.

MONEY MANAGEMENT	1	2	3	4	5
Borrowing money and arranging financing	☐	☐	☐	☐	☐
Keeping financial records	☐	☐	☐	☐	☐
Cash flow management	☐	☐	☐	☐	☐
Handling credit	☐	☐	☐	☐	☐
Buying insurance	☐	☐	☐	☐	☐
Reporting and paying taxes	☐	☐	☐	☐	☐
Budgeting	☐	☐	☐	☐	☐

continued

Managerial Skills Inventory — continued

Describe where and when you obtained this expertise.

_____

_____

_____

_____

MANAGING PEOPLE

	1	2	3	4	5
Hiring employees	☐	☐	☐	☐	☐
Supervising employees	☐	☐	☐	☐	☐
Training employees	☐	☐	☐	☐	☐
Evaluating employees	☐	☐	☐	☐	☐
Motivating people	☐	☐	☐	☐	☐
Scheduling workers	☐	☐	☐	☐	☐

Describe where and when you obtained this expertise.

_____

_____

_____

_____

DIRECTING BUSINESS OPERATIONS

	1	2	3	4	5
Purchasing supplies and raw materials	☐	☐	☐	☐	☐
Purchasing machinery and equipment	☐	☐	☐	☐	☐
Managing inventory	☐	☐	☐	☐	☐
Filling orders	☐	☐	☐	☐	☐
Managing facilities	☐	☐	☐	☐	☐

Describe where and when you obtained this expertise.

_____

_____

_____

_____

DIRECTING SALES AND MARKETING OPERATIONS

	1	2	3	4	5
Identifying different customer needs	☐	☐	☐	☐	☐
Developing new product and service ideas	☐	☐	☐	☐	☐
Deciding appropriate prices	☐	☐	☐	☐	☐
Developing promotional strategies	☐	☐	☐	☐	☐
Contacting customers and making sales	☐	☐	☐	☐	☐
Developing promotional material and a media program	☐	☐	☐	☐	☐

Describe where and when you obtained this expertise.

_____

_____

_____

_____

SETTING UP A BUSINESS

	1	2	3	4	5
Choosing a location	☐	☐	☐	☐	☐
Obtaining licences and permits	☐	☐	☐	☐	☐
Choosing a form of organization and type of ownership	☐	☐	☐	☐	☐
Arranging initial financing	☐	☐	☐	☐	☐
Determining initial inventory requirements	☐	☐	☐	☐	☐

Describe where and when you obtained this expertise.

_____

_____

_____

_____

_____

FIGURE 2.4   **SAMPLE BALANCE SHEET FORM**

Name: _____

BALANCE SHEET
as of

_____   _____   _____
(Month)   (Day)   (Year)

ASSETS

Cash & cash equivalents

Cash	_____	
Chequing/savings	_____	
Canada Savings Bonds	_____	
Treasury bills	_____	
Short-term deposits	_____	
Money market funds	_____	
Other	_____	
Subtotal		_____

Business/property

Investment property	_____	
Business Interests	_____	
Subtotal		_____

Registered assets

Registered Retirement Saving Plan (RRSP)	_____	
Employer's pension plan (Registered Pension Plan: RPP)	_____	
Registered Retirement Income Fund (RRIF)	_____	
Deferred Profit Sharing Plan (DPSP)	_____	
Other	_____	
Subtotal		_____

Personal Property

| Home | _____ | |
| Seasonal home | _____ | |

continued

Sample Balance Sheet Form — continued

Cars and/or other vehicles	_____	
Equipment	_____	
Collectibles (art)	_____	
Jewellery	_____	
Household furnishings	_____	
Subtotal		_____

Investments

Guaranteed Income Certificate (GIC) and term deposits	_____	
Mutual funds	_____	
Stocks	_____	
Bonds	_____	
Life insurance (cash surrender value)	_____	
Provincial stock savings plan	_____	
Subtotal		_____
TOTAL		_____ **(A)**

LIABILITIES
Short-term

Credit card debt	_____	
Personal line of credit, margin account	_____	
Instalment loans (e.g., car, furniture, personal loans)	_____	
Demand loans	_____	
Loans for investment purposes	_____	
Tax owing (income and property)	_____	
Other	_____	
Subtotal		_____

Long-term

Mortgage — home	_____	
Mortgage — seasonal home	_____	
Mortgage — investment property	_____	
Other	_____	
Subtotal		_____
TOTAL		_____ **(B)**

NET WORTH ANALYSIS
Liquid assets vs. short-term debt

Total assets	_____ (A)
Total liabilities	_____ (B)
Assets exceed debt by	_____
(Debt exceeds assets by)	_____
Debt-equity ratio (liabilities/net worth)	_____

Net worth (assets less total liabilities)   _____ **(A – B)**

FIGURE 2.5	PERSONAL LIVING EXPENSES WORKSHEET— DETAILED BUDGET*

1. REGULAR MONTHLY PAYMENTS
Rent or house payments (including taxes) $_____

Car payments (including insurance)   _____

Appliances/TV payments   _____

Home improvement loan payments   _____

Personal loan payments   _____

Health plan payments   _____

Life insurance premiums   _____

Other insurance premiums   _____

Miscellaneous payments   _____

Total $_____

2. FOOD EXPENSE
Food at home $_____

Food away from home   _____

Total $_____

3. PERSONAL EXPENSES
Clothing, cleaning, laundry, shoe repair $_____

Drugs   _____

Doctors and dentists   _____

Education   _____

Union and/or professional dues   _____

Gifts and charitable contributions   _____

Travel   _____

Newspapers, magazines, books   _____

Auto upkeep, gas, and parking   _____

Spending money, allowances   _____

Total $_____

4. HOUSEHOLD OPERATING EXPENSES
Telephone $_____

Gas and electricity   _____

Water   _____

Other household expenses, repairs, maintenance   _____

Total $_____

GRAND TOTAL
1. Regular monthly payments $_____

2. Food expense   _____

3. Personal expenses   _____

4. Household operating expenses   _____

Total Monthly Expenses $_____

---

*This budget should be based on an estimate of your financial requirements for an average month based on a recent 3- to 6-month period, and should not include purchases of any new items except emergency replacements.

FIGURE 2.6   ENTREPRENEURIAL ASSESSMENT QUESTIONNAIRE

	YES	NO
WHAT ABOUT YOU?		
1. Are you the kind of person who can get a business started and run it successfully?	___	___
2. Think about why you want to own your own business. Do you want it enough to work long hours without knowing how much money you'll end up with?	___	___
3. Does your family go along with your plan to start a business of your own?	___	___
4. Have you ever worked in a business similar to the one you want to start?	___	___
5. Have you ever worked for someone else as a supervisor or manager?	___	___
6. Have you had any business training in school?	___	___
WHAT ABOUT THE MONEY?		
7. Have you saved any money?	___	___
8. Do you know how much money you will need to get your business started?	___	___
9. Have you figured out whether you could make more money working for someone else?	___	___
10. Have you determined how much of your own money you can put into the business?	___	___
11. Do you know how much credit you can get from your suppliers — the people from whom you will buy?	___	___
12. Do you know where you can borrow the rest of the money needed to start your business?	___	___
13. Have you figured out your expected net income per year from the business? (Include your salary and a return on the money you have invested.)	___	___
14. Can you live on less than this so that you can use some of it to help your business grow?	___	___
15. Have you talked to a banker about your plans?	___	___
YOUR BUSINESS AND THE LAW		
16. Do you know what licences and permits you need?	___	___
17. Do you know what business laws you have to obey?	___	___
18. Have you talked to a lawyer about your proposed business?	___	___
HOW ABOUT A PARTNER?		
19. If you need a partner who has money or know-how, do you know someone who will fit — someone with whom you can get along?	___	___
20. Do you know the good and bad points about going it alone, having a partner, and incorporating your business?	___	___
WHAT ABOUT YOUR CUSTOMERS?		
21. Do most businesses in your community seem to be doing well?	___	___
22. Have you tried to find out how well businesses similar to the one you want to open are doing in your community and in the rest of the country?	___	___
23. Do you know what kind of people will want to buy what you plan to sell?	___	___
24. Do such people live in the area where you want to open your business?	___	___
25. Do you feel they need a business like yours?	___	___
26. If not, have you thought about opening a different kind of business or going to another neighbourhood?	___	___

Exploring New Business Ideas and Opportunities

In Stage Two you had an opportunity to evaluate your own potential for an entrepreneurial career from the standpoint of your personal fit with the requirements for success, the business skills required to start and run a business of your own, and the adequacy of your financial resources. Assuming that you feel you have the "right stuff" to continue to explore this career option, you will need an idea — the seed that will germinate and, hopefully, grow and develop into a profitable enterprise. This is the topic of Stage Three.

An idea is the first thing you will require to start a business. Ideas that succeed are difficult to find and evaluate, but they are critical to the entire process. It is rare for extraordinary amounts of money or effort to overcome the problems associated with what is fundamentally a bad idea.

While at the centre of every opportunity is an idea, not every idea represents a viable business opportunity. That relationship is illustrated below.

Initial New   Potential New   Decision to Start
Venture Ideas ●━━━━▶ Opportunities ●━━━━▶ a New Venture[1]

Some people may come up with any number of initial new venture ideas. After some additional thought and evaluation, they may recognize that some of their ideas are potential new venture opportunities. With even further thought and consideration they may then decide to start a new venture. Perhaps only one idea in a hundred will possess the elements required to make it a success. But how do you tell an idea from an opportunity? Harvard professor J.A. Timmons says *an opportunity has the qualities of being attractive, durable, and timely and is anchored in a product or service that creates or adds value for its buyer or end user.*[2] Many ideas for a prospective new business do not add much value for customers or users. To help you distinguish between a list of ideas and real opportunities you might start by asking yourself the following questions:

- Does the idea solve some fundamental consumer or business want or need?

- Is there a demand? Are there enough people who will buy the product to support a business and how much competition exists for that demand?

- Can the idea be turned into a business that will be *profitable*?

- Do you have the skills needed to take advantage of the opportunity? Why hasn't anyone else tried this concept? If anyone has, what happened to them?

In some instances what was felt to be a good idea was the key element stimulating an individual to think of going into business. In others it was the lack of an acceptable concept that was the principal factor holding back an aspiring entrepreneur. Perhaps you fall into this category. If so, it is important not to be impatient. It may take several years to fully develop and evaluate an idea that is suited to your particular circumstances and that you feel represents a real opportunity. Don't try to force the issue. Actively pursue a range of possible options, but wait until the right situation presents itself before investing your time and money.

There is no shortage of real opportunities. For example, the winners of the Business Development Bank of Canada's Young Entrepreneurs Awards for 2003 were involved in a wide range of different businesses,

---

1. R.P. Singh, G.E. Hills, and G.T. Lumpkin, "New Venture Ideas and Entrepreneurial Opportunities: Understanding the Process of Opportunity Recognition." Paper presented at the United States Association for Small Business and Entrepreneurship Annual Conference, 1999 (www.sbaer.uca.edu/Research/1999/USASBE/99usa657.htm).
2. J.A. Timmons, *New Venture Creation*, 4th ed. (Burr Ridge, IL: Irwin, 1994), p. 87.

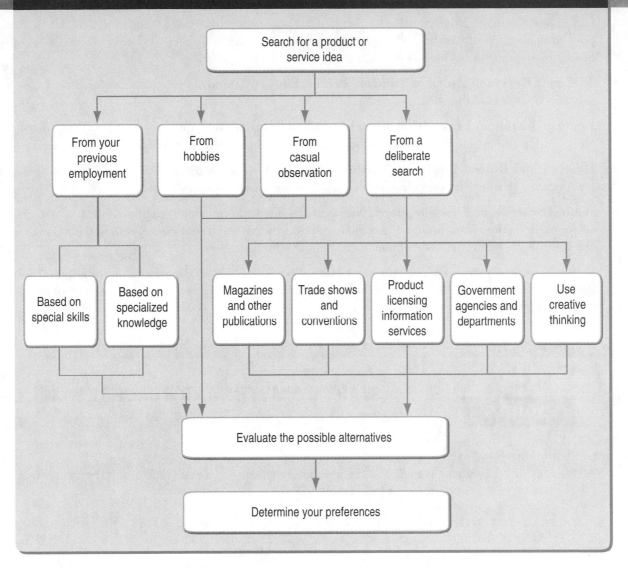

SEARCHING FOR IDEAS

Search for a product or service idea

- From your previous employment
- From hobbies
- From casual observation
- From a deliberate search

- Based on special skills
- Based on specialized knowledge
- Magazines and other publications
- Trade shows and conventions
- Product licensing information services
- Government agencies and departments
- Use creative thinking

Evaluate the possible alternatives

Determine your preferences

including information technology, corporate communications, retailing, construction materials, commercial security, packaged vacations, and a number of other very diverse businesses. For example:

- **Elana Rosenfeld and Leo Johnson, British Columbia**, roast and sell premium specialty coffee from around the world to cafes, gourmet food stores, and restaurants.

- **Jeff Bradshaw, Alberta**, co-owns and operates software and film production companies that create everything from corporate videos to television commercials to broadcast programming.

- **Cary and Shawn Schuler, Saskatchewan**, founded and operate an IT company focused mainly on consulting and product development.

- **Michael Rosenblat, Manitoba**, designed, patented, and manufactures temporary corrugated cardboard forms used in building concrete walls and floors and sells them through distributors across Canada and the United States.

- **Eric Grant-O'Grady, Ontario**, is one of the owners and operators of a company specializing in custom systems integration and the supply of robotics systems for the automotive, environmental, and other sectors.

- **Jean-Francois Rivest, Quebec,** designs, manufactures, and distributes a wide variety of kayaks and related accessories that are exported to more than 20 countries around the world.

- **Jason Murray, New Brunswick,** founded and operates the leading skateboarding and snowboarding retail store in the Maritimes.

- **Lawrence Conrad, Nova Scotia,** heads two companies that provide armed staff and vehicles to transport large amounts of cash to and from customer locations and uniformed and non-uniformed security guards to a variety of businesses.

- **Maureen Kerr and Amanda Stewart, Prince Edward Island,** offer customized golf packages for vacation travellers to the island.

- **Eugene Burton and Jason Critch, Newfoundland,** manufacture specialty crab traps and distribute other fishing supplies to customers in Canada, the United States, Norway, Ireland, and Greenland.

- **Heather and Robert Bourassa, Northwest Territories,** own and run a successful construction and maintenance business in a small, remote community well north of Yellowknife.

- **Jeanne Scarfe and Russ Sheppard, Nunavut,** founded and run a non-profit organization to promote sports participation, team-building, and other extra-curricular activities for the youth in their community and to raise the money to enable them to compete in other locations.

- **Dona Novecosky and Trevor Amiot, Yukon Territory,** own and operate a youth hostel for young travellers from around the world and a restaurant featuring such northern specialities as bison, musk ox, and Arctic char.[3]

Key points .... **START-UP MYTHS AND REALITIES** ....

Myth 1: I'm smart — I can just wing it.
Reality: Face it — you need a plan. One of the few things that small-business lenders, advisors, and consultants agree on is the need for a business plan.
Myth 2: I can do it on a shoestring.
Reality: While no one ever has enough money, having too little can spell doom. You have to have enough money for you and the company to survive until it can support itself.
Myth 3: No sweat. I have a great idea.
Reality: Great ideas are an important start for businesses but ideas alone won't get you far. You also need the resources, skills, and products to make a business grow. About 5 percent of the success equation is having a good idea.
Myth 4: I've got nothing better to do.
Reality: You cannot start a successful small business half-heartedly. The level of commitment associated with making a quick buck is a long way from the reality needed for success in starting a new business.
Myth 5: Maybe starting a business will help our marriage.
Reality: A risky bet. The stress involved in starting a business can amplify marital weaknesses.
Myth 6: A bad economy will mean fewer competitors.
Reality: Maybe. But it can also make the survivors more fierce competitors.
Myth 7: I'm mad as hell and I'm not going to take it anymore.
Reality: The frustration that you may feel with your current job can be a good rationale for starting your own business, but only if your anger is focused on finding a positive outcome.
Myth 8: If I can't think of anything else, I'll open a bar.
Reality: Despite common opinion, restaurants and bars are not easy businesses to start or run.

Source: Dave Kansas, "Don't Believe It," *The Wall Street Journal—Small Business,* October 15, 1993, p. R8.

---

3. Business Development Bank of Canada, "BDC Pays Tribute to Young Canadian Entrepreneurs," press release, October 20, 2003.

In Stage Three we will describe a number of sources from which you might obtain ideas for a prospective new venture and present a variety of techniques you can use to evaluate the conceptual, technical, and financial aspects of your idea to determine whether it might represent a real opportunity.

LONG-TERM EXPECTATIONS FOR YOUR BUSINESS

Whether your plans are to own and operate a business for a number of years or sell it shortly after it becomes operational, you will want to consider the long-term prospects of your venture. If you plan to keep the business, you are bound to have an interest in how it is expected to prosper; if you plan to sell the business, the prospective buyer will consider the long-term viability of the business in his or her purchase offer. So, either way, the long-term performance — the kind of firm your business may become — is important in evaluating alternatives. Opportunities with higher growth potential generally offer greater economic payoffs. However, those are not the only kind of payoffs that are important. Some small but stable ventures provide very enjoyable situations and lucrative benefits to their owners.

For purposes of assessing the expected long-term prospects of your venture, three types of possibilities should be considered:

1. Lifestyle ventures
2. Small, profitable ventures
3. High-growth ventures

LIFESTYLE VENTURES

These include most "one-man shows," mom-and-pop stores, and other lifestyle businesses such as gas stations, restaurants, drycleaning shops, and small independent retail stores. Typically, their owners make modest investments in fixed assets and inventory, put in long hours, and earn considerably less income than the average unskilled auto worker or union craftsperson. The profit in reselling these businesses tends to be quite low.

The operator of a lifestyle business often risks his or her savings to capitalize the enterprise, and works longer hours with less job security than the average employee. Most lifestyle businesses have a high risk of failure. Unless you are willing to put up with these inherent conditions, such types of businesses should probably be avoided in favour of staying with your job until a more attractive opportunity can be identified.

SMALL, PROFITABLE VENTURES

Small manufacturing firms, larger restaurants and retail firms, small chains of gas stations, and other multi-establishment enterprises commonly fall into this category. Usually they involve a substantial capital investment — $500,000 or more. Some owners put in long hours, others do not. Once established, many owners enjoy a comfortable living. The profit in reselling the business can be high to a buyer who sees both an attractive job and a profitable investment.

You might be surprised at how many small, virtually unnoticed businesses around your city or town have managed to provide a very comfortable living for their founders. Almost always there is a very particular reason that they are able to do so: a contract the entrepreneur was able to land at favourable terms; or a market that was unknown to others or too small to attract competitors, which therefore permitted a high profit margin; or special skills or knowledge on the part of the proprietor that enabled him or her to charge high rates for his or her time. The business's advantage may be its location, perhaps purchased for a low price many years earlier, or a patented process others are not able to copy. It may even be simply a brand that is protected by trademark and has become well known over time or through successful advertising.

HIGH-GROWTH VENTURES

Much rarer than lifestyle ventures or small, profitable ventures, but typically more highly publicized, are small firms that have the capability of becoming large ones. They include many high-technology companies formed around new products with large potential markets, and also some of the small, profitable firms that, due to such factors as having amassed substantial capital or having hit on a successful formula for operating, can be expanded many times. Ventures of this type are often bought and absorbed by larger companies. The potential for significant capital gain on resale of such a business can be substantial.

A key factor in starting a high-growth venture is choosing the right industry to enter. The rate of growth of the industry as a whole often plays a large role in determining the growth patterns of start-ups within it. In addition, however, there has to be some property of the business that can readily be multiplied by that company but cannot easily be duplicated by others for there to be significant growth potential. In franchising, for example, it can be a format for doing business that has proven exceptionally effective and can be taught. In high-technology firms, it is specialized know-how in creating something at a hard-to-reach frontier of engineering for which there is a demand. If a technology is common knowledge and not too capital-intensive, then companies providing it generally do not grow very rapidly.

SOURCES OF IDEAS FOR A NEW BUSINESS

In Stage Two it was suggested that your previous jobs, hobbies, personal experiences, and the like could provide you with some of the requisite business and technical skills needed to operate your own business. Similarly, your past work experience, hobbies, and acquaintances can provide a starting point for developing a list of business ventures you might wish to consider for further investigation. The following is a brief description of some of the sources most often used by entrepreneurs in search of new business opportunities.

YOUR JOB

Prior work experience is the most common source of new business ideas. It has been estimated that as many as 85 per cent of new businesses started are based on product ideas similar to those of prior employers of the founders. When you think about it, the attractions of starting a business in a field in which you have experience and expertise are obvious. You are already familiar with the products and services you will provide, you understand the competitive environment, you have some knowledge and understanding of customer requirements, you may already know several prospective clients, and so on.

Ideas from your previous employment can take several forms. For example, you might set yourself up as a consultant in some technical area using the background and experience you acquired in a previous job. You might develop a product or service for which your prior employer might be a prospective customer. You might even be interested in providing a product or service similar or related to that provided by your previous employer. In this last case you should check with a lawyer to ensure your plans do not violate the legal rights of that employer. You must be certain your actions do not infringe on any patent, trademark, or other proprietary rights, break any non-competition clause or other agreements you may have signed, involve the direct solicitation of your former employer's customers, or raise similar legal or ethical problems. Fergus Keyes, for example, was in the security business for over 30 years and held senior positions with a number of distributors of security products before losing his job as president of a Canadian company, due to a corporate merger. To him it seemed to be a natural step to set up his company in the same business. His firm, Panamsec.com Inc., achieved sales of over $400,000 in its first year of operation (Entrepreneurs in Action #6).

In other instances, the relationship with your previous employment situation may not be quite as direct as in Keyes' case. Judson Marcor, for example, had a strong interest in flying since he was very young. By the time he was 19 he already had his private pilot's licence and subsequently graduated from university with a degree in aeronautical studies. After flying small planes around northern Canada for five years he returned to school to complete a combination law degree/MBA at the University of Alberta. Despite a brief detour to article and practise law, with his strong interest and extensive background in aviation it is not surprising that he would be one of the principals involved in starting a business to offer a fractional ownership of a commercial aircraft to western Canadian companies (Entrepreneurs in Action #7).

YOUR HOBBIES

Some people are deeply involved with their hobbies, often devoting more time to them than to their regular job. There are many instances of such secondary interests leading to new business ventures. For example, serious athletes may open sporting goods stores, amateur photographers open portrait studios, hunters offer guiding services and run hunting lodges and game farms, pilots start fly-in fishing camps, philatelists open coin and stamp stores, and so forth.

Witness the case of Lee Rolfe in Entrepreneurs in Action #8. A self-admitted, long-time movie buff and previously the theatre and film critic for the now defunct *Winnipeg Tribune* newspaper, Rolfe invented a new

Panamsec.com Inc.: Security Products Distributor

President Fergus Keyes is justly proud of his business's success. Through concentrating on maintaining low overhead costs while building sales, this security products distributor is well on the way to achieving the company's long-term objective of "distributing security products around the world."

Panamsec doesn't install security systems; instead, the company represents a number of manufacturers and sells security products to dealers (companies that actually install the product) and to large industrial, commercial, and government operations that have their own in-house installation capabilities. Panamsec.com Inc.'s products include closed-circuit television systems, burglar and fire alarm systems, access control, home automation, and a host of similar security products.

In its first year of operation Panamsec's sales reached more than $400,000 (Canadian), which is pretty incredible for a company with a total staff of only three people. And the company is growing.

Keyes says, "In many ways, Panamsec.com Inc. is the type of business that we are seeing more and more in Canada. Small, efficient, and working in cooperation with other small businesses to be able to provide the same level of service that can be offered by any large organization. Technology today can certainly allow any small operation to have the 'look and feel' of a large company and can generally provide faster and more personalized service to its customer base.". . . .

Keyes has held senior positions with a number of North American and international security distributors since 1966. It seemed natural, he says, to start up his own security distributor operation when various mergers and acquisitions within the security industry resulted in the elimination of his last position as president of a large Canadian distributor. . . .

Panamsec knows the value of outsourcing and utilizes it fully. "Using the abilities of other small businesses dedicated to a specific function can allow a company to provide a service that in the past would have required a much larger investment," says Keyes.

For instance, a distribution business needs a warehouse for inventory and to ship and receive goods. Panamsec.com was able to find another small Canadian business called iZon Logistics in Oakville, Ontario, that receives, inventories, and ships all Panamsec.com products. Because of this outsourcing, Panamsec didn't have to invest in the costs and operation of its own warehouse — which was especially beneficial during the initial years of building the business. . . .

Panamsec.com Inc.'s slogan summarizes its long-term objective: "Distributing Security Products Around The World." To get there, the company is focusing on money and marketing in the short term.

"Not surprisingly," says Keyes, "for a small startup the biggest challenge is finding the operating capital needed to promote and expand the business." Thanks to increasing sales and profits, the company now has the financial documentation necessary to find financing. "With an updated business plan and two years of positive growth, we believe that we can now shop for money and look for the best terms possible."

Expanding Panamsec's marketing area is the company's other current goal. When Panamsec was in the startup phase, finding security product manufacturers that would allow the company to distribute its product line was the biggest challenge.

"Many manufacturers require minimum inventory to be purchased by the distributor, and Panamsec as a startup, without a track record and limited financial resources, had to concentrate on becoming a known distributor within the Canadian security industry to attract more and more manufacturers," says Keyes. . . . (www.panamsec.com)

game called *Flickers!*, based on movie trivia. He and several friends and relatives invested $20,000 to $25,000 to develop a prototype of the game and produce 100 or so copies that could be shown to interested parties. They plan to take these copies to a number of large toy and game trade shows in the United States in hope of interesting an established games manufacturer in producing and marketing their creation.

7   Entrepreneurs in action

Wanna Be a Jetsetter?

"We are the first company in Canada to offer fractional ownership of an airplane under a commercial certificate basis," says Judson Macor, a 33-year-old commercial pilot and president of AirSprint Fractional Ownership. "For $630,000, you can own a one-eighth interest in a Pilatus CP-12."

The concept of fractional ownership was originally conceived by American businessman Richard Santulli. The idea was simple; there were many individuals and corporations that couldn't rationalize the purchase of an entire jet but could afford part of one and the cachet of a private plane would still be theirs. "The manufacturers saw the light; instead of trying to sell a $16 million jet to an individual, you could open up a broader market by selling one-sixteenth of a jet for $1 million," says Macor.

Fractional ownership worked in the United States because U.S. Federal Aviation Administration regulations treated it as private ownership, instead of a commercial arrangement. "It meant less onerous crew duty terms, takeoff and landing restrictions, and maintenance schedules," says Macor.

Unfortunately, the same regulations weren't available in Canada. When you buy a portion of an aircraft in this country, Transport Canada does not consider it a private transaction, and owners must apply for the more stringent commercial operating certificate.

If there was anyone in Canada who was destined to make fractional ownership take flight however, it was Judson Macor. "I had the flying bug in me since I was five," he recalls. He obtained his private licence in high school, and by the age of 19 had qualified for his commercial pilot's ticket.

After high school, Macor attended the University of North Dakota, graduating in 1989 with a BSc in aeronautical studies. For five years, he flew Twin Otters and other small airplanes throughout northern Canada, before a downturn in the industry dried up work. Returning to school, he pursued a combined law degree/MBA at the University of Alberta. After graduating in 1997, he moved to Calgary and articled with a firm specializing in corporate law.

But, try as he might, Macor couldn't get the flying bug out of his system. When Phil Dewsnap, a friend from law school, called up and offered to help start a new company, Macor jumped at the chance. He quit his law job and, working from a spare bedroom in his house, the pair pored over various business plans, trying to decide what kind of company to start.

Knowing of the success of fractional ownership in the U.S., Macor and Dewsnap analyzed the Transport Canada rules and realized that they could make the concept work on a profitable economic basis within Canadian commercial regulations.

The key to their plan was the Pilatus CP-12 passenger plane. The Swiss-built turboprop is equipped with a 1,200 HP engine capable of transporting seven passengers and a quarter tonne of cargo for 3,500 kilometres at 500 km/hr. Designed to land and take off of very short, snow-covered gravel strips, it was ideal for northern Canadian destinations.

But, most of all, the price tag was under $5 million. "One quarter of a Pilatus 12 costs $1.26 million," he says. "That guarantees 200 hours per year of flight time. You pay a further $685/hr of flight time, and a monthly management fee of $6,900."

GREG GERLA PHOTOGRAPHY INC.

Macor and Dewsnap needed at least two aircraft to launch their endeavour. They contacted Bob MacLean in Edmonton, the western Canada distributor for the Pilatus, and struck up a 50/50 deal to merge their respective companies in exchange for two planes that MacLean owned. Macor then applied for the proper authorization and, after six months of paperwork, was finally granted commercial certification in May 2000.

The next step was to track down corporate clientele. AirSprint focused on western Canada-based companies with over $50 million in gross revenues,

150 employees, and a need to travel. "If you're flying less than 100 hours (per year), it's better to charter," says Macor. "If you're flying more than 500 hours, buy your own. The people who need 80 to 500 — that's who we're after."

AirSprint partly marketed their service based on cost comparisons to chartering. According to Macor, commonly quoted fares for a trip to Norman Wells, NWT, puts the cost of a charter in the $12,000 range, while the cost of a flight on your own plane, including monthly management fees, is under $8,000. "You only pay (the hourly fee) when you're onboard the aircraft," says Macor. "If it comes back empty, there's no extra charge. You don't pay holding fees for the aircraft or crew, either."

Soon after opening up for business in May, they managed to pre-sell their first aircraft. "Businesses like it because they get a huge tax deferral due to capital cost allowance," says Macor. "We minimize the effect of cash flow. The investment is also quite liquid, and you can sell anytime. The book value after five years is 95%."

Much to AirSprint's pleasant surprise, several individuals also stepped forward to buy portions. "Half of our clientele are high net-worth individuals who like the convenience of owning their own aircraft," says Macor. "We recently flew four and a half hours to Palm Springs. Compare that to showing up an hour in advance, and another hour at the other end clearing customs and collecting your baggage."

By the time AirSprint had their third plane delivered in August, it had been fully sold to fractional clients. "We have another one being delivered the second week of December, and we're pre-selling now," says Macor. He believes that there is a mature market for about 10 fractional ownership Pilatus aircraft in western Canada. "After that, we'll bring in jets with longer range." (www.airsprint.com)

Note: Some names and personal details have been changed to ensure anonymity.

Source: Gordon Cope, "Wanna Be a Jetsetter?" *Alberta Venture*, January/February 2001, pp. 109–110.

Many such ventures do very well, but there can be considerable conflict. Hobbies are typically activities that you and others are prepared to do at your own expense. This can exert downward pressure on the likely profitability of your business. As a result, margins are quite low in such areas as the production of arts and crafts; small-scale farming; trading in stamps, coins, and other collectibles; antique automobile restorations; and similar hobby-based operations.

PERSONAL OBSERVATION

For many people personal observation is the most practical way of identifying a business idea. Personal observations may arise from either casual observation or deliberate search.

CASUAL OBSERVATION

Often, ideas for a new product or service result from chance observation of daily living situations. This commonly occurs when people travel and observe product or service concepts being provided that are not yet available in the United States, Canada, or, perhaps, the person's local market area.

Restaurant themes and concepts, such as Thai, Mexican, health food, and salads, typically are established in most cities only after they have proven to be successful somewhere else. Sporting trends, such as sailboarding and rollerblading, and fashion colours and styles are also usually imported from outside the country.

For this type of observation to yield results, you have to recognize the need for a new type of product or service offering and then work out some kind of solution; for example, Brian Scudamore was astute enough to recognize that trash collection could be a growth industry (Entrepreneurs in Action #9). While still a teenager he printed cards and flyers and set up his own garbage disposal firm with a beat-up pickup truck. Since 1993 his business has grown to nearly $1.3 million in sales and he is looking to franchise his idea to other major centres across North America.

While he was a university student, Steve Debus observed that students wanted a casual pant that was congruent with their lifestyle. They often sat in front of a computer for hours on end, so wanted something that was comfortable and easy-wearing. They also wanted a pant they could wear during the day but still go

8 *Entrepreneurs in* action

Film Buff Hopes to Market New Movie-Trivia Game

It could have the makings of a good movie.

Film buff has a dream about inventing a game, takes dream to heart and invents movie-trivia game, game becomes an overnight sensation, inventor becomes rich and lives happily ever after.

OK, so maybe it's a little early for Winnipeg publisher and long-time film buff Lee Rolfe to be thinking movie scripts (which he isn't), but it's not outside the realm of possibilities, either.

You see, Rolfe did have a dream about inventing a new game and he did subsequently invent a movie-trivia game. Today he was to unveil his creation — *Flickers!* — at a three-day international toy and game inventors forum in Las Vegas. Time will tell if there's a storybook ending in the works here, or if *Flickers!* is just another seemingly good idea gone bad.

Rolfe isn't taking anything for granted at this point.

"We could have all kinds of interest, and we could have none," he admitted during an interview before leaving for Vegas. "We have no idea (what will happen)."

The "we" Rolfe refers to is himself and about 15 to 20 friends and relatives who have become shareholders in the new company (Eagle Games Ltd.) he recently formed to market his invention.

Rolfe estimates he and his fellow shareholders have ponied up between $20,000 and $25,000 during the last two and a half years to develop a prototype of the new game and produce about 100 copies that can be shown to interested parties.

Rolfe planned to take about 40 copies with him to Las Vegas. He's hoping that having a finished product to show to game-industry professionals, agents and buyers attending the forum will give him a leg up on some of the competition.

He's also hoping to score some bonus points for already having enough material to produce a sequel to *Flickers!* (*Flickers! II*). As well, Eagle Games has a number of other trivia games about theatre, television, Christianity and women also under development, Rolfe added.

"We don't want *Flickers!* to be viewed as a one-shot deal."

Rolfe owns his own publishing company (The Write Stuff) and has had a life-long interest in

movies. From 1974 to 1978, he was the theatre and film critic for the now-defunct *Winnipeg Tribune*.

With the invention of a movie-trivia game, "I sort of feel like I've come full circle!" he added with a laugh.

If there's strong interest in the game, Rolfe said he's not sure if Eagle Games will try producing and marketing the game itself, hire an agent to market it on its behalf or try to negotiate a licensing agreement with an established game manufacturer. He's hoping to get a better idea of what route to go once he's talked to some people at the Las Vegas show.

"It's more a matter of finding out what our options are and what might work the best and go from there," he added.

Rolfe believes this could be a perfect time to introduce a new movie-trivia game to the market because since the September 11, 2001, terrorist attacks on the United States, a growing number of people have been staying home and buying or renting movie videos. So it makes sense they might also have an interest in a trivia game about movies, he added.

The rules for *Flickers!* are simple: Each player rolls a coloured die and then is asked a question from a category of the same colour. The four categories of multiple-choice, question-and-answer cards include: actors and their roles; the Oscars; common bonds and quotable quotes.

Rolfe said he designed the game to be fun for the casual movie-goer, but also challenging for the avid film buff.

"I designed a bonus round where players with a better-than-average knowledge of movies can score extra points," he explained.

What sets his game apart from most other general movie-trivia games on the market, Rolfe suggested, is

that the element of chance has been eliminated. The game is won solely on a player's knowledge of movies. And it can be played with any number of adults, either individually or in teams.

Rolfe said even if he doesn't get the response he's looking for in Las Vegas, he won't give up his efforts to bring his invention to market. He noted there's another toy and games show being held next February in New York, which he described as "the mother of all toy shows."

"This (the Las Vegas forum) is not the be all and end all."

Source: Murray McNeill, "Film Buff Hopes to Market New Movie-Trivia Game," *Winnipeg Free Press*, September 5, 2003, p. B4. Reprinted with permission.

9 *Entrepreneurs in* action

Dial 1-800-GOT-JUNK

One person's trash is another one's treasure. That adage proved true for Brian Scudamore. The Vancouver native has developed a Midas touch when it comes to junk, turning a summer job into a million-dollar business.

Scudamore was just 18 when he was struck by the sight of a truck hauling away rubbish. "I've always been entrepreneurial," says Scudamore. "It just struck me that [trash collection] could be a growth industry." He quickly printed up cards and flyers and with a beat-up $700 pickup truck launched his own garbage-disposal firm, The Rubbish Boys. Despite the name, it was actually a one-man show that Scudamore ran during his summers off from university. It wasn't until 1993 that Scudamore went at it full-time.

The move into garbage disposal proved prescient, as Vancouver, like many other North American cities, has passed regulations that allow residents to turf just two bags of trash per week — forcing them to look for other alternatives when tackling big jobs such as renovations or yard work. From the get-go, Scudamore's plan was to differentiate himself from competitors by being more, well, professional.

PERRY ZAVITZ

"Service standards were missing," he says, "and the industry is notorious for people charging whatever they like. If you've got a Jag in the driveway, you'll pay more." Instead Scudamore — who changed the company name in 1998 to 1-800-GOT-JUNK? —

continued

Entrepreneurs in Action #9 — continued

puts a premium on service: he offers shiny trucks, uniformed drivers and a printed, up-front price list. Appointments are scheduled by a central office, and staff telephone customers for comments on their service. "Our approach really is different," he says, "and we get a lot of positive feedback about it."

Now Scudamore is taking that good will further afield. "We're planning to grow faster than we've grown," he says. He recently sold franchises in Seattle, Portland and Toronto. "We're expanding with other people and with other people's money," says Scudamore. "I believe that franchise owners have more of a drive to succeed than a corporate office does." Franchising is also a quick route to rapid growth, he says. "There are 30 major centres in North America that we want to be in by 2003 — and they are all markets that are larger than Vancouver." And that's not trash talk. (www.1800gotjunk.com)

Source: Hilary Davidson, "5 Entrepreneurs You Need to Know," *PROFIT*, June 1999, pp. 91–92. Reprinted with permission.

out in at night. They wanted something they could fall asleep in in their rooms but could still wear to class the next day without looking wrinkled. His answer was the "Exam Pant," which he initially sold for $20 each but has parlayed into a $2 million clothing design and marketing business employing 26 people. His company, Modrobes, has since expanded to include skirts, jackets, and hip bags, but his designs have not strayed from the basic premise on which the original Exam Pant was based — to provide young people with clothes that are comfortable, have a street-wise look, and are reasonably priced (Entrepreneurs in Action #10).

The observation may emerge from your own experience in the marketplace, be expressed by someone else who has recognized some opportunity or problem, or be the result of observing the behaviour of other people. Regardless of its source, this type of simple observation can be the source of numerous excellent new business ideas.

DELIBERATE SEARCH

While deliberate search may seem to be the most rational way of finding viable business ideas, in fact most new ventures do not start in this manner. The majority of business start-ups arise almost incidentally from events relating to work or everyday life. However, this approach should not be completely ignored, as it can be fruitful if you are committed to investigating the possibilities of starting a new business but lack the seed of any real, likely idea. For example, Mark Germain didn't know anything about the perfume business when he first set out to create a fragrance for his wife, Norma, who couldn't find a perfume she liked (Entrepreneurs in Action #11). However, he learned everything he could about the art of creating perfumes, consulting the "bibles of perfumery" and talking to as many experts as he could. That led him to the right people to help him develop a scent for Norma. As he became more involved in the process, he became increasingly excited about the commercial possibilities of launching a product to take on the major brands like Chanel and Nina Ricci, and he left his engineering job to work full-time on developing the perfume.

A deliberate search process can be initiated by consulting the following sources.

PUBLICATIONS

Reading business publications and other printed sources such as newspapers, specialty magazines, newsletters, and trade publications can provide ideas that might stimulate your entrepreneurial thinking. Some of the more important of these sources are listed below.

NEWSPAPERS AND MAGAZINES   *The Globe and Mail* (www.theglobeandmail.com), the *National Post* (www.nationalpost.com), and *The Wall Street Journal* (www.wsj.com) offer business and classified sections that provide a listing or make other reference to available small-business opportunities. A number of Canadian magazines such as *Canadian Business* (www.canadianbusiness.com), *PROFIT: The Magazine for Canadian Entrepreneurs* (www.profitguide.com), and the *Financial Post Magazine* (www.finpost.com), and U.S. publications such as *Inc.* (www.inc.com), *Entrepreneur* (www.entrepreneur.com), and *Fortune* (www.fortune.com) provide further descriptions of a range of business possibilities.

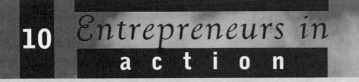

10 Entrepreneurs in action

Out of the Mainstream

Steven Debus wants you in his pants, and he's not afraid to tell you so. Clearly, the founder of Toronto-based Modrobes Saldebus Lounge Clothing Inc. knows a good catchphrase when he hears one. With eyebrow-raising slogans like "I want you in my pants" and "Saving the world one crotch at a time," the 29-year-old Debus has parlayed a lifelong interest in fashion into a $2-million clothing design and marketing business employing 26 people. He's shown that if you speak loudly enough in your customers' language, both consumers and conventional business partners will sit up and listen.

Debus formed Modrobes in 1995 to sell Exam Pants, a concept he'd developed as a business case study in university. Exam Pants were comfortable, easy-wearing pants designed by Debus for students who sit in front of computers for hours. "Students want a pant they can wear during the day and go out in at night," says Debus. "They want to be able to fall asleep in them and go to class the next day without the pant wrinkling."

Borrowing money from a relative to start, Debus went straight to his customers, touring universities with a table piled high with Exam Pants, which he sold for $20 apiece. He went wherever students congregated, such as the travelling Edgefest rock music festival. Debus stuck to his strengths — design and marketing — contracting out manufacturing.

Modrobes' line expanded to include skirts, jackets and hip bags. Most new product ideas came from the customers Debus was careful to stay close to. His designs included all his young clientele wanted: comfort, a streetwise look and reasonable prices — usually under $50.

Selling out of the back of a truck, though, only takes you so far. Debus wanted to break into retail. When sales calls didn't work, Debus tried the unconventional. "When I was in a town and people asked me where they could get the pants, I told them to call a certain local store," he recalls. "Then 30 or 40 people would call the store, and then the store would call me back." Small independent retailers picked up his line and their customers bought. By 1998, chains such as Athlete's World and Jean Machine came knocking. Today, Modrobes fashions are sold in 350 stores across Canada, including two company-owned outlets in Toronto that allow Debus to stay close to customers, his source of inspiration.

Despite the retail success, Debus remains committed to guerrilla marketing. Chains have asked him to do more traditional advertising, but he's ignoring them. He believes that his approach — creating a "wow factor" by designing cutting-edge clothes and speaking directly to his young customers in unconventional ways — drives sales. He prefers distributing Modrobes stickers students can put on their snowboards over conventional advertising. As long as his clothes sell, he says, the stores should be happy.

Debus won't comment on Modrobes' profitability except to say that the company is 100% self-financed and has zero bank debt. He hopes to build a $60-million company in five years by selling on the Net and in the U.S., where he believes his "wow factor" will work as it has here. Debus appeared at last summer's Woodstock '99 festival in Rome, N.Y., but he hasn't yet done formal planning for his entry into the American market.

Debus is stepping up his grassroots efforts. "We want to do our own tour," he says. "It would be like a house party, with bands, DJs and a fashion show rolled into one. We want to entertain." It will also give him another chance to tell people he wants them in his pants — and his skirts, and his jackets. (www.modrobes.com)

Source: Hilary Davidson, "Out of the Stream," *PROFIT*, November 1999, pp. 71–73. Reprinted with permission.

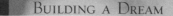

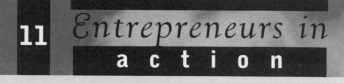

The Sweet Smell of Success

When Michel Germain went to register the name of his perfume with Canadian and U.S. trademark authorities back in 1990, he was pleasantly surprised: The name "Sexual" had never been registered to sell fragrance. It seems hard to believe. Scent, after all, has been an integral part of the human mating ritual for thousands of years, yet apparently no one had dared to commercially exploit its power by giving it such a provocative name. . . .

That kind of brazen creativity and marketing savvy has enabled a former electronic engineering technologist to come out of nowhere and take on some of the biggest fragrance brands — names like Calvin Klein and Ralph Lauren — in a fiercely competitive business. Since launching his perfumes in the fall of 1994 . . ., the Ottawa-based Germain, 38, has watched sales of his fragrances grow steadily into a business that brings in millions of dollars annually. It's quite a feat for what started out as a small, two-person operation, especially considering that Germain is up against all those beautiful bottles — as many as 250 women's fragrances and 130 men's — crowding the perfume counter.

Germain proudly reports that Sexual for women is consistently among the top 20 or so best-selling perfume brands in stores where it is sold. . . . But it's the men's fragrance, launched in 1996, that Germain points to as a clear badge of success. Not only is Sexual pour homme the fourth-best-selling men's scent at the Bay chain, says Germain, in July it became the No. 1 male fragrance at Bloomingdale's legendary 59th Street location in New York City. . . . In Canada, both the women's and men's lines of Sexual, as well as Germain's other perfume brand, Deauville, are available throughout the entire 100-store Bay chain. And now the scent of Germain's concoctions has reached as far as department stores in the Caribbean isles and the Arab nations of Dubai and Kuwait. . . .

But what makes Germain's story most remarkable, perhaps, is that he had no professional background in the perfume business before he jumped into it, nose-first. The impulse to get into the business came when he decided to concoct a fragrance for his wife, Norma, who couldn't find a perfume she liked. "I've always loved when a lady wears perfume," he says, "but unfortunately, my wife never wore a lot of it. One day, in frustration, I said 'I wish you would wear perfume.'" Norma replied that she would, "if she could find one that made her feel sexual and attractive, as if she were the only woman in the world," says Germain. Impressed by her boldness about what she wanted in a perfume, he promised to custom-make one.

Germain learned as much as he could about the art of creating perfumes, he says consulting the "bibles of perfumery" and talking to as many experts as he could, then finding the right people to help him develop a scent for Norma. As he became more involved in the process, he was increasingly excited by the possibilities of launching a commercial product, eventually leaving his engineering job to work on developing the perfume full-time. . . . Germain says, in total, he probably spent about $1 million developing Sexual, with the money coming mainly from family and friends. . . .

Germain's quest took him to New York in 1990, where he managed to convince International Flavors & Fragrances, the world's largest perfume-oil company, to help him create a new fragrance based on ingredients valued in ancient times for their supposed aphrodisiac qualities. He also enlisted the talents of renowned *parfumeurs* Sophia Grojsman and Carlos Benaim. . . .

Germain and his perfumers experimented with rare essences such as Egyptian jasmine, Indian sandalwood and Bulgarian red rose to create a strong (some would say "over-the-top," admits Germain) scent. He then took his fragrant formula to Bloomingdale's, figuring he might as well go big or go home. The initial response from Bloomie's execs, Germain says, was enthusiastic but cautious. They suggested he work in his home market first before trying to take on New York. . . . Germain took their advice. First he concentrated on developing demand for Sexual at Bay stores in Canada. Later, he set about improving the packaging to prepare his fragrance for the world market. He enlisted legendary French perfume bottle designer Pierre Dinaud, creator of the bottle for Calvin Klein's Obsession, to design a sleek, curvy flask for Sexual. . . .

Germain suggests that the test of a great perfume is the scent itself. But the secret of becoming a strong seller is good marketing — especially if you're a small outfit without the big bucks to spend on advertising. A widely recognized brand like Calvin Klein can ride the trends, says Germain, spending millions on launching one perfume, then moving on to the next one when the buzz dies down. But a smaller company has to have a strategy that can go the distance. So Germain focuses on in-store marketing — largely based on those "spritzer ladies" who offer free samples as you run the gauntlet of the department store cosmetics section. He relies on positive word of mouth to sell "one bottle at a time." And he uses exclusivity agreements with a small number of major retailers, which has the added benefit of focusing the distribution network on a few chains. "I don't have the infrastructure yet to be everywhere like the big names, so I focus on where I want to be most," says Germain. . . . (www.michelgermain.com)

Source: Zena Olijnyk, "The Sweet Smell of Success," *Canadian Business,* October 28, 2002.

NEWSLETTERS Thousands of newsletters are available, covering almost every conceivable subject. The information they contain is current and specialized, and can provide invaluable access to opportunities in any field. For further information, contact the reference librarian at your public library and ask for *Newsletters in Print* (Gale Research Company, www.gale.com). It lists every major publication.

TRADE PUBLICATIONS A list of available trade publications can be obtained from *Standard Rate and Data Service* (www.srds.com), *Canadian Advertising Rates and Data* (www.cardmedia.com), or similar publications available in most libraries. Trade magazines are usually the first to publicize a new product. In many cases the manufacturer is looking for help in distributing a new line. The ads will also provide information about potential competitors and their products. These trade publications are some of the best sources of data about a specific industry, and frequently print market surveys, forecasts, and articles on needs the industry may have. All this information can serve as a stimulating source of ideas.

INVENTORS' SHOWS, TRADE SHOWS, AND CONVENTIONS

INVENTORS' SHOWS These shows provide inventors and manufacturers with a place to meet to discuss potential products for the marketplace. Major inventors' shows are held annually in the larger cities throughout Canada and the United States. Information on upcoming shows may be available from online sources like InventNET, the Inventor's Network (www.inventnet.com/tradeshows.html), which provides a list of the major shows held throughout the United States.

TRADE SHOWS Shows covering the industry you want to enter can also be an excellent way to examine the products and services of many of your potential competitors. It can also be a way for you to meet distributors and sales representatives, learn of product and market trends, and identify potential products or services for your venture. Trade shows usually take place several times a year, in various locations. You will find trade show information in the trade magazines servicing your particular field or industry, or you could refer to the following sources:

- *Trade Shows Worldwide*, Gale Research Company (www.gale.com).
- Tradeshowbiz.com (www.tradeshowbiz.com) provides a detailed listing of trade shows and conventions in all areas of the economy that can be searched by industry.

CONVENTIONS Fairs or conventions are also an excellent place to stimulate your creative thinking. At a convention you are exposed to panels, speakers, films, and exhibitions. You also have an opportunity to exchange ideas with other people attending. Information on conventions and meetings scheduled to take place around the world can be obtained from:

- AllConferences.com (www.allconferences.com) is a directory focusing on conferences, conventions, trade shows, and workshops. The information ranges from specialized scientific, medical, and academic conferences to all kinds of general events.

PATENT BROKERS AND PRODUCT LICENSING INFORMATION SERVICES

An excellent way to obtain information about the vast number of new product ideas available from inventors, corporations, or universities is to subscribe to a service that periodically publishes data on products offered for licensing. Licensing means renting the right to manufacture or distribute a product within agreed rules or guidelines. For example, you might purchase the right to manufacture T-shirts and sweaters with the logo of Batman, Dilbert, or other popular fictional characters, or use the trademark of a popular product such as Labatt's or Coca-Cola on similar apparel. The owner of the licence retains ownership and receives a royalty or fixed fee from you as the licensee. Here are some of the information services you can contact to locate product or service licensing opportunities:

National Technology Index
Industry Canada
Innovation and Policy Branch
C.D. Howe Building
235 Queen Street
Ottawa,Ontario K1A 0H5
(strategis.ic.gc.ca/sc_innov/nti/engdoc/search.html)

Government Inventions Available for Licensing
National Technical Information Service (NTIS)
U.S. Department of Commerce
Springfield, VA 22161
(www.ntis.gov)

Also:

The World Bank of Licensable Technology available through
The Canadian Innovation Centre
Waterloo, Ontario
(www.innovationcentre.ca)

The Canadian Intellectual Property Office administers the Canadian Patent Database (patents1.ic.gc.ca) as one vehicle for inventors and entrepreneurs to get together. This database includes the full content of all patent files including an indication of which patent-holders wish to make their patents available for sale or licensing. For more information, contact:

Canadian Intellectual Property Office
Place du Portage I
50 Victoria Street
Hull, Quebec K1A 0C9
(cipo.gc.ca)

FRIENDS, ACQUAINTANCES, AND OTHER SOCIAL CONTACTS

Discussions with those you know should not be overlooked as a source of insight into needs that might be fulfilled by a new venture. Comments such as "wouldn't it be nice if someone came up with something to do away with …" or "what this place needs is …" and other complaints and observations can provide a number of potential ideas.

FEDERAL AND PROVINCIAL GOVERNMENT AGENCIES AND DEPARTMENTS

Industry Canada, the provincial departments of economic development, the Business Development Bank (BDC), university entrepreneurship centres, small-business development centres, community colleges, and various other federal and provincial government agencies are all in the business of helping entrepreneurs by means of business management seminars and courses, advice, information, and other assistance. See the listing of Some Useful Contacts in the For Further Information section at the back of this book. You can also get feedback on the viability of your business idea, or even suggestions. The cost in most cases is nominal.

Numerous other government agencies, such as the Canada Business Services Centres of Industry Canada (www.cbsc.org) also have publications and resources available to stimulate ideas for new business opportunities. Your public library can provide you with further information on all the government departments relevant to your area of interest. It is possible to get your name on mailing lists for free material, or even a government source list so that others can find out about goods or services that you may want to provide.

USE CREATIVE THINKING

Tremendous opportunities can materialize from the simple exchange of ideas among a number of people. A variety of analytical techniques and creative thinking concepts can be used to facilitate this exchange. They help to generate and subjectively evaluate a number of prospective new business opportunities. These include such approaches as the use of decision trees, force field analysis, Plus/Minus/Interesting (PMI) assessment — and similar concepts (see www.mindtools.com/page2.html). Perhaps the most popular approach used for this purpose is "brainstorming."

Brainstorming is a method for developing creative solutions to problems. It works by having a group of people focus on a single problem and come up with as many deliberately unusual solutions as possible. The idea is to push the ideas as far as possible to come up with distinctly creative solutions. During a brainstorming session there is no criticism of the ideas that are being put forward—the concept is to open up as many ideas as possible, and to break down any previously held preconceptions about the limits of the problem. Once this has been done the results of the brainstorming session can be explored and evaluated using further brainstorming or other analytical techniques.

Group brainstorming requires a leader to take control of the session, encourage participation by all members, and keep the dialogue focused on the problem to be resolved. It is helpful if participants come from diverse backgrounds and experiences, as this tends to stimulate many more creative ideas. A brainstorming session should be fun as the group comes up with as many ideas as possible from the very practical to the wildly impossible, without criticism or evaluation during the actual session.

Ross McGowan and his friends used a brainstorming session to generate ideas for a prospective golf-related business they might start. Eventually someone hit on the idea of establishing a golf-training centre devoted entirely to the short game (Entrepreneurs in Action #12). From there they were able to go out and do a market analysis to see if the concept had any potential and the nature and extent of the competition. That analysis revealed that outside of one school in Florida, no one had thought to open a short game facility anywhere in North America and there seemed to be a tremendous need for such a centre. That was the motivation McGowan and his group needed to move forward with the implementation of their plan and the opening of their first centre.

However, not all ideas, even good ones, necessarily succeed. The Short Game facility in Winnipeg closed for good early in the summer of 2002. The concept definitely seemed to work but the owners miscalculated the length of the season. Rather than an April-to-October season as they expected, they discovered their season was really from May to the end of July. Manitoba golfers were just not interested in practising in August and September. They were principally interested in getting their real games in. All was not lost however. The U.S. Short Game rights were sold to a group looking to open a facility in Las Vegas, which has a much longer season.

The following is an example of a modified brainstorming exercise that you could use to help identify opportunities you might choose to develop for a new business.

A FOUR-STEP PROCESS

1. Meet with someone you trust (a close friend, relation, or other person) for one hour. With this individual discuss your strengths, weaknesses, personal beliefs, values, and similar topics. In other words, focus on what you enjoy doing because you do it well (jobs, hobbies, sports, pastimes, etc.) and where your limits are in terms of interests, ethics, capabilities.

2. After considering your strengths and weaknesses, pick the activity (job, hobby, etc.) that you enjoy the most. Think of a number of problem areas that affect you when you engage in that activity. Then meet with a group of personal acquaintances (3–5) and actively brainstorm a number of potential products or services that could solve those problems (no criticism or negative comments). In an hour you should be able to come up with 80–100 potential product/service ideas.

Short Game, Big Ideas

Helping players get up and down appears to be on the upswing these days. That's what a group of golf-minded Winnipeggers guessed would be the case a little over four years ago.

Intent on starting a golf-related business but unsure about what that enterprise might be, the group convened a brainstorming session to determine what form their prospective business should take. Eventually, someone finally hit on an idea — why not open a golf training centre devoted entirely to the short game?

"The concept evolved from an idea put forth by one of our Toronto-based partners, Richard Donnelly," explained Ross McGowan, president of Winnipeg-based Short Game Golf Corporation. "The next step was to go out and do a market analysis to see if it had any potential."

What that analysis revealed was that outside of Dave Pelz's short game school in Boca Raton, Fla., no one had thought to open a short game-only practice facility anywhere in North America. Furthermore, the research showed that an untapped continental market of over 30 million golfers was there for the taking. And there was more, said McGowan.

"Our research also uncovered some other facts that underscored the need for a short game facility. First, 80 per cent of a golfer's handicap is created from 60 yards and in. Second, 65 per cent of the strokes taken in an average round occur from 60 yards and in. We also found that putting makes up 43 per cent of the strokes in an average round of golf."

Elated by its discovery, the group knew that it had to move fast to take advantage of the niche opportunity it had unearthed. The first step was to find a backer for the project.

"We got things started in the summer of 1995," recalls McGowan. "We went to Charlie Spiring (president and CEO of Wellington West, a Manitoba-based investment firm) to put together the initial financing to get the company going. After that, it was a matter of determining how to design the facility, and conducting site selection."

Although it took 14 months to refine the concept and find a suitable location, the wait proved to be worthwhile. A 3.8-acre parcel of land was purchased in South Winnipeg, and by May 1997, the first PGX Short Game and Golf Training Centre was open for business.

Though confident in its product, the group, which had grown to 12 partners, approached the opening with a cautious optimism. Winnipeg, after all, carries a reputation for being one of the toughest test markets in the country, so where better to make a trial run, noted McGowan.

"Winnipeg is a representative example of a mid-sized city, and the originating partners are from Winnipeg, as well. Plus there's the saying: 'If it works in Winnipeg, it will work anywhere,'" said McGowan, referring to the thrifty spending habits of the city's residents.

Apparently, Winnipeggers have liked what they've seen.

"The reception has been excellent and is continuing to build in a positive way," McGowan said. "Membership has increased in each of the three years, and we expect to keep building on that."

The major reason for the centre's success lies in its thoughtful layout. The complex contains four large USGA-standard greens, two silica sand bunkers, and two large water hazards. Both the greens and surrounding terrain have been contoured to provide golfers with similar conditions they would face during a typical round of golf. The emphasis is clearly on finesse, as no shot measures longer than 60 yards. Hitting stations are strategically placed around the greens to provide a variety of challenges and ensure no one shot is the same. . . .

Unlike other practice facilities that leave customers to their own devices, there is plenty of expert advice readily available at the Short Game Centre. Each of the six major hitting stations features a video kiosk, where instruction on any facet of the short game is only a touch of a video screen away.

While the short game concept provides the average public player an opportunity to refine what is traditionally the worst part of his or her game, McGowan is also cognizant of the fact that the facility makes a great venue to stage corporate golf outings.

"Corporate events are a huge part of our business in Winnipeg, and we see it being no different elsewhere," he said. "Staging an event at a centre is an excellent alternative to a golf tournament. It's less costly and everyone is in one place. We close the centre down from 4–8 p.m., put on a nine-hole challenge along with a skills competition, and then cap off the day with a barbeque and drinks. Our goal is to have 40 corporate outings this year. We already had 25 booked by May."

The Short Game Centres [will also] get into the retail side of the game, something McGowan sees as a natural progression.

"We need to provide a full-service retail operation with custom-fitting of wedges and putters. Of course, there will be nuances unique to each market area. Seeing as we specialize in short game instruction, the next step is to specialize in fitting short game equipment."

While McGowan and his cohorts want to take the concept worldwide, their main goal remains a simple one.

"Where Dave Pelz is the Rolls Royce of the short game business, we want to be the Henry Ford of the short game. We want to give the average golfer access to the finest golf and training facility in the world."

Source: Todd Lewys, "Short Game, Big Ideas," *Score*, August/September 2001, p. 29. Reprinted with permission of *SCOREGolf* Magazine.

3. Take this list of potential ideas back to the same person you met with in (1). Reflect back on what you previously identified as your strengths and weaknesses and use that information to develop a framework to narrow the 80–100 ideas down to what you think are the five best new business ideas for you.

4. By yourself, take the five ideas and refine them down to the *one* that you feel relates most closely to your individual interests. Answer the following questions about that top idea:

    - Why did you select it?
    - Where did the idea come from?
    - What are the principal characteristics or attributes of the idea?
    - In what context did it come up during the brainstorming session?
    - What is your ability to carry out the idea?
    - What resources would you need to capitalize on the idea?
    - How profitable is a business venture based on the idea likely to be?
    - Who else might you need to involve?
    - What do you feel is the success potential of the idea you have proposed on a scale of 1 to 5 (with 5 being a very profitable venture)?[4]

The range of sources discussed here is certainly not exhaustive. Through careful observation, enthusiastic inquiry, and systematic searching, it is possible to uncover a number of areas of opportunity.

As you go about this kind of search it is important to write down your ideas as they come to mind. If you don't, a thought that might have changed your life may be lost forever.

WHERE DO NEW VENTURE IDEAS COME FROM?

A survey of over 300 entrepreneurs asked them to provide the sources of the initial ideas for their business. The results are shown in Table 3.1.

Prior experience was by far the most important source of new venture ideas that led to the founding of these firms (73 per cent). However, social contacts were also very important in identifying the ideas on which their businesses were based. A large percentage of entrepreneurs identified business associates (32.8 per cent) and friends and family (19.1 per cent) as important sources of the ideas for their business.

A substantial percentage also reported that they had seen a similar business somewhere else and used that as the basis for their firm (25.8 per cent). Most of those who reported that they had seen a similar business somewhere else also based their business on their prior personal experience. This indicates that that by far the majority of entrepreneurs model their firms in some way on companies in which they have previously worked; for example, after working for some information technology company, these individuals may have realized they could provide some aspect of that or a similar service to clients themselves or provide a service to their employer and similar companies on a contract basis. Working in an industry provides individuals with information and access to professionals within that industry that can help them identify new venture opportunities.

---

4. I would like to thank Vance Gough of Mount Royal College for permission to include this exercise.

TABLE 3.1	WHERE ENTREPRENEURS GET THE IDEAS FOR THEIR NEW VENTURES[5]

SOURCE OF IDEA	PER CENT OF RESPONDENTS*
Prior business experience	73.0%
Business associates	32.8%
Saw a similar business somewhere else	25.8%
Suggestion by friends or relatives	19.1%
Hobby/personal interest	17.2%
Personal research	11.3%
It just came to mind	10.9%
Saw something in a magazine/newspaper	2.3%
Saw or heard something on radio/television	0.4%
Other sources	4.7%

*Sums to more than 100% since respondents could indicate more than one source.

AREAS OF FUTURE OPPORTUNITY

In searching for a unique business idea the best thing to keep in mind is the dynamic changes taking place within our society, our economy, and our everyday way of doing things. These changes are usually difficult to get a handle on and it is hard to understand their implications for new business possibilities, but they represent the principal areas of opportunity available today. If you think about it for a minute, most of the major growth areas in business — such as computers and information technology; cable television systems; fast food; a wide range of personal services; and direct selling by mail, telephone, and television — did not even exist just a few years ago. But now they are so commonplace we take them for granted. Getting information on emerging trends and assessing their implications for various business situations can be a major road to significant business success.

What can we expect in the future? No one has a crystal ball that can predict these changes with 100 per cent accuracy, but many books and business publications provide projections of future trends and changes that could be useful to the insightful observer. For instance, Faith Popcorn, the consumer-trend diva who first labelled the "cocooning" trend, has identified a number of others that she sees being reflected in modern North American society. These include:

- **99 Lives** Too fast a pace and too little time causes societal schizophrenia and forces us to assume multiple roles. Popcorn says that time is the new money — people would rather spend money than time — and predicts that by 2010, 90 per cent of all consumer goods will be home-delivered.

- **Anchoring** A reaching back to our spiritual roots, taking what was secure from the past to be ready for the future. Popcorn notes that more and more people are returning to traditional Western religions, feeling that religion is an important part of their lives, or are exploring non-Western alternatives in their search for spirituality and healing.

- **AtmosFEAR** Polluted air, contaminated water, and tainted food stir up a storm of consumer doubt and uncertainty. Headlines scream about E. coli, mad cow disease, anthrax threats, and other environmental problems. Bottled water has become a billion-dollar business in North America alone.

- **Being Alive** Awareness that good health extends longevity and leads to a new way of life. Look at the tremendous surge in the sales of organic products and herbal additives and remedies, and the popularity of fitness clubs and gyms, acupuncture, magnets, meditation, and other forms of alternative medicine.

5. Singh, Hills, and Lumpkin (1999).

FYI FOR YOUR INFORMATION

TOP 10 BUSINESS OPPORTUNITIES FOR 2003

1. **Organics** Smart foods for health-conscious consumers
2. **Consulting** Selling your business acumen
3. **Wireless world** Devices and software enabling businesses to profit from wireless technologies
4. **Green power** Helping businesses and consumers cut energy costs and pollution
5. **Fountain of youth** Keeping boomers young
6. **Computer interfaces** Efficient ways to input information
7. **"Seniorizing the home"** Devices to help the aged live in their own homes
8. **Explaining technology** Helping people deal with the ever more complex technologies in their daily lives
9. **Many worlds** Helping businesses sell to diverse cultures
10. **Living slim** Selling ways to lose weight — or to live with it

Source: *PROFIT*, December–January 2003, p. 19.

- **Cashing Out** Working women and men, questioning personal/career satisfaction and goals, opt for simpler living. Stressed consumers, she says, are searching for fulfilment and simplicity but going back to basics in their lifestyles, consciously opting for more leisure time or getting out of the rat race by starting a home-based or other small business.

- **Clanning** Belonging to a group that represents common feelings, causes, or ideals; validating one's own belief system. People are banding together to form common-interest clubs, groups, and other organizations where they can share opinions, beliefs, complaints, or whatever else they are feeling with other like-minded individuals.

- **Down-Aging** Nostalgic for their carefree childhood, baby boomers find comfort in familiar pursuits and products from their youth. Music, automobile brands, movies, and a variety of other names and products from the 1960s and 1970s are all being resurrected in response to this demand.

- **Egonomics** To offset a depersonalized society, consumers crave recognition of their individuality. This has created opportunities for improved customer service by increasingly recognizing the specific needs of individuals or for the "ultracustomization" of products and services to the specific requirements of particular customers.

- **EVEolution** The way women think and behave is impacting business, causing a marketing shift away from a traditional, hierarchical model to a relationship model. As Popcorn notes, women have far more financial influence then has traditionally been recognized. They own one-third of all North American businesses and control 80 per cent of all household spending in the country. As a consequence, marketing to them in an appropriate manner can mean a significant business opportunity.

- **Fantasy Adventure** The modern age whets our desire for roads untaken. Exotic theme hotels in Las Vegas are exploding, theme parks are booming, cruise lines are expanding, adventure and eco-tourism are growing, and theme rooms and suites in hotels are becoming increasingly popular as people strive to satisfy their exotic fantasies.

- **Icon Toppling** A new socioquake transforms mainstream North America and the world as the pillars of society are questioned and rejected. Increasingly sceptical consumers are ready to bring down the long-accepted monuments of business, government, and society. Large companies no longer hold our trust. Loyalty to a single employer has gone the way of the dinosaur. Governments are now a reminder of cynicism and distrust. And the views of doctors, lawyers, and other professionals are no longer accepted without question.

- **Pleasure Revenge** Consumers are having a secret bacchanal. They're mad as hell and want to cut loose again. They are tired of being told what's good for them, so are indifferent to rules and regulations and want to enjoy some of the more "forbidden" aspects of life. Steakhouses, martini bars, and similar diversions are all popular reflections of this trend.

- **Small Indulgences** Stressed-out consumers want to indulge in affordable luxuries and seek ways to reward themselves. Premium-priced products such as ice cream, sunglasses, chocolate, liqueur, and similar items have become one way for consumers to reward themselves at moderate expense at the end of a hard day or week.

- **SOS (Save Our Society)** The country has rediscovered a social conscience of ethics, passion, and compassion. We are seeing more corporations make a commitment to return some proportion of their profits to the community; consumers are becoming more responsive to companies that exhibit a social conscience attuned to ethical concerns, education, or the environment; and there has been a dramatic increase in the popularity of "ethical" mutual funds.

- **Vigilante Consumer** Frustrated, often-angry consumers are manipulating the marketplace through pressure, protest, and politics. Consumers seek real products, benefits, and value. When they are disappointed, they can be formidable enemies. At any one time there are typically a number of boycotts in progress against some company. This has really been facilitated by the growth of the Net, where consumers can set up chat rooms, news groups, and Web sites to carry on their complaint against some particular company or brand.[6]

The kind of social changes mentioned by Popcorn help define the future orientation of our society and can all spell potential opportunity for an aggressive entrepreneur.

In a similar vein, Canadian Shirley Roberts, in her book *Harness the Future: The 9 Keys to Emerging Consumer Behaviour*, says that the future will be bright for those entrepreneurial companies that move first out of the gate just as demand starts to rise for products and services to meet consumers' changing needs. That, she says, means figuring out tomorrow's buyers today.

Predicting consumer demand, Roberts feels, lies in understanding the nine drivers of consumer behaviour:

1. Demographics
2. The economy
3. Technology
4. Globalization
5. Government
6. Environmental issues
7. Wellness
8. The retail environment
9. The consumer psyche[7]

For example, rising personal health concerns as reflected in the "Being Alive" trend mentioned by Popcorn mean future consumers will take a more proactive approach to maintaining their personal wellness. In addition, trends like increasing globalization are exposing more people to products and cultures, and changing their tastes as a result.

Any one of these trends could represent an area of significant opportunity for an observant individual. Keeping on top of these shifts can provide the inspiration for many significant new business opportunities. As the futurist John Naisbitt has said, "trends, like horses, are easier to ride in the direction they are going."

SOME SPECIFIC IDEAS AND CONCEPTS FOR THE FUTURE

In view of all these evident trends, a number of specific business ideas are expected to do well in the marketplace of the future. Roberts, for example, provides a list of her predictions for the best businesses for the future:

1. Self-diagnostic medical tools
2. Affordable organic foods

6. F. Popcorn and L. Marigold, *Clicking: 17 Trends That Drive Your Business — and Your Life* (New York: HarperBusiness, 1998).
7. Shirley Roberts, *Harness the Future: The 9 Keys to Emerging Consumer Behaviour* (Toronto: John Wiley and Sons Canada, Ltd., 1998).

3. Educational books, videos, and CD-ROMs

4. Technology-training centres

5. Customized information services

6. Anti-aging cosmetics

7. Pet-related products and services

8. Financial services tailored to women

9. Activewear for aging adults

10. Home-safety devices[8]

The list that follows will expand on some of the possible implications of these trends and give you some idea of specific businesses they indicate should be potential opportunities. The list is by no means complete, but it will give you a few things to think about.

BIOTECHNOLOGY will become a significant growth area as we expand our knowledge of genetic engineering. The world population is exploding, and feeding these additional people with our existing land base will require biotechnological intervention. There will be many business opportunities in agriculture, landscaping, and other food-related industries. Biotechnology will also come into play in products to extend and improve the quality of human life. Possible new venture opportunities include:

- Blood tests to screen for genetic diseases
- Genetic engineering and the development of alternative medicines
- Bionic parts and artificial replacement organs
- DNA modifications to improve disease resistance or increase plant and animal yields
- Implantable microchips in animals

THE INTERNET is growing explosively and interest is likely to continue to be strong despite the recent problems and failures of a number of business-to-consumer (B2C) Web-based companies. These were largely situations where the business model had not been well defined and developed, where the business operators had underestimated the financial and technical resources required to get their business to the break-even point, or that were simply poorly managed and the financial reserves that were available for them to get the business off the ground were squandered. Despite this shakeout, use of the Internet continues to grow rapidly and e-commerce still presents a large number of potential opportunities for either new or existing businesses. Many forecasters predict that business-to-business (B2B) e-commerce will grow more than 10 times faster then B2C commerce, so most of the attractive opportunities are likely to be found in this arena.

There is no doubt the Internet will continue to change the way we communicate and conduct business. Regardless of whether your venture is Web-based or not, you will still likely have a Web page for customer support and communication, to complement your advertising and marketing program, to offer product information, to conduct research and obtain competitive intelligence, or to network with other business owners. New venture opportunities using the Net could include:

- Designing, hosting, and maintaining Web sites
- Internet marketing consulting services
- Software development for very specific applications
- Selling specialty products such as small-business equipment, health-related equipment and supplements, cosmetics and anti-aging products, home-delivered meals and specialty foods, gaming services and related products, travel and leisure products and services, multimedia packages and programs, and a wide range of other products that serve narrow markets around the globe, 24 hours a day, 7 days a week.

TRAINING AND PROFESSIONAL DEVELOPMENT is also an important growth area, particularly in regards to corporate, consumer, and computer training. The explosion in Internet usage, new technology and operating systems, and modified software programs will continue to fuel the need for training to keep computer skills

8. As reported in "Know Thy Next Customer," *PROFIT*, December–January 1999, p. 40.

WHY AN E-BUSINESS TODAY?

1. The Internet is the fastest-growing market opportunity today, promising a remarkable growth curve for entrepreneurs who like to think big.
2. The Net can make things better, faster, and cheaper, all in one place.
3. The number of Canadians with access to the Internet is soaring and they represent an affluent group.
4. The Web loves entrepreneurs, particularly women, because it's an ideal equalizer. It allows the breakdown of gender, geographic, and other barriers and enables small businesses to compete against big firms.
5. E-commerce makes your domestic market everyone's export market. It blurs the distinction between domestic and international markets.

Source: Based on Royal Bank, *Champions: Breakthroughs and Resources for Women Entrepreneurs*, Summer 2000.

current. In addition, more and more small businesses are becoming computerized and need the support. Consumers are also looking to renew and improve themselves, and seminars and other educational programs designed to facilitate this personal growth are likely to do well. Some specific training and development opportunities include:

- Customized on-site computer training and centralized computer training centres
- Image consultants
- Professional organizers
- Videoconferencing specialists
- Programming consultants
- Personal financial planning programs
- Internet-based training and educational programs

MAINTAINING "WELLNESS" is an emerging theme that will create a growing demand for a variety of fitness and health-related products. People are focusing on experiencing a better quality of life by shaping up and healing their minds and bodies. New venture opportunities exist in the following areas:

- Healthier and organically grown food products
- Alternative medicine and homeopathic remedies
- Spas and cosmetic surgery centres
- Holistic health clubs and fitness centres
- Holistic healing and the use of ancient remedies
- Stress relief programs
- Restaurants emphasizing low-fat and other types of "healthy" foods

PERSONAL INDULGENCE is almost the opposite of the "wellness" trend, with people wanting to reward themselves periodically with small, affordable luxuries. New venture opportunities here could include:

- Individual portions of gourmet foods
- Specialty ice cream and other exotic desserts
- Specialty coffee, tea, and wine shops
- Outlets for specialty breads, bagels, and other baked goods
- Exotic meats such as elk, wild boar, bison, ostrich, and venison
- Bed-and-breakfast places or small hotels with specialty services
- Aromatherapy

FYI FOR YOUR INFORMATION

With the ever-increasing popularity of e-business, here are a few Web sites you might want to check out for more information on doing business on the Internet:

E-Business Info-Guide   A document designed to help you navigate through the different government programs, services, and regulations that deal with electronic commerce, and identify those of interest.
(www.cbsc.org/english/search/display.cfm?CODE=2842&Coll=FE_FEDSBIS_E)

ebiz.enable   All the information you need to help your business get started on the Internet.
(strategis.ic.gc.ca/epic/internet/inee-ef.nsf/vwGeneratedInterE/Home)

E-Commerce—Exploring Your Options   An overview of what you need to know to set up an online store to do business on the Internet.
(www.cbsc.org/english/search/display.cfm?Code=4021&Coll=FE_FEDSBIS_E)

E-Future Centre   All the information, contacts, and advice you need to make more informed e-business decisions. Primarily directed toward Alberta businesses, but the information is useful to anyone.
(www.e-future.ca/about/index.asp)

Webmonkey E-Commerce Tutorial   A tutorial that will show you how to generate a realistic e-business plan; create a site design that caters to your online customers; deal with things like credit cards, tax, shipping, and security; and decide whether you should build, buy, or rent an e-commerce solution to manage your site's transactions.
(webmonkey.wired.com/webmonkey/e-business/building/tutorials/tutorial3.html)

CHILDREN'S PRODUCTS AND SERVICES will increase in demand with an increasing birth rate due to the "echo" from the baby boom, two-income families, and single-parent households trying to balance work and home. Young people, including teens and pre-teens, have also become a significant market in their own right, with considerable exposure to conventional media and billions of dollars of discretionary income of their own. In addition, parents and grandparents increasingly want their children and grandchildren to have "everything" and are prepared to pay for the "best." New business opportunities in this area include:

- Childcare centres and camps
- Juvenile safety products
- Fitness centres and play zones for kids
- Healthy food products for infants and children
- Home health care for newborns
- Designer clothing for children
- Educational toys, games, and puzzles
- Programs for children with learning disabilities
- Children's bookstores

HOME HEALTH SERVICE AND ELDERCARE will continue to be a rapidly growing market with the aging of the baby boomers and the ever-increasing costs and declining quality of health care. Opportunities for businesses in this area include:

- Home health care providers such as physiotherapists, occupational therapists, and nursing assistants
- Door-to-door transportation services for the elderly
- Homemaking services

- Daycare centres for the elderly
- Seniors' travel clubs
- Independent, residential, and assisted-living centres
- Products and services for the physically challenged

WORK-AT-HOME PRODUCTS AND SERVICES will grow in popularity as the stay-at-home-and-work trend continues to sweep the country. Increasing numbers of telecommuters from the corporate world and home-based entrepreneurs want to provide a comfortable, secure environment for themselves to work effectively from home. Opportunities for new business ventures include:

- Decorating and furnishing of home offices
- Home safety and protection devices
- Home-office furniture and technical equipment
- On-site equipment repair services
- Home delivery services for office equipment, furniture, and supplies

PET CARE AND PAMPERING represents a significant market opportunity as well for specialized care products and services. Some opportunities for businesses here include:

- Pet daycare centres and hotels
- Pet snacks and treats
- Home grooming services for pets
- 24-hour veterinary care
- Entertainment products and videos for pets
- Baked products for dogs
- Pet furniture and clothing stores
- Restraining systems for pets

RETAIL BOUTIQUES with narrow sales niches will increase in number as the category-killer box stores and discount department stores expand across the country and come to dominate most conventional retail markets like building materials, lawn and garden supplies, books, computers and office supplies, consumer electronics, food products, music, video rentals, and other categories. Opportunities for one-of-a-kind stores include:

- Second-hand goods
- Optometry
- Bakery cafés
- Specialty shoe stores
- Home decorating
- Birding
- Gardening centres
- Stress relief
- Paint-your-own pottery and similar craft stores
- Travel-related products and services
- Homeopathic remedies
- Microbreweries

PERSONAL SERVICES OF ALL TYPES will grow in popularity as people spend more time at work and have fewer leisure hours. As a result they will be willing to pay others to run their errands and handle many time-consuming home and family-related matters. Providers of these personal errand services could perform a variety of tasks such as grocery shopping, picking up laundry, buying theatre tickets, having shoes repaired, and other jobs. They could also arrange for the repair and servicing of cars, take care of pets, choose gifts, consult on the selection of clothes, and handle similar personal matters. Other opportunities in this area include:

- Personal concierge service
- Gift services
- Pickup and delivery service for guests and clients
- Rent-a-driver
- Rent-a-chef
- Personal escort service

SHERMAN'S LAGOON

© Jim Toomey. Reprinted with special permission of King Features Syndicate.

However, Roberts feels that the terrorist attacks of 9/11 have dramatically affected a number of her key drivers of consumer behaviour and, as a result, the behaviour of Canadian consumers and others around the world will change significantly, perhaps for a long time.[9] Obviously the travel, tourism, hotel, and conference businesses have been severely impacted and have yet to fully recover from the shock of the attacks, but Roberts sees a general shift from an indulgent society with endless wants focused on enjoying the pleasures in life to a nation of "fort builders" hunkering down and going back to basics. Now we just want to be safe and are reassessing our priorities in terms of how we want to spend our money.

Some specific businesses that Roberts predicts will do well as a result of this change include:

- The telecommunications industry as the demand for teleconferencing, Internet services, long-distance, and other telecommuting tools increases.
- TV viewership should increase as well as the demand for home videos, newspapers, and magazines as consumers spend more time in their "forts."
- Back-to-basics retailers like Wal-Mart and Canadian Tire will continue to do well. Family apparel necessities will be in high demand but high fashion will take a nosedive.
- A return to family values will turn religious holidays into larger events, which should be good news to a variety of retailers. Greeting card sales will see an upsurge as well.
- Small home repairs and improvements, as well as home electronics upgrades, will be popular but not major renovations that require a large capital outlay as families add comfort to their "forts."
- Small indulgent luxuries will get a boost as consumers try to forget their troubles for just a little while. Fine chocolates, flowers, better wines, and fragrances should increase in demand.
- Consumers will postpone their purchases of new cars but the demand for auto repairs will increase as more people choose to drive rather then fly.
- Grocery stores will recapture a larger share of the food dollar from restaurants as consumers spend more time in their "forts." Casual and fining dining will be hardest hit but lower-priced family and quick-service restaurants should still see business as usual.

9. Shirley Roberts, "Terrorist Attack Shifts Consumer Psyche from Experience Seekers to Fort Builders," *Trends & Insights*, Market-Driven Solutions Inc. (www.marketdrivensolutions.com/trends.htm), accessed August 18, 2004.

- Safety will be a higher priority, so home security systems, security guard services, and cellphones should see an increase in demand.

Trend watcher Mike Lipkin generally agrees with Roberts' assessment of today's environment. He points to five social trends that can lead to booming business opportunities:

1. **The Fear Factor** The rate of change and the magnitude of crises facing society today are making people more afraid than ever. This will provide an opportunity for products and services that provide people with physical or emotional peace of mind, such as alarm systems, security services, emergency preparedness kits, and stress counselling.

2. **Complicated Is Out** People generally want things made simple. They want to be able to get an item and understand it immediately. This will create a demand for such services as information gathering and processing services, personalized financial services, and personal planners and organizers.

3. **Loss of Self** People are less willing to trust themselves and their judgement, and are becoming increasingly sceptical and cynical about the world and its institutions. They seek someone or something that gives them a sense of direction and inclusion. Opportunities will exist for anything that makes people feel in control or good about themselves such as inspirational posters, music, books such as the *Chicken Soup* series, alternative ways to connect with a higher power such as yoga or meditation courses, communication and confidence training programs, and any kind of loyalty program.

4. **We're No. 1** People are less willing to put duty and obligation above personal gratification and beautification. Attractive homes and bodies provide a degree of escape from an increasingly demanding world. Anything that helps enhance people's homes, quality of life, physical health, or attractiveness (such as interior decoration and renovation, cooking lessons, gourmet kitchen appliances, and spa treatments) is likely to do well.

5. **Too Pooped to Participate** People no longer have the time, energy, or inclination to pursue ongoing personal development and education. This will create opportunity for anything that facilitates personal development without great effort, such as Internet dating or support groups, business networking clubs, outlets that cater to safe social interaction such as Starbucks or Chapters, and mentorship programs.[10]

These are just a few of the possibilities that are available to you for starting a business of your own. Becoming a successful entrepreneur means becoming a trend-spotter so that you are aware of potential sources of opportunity. To this end you must be observant, listen to other people, and ask lots of questions. Keeping abreast of these changes will help you identify any number of prospective business opportunities.

EVALUATING YOUR IDEAS

As you have seen, generating ideas for a prospective new business is a relatively simple procedure — the end result of which is a number of potential business opportunities that may, or may not, have a chance of becoming successful ventures.

Discovering ideas is only part of the process involved in starting a business. The ideas must be screened and evaluated, and a selection made of those that warrant further investigation. It is essential that you subject your ideas to this analysis to find the "fatal flaws" if any exist (and they often do). Otherwise, the marketplace will find them when it is too late and you have spent a great deal of time and money.

But how can you determine which ideas you should evaluate? Of the multitude of possible alternatives, which are likely to be best for you? Knowles and Bilyea suggest that you think of the process of selecting the right opportunity for you as a huge funnel equipped with a series of filters. You pour everything into this funnel — your vision, values, long-term goals, short-term objectives, personality, problems, etc. — and a valuable business idea drains out the bottom.[11] This opportunity selection process contains six steps:

1. Identify your business and personal objectives.
2. Learn more about your favourite industries.

---

10. S. Baillie, "The Times They Are A-Changing," *PROFIT*, December 2003, p. 26.

11. Ronald A. Knowles and Cliff G. Bilyea, *Small Business: An Entrepreneur's Plan*, 3rd Canadian ed. (Toronto: Harcourt Brace & Company, 1999), p. 55.

3. Identify promising industry segments.

4. Identify problem areas and brainstorm solutions.

5. Compare possible solutions with your objectives and opportunities in the marketplace.

6. Focus on the most promising opportunities.

STEP 1: IDENTIFY YOUR BUSINESS AND PERSONAL GOALS

List your personal and business goals. What do you want from your business? Money? Personal fulfilment? Independence? To be your own boss? Freedom? Control over your own destiny? Think back to what stimulated your interest in thinking about going into a business of your own in the first place. List everything you would like to accomplish and what you expect your business to be able to provide.

At this stage it might help to meet with someone whom you trust — a close friend, relation, or other person — for an hour or so. With this individual you can discuss your strengths and weaknesses, goals, values, ethical standards, and similar personal issues. She or he can help you focus your goals and refine your thinking in relation to what you enjoy doing, what you are good at, and where your limits are in terms of interests and capabilities.

STEP 2: RESEARCH YOUR FAVOURITE INDUSTRIES

As you considered the variety of trends we discussed earlier in this Stage, there were undoubtedly a number of possibilities that captured your interest. Now you should explore a couple of these situations in more detail. These industries should be ones that interest you and about which you have some first-hand knowledge. They could be food service, travel, manufacturing, retailing, construction, or whatever.

After you have picked your industries, investigate all the information you can find about them from business publications, government agencies and departments, trade magazines, the Internet, and similar sources. The Industry Canada Web site (www.ic.gc.ca) and online databases such as ABI/Inform and Canadian Business and Current Affairs (CBCA) available at your local university library can point you to hundreds of articles related to almost any field. Focus on such areas as the history of the business, the nature and degree of competition, recent industry trends and breakthroughs, number and distribution of customers, and similar topics. It will help to write a brief industry overview of each situation after you have completed your investigation.

STEP 3: IDENTIFY PROMISING INDUSTRY SEGMENTS

With a thorough understanding of one or more industry situations you are now in a position to identify possible market segments where you think you could survive and prosper. Profile your typical target customer — a person or business who needs a particular product or service you could provide.

If you are looking at the consumer market, identify what this prospect will look like in terms of demographic factors such as age, gender, location, income, family size, education, and so on, and in terms of psychographic and other factors such as interests, values, lifestyle, leisure activities, and buying patterns. If you are looking at a commercial/industrial market, use company size, industry, geographic location, number of employees, and so on.

STEP 4: IDENTIFY PROBLEM AREAS AND BRAINSTORM SOLUTIONS

Identify the problem areas for some of these groups of customers that you feel are currently being met ineffectively. What "gaps" are there in terms of the needs of these customers that you feel you can address? Get together with a group of people who know something about business and the industry. Try to actively brainstorm a list of products and services that could represent potential ways to solve these problems. Keep your discussion positive. Let your imagination roam. Don't be concerned with the merits or demerits of an idea at this stage. Just try to make note of as many potential ideas as you can. You should be able to come up with 80–100 or more prospective ideas in an hour.

Refine your list. Try to narrow it down to the five or ten best ideas for you based on your interests, goals and objectives, strengths and weaknesses, and available resources.

STEP 5: COMPARE POSSIBLE SOLUTIONS WITH YOUR OBJECTIVES AND OPPORTUNITIES IN THE MARKETPLACE

Richard Buskirk of the University of Southern California has designed a framework you can use to evaluate the pros and cons of your potential business ideas.[12] It is built around what he calls the "Ideal" or "Model" business. The framework contains 19 distinct factors that affect the chances of success for any new business. Very few ideas will conform precisely to the specifications of the model, but the more a business idea deviates from the "ideal," the more difficulties and greater risks you will encounter with that venture. Testing your concepts against the model will also help identify the areas in which you might expect to have difficulties with your business.

The model is presented in Table 3.2. Let us briefly discuss each of the factors listed.

REQUIRES NO INVESTMENT If you don't have to put any money into your business, then you can't lose any if it fails. You lose only the time you have invested. The more money that must be committed to the venture, the larger the risk and the less attractive the business becomes. Some new businesses, such as fancy theme restaurants, may require so much initial capital there is really no way they can be financially profitable. Smart businesspeople tend to avoid businesses that require a large investment of their own money.

HAS A RECOGNIZED, MEASURABLE MARKET The ideal situation is to sell a product or service to a clearly recognized market that can be relied on to buy it. This may require doing a preliminary investigation of the market acceptance of your idea or concept. Look for some market confirmation of what you propose to offer before proceeding any further.

A PERCEIVED NEED FOR THE PRODUCT OR SERVICE Ideally, your intended customers should already perceive a need for what you intend to sell them. They should know they need your product or service now, thus simplifying your marketing efforts. If they don't recognize their need, you have to first persuade them they need the product and then convince them to buy it from you. Try to avoid products or services that require you to educate the market before you can make a sale.

A DEPENDABLE SOURCE OF SUPPLY FOR REQUIRED INPUTS Make certain you can make or provide what it is you plan to sell. Many businesses have failed because they were unable to obtain essential raw materials or components under the terms they had originally planned. Sudden changes in price or availability of these key inputs can threaten the viability of your entire venture. Large corporations commonly try to directly control or negotiate long-term contracts to assure reliable and consistent supplies. You have to be just as concerned if there are only one or two sources for the materials you require.

NO GOVERNMENT REGULATION The ideal business would not be impacted at all by government regulation. This is impossible in today's world, but some industries are more subject to government involvement than others. Food, drugs, financial services, transportation, communications, etc., are all examples of businesses that require extensive government approval. If your business falls into this category, make sure you understand how government regulations will affect you in terms of time and money.

REQUIRES NO LABOUR FORCE The ideal business would require no labour force. This is possible in one-person operations — the "one-man show." Once you hire an employee you have a lot of government paperwork to deal with relating to Employment Insurance, Canada Pension, and other legal requirements. You are also subject to a broad range of regulations concerning such things as occupational health and safety, human rights, and pay equity. Few small-business operators enjoy dealing with these requirements, and they can be quite time-consuming. If your business demands the hiring of additional employees you must be prepared to take on the responsibility for managing these people effectively.

PROVIDES 100 PER CENT GROSS MARGIN While virtually no businesses provide a 100 per cent gross margin, the idea is that the larger the gross margin, the better the business. Gross margin is what you have left after paying the *direct* material and labour costs for whatever it is you are selling. For example, say you are running an appliance repair business. A typical service call takes one hour, for which you charge the customer $50. However, this call costs you $15 in direct labour and $5 in parts and materials; therefore, your gross margin is $30, or 60 per cent. Service industries like this generally have larger gross margins than manufacturing businesses.

12. Richard Buskirk, *The Entrepreneur's Handbook* (Los Angeles: Robert Brian, Inc., 1985), pp. 41–45.

TABLE 3.2	CHARACTERISTICS OF THE "IDEAL" BUSINESS

- Requires no investment
- Has a recognized, measurable market
- A perceived need for the product or service
- A dependable source of supply for required inputs
- No government regulation
- Requires no labour force
- Provides 100 per cent gross margin
- Buyers purchase frequently
- Receives favourable tax treatment
- Has a receptive, established distribution system
- Has great publicity value
- Customers pay in advance
- No risk of product liability
- No technical obsolescence
- No competition
- No fashion obsolescence
- No physical perishability
- Impervious to weather conditions
- Possesses some proprietary rights

In businesses with low gross margins, small errors in estimating costs or sales can quickly lead to losses. These businesses also tend to have a high break-even point, making it very difficult to make a lot of money. High-margin businesses, on the other hand, can break even with very small sales volumes and generate profits very quickly once this volume of business is exceeded.

BUYERS PURCHASE FREQUENTLY The ideal business would provide a product or service that customers purchase very frequently. This gives you more opportunities to sell to them. Frequent purchasing also reduces their risk in case your offering doesn't live up to their expectations. You are much more likely to try a new fast-food restaurant that has opened in town than you are to purchase a new brand or type of washing machine, fax machine, home theatre system, or other such item.

RECEIVES FAVOURABLE TAX TREATMENT Firms in certain industries may receive tax incentives such as accelerated depreciation on capital assets, differential capital cost allowances, investment tax credits, or various other tax breaks. The ideal business will receive some sort of favourable or differential tax treatment. This sort of advantage can make your business more profitable and attractive to other investors should you require outside capital.

HAS A RECEPTIVE, ESTABLISHED DISTRIBUTION SYSTEM Ideally, your business would sell to established middlemen and distributors who are eager to handle your product. If you have to develop a new method of distribution or are unable to obtain access to an existing one, getting your product to market can be a long and costly process. If traditional wholesalers and retailers are not prepared to carry your line, achieving any reasonable level of market coverage can be extremely difficult.

HAS GREAT PUBLICITY VALUE Publicity in magazines, in newspapers, and on television has great promotional value, and what's more, it's free. If your offering is sufficiently exciting and newsworthy, the resulting publicity may be sufficient to ensure a successful launch for your business. The publicity given to fashion concepts like Modrobes, the radio and television coverage of Al Pooper Scoopin', a business to clean up the "doggie doo" in one's backyard, and favourable reviews of local restaurants by newspaper food critics are all examples of tremendously helpful public notice of new products.

CUSTOMERS PAY IN ADVANCE A major problem facing most new businesses is that of maintaining an adequate cash flow. Typically, small firms are chronically short of cash, the lifeblood they require to pay their employees, their suppliers, and the government on an ongoing basis. The ideal business would have customers who pay in advance. This is in fact the case for many small retail service firms, the direct-mail industry, and manufacturers of some custom-made products. Businesses where customers pay in advance are usually easier to start, have smaller start-up capital requirements, and don't suffer the losses due to bad debts incurred on credit sales.

NO RISK OF PRODUCT LIABILITY   Some products and services are automatically subject to high risk from product liability. Anything ingested by the customer, amusement facilities such as go-cart tracks and water slides, and many manufactured products that possibly could cause injury to the user — all are loaded with potential liability. Liability can occur in unexpected situations, such as the serious injury recently sustained by a golfer whose golf club shattered and impaled him in the chest.

Try to avoid such high-risk businesses, or take every precaution to reduce risk, and carry lots of insurance.

NO TECHNICAL OBSOLESCENCE   The ideal product or service would not suffer from technical obsolescence. The shorter the product's expected technical life expectancy, the less desirable it is as an investment. Products like popcorn, shampoo, garden tools, and electric drills seem to have been with us for as long as most of us can remember. On the other hand, the DVD player, MP3 player, and laptop computer are of recent origin and are undergoing rapid technological transformation. Businesses built around these products are extremely risky for smaller firms and have a very high probability of failure.

NO COMPETITION   Too much competition can be a problem, since aggressive price competitors can make it very difficult for you to turn a profit. Not having any competition can certainly make life much easier for a new small business. But if you ever find yourself in this happy situation, you should ask yourself why. True, your offering may be so new to the marketplace that no other firms have had a chance to get established. But maybe it is just that other firms have already determined there really is no market for what you are planning to provide.

NO FASHION OBSOLESCENCE   Fashion products usually have extremely short life cycles. You must be sure you can make your money before the cycle ends, or be prepared to offer an ongoing series of acceptable products season after season, if you hope to build your business into a sizeable enterprise. Fashion cycles exist not only for clothing and similar products but also for items like toys — witness what happened with the hula hoop, Wacky Wall Walker, Rubik's Cube, and Cabbage Patch dolls.

NO PHYSICAL PERISHABILITY   Products with a short physical life have only a limited window available for their disposition. This applies not only to most food items but also to a wide variety of other goods such as photographic film. If your product is perishable, your business concept must include some method of selling your inventory quickly or a contingency plan to dispose of aged merchandise before it spoils.

IMPERVIOUS TO WEATHER CONDITIONS   Some businesses are, by their very nature, at the mercy of the weather. If the weather is right for them, they prosper; if not, they may go broke. Pity the ski resort owner without any snow, the waterslide operator with a year of unseasonably cold weather, the beach concession during a summer of constant rain, the market gardener in the midst of an unexpected drought. The ideal business would not be impacted by these unpredictable changes in the weather.

POSSESSES SOME PROPRIETARY RIGHTS   The ideal business would possess significant proprietary rights that give it some unique characteristic and protection against competition. These rights can be in the form of registered patents, trademarks, copyrighted material, protected trade secrets, licensing agreements that provide some sort of exclusive manufacturing arrangements, or perhaps rights for exclusive distribution of certain products in particular markets. Gendis Corporation, for example, was largely built on the rights to distribute first Papermate pens and then Sony products in Canada on an exclusive basis.

Of the ideas that you have generated you might want to pick three and evaluate each of them against the factors described in the Buskirk model in Figure 3.1. This evaluation will illustrate how well these ideas fit with all the characteristics of the "ideal" business. How would you rate each idea on each of Buskirk's 19 factors? On the basis of this evaluation, which of these ideas do you feel represents the most significant new venture opportunity for you? Can you justify your response? Did the idea you picked score less than five on any of Buskirk's factors? If so, can you think of any way to overcome the situation or find other solutions to the problem?

For a more formal evaluation of an invention, software concept, or other innovative idea, the Canadian Innovation Centre will conduct a comprehensive assessment to assist you in the decisions you must make regarding your idea. For more information, contact Canadian Innovation Centre, 1A-490 Dutton Dr., Waterloo, Ontario N2L 6H7; phone 1-800-265-4559 or (519) 885-5870 (www.innovationcentre.ca).

FIGURE 3.1   COMPARE YOUR IDEAS TO THE "IDEAL" BUSINESS

Directions: Evaluate your concept in comparison with a model business by indicating how well each of the ideal characteristics below applies to your concept. Use a scale from 1 to 10, where 1 means the ideal trait is not at all true for your concept, and 10 means it is perfectly true.

FIT WITH MODEL BUSINESS

Requires no investment	1	2	3	4	5	6	7	8	9	10
Has a recognized, measurable market	1	2	3	4	5	6	7	8	9	10
A perceived need for the product or service	1	2	3	4	5	6	7	8	9	10
A dependable source of supply for required inputs	1	2	3	4	5	6	7	8	9	10
No government regulation	1	2	3	4	5	6	7	8	9	10
Requires no labour	1	2	3	4	5	6	7	8	9	10
Provides 100 per cent gross margin	1	2	3	4	5	6	7	8	9	10
Buyers purchase frequently	1	2	3	4	5	6	7	8	9	10
Receives favourable tax treatment	1	2	3	4	5	6	7	8	9	10
Has a receptive, established distribution system	1	2	3	4	5	6	7	8	9	10
Has great publicity value	1	2	3	4	5	6	7	8	9	10
Customers pay in advance	1	2	3	4	5	6	7	8	9	10
No risk of product liability	1	2	3	4	5	6	7	8	9	10
No technical obsolescence	1	2	3	4	5	6	7	8	9	10
No competition	1	2	3	4	5	6	7	8	9	10
No fashion obsolescence	1	2	3	4	5	6	7	8	9	10
No physical perishability	1	2	3	4	5	6	7	8	9	10
Impervious to weather conditions	1	2	3	4	5	6	7	8	9	10
Possesses some proprietary rights	1	2	3	4	5	6	7	8	9	10

Total points =
160–190 = A concept; 130–159 = B; 110–129 = C; 80–109 = D; Below 80, drop concept.

After completing this evaluation, does it make sense to proceed with the venture?
Explain your answer.

STEP 6: FOCUS ON THE MOST PROMISING OPPORTUNITIES

Which of the ideas you have evaluated seems to be the best fit with the "ideal" business and is most consistent with your goals and values? This is probably the one you should be looking to pursue. However, no matter how exhaustive your evaluation, there is no guarantee of success. The challenge is to do the best you can in conducting an assessment of each of your principal ideas, knowing that at some point you will have to make a decision with incomplete information and less than scientific accuracy. As a good friend of mine commented during a dinner speech not long ago, "Entrepreneurship is like bungee jumping. Both require an act of faith."

DECIDING HOW TO PROCEED

Once satisfied you have identified an idea that represents a significant business opportunity, you must determine the best way to proceed. There are all sorts of *entry strategies* — ways people start new enterprises.

Reflecting on these alternatives and judging how they fit with your specific idea and your particular abilities and circumstances will enable you to turn them into real opportunities. No general rules have been developed to guarantee success, or even to indicate which concepts and strategies will work best in different situations, but being aware of the possibilities will give you a clearer picture of the job you need to do to succeed.

BUY A BUSINESS

One possibility is to find a business presently operating in your area of interest, buy it, and take over its operations. You may want to buy the business either because it is already quite successful but the current owners want to get out for some reason, or because the business is not doing very well under the current owners and you feel you can turn it around.

This can be a good entry strategy. A good deal of time and effort are involved in the start-up phase of any business. This stage can be bypassed when you buy a going concern. You also acquire a location, customers, established trade relationships, and a number of other positive elements.

These advantages don't come for free, however. Buying an existing business may cost you more than getting into a similar business on your own. The current owner may expect to receive "goodwill" for certain assets already acquired or the effort devoted to the business so far. You may also inherit some problem, such as obsolete equipment, the bad image and reputation of the previous owners, or labour difficulties.

For a more complete discussion of this entry strategy, refer to Stage Four of this book.

ACQUIRE A FRANCHISE

Another alternative is to buy the rights to operate a business that has been designed and developed by someone else, i.e., to acquire a *franchise*. Under a franchise agreement, an established company, the *franchisor*, with one or more successful businesses operating in other locations, provides assistance to a new firm in breaking into the marketplace. In return, the new owner, or *franchisee*, pays a fee for the assistance, invests money to set up and operate the business, pays a percentage of sales as a royalty to the franchisor, and agrees to operate the business within the terms and conditions laid out in the franchise agreement.

The assistance provided by the franchisor can take many forms, such as:

- The right to use the franchisor's brand names and registered trademarks
- The right to sell products and services developed by the franchisor
- The right to use operating systems and procedures developed by the franchisor
- Training in how to run the business
- Plans for the layout of the business facilities and the provision of specialized equipment
- A regional or national advertising program
- Centralized purchasing and volume discounts
- Research and development support

While the failure rate of franchised businesses is reported to be lower than that for independently established firms, there are a number of disadvantages associated with the concept.

For more detailed information, refer to Stage Five of this book.

START A BUSINESS OF YOUR OWN

The third and probably most common means of getting into business for yourself is to start a business of your own from scratch. This is the route most frequently travelled by the true entrepreneur who wants a business that is really his or her own creation. Starting your own business can take many forms and involve a variety of entry strategies. While we are unable to discuss all the possibilities here in any detail, a few alternatives will be mentioned to get you thinking about their fit with your particular situation. Some of the possibilities available for you are:

1. Develop an entirely new product or service unlike anything else available in the market.
2. Acquire the rights to manufacture or sell someone else's product or use someone else's name or logo under licence. These rights could be exclusive to a product category, a geographic area, or a specific market.
3. Find a customer who wants to buy something. Then create a business to make that sale or serve that need.
4. Take a hobby and develop it into a business.
5. Develop a product or service similar to those currently on the market but that is more convenient, less expensive, safer, cleaner, faster, easier to use, lighter, stronger, more compact, or has some other important, distinguishing attribute.

6. Add incremental value to a product or service already available by putting it through another production process, combining it with other products and services, or providing it as one element in a larger package.

7. Become an agent or distributor for products or services produced by someone else. These may be domestically produced or imported from other countries.

8. Open a trading house or become a selling agent for Canadian firms who may be interested in selling their products or services abroad.

9. Develop a consulting service or provide information to other people in a subject area you know very well.

10. Become a supplier to another producer or large institutional customer. Large organizations require an extensive range of raw materials, supplies, and components to run their business. A small portion of their requirements could represent a significant volume of sales for you. This type of "outsourcing" is an excellent opportunity to pursue either through a contract or a strategic alliance with a larger organization.

11. Identify a situation where another firm has dropped what may be profitable products or product lines. They may have abandoned customer groups or market segments that are uneconomic for them to serve effectively but that may still be quite lucrative for a smaller company.

12. Borrow an idea from one industry or market and transfer it to another. A product or service that has been well accepted in one situation may well represent a substantial opportunity in other circumstances as well.

13. Look for opportunities to capitalize on special events and situations or unusual occurrences. You may be able to "piggyback" your business onto these situations.

Video Case #3

Java Nook

Summary

When considering a new business idea there is a lot to consider. When Annette Levigne thought of opening a coffee shop, she jumped right in and didn't try to assess long-term implications, strategy, total launch costs, etc. She found that getting the idea and choosing a name is the easy part of starting a business.

Questions for Discussion

1. Where did Levigne get her business idea? Where else can business ideas come from?

2. Levigne is the mother of six and very busy. Did she have too much going on in her personal life to start a new business? What could she have done to make things run more smoothly?

3. How can you accurately estimate start-up costs? Is it better to be optimistic or pessimistic in your estimates?

4. Should the Java Nook have expanded three weeks into its operation? What are some pros and cons of expanding so quickly?

Buying a Business

Stages Two and Three of this book have provided you with a means of evaluating your personal potential for an entrepreneurial career and a procedure for generating and evaluating the basic attractiveness of an idea on which to base your own business. The obvious route to self-employment is to start a business of your own based on this idea. Another route that should be explored is that of buying an existing firm. For many people this may even be their preferred course of action. How do you decide which route to take?

Stage Four discusses the various aspects that should be evaluated in considering whether you should start a new business or buy an existing one.

ADVANTAGES AND DISADVANTAGES OF BUYING AN EXISTING BUSINESS

The case for buying an existing firm, as against setting up a new one of your own, is not clear-cut either way. Each situation must be decided on its merits. There are distinct advantages and disadvantages to each course of action. You must consider how well your personal preferences fit into each of these options.

REASONS FOR BUYING AN ESTABLISHED BUSINESS

Here are some reasons why one *should* consider buying an established business:

1. Buying an existing business can reduce the risk. The existing business is already a proven entity. And it is often easier to obtain financing for an established operation than for a new one.
2. Acquiring a "going concern" with a good past history increases the likelihood of a successful operation for the new owner.
3. The established business has a proven location for successful operation.
4. The established firm already has a product or service that is presently being produced, distributed, and sold.
5. A clientele has already been developed for the product or service of the existing company.
6. Financial relationships have already been established with banks, trade creditors, and other sources of financial support.
7. The equipment needed for production is already available and its limitations and capabilities are known in advance.
8. An existing firm can often be acquired at a good price. The owner may be forced to sell the operation at a low price relative to the value of the assets in the business.

DISADVANTAGES OF BUYING AN ESTABLISHED BUSINESS

Here are some reasons why one may decide not to buy an existing business:

1. The physical facilities (the building and equipment) and product line may be old and obsolete.
2. Union/management relationships may be poor.
3. Present personnel may be unproductive and have a poor track record.

BUYING A BUSINESS

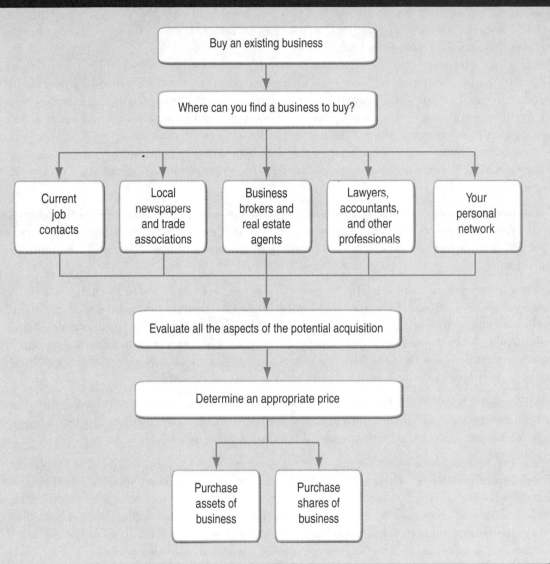

Buy an existing business

↓

Where can you find a business to buy?

- Current job contacts
- Local newspapers and trade associations
- Business brokers and real estate agents
- Lawyers, accountants, and other professionals
- Your personal network

↓

Evaluate all the aspects of the potential acquisition

↓

Determine an appropriate price

- Purchase assets of business
- Purchase shares of business

4. The inventory may contain a large amount of "dead" stock.

5. A high percentage of the assets may be in poor-quality accounts receivable.

6. The location of the business may be bad.

7. The financial condition of the business, and its relationships with financial institutions, may be poor.

8. As a buyer, you inherit any ill will that may exist toward the established firm among customers or suppliers.

9. As an entrepreneur, you have more freedom of choice in defining the nature of the business if you start one of your own than if you purchase an existing firm.

As you can see, there are both pluses and minuses in choosing to acquire an established business. You should view this option in terms of whether it will enable you to achieve your personal objectives. How do these advantages/disadvantages compare with those of starting a new business of your own? In buying an existing business do you see a reasonable opportunity to succeed? No one else can really advise you what to do. Instead, you must "do your own thing" and match the alternatives with your abilities and interests.

HOW TO FIND THE RIGHT BUSINESS TO BUY

Just finding a business to buy is easy. Dozens are listed every day in the "Business Opportunities" classified section of your local newspaper as well as the major business newspapers. However, what tends to be found in these classified sections are mostly hotel, motel, restaurant, and franchise propositions, which are largely high-risk, low-profit ventures generally unattractive to investors. Many of these are failing businesses that their current owners are trying to unload.

Seeking out a business acquisition to match your desires and experiences can be a very time-consuming and difficult process. Hundreds of businesses change hands every year, so it should be possible to find one that appeals to you if you are sufficiently determined and persistent. However, rather than being sold as a result of an advertisement in some newspaper, most businesses are sold to people who had some active business relationship with the company when it became available. It is usually not sufficient for an individual determined to acquire a business to sit and wait for the right opportunity to come along. You must go looking.

There are basically five different sources through which you may obtain information regarding attractive companies to buy:

1. **Your present business activity** Acquisition candidates may include present or potential competitors of your current employer, suppliers, customers, and perhaps even your present employer. These situations probably provide the best match between your experience and strengths and the unique requirements of the business.

2. **Direct independent contact** This may involve making "cold calls" on firms that look good or in which you have an interest; such firms may be identified from Chamber of Commerce directories and trade association membership lists. Another way is to place "Acquisition Wanted" advertisements in several major newspapers. In addition, despite what has been said earlier, you may wish to follow up on some advertisements in the "Business Opportunities" section of the major financial papers. Every now and then an advertisement may appear in these sections that would warrant your consideration.

3. **Middlemen** These include business brokers and commercial real estate agents. These individuals are professionals who work at bringing buyers and sellers together for a commission. The commission, typically payable by the seller, varies with the size of the deal but may be as high as 10 per cent of the negotiated purchase price.

4. **Confidential advisors** These include the loans officer at your bank, securities brokers, professional accountants, and lawyers. These advisors are often aware of what businesses are or may soon be available for sale. These sources may be difficult to use, however, because their information is shared mostly with other clients with whom they have developed some relationship over time. In many cases it may be necessary for you to have gained the confidence of the source over an extended period.

5. **Other sources** These include venture capital firms, personal friends and acquaintances, and insurance brokers and agents. Essentially you should consider all individuals within your personal network of business contacts who may have access to information on attractive businesses for sale. This requires letting many of these people know about your search and the kind of business for which you are looking. You will need to keep reminding them about your interest, so that when the information comes along there is a good probability that it will make its way back to you. This was how Jim Iredale came to buy Ware House Hobbies (Entrepreneurs in Action #13).

Which of these sources you should utilize depends on many factors, such as the time you have available, whom you know within the business community, and the kind of company you are looking for. You should experiment with each of these sources and decide on the one or two that work best for you.

IMPORTANT FACTORS TO CONSIDER

An essential requirement for the successful purchase of an existing firm is knowing how to assess and evaluate the operation. This is a complicated process, so you are well advised to have professionals such as an accountant, lawyer, or business evaluator assist you in negotiations when considering buying a business. As a potential buyer, you should also have a good understanding of the nature of the target business and the

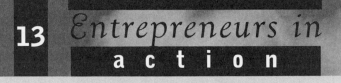

13 *Entrepreneurs in* action

Model Railroader Makes Tracks

Jim Iredale is what you might call an entrepreneur by chance.

Three years ago, Iredale was holding down a regular nine-to-five job as a Winnipeg accountant/comptroller when the owner of a hobby shop he frequented — Ware House Hobbies — mentioned that he was looking for someone to buy his business.

Although he'd never harboured any entrepreneurial aspirations, the avid model railroader said he became intrigued by the notion of owning his own hobby shop.

He also realized that after 13 years as an accountant/comptroller, he was growing tired of just working with numbers. He wanted to work with people, too.

So after kicking the idea around for a couple of months, Iredale took the plunge. He quit his job, bought Ware House Hobbies, and he and his wife, Bev, became full-time small-business operators. "This was a situation that could not easily be repeated. It was the right opportunity at the right time."

Iredale said he's also surprised at how well the business has done.

"I thought I was buying a small, sleepy little business and that appealed to me," he said. "But it didn't turn out to be a slow, sleepy business at all. It's very busy."

So busy, in fact, that earlier this month he and Bev moved the store into larger quarters at 1870 Portage Ave. They've also hired a part-time helper.

The new store is twice the size of the old one, and gives them more room to display the more than 5,000 model railroad-related items they keep in stock. It also gives them room to expand their mail-order operations and their doll houses and miniatures department.

On the mail-order front, Iredale said, although the bulk of the orders come from rural Manitoba, Saskatchewan and northwestern Ontario, the shop also regularly receives orders from as far as B.C. and the Northwest Territories.

In fact, mail-order sales now account for about 20 per cent of the shop's total sales, he added.

WAYNE GLOWACKI/WINNIPEG FREE PRESS. REPRINTED WITH PERMISSION.

"I'm not making as much money as I used to make as an accountant," he conceded. "But there are other rewards. I like my lifestyle a lot better."

Source: Murray, McNeill, "Model Railroader Makes Tracks After Turning Hobby Into Career," © *Winnipeg Free Press*, October 22, 1996, p. B1. Reprinted with permission.

industry in which it competes to be able to assess its future performance, strengths, weaknesses, unexploited market opportunities, and other factors. Learning about a business after the fact can be a sure recipe for failure. A number of basic factors must be considered in determining the value of the business to you. Some of these are more complex and involved than others, but each one must be carefully investigated and studied. The most important of these concerns are discussed below.

WHY IS THE BUSINESS FOR SALE?

You should have this question in mind at all times during the evaluation of a possible acquisition. When the owner of a business decides to dispose of it, the reason presented to the public may be somewhat different from the facts of the situation. Owners may be quite willing to express some reasons for wanting to sell their businesses. They wish to retire, or they want to move to another city, or illness is pressuring the owner to leave the business. But there are a number of others that the current owner may not be quite so likely to volunteer. For example, the owner may be experiencing family pressures or marital problems, or perhaps the owner sees a better business opportunity somewhere else. None of these reasons is cause for concern. But what if the company needs more financing than the owner can raise, or the current market for the firm's products is depressed? What if competitors are moving in with more effective products or methods, or the current plant and equipment is worn out or obsolete, and the firm is no longer able to compete successfully? And what if the firm is having to contend with new government regulations that are creating some difficulties, or certain key employees are leaving the firm to set up a similar business of their own?

As you can see, there are many possible reasons why a business may be up for sale. It is important that you retain a sceptical attitude, because behind each of the offered explanations may be a number of hidden ones. A sceptical attitude forces you to examine the situation from all angles and not necessarily accept at face value everything you are told. When the real reasons for selling are factors that may lead to the eventual collapse of the company, the present owner may be hard-pressed to justify your purchase of the enterprise.

This is not to say that all businesses for sale are bad buys. Many companies are sold for very plausible and honest reasons. However, to keep from losing your shirt as well as your savings, a detailed evaluation should be conducted to determine the true character of the business.

FINANCIAL FACTORS

An analysis of the financial statements of the firm being sold, preferably with the help of a professional account-ant, can help you assess its current health. You should not fall into the trap, however, of accepting these state-ments as the absolute truth. Even in those situations where the statements have been audited, many accounting techniques allow business owners to present a less than accurate picture of the financial situation of their company. You must be careful to ensure that the statements have not been biased in favour of the seller.

The most important financial factors are: (1) the trend in profits, (2) ratio analysis, (3) the value of the business's tangible assets, (4) the value of the business's intangible assets, and (5) cash flow. Let us discuss each in turn.

THE TREND IN PROFITS

A study of the records of the business will indicate whether sales volume and profits have been increasing or decreasing. If they have been going up, it is useful to know which departments within the business, or products within the firm's product line, have accounted for this increased sales and/or profitability.

If sales and profits are declining, the question may arise as to whether this is due to a failure by the firm to keep up with the competition, to its inability to adjust to changing circumstances, or perhaps to a lack of selling effort. Some experience with this type of business situation, plus a few questions directed to appropriate sources, may elicit an explanation.

RATIO ANALYSIS

For every size and type of business there are certain financial ratios that have become generally accepted as reasonable for that kind of operation. Some information on these ratios is collected and published by trade organizations and associations such as the National Retail Hardware Association or the National Association of Retail Grocers. Ratios have also been developed by various manufacturers for use by retailers that handle their product lines. Ratios for firms in a wide variety of retail, service, and manufacturing sectors are pub-lished by Dun & Bradstreet (www.dnb.com), the Risk Management Association (formerly Robert Morris Associates) (www.rmahq.org), and other companies. Industry Canada, as part of its Performance Plus Small-Business Profiles Web site (sme.ic.gc.ca), can provide information as well. A study of the ratios of any busi-ness offered for sale, compared with standard ratios for that industry and size of company, will quickly indicate any discrepancies. These discrepancies may be due to mismanagement, neglect, carelessness, or perhaps even the lack of appropriate financing. The most frequently considered ratios are:

1. **Current ratio** The current ratio is defined as current assets divided by current liabilities. It is a measure of short-term solvency. Current assets normally include cash, marketable securities, accounts receivable, and inventories. Current liabilities consist of accounts payable, short-term notes payable, income taxes payable, and accrued expenses. A general rule of thumb is that a current ratio of 2:1 could be considered satisfactory for a typical manufacturing business. Service firms typically have a lower ratio, since they tend

to have less inventory. However, as with any rule of thumb, extreme care should be exercised in evaluating this ratio. A cash-poor firm may be unable to pay its bills even though its ratio appears to be acceptable. On the other hand, many businesses with a current ratio less than the rule of thumb are quite solvent.

Too high a ratio can indicate the business is not utilizing its cash and other liquid assets very efficiently; too low a ratio may raise questions about the firm's ability to meet its short-term obligations. In practice, however, what is more important than the absolute level of the current ratio is how the ratio is changing over time. An improving current ratio would tend to indicate improved short-term financial solvency unless the business is building up excessive or obsolete inventories.

$$\text{Current Ratio} = \frac{\text{Current Assets}}{\text{Current Liabilities}}$$

2. **Quick ratio** The quick ratio is obtained by dividing current liabilities into current assets minus inventories. The quick ratio can be used to estimate the ability of a firm to pay off its short-term obligations without having to sell its inventory. Inventories tend to lose their value faster than other assets if disposed of in a hurry. The quick ratio is probably a more valid test of the firm's ability to meet its current liabilities and pay its bills than the current ratio.

$$\text{Quick Ratio} = \frac{\text{Current Assets} - \text{Inventories}}{\text{Current Liabilities}}$$

3. **Debt to net worth** The debt-to-net-worth ratio indicates the firm's obligations to its creditors relative to the owner's level of investment in the business. Debt includes current liabilities, long-term loans, bonds, and deferred payments; the owner's net worth includes the value of common stock, preferred stock, any capital surplus, and retained earnings. Any outstanding shareholders' loans to the business should be considered part of the owner's net worth rather than as part of the business's present debt. This ratio is commonly used by creditors to assess the risk involved in lending to the firm. For example, if the debt-to-net-worth ratio is too high, say about 2:1 or 3:1, you may find it difficult to borrow additional funds for the business. Too low a ratio, on the other hand, may indicate the business is not being operated very efficiently and some profits are being sacrificed.

$$\text{Debt-to-Net-Worth Ratio} = \frac{\text{Total Outstanding Current and Long-Term Debt}}{\text{Net Worth}}$$

4. **Gross profit to sales** This ratio is determined by dividing gross profit or gross margin by net sales. Gross profit is determined by deducting costs of goods sold from net sales. No general guidelines exist for this ratio, or even among companies within an industry, as it can vary substantially.

$$\text{Gross-Profit-to-Sales Ratio} = \frac{\text{Gross Profit}}{\text{Net Sales}}$$

5. **Net profit to sales** This ratio is calculated by dividing net profit by net sales. You may use net profit either before or after taxes. As with the previous ratio, no general guidelines exist because of the variability among companies and industries. This figure can be as low as 1 per cent or less for retail food stores and supermarkets, and as high as 8 or 9 per cent in some service sectors.

However, you might evaluate how these ratios compare with those of other, similar companies or how they have been changing over time. If the ratio has recently been declining, why? This may indicate that the firm's costs have been increasing without a commensurate increase in prices, or perhaps competition may have increased and the company is forced to keep its prices low in order to compete.

$$\text{Net-Profit-to-Sales Ratio} = \frac{\text{Net Profit (Before or After Taxes)}}{\text{Net Sales}}$$

6. **Return on assets** This ratio is determined by dividing net profit (before or after taxes) by total assets. It is an excellent indicator of whether all the firm's assets are contributing to its profits and how effectively the assets are being employed — the real test of economic success or failure. Unfortunately, this is not an easy ratio to apply, because it is a measure of the movement of assets in relation to sales and profits during a particular period of time. The methods used by accountants to determine the level of total assets in the business can have a great effect on this ratio, and there are no real general or convenient rules of thumb for finding out whether the current return on assets is acceptable.

$$\text{Return on Assets} = \frac{\text{Net Profit (Before or After Taxes)}}{\text{Total Assets}}$$

7. **Sales to inventory** This ratio is determined by dividing annual net sales by the average value of inventories. This does not indicate actual physical turnover since inventories are usually valued at cost while sales are based on selling prices, including markups, but this ratio does provide a reasonable yardstick for comparing stock-to-sales ratios of one business with another or with the average values for the industry.

$$\text{Sales-to-Inventory Ratio} = \frac{\text{Net Sales}}{(\text{Beginning Inventory} + \text{Ending Inventory})/2}$$

8. **Collection period** To determine the average collection period for the business's outstanding accounts receivable, annual net sales are divided by 365 days to determine the business's average daily credit sales. These average daily credit sales are then divided into accounts receivable to obtain the average collection period. This ratio is helpful in assessing the collectability of any outstanding receivables.

$$\text{Average Collection Period} = \frac{\text{Accounts Receivable}}{\text{Net Sales}/365}$$

All these ratios are calculated from information on the firm's income statement or balance sheet. Figures 4.1 and 4.2 illustrate simplified financial statements for a hypothetical firm called The Campbell Co. The value of each of these ratios for that company would be as follows:

1. Current ratio $= \dfrac{\$158,000}{\$95,000} = 1.66$

2. Quick ratio $= \dfrac{\$78,000}{\$95,000} = 0.82$

3. Debt to net worth $= \dfrac{\$135,000}{\$50,000} = 2.70$

4. Gross profit to sales $= \dfrac{\$133,000}{\$425,000} = 0.31$ or 31%

5. Net profit to sales $= \dfrac{\$13,500}{\$425,000} = 0.03$ or 3%

6. Return on assets $= \dfrac{\$13,500}{\$185,000} = 0.07$ or 7%

7. Sales-to-inventory ratio $= \dfrac{\$425,000}{(\$75,000 + 80,000)/2} = 5.48$

8. Average collection period $= \dfrac{\$53,000}{\$425,000/365} = 45$ days

It would appear from these ratios that The Campbell Co. is in reasonably sound shape financially. Its debt-to-net-worth ratio is within acceptable limits and the business is quite solvent, as indicated by the current and quick ratios. The other ratios are more difficult to evaluate, but they would be quite acceptable for firms in many lines of business.

To illustrate the range of possible values for each of these ratios, some typical examples for Canadian companies in a number of industries are shown in Table 4.1. Notice that there can be considerable variation in the value of each ratio within economic sectors as well as between sectors. Within a sector these ratios represent an average for each industry code and, therefore, may be somewhat misleading. These figures include a range of firms, some of which may be doing extremely well and others that may be on the verge of bankruptcy. The variations from sector to sector are largely due to structural differences that impact the financial profile of firms in each line of business in quite different ways.

This data as well as other detailed financial and employment data on small businesses by industry in Canada is available from the Performance Plus Small-Business Profiles database of Industry Canada at sme.ic.gc.ca. These profiles are usually produced every two years, with 2000 being the most current available. These data can provide performance benchmarks for the financial planning of both start-up and established businesses.

FIGURE 4.1   EXAMPLE OF SIMPLIFIED BALANCE SHEET

THE CAMPBELL CO. BALANCE SHEET
AS OF DECEMBER 31, 200Y

ASSETS (000s)

Current Assets
Cash		$ 25
Accounts receivable		53
Inventory		80
Total current assets		$ 158 (A)

Fixed Assets
Machinery	$ 40	
Less: Accumulated depreciation	25	15
Equipment and fixtures	30	
Less: Accumulated depreciation	18	12
Total fixed assets		27 (B)
Total Assets (C = A + B)		**$185 (C)**

LIABILITIES AND OWNER'S EQUITY

Current Liabilities*
Accounts payable	$ 60	
Notes payable	35	
Total current liabilities		95

Long-Term Liabilities
Notes payable†	$ 40	
Total long-term liabilities		40
Total liabilities		$135 (D)

OWNER'S EQUITY
Capital investment		20
Retained earnings		30
Total owner's equity		50 (E)
Total Liabilities and Owner's Equity (F = D + E)		**$185 (F)**

*Debt is due within 12 months.
†Debt is due after 1 year.

FIGURE 4.2   EXAMPLE OF SIMPLIFIED INCOME STATEMENT

THE CAMPBELL CO.
INCOME STATEMENT
FOR YEAR ENDING DECEMBER 31, 200Y

(000s)

Gross sales	$428		
Less: Returns	3		
Net Sales		**$425**	**(A)**
Cost of goods sold:			
Beginning inventory	$ 75		
Plus: Net purchases	297		
Cost of goods available	372		
Less: Ending inventory	80		
Cost of Goods Sold		292	**(B)**
Gross Profit (C = A − B)		$133	**(C)**
Selling Expenses		$ 29	**(D)**
Administrative expenses:			
Office salaries	$ 60		
Interest	9		
Depreciation	10		
Other administrative expenses	7		
Total Administrative Expenses		86	**(E)**
Profit Before Income Tax (F = C − D − E)		$ 18	**(F)**
Income Tax (G = 25% of F)		4.5	**(G)**
Net Profit (G = F − G)		$ 13.5	**(H)**

Keep in mind that financial ratios are open to wide interpretation and should be relied on to get only a general perspective of the relative financial health of the business, to measure the financial progress of the business from one time period to another, or to flag major deviations from an industry or sector norm.

VALUE OF TANGIBLE ASSETS

In assessing the balance sheet of the prospective acquisition, you must determine the actual or real value of the tangible assets. A physical count of the inventory must be taken to determine if the actual level corresponds to the level stated on the balance sheet. This inventory must also be appraised in terms of its age, quality, saleability, style, condition, balance, freshness, etc. Most large inventories will have some obsolescence. You must determine whether the present inventory is consistent with current market conditions. Also, take care that the seller does not sell this inventory after you have checked it. Any consignment goods in inventory should be clearly identified as well. This evaluation is best performed by someone with considerable experience in the industry involved. Perhaps you can hire the services of the owner of a similar but non-competing firm to assist you in this appraisal.

You must also check the age of any outstanding accounts receivable. Some businesses continue to carry accounts receivable on their books that should have been charged off as bad debts, resulting in an overstatement of the firm's profit and value. Generally, the older the receivables, the lower their value. Old outstanding accounts may reveal a slack credit policy by the present owner. These old accounts will have to be discounted in determining the present value of the business.

The fixed assets of the business must also be scrutinized. You should determine if the furniture, fixtures, equipment, and building are stated at their market or depreciated value. Some questions you should ask include: How modern are these assets? Are they in operating condition? How much will it cost to keep these assets in operation? Are the assets all paid for? You must be aware of any liens or chattel mortgages that may

| TABLE 4.1 | KEY BUSINESS RATIOS IN CANADA — CORPORATIONS | | | | | | | |

SIC Category	Line of Business	I Current Ratio (Times)	III Debt/ Net Worth (Times)	IV Gross Profit/ Sales (%)	V Net Profit/ Sales (%)	VI Return on Assets (%)	VII Sales to Inventory (Times)	VIII Collection Period (Days)
Z0000	TOTAL ALL INDUSTRIES	1.3	3.3	33.7	3.1	6.2	12.5	39.4
J0000	RETAIL TRADE	1.5	3.1	19.1	1.0	4.9	7.0	14.9
J6511	Book & Stationery Stores	1.4	2.4	19.6	1.6	6.4	5.4	17.9
J6130	Women's Clothing Stores	1.3	4.1	22.5	0.8	4.7	5.6	13.2
J6520	Florists, Lawn and							
	Garden Centres	1.2	—	25.3	1.1	7.4	9.4	22.2
J6230	Household Furnishing Stores	1.3	4.4	22.0	0.9	4.1	4.9	15.3
J6110	Shoe Stores	1.7	7.0	22.8	—	—	2.8	3.8
	FOOD AND BEVERAGE							
Q9200	SERVICES	1.0	16.0	33.1	-0.8	1.1	53.9	5.1
Q9221	Taverns, Bars and Night Clubs	0.9	7.2	34.8	0.8	5.7	37.2	5.2
Q9211	Restaurants, Licensed	1.0	34.9	31.0	0.4	3.7	52.6	4.4
Q9212	Restaurants, Unlicensed	1.0	12.4	37.0	-6.7	-8.4	50.2	—
I0000	WHOLESALE TRADE	1.5	2.8	17.5	1.9	5.5	7.9	49.2
I5210	Food	1.3	2.2	12.8	1.3	4.7	18.1	31.9
I5610	Metal and Metal Products	1.4	0.9	25.0	6.5	11.6	10.6	46.0
I5110	Petroleum Products	1.3	4.1	16.9	3.1	8.9	28.0	48.8
E0000	MANUFACTURERS	1.4	2.3	24.2	3.3	7.1	9.2	56.8
E1070	Bakery Products	1.3	7.5	23.2	1.3	5.8	17.5	15.6
E2440	Women's Clothing	1.4	12.6	18.7	—	—	15.5	50.9
E1030	Fruit and Vegtable Industries	1.8	1.4	21.3	—	—	2.4	49.6
E3070	Heating Equipment	2.2	0.6	23.7	—	—	5.2	71.7
E3090	Other Metal Fabricating	1.6	1.7	25.8	5.4	10.2	11.3	63.5
E2512	Sawmill and Planing Mill							
	Products	2.0	1.5	21.1	4.0	9.9	4.4	43.7
F0000	CONSTRUCTION INDUSTRIES	1.5	7.4	25.6	2.6	5.1	9.6	47.6
F4010	Residential Building	1.4	-7.9	14.4	1.4	3.2	5.0	32.3
M0000	BUSINESS SERVICES	1.1	2.0	45.7	7.7	10.5	226.3	62.0
R9730	Funeral Services	1.0	2.5	60.2	8.3	4.4	95.8	47.8
Q9111	Hotels and Motor Hotels	0.6	—	48.8	1.8	5.6	69.7	6.9
R9650	Sports and Recreation Clubs	1.0	4.4	52.8	-0.8	2.6	24.0	21.5
G0000	TRANSPORTATION AND							
	STORAGE	1.1	2.7	58.4	3.4	8.0	356.3	39.2
H4811	Radio Broadcasting	1.0	1.5	50.6	2.9	4.9	—	77.8
G4581	Taxicab Industry	1.1	1.8	55.2	1.6	4.1	—	26.2
G4560	Truck Transport	1.0	3.0	59.1	3.0	8.4	781.5	37.1

Source: Key Business Ratios in Canada — Corporations: Calculations partially based on data from the Industry Canada Performance Plus Web site (strategis.ic.gc.ca/epic/internet/inpp-pp.nsf/en/h_pm00000e.html), accessed January 10, 2004.

have been placed against these assets. This pledging of assets to secure a debt is a normal business practice; however, you should know about any such mortgages. Other liabilities such as unpaid bills, back taxes, back pay to employees, and so on, may be hidden; you must be aware of the possibility of their existence, and contract with the seller that all claims not shown on the balance sheet will be assumed by him or her.

VALUE OF INTANGIBLE ASSETS

In addition to the more obvious physical goods and equipment, certain intangible assets may also have a real value to a prospective purchaser. Among the most important of these are goodwill; franchise and licensing rights; and patents, trademarks, and copyrights.

You must be very realistic in determining what you can afford or are prepared to pay for goodwill. Is the public's present attitude toward the business a valuable asset that is worth money, or is it a liability? Typically, few businesses that are for sale have much goodwill value. Is any goodwill associated with the business personal to the owner or largely commercial due to the location, reputation, and other characteristics of the business? If largely personal, this goodwill may not be transferable to a new owner, so you should not pay very much for it. Many business owners, however, often have very unrealistic and inflated ideas of the goodwill associated with their business because they have built it up over the years with their own "sweat equity" and, therefore, are not very objective. So you should be careful, and talk to customers, suppliers, neighbours, employees, and perhaps even competitors, to determine if this level of goodwill does actually exist.

In fact, quite often things are not always as they appear. When Jeanne Lawrence bought what she thought was a reputable and thriving fashion design business and retail store, she expected business to carry on as usual. It was only after she had taken over the firm that she discovered the company's once reputable name had become tarnished in the past year. She was bombarded with a litany of customer-service complaints ranging from poor workmanship, to ill-fitting clothing, to people who had paid in full for work that hadn't been done. The situation was so bad she was spending all the money she was taking in on new business repairing the damage that had been done before she took over the company. Eventually Lawrence realized that she could repair the merchandise that had been sold before she took over but she couldn't repair the reputation of the business, so she changed the name (Entrepreneurs in Action #14).

If franchise, licensing, or other rights are involved in the business, you should make certain that you understand the terms and conditions associated with such rights, and that these rights will be transferred to you on acquisition of the company. An effort should also be made to determine the market value of any patents, trademarks, or copyrights the company may hold, and make sure these are part of the sale — i.e., do not remain with the current owner on completion of the transaction.

CASH FLOW

You must also observe the cash flows generated by the operation. A business can be very profitable but chronically low in cash due to overly generous credit terms, excessive inventory levels, or heavy fixed-interest payments. You must assure yourself that on your entry into the business you will have sufficient inflows of cash to meet your cash outflow requirements. Constant cash problems can indicate that the business is possibly being run by ineffective management or that the firm's resources have generally been badly allocated. You must ask yourself if you have the know-how to overcome this misallocation of resources. If the firm's cash flow is very low and the long-term debt is quite high, the business may be eating up its capital to pay the debt, or possibly defaulting on its debt. If you are to contend with such issues, you may have to increase the firm's debt or be prepared to invest more capital in the business to ease the cash flow problem.

MARKETING CONSIDERATIONS

The previous section dealt with the internal aspects of the firm's profitability; there has been no discussion of the external determinants of these conditions. But you must be concerned with analyzing markets, customers, competition, and various other aspects of the company's operating environment.

You must carefully examine the company's current market situation. Each market segment served by the firm must be analyzed and understood. Studying maps, customer lists, traffic patterns, and other factors can help you to determine the normal market size for the business. Once the market and its various segments are understood, the composition of these segments should be determined to identify the approximate number of customers in the total market. As a buyer, you should be concerned with:

1. The company's trading area
2. Population demographics
3. The trend and size of the market

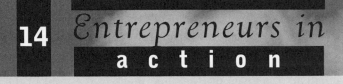

14 Entrepreneurs in action

Buyer Beware Doesn't Apply Only to Customers

CLOTHING STORE OWNER BOUGHT BAD REPUTATION

When Jeanne Lawrence bought a reputable and thriving company this year, she expected business would carry on as usual.

Lawrence bought a fashion design and retail store earlier this fall that specializes in made-to-order evening wear, bridal gowns and daytime apparel. Clothing ranges from $100 lingerie sets to $2,000 evening gowns. Lawrence is a designer with 25 years' experience and has also operated a store before.

SERVICE COMPLAINTS

But when she took over from the previous owner she was bombarded with a litany of customer service complaints. So many in fact that she says she's spending all the money she's taking in on new business repairing damage done before she took control.

"I've been trying to repair the reputation this place had at one time," says Lawrence.

Lawrence says customer complaints range from poor workmanship, to poor-fitting clothing, to people who paid in full for work that hadn't been done. Since she has taken over, Lawrence discovered the business's once reputable name has fallen in the last year.

Lawrence estimates about 75 per cent of the clientele was lost in the last year or two.

"Complaints were never redressed. I've been contacted by the Better Business Bureau with horror stories."

Lawrence wouldn't reveal the purchase price of the business but said it was considerable. She said she thought she was also buying the goodwill that went with the company's name.

"To buy a name that's reputable — that doesn't come cheap," she comments.

Marty Eakins is a partner with the Winnipeg office of KPMG. Eakins says when buying a business, it's very much caveat emptor.

"The whole notion of due diligence is critical."

He says that means hiring an experienced financial person to review financial statements both current and past. But Eakins says even at that, no firm can give 100 per cent assurance that what you're buying is solid gold.

Lawrence says she had her accountant look at the books (her accountant recommended she buy the company). And financially, the business was solid. It was the company's reputation that wasn't what she expected.

Eakins says goodwill is difficult to assess. In purely financial terms, goodwill is the excess of the purchase price over the tangible assets. Eakins says if a company has assets valued at $500,000 and someone pays $1 million, then the goodwill they've purchased is $500,000.

Eakins says prospective buyers should learn as much about the business they're buying as possible, looking at macroeconomic factors such as the industry and the national economy as well as the business itself. He says checking customer lists and talking to a few customers is also helpful.

WAYNE GLOWACKI/WINNIPEG FREE PRESS. REPRINTED WITH PERMISSION.

Lawrence is sticking with the business, but she's already made changes. Along with her associate, designer Karen Dolan, she's bringing in more seasonal wear and gift items. Lawrence says they've even started selling ready-to-wear that's 80 per cent completed and then can be altered to the individual.

CHANGED THE NAME

Most importantly, Lawrence realizes that she can repair merchandise sold previously, but she can't repair the reputation associated with the name. So the store name has been changed to Loiselle.

Unfortunately, Lawrence has spent so much money fixing mistakes that for the moment she can't afford a new sign.

Source: Paul McKie, "Clothing Store Owner Bought Bad Reputation," © *Winnipeg Free Press*, December 1, 1997, p. B5. Reprinted with permission.

4. Recent changes in the market

5. Future market patterns

All these factors help in determining whether the firm's market area is changing, or there is a declining relevant population, or technological or other changes may be creating an obsolete operation.

This kind of information can assist you in assessing trends in the level of the business's market penetration. For example, if its market share has been increasing, then perhaps you should anticipate further growth. But if the business's market penetration has been declining or static, you should be aware that something could be wrong with the operation. It may be that the business is nearing the end of its life cycle. A shrewd seller, aware that the operation is approaching a natural decline, may be bailing out.

At the same time, a business that is not presently being marketed very well may represent a significant opportunity with the right management. John and Elisa Tait bought a store, Elements of Nature, that was little more than a museum gift boutique (Entrepreneurs in Action #15). Sales were often as low as $50 per day. During the first five years, they turned the business around so that in-store sales grew to as much as $4,000 on some days and developed a thriving Web-based business as well, attracting orders from all over the world. The business has become so successful the Taits have expanded to Calgary where they can pursue not only new business opportunities but more personal interests as well.

Competition facing the business must also be evaluated and understood. First and foremost, you should make sure that the present owner will not remain in competition with you. Very often an owner will dispose of a business only to open up a similar operation. If the business is largely based on the personality and contacts of the owner, you may be hard-pressed to maintain the necessary rapport with customers, suppliers, and financial sources. A legal agreement may help ensure that the vendor will not go on to compete with you.

Another aspect of assessing competition is to look at that presently faced by the firm. You should be aware of the business's major competitors and what trends can be foreseen in the nature of their activity. Most of this information can be obtained either from direct observation or by talking with other people in the business.

Other aspects of the environment also should not be overlooked. You must be tuned in to developments in the economy, changes in technology, government policy and regulations, and trends in society at large that can affect your business situation. Your banker or other professionals may be able to tell you what the experts are saying about such variables. Both national and regional economic factors must be studied to develop accurate projections as to the size of the market opportunity available to the business.

HUMAN FACTORS

When a business is being purchased, personnel must be considered equal in importance to financial and marketing factors, because usually it is desirable to retain certain key people to provide some continuity. As a prospective buyer, you should assess the value of the company's personnel and try to become acquainted with the attitudes of the present employees. For example, will key employees continue to work for the firm under your management? If these key people are likely to leave, you must anticipate the consequences.

Both the quality and the quantity of trained personnel must be evaluated. The skill level of the employees has some bearing on the sale value of the business. Highly trained staff, for example, can increase the seller's bargaining power. On the other hand, inefficient and poorly trained staff may permit you to negotiate a lower purchase price because of the long-term expense involved in retraining or hiring additional employees.

OTHER CONCERNS

In assessing a business to buy, you will also have to take into account a number of other factors. These include various legal considerations as well as past company policies. The legal aspects of doing business are becoming increasingly more complex and the use of a lawyer is practically a fact of business life. A lawyer can help you in such areas as deciding on an appropriate form of legal organization; identifying real estate documents such as zoning restrictions and covenants that may put you at a disadvantage; labour laws and union regulations; complying with all licensing and permit requirements; the transferability of intangible assets such as copyrights, patents, dealerships, and franchises; and whether buying the shares or the assets of the firm is the most advantageous way of purchasing the company.

You should also have some understanding of the historical practices of the firm relating to employees, customers, and suppliers if future policies are to enhance your opportunities for business growth. An evaluation

15 Entrepreneurs in action

Kids-stuff connoisseurs find a niche in Calgary

John and Elisa Tait weren't monkeying around when they decided to take their Winnipeg toy store's concept out west.

The owners of Elements of Nature, located adjacent to the Manitoba Children's Museum, saw both a business and personal opportunity in Calgary.

Not only would the mountain bike addicts be able to get their fix in the nearby Rockies, but the Taits felt they could fill a void in the toy store market.

"We looked at Calgary and were amazed at how few stores there were in the marketplace. We were really encouraged by some of our suppliers. They told us if we opened a store in Calgary, we'd kick butt," said John Tait in an interview.

In April, the Taits moved west and, a month later, they opened The Discovery Hut in the Chinook Centre mall. The 2,400-square-foot store has a tropical theme similar to the slightly smaller Elements of Nature and likewise comes complete with scores of toy monkeys on the walls and world-beat music on the stereo.

Tait said such a move wouldn't have been possible if it weren't for the success of Elements of Nature. When they bought the store five years ago, it was more of a museum gift boutique. Customers were scarce and sales of some of its goods, such as rocks and magnifying glasses, were even more scarce, sometimes as little as $50 per day.

Slowly, the store was transformed into an interactive, bright, upbeat destination specializing in high-quality and educational toys such as Beanie Baby plush dolls, the Thomas the Tank Engine line, Brio Trains from Sweden, Felt Kids, Lamaze toys for infants and more than 2,000 CDs, tapes and videos of children's music, featuring the likes of local stars such as Al Simmons, Fred Penner and Heather Bishop.

As quickly as Elements of Nature sales have grown — to as much as $4,000 per day — its website business (www.elementsofnature.com) has grown even faster.

Eilef Ausland, Elements' manager, said web sales are consistently up more than 60 per cent year-over-year.

"This Christmas, we'll need to double our staff levels. It's going to be crazy," he said in an interview, as he thumbed through the day's Internet orders from Poland, England, California, Illinois, Ohio and Vancouver.

Tait said The Discovery Hut website is under construction but once it is up and running, its orders will be filled from his Winnipeg shipping hub.

Both Ausland and Tait agree that the biggest challenge facing a specialty toy store is carving out a niche in the face of big box retailers such as Toys R Us and Wal-Mart.

"Traditionally, we stay away from their product lines," Tait said. "Most of their products are from major suppliers and a lot of them are war-related or violent toys. We focus on toys that provide a real quality playing and learning experience for kids."

Terry Napper, manager of the Chinook Centre, said thus far The Discovery Hut has proven to be an excellent fit for the mall, which recently underwent a $300-million facelift.

"We have a lot of families that shop here. This store is bang-on for what we need. This concept would work in 70 to 80 per cent of the shopping centres in the country," he said in an interview.

"Most malls have either a Toys R Us or Zellers or Wal-Mart with a strong toy department, but very few have educational toys, which suit a lot of the public."
(www.elementsofnature.com)

Source: Geoff Kirbyson, "Kids-stuff connoisseurs find a niche in Calgary," *Winnipeg Free Press*, August 20, 2001, p. B5. © *Winnipeg Free Press*. Used with permission.

of these practices and policies will determine if you should continue with past practices or make modifications. If you fail to make this evaluation, you may eventually find yourself in a situation where you have to continue policies that are ill-advised in the long run. For example, it may be necessary to tighten credit policies or make a change in labour practices, even though this may cause a short-term loss of customers or employees.

KEY POINTS TO CONSIDER IN BUYING A BUSINESS

- Take your time and verify the information you are given before you commit yourself.
- Don't fall in love with the business before you do your homework.
- Be careful not to pay too much for goodwill.
- Buy a business within an industry you know well, with a product or service you are comfortable selling.
- Buy based on the return on investment not the price.
- Don't use all your cash for the purchase and then run into cash flow problems.
- Investigate before you buy.

Source: "Buying a Business: Questions to Answer Before You Buy" (www.cbsc.org/manitoba/index.cfm?name=buying), accessed December 26, 2001.

HOW TO DETERMINE AN APPROPRIATE PRICE TO PAY FOR A BUSINESS

Buying a business is a serious matter involving a substantial financial and personal investment. A business bought at the wrong price, or at the wrong time, can cost you and your family much more than just the dollars you have invested and lost. After you have thoroughly investigated a business opportunity according to the factors in the previous section, weighed the wealth of information you have gathered, and decided that your expectations have been suitably fulfilled, a price must be agreed upon with the seller.

Valuing a business is a very complex procedure, so it is impossible to do it justice here. Any explanation short of an entire book is probably insufficient. The process takes into account many variables and requires that you make a number of assumptions. Determining an appropriate price to pay for a business is a very technical process. If you are trying to make this determination on your own, you should either have a sound knowledge of general accounting principles or use the services of a professional accountant or business valuation expert who has taken formal training and is accredited by the Canadian Association of Business Valuators.

Setting the purchase price for a going concern typically involves two separate kinds of evaluations:

1. **Balance sheet methods** — evaluation of the firm's tangible net assets
2. **Earnings-based methods** — evaluation of the firm's expected future earnings

The balance sheet methods are generally less reliant on estimates and forecasts than the earnings-based methods; however, it should be remembered that balance sheet methods totally ignore the future earnings capability of the business.

BALANCE SHEET METHODS

This approach calls for making some evaluation of the assets of the business. It is used most often when the business being valued generates its earnings primarily from its assets, as with retail stores and manufacturing companies.

There are a number of balance sheet methods of evaluation including *book value, modified or adjusted book value*, and *liquidation value*. Each has its proper application, but the most useful is the adjusted book value method.

BOOK VALUE

If the company has a balance sheet, the quickest means of determining a valuation figure is to look at its net worth as indicated there. You simply take the total assets as shown in the financial statement and subtract total liabilities to get the *net book value*. The advantage of this method is that for most firms the numbers are readily available.

Its drawbacks, however, are numerous. The company's accounting practices will have a big impact on its book value. Similarly, book value does not necessarily reflect the fair market value of the assets or the liabilities. For example, buildings and equipment shown on the balance sheet may be depreciated below their actual market value, or land may have appreciated above its original cost. These differences will not be reflected on the company's balance sheet. Despite these drawbacks, however, net book value may be useful in establishing a reference point when considering the asset valuation of a business. This approach is illustrated in section I of Figure 4.3 on the basis of the balance sheet for The Campbell Company presented in Figure 4.1, and shows a value of $50,000.

ADJUSTED BOOK VALUE

The adjusted book value method is the most useful balance sheet method. It is simply the book value adjusted for differences between the stated book value and the fair market value of the business's fixed assets and liabilities. Adjustments are most frequently made to the book values of the following items on the balance sheet:

- Accounts receivable—often adjusted downward to reflect the fact that some receivables may be uncollectable.

- Inventory—usually adjusted downward, since some of it may be dated or stale and difficult to sell off at prices sufficient to cover its cost.

- Real estate—often adjusted upward since it has commonly appreciated in value since being acquired by the business.

- Furniture, fixtures, and equipment—adjusted upward if they are relatively new and have been depreciated below their market value or adjusted downward if they are older and worn out or technologically obsolete.

This refinement of the plain book value approach still has a number of drawbacks, but it does give a more accurate representation of the value of the company's assets at current market value than book value does. The application of this method is illustrated in section II of Figure 4.3, and shows a value of $85,000.

LIQUIDATION VALUE

A third approach is to go beyond the books of the company to get a more detailed evaluation of specific assets. Generally this involves determining the *liquidation value* of the assets or how much the seller could get for the business or any part of it if it were suddenly thrown onto the market. This approach is ordinarily a highly conservative evaluation and, as such, is frequently useful in determining the lowest valuation in a range of values to be considered. The liquidation value approach is presented in section III of Figure 4.3, and shows a value of $43,000. Note that the liquidation value of the firm's fixed assets may be considerably less than their appraised market value, largely due to the distress nature of their disposition.

INCOME STATEMENT METHODS

Although a balance sheet method is often the approach to valuing a business that can be prepared most easily, it is more common to use an income statement method, particularly for service-type businesses. In most cases a going concern is much more than just the sum of its physical assets. Income statement methods are more concerned with the profits or cash flow produced by the assets of the business rather than the assets themselves.

While the cost of reproducing or liquidating the business assets can be closely determined, the cost of duplicating the firm's experience, management, technical know-how, and reputation is not so easily determined. These intangible factors will be reflected in the firm's past and expected future earnings.

To study past earnings trends, it is important to select a time period that is true and representative. A period of five years is generally considered to be an appropriate length of time to observe an earnings trend; however, economic cycles and other factors must be taken into consideration.

Once earnings have been determined, various approaches can be used to determine an appropriate price. One approach is a simple *capitalization of an average of past profits or capitalization of earnings*. In this method, the profits for a selected period of years are adjusted for unusual items and an appropriate capitalization rate is applied to the average profit level derived. (See Figure 4.4, and section I of Figure 4.6.)

FIGURE 4.3   APPLICATION OF BALANCE SHEET METHODS

BUSINESS VALUATION — THE CAMPBELL CO.
BALANCE SHEET METHODS

(000s)

I. NET BOOK VALUE

Total stockholders' equity*	$ 50
Net Book Value	**$ 50**

II. MODIFIED BOOK VALUE

Net book value	$ 50
Plus:	
Excess of appraised market value of building and equipment over book value	25
Value of patent not on books	10
Modified Book Value	**$ 85**

III. LIQUIDATION VALUE

Net book value	$ 50
Plus:	
Excess of appraised liquidation value of fixed assets over book value	9
Less:	
Deficit of appraised liquidation value of inventory over book value	(5)
Deficit due to liquidation of accounts receivable	(3)
Costs of liquidation and taxes due upon liquidation	(8)
Liquidation Value	**$ 43**

*Item E from Figure 4.1.

FIGURE 4.4   EXAMPLE OF SUMMARY OF EARNINGS SHEET

THE CAMPBELL CO.
SUMMARY OF EARNINGS FOR PAST FOUR YEARS

Year	Earnings After Taxes (000s)
200Y	$13.5
200Y–1	12.1
200Y–2	10.8
200Y–3	7.2
200Y–4	4.6

A variation on this method is to weight the earnings of prior years to give greater emphasis to more recent profit levels (for example, the most recent year is given a weight of 5, the previous year 4, the next previous year 3, and so on).

The major advantage of this approach is that it is easy to use. However, the selection of an appropriate capitalization rate or multiple to apply to past or expected future earnings is not a simple, straightforward process. For illustrative purposes we have selected a desired rate of return of 16 per cent, or approximately six times the earnings shown in Figure 4.6.

The rate that can be earned on secure investments usually serves as the "base" rate or minimum capitalization rate that would be used. The chosen capitalization rate is really an assessment of the risk you perceive to be related to the business in comparison to the risk related to obtaining the "base" rate. It is an indication of the rate of return you are prepared to accept for assuming that risk in relation to the rates of return you could earn from other, more secure investments such as bonds, guaranteed income certificates, etc.

The selection of a capitalization rate can have a large impact on your evaluation of a business. If, for example, your desired rate of return is increased from 16 per cent to 20 per cent in Figure 4.6, the estimated value of The Campbell Co. based on capitalization of its past earnings would be reduced from $60,000 to $48,000. The estimated values using discounted future earnings and discounted cash flow would be similarly reduced if we were to use a 20 per cent rather than a 16 per cent expected rate of return.

The *discounted future earnings* approach requires estimating after-tax earnings for a number of years in the future as well as determining an appropriate rate of return for the investor. Each future year's earnings are then discounted by the desired rate of return. A higher discount rate might be considered in this case since the estimates are based on projections of future earnings rather than historical results and may be very subjective in nature. In addition, since net earnings, after tax, are used as the basis for the projection, the discount rate used should be net of tax as well. The sum of these discounted values is the estimated present value of the company (Figure 4.5 and section II of Figure 4.6).

FIGURE 4.5   EXAMPLE OF PROJECTED INCOME SHEET

THE CAMPBELL CO.
PROJECTED FIVE-YEAR EARNINGS AND CASH FLOW

Year	Projected Earnings After Taxes (000s)	Projected Cash Flow (000s)
200Y+1	$14.0	$16.9
200Y+2	16.8	21.1
200Y+3	20.2	26.4
200Y+4	24.2	33.0
200Y+5	29.0	41.2

Assumptions:
1. Earnings are expected to grow at a rate of 20% per year.
2. Cash flow is expected to grow at a rate of 25% per year.

The advantage of this approach is that future earnings potential becomes the principal investment criterion, taking into account the time value of money. The principal disadvantage is that in many situations, future earnings cannot be projected with any real accuracy because of the uncertainties of the operating environment and the marketplace.

The *discounted cash flow* approach is the valuation method most commonly used for smaller, privately held businesses. It is essentially the same as the discounted future earnings approach, except that future anticipated cash flows rather then earnings are used to determine the valuation, as can be seen in section III of Figure 4.6. The difference between earnings and cash flow is that cash flow includes a number of non-recurring and non-cash items that may be reflected in the income statement such as:

- The net profit or loss of the business
- Any salary paid to the owner in excess of what a comparable manager might be paid
- Any perks or discretionary benefits paid to the owner such as a car allowance, travel and entertainment expenses, personal insurance, etc.
- Interest payments unless they will be assumed by the buyer
- Any non-recurring expenses such as legal or other fees
- Non-cash expenses such as depreciation and amortization

Like the discounted future earnings approach, this method of valuation also depends on highly uncertain estimates and assumptions. Many people feel, however, that this method typically provides the most reasonable estimate of a company's value. Both of these approaches require detailed year-to-year forecasts that can result in data that have the illusion of precision, but in fact may be quite speculative and unreliable.

FIGURE 4.6   APPLICATION OF EARNINGS METHODS

BUSINESS VALUATION — THE CAMPBELL CO.
EARNINGS METHODS

I. CAPITALIZATION OF EARNINGS

Average Earnings Over Past Five Years (Figures 4.2 and 4.4) (000s)	
200Y–4	$ 4.6
200Y–3	7.2
200Y–2	10.8
200Y–1	12.1
200Y	13.5
Total	$48.2 in the previous 5 years

Average Earnings = $9.6
Divided By: Investors' desired rate of return = 16%*
Value of Company Based on Capitalization of Past Earnings = 9.6 x 100/16 = $60.0

II. DISCOUNTED FUTURE EARNINGS

Projected After-Tax Earnings (Figure 4.5) (000s)	x	Present Value Factor Assuming 16% Return	=	Present Value of After-Tax Earnings (000s)
200Y+1	$ 14.0		0.862	$12.1
200Y+2	16.8		0.743	12.5
200Y+3	20.2		0.641	13.0
200Y+4	24.2		0.552	13.4
200Y+5	29.0		0.476	13.8
Total $104.2			**Total**	$64.8

Value of Company Based on Discounted Future Earnings = $64.8

III.   DISCOUNTED CASH FLOW

Projected Cash Flow (Figure 4.5) (000s)	x	Present Value Factor Assuming 16% Return	=	Present Value of Cash Flow (000s)
200Y+1	$ 16.9		0.862	$14.6
200Y+2	21.1		0.743	15.7
200Y+3	26.4		0.641	16.9
200Y+4	33.0		0.552	18.2
200Y+5	41.2		0.476	19.6
Total $138.6				$85.0

Value of Company Based on Discounted Cash Flow = $85.0

*The actual rate of return to use depends upon your cost of capital, as well as the perceived risk inherent in the investment.

Each of these evaluation methods is illustrated in Figure 4.6 for the case of Campbell. The following assumptions are reflected in these calculations:

1. Future earnings are estimated with new management in place.

2. Earnings are expected to grow at a rate of 20 per cent per year.

3. The income tax rate, including federal and state or provincial income taxes, is 20 per cent.

4. Your desired return on investment is 16 per cent.

As illustrated in Figure 4.7, the values of The Campbell Company vary widely according to the valuation method used. The actual value of the company will depend on which method is most appropriate for the circumstances. For example, the seller will argue that the valuation method yielding the highest value — modified book value or discounted cash flow — is the most appropriate one. However, you would argue that the one reflecting the lowest value for the business — liquidation value — is probably the most appropriate. The price actually agreed on will result from extensive negotiation between you and the prospective seller, and will involve considering not only these formal evaluation methods but a host of other business and personal considerations as well.

FIGURE 4.7	CAMPBELL CO. VALUATIONS ACCORDING TO DIFFERENT METHODS

Method	Estimated Value (000s)
Net book value (Figure 4.3, I)	$50.0
Modified book value (Figure 4.3, II)	85.0
Liquidation value (Figure 4.3, III)	43.0
Capitalization of earnings (Figure 4.6, I)	60.0
Discounted future earnings (Figure 4.6, II)	64.8
Discounted cash flow (Figure 4.6, III)	85.0

RULE-OF-THUMB APPROACHES

In some situations, especially the purchase of service industries, certain rules of thumb have been developed to serve as useful guides for the valuation of a business. They typically rely on the idea of a "price multiplier." One common rule of thumb in firms where there are substantial assets is to add up:

(the fair market value of the company's fixed assets) +
(the owner's cost of current inventory) +
(approximately 90 per cent of what appear to be good accounts receivable) +
(a percentage of the company's net income before taxes as goodwill) =
Approximate Value of the Business

In companies where there are relatively few tangible assets, another rule of thumb is to calculate the selling price as a percentage of the net or gross annual receipts of the business. This method is illustrated in Table 4.2 for various types of businesses.

One word of advice, however. Many valuation professionals discourage the use of such rule-of-thumb formulas. They contend that the formulas don't address many of the factors that impact a business's actual value and rely on a "one size fits all" approach when no two businesses are ever actually alike. These rule-of-thumb formulas do, however, give you an easy way to at least get a ballpark figure on what a business might be worth. But keep in mind that using one of these rules of thumb does not mean that the balance sheet and the income statement for the business can be ignored. These rules are merely a starting point for business valuation and must be reviewed in the context of the other business factors discussed earlier in this section.

TABLE 4.2   RULES OF THUMB FOR VALUING A SMALL BUSINESS

Type of Business	"Rule of Thumb" Evaluation
Accounting Firms	100–125% of annual revenues
Auto Dealers	2–3 years' net income + tangible assets
Book Stores	15% of annual sales + inventory
Coffee Shops	40–45% of annual sales + inventory
Courier Services	70% of annual sales
Daycare Centres	2–3 times annual cash flow
Dental Practices	60–70% of annual revenues
Employment and Personnel Agencies	50–100% of annual revenues
Florists	34% of annual sales + inventory
Food/Gourmet Shops	20% of annual sales + inventory
Furniture and Appliance Stores	15–25% of annual sales + inventory
Gas Stations	15–25% of annual sales + equip./inventory
Gift & Card Shops	32–40% of annual sales + inventory
Grocery Stores	11–18% of annual sales + inventory
Insurance Agencies	100–125% of annual commissions
Janitorial and Landscape Contractors	40–50% of annual sales
Law Practices	40–100% of annual sales
Property Management Companies	50–100% of annual revenues
Restaurants (non-franchised)	30–45% of annual sales
Sporting Goods Stores	30% of annual sales + inventory
Travel Agencies	40–60% of annual commissions

Source: Excerpted from *2003 Business Reference Guide* (Wilmington, NC: Business Brokerage Press)

WHAT TO BUY — ASSETS OR SHARES?

The acquisition of a business may be structured under one of two basic formats:

1. You can purchase the seller's stock or shares in the business.
2. You can purchase part or all of the business's assets.

Although these alternatives are treated somewhat the same for financial reporting purposes, the tax consequences can differ significantly. A major consideration in the purchase or sale of a business may be the effect on the tax liability of both the buyer and the seller. The "best" form of a particular transaction will depend on the facts and circumstances of each case. Since the tax implications of acquiring or disposing of a business can be very complex, and a poorly structured transaction can be disastrous for both parties, it is suggested that you seek competent tax advice from your accountant or lawyer regarding this matter. Another factor to consider in deciding whether to buy assets or shares is "contingent liabilities." If assets are acquired, in most instances the buyer takes no responsibility for any contingencies that may arise subsequent to the sale such as lawsuits, environmental liabilities, or tax reassessments.

In some cases there may not be any choice. If the company is a sole proprietorship, for example, there are no shares, only assets and liabilities accumulated in the course of doing business that belong to the proprietor personally. So when acquiring the company, you and the owner must decide which of these assets and liabilities are to be transferred and which are to stay with the present owner. You may feel that some of the assets are not really essential to carry on the business and the seller may desire to keep something — often the real estate, which you may be able to lease rather than buy from him. This may be one way of reducing the cost of the business to you. These are matters that would have to be discussed in detail between you and the prospective seller.

A CASE STUDY—THE BROWN CO.

On Dave Brown's 65th birthday, he decided to sell his business, The Brown Co., a manufacturer and importer of specialty leather products. Dave had worked hard all his life, and now he wanted time to travel. But he didn't know where to start in setting a price for his business. His lawyer suggested he contact a valuation firm to find out what his business was worth.

The valuation expert, George Smith, asked Brown to describe his business and its strengths and weaknesses. He also asked for such items as balance sheets, cash flow statements, and income statements for the past five years.

The Brown Co.'s Profile

The Brown Co., while somewhat cyclical, had a history of consistent profitability. The past year had provided an income of roughly $100,000 before taxes. Brown pays himself an annual salary of $100,000.

The Brown Co. has a stable and diverse customer base as well as an excellent reputation for quality service and product delivery. Its exclusive contracts with certain key suppliers also provide The Brown Co. with a significant competitive advantage over its rivals.

Valuation Approaches

After considering all the information Brown provided and making his own investigation, Smith considered the two classic approaches to determining a value for the business:

THE INCOME APPROACH This method capitalizes or discounts the company's expected earnings stream. One of the best approaches is discounted cash flow analysis, which estimates the present value of the future stream of net cash flows expected to be generated by the business. The net cash flows are forecast for an appropriate period and then discounted to present value using a discount rate that reflects the risks of the business.

THE ASSET APPROACH This method considered the value or replacement cost of the company's assets as an indication of what a prudent investor would pay for this opportunity.

Using the Approaches

Smith used the discounted cash flow approach to provide what he thought was a realistic assessment of the business's expected selling price. He did not employ the asset approach because he felt a going concern business like The Brown Co. has significant "goodwill" value, such as brand equity or established customer relationships, which are very difficult to account for using the asset method.

To determine a value for The Brown Co., Smith first estimated the present value of future net cash flows. Cash flow forecasts require analysis of all variables influencing revenues, expenses, and capital investment. While projections of future operating results can sometimes be difficult to forecast reliably, The Brown Co. had a history of stable sales and profitability, both growing at an annual rate of about 3 per cent. Smith therefore chose the most recent 12 months' results as his base-year forecast.

Computing Cash Flow

To obtain an accurate basis for his forecast, Smith first adjusted the income statement. As shown in Table 4.3, he added back into the net profit the difference between Brown's salary of $100,000 and a more typical manager's salary of $50,000 to run such a business. He also added back interest expenses because existing financing arrangements typically don't affect the value of a company unless they are going to be assumed by the buyer.

He then subtracted taxes at The Brown's Co.'s average effective federal and provincial tax rate of 20 per cent and calculated the company's after-tax operating profitability.

Smith next added back depreciation expense, a non-cash expense of $25,000. He then subtracted the average annual capital expenditures, estimated at $35,000, and the $5,000 average increase in working capital, such as accounts receivable, needed to finance The Brown Co.'s revenue growth.

Brown was a mechanical engineer by training and had collected a quantity of machinery not really needed in the business's operations. So, Smith had these hard assets appraised by an external firm that specialized in that business, with a resulting value of $50,000. He then added the appraised value of this excess machinery, which could be sold separately, to the total value of The Brown Co.'s operations.

Return on Investment

Would you buy a business if you could make as much simply by investing your money? Of course not; the

continued

What's a Business Worth? — continued

risk in owning a business is much greater. So, Smith considered the fact that buyers expect to receive a higher return on the business than on more passive investments such as certificates of deposit and real estate. The valuation expert defines the rate at which cash flows were discounted as a competitive rate of return for The Brown Co. given its inherent risk factors. Smith also examined the rates of return of comparable publicly held companies. Based on this analysis, Smith concluded 16 per cent was a fair cost of capital to use to discount The Brown Co.'s after-tax net cash flow.

The discounted cash flow valuation conclusion for The Brown Co. was approximately $800,000, consisting of $750,000 for the company's operations and $50,000 as the value of the excess machinery.

Happy Endings

Brown was pleasantly surprised by the final valuation. But, as Smith told him, a valuation is one thing, but the actual selling price can be quite another. He suggested that Brown ask $850,000 for the business including the extra equipment but to be prepared to accept less, or possibly assist the buyer with some financing. Brown agreed, and at Smith's suggestion also offered to stay on for a few months after the sale to ensure a smooth management transition.

What was the actual price? After about nine months, The Brown Co. was sold for $820,000. The price was slightly greater than the valuation number due to the favourable terms Brown gave the buyer. He agreed to accept $300,000 in cash, provided a

TABLE 4.3 The Brown Co. Base-Year Adjustments and Valuation	
Income before taxes	$100,000
Excess salary	50,000
Interest on financing	25,000
Adjusted pretax income	175,000
Taxes at 20%	(35,000)
Adjusted profit after tax	140,000
Plus depreciation	25,000
Less working capital invest.	(5,000)
Less capital expenditures	(35,000)
Total adjusted base-year free cash flow	$125,000
Present value of discounted cash flow	$750,000
Plus excess machinery	50,000
Total value of The Brown Co.	$800,000

promissory note to the buyer for another $300,000 at 7 per cent and the remainder was the buyer's assumption of The Brown Co.'s outstanding $220,000 of long-term debt and accrued expenses.

Source: Adapted from "What's My Company Worth? A Case Study—'Colombo Company,'" BVS (www.bvs-inc.com), accessed February 2002.

FINANCING THE PURCHASE

PERSONAL EQUITY

Any number of sources of financing can be used to purchase a business. Because you are buying something that already exists and has a track record, you may find this financing easier to obtain than if you were starting a business from scratch. However, the place to begin is with your own personal equity. In most transactions, anywhere from 20 to 50 per cent of the money needed to purchase a business comes from the buyer and his or her family and close friends. The notion of buying a business by means of a highly leveraged transaction with a minimum amount of up-front cash is not a reality for most buyers.

SELLER FINANCING

If you do not have access to enough cash to make the purchase you might consider asking the seller to finance part of the purchase. This is very common in the sale of many small businesses. The seller's willingness to participate will be influenced by his or her own requirements, such as tax considerations or cash needs. For example, the seller might carry a promissory note for part of the purchase price, or you might lease rather than buy a portion of the facilities, equipment, or other assets. Another option is that you may be able to get the seller to agree to tie repayments to the actual performance of the business after the sale. Terms offered by sellers are usually more flexible and often more favourable than those available from a third-party lender

FYI FOR YOUR INFORMATION

Buying a Business An overview of the pros and cons, and the key questions you need to ask yourself about buying a business. (www.cbsc.org/english/search/display.cfm?CODE=4009&Coll=FE_FEDSBIS_E)

How to Buy a Business—Checklist The steps you need to take in evaluating a business that is for sale. (www.cbsc.org/alberta/search/display.cfm?Code=8004&coll=AB_PROVBIS_E)

Financing the Business Acquisition A discussion of where to get the money to finance the acquisition of a business (from a U.S. perspective). (businessbookpress.com/articles/article144.htm)

Business Valuation Methods An overview of several of the basic methods of evaluating a business. (home3.americanexpress.com/smallbusiness/resources/starting/valbiz.shtml)

like a bank. In addition, there may be some real advantages to the sellers since many of these options will provide them with a steady source of revenue instead of a lump sum payment, so they don't immediately face a tax liability on any capital gains realized from selling the business.

THIRD PARTIES

Banks and other lending institutions may provide a loan to assist in the purchase of a business, although the rate of rejection tends to be quite high on these transactions. When a bank will consider financing an acquisition, its focus tends to be on the physical assets associated with the transaction. The bank might, for example, provide financing for up to 50 to 75 per cent of the value of any real estate, 75 to 90 per cent for any new equipment acquisitions, or 50 per cent of any inventory. The only other assets that might be attractive are the accounts receivable, which it may finance to 50 or 60 per cent as well.

With any of these financing options, buyers must be open to creative solutions. They must also be prepared to take some risks. There is no sure thing, even though the business may appear to have had a long and successful operating history.

A WORD OF WARNING

As you have seen, there are a lot of things you need to worry about in buying an existing business, including undisclosed debts, overstated earnings, poor employee relations, overvalued inventory, and potential lawsuits. Therefore, you should have a good accountant and an attorney on your team for all but the simplest business acquisitions. The lawyer can either represent you in the actual negotiations or just serve as your coach, and can also act as your trustee in handling the exchange of money. It a good idea, if possible, to retain a lawyer who is very familiar with the tax aspects of business transfers, as this can often save you a lot of money. In addition, if you are buying a business for more than the value of its tangible assets, you should consider consulting with a professional business appraiser who has some experience in valuing businesses in the same industry.

STRIKING A DEAL

When the negotiations to acquire a business actually begin, you will discover that the value you may have assigned to the business during your assessment process serves as a useful benchmark to begin the negotiations but it is not likely to be the final purchase price. At this point, a number of intangibles may enter the process, and depending on the factors that motivate each party to the deal, the final purchase price may be higher or lower than the price you calculated during the valuation process. At the end of the day, a good deal is one where both parties are satisfied with the price and other terms of the deal.

The question is: How can you negotiate this type of "win–win" scenario? Here are a few things to consider:

1. As a buyer, you must know the highest amount you are willing to pay for the business before negotiations start.

2. Avoid confrontational language that will offend the other party and shut negotiations down; stick to calm, factual reasoning and arguments as you negotiate back and forth.

3. When entering negotiations, it is important to understand that intangible assets can drive up the price of a business. Sellers typically want to allocate as much to goodwill as possible so they will be better off for tax purposes, while you may want to minimize the amount allocated to goodwill and maximize the amount allocated to tangible assets, which depreciate at a faster rate.

4. As the buyer, if you are firm on one point such as the purchase price or the allocation of goodwill, then you should look for other areas where you can be flexible, like vendor financing, in order to facilitate the closing of the deal.

5. If the deal isn't working, always be willing to walk away.[1]

TAKING OVER A FAMILY BUSINESS

Another route to entrepreneurship for you may be taking over or joining a family business, perhaps a firm founded by your parents or grandparents. In fact, many family leaders actively strive to continue the family involvement in their businesses over several generations. This is a situation that has some unique opportunities and risks.

Family businesses are characterized by having two or more members of your family who may already control, are directly involved in, or own the majority of a business. It is estimated that roughly 80 per cent of all businesses in North America are family businesses. What distinguishes these firms from non-family businesses is:

1. The interrelationship between family members interacting with each other and interacting with the business

2. The complex issue of succession planning

As illustrated in Figure 4.8, a family business can be thought of as an integrated system with three different subsystems, each with its own boundaries that separate it from the other subsystems. These three overlapping perspectives must be integrated to facilitate effective functioning of the entire system, and a change in one subsystem has ramifications for both of the other subsystems. This is further complicated by the fact that the major subsystems—family and business—are fundamentally different.

For example, if we think for a moment about the values of a typical family, they would include such things as unconditional acceptance of each member, permanent relationships, and a nurturing environment intended to foster the well-being of the entire group. This is basically an emotion-based system as shown in Table 4.4. On the other hand, a business system tends to be goal- and task-focussed, and all about making money. It values qualities like competence, productivity, and performance, and tends to be task-based in its orientation. So, at a very basic level, these two subsystems have widely divergent goals and values. What makes a family business so challenging is that family members have to find a way to make these two differing subsystems coexist, so that family members not only work effectively together but do so in the best interests of the business.

This situation can become further complicated when the third subsystem—ownership—is factored into the equation. The ownership group may include both family and non-family members who may or may not also be actively involved in managing the business. In addition, these individuals can have totally different experiences and expectations of the system that need to be factored in.

Figure 4.8 also depicts the interaction of these three subsystems to create seven possible sets of circumstances in which you might find yourself in relation to a family-owned enterprise:

1. A family member who neither works in the business nor is a shareholder

2. A non-family member who works in the business but is not a shareholder

---

1. M. Collins and J. King, *A Comprehensive Guide to Buying a Business in Canada*, CanadaOne Toolkit (www.canadaone.com/tools/buy_a_biz/section3e.html), accessed August 18, 2004.

FIGURE 4.8	A SYSTEMS VIEW OF FAMILY BUSINESS

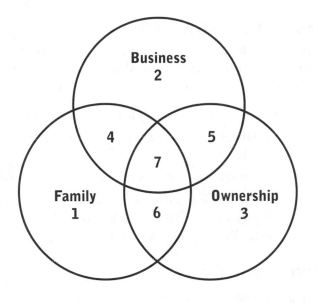

Source: M.Voeller, L. Fairburn, and W. Thompson, *Exit Right: A Guided Tour of Succession Planning for Families-In-Business Together* (Toronto: Summit Run Inc., 2000), p. 15

TABLE 4.4	MAJOR DIFFERENCES BETWEEN A BUSINESS SYSTEM AND A FAMILY SYSTEM

BUSINESS SYSTEM	FAMILY SYSTEM
Task-based system	Emotion-based system
Mission: To produce goods/services profitably	Mission: To nurture offspring into competent adults
Competency prevails	Equality rules
Acceptance is based on performance	Acceptance is unconditional
Relationships are temporary and contractual	Relationships are permanent
Power: Based on authority and influence	Power: Based on generational stage/birth order

Source: Adapted from M.Voeller, L. Fairburn, and W. Thompson, *Exit Right: A Guided Tour of Succession Planning for Families-In-Business Together* (Toronto: Summit Run Inc., 2000), p. 14.

3. A non-family shareholder who does not work in the business
4. A family member who just works in the business
5. A non-family shareholder who works in the business
6. A family member who is a shareholder but doesn't work in the business
7. A family member who owns shares and works in the business

Individuals in different circumstances will have totally different experiences and expectations for the business as a whole, yet all of them are in a position to significantly impact the ongoing success of the enterprise. These different needs and expectations need to be taken into account in managing the business.

THE QUESTION OF SUCCESSION

It is generally conceded that the most important issue facing most family businesses is the question of succession. Death or retirement of the founders or principals of all businesses is inevitable, yet most family firms lack any kind of clear succession plan. There are three main reasons for this omission:

1. The owners are often too busy keeping their business alive and operating to plan for their own departure.
2. The owners don't have any confidence in the ability of their children or the relatives who might replace them to continue to run the business.
3. The owners do not see the perpetuation of their business in the family as a major concern.

This lack of a succession plan can create difficulties for a number of people, including family members, bankers, employees, managers, lawyers, spouses, and friends. Planning with foresight for succession can create a much more favourable transition than trying to implement these changes after the fact.

PLANNING A SUCCESSFUL TRANSITION

A number of important issues must be considered in developing a successful succession plan, including:

1. **Understanding the context for the transition** Several key aspects that contribute to a successful succession plan include the timing, the type of business, the hopes and desires of the principal owner, and environmental considerations.

Timing

The earlier the owner starts to plan for a successor, the better the chance of getting the right person. Otherwise death, illness, or other issues can create a major problem for the business if a contingency plan is not in place.

Type of Business

Some owners may be easy to replace. With others it may be a lot more difficult. Situations that require a high level of technical expertise or where the business has been built on the principal owner's personal network of connections may make transition difficult. However, finding someone to run a business that requires minimal knowledge or experience may not be very difficult.

The Hopes and Desires of the Principal Owner

Family business succession includes the transfer of ethics, values, and traditions, as well as transfer of the actual business. A successor is typically expected to share these standards and continue adherence to them in the business.

Business Environment Considerations

The business environment usually changes over time and often an accompanying change is needed at the top to address these changing circumstances. It is critical to ensure that the successor and the environment have the "right fit" if a change in leadership is to be effective.

2. **Identifying the Qualities Needed in a Successor** Successful successors may need to possess a number of qualities or characteristics. Some of the more common of these characteristics include:
   - Knowledge of the business or the ability to acquire that knowledge within an acceptable time frame
   - Honesty and the basic capacity to operate the business successfully
   - Good health
   - Energy and perceptiveness

- A genuine enthusiasm for the business
- A personality compatible with the requirements of the business
- A high level of perseverance
- Stability, maturity, and aggressiveness
- Problem-solving skills and resourcefulness
- The ability to plan and organize
- The ability to help other people to develop
- A general agreement with the owner's basic philosophy about the business[2]

If it is difficult to identify an individual with all these traits, emphasis should be placed on selecting a successor with the capacity to develop most of these characteristics within a reasonable time frame.

3. **Implementing the succession plan** A number of important steps can be followed in the successful implementation of a succession plan, including:

Grooming an Heir

In some cases the heir apparent to take over the business may be obvious or the principal owner may pick a successor and let it generally be known in order to be able to openly help that person to develop. In others, the owner may hesitate to actually announce a choice. While one family member may appear to have the inside track, there may be a number of other possibilities and no one knows for sure who will get the job. Even if the successor has been chosen, it is not uncommon for the owner to have difficulty delegating the authority needed to effectively help that person develop the skills required to take over the business.

Family Acceptance of the Plan

Whatever succession plan is developed requires the general acceptance of the rest of the family. A detailed discussion with all family members about their expected duties, obligations, and responsibilities is imperative to the success of the plan. All those who will be most affected by the plan need to be included, so that hopefully the plan will gain their general acceptance and support.

A "family council" may be effective for this purpose — a formal, periodic meeting where family members share information, discuss issues, and make decisions about matters that affect them as a group. The family council should include all family members, regardless of their roles in the business, and usually also involves those who may not have a direct involvement in the business but who are nevertheless impacted by its direction and success.[3] It can be a valuable tool for enhancing family relationships and improving communication about the business.

The Use of Outside Assistance

Developing a succession plan and running a family business in general is a complex task involving complicated financial matters, buy–sell agreements and other legal issues, the resolution of conflict among family members, and a lot of other specialized tasks that are best handled by outside consultants and advisors. These may include expert consultants such as accountants, lawyers, financial planners, industrial psychologists, and others who have a specialized field of knowledge that can be useful for resolving a particular kind of problem.

This phase might also include "process" consultants or facilitators who help the family members to see the entire picture and move toward their broader-based goals in a coordinated way. For example, most experts recommend using a facilitator skilled in dealing with family dynamics and conflict, in conjunction with family council meetings.

---

2. R.M. Hodgetts and D.F. Kuratko, *Effective Small Business Management*, 6th ed., The Dryden Press Series in Entrepreneurship (Orlando, FL: Harcourt Brace College Publishers, 1997), p. 65.
3. M. Voeller, L. Fairburn, and W. Thompson, *Exit Right: A Guided Tour of Succession Planning for Families-In-Business Together* (Toronto: Summit Run Inc., 2000), p. 33.

THE ENDURING TRAITS OF SUCCESSFUL FAMILY FIRMS

Many people argue against family members working together in a business, yet numerous business dynasties have been created by family firms. One famous business consultant, David Bork, recommends recognizing some of the "enduring traits" that successful family firms have exhibited over the years:

1. Shared values about people, work, and money
2. Shared power by respecting one another's talents and abilities
3. Traditions that set them apart from other families
4. Willingness to learn and grow and an openness to new ideas
5. Engaging together in other activities besides business to maintain relationships
6. Genuine caring for other family members
7. Mutual respect and trust for other family members
8. Assisting and supporting one another through times of grief, loss, pain, and shame
9. Respect for one another's privacy
10. Well-defined interpersonal boundaries to avoid conflict between family members

Source: S. Nelton, "Ten Keys to Success in Family Business," *Nation's Business*, April 1991, pp. 44–45.

HOW CAN YOU PREPARE FOR RUNNING THE FAMILY BUSINESS?

If you are involved in a family business, you can't start too soon to prepare yourself for your future role in that business. Some important steps in this preparation include:

- **Tell others of your interest in being involved in the family business** Don't keep your aspirations secret. Announce your goals to others and look to them for assistance, advice, and support in helping you achieve them. It is especially important that your intentions be made clear to the principal stakeholders in the business such as parents, siblings, and employees.

- **Take responsibility for your personal development** This might include an informal apprentice-ship in the business, perhaps starting with summer and part-time jobs. You should also consider an appropriate educational program, perhaps taking a diploma or degree in business or a related field so that you understand the general parameters of operating a company.

- **Gain experience outside the family business** Working for another firm outside the family enterprise, even in another industry, can be an effective way of gaining valuable experience and building your credibility as a manager or the boss in your own business. It can also be a useful learning experience, as you have an opportunity to see different management styles, observe different operating techniques, and solve different problems — valuable skills that you can bring back to the family business. It is also an opportunity to obtain accountability training by holding positions that teach responsibility and provide important opportunities for decision making.

- **Build relationships** Build contacts with individuals who are part of the family business's current network, including customers, suppliers, lawyers, bankers, and other professional advisors. These connections are often made in community-service settings and social situations such as sporting events, at the golf club, or in similar circumstances. You might also start building up your own network through school alumni and membership in the Chamber of Commerce, service clubs, professional associations, and other organizations.

- **Avoid family feuds** Work with other members of the family, not against them. Learn to blend family traditions and values with your future business goals. This will help pave the way for a smooth transition when a clear takeover plan is in place.

FYI FOR YOUR INFORMATION

CAFE The Canadian Association of Family Enterprise (CAFE), is a not-for-profit national organization dedicated to promoting the well-being and understanding of families in business. There are CAFE chapters in most major business regions from British Columbia to Nova Scotia. CAFE offers an outsider's perspective and an insider's understanding of family businesses. Its objective is to educate, inform, and encourage its members in areas of unique interest to family businesses, through a program of activities that provide sources of information and professional advice. (www.cafenational.org)

CHECKLIST FOR A BUSINESS ACQUISITION

Should you start a new business or buy an existing one? At this point in your deliberations, this is the critical question. The material in the Business Acquisition Questionnaire, Figure 4.9, will aid you in making this choice.

If, after answering the questions in Part A, you decide to enter an established business rather than to start one of your own, then you should proceed to the questions in Part B. You may want to reproduce these pages and answer the same questions for several businesses you have in mind. Go through the questionnaire and answer the questions concerning each business as conscientiously as you can.

FIGURE 4.9	BUSINESS ACQUISITION QUESTIONNAIRE

PART A

Before deciding whether you will purchase an established business, you need to give consideration to the positive and negative features of this alternative. You should rate each point in the questionnaire as you perceive its significance and importance to you.

1. How would you define the nature of the business in which you are interested?

   _____

   _____

   _____

2. How important are each of the following factors to you in electing to buy an established business? Indicate the importance of each factor to you on a scale ranging from 0 (not important at all) to 10 (extremely important):

   a. Having a business with a proven performance record in sales, reliability, service, and profits _____

   b. Avoiding the problems associated with assembling the composite resources — including location, building, equipment, material, and people _____

   c. Avoiding the necessity of selecting and training a new workforce _____

   d. Having an established product line/service _____

   e. Avoiding production problems typically associated with the start-up of a new business _____

   f. Having an established channel of distribution to market your product/service _____

   g. Having a basic accounting and control system already in place _____

   h. Avoiding the difficulty of having to work out the "bugs" that commonly develop in the initial operation of a new business _____

   i. Having established relationships with suppliers and financial institutions _____

   j. Being able to acquire the assets of the business for less than their replacement value _____

   Total _____

continued

Business Acquisition Questionnaire — continued

3. In checking back over the points covered in question 2, the closer your total score on all items is to 100, the more purchasing an established business is likely to be of interest to you as a means of going into business for yourself.

PART B

The following is a set of considerations to be assessed in evaluating an established business. Your responses, information from the present owner, and other information concerning the status of the business should guide you to a comfortable decision as to whether this business is for you.

1. Why Is the Business for Sale?

_____

_____

_____

_____

2. Financial Factors

   a. Recent sales trend:

      _____ Increasing substantially

      _____ Increasing marginally

      _____ Relatively stable

      _____ Decreasing marginally

      _____ Decreasing substantially

   b. Recent trend in net profit:

      _____ Increasing substantially

      _____ Increasing marginally

      _____ Relatively stable

      _____ Decreasing marginally

      _____ Decreasing substantially

   c. Are the financial statements audited?

      Yes _____ No _____

   d. Apparent validity of financial statements:

      Accurate_____Overstated _____Understated_____

      Check the following:
- Relationship of book value of fixed assets to market price or replacement cost
- Average age of accounts receivable and percentage over 90 days
- Bad debts written off in the past 6 months, 12 months

   e. Ratio analysis: _____

	Industry Standard	This Company Year To Date	Last Year	Two Years Ago
Current ratio	_____	_____	_____	_____
Quick ratio	_____	_____	_____	_____
Debt-to-net-worth ratio	_____	_____	_____	_____
Gross-profit-to-sales ratio	_____	_____	_____	_____
Net-income-to-sales ratio	_____	_____	_____	_____
Return on assets	_____	_____	_____	_____

3. **Tangible Assets**

   a. Are the land and buildings adequate for the business?
   Yes _____ No _____

   b. Is the location acceptable?
   Yes _____ No _____

   c. Is the machinery and equipment worn and out of date?
   Yes _____ No _____

   d. How does it compare with the latest available?

   _____

   _____

   _____

   e. What is the maintenance status of the plant and equipment?
   Excellent _____ Good _____ Fair _____ Poor _____

   f. Is the plant of sufficient size and design to meet your current and projected requirements?
   Yes _____ No _____

   g. Does the plant appear to be well laid out for the efficient use of people, machines, and material?
   Yes _____ No _____

   h. What is the approximate value of the company's inventory?
   Raw material $ _____
   Work-in-process $ _____
   Finished goods $ _____
   Total   **$ _____**

   i. Does the inventory contain a high proportion of obsolete or "dead" stock?
   Yes _____ No _____

4. **Intangible Assets**

   a. Does the company name or any of its trade names have any value?
   Yes _____ No _____

   b. What kind of reputation does the business have with its customers?
   Positive _____ Neutral _____ Negative _____

   c. What kind of reputation does the business have with its suppliers?
   Positive _____ Neutral _____ Negative _____

   d. Are any franchise, licensing, or other rights part of the business?
   Yes _____ No _____

   Are they included in the deal?
   Yes _____ No _____

   e. Are any patents, copyrights, or trademarks part of the business?
   Yes _____ No _____

   Are they included in the deal?
   Yes _____ No _____

5. **Marketing Factors**

   Is the market for the firm's product/service:
   _____ Increasing?
   _____ Stable?

continued

Business Acquisition Questionnaire — continued

_____ Declining?   If *declining*, this is principally attributable to:

    _____ a. Decreasing demand due to lower popularity
    _____ b. A changing neighbourhood
    _____ c. A declining target population
    _____ d. Technological change
    _____ e. Lack of effort by present owner
    _____ f. Other factors

6. Human Factors

a. Is the present owner in good health?
Yes _____ No _____

b. Does the present owner plan to establish a new business or acquire another business that would compete with yours?
Yes _____ No _____ Uncertain _____

What are the intentions of the present owner?

_____

_____

_____

c. How efficient are current personnel?

    i. What is the rate of labour turnover? _____%

    ii. What is the rate of absenteeism? _____%

    iii. What proportion of production is completed without rejects? _____%

    iv. Can you accurately determine the cost of producing an individual unit of the product or service? Yes _____ No _____

    v. How has this changed in the past year?
    Increased _____ Stayed the same _____ Decreased _____

d. Has a union recently won an election to serve as a bargaining agent for the company's employees?
Yes _____ No _____

e. Will most of the key employees continue to work for the firm under your management?
Yes _____ No _____

f. Will you have to incur considerable costs in retraining or hiring additional employees?
Yes _____ No _____

7. Other Considerations

a. Are there any zoning restrictions or caveats on the property that may put you at a competitive disadvantage?
Yes _____ No _____

b. Can you satisfy all the federal and provincial licensing and permit requirements?
Yes _____ No _____

c. Have you considered what would be the most advantageous way of purchasing the company?
Buy shares _____ Buy assets _____ Don't know _____

d. Have you had a lawyer and an accountant review the material you received from the vendor and any other information you may have regarding the business?
Lawyer   Yes _____ No _____
Accountant   Yes _____ No _____

8. **Your Evaluation of the Business**

What have you determined to be the approximate value of the business based on the following valuation approaches?

a. Net book value $ _____

b. Modified book value $ _____

c. Liquidation value $ _____

d. Capitalization of past earnings $ _____

e. Discounted future earnings $ _____

f. Discounted cash flow $ _____

The areas covered by this checklist are not meant to be exhaustive; they are presented merely to guide and stimulate your own thinking about buying an existing business. The more information you can compile to assist you in making this decision the better.

Video Case #4

The Glove Lady

Summary

Mary Elizabeth Coleman has survived being downsized, and managed to turn her passion for gloves into a business. But the fledgling entrepreneur is learning just how much the constant need for cash will rule her business life and impact the decisions she can make to grow her business.

Questions for Discussion

1. What difficulties does Coleman face by keeping her business in her small basement?

2. What problems do small entrepreneurs like Coleman face in obtaining financing?

3. Why might it not be advisable for her to diversify her product line at the present time?

4. What factors are critical to consider when investigating the purchase of an existing business?

5. What would you recommend Coleman do next?

Considering a Franchise

In addition to exploring the possibilities of starting your own business or buying an existing one, you may want to investigate the opportunities presented by *franchising*. Canada is said to be the franchise capital of the world: This sector is estimated to employ 1 million people and register sales of $100 billion a year, or almost 50 per cent of total retail sales in the country. Over 1,300 franchisors have nearly 64,000 outlets, giving Canada more franchised units per capita than any other place on the planet.[1]

Franchising allows you to go into business for yourself and at the same time be part of a larger organization. This reduces your chances of failure, because of the support that the established company can provide. If this appears to be an attractive situation, then a franchise may be the answer for you. Let's look at what this means in the context of starting a business of your own.

AN INTRODUCTION TO FRANCHISING

Franchising has often been referred to as an industry or a business. However, it is neither. It can best be described as *a method of doing business* — a means of marketing a product and/or service that has been adopted and used by a wide variety of industries and businesses.

WHAT IS FRANCHISING?

There is no single, simple definition of franchising. For example, Statistics Canada defines it as *a system of distribution in which one enterprise (the franchisor) grants to another (the franchisee) the right or privilege to merchandise a product or service.* The International Franchise Association, the major trade association in the field, defines it as *a continuing relationship in which the franchisor provides a licensed privilege to do business, plus assistance in organizing, training, merchandising, and management in return for consideration from the franchisee.* These are just two of the many definitions that have been offered.

Regardless of the formal definition, however, it is best to think of franchising as a legal and commercial relationship between the owner of a trademark, trade name, or advertising symbol and an individual or group of people seeking the right to use that identification in a business. A franchisee generally sells goods and services supplied by the franchisor or that meet the franchisor's quality standards. Franchising is based on mutual trust and a legal relationship between the two parties. The franchisor provides business expertise such as a proven product or service offering, an operating system, a marketing plan, site location, training, and financial controls that otherwise would not be available to the franchisee. The franchisee brings to the franchise operation the motivation, entrepreneurial spirit, and often the money to make the franchise a success.

Virtually all franchise arrangements contain the following elements:

1. A continuing relationship between two parties
2. A legal contract that describes the responsibilities and obligations of each party
3. Tangible and intangible assets (such as services, trademarks, and expertise) provided by the franchisor for a fee
4. The operation of the business by the franchisee under the franchisor's trade name and managerial guidance

---

1. C. Clark, "The New Face of Franchising," *PROFIT*, December/January 2000, p. 37.

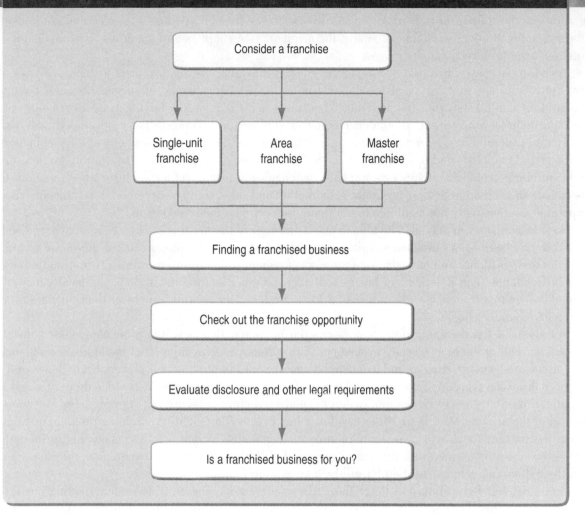

INTERESTED IN A FRANCHISE?

Consider a franchise

Single-unit franchise → Area franchise → Master franchise

Finding a franchised business

Check out the franchise opportunity

Evaluate disclosure and other legal requirements

Is a franchised business for you?

Franchise arrangements can be subdivided into two broad classes:

1. **Product distribution arrangements**, in which the dealer is to some degree, but not entirely, identified with the manufacturer/supplier
2. **Entire-business-format franchising**, in which there is complete identification of the dealer with the supplier

In a *product distribution arrangement*, the franchised dealer concentrates on one company's product line, and to some extent identifies his or her business with that company. Typical of this type of franchise are automobile and truck dealers, gasoline service stations, and soft drink bottlers.

Entire-business-format franchising is characterized by an ongoing business relationship between franchisor and franchisee that includes not only the product, service, and trademark, but the entire business format — a marketing strategy and plan, operating manuals and standards, quality control, and continuing two-way communications. Restaurants, personal and business services, rental services, real estate services, and many other businesses fall into this category.

Entire-business-format franchising has been primarily responsible for most of the growth of franchising since 1950. Most of our comments will relate to this form of franchising.

ADVANTAGES OF FRANCHISING

As has been pointed out, franchising is one means for you (the *franchisee*) to go into business for yourself, yet at the same time be part of a chain, with the support of an established company (the *franchisor*) behind you. This can enable you to compete with other chains through the use of a well-known trademark or trade name. In addition, the franchisor may provide you with assistance in such areas as site selection, equipment purchasing, national advertising, bookkeeping, the acquisition of supplies and materials, business counselling, and employee training.

As a franchisee you will have the opportunity to buy into an established concept with reduced risk of failure. Statistics show that a typical franchisee has an 80 per cent chance of success. Several factors may explain this result. First, your risk is reduced because you are supposedly buying a successful concept. This package includes proven and profitable product or service lines, professionally developed advertising, a known and generally recognized brand name, the standardized design or construction of a typical outlet, and a proven and market-tested operating system. Second, you are often provided with training for your new job and continuing management support. You have the ongoing assistance of a franchisor who can afford to hire specialists in such areas as cost accounting, marketing and sales, and research and development. These are important assets usually not available to the small, independent businessperson.

As a franchisee you may also be able to take advantage of the lower cost of large-scale, centralized buying. You may be able to purchase supplies at reduced cost, since the franchisor can purchase in bulk and pass the savings along. You may also have access to financing and credit arrangements that would not otherwise be available to an independent business. Banks and other lending institutions are usually more willing to lend money to a franchisee who has the backing of a large, successful franchisor than they are to a completely independent business.

A franchisee has the opportunity to acquire a proven system that has already been developed, tested, and refined, with all of the bugs already worked out. This allows you to avoid a lot of the start-up problems typically associated with starting an independent business. For example, football players Khari Jones and Wade Miller of the Winnipeg Blue Bombers had been big fans of Booster Juice products since they stumbled across an outlet three years ago in Edmonton, so they opened a franchise of their own (Entrepreneurs in Action #16). As part of the arrangement, both Miller and Jones had to attend an eight-day training program in Edmonton to learn everything there is to know about running such an outlet, including how to make their principal product — the smoothie. Armed with this background and Miller's prior business experience, they are optimistic that their shopping centre-based outlet will be a great success.

Similarly, Jeff Pylypchuk and Peter Tofinetti considered opening an independent cycling business but opted for a franchise instead, and were glad they did. Their Cyclepath franchise was profitable almost immediately and they credit much of this success to the franchise system. By buying into a franchise they were immediately set up with a complete system and had the advantage of being associated with a larger brand name company (Entrepreneurs in Action #17).

DISADVANTAGES OF FRANCHISING

While franchising has a considerable number of advantages, there are also several disadvantages of which you should be aware. One of the principal complaints is the degree of control that franchisors exert over their franchisees. While you will be an independent businessperson, in effect you do not have complete autonomy and must operate within the operating system as defined by the franchisor. You are usually in a subordinate position to the franchisor and must abide by the often extremely rigid terms and conditions of the franchise agreement. All franchise contracts give the franchisor either an open right to terminate the contract or the right to terminate upon breach of the agreement. As a result, you may find yourself in a weak bargaining position.

Franchisees also have certain reporting obligations to the franchisor and may be subject to frequent inspection and constant supervision. To fit comfortably into such an arrangement, you must accept the necessity of such controls. These restrictions, however, may be unacceptable to some individuals. You must seriously assess your personal suitability for the role of a franchisee.

Another disadvantage of franchising is that the cost of the services provided to you by the franchisor is based on your total sales revenue. These costs can amount to 10 per cent or more of your total revenue or an even larger share of your profits. A related complaint is that the markup franchisors may add to the

16 Entrepreneurs in action

Bombers Big on Beverages

OK, let's think about how this might play out.

Jones steps back, hands off to Miller, who bulls his way to the front counter and drops the smoothie into the hands of a waiting customer.

Yeah. Yeah. That could work. And that's exactly what Winnipeg Blue Bombers quarter-back Khari Jones and running back Wade Miller were thinking when they recently opened a new Booster Juice franchise in the St. Vital Shopping Centre.

"For one thing, we're pretty good friends off the field," Jones explained during an interview yesterday. "We were golfing partners, and we knew we were both interested in doing something like this."

For another thing, while Jones may be a raw rookie when it comes to running a business, Miller has five years' experience under his belt as co-owner of two other successful businesses in the city — Elite High Performance Sports Injuries Centres (two of them) and Pinnacle Staffing Inc. So it wasn't like they'd be walking into this blindfolded.

And finally, they've both been big fans of Booster Juice products since they stumbled on an outlet about three years ago in Edmonton, where the retail chain got its start.

"It's something that's nutritious and good tasting, so we don't have any problems talking to kids about it," Jones said of the Booster Juice products, which include fresh-squeezed fruit and vegetable juices and smoothies — a Slurpee-type drink made from fresh fruits and fruit juices, non-frozen sorbets, hand-made yogurts and nutritional supplements.

OK, so it sounds like a good game plan, but have they been able to execute it? According to the two players, the answer is a resounding "Yes!"

"We've been very busy," Jones said.

"It's been very good," Miller said.

As is fitting for a couple of football players, Jones and Miller had to attend an eight-day training camp with Booster Juice in Edmonton before they opened their own juice bar. They learned pretty well everything there is to know about running a Booster Juice outlet, including how to make smoothies.

With staff of 10 to 14 employees, the two football players and their two silent partners don't need to be at the store on a daily basis. But Jones and Miller said they still like to drop in every now and then and sling some smoothies, wash some dishes, or whatever.

Wade Miller (left) and Khari Jones

Because it's not widely known that he and Miller are co-owners of the juice bar, Jones said he's caught more than a few customers by surprise when working behind the counter.

"We have this big football picture of us hanging at the front of the store. I just point up to the picture and say, 'Yeah, it's me. I just don't have my helmet on,'" he said with a chuckle.

If there's one area where the two new partners don't seem to be in agreement, it's the sometimes-thorny issue of who's the boss in this new venture.

"He's the quarterback, so he's obviously the boss," Miller said without hesitation. But when Jones heard that, he burst out laughing.

"No, no, it doesn't work like that," he explained. "He's definitely a big part of everything that goes on and he knows it.". . . . (www.boosterjuice.com)

Source: Murray McNeill, "Bombers big on beverages," *Winnipeg Free Press,* December 10, 2003, p. C8. Reprinted with permission.

17   Entrepreneurs in action

The Franchise Biz

Lifelong best friends Jeff Pylypchuk, 29, and Peter Tofinetti, 30, never thought they could turn their love of bike riding into a business. Just four years ago, the two were "socking away" cash at menial jobs in Thunder Bay, Ontario — Pylypchuk, waiting tables and Tofinetti, hawking insurance. Today, their bike shop, Cyclepath, pulls in an impressive $750,000 a year in sales.

How did they do it? By purchasing a franchise business that matched their interests.

"We started cycling together — road racing — when we were about 13, and we had always been unimpressed with the service we received in bike shops," says Pylypchuk. "So, we thought about starting our own business."

With their combined savings of about $75,000, Pylypchuk and Tofinetti considered opening an independent business, but that meant starting from scratch — coming up with a store name, finding real estate and attracting customers. Then they discovered Cyclepath, which, at the time, was a successful bicycle franchisor with 50 franchises. After extensive research, which included calling other franchisees, Pylypchuk and Tofinetti decided to buy into the system. They paid $40,000 for their franchise, and took out a small business loan to help with expenses such as rent and merchandise. "It just took off from there," says Pylypchuk.

Did it ever. Their Cyclepath franchise opened in 1996 and was almost immediately profitable. Halfway through its second year, the store was pulling in half a million dollars, "which is double what we ever imagined," says Tofinetti.

They credit their success, in part, to the franchise system. "There was good advertising support by a professional ad agency. The store looked polished; you could tell a lot of research had gone into these stores," says Pylypchuk. "There were a lot of things we could have figured out over time, but by buying into a franchise, we basically bought the package and, boom, we were set up."

Therein lies the lure of the franchise business: it's the same adrenaline rush that comes with starting an independent business, but with the instantaneous advantage of being associated with a larger brand name company.

However, if you're considering plunking your savings on a franchise, know that it can be a complex and risky proposition, but one that can be immensely rewarding. Just ask Jeff Pylypchuk: "The coolest thing is working with a product that is more than just a means to make money. Sometimes we'll just get up and go for a ride in the bush. Had we opened a doughnut franchise, I think after five years I'd be going nuts," he says. "Ultimately, it is about buying into a product that you enjoy." (realm.net)

Excerpted with permission from *Realm: Creating Work You Want™*, Fall 2000, published by YES Canada-B.C. Available online or in print by calling 1-877-REALM-99. For more information, phone: (604)435.1937; fax: (604)435-5548; e-mail: info@realm.net.

products you must buy from them can increase your operating costs, particularly if equally good products could be purchased elsewhere at lower prices. While you might initially feel that your operating costs are likely to be lower as a result of the franchisor's central purchasing program, it may not become apparent until later that you are actually paying a huge markup on the material, equipment, and supplies you acquire.

Acquiring a franchise is not necessarily a licence to print money. Besides an initial franchise fee, you will probably also have to make periodic royalty payments and advertising contributions based on a percentage of your gross revenues. Even with these expenditures, you still run the risk of not achieving the expected sales, and thus the profit that the franchisor stated was possible.

It should also be remembered that the benefits available through franchising have not always materialized. Franchisors have not always supplied the services they promised or truthfully disclosed the amount of time and effort the franchisee would have to commit to the franchise. Termination policies of many franchisors have given franchisees little or no security in many cases.

TYPES OF FRANCHISES

FRANCHISE FORMATS

There are three major ways a franchise can be formatted:

1. **Single-unit franchise** This is the most popular and simplest format. In it, the franchisor grants you the right to establish and operate a business at a single location. This has been the most popular means of franchise expansion and the method by which many independent entrepreneurs have become involved in franchise distribution.

2. **Area franchise** This format involves a franchisor's granting you the right to establish more than one outlet within a specified territory. This territory can be as large as an entire province or state, or even a country, or it can be as small as part of a city. To assure that this territory is adequately serviced, the franchisor will usually require the construction and operation of a specific number of outlets within a period of time. Area franchising may be a means of achieving certain economies of scale, and perhaps a lower average franchise cost. On the other hand, it requires a larger total capital outlay for plant and equipment. Area franchisees with a large number of outlets can sometimes acquire greater financial strength than their franchisors. This has happened in a number of instances in the fast-food industry.

3. **Master franchise** In this format, a franchisor grants you (the *master franchisee*) the right, not only to operate an outlet in a specific territory, but also to sell subfranchises to others within that same territory. Granting master franchises is the fastest way for a franchisor to expand, but it is also very complex and results in a division of fees and royalties between the franchisor and subfranchisor. A master franchisee may not need as much initial capital as an area franchisee, but he or she must learn not only how to open and operate a franchise business but also how to sell franchises.

RANGE OF AVAILABLE FRANCHISES

It is interesting to note that several of these franchisors, such as Dunkin' Donuts and Baskin-Robbins, have dramatically decreased the number of franchised outlets they have in Canada over the previous four to five years. Others, including Curves and Quizno's, are still growing very rapidly.

To give you an idea of the current scope of franchising, the 2004 *Franchise Annual Directory* (www.infonews.com) provides information on over 1,300 Canadian listings in 69 different product/service categories. The range of possibilities available to a prospective franchisee includes opportunities in the following areas:

- Accounting and tax services
- Allergy control
- Automotive rental and leasing
- Automotive muffler shops
- Beverages
- Building products and services
- Cleaning products and services
- Dating services
- Employment services
- Financial services
- Florist shops
- Food: candy, popcorn, snacks
- Food: convenience stores
- Food: restaurants
- Formal wear
- Furniture refinishing and repair
- Hairstyling and cosmetics
- Home furnishings: retail and sales
- Home inspection
- House-/pet-sitting services
- Lawn and garden care
- Moving services
- Pest control
- Photo, framing and art
- Printing and copying services
- Real estate services
- Schools and teaching
- Sport and recreation
- Tanning salons
- Travel
- Video and audio sales
- Water treatment
- Wedding-related services

At the individual franchisor level, the top 10 franchise organizations in 2004, based on an evaluation by *Entrepreneur* magazine, are shown in Table 5.1.

TABLE 5.1   TOP 10 FRANCHISE ORGANIZATIONS IN 2004*

Company	Description	Web Site	Number of Outlets		
			Franchised Total	Franchised Canada	Corporately Owned
1. Subway	Submarine sandwich restaurant chain	www.subway.com	19,237	1,803	1
2. Curves	Women-only fitness centres	www.buycurves.com	5,833	498	0
3. Quizno's Franchise Co.	Quick-service sandwich shop	www.quiznos.com	2,423	213	5
4. 7-Eleven Inc.	Convenience store chain	www.7-eleven.com	21,887	0	2,547
5. Jackson Hewitt Tax Service	Income tax preparation service	www.jacksonhewitt.com	3,709	0	516
6. The UPS Store	Business, communication, and postal service centres	www.theupsstore.com	4,631	263	0
7. McDonald's	Hamburgers, chicken, salads	www.mcdonalds.com	22,116	843	8,065
8. Jani-King	Commercial cleaning	www.janiking.com	10,349	524	25
9. Dunkin' Donuts	Doughnut shop	www.dunkindonuts.com	5,835	108	0
10. Baskin-Robbins USA Co.	Ice cream and frozen yogurt shop	www.baskinrobbins.com	5,105	150	0

* *Entrepreneur*, "25th Annual Franchise 500," January 2004. The evaluation is based on such factors as financial strength and stability, growth rate, size of the system, number of years in business, length of time franchising, start-up costs, litigation, percentage of terminations, and whether the company provides financing. (www.entrepreneur.com)

Within this broad spectrum of available opportunities, the most popular areas have been fast food (take-out/sit-in), food retail (candy, coffee, yogurt, etc.), automotive products and services, and business-related/communication services.

CANADIAN LEGISLATION AND DISCLOSURE REQUIREMENTS

Many U.S. states have laws and regulations governing franchise companies, but the same is not true of Canada. Only Alberta and Ontario have legislation specifically relating to franchise disclosure, although other provinces are expected to soon adopt similar legislation. The legislation in both provinces is quite similar in that it requires franchisors (with some exceptions) to provide prospective franchisees with a disclosure document containing a lot of information that otherwise would be very difficult for the prospective franchisee to obtain. This information includes:

- the business background of the directors and officers of the franchisor
- details of any litigation against the franchisor

- details of bankruptcy, insolvency, or criminal proceedings against the franchisor or its directors
- the names and addresses of existing and former franchisees
- the particulars of any advertising fund expenditures
- a set of financial statements.

This information must be provided to the franchisee at least 14 days before signing any franchise agreement or paying any money to the franchisor. Otherwise the franchisee may have recourse to rescind the franchise agreement. For example, 3 for 1 Pizza and Wings (Canada) Inc. was found in violation of Ontario's franchise law by not providing a full package of disclosure information and ordered to repay $35,000 to a man who backed out of a deal. This was the second time the company was ordered to pay refunds after a judge concluded the company had not provided sufficient disclosure.[2] The basic principle behind the legislation is that everyone entering into a franchise arrangement should have access to all the information necessary to make an informed decision. The presumption is that both parties "act in good faith and in accordance with reasonable commercial standards."

Prior to the recent passage of these regulations, Canada was known as the "Wild West" of franchising. The passage of these and similar laws may prevent further situations like that of Fereshteh Vahdati and her husband in Entrepreneurs in Action #18. They spent more than $100,000 to buy a Toronto pizza franchise and another $100,000 in legal costs in a court battle against the pizza-chain owner, and ended up losing it all.

In all other provinces, franchisors are still under no legal obligation to provide any specific information or file any material with a government agency or department. As a prospective franchisee, you are on your own for the most part. If your potential franchisor does operate in Alberta or Ontario, however, you should request a copy of the disclosure material they are obliged to provide to prospective franchisees in those provinces, although you may not be entitled to the same length of time for deliberation or legal recourse.

THE U.S. SITUATION

Since 1979 the U.S. Federal Trade Commission (FTC) has required that every franchisor offering franchises in the United States have a *disclosure statement* called a "Uniform Franchise Offering Circular" (UFOC) ready to offer a prospective franchisee. A copy of any disclosure statement can be obtained from the Federal Trade Commission, Washington, DC 20580 (www.ftc.gov). This document discloses 20 categories of information:

1. Identifying information about the franchisor
2. Business experience of the franchisor's directors and key executives
3. The franchisor's business experience
4. Litigation history of the franchisor and its directors and key executives
5. Bankruptcy history of the franchisor and its directors and key executives
6. Description of the franchise
7. Money required to be paid by the franchisee to obtain or commence the franchise operation
8. Continuing expenses to the franchisee in operating the franchise business that are payable in full or in part to the franchisor or to a person affiliated with the franchisor
9. A list of persons who represent either the franchisor or any of its affiliates, with whom the franchisee is required or advised to do business
10. Real estate, services, supplies, products, inventories, signs, fixtures, or equipment that the franchisee is required to purchase, lease, or rent, and a list of any persons with whom such transactions must be made
11. Descriptions of consideration paid (such as royalties, commissions, etc.) by third parties to the franchisor or any of its affiliates as a result of a franchisee's purchase from such third parties
12. Description of any franchisor assistance in financing the purchase of a franchise
13. Restrictions placed on a franchisee's conduct of the business
14. Required personal participation by the franchisee

---

2. J. Daw, "3 for 1 Pizza & Wings ordered to repay $35,000," *Toronto Star*, May 31, 2003, p. C3.

18 Entrepreneurs in action

Taken to the Cleaners

Fereshteh Vahdati and her husband spent more than $100,000 to buy a Toronto pizza franchise, invested thousands more on various fees — and worked 17 hours a day.

Their payoff?

"We didn't make any money," said a despondent Vahdati on Thursday.

"Everything goes to (the chain) . . . These people cheat us and we've lost everything."

Vahdati said she and her husband spent $100,000 on legal costs in a fruitless court fight against the pizza-chain owner.

The couple immigrated to Canada eight years ago and heard about the business from a community newspaper here.

The owner asked them to pay a 10 per cent royalty and four per cent of sales for advertising, Vahdati said.

But after they bought the stores, they were told they also had to spend $65,000 a year to buy flyers from the owner.

They eventually ran out of money and the company seized the stores from them, Vahdati said.

Source: Adapted from Tom Blackwell, "New Bill Aims to Protect Franchise Owners," *Canadian Press NewsWire*, December 3, 1998. Used with permission.

15. Information about termination, cancellation, and renewal of the franchise
16. Statistical information about the number of franchises and their rate of termination or failure
17. Franchisor's right to select or approve a site for the franchise
18. Training programs for the franchisee
19. Celebrity involvement with the franchise
20. Financial information about the franchisor

The FTC regulations also require that if the franchisor makes any claims regarding the level of earnings you might realize as a result of owning its franchise, a reasonable basis must exist to support the accuracy of these claims. When such claims are made, the franchisor must have prepared an "Earnings Disclosure Document" for prospective franchisees, explaining the basis and material assumptions on which the claims are made.

If the franchise you are investigating currently operates in the United States, this information should be readily available.

THE FRANCHISE AGREEMENT

Because two independent parties participate in a franchise relationship, the primary vehicle for obtaining central coordination and control over the efforts of both participants is a formal contract. This *franchise agreement* is the heart of the franchise relationship. It differs from the typical contract in that it contains restrictive clauses peculiar to franchising that limit your rights and powers in the conduct of the business. Franchisors argue that these controls are necessary to protect their trademark and to maintain a common identity for their outlets.

A franchise agreement should cover a variety of matters. There should be provisions that cover such subjects as:

- The full initial costs, and what they cover
- Use of the franchisor's trademarks by the franchisee
- Licensing fees

- Land purchase or lease requirements
- Building construction or renovation
- Equipment needs
- Initial training provided
- Starting inventory
- Promotional fees or allowances
- Use of operations manuals
- Royalties
- Other payments related to the franchisor
- Ongoing training
- Cooperative advertising fees
- Insurance requirements
- Interest charges on financing
- Requirements regarding purchasing supplies from the franchisor, and competitiveness of prices with those of other suppliers
- Restrictions that apply to competition with other franchisees
- Terms covering termination of the franchise, renewal rights, passing the franchise on to other family members, resale of the franchise, and similar topics

In considering any franchise proposition, you should pay a great deal of attention to the franchise contract. Since it is a key part of the relationship, it should be thoroughly understood. The rest of this section discusses the evaluation of an agreement for a single-unit franchise within a business-format franchise system. It is important to realize, however, that this is not a "typical" franchise agreement; there is really no such thing. While agreements may follow a fairly standard approach in terms of format, they do not do so in terms of content. Every agreement is specially drafted by the franchisor to reflect its particular objectives and the future of the business.

OBLIGATIONS UNDERTAKEN BY THE FRANCHISOR

The obligations undertaken by the franchisor may include any or all of the following:

1. To provide basic business training to you and your employees. This includes training in bookkeeping skills, staff selection, staff management, business procedures, and the systems necessary to control the operation. In addition, the franchisor may provide you with training relating to the operational aspects of the business.

2. To investigate and evaluate sites for the location of your franchise. You will be advised as to whether or not the site meets the franchisor's standards and what sort of performance might be expected at that location. In addition you may be assisted in the design and layout of your franchise operation.

3. To provide either the equipment or the specifications for any necessary equipment and furniture you require.

4. To provide promotional and advertising material to you, and some guidance and training on marketing and promotional principles.

5. The franchisor may provide you with a statement indicating the amount of opening inventory required, and may make arrangements for you to purchase inventory either from the franchisor's own purchasing department or from particular suppliers established for this purpose.

6. The franchisor may provide you with on-site assistance for the opening of your franchise outlet. Quite often the franchisor will provide a team of two to three people to assist you in getting the business off the ground.

7. The franchisor may also provide business operating manuals explaining the details of operating the franchise system and a bookkeeping/accounting system for you to follow. There may also be additional support through such things as business consultation, supervisory visits to your premises, and staff retraining.

OBLIGATIONS IMPOSED ON A FRANCHISEE

Your obligations as a franchisee may require you to do any or all of the following:

1. Build your franchise outlet according to the plan or specifications provided by the franchisor
2. Maintain construction and opening schedules established by the franchisor
3. Abide by the lease commitments for your franchise outlet
4. Observe certain minimum opening hours for your franchise
5. Pay the franchise fees and other fees specified in the franchise agreement
6. Follow the accounting system specified by the franchisor and promptly provide financial reports and payments of amounts due
7. Participate in all regional or national cooperative advertising and use and display such point-of-sale or advertising material as the franchisor stipulates (this would include having all your advertising materials approved by the franchisor)
8. Maintain your premises in clean, sanitary condition and redecorate when required to do so by the franchisor
9. Maintain the required level of business insurance coverage
10. Permit the franchisor's staff to enter your premises to inspect and see whether the franchisor's standards are being maintained
11. Purchase specific goods or services from the franchisor or specified suppliers
12. Train all staff in the franchisor's method and ensure that they are neatly and appropriately dressed
13. Obtain the franchisor's consent before assigning the franchise contract to another party
14. Maintain adequate levels of working capital and abide by the operations manual provided by the franchisor

These are only examples of some of the obligations you might expect to incur. There will probably also be clauses involving bankruptcy, transfer of the business, renewal of the contract, and provisions for the payment of royalties and other financial considerations.

FRANCHISE FEES AND ROYALTIES

In most cases you will be required to pay an initial franchise fee on signing the franchise agreement. This fee generally pays for the right to use the franchisor's trade name, licences, and operating procedures; some initial training; and perhaps even assistance in site selection for your franchise outlet. The amount of the fee varies tremendously, according to the type of franchise business. For a large restaurant operation or hotel, for example, the fee may be as high as $50,000 or $60,000, but for a small service franchise (such as maid service or lawn care) it may be only $5,000 to $10,000. This fee is not all profit for the franchisor, as it must go to pay for franchisee recruitment, training, assistance with site selection, and other services normally provided to you. Some franchisors will charge a separate training fee, but this is usually established merely to recover the cost of providing the training to you and your employees.

In addition to this initial fee, ongoing fees may also be provided for in the franchise agreement. These will generally consist of royalties payable for ongoing rights and privileges granted by the franchisor. Royalties are usually calculated as a percentage of the gross sales, not profits, generated by your franchise. They may be paid either weekly, monthly, or quarterly, and represent the main profit centre for most franchisors. These royalties must continue to be paid even though the franchise may be losing money. For a fast-food franchise, typical royalties range from 3 per cent to 8 per cent. For some service franchises, the royalty may run from 10 to 20 per cent or even higher.

While some franchisees come to resent having to continue to pay ongoing royalties to their franchisor, this payment may be preferable to the franchisor charging a higher initial fee to the franchisee. Ongoing royalty payments at least imply a continuing commitment to the success of the franchise by the franchisor, to the ultimate benefit of both parties.

As well as royalty fees, many franchise agreements require you to contribute a proportion of your business's gross revenues to a regional or national cooperative advertising fund. This contribution may be an additional

2 to 4 per cent of gross sales. These payments are used to develop and distribute advertising material and to run regional and national advertising campaigns. These, too, are typically not a source of profit for the franchisor.

The administration of these advertising funds has often been the subject of considerable concern to franchisees and one of the areas of greatest dispute between franchisors and franchisees. The advertising fund should be maintained as a separate trust account by the franchisor and not intermixed with its general operating revenues. The purpose of this fund should be specified in the franchise agreement. In addition, the agreement should also state how and by whom the fund will be administered.

In addition to requiring you to support a regional or national advertising program, a franchisor may require you to support your own local advertising. Typically you must spend a specific amount on a periodic basis, calculated either on the basis of a percentage of gross sales or in terms of a fixed amount. Local advertising devised by you will normally require the prior approval of the franchisor.

In some cases the franchisor also provides you with special services such as bookkeeping, accounting, and management consulting services, which are billed on a fee-for-service basis. Before acquiring a franchise you should be sure that you understand all the fees that will be payable, including any extra fees that may not be mentioned in the franchise agreement.

PURCHASE OF PRODUCTS AND SUPPLIES

A key element in the success of many franchise organizations is the sameness of each of the franchise outlets. Therefore, franchisors will work to ensure the maintenance of a certain quality of product or service and to make sure that uniform standards are employed throughout their system. Consequently, many franchisors, in an attempt to exercise complete control over their operation, require you to purchase products and services from them or from designated sources. In some cases the approved suppliers may include affiliates of the franchisor. You may also be able to purchase items from other sources of supply, provided the franchisor has approved each of those sources in advance.

If the franchisor exerts tight control over such supplies, you should try to ensure beforehand that supplies are going to be readily available when required, that they are sold to you at fair market value and on reasonable terms, and that you have the ability to choose alternative sources for any non-proprietary items if the franchisor or the designated supplier is unable to provide them to you when required.

Many franchisors earn a profit from providing supplies to their franchisees. Often, however, because franchisors exercise enormous buying power they can supply goods and services at prices and under terms that are better than those you could negotiate for yourself. You should shop around to compare prices for comparable merchandise. If the prices being charged by the franchisor are out of line, this added cost can dramatically affect your business's future earnings.

Volume rebates are often paid to franchisors by suppliers of particular products. Rather than pocket the money themselves or distribute it back to their franchisees, some franchisors will contribute this to the advertising fund. As a potential franchisee you should ask how these rebates will be handled, as a considerable amount of money may be involved.

LEASED PREMISES

Many franchise operations require the use of physical facilities such as land and buildings. When these premises are leased rather than owned by the franchisee, there are a number of ways in which this lease arrangement can be set up:

1. The franchisor may own the land and/or buildings and lease it to you.
2. You may lease the land and/or building directly from a third party.
3. You may own the property, sell it to the franchisor, and lease it back under a *sale leaseback* agreement.
4. A third party may own the property and lease it to the franchisor, who then sublets it to you.

The franchise agreement should spell out who is responsible, you or the franchisor, for negotiating the lease, equipping the premises, and paying the related costs. If a lease is involved, its terms and renewal clauses should be stated and should correspond with the terms of the franchise. You must be careful not to have a 20-year lease on a building and only a 5-year franchise agreement, or vice versa.

Franchisors generally want to maintain control of the franchise premises. Accordingly they will often own or lease the property on which the franchise business is located, and then sublet these premises to you. In other situations the franchisor may assign a lease to you subject to a conditional reassignment of the lease back to the franchisor on termination of the franchise for any reason.

With respect to other leasehold improvements, you may also be required to purchase or lease from the franchisor (or from suppliers designated by the franchisor) certain fixtures, furnishings, equipment, and signs that the franchisor has approved as meeting its specifications and standards.

TERRITORIAL PROTECTION

In many cases the franchise agreement provision with respect to your territory and protection of that territory may be subject to considerable negotiation prior to inclusion in the agreement. You will generally want to have the franchisor agree not to operate or grant a franchise to operate another franchised outlet too close to your operation. This restriction may be confined to a designated territory, or may be confined to a predetermined geographic radius from your premises.

Franchisors, on the other hand, like to see exclusive territorial protection kept to a minimum. As a result, some franchisors may restrict the protection provided to you to a grant of first refusal to acquire an additional franchise within your territory, or may subject you to a performance quota in terms of a prescribed number of outlet openings in order to maintain exclusivity within your territory. Another approach taken by some franchisors is to limit exclusivity to a formula based on population, with the result that when the population within your territory exceeds a certain number, the franchisor may either itself operate, or grant a franchise to operate, an additional outlet in the territory.

Some questions you might like to have answered in the franchise agreement are as follows:

1. Exactly what are the geographic boundaries of your territory, and are they marked on a map as part of the contract?
2. Do you have a choice of other territories?
3. What direct competition is there in your territory, and how many more franchises does the franchisor expect to sell in that area within the next five years?
4. If the territory is an exclusive one, what are the guarantees of this exclusivity?
5. Even with these guarantees, will you be permitted to open another franchise in the same territory?
6. Can your territory be reduced at any time by the franchisor?
7. Has the franchisor prepared a market survey of your territory? (If so, ask for a copy of it and study it.)
8. Has the specific site for the franchise within the territory been decided on? (If not, how and when will this be done?)

TRAINING AND OPERATING ASSISTANCE

Virtually every franchise agreement deals with the question of training the franchisee. Training programs may involve training schools, field experience, training manuals, or on-location training.

The franchise agreement should have some provision for an initial training program for you, and should specify the duration and location of this training and who is responsible for your related transportation, accommodation, and living expenses. This initial training is generally provided for you and the managers of your franchise business. The franchisor will usually require you and your managers to complete the training program successfully prior to the opening of your franchise business. If for some reason you should fail to complete the training program, the franchisor often reserves the right to terminate the agreement and refund all fees, less any costs incurred.

Many franchise agreements also provide for start-up advisory training at the franchise premises prior to or during the opening of the business. This typically involves a program lasting a specified number of days. The agreement should indicate who is expected to bear the cost for such start-up training, including who will be responsible for the payment of travel, meals, accommodation, and other expenses of the franchisor's supervisory personnel.

The franchise agreement may also make reference to periodic refresher training. It should specify whether attendance at such programs is optional or mandatory. If it is mandatory, you should ensure that a specified maximum number of such programs is indicated for each year of the franchise agreement. The duration and location of these programs should also be specified.

Most franchisors want tight control over the day-to-day operations of the franchise, and accordingly they provide extensive operating assistance to their franchisees. This assistance is often in the form of a copyrighted operations manual that spells out, procedure by procedure, how you are expected to run the business. The manual will include such information as the franchisor's policies and procedures, and cover such details as the hours you must remain open, record-keeping methods and procedures, procedures for hiring and training employees, and, in a restaurant franchise, such matters as recipes, portion sizes, food storage and handling procedures, and menu mix and prices. The franchise agreement may also indicate that operating assistance will be provided in relation to:

1. The selection of inventory for your franchise business

2. Inspections and evaluation of your performance

3. Periodic advice with respect to hiring personnel, implementing advertising and promotional programs, and evaluating improvements in the franchise system

4. Purchasing goods, supplies, and services

5. Bookkeeping and accounting services

6. Hiring and training of employees

7. Formulation and implementation of advertising and promotional programs

8. Financial advice and consultation

9. Such additional assistance as you may require from time to time

CONTRACT DURATION, RENEWAL, AND TERMINATION

The duration of your franchise agreement may be as short as one year or as long as 40 to 50 years. However, the majority of franchise contracts run from 10 to 20 years. Most agreements also contain some provision for renewal of the contract. Be sure you understand these renewal provisions and what the terms, conditions, and costs of renewal will be. Renewal provisions commonly contain requirements for the payment of additional fees and upgrading of the franchise facilities to standards required by the franchisor at that time. The cost of upgrading is usually borne by the franchisee.

You should be aware, however, that not all agreements necessarily contain provisions for their renewal at the expiration of the initial term. Some agreements merely expire at the end of this term, and the rights revert to the franchisor.

The part of the franchise agreement usually considered most offensive by many prospective franchisees are those sections relating to termination of the agreement. Franchisors typically wish to develop a detailed list of conditions in which you might be considered in default of the agreement. *Events of default* typically fall into two categories: (1) critical or material events that would allow for termination of the agreement without notice by the franchisor and (2) events about which you would first be given written notice, with an opportunity to correct the situation.

Most franchise agreements also allow the franchisor the right, on termination or expiration, to purchase from you all inventory, supplies, equipment, furnishings, leasehold improvements, and fixtures used in connection with the franchise business. The method of calculating the purchase price of such items is entirely negotiable by the parties prior to the execution of the franchise agreement. This has been another area of considerable disagreement between franchisors and franchisees.

When renewing franchise agreements, many franchisors do not require the payment of an additional fee, but they may require franchisees to pay the current, and usually higher, royalty fees and advertising contributions. These increases, of course, reduce your income. In addition, the franchisor may require you to make substantial leasehold improvements, update signage, and make other renovations to your outlet to conform to current franchise system standards. These capital expenditures can be expensive, so it should be clear from the beginning what improvements might be required on renewal.

SELLING OR TRANSFERRING YOUR FRANCHISE

With respect to the transfer or sale of your franchise, most franchise agreements indicate that you are granted rights under the agreement based on the franchisor's investigation of your qualifications. These rights are typically considered to be personal to you as a franchisee. The contract will usually state that transfers of ownership are prohibited without the approval of the franchisor, but you should attempt to have the franchisor agree that such consent will not be unreasonably withheld.

For self-protection, you should be sure that the agreement contains provisions for the transfer of the franchise to your spouse or an adult child on your death. Also, it should be possible to transfer the franchise to a corporation that is 100 per cent owned by you and has been set up solely to operate the franchise. These transfers should be possible without the payment of additional fees.

Most franchisors, however, require transfer of your franchise to an external party who meets their normal criteria of technical competence, capital, and character.

Another common provision is for the franchisor to have a *right of first refusal* — the option to purchase your franchise in the event that you receive an offer from an independent third party to acquire your rights. In such a situation you may be required to first offer such rights back to the franchisor under the same terms and conditions offered by the independent third party. If the franchisor declines to acquire your rights within a specified period of time after receipt of your notice of such an offer, you can proceed to complete the sale or transfer to the third-party purchaser.

One problem with this right of first refusal is the response time the franchisor has to exercise this right. In some agreements the allowable period is several months, during which the third-party buyer is left on hold. In your original agreement, you should try to negotiate for a more reasonable period of 15 to 30 days for the exercise of this right of first refusal.

By anticipating these and other problems during the initial negotiations, you may be able to avoid future difficulties and enhance the marketability of your franchise.

SOME EXAMPLES

As mentioned above, the specific terms included in a franchise agreement can vary substantially from situation to situation. For example, under the terms of the Enviro Masters Lawn Care (www.enviromasters.com) franchise agreement for its organic and environmentally considerate lawn care service franchise, franchisees pay $15,000 to $25,000 for an initial franchise fee plus a monthly royalty of 5 per cent of gross sales and 2 per cent of gross sales for the corporate advertising program. The minimum total investment required to get into the business is $25,000, with a total average investment of around $35,000. For this fee the franchisee receives the use of the company's trademark and trade names. The company also provides training, marketing support, and field training in turf management and similar areas.

In contrast, franchisees of Quizno's Classic Subs (www.quiznos.com) can expect to make a total investment of around $200,000 to open a typical outlet. This includes the company's standard franchise fee of $25,000. In addition, franchisees will need further funds for deposits of various types and money for working capital. Royalties amount to 7 per cent of gross sales paid monthly, and the advertising contribution is a further 4 per cent (1 per cent for national advertising and 3 per cent for expenditures in the local market). Of this amount, franchisees should have at least $60,000 in unencumbered cash. The rest may be financed through one of the national banks' franchise programs with the assistance of the company. Franchisees receive 22 days of intensive initial training, assistance in site selection and lease negotiations, pre-opening and ongoing operational support, and national, local, and grand opening store marketing programs.

The Keg Steakhouse and Bar (www.kegsteakhouse.com) bills itself as Canada's leading steakhouse. A typical new, stand-alone Keg restaurant requires an investment of over $1.8 million to build the facility and cover the necessary start-up costs. This includes the franchise fee of $50,000. Franchisees also pay a royalty of 5 per cent of their gross sales each month and contribute 2.5 per cent to a corporate advertising fund. This enables them to use the "Keg" brand name on their restaurant and the company provides them with training and other support before they open their location, and ongoing support in accounting, marketing, menu development, personnel management, and financial planning.[3]

A sampling of some other popular franchisors indicating their initial franchise or dealership fee, royalty rate, required advertising contribution, and their approximate total average investment to open a typical outlet is shown in Table 5.2.

---

3. For further information on these and other franchise opportunities, see *The Franchise Annual Directory* published by Info Franchise News Inc. (12 Church Street, P.O. Box 755, St. Catharines, Ontario L2R 6Y3: www.infonews.com) and *The Canadian Franchise and Dealership Guide* published by the New Business Centre (5100 South Service Road, Unit 55, Burlington, Ontario L7L 6A5: www.newbusinesscentre.com).

TABLE 5.2   A SAMPLING OF CANADIAN FRANCHISORS

Franchisor	Number of Owned Units In Canada	Number of Franchisees/ Dealers In Canada	Initial Fee	Royalty	Advertising Program	Approximate Investment Required	Web Site
Boston Pizza	1	100	$45,000	7%	2.5%	$650,000 – 750,000	www.bostonpizza.com
Dollar Thrifty Rent-a-Car	56	96	$5,000 – 100,000	8%	—	$60,000 – 250,000	www.thrifty.com
Great Canadian Dollar Store	—	140	$15,000	4%	—	$100,000	www.dollarstores.com
Molly Maid	—	160	$14,000	6%	—	$14,000 + $4,000 working capital	www.mollymaid.com
Dairy Queen Canada	—	520	$35,000	4%	—	$450,000 – 1,200,000	www.dairyqueen.com
We Care Home Health Services	2	51	$40,000	5%	2%	$100,000	www.wecare.ca
McDonald's Restaurants of Canada	344	771	$45,000	17% includes rent, service fees, and advertising	—	$600,000 – 800,000	www.mcdonalds.com
Midas Muffler	20	230	$25,000	5%	5%	$225,000	www.midas.com
Domino's Pizza	—	206	$25,000	5.5%	4%	$150,000	www.dominos.com
Second Cup Coffee Co.	6	400	$25,000	9%	2%	$300,000 – 350,000	www.secondcup.com
Tim Hortons	145	1,553	$50,000	3%	—	$350,000 – 400,000	www.timhortons.com
Kwik Kopy Printing	3	67	$29,500	6%	3%	$200,000 + working capital	www.kwikkopy.ca
Shred-It	12	56	$55,000	5%	1.5%	$350,000	www.shredit.com

Source: Adapted from *The Franchise Annual Directory* 2004, Info Franchise News Inc.

BUYING A FRANCHISE

FINDING A FRANCHISE BUSINESS

Perhaps the most common source of preliminary information regarding available franchises is newspaper advertisements. Major business newspapers such as the *National Post* and *The Globe and Mail* all have special sections devoted to franchise advertisements. The "Business" or "Business Opportunities" section of the classified advertisements in your local newspaper can also be an important place to look for prospective franchise situations. Business journals and trade magazines may also contain ads for many franchise organizations. Recommendations from friends, trade shows and seminars, and business opportunity shows often held in our larger cities can also be excellent means of contacting franchisors.

Another important source of information is franchise directories, which list franchisors' names and addresses along with information on the type of franchise offered, the costs involved, and other useful information. Some helpful directories include *The Franchise Annual Directory* and *The Canadian Franchise and Dealership Guide* (see footnote 3).

OUT-OF-THE-ORDINARY FRANCHISE OPPORTUNITIES

If fast food, oil changes, and lawn care are not your idea of an exciting business, here are some examples of new, imaginative, and unique franchise opportunities that threaten to put an entirely new face on the industry:

- **Easyriders** Franchise stores that sell new, used, and custom motorcycles, parts and accessories, and fashion motorcycle apparel (www.easyriders.com)
- **Cutie Pies Co.** A home-based business bronzing baby handprint/footprint keepsakes (www.cutiepies.net)
- **Flamingo a Friend** Place plastic animals — flamingos, cows, pigs, etc. — in yards for special events like birthdays, anniversaries, graduation, etc. (www.flamingoafriend.com)
- **Impressions on Hold International** Custom-write and -produce "on hold" advertising messages for business phone systems to increase the productivity of on-hold time for their customers (www.impressionsonhold.com)
- **Flyaway Indoor Skydiving** Closed system indoor vertical wind tunnel in which participants perform skydiving maneuvers (www.flyawayindoorskydiving.com)
- **Pointts** Defence services for people facing charges for traffic violations (www.points.com)

Source: *The Franchise Annual Directory* 2004, Info Franchise News Inc.

CHECKING OUT THE FRANCHISE OPPORTUNITY

After sifting through the various choices available, most prospective franchisees narrow their selection down to one or two possibilities. The next step is requesting a promotional kit from each of these franchisors. Normally this kit contains basic information about the company — its philosophy, a brief history, a listing of the number of outlets, where they do business, etc. Most kits also contain an *application form* requesting your name and address, information about your past business experience, the value of your net assets, and other data; for the process to continue with the franchisor, you must complete it in detail. The form may have any one of a number of titles:

- Confidential Information Form
- Personal History
- Confidential Application
- Franchise Application
- Pre-Interview Form
- Qualification Report
- Credit Application
- Application for Interview Form
- Request for Interview

Regardless of which of these titles is used, they are all different ways of describing the same thing and request much the same information. For example, you may be asked for:

1. Personal data such as your name, address, telephone number, age, health and physical impairments, marital status, number of dependants, and the names of any fraternal, business, or civic organizations to which you might belong

2. Business data such as your present business, your position, the name and address of your employer, how long you have been involved in this business, your present annual salary, and any previous business history you may have, and the name and address of your bank

3. Professional references from your bank manager, for example, and any other references you may care to provide

4. Financial data such as your average annual income for the past five years and a total declaration of your current assets and liabilities to establish your net worth

5. Additional data that relate to your particular interest in the franchise

The application form normally requires you to provide a deposit, typically in the range of $2,000 to $5,000. In most cases the form will state that this deposit will be credited toward the initial franchise fee without interest or deduction if the transaction proceeds. However, you should make sure that if you are turned down, all or most of this deposit will be refunded, especially if it is a large amount of money and the franchise is new and unproven.

If your application is approved, the franchisor will interview you to determine your suitability as a franchisee. The focus of this interview will be on assessing your capability according to various objective criteria that have been established by the franchisor. Every franchisor has its own established criteria based on previous experience with various kinds of people. For example, many franchisors will not consider absentee owners and refuse to grant franchises strictly for investment purposes. They feel that the success of their system rests on the motivation created by individually owned and managed outlets.

The personal characteristics desired by the franchisor will vary with the type of business. For example, a different level of education is necessary to operate a management consulting service than is needed to operate a carpet cleaning firm. Research on these selection criteria indicates that many franchisors tend to rank them in the following order:

1. Credit and financial standing
2. Personal ability to manage the operation
3. Previous work experience
4. Personality
5. Health
6. Educational background

While other factors may also be considered by particular franchisors, these criteria tend to dominate the selection process.

This interview is also an opportunity for you to raise questions about the franchisor's financial stability, trademark protection policy, the ongoing services provided to franchisees, information regarding any financial packages that may have been arranged with particular banks, the names and addresses of current franchisees, and any other questions that may occur to you. This is an opportunity for you and the franchisor to assess each other and see if you can work together on a long-term basis.

At this interview, the franchisor will also provide you with a copy of the franchise agreement. At this point, you must evaluate all the available information with the help of an accountant, your bank manager, and a lawyer to ensure that you feel comfortable with the franchisor and that you are happy your investment is secure. If you have any remaining questions or doubts, now is the time to resolve them. Then, if you are still not completely sure in your own mind that you wish to proceed, you should ask for a refund of your deposit.

Well-established and popular franchisors are unlikely to change their arrangements or legal documentation very much in response to a prospective franchisee's requests. They have successful systems in which many would-be franchisees would like to participate. For them, it's a seller's market.

If one of these franchisors accepts you as a franchisee, you may have to make up your mind very quickly. It is important to be decisive. If you are comfortable with the franchisor and the franchise agreement, you should be ready to sign. If not, you should ask for a refund and pursue other opportunities.

Some franchisors will expect you to sign the contract right away. Others wait until they have found a suitable location for your outlet, usually within a predetermined period of time. In some cases, it can take weeks, perhaps even months, for a suitable site to be found or a lease negotiated before you actually sign. It should also be remembered that popular franchisors often have long waiting lists of prospective franchisees, so that one or more years can pass before you will be in business.

FRANCHISE FINANCING

One of the first steps in evaluating any franchise opportunity is to determine the total cost of getting into the business. This could include the initial franchise fee, equipment costs, start-up inventories and expenses, and initial working capital requirements. This total commitment can be substantial. A study released by the International Franchise Association in the United States indicated the following average initial investment to start a franchised outlet by industry category. These figures are in U.S. dollars and do not include the cost of real estate.[4]

Baked goods	$195,000
Business services	$86,000

---

4. "The Profile of Franchising: A Statistical Abstract of 1998 UFOC (Uniform Franchise Offering Circulars) Data," International Franchise Association Educational Foundation, Inc., Washington, D.C., February 2000.

Fast food	$183,000
Lodging	$2,100,000
Printing	$232,000
Restaurant	$478,000
Service business	$158,000
Sports and recreation	$386,000
Travel	$56,000

You must also determine how much of this amount must be put up as an initial investment and what kind of terms might be arranged for handling the balance. Most franchisors expect the franchisee to put up 30 to 50 per cent of the total franchise package cost as an initial investment. You must ask yourself whether you have enough unencumbered capital to cover this amount.

Financing of the remainder can sometimes be done through the franchisor, or the franchisor may have previously arranged a standardized financing package for prospective franchisees through one of the major banks or trust companies. Subway, the successful submarine sandwich franchise, offers its new franchisees financing via an in-house equipment leasing program. Compucentre also has arranged an in-house financing program for franchisees in conjunction with a couple of the major banks. These programs may be somewhat more expensive for the franchisee than arranging an independent bank loan, but they can be more convenient.

The initial investment required for a restaurant franchise can be substantial. A typical fast-food take-out restaurant such as Koya Japan has an initial franchise fee of $25,000 and an average total investment of $175,000. The cost of a full-service restaurant such as Swiss Chalet Chicken & Ribs includes a franchise fee of $75,000 and a total investment ranging from $1.1 million to $1.4 million. In these cases, equipment and leasehold improvements tend to make up the largest component of the total cost.

In the retail sector, the size of the total investment will vary depending on the nature and location of the outlet. For example, a video store like Jumbo Video will require a franchise fee of $50,000 and a total investment of roughly $400,000, with the franchisee having to provide $150,000 in cash. A computer store like Compucentre has a franchise fee of $25,000 with an average investment of $275,000, while a retail building supply dealership like Windsor Plywood has an initial fee of $35,000 and a total required investment up to $1 million. Most of these investments are typically in inventory.

Key points

WHAT DOES IT COST TO OPEN A FRANCHISE ?

The estimated costs to open a Joey's Only Seafood Restaurants/Tennessee Jack's Rotisserie Chicken N' Ribs are (based on approximately 204 square metres, in Canadian dollars):

Franchise fee	$25,000
Opening promotion fee	5,000
Leasehold improvements	90,000–130,000
Smallwares	9,000
Furniture, fixtures, and kitchen equipment	105,000–120,000
Miscellaneous	6,000
Food and supplies	11,000
TJ Foods opening supplies	11,000
Training and pre-opening expenses	11,000
Deposits	4,000–10,000
Total Estimated Cost to Open	**$277,000–338,000**

Source: Joey's Only (www.joeys-only.com/contact.htm), accessed July 3, 2004.

The investment required for a service franchise is usually much lower. Many service franchises can be established for a total investment of less than $50,000. For example, Jani-King Canada, the world's largest commercial cleaning franchise, offers its franchises for a fee ranging from $9,900 to $24,900 depending on the territory, with a nominal additional amount of financing for equipment, supplies, and initial working capital. A residential cleaning and maid service franchise like Molly Maid can be established for a franchise fee of $14,000 plus $4,000 to $5,000 in working capital. At the other extreme, opening a franchised hotel or motel may involve a total investment of several million dollars, although the initial amount of money required may be much less since the land and buildings for the hotel or motel can often be externally financed.

Key points

ADVICE WHEN CONSIDERING A FRANCHISE OPTION

- Do your own research, and take your time.
- Don't be afraid to cold-call current franchisees (especially those in other provinces) and ask them all kinds of questions.
- Try to talk to former franchisees whose business went under. The more reputable franchisors may help you with names and numbers.
- Talk to knowledgeable people in the franchising sector to get the latest word on the organization you're thinking of joining, and what it's like to work with.
- Have an experienced franchise lawyer review your contract.
- If you still want to jump into the world of franchising, assume that nothing will ever again work the way you are used to. The best you can hope for is to reduce the number of "omigawd" surprises you are going to have to face.

Source: M. Stern, "Franchise Fairy Tales," *Canadian Business*, June 23, 2003, p. 30.

FUTURE TRENDS IN FRANCHISING

A number of trends have emerged in the past few years that will positively impact franchising opportunities, and they are likely to continue. Among the most important are:

1. **Increasing emphasis on senior care** As North America ages with the maturing of the baby boomers, it is predicted that eldercare will replace child care as the number-one social issue. As they age, many seniors want to stay in their own homes, so any business that will provide them with companionship, extra help around the house, or assistance in performing their daily activities, such as personal care and meal preparation, is likely to succeed.

2. **Child care and education** Increasingly, people want their children to have fun, become better educated, or get other forms of enrichment or special attention, and they are prepared to pay for it.

3. **Technical support** With the continual dependence of people and businesses on increasingly complex technology, advice is often needed on what to buy and what not to buy, how to handle repairs and upgrades, as well as solutions for various technological problems.

4. **Pet care** More and more, pets are being considered part of the family and companies are springing up to provide a range of services, such as boarding facilities, cleaning and grooming, pet training, and feeding and general care services.

5. **Home improvements** Consumers are increasingly spending more on their dwellings, which has created an explosion of franchisors providing a broad range of services, such as general building services, kitchen remodelling, handyman services, interior decorating and painting, and electrical and plumbing services.

6. **Fitness** Fitness and obesity have received considerable coverage in the media, fuelling consumer interest in improved diet and exercise regimes. Gyms and fitness centres have been at the centre of this trend, particularly facilities that have emphasized women-only services.

7. **Restaurants** Restaurants of all types are expected to continue to be a very popular sector of franchising. Concepts such as Asian and healthy fast food, specialty ice cream, and neighbourhood coffeehouses continue to grow.

FYI FOR YOUR INFORMATION

For more information on franchising you might check out the following sources:

Canadian Franchise Association (www.cfa.ca)

International Franchise Association Check out its "Consumer Guide to Buying a Franchise." (www.franchise.org)

Franchise Conxions A Canadian-based franchise and small-business consulting firm that offers a wide range of services to the franchise industry. (www.franchise-conxions.com)

Checklist for Franchisees: Canada Business Service Centres (www.cbsc.org/english/search/display.cfm?CODE=4010&Coll=FE_FEDSBIS_E)

FranNet, The Franchise Connection A collection of resource materials and articles that have been featured in various franchise-related magazines and publications. (www.frannet.com/Research)

Canadian Franchise Opportunities An online directory of franchises and franchise business services. (canada.franchiseopportunities.com)

The Franchise Annual Online An online version of *The Franchise Annual Directory* with an extensive listing of available franchises. (www.infonews.com/online.html)

EVALUATING A FRANCHISE — A CHECKLIST

The checklist shown in Figure 5.1 can serve as an effective tool for you to use in evaluating a franchise opportunity. When reading through the questions, you will notice that some of them require you to do a little homework before you can reasonably respond. For example, you and/or your lawyer will have to review the franchise agreement to assess the acceptability of the various clauses and conditions. You will also have to give some thought to how much capital you have personally and where you might raise additional financing.

Some questions call for further research. Ask the franchisor for the names and addresses of a number of current franchisees. Select a sample of them and contact them to discuss their views of the franchisor and the franchise agreement. Make certain your interview takes place without the franchisor or his or her representative present. Check the length of time that the franchisee has operated in that particular location in comparison to the length of time that franchise has been in existence. If there is a difference, try to determine what happened to the earlier franchisee(s). If you have been provided with pro forma financial statements or other information by the franchisor indicating the level of sales and financial performance you might expect, ask these franchisees to confirm that these statements are reasonably close to reality. In addition, what you may feel you require in terms of training, advertising and promotion support, and ongoing operating assistance may be a function of the type of franchise you are evaluating.

Make a copy of this checklist for each franchise you intend to evaluate. By using a similar outline to assess each opportunity, it will be much easier for you to compare them.

FIGURE 5.1   CHECKLIST FOR EVALUATING A FRANCHISE

THE FRANCHISOR

1. What is the name and address of the franchise company?
   Name _____
   Address _____
   _____

2. The franchise company is: Public _____ Private _____

3. What is the name and address of the parent company (if different from that of the franchise company)?
   Name _____
   Address _____
   _____

4. The parent company is: Public _____ Private _____

5. On what date was the company founded and when was the first franchise awarded?
   Company founded _____ First franchise awarded _____

6. How many outlets does the franchise currently have in operation or under construction?
   a. Of these outlets, how many are franchised and how many are company-owned?
      Franchised _____ Company-owned _____
   b. How many franchises have failed?
   c. How many of these failures have been within the past two years?
   d. Why did these franchises fail?
      Franchisor's reasons _____
      _____
      _____
      Franchisee's reasons _____
      _____
      _____

7. How many new outlets does the franchisor plan to open within the next 12 months? Where will they open?
   How many _____ Where _____
   _____

8. a. Who are the key principals in the day-to-day operation of the franchisor's business?

Name	Title	Background
_____	_____	_____
_____	_____	_____
_____	_____	_____
_____	_____	_____

   b. Who are the directors of the company, other than those individuals named above?

Name	Title	Background
_____	_____	_____
_____	_____	_____
_____	_____	_____
_____	_____	_____

continued

Checklist for Evaluating a Franchise — continued

   c. Who are the consultants to the company?

Name	Title	Background
_____	_____	_____
_____	_____	_____
_____	_____	_____
_____	_____	_____

THE FRANCHISE

1. Fill in the following data on each of several present franchisees.

Franchise 1

Owner_____

Address _____

_____

Telephone _____

Date started_____

Franchise 2

Owner_____

Address _____

_____

Telephone _____

Date started_____

Franchise 3

Owner_____

Address _____

_____

Telephone _____

Date started_____

2. Has a franchise ever been awarded in your area?   Yes _____ No _____
   a. If Yes, and it is *still in operation*, provide details.

Owner_____

Address _____

_____

Telephone _____

Date started_____

   b. If Yes, and it is *no longer in operation*, provide details.

Person involved_____

Address _____

Date opened_____

Date closed_____

Reason for failure_____

3. Is the product or service offered by the franchise:

    a. Part of a growing market?   Yes _____ No _____

    b. Needed in your area?   Yes _____ No _____

    c. Of interest to you?   Yes _____ No _____

    d. Safe for the consumer?   Yes _____ No _____

    e. Protected by a guarantee or warranty?   Yes _____ No _____

    f. Associated with a well-known trademark or personality?   Yes _____ No _____

    g. Accompanied by a trademark that is adequately protected?   Yes _____ No _____

4. Will you be acquiring:

    a. A single-unit franchise?   _____

    b. An area franchise?   _____

    c. A master franchise?   _____

5. The franchise is: Exclusive _____ Non-exclusive _____

6. What facilities will be required and will you have to own or lease?

    a. Business can be operated out of home? Yes _____ No _____

    b. Facilities required:

	Yes	*No*	*Own*	*Lease*
Office	_____	_____	_____	_____
Retail outlet	_____	_____	_____	_____
Manufacturing facility	_____	_____	_____	_____
Warehouse	_____	_____	_____	_____
Other (specify)	_____	_____	_____	_____

7. Who will be responsible for:

	Franchisor	*Franchisee*
a. Location feasibility study?	_____	_____
b. Facility design and layout?	_____	_____
c. Construction?	_____	_____
d. Furnishing?	_____	_____
e. Arranging financing?	_____	_____

FRANCHISE COSTS

1. Is a forecast of expected income and expenses provided? Yes _____ No _____

    a. If Yes, is it:

        i. Based on actual franchisee operations? _____

        ii. Based on a franchisor-owned outlet? _____

        iii. Based strictly on estimated performance? _____

    b. If Yes, does the forecast:

        i. Relate directly to your market area? Yes _____ No _____

        ii. Satisfy your personal goals? Yes _____ No _____

        iii. Provide for an acceptable return on investment? Yes _____ No _____

        iv. Provide for an adequate level of promotion and personal expenses? Yes ____ No ____

continued

Checklist for Evaluating a Franchise — continued

2. How much money will it require to get started in the business? Itemize.

Item	*Amount*
a. Franchise fee	$ _____
b. Franchisor-provided services	_____
c. Supplies and opening inventory	_____
d. Real estate	_____
e. Machinery and equipment	_____
f. Furniture and fixtures	_____
g. Opening expenses	_____
h. Other	_____
Total Initial Investment	$ _____ **(A)**

3. How much other money will be required:

a. To defray operating losses for first few months of operation? $ _____ **(B)**

b. To cover your personal expenses for the first year of operation? $ _____ **(C)**

4. Total financial requirements (A + B + C = D) $ _____ **(D)**

5. How much of these total financial requirements do you personally have available? $ _____ **(E)**

6. If the franchisor provides any financial assistance:

a. How much? $ _____ **(F)**

b. What does this represent as a percentage of your total estimated costs? _____ %

c. What is the interest rate on this financing? _____ %

d. When does the money have to be paid back? _____

7. Where will you be able to obtain the rest of the required funds? Specify sources from the following list:

a. Banks, credit unions, or other financial institutions	$ _____
b. Finance companies	_____
c. Friends, relatives, and neighbours	_____
d. Other private sources	_____
e. Leasing arrangements	_____
f. Suppliers' credit	_____
g. Government assistance programs	_____
h. Other (specify)	$ _____
Total	$ _____ **(G)**

8. Total funds available from all sources (E + F + G = H)

Grand Total $ _____ **(H)**

9. How do the funds available compare with your total estimated requirements? (D − H) $ _____

THE FRANCHISE AGREEMENT

1. Have you obtained a copy of the franchise agreement? Yes _____ No _____

2. Have you given a copy to your lawyer and accountant to review?

Lawyer   Yes _____ No _____

Accountant   Yes _____ No _____

3. Does the agreement contain clauses that relate to the following areas and activities and are the specified terms and conditions acceptable or unacceptable to you?

	Yes	No	If Yes Acceptable	If Yes Unacceptable
a. Franchise fee	_____	_____	_____	_____
b. Commissions and royalties	_____	_____	_____	_____
c. Purchase of products and supplies	_____	_____	_____	_____
d. Lease of premises	_____	_____	_____	_____
e. Territorial protection	_____	_____	_____	_____
f. Training assistance	_____	_____	_____	_____
g. Termination	_____	_____	_____	_____
h. Renewal	_____	_____	_____	_____
i. Selling and transferring	_____	_____	_____	_____
j. Advertising and promotion	_____	_____	_____	_____
k. Operating assistance	_____	_____	_____	_____
l. Trademark protection	_____	_____	_____	_____

RUNNING YOUR FRANCHISE OPERATION

1. Does the franchisor provide you with an initial formal training program? Yes _____ No_____

If Yes: a. How long does it last? _____days

b. Is cost included in the franchise fee? Yes_____No_____Partially _____

If No or Partially, specify how much you will have to pay for:

- i. Training course $ _____
- ii. Training materials   _____
- iii. Transportation   _____
- iv. Room and board   _____
- v. Other   _____

Total Costs $ _____

c. Does the training course cover any of the following subjects?

- i. Franchise operations   Yes _____ No _____
- ii. Sales   Yes _____ No _____
- iii. Financial management   Yes _____ No _____
- iv. Advertising and promotion   Yes _____ No _____
- v. Personnel management   Yes _____ No _____
- vi. Manufacturing methods   Yes _____ No _____
- vii. Maintenance   Yes _____ No _____
- viii. Operations   Yes _____ No _____
- ix. Employee training   Yes _____ No _____
- x. Other (specify) _____
        _____Yes _____ No _____

2. How do you train your initial staff?

a. Is the training program provided by the franchisor? Yes _____ No _____

b. Does the franchisor make a staff member available from head office to assist you? Yes_____ No_____

continued

Checklist for Evaluating a Franchise — continued

    c. What materials are included in the staff training program?

_____

_____

_____

3. Is there any requirement for you to participate in a continuing training program?

Yes _____ No _____

If Yes:

    a. Who pays the cost of this program?   Franchisee_____ Franchisor _____

    b. If you have to pay for this continuing training, how much does it cost? $ _____

4. Is the product or service of the franchise normally sold by any of the following means?

a. In customer's home — by appointment	Yes _____	No _____
b. In customer's home — by cold-calling	Yes _____	No _____
c. By telephone	Yes _____	No _____
d. In a store or other place of business	Yes _____	No _____
e. At customer's business — by appointment	Yes _____	No _____
f. At customer's business — by cold-calling	Yes _____	No _____
g. By direct mail	Yes _____	No _____
h. Other (specify) _____	Yes _____	No _____

5. How do you get sales leads and customers?

a. Provided by franchisor	Yes _____	No _____
b. Self-generated	Yes _____	No _____
c. Through advertising	Yes _____	No _____
d. By direct mail	Yes _____	No _____
e. By telephone	Yes _____	No _____
f. Through trade shows	Yes _____	No _____
g. Other _____	Yes _____	No _____

6. Give a brief profile of the types of customers you feel are the best prospects for the products or services offered by the franchise.

_____

_____

_____

7. a. What is the national advertising budget of the franchisor? $ _____

    b. How is this budget distributed among the primary advertising media?

TV	% _____
Radio	_____
Newspaper	_____
Outdoor	_____
Magazines	_____
Direct mail	_____

Other (specify)   _____

Total   **100%**

8. What kind of advertising and promotion support is available from the franchisor for the local franchisee?

	Yes	*No*	*If Yes, Cost*
a. Prepackaged local advertising program	_____	_____	$ _____
b. Cooperative advertising program	_____	_____	$ _____
c. Grand-opening package	_____	_____	$ _____

9. Do you need the services of an advertising agency?   Yes _____ No _____

10. a. Who are your principal competitors? Name them in order of importance.

    1. _____

    2. _____

    3. _____

    b. Describe what you know about each and how each compares with your franchise.

Competitor 1

Owner _____

Address _____

_____

Description _____

_____

_____

Competitor 2

Owner _____

Address _____

_____

Description _____

_____

_____

Competitor 3

Owner _____

Address _____

_____

Description _____

_____

_____

11. What operating assistance is available from the franchisor if you should need it?

a. Finance and accounting	Yes _____	No _____
b. Advertising and promotion	Yes _____	No _____
c. Research and development	Yes _____	No _____
d. Sales	Yes _____	No _____
e. Real estate	Yes _____	No _____

continued

Checklist for Evaluating a Franchise — continued

f. Construction   Yes _____ No _____

g. Personnel and training   Yes _____ No _____

h. Manufacturing and operations   Yes _____ No _____

i. Purchasing   Yes _____ No _____

j. Other (specify)   Yes _____ No _____

12. Does the franchisor have a field supervisor assigned to work with a number of franchises?
Yes _____ No _____

If Yes: a. How many franchises is she/he assigned to?

b. Who would be assigned to your franchise?

Name_____

Address_____

_____

Telephone_____

Video Case #5

Reading the Fine Print

Summary

A franchise would seem like a good fit for a budding entrepreneur — right? Not so, according to former Second Cup franchisee Paul Dahlin. After a disagreement between Second Cup and his landlord over the cost of his lease, Second Cup decided to vacate the building and left Dahlin without a franchise, and out the $150,000 he had invested in the business.

Other entrepreneurs have also learned hard lessons from the fine print in their franchise agreements. Dale Hunt purchased one Robin's Donuts location and then another farther down the street. After they became successful, his cost of supplies increased. He thought he could charge more for the products he sold, but that did not please the franchisor. In the end, he sold both his locations at a loss and sued Robin's Donuts for breach of contract.

Questions for Discussion

1. What grounds could a franchisee have to sue a franchisor?

2. Who has the most control in the franchisee–franchisor relationship? Why?

3. What are the benefits of opening a franchise from the franchisee's point of view?

4. What important lessons can be learned from the experience of these franchisees?

5. Why would a franchisor not want someone with an entrepreneurial spirit to become one of its franchisees?

Conducting a Feasibility Study

Part 1: Technical and Market Assessment

So far, we have considered and evaluated your new venture primarily from a conceptual point of view. That is, we have concentrated on the following questions:

1. What product/service businesses would you be interested in pursuing?
2. How attractive are these venture ideas?
3. What options should you consider in getting into a business of your own?

Now, in Stage Six, a step-by-step process will be presented to help you transform your chosen venture concept from the idea stage to the marketplace. This is accomplished by means of a *feasibility study* to determine the probability of your product or service idea successfully getting off the ground by subjecting it to solid analysis and evaluation. You must put your ideas through this type of evaluation to discover whether they contain any fatal flaws that are likely to impact their viability. Sometimes people get all excited about the prospects of a new business without thoroughly researching and evaluating its potential. Some time later they may discover that while the idea was good, the market was too small, the profit margins too narrow, the competition too tough, the financing insufficient, or there are other reasons that cause the business to fail. If the individuals involved had thoroughly researched their idea and conducted a feasibility study before starting, many of these failed businesses would never have been started in the first place.

A feasibility study is the first comprehensive plan you need in contemplating any new venture. It proves both to yourself and others that your new venture concept can become a profitable reality. If the feasibility study indicates that the business idea has potential, then you can proceed to write a business plan. A typical feasibility study considers the following areas:

1. The concept for your venture
2. An assessment of your market
3. The technical feasibility of your idea
4. The supply situation
5. Cost–profit analysis
6. Your plans for future action

The first four of these topics will be discussed in this Stage; the last two will be addressed in Stage Seven. Much of the same information can be incorporated into your subsequent business plan (see Stage Eleven) if it appears that your venture warrants commercial development.

The contents of a typical feasibility study are outlined in Figure 6.1 on page 146. You can use this guide to assist you in evaluating the feasibility of your new venture idea.

YOUR VENTURE CONCEPT

It is critical that you be able to clearly and concisely explain, verbally, the principal concept underlying your venture — what sets it apart from other businesses of similar character. This is what is sometimes called your

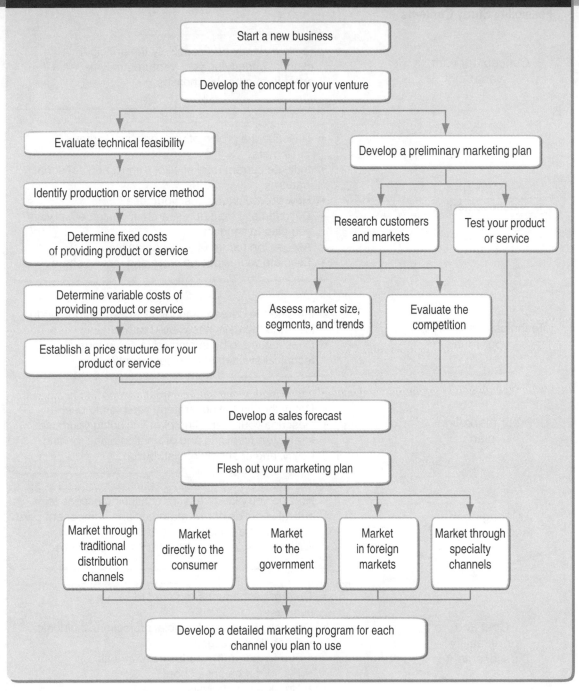

FEASIBILITY STUDY — PART 1

- Start a new business
- Develop the concept for your venture
  - Evaluate technical feasibility
    - Identify production or service method
    - Determine fixed costs of providing product or service
    - Determine variable costs of providing product or service
    - Establish a price structure for your product or service
  - Develop a preliminary marketing plan
    - Research customers and markets
      - Assess market size, segments, and trends
      - Evaluate the competition
    - Test your product or service
- Develop a sales forecast
- Flesh out your marketing plan
  - Market through traditional distribution channels
  - Market directly to the consumer
  - Market to the government
  - Market in foreign markets
  - Market through specialty channels
- Develop a detailed marketing program for each channel you plan to use

"elevator pitch"—a conversation that begins when the elevator door closes and ends when the door opens at your floor. That means you have only a few seconds to capture your listener's interest, so you had better be able to explain your concept quickly, completely, and confidently. If you have difficulty explaining to other people precisely what your business proposes to do, it is a clear sign that your concept still needs development and refinement.

An idea is not yet a concept, only the beginning of one. A fully developed concept includes not only some notion as to the product or service the business plans to provide, but also a description of the proposed pricing strategy, promotional program, and distribution plans. It will also consider such aspects of the business as what is unique or proprietary about your product or service idea, any innovative technology involved in its production or sale, and the principal benefits it is expected to deliver to customers.

FIGURE 6.1   A TYPICAL FEASIBILITY STUDY

Feasibility Study Contents

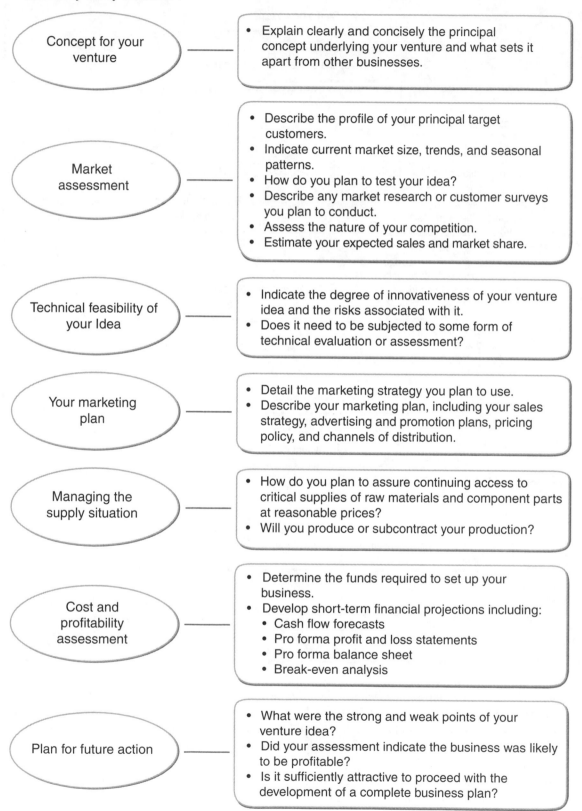

Developing a good description of your concept can be difficult. Many concepts are too broad and general, not clearly communicating the really distinctive elements of the venture — for example, "a retail sporting goods outlet" or "a tool and equipment rental store." Other concepts may use words like "better service," "higher quality," "new," "improved," or "precision machined," which are either ambiguous or likely to have different meanings for different people. It is much better to have a detailed, clear, definitive statement — for example, "a retail outlet providing top-of-the-line hunting and fishing equipment and supplies for the serious outdoors person" or "a tool and equipment rental business for the professional, commercial, and residential building contractor." Such descriptions are easier to visualize and allow the uninformed to really understand what it is you propose to do.

Your business concept is not necessarily etched in stone. It may need to change and evolve over time as you come to better understand the needs of the marketplace and the economics of the business. Sharpening and refining of your concept is normal and to be expected.

TECHNICAL FEASIBILITY

You should keep in mind that not all businesses are started on the basis of new or original ideas. Many, in fact, merely attempt to copy successful ventures. To simplify matters, all product and service ideas can be placed along a continuum according to their degree of innovativeness or may be placed into one of the following categories:

1. **New invention** This is something created for the first time through a high degree of innovation, creativity, and experimentation. Examples include fibre optics, hydrogen-fuelled vehicles, bionic prostheses for replacement arms and legs, WiMax and other wireless technologies, and radio frequency identification systems.

2. **Highly innovative** This term means that the product is somewhat new and as yet not widely known or used. Examples are MP3 players, cellphones integrated with cameras and full text keyboards, wide-ranging consumer products incorporating GPS technology, and non-invasive testing techniques for various kinds of cancer.

3. **Moderately innovative** This refers to a product that is a significant modification of an existing product or service or combines different areas of technology, methods, or processes. Examples include microprocessors used to control automobile fuel injection systems or single-person cars. The term could also refer to such ideas as the redesign of bicycles to make them easier to ride by handicapped or physically disabled people, thus developing a new market.

4. **Slightly innovative** This term means that a small, yet significant, modification is made to an established product or service, as in larger-scale or more exotic recreational water slides.

5. **"Copycatting"** This is simply imitating someone else's business idea.

The degree of innovation inherent in a business idea has strong implications for the risk, difficulty in evaluation, and profit potential of the venture. *Risk* refers to the probability of the product or service's failing in the marketplace. *Evaluation* is the ability to determine its worth or significance. *Profit potential* is the level of return or compensation that you might expect for assuming the risks associated with investing in this business.

In general, the following relationships hold:

1. New inventions are extremely risky and difficult to evaluate, but if they are accepted in the marketplace they can provide enormous profits.

2. For moderately innovative and slightly innovative ideas, the risks are lower and evaluation is less difficult, but profit potential tends to be more limited.

3. In the "copycat" category, risks are often very high and profit potential tends to be quite low. Such businesses usually show no growth, or very slow growth, and there is little opportunity for profit beyond basic wages.

Every new product must also be subject to some form of evaluation to ensure that the benefits intended for prospective customers can indeed be delivered. In developing a working prototype or an operating model of a product with this criterion in mind, some of the most important technical rquirements to consider include the:

- Functional design of the product and the attractaiveness of its appearance
- Flexibility of the product in permitting ready modification of its external features to meet customer requirements or competitive pressures

- Durability of the materials from which the product is made
- Expected product reliability under normal operating circumstanstances
- Safety of the product under normal operating conditions
- Expected rate of obsolescence
- Ease and cost of maintenance
- Ease and cost of processing or manufacture
- Ease of handling and use by the customer

If a product doesn't fare well on some of these requirements, it should be reworked until it does.

One key approach for testing a new product is to subject it to the toughest conditions that might be experienced during actual use. In addition to this kind of test there may be standard engineering tests to which the product will have to be subjected to receive Canadian Standards Association (CSA) (www.csa.ca) or Underwriters Laboratory (UL) (www.ul.com) certification. You might also undertake an evaluation of alternative materials from which the product could be made. Further assistance in conducting a technical evaluation may be available from various agencies of your provincial government as well as some colleges and universities and the Canadian Innovation Centre (www.innovationcentre.ca).

MARKET ASSESSMENT

Assessing the potential market for your concept is a critical part of any feasibility study. At the very least, you need to demonstrate that a market does in fact exist, or there is not much point in developing a full-scale business plan. In some cases the potential market may be large and obvious; in others, considerable research and investigation may be required to demonstrate there is likely to be any significant level of demand. It is essential to determine that a sufficiently large market exists to make the concept financially viable.

WHO IS YOUR CUSTOMER?

To tailor your marketing program to the needs of your market, you must have a very clear idea of who your customers are likely to be. To do this you will need to gather some information in the marketplace. The more information you have about your target market, the better you will be able to develop a successful marketing plan.

TYPES OF MARKETS

The first thing to recognize is that the term "market" does not refer to only a single type of possible customer. A number of different types of markets exist such as:

1. **The consumer market** Individual users of products and services such as you and I

2. **The institutional market** Organizations such as hospitals, personal care homes, schools, universities, and similar types of institutions

3. **The industrial market** Other firms and businesses in your community and across the country

4. **The government market** Various agencies and departments of the municipal, provincial, and federal governments

5. **The international market** Markets similar to the above examples outside the national boundaries of the country

WHAT IS *YOUR* MARKET?

Very few businesses initially operate in all of these markets. Most analyze the possibilities available to them in each situation to determine which offers the best potential. This involves asking such broad questions as:

1. How big is the market?
2. Where is it located geographically?
3. How fast is it growing?

4. What organizations and/or individuals buy this kind of product or service?

5. Why do they buy it?

6. Where and how do they buy it?

7. How often do they buy it?

8. What are their principal requirements in selecting a product or service of this type?

To determine which of these markets is likely to represent the best opportunity for you, you need to understand just what your product or service has to offer to a group of people or businesses. To do this, you need to understand the primary features of your product or service offering and the benefits it can provide. A *feature*, for example, is some characteristic of a product or service that is part of its basic make-up, while a *benefit* is what motivates people to actually buy it. If an automobile has air bags or anti-lock brakes, they are features of the car, but the benefit they provide to the consumer is increased safety. By knowing what your product or service has to offer in terms of features and what will make customers buy it, you can begin to determine characteristics that may be common across the members of your potential market. This kind of assessment will serve to identify some broad areas of opportunity for you.

SEGMENT YOUR MARKET

It is natural to want to target as many people and groups as possible with your business offering. However, in most circumstances it is not very practical to do so. For example, you are not likely to have the promotional budget to be able to communicate effectively with many different groups at once. Even if you had a large enough promotional budget, your promotional message would not likely talk directly to any one group, thus having much less impact. So, in addition to doing the broad analysis described above, you also need to question whether within these major market types there are groups of potential customers with different preferences, requirements, and purchasing practices, or that are concerned about different benefits. For example, toddlers, teenagers, businesspeople, and older adults all have quite different clothing needs although all are members of the consumer market. Retailers, designers, and manufacturers must take these different needs into account when developing and marketing their product lines. Each of these groups should be considered a separate *target market*. This process of breaking down large, heterogeneous consumer or industrial markets into more homogeneous groups is known as *market segmentation*. Most markets can be segmented on the basis of a number of variables:

1. **Geographic location** such as part of a city or town, county, province, region, or country. If you are selling farm equipment, geographic location is obviously a major factor in segmenting your target markets since your customers will be located in particular rural areas. Climate is a commonly used geographic segmentation variable that affects industries such as sporting equipment, lawn and garden equipment, snowblowers and snowmobiles, and heating and air-conditioning equipment. If this is a factor in your business, you need to identify the geographic area where your market is located and identify the specific boundaries within which you will do business.

2. **Demographic description** such as age, gender, marital status, family size, race, religion, education level, income, and occupation. Non-consumer markets might be classified on the basis of their total purchases or sales, number of employees, or type of organizational activity. Choose those demographic characteristics of your target market that relate to their interest, need, and ability to purchase your product or service. For example, a market for luxury condominiums would include professional married couples approximately 35 to 55 years old with incomes of more than $100,000 and either no children or grown children. Similarly, a company like Modrobes might describe its target market as single young men and women between 18 and 25 who are still in school, with incomes under $20,000.

3. **Psychographic or sociological factors** such as lifestyle, status, timing and means of purchasing, and reasons for buying products or services similar to yours. The desire for status or enhanced appearance, the pursuit of fun and excitement, or the desire to be socially responsible and environmentally conscious are all examples of these kinds of variables. Many products — like a variety of extreme sports such as skydiving and bungee jumping, organically grown foods, and environmentally friendly insect control methods — would appeal or not appeal to different people largely on the basis of these types of factors.

RESEARCH YOUR MARKET

WHAT IS MARKET RESEARCH?

Market research can be defined as the gathering, processing, reporting, and interpretation of market information. Small businesses typically conduct less market research than larger ones, but it is essential that all businesses engage in this process to some degree to prepare a realistic marketing plan. The market research process involves four basic steps:

1. Define the need for information
2. Search for secondary data
3. Gather primary data
4. Interpret the information

We will discuss each of these steps as they relate to obtaining the information you will require to put together your market assessment.

DEFINE THE NEED FOR INFORMATION

Before you take the time to gather any data, you need to first decide how you are going to use the information and what you need to demonstrate or show with the information. For example, do you need to:

- Estimate the total expected size of the market for your product or service and the nature and extent of any trends in expected demand?
- Determine the expected level of demand for your product or service?
- Provide a description of who you feel will be your primary customer?
- Outline how your customers are expected to buy your product or service and with what frequency?
- Understand the nature and extent of the competition you may face in the marketplace?

SEARCH FOR SECONDARY DATA

The easiest place to start to try to answer these questions is by searching through available sources of secondary data. Secondary data comprise information that others have put together relating to your industry and/or your customers. Using secondary data is usually considerably less expensive than gathering new information so you should exhaust all readily available sources of secondary information before moving on to gather new data of your own.

Secondary data can come from a tremendous variety of sources. Often they may not exist in the exact form you require but by combining data from a number of secondary sources you may be able to compile the information you require, and at much lower cost than going out and gathering your own information.

SOURCES OF SECONDARY MARKET INFORMATION

There are a number of sources you might consult to get a handle on the approximate size of the market you are considering entering. Some of these sources are Statistics Canada publications; various industry reports, trade journals, and investment journals; and financial statements of your leading competitors. You must be careful to make some provision for error in your estimate of market size. Most of the information sources you will consult will not be able to provide complete up-to-date figures, and forecasts of future sales are always subject to error. Statistics Canada, for example, breaks the country up into 36 Census Metropolitan Areas (CMAs) (www12.statcan.ca/english/census01/home/index.cfm). For each CMA there are a series of referenced maps providing an index for which it is possible to get a tract number for almost any neighbourhood in the country. From this tract number you can get a detailed breakdown of the number of people and their characteristics within a single local neighbourhood or for a combination of tracts comprising a region of a city or for the entire metropolitan area. This data can be a valuable resource, providing a wide variety of information on a large number of geographic markets. The major drawback, however, is that it is largely derived from census data and may be a little stale. This should not be surprising, given the constantly changing tastes of consumers and ongoing technological advancement.

Following are listings of some of the more popular sources of market information. Much of this material is available at your local public, college, or university library.

INDUSTRY AND TRADE ASSOCIATIONS In most situations the best place to start is with the industry or trade associations for the industry in which your business will compete. For example, if you were thinking of starting a retail sporting goods store, you could find a lot of data on the industry and other useful information available from a number of industry associations, depending on your particular emphasis. Some examples are:

- Bicycle Trade Association of Canada (www.btac.org)
- Canadian Sporting Goods Association (www.csga.ca)
- National Spa & Pool Institute of Canada (www.nspi.org)
- National Sporting Goods Association (www.nsga.org)
- SGMA International (www.sgma.com/index.html)

Similarly, a lot of useful information related to establishing a business to grow and distribute a variety of organic fruits and vegetables could be obtained from the following organizations, among others:

- Canadian Organic Growers (www.cog.ca)
- Certified Organics Association of British Columbia (www.certifiedorganic.bc.ca)
- Canadian Organic Advisory Board (www.coab.ca)
- Organic Producers Association of Manitoba (www.opam.mb.ca)
- Organic Crop Improvement Association (www.ocia.org)
- The National Organic Program (www.ams.usda.gov/nop/indexIE.htm)

Virtually all of these organizations have Web sites where you may be able to access market studies, cost-of-doing business reports, industry fact sheets, and other statistical data that can help you research the potential market for your business.

TRADE PUBLICATIONS Just to give you an idea of the number and diversity of the trade publications produced in Canada, take a minute to review Table 6.1. It is by no means a listing of all trade-oriented publications, merely a sampling of the range of material available to you. Depending on the nature of your new venture, any one or more of innumerable publications could represent a source of market-related information or a means for you to communicate with potential customers.

GENERAL PUBLICATIONS In addition to trade publications there are numerous general publications that can be extremely useful in compiling relevant market data. Some of the more important of these are listed in Table 6.6 on page 180. In addition to all these publications, other sources that you should look to for information include:

1. Your local Chamber of Commerce
2. Your city or municipal government
3. Local or regional development corporations
4. District school board offices
5. Provincial government offices
6. Downtown business associations
7. Shopping centre developers
8. Advertising agencies
9. Newspapers, and radio and television stations
10. Competitors
11. Sales representatives and trade suppliers
12. Similar businesses in another location
13. Other business associates

CANADA BUSINESS SERVICE CENTRES

One prospective source of market information that should not be overlooked is your provincial Canada Business Service Centre (CBSC: www.cbsc.org). The CBSCs are a collaborative effort of federal, provincial, and private sector organizations, designed to provide businesspeople with access to a wide range of

TABLE 6.1   SOME CANADIAN TRADE PUBLICATIONS

Aerospace & Defence Technology	Canadian Mining Journal	Industrial Product Ideas
Applied Arts	Canadian Music Trade	Jobber News
Architecture Concept	Canadian Oil & Gas Handbook	Lighting Magazine
Atlantic Fisherman	Canadian Pharmaceutical Journal	Luggage, Leathergoods & Accessories
Aviation Trade	Canadian Pool & Spa Marketing	L'Automobile
Bakers Journal	Canadian Premiums & Incentives	Machinery & Equipment MRO
Bath & Kitchen Marketer	Canadian Security	Masthead
Benefits Canada	Canadian Vending	Medicine North America
Boating Business	Computer Dealer News	Modern Purchasing
Bodyshop	Construction Canada	Motel/Hotel Lodging
Building Renovation	Cosmetics	Office Equipment & Methods
Business to Business Marketing	Dental Practice Management	Plant Engineering & Maintenance
CAD/CAM & Robotics	Design Engineering	Plastics Business
Canadian Apparel Manufacturer	Eastern Trucker	Quill and Quire
Canadian Beverage Review	Electrical Equipment News	Sanitation Canada
Canadian Building Owner & Property Manager	Farm Equipment Quarterly	Service Station & Garage Management
Canadian Doctor	Fleur Design	Shopping Centre Canada
Canadian Food & Drug	Floor Covering News	Software Report
Canadian Forest Industries	Food in Canada	Sports Business
Canadian Funeral News	Food & Drug Packaging News	The Bottom Line
Canadian Grocer	Footwear Forum	The Business and Professional Woman
Canadian Hairdresser	Fur Trade Journal	The Western Investor
Canadian Heavy Equipment Guide	Gardenland	Trade Asia Magazine
Canadian Hotel & Restaurant	Gifts and Tablewares	Transportation Business
Canadian Industry Shows & Exhibitions	Greenhouse Canada	Visual Communications
Canadian Jeweller	Group Travel	Water & Pollution Control
Canadian Machinery & Metalworking	Hardware Merchandising	Woodworking
	Health Care	
	Industrial Distributor News	

information on government services, programs, and regulations. Each CBSC offers a broad range of products and services tailored to meet the needs of its particular clients. These include:

- Toll-free telephone information and referral service
- Business Information System (BIS) database containing information on the services and programs of the participating departments and organizations
- info-FAX service: Condensed versions of the BIS products, accessed through an automated FaxBack system
- info-Guides: A set of documents that provide brief descriptions of services and programs related to a particular topic (e.g., exporting, tourism)
- Other business services, which could include interactive diagnostic software, videos, business directories, how-to manuals, CD-ROM library search capability, and external database access

CBSCs are located in one major urban centre in each province. A complete listing of the location of each centre and the numbers for telephone referral and FaxBack service at each site can be found in the listing of Useful Contacts in the For Further Information section at the back of this book.

THE INTERNET

Another place where you may be able to find a good deal of information about any idea you plan to pursue is the Internet. Not everything is available on the Internet yet, but with a little practice even new users can skim the Net's millions of Web pages and thousands of newsgroups for topics of general interest or to help find precise pieces of specific data.

The job of culling information from the millions of Web pages has been simplified by the development of a variety of search tools that enable the user to rapidly search through directories or the nooks and crannies of the Web itself to create indexes of information related to a particular topic.

Internet directories such as Yahoo! enable you to search for Internet sites by category. For example, if you are looking for Web sites on a particular topic such as "home-based business," a particular company or business such as "Spin Master Toys" or "Take-A-Boo Emporium," or if you are looking for a general subject guide to resources available over the Internet, you should probably use a directory. Yahoo! Canada (www.yahoo.ca), for example, contains millions of Web sites organized into a number of categories such as travel, food, and sports, as well as hundreds of subcategories.

Search engines are sites that contain the contents of millions of pages of information from throughout the Web, and are used to find pages containing specific words or phrases. Google (www.google.ca) is one of the most popular. These search engines send out software agents or "spiders" that explore the entire Internet instead of just the Web pages that have been indexed for the directory. The problem with this approach, however, is that some of these search engines are not very discriminating. Sorting through the thousands of matches that may result from any search can be a real chore.

The differences between search engines and directories, however, are becoming very clouded. Each type of search site is taking on more of the characteristics of the other so that directories now include search engines and search engines now include directories. You need to understand the basic characteristics of each type of tool since you will be using both when making any search for information on the Internet, often on the same site.

The major search engines and directories are listed in the FYI box on page 154. In addition to these basic tools there are a number of other search tools you should consider as well. These include:

- **All-in-one or "parallel" search engines** such as MetaCrawler (www.metacrawler.com), Dogpile (www.dogpile.com), or Ask Jeeves (www.askjeeves.com). These search engines simultaneously submit your search request to several other search engines and combine the results into one report.

- **Specialized search engines** such as About.com (www.about.com) and Search.com (www.search.com), which will provide you with access to hundreds of other specialized search engines, and Strategis (strategis.gc.ca), the Industry Canada Web site that provides access to almost everything you need to know about starting and running a business in Canada.

- **Search accelerators** such as Copernic 2001 (www.copernic.com), WebFerret (www.ferretsoft.com), and BrightPlanet's Deep Query Manager (brightplanet.com/products/dqm.asp). These programs simultaneously query several search engines for the words or phrases you are searching for and summarize the results in a simple, easy-to-read format. Most of these accelerators are sold as separate programs to be installed on your computer.

- **Subject guides** can be an excellent source of information about a particular topic since someone who has a lot of knowledge about a subject has usually prepared the index. There are literally thousands of subject guides that contain links to a number of other Web sites. Many of them can be found by searching in directories like Yahoo! or Google. Some of the best ones for information relevant to small business include the Web sites of the Canadian Youth Business Foundation (CYBF) (www.cybf.ca), *PROFIT* magazine (www.profitguide.com), and EntreWorld (www.entreworld.com). These guides can be excellent starting points to begin your search for more specific information.

- **Commercial research databases** such as Micromedia ProQuest (www.micromedia.ca), MSN Encarta (encarta.msn.com), and Northern Light (www.northernlight.com). These databases contain information from newspapers, magazines, journals, and other hard-to-find information sources and make it available for a fee. This can be a flat fee per month, a per document charge, or a combination of a monthly/annual fee and a per document charge.[1]

Most search engines provide basic instructions as to how to initiate a search as part of their home page. For a beginner, it all starts with you entering a "query." A "query" consists of one or more keywords — a company name, a city or country, or any other topic likely to appear either in the title or the body of a Web page. Most

---

1. For a more detailed discussion of the use of these search tools see Jim Carroll and Rick Broadhead, *Canadian Internet Directory and Research Guide* (Toronto: Stoddart Publishing Co. Ltd.).

search programs employ Boolean logic, expanding or limiting a search by including "and," "but," and "or" as part of the search process. The more precise your query, the better. For example, if you are interested in a topic like antique automobiles, typing in "antique automobiles" instead of just "automobiles" will direct you to information regarding older cars, although you may also get sites for antique dealers in general and other related subjects.

With most search engines the process starts with a click of your mouse once you have entered your query. Within seconds, a list of matches is produced, usually in batches of 10, with a brief description and a link to the home page. A further click on one of the matches gets you to that page or Usenet group.

There are a number of fundamental problems you need to be aware of in gathering research information off the Net. First, the quality of some of the information may be of questionable value or use. There is a lot of useless information online since literally anyone can create a Web site. Second, the information you come across may be misleading. Since anyone can set up a Web site and publish information, fraud and misrepresentation have become real problems. Third, the information may be out of date. There is no assurance that information on the Web is the most recent or reflects current research or theory.

To use the Web for research purposes it is essential that you take the time to learn how to do it effectively. Most of us simply do not take the time to learn this skill. We simply connect to the Internet, call up our favourite search engine, plug in a couple of key words, and do a search. Then we begin browsing through the results and start to surf many of the sites that come up. We then give up some time later, very frustrated and without having found much relevant information.

Professional researchers, on the other hand, think carefully about the information they are looking for. They plan a specific search strategy and decide which search terms might be the most effective in finding the information they are searching for. It is only then that they log onto the Internet to conduct a preliminary search. Based on what they find, they will try some other terms and use other search engines, continually refining their search as they go. Eventually they are likely to find just what they are looking for.

As you can see, the first approach is entirely hit and miss while the other involves some careful thought and planning and is likely to be much more effective.

FYI FOR YOUR INFORMATION

Here is a list of the major search engines on the World Wide Web that can be useful for research purposes:

Google	www.google.ca
About	www.about.com
AltaVista	www.altavista.com
Excite	www.excite.com
HotBot	www.hotbot.com
Looksmart	www.looksmart.com
Lycos	www.lycos.ca
Northern Light	www.northernlight.com
WebCrawler	www.webcrawler.com
Yahoo!	www.yahoo.ca
Alltheweb	www.alltheweb.com
Kart00	www.kartoo.com

GATHER PRIMARY DATA

Doing your own research — called primary research — may be the best way to get the most current and useful information regarding your potential market. A number of techniques can be used to obtain primary data. These can be classified into two basic research approaches: observational methods and questioning methods.

OBSERVATIONAL METHODS This is the gathering of primary data by observing people and their actions in particular situations. It may entail such approaches as observing the behaviour of shoppers in a store as they go about purchasing a range of different products, or counting traffic flows through a mall or past a particular location, or observing patterns in traffic flows around a store or other facility.

QUESTIONING METHODS These include both the use of surveys and experimentation that involves contact with respondents. Survey research involves the systematic collection of data from a sample of respondents to better understand or explain some aspect of their behaviour. This data collection can occur by personal contact, through the mail, by telephone, or on the Internet. In addition, the information may be gathered from people individually as in an individual interview or in a group such as a focus group.

Survey research is the most widely used method of primary data collection. Its principal advantages are its relatively low cost and flexibility. It can be used to obtain many different kinds of information in a wide variety of situations.

However, there are also some problems associated with survey research. Constructing a good survey is not necessarily an easy thing to do. Sometimes people are unable or unwilling to answer survey questions, so the response rate is not always as high as you might like to see. In addition, a number of technical issues relating to survey research, such as appropriate sample size, reliability, validity, and statistical significance, need to be considered as well. These issues go beyond the scope of this book but definitely need to be considered when gathering any primary data. Before rushing out to conduct a survey, however, it is a good idea to formulate a systematic research design that addresses the following issues:

Problem statement   1. What is the decision you have to make?

2. What information will assist you in making that decision?

Questionnaire design   1. Precisely what information do you want to collect in the interviews?

2. What interview questions will get you that response from respondents?

3. How should those questions be phrased?

4. How are you going to contact prospective respondents?

Sampling procedure   1. Who should your respondents be?

2. How many respondents should you use?

Data analysis   How will you tabulate, summarize, and analyze your data?

There are also some general guidelines you can follow to help you design effective questionnaires:

- Pre-test the survey on a small group of people to ensure that respondents clearly understand your questions.
- Make certain you are actually asking the right questions to get the information you need.
- Decide how you intend to use the information you will obtain when designing the questionnaire.
- Keep your survey concise and readily understandable.
- Ask direct questions that relate specifically to the topic in which you are interested.
- If you are providing respondents with a finite range of possible answers (as with a Likert-type scale), try to provide a maximum of five possible responses.
- Make sure your questions can be answered easily by your respondents.
- Don't offend anyone.
- Don't mislead respondents about the purpose of your survey.
- Don't answer the questions for them by prompting them for answers.
- Give respondents sufficient time to provide an appropriate response.
- Don't bias their responses by personally reacting to any answers, either positively or negatively.
- Ask all personal information at the end of the survey so the respondent is not discouraged from replying
- Always be courteous; remember they are doing you a favour.

An example of a relatively simple survey developed by a woman who wanted to open a fitness centre and offer one-on-one training is illustrated in the Key Points box on page 156.

MARKET-TESTING YOUR IDEA

In addition to obtaining information from prospective customers, there are also a number of primary research methods you can use to gauge likely market reaction to your particular concept or idea. These techniques are

Key points ········· FITNESS CENTRE QUESTIONNAIRE ·········

1. Do you exercise regularly?   YES ___ NO ___
   If NO, please go to Part A.
   If YES, please go to Part B.

PART A. PLEASE CHECK YOUR REASONS FOR NOT EXERCISING:

___ Lack of time   ___ Lack of motivation   ___ Cost
___ No convenient fitness centres   ___ Medical reasons
___ Other. Please specify _____

PART B. CHECK THE TYPE OF EXERCISE YOU DO:

___ Aerobic   ___ Nautilus   ___ Free weights   ___ Yoga
___ Pilates   ___ Tai Chi   ___ Running   ___ Swimming
___ Other. Please specify _____

2. Are you: ___ Male ___ Female

3. What is your age group?
   ___ Under 25   ___ 26–35   ___ 36–50   ___ Over 50

4. Where do you normally exercise?
   ___ At home   ___ Fitness centre
   ___ Other. Please specify _____

5. How far do you live from (location of proposed centre)?
   ___ Nearby   ___ 5–10 kms   ___ over 10 kms

6. Do you think your community needs a new fitness centre?   YES ___ NO ___

7. Would you be interested in one-on-one training?   YES ___ NO ___

8. Do you have any comments or suggestions about the need for a fitness centre in your community?

Source: Adapted from "How to Prepare a Market Analysis," Edward Lowe Foundation, *Entrepreneurial Edge* (edge.lowe.org).

more subjective and cannot be analyzed statistically. However, most of them provide instant feedback. Usually one opinion leads to another so that overall you will receive some interesting and useful information. These techniques include prototype development, obtaining opinions from prospective distributors, comparing your idea directly with competitors' offerings, conducting in-store tests, and demonstrating at trade shows.

One or more of these techniques can be used to assess how the market is likely to react to your concept or idea. For example, the young owners of Spin Master Toys used a variety of methods to refine and test the idea behind their initial product — the Air Hog, a World War II-era toy jet fighter that flies on compressed air (Entrepreneurs in Action #19). The English inventors who developed the concept had put together a crude prototype to demonstrate the idea. It was described as "a Canada Dry ginger ale bottle with foam wings" and didn't fly. Subsequent prototypes "flew some of the time — kind of" until after myriad versions, a year and a half, and half a million dollars later they finally had what appeared to be a market-ready product.

At the same time as this product development was taking place, one of the owners took an early prototype of the product to a buyer for Canadian Tire stores. The response was very positive and while the company was

19 Entrepreneurs in action

Cashing in on Kids

Like a pilot in a death spiral, Ben Varadi was having one of those gut-checking moments. As head of product development for Spin Master Toys, he had flown last January to Scottsdale, Ariz., to film a commercial for a new product that had a lot riding on it. Even though Spin Master had yet to put it in production, the Air Hog promised to be a coup not only for the budding Toronto-based company, but for the industry as a whole: a toy airplane that would run on compressed air rather than gas or rubber bands, and would fly for hundreds of yards rather than piddling out after just a few. In theory, at least, this is what should have happened: the weather should have been cloudless and dry (Varadi chose Arizona as a location because it hardly gets any rain), and the prototype should have flown through the air with the greatest of ease.

So Varadi and the crew are out on a Holiday Inn golf course in Scottsdale — and the sky is cloudy. . . . They get set to fire up the Air Hog, a purple-and-yellow flying machine that otherwise resembles a World War II-era fighter plane. The sophisticated air-compressor engine is primed, the cameras are rolling, the tousle-haired kid hired to star in the ad lets the Air Hog go and — well, a mere four seconds later, the toy's sputtering film début comes to an end on the hard track of the fairway. Crash and burn, baby.

It's a rule in toy advertising that you can't make a product appear to do things in a commercial that it can't do in reality. Trouble was, as with most new toys in the preproduction stage, the Air Hog's abilities were still unknown. Varadi, who's 28, and his Spin Master cohorts, president Anton Rabie and CEO Ronnen Harary, both 27, knew what it was *supposed* to do; they just weren't quite sure that it could actually do it. "Until you're in production, all you've got are theories," Varadi says. "You can spend all this money and at the end of the day, it still doesn't work."

So your company is spending $100,000 filming this commercial — and the Air Hog is performing like a pig. What do you do? You get creative. You shoot the commercial, cutting shots of the plane's brief flights so that it looks like it's flying 100 yards a pop, like it's twisting and turning through the air just the way you want it to. There's nothing dishonest about that — as long as the product, once it's on the market and the object of every 10-year-old boy's

desire, lives up to its billing. "So we had a challenge," Varadi says. "We had to make the thing fly like it did in the commercial."

The inverted logic must have worked, because the Air Hog is soaring these days. In an industry dominated by giants such as Hasbro, Mattel and Irwin, five-year-old Spin Master Toys seems to have come up with a bona fide hit. . . .

The Air Hog has been flying off the shelves of U.S. specialty stores such as FAO Schwarz and Noodle Kidoodle. Since June, Spin Master has sold 350,000 Air Hogs to retailers. By next August, Rabie, Harary and Varadi expect to sell a million more. Not bad for a product that the major toy companies thought would never fly. And the TV commercial hasn't even aired yet. . . .

THOMAS FRICKE PHOTOGRAPHY

The history of Spin Master Toys is part Wright brothers, part Roots — a tale of what happens when innovation meets savvy marketing. Childhood pals who met at summer camp a few years after their families moved to Toronto from South Africa, Rabie and Harary both attended the University of Western Ontario in London, where the future company president studied business and Harary took political science. While at school, where they also met biz-student Varadi, the pair established a business under the name Seiger Marketing. Their idea: a campus poster

continued

Cashing in on Kids — continued

adorned with frosh-week photos and advertising from local businesses. After graduating, Rabie and Harary, then 23, had $10,000 in their pockets from poster sales; all they needed was a product. And when Harary's grandmother brought back a novelty gift from Israel in 1994 — a sawdust-filled stocking with a face that sprouted grass for hair — they knew they had found it. The Earth Buddy was born.

With the Earth Buddy's vaguely environmental cachet, Rabie figured it would be a perfect fit for the urban-adventurer image espoused by Roots Canada Ltd., a company founded by Michael Budman and Don Green (who, coincidentally, also met at summer camp). Budman bit, allowing Rabie and Harary to test-market the nouveaux Chia Pets in Roots stores. The little guys were, in short, a hit. In the U.S., K-Mart ordered 500,000 Buddies. Operations moved from Harary's kitchen to a factory staffed by 200 employees working around the clock. In six months, the Earth Buddy generated $1.8 million in sales. That's a lot of sawdust and socks.

One hit wonder? No way. In 1994 the company launched a three-rod juggling game called Spin Master Devil Sticks — a higher-tech version of a product Harary sold from the back of his VW Microbus at Grateful Dead concerts when he was 17. In the spring of 1995, the Devil Sticks became the No. 1 non-promoted toy in Canada, selling more than 250,000 units in six months. It broke the company into the U.S., positioning it for continent-wide distribution, and it gave Rabie and Harary's business a new name — Spin Master — which has proven to be appropriate in more ways than one.

The Air Hog flew onto the scene in February 1996, at the Toy Fair, an annual get-together in New York that attracts hundreds of toymakers, retailers and inventors. There, Varadi was approached by inventors from the English firm Dixon-Manning Ltd., who pitched an idea they had for a plane that ran on air power. Varadi and Harary arranged to meet with Dixon-Manning at 5 p.m. that day to discuss details, but when they arrived, they found the inventors had optioned the concept for 30 days to a major U.S. toy company. "So I made a note to call them in 30 days and see if they passed — and sure enough, they did," recalls Harary. "And when [Dixon-Manning] sent the item to us, I saw why."

Basically, the prototype the inventors sent to Toronto was, Harary says, "a Canada Dry ginger ale bottle with foam wings — it still had the label on it." But the partners at Spin Master saw opportunity. "The one thing that did appeal to me wasn't so much the item itself as the state of the category," Varadi says. Here's the reason: the toy-airplane market didn't have a middle. On the top end were gasoline-powered planes that sold for $80 and up; on the low end were $3 rubber-band-and-balsa-wood "aircraft." Varadi figured that, in that niche market, "there's got to be something in the middle." And the air-pressure technology was something new, holding out the promise of a whole line of toys that ran off its simple-sounding, but hard-to-produce, pneumatic engine. "If we could pull this off, we'd be like pioneers in this category," Varadi says. "We also realized that this would elevate the level of the company in terms of how people saw us."

The trio started talking to buyers within two months of taking on the project in July 1996. Harary took a prototype to a Canadian Tire buyer in October, who said she would place "a big order" — *if* he could ship it for spring. "I had this nagging feeling, what if we make this commitment and can't keep it — will it risk the reputation of the company?" he says. "I looked them in the face and said, 'I don't think we can make it.' No one wants to turn down a challenge, but it was probably one of the best things we've done." Egos still intact, the boys now had confidence that retailers were behind their product. But talking to the buyers led to another revelation: Hasbro, Mattel and, as Varadi says, "everybody and his uncle" had turned down the Air Hog. "You're thinking, if a company like Hasbro turned it down, what were they thinking that we were missing?"

That was gut check No. 1. And for a time, it must have seemed that the no-takers were right. The first prototype Spin Master received from Dixon-Manning didn't fly; the second "flew some of the time — kind of," Harary says.

The three had planned on the development phase taking six months. It ended up taking a year and a half. . . . Rabie remembers getting frantic eureka-style calls from Harary and Varadi, who would be out in a park somewhere testing one of myriad versions of the Air Hog. "There's been another breakthrough!" Varadi would proclaim. Rabie would run out to the park with a camcorder to make a tape to show buyers and — it wouldn't fly, again. "It was Murphy's Law," Rabie says. Meanwhile, focus-group results with actual kids were disastrous: they couldn't figure out the plane's air-pump system, they turned the propeller the wrong way — you name it. Rabie and his team came up with two solutions. One was to set up a 1-800 help line for fledgling pilots; the other was to produce an instructional video (now included with every Air Hog). By showing the video, Varadi says, "we went from a terrible focus group, where one out of five could do it, to a focus group where every kid could do it." . . . .

. . .The next step was to make the moulds for all the parts and set up the machinery to manufacture the planes — a tooling-up that would cost $100,000. Time for another gut check. "It's easy to make one thing work," Harary says, "but to make half a million things work is a totally different ball game." Rabie, Harary and Varadi decided it was time to fly or get off the plane. But would it work? "When we made the decision to go ahead with it, we didn't know," Rabie says, "We just said, "OK, we're going to tool and debug."

Since it's an outdoor toy, the Spin Masters figured it would be ideal for a spring début. So they made the ad in Arizona, fixed the design bugs and simultaneously tested two distribution paths in Minneapolis: specialty chains such as Noodle Kidoodle, which concentrate on high-end educational toys, and Target department stores in the area. With air support from the commercial, the plane beat expectations under both retailing models, selling more than 25 units per store per week (8 to 12 units in that price category is considered good). In the end, Spin Master decided to stick with a conservative distribution plan, leaving the Air Hog in specialty stores and as a Sears catalogue item for a year, then releasing it in the mass market with a national ad campaign the following spring through major retailers. . . . (www.spinmaster.com)

Source: Adapted from Shawna Steinberg and Joe Chidley, "Fun for the Money," *Canadian Business*, December 11, 1998, pp. 44–52. Reprinted with permission.

not prepared to meet the time lines for delivery required by the buyer and turned down the sale, the experience did confirm that retailers would be behind their product if they could produce an acceptable, working version.

The company also conducted some focus groups with actual kids to see what they thought of the Air Hog and to assess their ability to use it properly. The initial results were disastrous. The kids couldn't figure out the plane's air-pump system, they turned the propeller the wrong way, and had a variety of other problems. To overcome these difficulties, the company came up with a couple of solutions. One was to set up a toll-free number to serve as a help line for kids experiencing problems. The other was to include an instructional video with every Air Hog, explaining the proper way to use the toy.

All this testing seems to have paid off. Three hundred and fifty thousand Air Hogs literally flew off the shelves of major U.S. retailers over that season.[2]

But could Spin Master follow up on the tremendous success it was able to achieve with the Air Hog? So far, its product line has expanded to include a number of other big hits, such as the Hydro Vector Rocket, Sky Shark and e-Charger planes, Flick Trix replica sports bikes, the Road Ripper air-pressured cars, Shrinky Dinks children's keepsakes, Catch-A-Bubble catch-and-stack bubbles, the ICEE Maker, Teenage Mutant Ninja Turtle toys, Wiggles characters, B-Boyz dance figures, and Mighty Beanz collectible plastic jumping beans, among other successful creations. Along the way, the company has continued to rely on the same kind of grass-roots marketing that jump-started the Air Hog: product demonstrations, unique public relations campaigns, and cultivating relationships with journalists, retailers, and other leaders in the toy industry.[3]

DEVELOPING A PROTOTYPE   A *prototype* is a working model of your product. If you are considering selling a product that, when mass-produced, could cost you $5 per unit to manufacture, prototypes may cost you hundreds of dollars each. However, this could be an inexpensive investment, because with just one prototype you can get photographs, make up a brochure or flyer, show the idea to prospective buyers, and put out publicity releases. You don't need a thousand or 10 thousand units at this stage.

Even though you are interested in producing only a few units at this point, it is still important to get manufacturing prices from a number of (around five) different suppliers. You should find out how much it will cost to produce various quantities of the product (1,000 units, 5,000 units, 10,000 units) and what the terms, conditions, and costs of the production process would be. Once you have this information you will be able to approach buyers and intelligently and confidently discuss all aspects of the product.

OBTAINING OPINIONS FROM PROSPECTIVE DISTRIBUTORS   A second way to test your product idea is to ask a professional buyer's personal opinion. For example, most major department stores and other retail chains are organized into departments, each department having its own buyer. After arranging to see the buyer representing the product area in which you are interested, arm yourself with the cost information you received from potential suppliers. Remember, a buyer is a very astute person. He or she has seen thousands of items before yours,

2. Shawna Steinberg and Joe Chidley, "Fun for the Money," *Canadian Business*, December 11, 1998, pp. 44–52.
3. Kara Kuryllowicz, "Air Hogs, the Sequel!" *PROFIT*, September 1999, p. 10, and Kali Pearson, "Why Didn't I Think of That?" *PROFIT*, May 2001, pp. 28–34.

and in most cases will be able to tell you if products resembling yours have ever been on the market, how well they sold, what their flaws were, etc. You can get a tremendous amount of free information from a buyer, so it is advisable to solicit his or her independent opinion before you become too involved with your product.

COMPARING WITH COMPETITORS' PRODUCTS   Most of us have only limited exposure to the vast array of products available in the marketplace and so could end up spending a lot of money producing a "new" product that is already being marketed by someone else. Test your product idea by comparing it with other products already on the market, before you invest your money.

ONE-STORE TEST   Another way to test your product is to run a one-store test. This can be done by arranging with a store owner or manager to put a dozen units of your product on display. The purpose of this test is to learn what the public thinks about your product. You can often get the store owner's cooperation, because the store doesn't have to put any money up front to purchase your product. However, problems can be associated with such tests. If you are very friendly with the owner, he or she may affect the results of the test in your product's favour by putting it in a preferred location or by personally promoting it to store customers. You should request that your product be treated like any other, because you are looking for unbiased information.

Also, you should keep in mind that one store does not constitute a market; the one store in which you test may not be representative of the marketplace in general. Nevertheless, the one-store test is a good way to gather information on your product.

TRADE SHOWS   Another excellent way to test your product idea is at a trade show. It makes no difference what your field is — there is a trade show involving it. At a trade show you will have your product on display and you can get immediate feedback from sophisticated and knowledgeable buyers — people who know what will sell and what will not. There are approximately 15,000 trade shows in Canada and the United States every year, covering every imaginable product area, so there is bound to be one that could serve as a reasonable test site for you.

CONDUCTING A CUSTOMER SURVEY

A critical factor in successfully launching a new venture is understanding who your customers are and what needs your product or service might satisfy. It is important to consider that not all potential customers are alike or have similar needs for a given product. For example, some people buy a toothpaste primarily to prevent cavities, while others want a toothpaste that promotes whiter teeth, fresher breath, or "sex appeal," or has been designed specifically for smokers or denture wearers. You have to determine which of these segments (i.e., cavity prevention, whiter teeth, etc.) your product or service can best satisfy.

As previously mentioned, most major markets can be broken down into more homogeneous groups or *segments* on the basis of a number of different types of variables. In developing a plan for your proposed business venture you must consider who your potential customers are and how they might be classified, as in the toothpaste example, into somewhat more homogeneous market segments. You should be clear in your own mind just which of these segments your venture is attempting to serve. A product or service that is sharply focused to satisfy the needs and wants of a specifically defined customer group is typically far more successful than one that tries to compromise and cut across the widely divergent requirements of many customer types. Small businesses are often in a position to search for "holes" in the market representing the requirements of particular customer types that larger companies are unwilling or unable to satisfy. Figure 6.2 on page 183 provides a framework you can complete to develop a market profile of your prospective customer.

To be successful, you should seek a *competitive advantage* over other firms — look for something especially desirable from the customer's perspective, something that sets you apart and gives you an edge. This may be the quality of your product, the speed of your service, the diversity of your product line, the effectiveness of your promotion, your personality, your location, the distinctiveness of your offering, or perhaps even your price.

To accomplish all this may require some basic market research. This might be thought of as one of the first steps in testing your product or service idea with potential customers.

Since you will want to provide as good a description of your offering as possible (preferably via a prototype), personal, face-to-face interviews are the best method for gathering the information. Figure 6.3 on page 184 provides an outline for a survey you might conduct. It would be wise to interview at least 30 to 40 potential customers to help ensure that the responses you receive are probably representative of the marketplace in general. This approach can be used effectively for either consumer or industrial products/services.

This customer survey will provide you with important information that will allow you to further develop and fine-tune your marketing strategy. For example, if you discover that the most customers will pay for your

DO-IT-YOURSELF MARKET RESEARCH

Here are some things you should keep in mind when doing your own market research.

1. In conducting a survey, your information will be only as good as your sample. To be useful, your sample group needs to be relevant to and representative of your target population.

2. Design your survey or questionnaire carefully. Make sure it's focused specifically on the information you need to know.

3. Keep your survey or questionnaire as short as possible, preferably a single page.

4. Always provide some opportunity for the respondent to provide detailed answers.

5. Work out how you intend to record the information and analyze the data as you are developing the questionnaire.

6. Before you administer the survey, establish the criteria that you will use to make decisions based on the information obtained from the survey.

7. Remember, market research is needed at all stages of a business's life to keep you in touch with your customers and their needs and desires.

Source: ©J. Susan Ward, 2001 (sbinfocanada.about.com); licensed to About.com, Inc. (www.about.com). Used by permission. All rights reserved.

product is $10 and you had planned on charging $12, you will have to reconsider your pricing strategy. Similarly, if customers prefer to purchase products like yours by mail, you will have to keep that in mind as you set up a distribution system. The responses to each of the questions posed in the survey should be analyzed and their impact on areas of marketing strategy noted. These will be brought together later in your preliminary marketing plan.

INTERPRET THE INFORMATION

Once this secondary and primary data have been gathered, they must be analyzed and translated into usable information. The research needs to aid you in making management decisions related to such issues as:

- Who should be your customer?

- What product or service should you be selling?

- What is the total size of your potential market and how can it be broken down?

- Who are your competitors and what are their strengths and weaknesses?

- What is your estimated sales forecast?

- Where should you locate your business?

- How should you promote, price, and distribute your product?

Some conclusions based on the analysis of this data may be obvious. Others may be more difficult to decipher or you may feel the data you need to answer the question are just not available. Nonetheless market research can provide you with some of the information you need to be more proactive and help you decide what you should be doing in the future rather than just relying on what has happened in the past.

ESTIMATING TOTAL MARKET SIZE AND TRENDS

A large part of market assessment is determining the volume of *unit sales* or *dollar revenue* that might flow from a market and what proportion of this you might expect to capture. At first glance "unit sales" seems to mean simply how many potential customers there are in the market for your product/service. However, this would overlook the possibility that some customers may buy more than one unit of the product/service. Estimates of total market size must take these *repeat purchases* into account. Total demand is determined by multiplying the number of customers who will buy by the average number of units each might be expected to purchase. To determine the total market size in dollars, simply multiply this total number of units by the average selling price.

Figure 6.4 on page 185 provides a form you can complete to estimate the approximate total market size (past, present, and future) and the expected trends for your product/service type.

THE NATURE OF YOUR COMPETITION

Unless your product or service is a "new to the world" innovation, which is unlikely, it will have to compete with other products or services that perform a similar function. In the customer survey, your respondents probably identified the names of a number of firms that offer products or services designed to meet the same customer needs as yours. Now you must ask specific and detailed questions concerning your likely competition. The answers will help you get a better understanding of the sales and market share you could achieve, and changes or improvements you should make in your marketing program (pricing, promotion, distribution, etc.).

"Business is lousy. Maybe I should have done more market research first."

© Randy Glasbergen. Reprinted with permission from www.glasbergen.com

You should also be on the lookout for areas where you can gain a sustainable competitive advantage. In other words: Can you provide the best-quality, the lowest-cost, the most innovative, or the better-serviced product?

Figure 6.5 on page 185 provides a form to help you organize your evaluation of your competitors. Fill out a copy of this form for each major competitor you have identified. Unfortunately, competitors will probably not cooperate in providing you with this information directly. Sources that can be useful in getting the information, however, include published industry reports, trade association reports and publications, corporate annual reports, and your own personal investigation.

DEVELOPING A SALES FORECAST

Sales forecasting is the process of organizing and analyzing all the information you have gathered in a way that makes it possible to estimate what your expected sales are likely to be. Your sales forecast will probably be one of the most difficult and yet the single most important business prediction you ever make. If you get it wrong, the error can lead to plenty of unsold inventory and problems generating sufficient cash to keep the business going or to a number of disappointed customers.

But how do you get it right? One way is to consider the following formula:

Sales Forecast = Total Estimated Market Size x Estimated Growth Rate x Market Share Target

ESTIMATING MARKET SIZE

Fairly accurate market data are available from trade associations and other secondary sources for certain industries. However, companies in many other industries have to operate without any concrete information concerning the total size of the market for their products or services. Nonetheless, information on market size is vital to develop a meaningful marketing plan.

It is especially important when introducing new products that you have a good estimate of the size of the total market, but this is exactly the situation for which obtaining an accurate forecast is most difficult. For example, suppose that you were considering setting up a distribution business to sell garbage bags and shopping bags made from recycled plastic (polyethylene) in Halifax. To estimate the total potential market that might be available you would need to know the total demand for such products in the four Atlantic provinces, if that was how you had geographically defined you market. In addition, you would also be interested in determining the size of the various segments of the market. Three obvious segments that should be considered might be: (1) garbage bags for household use sold by retail stores; (2) heavy-duty garbage bags sold in bulk for commercial and industrial use; (3) printed plastic shopping bags for independent retail stores and chains. You may not wish to compete in the entire market but decide to focus on the needs of one particular segment, such as printed shopping bags for chain stores.

It is usually much easier to determine market data for established products. Data on total market sales may already exist or they can be developed using either a *top-down* or a *bottom-up* approach.

TOP-DOWN APPROACH

The top-down approach utilizes published data on statistics such as total market size and weights them by an index that may be some factor such as the percentage of the population within your designated geographic area. For example, our distributor of plastic bags needs an estimate of the total size of the potential market for these bags in Atlantic Canada. Since the four Atlantic provinces account for approximately 10 per cent of the total Canadian population, a rough estimate of the size of the plastic bag market in that region would be 10 per cent of the total Canadian market. Data concerning the entire Canadian market may be available from sources such as Statistics Canada or from trade associations or other industry sources. One word of caution, however, in using this approach: This estimate of the total market for plastic bags in the Atlantic provinces is accurate only if usage patterns of plastic bags are the same in that region of Canada as they are in the country as a whole.

BOTTOM-UP APPROACH

The bottom-up approach involves aggregating information from the customer level to the total market level. Information on past or current purchase or usage of a product or service may be collected from a sample of customers by a mail or telephone survey or through personal interviews. For frequently purchased consumer products, like plastic garbage bags, for example, the survey may simply ask how much of the product is used either by individuals or the entire household during an average week or month. These individual or household statistics are then aggregated based on population or household statistics that are available from Statistics Canada and other sources to develop an estimate of the total size of the potential market. An overview of both these approaches is illustrated in the following Key Points box.[4]

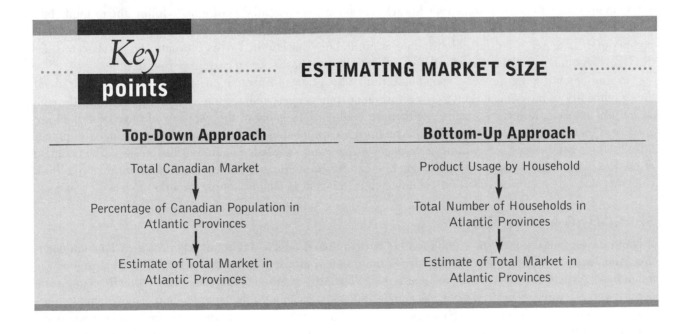

Key points

ESTIMATING MARKET SIZE

Top-Down Approach	Bottom-Up Approach
Total Canadian Market	Product Usage by Household
↓	↓
Percentage of Canadian Population in Atlantic Provinces	Total Number of Households in Atlantic Provinces
↓	↓
Estimate of Total Market in Atlantic Provinces	Estimate of Total Market in Atlantic Provinces

4. Adapted from J.G. Barnes, *Research for Marketing Decision Making* (Toronto: McGraw-Hill Ryerson Ltd., 1991), pp. 84–94.

For your business plan, these sales estimates for your first year of operation should be monthly, while the estimates for subsequent years can be quarterly. A serious miscalculation many aspiring entrepreneurs make is to assume that because their new product or service appeals to them, other consumers will buy it as well. It is important to be aware of this tendency. This type of thinking is often reflected in what is known as the "2 per cent syndrome." This syndrome follows a line of reasoning such as, "The total market for a product is $100 million. If my firm can pick up just 2 per cent of this market, it will have sales of $2 million per year."

There are, however, two things wrong with this line of reasoning. The first is that it may be extremely difficult for you to capture 2 per cent of this market unless your business has a unique competitive advantage. The second is that a 2 per cent market share may still be unprofitable, since competing firms with greater market share may benefit from *economies of scale* — lower unit cost due to mass production — and other cost advantages unavailable to your firm.

A number of external factors can affect your sales, including:

- seasonal changes
- holidays
- special events
- political activities and events
- general economic conditions
- weather
- fashion trends and cycles
- population shifts
- changes in the retail mix

In addition, a number of internal factors must be considered, such as:

- level of your promotional effort
- your ability to manage inventory levels effectively
- the distribution channels you decide to use
- your price level relative to the competition
- any labour and personnel problems you might encounter

It is impossible to predict all these situations but you should try to take them into account in developing your sales forecast.

One approach to gaining some insight into your business's potential market is to follow the example laid out in Figure 6.6 on page 187. Refer to the *market profile* you developed in Figure 6.2. How do you feel your prospective customers would decide whether or not to buy your offering? This estimate should also consider the likely frequency and volume of a typical customer's purchases over a certain period of time.

In implementing this process, you should think about how prospective customers will likely hear about the opportunity to buy your product/service, whether from a salesperson, from an advertisement, or through a chain of intermediaries. Estimates can then be made of how many of the people you have described are good prospects and, consequently, what your total sales volume might be. This can be an "armchair" procedure involving the use of some library references or personal knowledge of similar businesses. The estimate of market potential developed using this method can be quite crude; however, it is important that you think your way through such a process and not sidestep it in favour of simply hoping a market exists for you.

SELECTING A LOCATION

It is often said that the three most important factors in the success of any retail business are "location, location, and location." Every new business faces the problem of where to locate its facilities. This problem is much more critical to retailers than to other types of businesses. Much of their business typically comes from people who are walking or driving by. As a consequence, a customer's decision to shop or not shop at a particular store may depend on such factors as what side of the street you are on, ease of access and egress, availability of parking, or similar concerns. This means that in determining the best location for your business you will have to concern yourself with a variety of issues.

1. **Zoning regulations** Zoning bylaws govern the kind of activities that can be carried on in any given area. Classifications vary from locality to locality, but many municipalities categorize activities as residential, commercial office, commercial retail, institutional, and industrial. When considering a location, make certain the business activities you plan to pursue are permitted under the zoning restrictions for that area.

2. **Municipal licences and taxes** Businesses must typically buy a municipal business licence. In the city of Winnipeg, for example, more than 115 types of businesses require a licence, which costs from $15 to over $2,000. In general, businesses in some amusement fields or that affect public health and safety require a licence.

    Businesses, like homeowners, must usually pay a business tax — a tax assessed as a percentage of the rental value of the premises or on the basis of a standard assessment per square foot of space utilized. These requirements vary from municipality to municipality.

3. **Municipal services** You should make sure that municipal services such as police and fire protection, adequate sewer and water supplies, public transit facilities, and an adequate road network are available to meet your business's requirements.

4. **Other considerations** Other things to consider are such site-specific issues as:
   - cost
   - the volume and timing of traffic past the location
   - the nature of the location, whether on a downtown street, in a strip mall, or in an enclosed mall
   - the nature of the area surrounding your location and its compatibility with your business
   - the kind and relative location of surrounding businesses
   - the volume of customer traffic generated by these other firms and the proportion that might "spin off" to your store
   - the growth potential of the area or community
   - the number and location of curb cuts and turnoffs

Figure 6.7 on page 188 provides a rating form you can use to help choose the most favourable location for a retail business.

Most of these same location factors also apply to service businesses, although perhaps not to the same degree. If your service business requires you to visit prospective customers at home or place of business, a central location providing easy access to all parts of your market area may be preferred.

Location has a quite different meaning for manufacturing firms. Manufacturers are principally concerned about locating their plant where their operations will be most efficient. This means considering such issues as:
   - General proximity to primary market areas
   - Access to required raw materials and supplies
   - Availability of a suitable labour force
   - Accessibility and relative cost of transportation and storage facilities
   - Availability and relative cost of power, water, and fuel supplies
   - Financial incentives and other inducements available from municipal, provincial, or federal government agencies

The importance of each of these factors in the location decision will depend on the nature of your manufacturing business and your own preferences and requirements.

BUYING OR LEASING FACILITIES

Many new businesses already own or decide to purchase the land and building in which their ventures or the machinery and equipment they will require to operate are located. With today's extremely high costs, however, this may not be a wise decision. The majority of new firms are not principally in the business of speculating in real estate and should not acquire their own property. During their early stages most businesses tend to be short of cash and many have failed because they had their capital tied up in land and buildings when it could have been more effectively used to provide needed working capital for the business itself. In addition, a business that owns its own building may be more difficult to sell at a later date, since a smaller number of potential buyers will have enough capital to buy both the business and the property. While building your own facility enables you to more carefully tailor the property to the specific requirements of your business, it tends to be a much more costly alternative.

If you are planning to rent or lease your facilities it is a good idea to have your lawyer review the terms and conditions of the agreement. You will want to ensure satisfactory arrangements in such matters as:

1. **The duration of the agreement** A business lease can last a year, three years, five years, or any other mutually agreed-on term. A short-term lease may be preferable if your situation is likely to change soon. However, the lease conditions can be a valuable asset of your business, and a short-term lease may reduce the sale value of your business (if you ever sell it) because of loss of the goodwill associated with maintaining your present location. The ideal lease arrangement should enable you to stay in the location for some time, in case your venture is successful, but give you the flexibility to move after a reasonable period of time if it doesn't work out.

    You also need to consider the terms and conditions for renewing the lease. Are there provisions for automatic renewal? Is there a maximum to any rent increase applied on renewal of your lease?

2. **The rent** Rental costs for commercial property are commonly stated in terms of the annual cost per square foot of floor space. For example, a 1,500-square-foot location rented for $8 per square foot will cost $12,000 per year, or $1,000 per month. This may be a *net lease*, in which you pay a single monthly fee that is all-inclusive (rent, utilities, maintenance costs, property taxes, etc.), or a "net-net-net" or *triple net lease*, in which you pay a base rent plus a share of all the other expenses incurred by the landlord in operating the building. In the latter situation your operating costs may fluctuate each year because of changing tax, maintenance, insurance, and other costs.

    In retail shopping malls, *participating* (or *percentage*) *leases* are common. Instead of a fixed monthly rent, the landlord receives some percentage of your sales or net profit. There are several types of participating leases. You may pay either a percentage of the total monthly sales of your business, a base rent plus some percentage of your gross sales, or a percentage of your net profit before interest and taxes. Shopping centre leases can be quite complex documents, so be certain to check with your accountant and lawyer before committing yourself.

3. **The ownership of any additions or improvements you might make to the facilities** Under the terms of most leases, all improvements and fixtures that you add to the premises are considered as belonging to the landlord. They immediately become part of the building and cannot be removed without his or her consent. If you need to install expensive fixtures to launch your business, you should try right up front to negotiate permission to remove specific items.

4. **Any restrictions on the use of the property** Most leases specify the kind of business activity you can carry on in the location. Before signing, you should think not only about the activities you now plan to engage in, but also about those you might wish to engage in in the future. Many leases also contain a non-competition clause to protect you from competitive firms coming into the premises and taking away your business.

5. **Whether you are permitted to sublet some or all of the property to a third party** This is commonly permitted, but only with the prior written consent of the landlord, and it is subject to any use restrictions and non-competition clauses in your agreement.

    A closely related issue is your ability to assign any remaining time left on your lease to another party. If you decide to sell your business, this can be an attractive part of the package. In some cases, assignment of the lease is not permitted; in others, an assignment may be acceptable with the prior written consent of the landlord, which may then not be unreasonably withheld.

6. **The nature of any default and penalty clauses** The lease will spell out the situations that constitute a breach of its conditions and the recourse available to the landlord. Obvious grounds for default include failure on your part to pay the rent, the bankruptcy of your business, violation of the use conditions or non-competition clauses, and so on. Should you default on the lease, the landlord may be able to claim accelerated rent for the time remaining on the lease. For example, if you were to move out two years before your lease expires, the landlord may claim the full two years' rent. In this situation, however, the landlord legally must try to limit his or her damages by renting out your space to another party as soon as possible.

Your lease may or may not contain a *penalty clause* limiting your exposure should you breach the lease. A penalty of three months' rent is common in many situations, although the landlord will want you or the directors of an incorporated business to sign personal guarantees for the amount of the penalty.

HOME-BASED BUSINESSES

For many kinds of businesses, working out of the home has become a very popular and attractive option. There are a number of advantages to running your business out of your home, the most obvious of which is the cost.

Not only can you save on the rent for your business premises by operating in this manner, but the Canada Revenue Agency will also let you write off part of your home expenses for income tax purposes. Possible write-offs are utility costs, mortgage interest, municipal taxes, and other expenses related to maintaining that part of your premises used for your business. You can also save on the cost and time of travelling to and from work every day, and you have greater flexibility in planning and organizing your work and personal life. In addition, a home-based business may have a number of other benefits such as letting you wear more comfortable clothes and giving you more time to look after and be with your family. There are, however, a number of disadvantages.

1. It takes a lot of self-discipline to sustain a regular work schedule and resist distractions from family, friends, television, and other sources. You may find that there are too many interruptions to work effectively, that you tend to mix work with family life too much, or become distracted by household chores. Conversely, you may find it very difficult to get away from your work when you would like to, since it is so close at hand, and you may have trouble quitting after a full day.

2. Suppliers and prospective customers may not take you as seriously. You may have to rent a post office box or make other arrangements to give the appearance of operating from a more conventional commercial location.

3. The space available in your home may not be appropriate for your business, and you may not have access to facilities and equipment such as computers and fax machines that you need to conduct your business effectively.

4. If your house is in a typical residential area, operating a business from your home will probably contravene local zoning bylaws.

    It is true that most municipal governments have become reasonably flexible in this regard and do not go looking for violations; they will, however, respond to complaints from immediate neighbours and others in the vicinity. It is a good idea to check with these people before starting any kind of visible business activity from your home. Activities that may lead to complaints are posting a large sign on the front lawn; constant noise; a steady stream of customers, suppliers, or others in and out of your home; or the clutter of parked vehicles in your yard or on the street.

In the end, operating a home-based business is really a very personal decision. From a practical perspective, you can probably do what you want, as long as no one complains. However, this mode of operation is not suitable for all types of businesses, and for many people may not be a comfortable decision.

FLESHING OUT YOUR MARKETING PROGRAM

The purpose of this section is to bring together what you have learned about the total market potential for your product or service, customer attitudes toward your particular offering, and the nature of the competitive environment you will be facing. The goal is to put down on paper a preliminary marketing strategy or plan for your new venture concept. This involves making some decisions regarding what you feel is an appropriate *marketing mix* for your business. Put simply, the principal ingredients of your marketing program that must be blended together to form your overall strategy can be grouped under the following headings:

1. Product or service offering
2. Pricing program
3. Promotional plans
4. Method of distribution

PRODUCT OR SERVICE OFFERING

The product area involves the planning and development of the product or service you are planning to offer in the marketplace. This involves defining the breadth and depth of your offering, the length of your line, how it will be packaged and branded, the variety of colours and other product features, and the range of complementary services (delivery, repair, warranties, etc.) that will be made available to the customer.

PRICING PROGRAM

Your pricing strategy involves establishing the right base price for your offering so that it is appealing to customers and profitable to you. This base price may be adjusted to meet the needs of particular situations, such as to encourage early acceptance of your offering during its introductory stages; to meet aggressive or exceptional competition; to provide for trade, functional, seasonal, and other discounts; or to introduce your product/service into new market situations.

A number of approaches can be used to determine a base price for your planned market offering. These include *cost-based pricing*, *value-based pricing*, and *competition-based pricing*.

COST-BASED PRICING

One of the most commonly used strategies by retailers and small manufacturers is *cost-based pricing or markup pricing*. The cost of your product or service is determined and used as the base, and then a markup is added to determine what your selling price should be. *Markups* are generally expressed as a percentage of the selling price — for example, a product costing $2.50 and selling for $5 has a 50 per cent markup.

To illustrate, let's assume you've come up with a new formula for an automobile engine treatment that will be sold through auto parts jobbers to service stations for use in consumers' cars. Table 6.2 illustrates what the price markup chain for this product might look like.

As you can see, in this illustration a product with a factory cost of $1.50 has a retail selling price of $5 to the final consumer. The markup percentages shown here are merely examples of a typical situation, but in most wholesale and retail businesses, standard markups tend to prevail in different industry sectors. Food products and other staple items usually have a low unit cost and high inventory turnover, so the markups tend to be fairly low, 15 to 25 per cent; products such as jewellery and highly advertised specialty products typically have higher markups, perhaps as much as 50 or 60 per cent or even more.

This type of markup pricing is simple and easy to apply and can be very successful if all competitors have similar costs of doing business and use similar percentages. On the other hand, this approach does not take into account variations in the demand for the product that may occur with a different final price. For example, how much more or less of the engine treatment would be sold at a price of $4 or $6 rather than the $5 price determined by the standard markup chain?

TABLE 6.2   PRICE MARKUP CHAIN

	Per Bottle	Markup
Direct factory costs	$1.00	
Indirect factory costs	0.50	
Total factory cost	$1.50	
Manufacturer's markup	0.50	25%
Manufacturer's selling price	$2.00	
Jobber's markup	0.50	20%
Jobber's selling price	$2.50	
Service station markup	2.50	50%
Service station selling price	$5.00	

Most manufacturers do not employ markup pricing in the same way that many wholesalers and retailers do. However, if you plan to manufacture a product that will be sold through wholesalers and various types of retail outlets, it is important for you to know the markups these distributors will likely apply to your product. For instance, in the above example if the manufacturer of the engine treatment thinks $5 is the right retail price, he or she can work backwards and determine that it must be able to sell profitably to the jobbers for $2 to succeed. If that is not possible, perhaps the overall marketing strategy for the product should be reconsidered.

VALUE-BASED PRICING

Instead of using costs, more and more companies are basing their prices on their estimate of the market's perceived value of their market offering. This is particularly true in determining the most appropriate price to charge in a service business. This perceived value is the overall value the customer places on a product or service. The process begins by analyzing customer needs and value perceptions. This may involve much more than just the basic product or service itself and include other features such as availability, image, delivery, after-sales service, warranty considerations, and other issues. With this approach the price is set by determining the price that people are willing to pay while making sure that you can still cover all your costs.

The way businesses are able to price more effectively on "value" is by differentiating themselves in some way from the competition. This differentiation can be based on any number of factors such as promotion and advertising, availability, or the addition of value-added services. People are prepared to pay more for products produced by name designers such as Bill Blass, Calvin Klein, or Tommy Hilfiger, for example, than they are for similar items produced by others. Similarly a computer store that provides emergency service to customers on a 24/7 basis might be able to charge more for its computers or extended warranty package than an outlet that is open only from 9:00 a.m. to 6:00 p.m. five days a week.

COMPETITION-BASED PRICING

In some situations consumers base their judgements of a product's or service's value on the prices that competitors charge for similar offerings. You might decide to base your price largely on competitors' prices with less attention to your own costs or expected demand. For example, you might decide to charge the same, more, or less than your principal competitors. Some of this may depend on the image you are trying to achieve in the marketplace. If you want to create an image of a bargain or discount operation such as Dollar Store Plus or Ultracuts, for example, then your prices should be consistent with that image. Similarly, if you are trying to establish an image of a luxury operation such as Holt Renfrew or an exclusive hair salon, people may be prepared to pay more and your prices should be consistent with that position. Your target market might not be attracted to a cheaper product or service.

In addition to establishing a base price for your product or service line, you may permit some customers to pay less than this amount in certain circumstances or provide them with a discount. The principal types of discounts are quantity discounts, cash discounts, and seasonal discounts. *Quantity discounts* are commonly provided to customers who buy more than some minimum quantity or dollar value of products or services from you. This discount may be based either on the quantity or value of each individual order (non-cumulative) or on the total value of their purchases over a certain period of time, such as a month (cumulative).

Cash discounts are based on the typical terms of trade within an industry and permit customers to deduct a certain percentage amount from the net cost of their purchases if payment is made in cash at the time of purchase or full payment is made within a specified number of days. Different types of businesses have their own customary cash discounts. For example, a typical discount is expressed as "2/10 net 30." In this situation, a customer who is invoiced on October 1 for an outstanding bill of $2,000 need pay only $1,960 if payment is made before October 10. This is a 2 per cent cash discount for making payment within the 10 days. Otherwise the full face value of the invoice ($2,000) is due by October 31, or 30 days after the invoice date.

Seasonal discounts of 10 per cent, 15 per cent, 20 per cent, or more on your normal base price may be offered to your customers if their purchases are made during your slow or off-season. This gives you a method of moving inventories that you may otherwise have to carry over to the following year or of providing your dealers, agents, and other distributors with some incentive to stock up on your products well in advance of the prime selling season.

PROMOTIONAL PLANS

The budget that you allocate for the promotion of your new venture must be distributed across the following activities:

1. Advertising
2. Personal selling
3. Sales promotion
4. Public relations

Each of these activities differs along a number of important dimensions, such as their cost to reach a member of the target audience and the degree of interaction that can take place with that audience. Table 6.3 summarizes how these activities compare on a number of different criteria.

TABLE 6.3   A COMPARISON OF VARIOUS PROMOTIONAL ACTIVITIES

	Advertising	Sales Promotion	Public Relations	Personal Selling
Cost per Audience Member	Low	Low	Very Low	Very High
Focus on Target Markets	Poor to Good	Good	Moderate	Very Good
Ability to Deliver a Complicated Message	Poor to Good	Poor	Poor to Good	Very Good
Interchange with Audience	None	None	Low to Moderate	Very Good
Credibility	Low	Low	High	Moderate to High

Source: Adapted from Gerald E. Hills, "Market Opportunities and Marketing," in William D. Bygrave, *The Portable MBA in Entrepreneurship,* 2nd ed. (Hoboken, NJ: John Wiley & Sons, Inc., 1999). This material is used by permission of John Wiley & Sons, Inc.

The distribution of your expenditures should be made to obtain the maximum results for your particular circumstances. It is impossible to generalize about the optimum distribution of your dollars to each of these activities. Different businesses use quite different combinations. Some companies put most of their money into hiring a sales force and their sales promotion program; others put most of their budget into a media advertising campaign. The proper combination for you will depend on a careful study of the relative costs and effectiveness of each of these types of promotion and the unique requirements of your business.

We often think of promotion as being directed strictly toward our final prospective customer, and in fact the largest share of most promotional activity is channelled in that direction. However, promotion can also be used to influence your dealers, your distributors, and other members of your distribution channel. This may persuade them to adopt your offering more rapidly and broaden the breadth of your distribution coverage.

ADVERTISING

Advertising is one of the principal means you have of informing potential customers about the availability and special features of your product or service. Properly conceived messages presented in the appropriate media can greatly stimulate demand for your business and its offerings. A wide range of advertising media is available to carry your messages, of which the most important are those listed in Table 6.4. Which of these media you should choose for your advertising program will depend on the consumers you are trying to reach, the size of the budget you have available, the nature of your product or service, and the particular message you hope to communicate.

TABLE 6.4	THE MOST COMMON ADVERTISING MEDIA

1. MAGAZINES
- a. Consumer magazines
- b. Trade or business publications
- c. Farm publications
- d. Professional magazines

2. NEWSPAPERS
- a. Daily newspapers
- b. Weekly newspapers
- c. Shopping guides
- d. Special-interest newspapers

3. TELEVISION
- a. Local TV
- b. Network TV
- c. Special-interest cable TV

4. RADIO
- a. Local stations
- b. Network radio

5. DIRECTORY
- a. Yellow Pages
- b. Community
- c. Special-interest

6. DIRECT MAIL ADVERTISING
- a. Letters
- b. Catalogues

7. OUTDOOR ADVERTISING
- a. Billboards
- b. Posters

8. TRANSPORTATION ADVERTISING
- a. Interior car cards
- b. Station posters
- c. Exterior cards on vehicles

9. POINT-OF-PURCHASE DISPLAYS

10. ADVERTISING NOVELTIES AND SPECIALTIES

11. THE INTERNET

SHERMAN'S LAGOON

©Jim Toomey. Reprinted with special permission of King Features Syndicate.

ADVERTISING ON THE INTERNET One form of advertising that is rapidly increasing in popularity is the use of the Internet. The World Wide Web is open for business and small firms, particularly retail businesses, are jumping aboard in ever-increasing numbers. Before joining this throng, however, you should consider whether a Web presence will really serve your business interests. If so, you need to formulate a clear strategy or plan, rather than just developing another Web page to join the millions that already exist on the Net.

Martin and Andrea Swinton (Entrepreneurs in Action #20), for example, have used the Web very successfully to develop their antique business in Toronto. They didn't just throw up a Web site and hope for the best. Their initial approach was experiment by listing a number of items on eBay to test the response of the electronic marketplace to their overall business idea. A positive response there led them to develop their own Web site to demonstrate some of the merchandise they had available in their store, as well as link up to their items for auction on eBay. Their site complements the more traditional advertising and promotion they have

20 *Entrepreneurs in* **a c t i o n**

Take-A-Boo Emporium

Take-A-Boo Emporium is an eclectic antique store in Toronto, Ontario, owned and operated by Martin and Andrea Swinton, a husband-and-wife team.

Martin and Andrea have successfully operated their antique store for four and a half years now, and are justly proud that they're not only still in business, but growing. As Andrea says, "Retail is a tough business. Several retailers have come and gone in our neighbourhood within the time that we've been open."

One of the reasons for the success of Take-A-Boo Emporium is Martin and Andrea's solid partnership. As anyone who's ever been a part of one knows, a partnership is one of the most difficult business relationships to maintain. Andrea and Martin's partnership is so successful because their expertise complements each other perfectly.

"Martin and I have different strengths and we take advantage of it," Andrea says. "Martin is the salesperson, the antiques expert, and the 'guy up front.' I'm the business side of it. He sticks to what he does best and so do I."

A life-long lover of antiques, Martin has traveled extensively through Europe, India, and Southeast Asia. He graduated from the University of Toronto with a degree in archeology and anthropology (specializing in Chinese art and pre-Columbian art). His personal areas of collection include Asian art, European furniture, and the Arts & Crafts movement. He collects old phonographs and replicas of antique cars. Before opening Take-A-Boo Emporium, Martin worked as an antiques appraiser at an auction house.

Andrea holds a Bachelor of Arts degree from Queen's University. She brings experience in marketing, communications, and public relations to the company. . . .

RISING TO THE CHALLENGE OF BUSINESS PROMOTION

While many people think that finding antiques is the hardest part of Andrea and Martin's business, it isn't. Finding inventory is easy, as Andrea and Martin buy from a network of other antique dealers, do estate sales, and do consignment.

The hardest part of starting Take-A-Boo was finding customers. Like many small businesses, Take-A-Boo Emporium had no advertising budget when it opened (and still doesn't). Andrea and Martin have both spent many hours promoting the business. Rising to the challenge of business promotion means exploring a variety of promotion ideas and constantly searching for new business promotion opportunities.

Andrea regularly sends out press releases to home decor magazines, newspaper editors, and television producers. These efforts have paid off with mentions in local community newspapers. For instance, a June window display that included wedding photos of local residents was featured in a local newspaper.

"It was a nice way to tie in the community and generate awareness at the same time," Andrea says.

Take-A-Boo Emporium's second anniversary street party in June was another promotion idea that was a big hit with local customers and helped raise the business's profile in the community. The party included bubble-blowing for the kids and free caricatures for customers.

The company's promotion efforts on local television have also been very successful, bringing customers to the store and building credibility. Martin has appeared as an antiques expert on *Toronto Living* and appears regularly on the Rogers Community Television program *Daytime*. When he appeared on *Breakfast Television* on Citytv, two customers who called in to the shop while Martin was on the air bought items from Take-A-Boo Emporium. Now there's great customer response!

Andrea has also often discussed story ideas with *The Globe and Mail*, the *National Post*, and a variety of home magazines. While nothing national has panned out yet, Andrea is hopeful. "Making the contact is the first part. Generating publicity takes time. The seed planted today will blossom next spring into a story.". . . .

FROM eBAY TO WEB SITE

One phase of Take-A-Boo Emporium's continued growth is its Web site, www.Takeaboo.com.

Take-A-Boo Emporium sells unique, one-of-a-kind items. Andrea describes their store as "a return to an old-style shopping experience. From Arts & Crafts furniture to Tibetan and Chinese artifacts, to French washstands, Take-A-Boo Emporium has something for everyone.

"However, the chance of a collector of Chinese antiquities, for instance, walking in off the street and buying something is very small. The company needed a way to reach those collectors (and buyers) of such unique items. The Internet was an obvious marketing vehicle for selling antiques.

Instead of immediately throwing up a Web site and hoping for the best, though, Andrea and Martin decided to test the electronic marketplace first, using eBay to test their business idea. At the end of 2000, they posted six items on eBay, and sold four of them.

These positive eBay results led to developing their own Web site, so they could link to their eBay auctions and hopefully generate more business for the retail antique store. "Our Web site," Andrea says, "has made the world our marketplace."....

Andrea and Martin have successfully met the retailing challenge of selling antiques, combining their expertise with ongoing marketing efforts to meet their goals.

"Our business philosophy is to provide antiques at a fair price," Andrea says. "We're in the antique-selling business, not the antique-storing business. We price things to move." (www.Takeaboo.com)

done, such as sending out press releases, developing effective window displays, hosting neighbourhood street parties, and appearing on local television, and has enabled them to reach antique collectors all over the world.

If you decide to proceed with implementing a Web site, remember that the Web is not a passive delivery system like most other media but is an active system where the user expects to participate in the experience. Your virtual storefront must be genuinely interesting and the interactivity of the Web should be used to your advantage to attract and hold the ongoing interest of your target consumers.

Opening a successful Web site is not as complicated as it may appear, but it can be expensive to do the job right. You can do it yourself or enlist the expertise of a multimedia production house. Production costs depend entirely on the size and interactivity of your site, running anywhere from $500 on the cheap to $100,000 for a full-blown corporate site. Maintenance costs are minimal but materials and other aspects of the site's operation should be updated regularly, such as once a month.

Once your page is developed, it is important that you get a domain name and file a registration request. You will also want a reliable Web server to house your site. Try to get as many links leading to your site as possible by listing with directories, hotlinks, and so on where consumers will be able to find you quite easily. You might also give some consideration to joining a cybermall, such as the RES Cybermall (www.res.ca).

PERSONAL SELLING

Personal selling involves direct, face-to-face contact with your prospective customer. A personal sales-person's primary function is usually more concerned with obtaining orders than informing your customers about the nature of your offering, as in the case of advertising. Other types of salespeople are principally involved in providing support to different components of your business or filling routine orders rather than more persuasive kinds of selling. The basic steps involved in the selling process are as follows:

1. **Prospecting and qualifying** Identifying prospective customers
2. **The sales approach** The initial contact with the prospective customer
3. **Presentation** The actual sales message presented to a prospective customer
4. **Demonstration** of the capabilities and features or most important characteristics of the product or service being sold
5. **Handling any objections or concerns** the prospective customer may have regarding your offering
6. **Closing the sale** Asking the prospective customer for the order
7. **Post-sales activities** Follow up to determine if customers are satisfied with their purchase and to pursue any additional possible sales

SALES PROMOTION

Sales promotion includes a broad range of promotional activities other than advertising and personal selling that stimulate consumer or dealer interest in your offering. While advertising and personal selling tend to be ongoing activities, most sales promotion is sporadic or irregular in nature. Sales promotion includes activities related to:

1. Free product samples
2. Discount coupons
3. Contests
4. Special deals and premiums
5. Gifts
6. Special exhibits and displays
7. Participation in trade shows
8. Off-price specials
9. Floats in parades and similar events

As you can see, sales promotion consists of a long list of what are typically non-recurring activities. They are intended to make your advertising and personal selling effort more effective and may be very intimately involved with them. For example, your advertising may be used to promote a consumer contest, or certain special deals and incentives may be offered to your salespeople to encourage them to increase their sales to your dealers or final consumers. These activities can be an effective way for businesses with a small budget and some imagination to reach potential sales prospects and develop a considerable volume of business.

PUBLIC RELATIONS

Public relations relates to your business's general communications and relationships with its various interest groups such as your employees, stockholders, the government, and society at large, as well as your customers. It is concerned primarily with such issues as the image of you and your business within the community rather than trying to sell any particular product or service. Publicity releases, product introduction notices, news items, appearances on radio and television, and similar activities are all part of your public relations program.

METHOD OF DISTRIBUTION

Your channel of distribution is the path your product or service takes to market. Physical products typically follow one or more complex paths in getting from the point at which they are produced to the hands of their final consumer. These paths involve the use of several different kinds of wholesalers and retailers who perform a variety of functions that are essential to making this flow of products reasonably efficient. These functions include buying, selling, transporting, storing, financing, and risk-taking.

Distribution channels consist of channel members that are independent firms that facilitate this flow of merchandise. There are many different kinds, and they have quite different names, but the functions they perform may not be that dramatically different. For example, wholesalers are generally classified according to whether they actually take title or ownership of the products they handle (*merchant wholesalers*) or not (*agents*). Merchant wholesalers are further classified as *full-service*, *limited-function*, *drop shippers*, *truck wholesalers*, and *rack jobbers*. Agents are commonly referred to as *brokers*, *manufacturer's agents*, *selling agents*, *food* or *drug brokers*, etc. For small manufacturers, all of these types of wholesalers, alone or in combination, represent possible paths for getting their product to market.

Retailers, too, cover a very broad spectrum, starting with the large department stores that carry a broad product selection and provide an extensive range of customer services; through specialty stores such as electronics, men's clothing, and furniture stores; on down to discount department stores, grocery stores, drug stores, catalogue retailers, and convenience stores. All represent possible members that could be included in your channel of distribution.

In addition to opportunities for marketing your products or services in conjunction with these traditional and conventional distribution channel members, you should not overlook more unconventional possibilities for reaching your potential customers. For example, over the past few years we have seen tremendous growth of various forms of non-store retailing, including:

1. Mail-order catalogues
2. Direct response advertising on television and in newspapers and magazines
3. Direct selling door to door
4. Party plan or home demonstration party selling
5. Direct-mail solicitations
6. Vending machines
7. Trade shows
8. Fairs and exhibitions
9. The Internet

Toad Hall Toys, for example, is a small independent toy store in downtown Winnipeg, known for its wide and unique selection of children's toys (Entrepreneurs in Action #21). Toad Hall specializes in specialty, often hard-to-find items and serves as an alternative to the large chains that commonly carry only the more popular items advertised on television. The company was considering developing a mail-order catalogue to send to prospective customers when it realized that the Internet could be a much less expensive way to go. The initial Toad Hall site was created in-house and is still maintained and updated on a daily basis by the company. Over the past couple of years, its Web business has developed into a key component of its overall business strategy, and the company receives orders from all over the world, including the United States, Europe, South America, and Asia. Toad Hall is now considered one of the most successful online retailers in Manitoba.

You should also be aware of market opportunities that may exist for your venture in foreign markets. These may be accessed by direct exporting, using the services of a trading company, licensing or franchising a firm in that market to produce and sell your product or service, setting up a joint venture with a local firm, or some similar strategy.

DEVELOPING A PRELIMINARY MARKETING PLAN

Figure 6.8 on page 190 presents a framework to help you prepare a preliminary marketing plan for the product or service idea behind your prospective venture. It will guide you through the process and indicate the kind of information you will need to do a thorough job. It will get you thinking about the size and nature of the market opportunity that may exist for your concept or idea. It will also focus your thoughts on the marketing program you will require to take advantage of the opportunity and achieve your personal goals. The marketing plan is a key part of your feasibility study and your subsequent business plan. Much of the work you do here can be incorporated into your business plan.

Keep in mind, however, that marketing plans are not static documents. Businesses normally have to reformulate their marketing strategy several times over their active life. Economic conditions change, additional competitors come onto the scene, and customer's interests and requirements change. Consequently, the business must plan marketing programs appropriate to each stage in its development. For example, Scott and Bruce identified five stages in the growth of a typical small business: inception, survival, growth, expansion and maturity.[5] The basic features of each stage are different and the objectives of the business's marketing plan will vary as well. Table 6.5 provides an overview of some of the basic features of each stage and how the firm's marketing efforts may need to be modified to address the principal issues typical of each stage.

MANAGING THE SUPPLY SITUATION

A key factor in the success of any new venture is some assurance of continuing access to critical supplies of raw material and component parts at reasonable prices. Many new businesses have floundered due to changing supply situations that impacted their ability to provide products of acceptable quality or that drastically increased their costs of production. These conditions are seldom correctable and tend to be terminal

---

5. M. Scott and R. Bruce, "Five Stages of Growth in Small Business," *Long-Range Planning*, June 1987, pp. 45–52.

21 Entrepreneurs in action

Toad Hall Toys

Perhaps the most well-known of all the Manitoba-based businesses using e-commerce is Toad Hall Toys. Toad Hall is a 25-year-old family-run business. Located in Winnipeg's historical exchange district, Toad Hall is known for its wide and unique selection of children's toys. Dan Aysan, who owns the toy store, states that Toad Hall is an alternative to the nation-wide chains that carry many of the popular items advertised on television. Toad Hall carries products in small quantities and offers more specialty, unique or hard-to-find items.

THE E-PRODUCT

In the mid-90s the company wanted to develop a catalogue of toys and saw that the Internet was becoming available to more people. The Internet looked like it might be a less expensive way of creating and distributing the Toad Hall catalogue. From that point on, Toad Hall has not stopped! The initial Toad Hall Toys Web site cost $500 to produce in-house versus the projected cost of $100,000 to complete production and distribution of a standard, full-colour catalogue.

The initial site was created in-house and is updated on a daily basis. The company feels that it was, and still is, extremely important to have the ability to update and maintain the site within Toad Hall. This ensures that the company has the ability to guarantee that all of the products on the site are current. In-house maintenance and updates also keep the associated costs in line.

Although much of the work for the Toad Hall site was performed in-house, the company still had to secure a Web site host. The Toad Hall decision to select a particular company was based primarily on reliability, because the site had to be up and running all the time. It was also important that the service provider use the latest technology and equipment, as Toad Hall wanted to ensure its customers had fast access to its site at all times.

Toad Hall receives orders from around the world including the United States, Europe, South America and Asia and feels that it is especially important to be registered with all the search engines possible.

Toad Hall regularly tracks the search engines to ensure that Toad Hall's name appears. The company also spent money, a modest amount relative to the success rate, to use the search engine registration services on a regular basis. Free listings are also taken advantage of to promote the site and this has proven to be a winning strategy. . . .

WHERE ARE THEY NOW?

The company is extremely pleased with the growth of its Web site sales. In fact, its Web business is a key component of the company's overall business strategy, as it has set specific financial objectives for its Web sales in the same manner as it has sales targets for its in-store sales.

Toad Hall's next objective is to integrate its inventory and back office accounting programs with its e-commerce programs. At present, this is not an easy task as the company's in-store inventory system is not yet able to cleanly integrate with the e-commerce transaction processing services. Another challenge for Toad Hall to look forward to! . . . .

Toad Hall recommends that companies investing in e-commerce services remember that customer service is key. Look for the best in suppliers, including Internet service providers and shipping/courier services. In today's economy, customers are only a mouse click away from choosing another company, so servicing customers beyond their expectations is a must. In-house technical expertise is important to be able to update and maintain your own Web site on your own time.

If you ask most people, Toad Hall is the most successful online retailer in Manitoba, demonstrating what unique products, hard work and an enthusiasm for the Internet will do! (www.toadhalltoys.com)

Source: Canada Business Service Centres Web site (www.cbsc.org/manitoba/index.cfm?name=displaybis&coll=MB_PROVBIS_E&Code=6314), accessed February 22, 2004.

TABLE 6.5	A MODEL FOR SMALL BUSINESS GROWTH				
	Stage 1 Inception	**Stage 2 Survival**	**Stage 3 Growth**	**Stage 4 Expansion**	**Stage 5 Maturity**
Key Issue	Obtaining customers	Increasing competition	Expansion into new products or markets	Greater external emphasis	Finding growth opportunities
Product and Market Research	None	Little	Some new product development	New product development, market research	Production innovation
Product Market	Single basic product line	Single product line and market but greater scale	Broader but limited product line, single market	Extended range of products, broader markets	Contained product lines, multiple markets
Emphasis of Marketing Plan	Limited channels of distribution, cost-plus pricing, heavy sales promotion	Reach expanding markets, broader channels of distribution	Emphasis on cost-efficiency, penetration pricing, build market awareness and distribution	Greater focus on customer needs and adapting the marketing plan (including promotion) to meet those needs	Major investment in the marketing effort, phase out weak products, cut prices, focus on profitable niches

Source: M. Scott and R. Bruce, "Five Stage of Growth in Small Business," *Long-Range Planning*, June 1987, pp. 45–52.

for the smaller firm. It is critical that you investigate the range of possible sources for these key elements well in advance of starting your venture.

Assessing your supply situation requires an understanding of the manufacturing cycle for your product or service and an in-depth appreciation of the market for equipment, materials, and parts. One strategy being followed by more and more smaller firms is to subcontract their production requirements instead of making their own products. This strategy has a number of significant advantages:

- Your business can use the subcontractor's money instead of having to raise the funds to build your own production facilities.

- You can take advantage of the expertise and technical knowledge possessed by the subcontractor without having to develop it yourself.

- Using a subcontractor may enable you to bring your business on stream more rapidly. There is no need to delay while your production facilities are being built and broken in.

- You can concentrate your time on developing a market for your products and running your business rather than on trying to produce a satisfactory product.

- You may be able to benefit from the reputation and credibility of the subcontractor; having your products produced by a firm with an established reputation will rub off on your business.

- A reliable subcontractor can also keep you up to date with technical advances in that field so that your products don't become obsolete.

- Perhaps the most important advantage of using a subcontractor is that it establishes your costs of production in advance, reducing the uncertainty and unpredictability of setting up your own facilities. A firm, fixed-price contract from a reliable subcontractor nails down one of your most important costs of doing business and facilitates your entire planning process.

FYI FOR YOUR INFORMATION

The following are some helpful Web sites for developing your marketing plan:

From Idea to Market: How to Get Your Product on the Shelf through Market Research
A summary overview of marketing and market research and how this information is crucial for your idea or venture to succeed. (www.cbsc.org/manitoba/index.cfm?name=idea)

Online Small Business Workshop A six-session online workshop covering much of the information you need to consider when starting a regular business or an e-business. (www.cbsc.org/osbw)

Market Research—Where to Find the Information You Need A comprehensive list of some the key market research resources available. (http://www.cbsc.org/alberta/tbl.cfm?fn=market_source)

Business Information by Industrial Sector A comprehensive overview of Canadian business information by industry sector. (strategis.ic.gc.ca/sc_indps/engdoc/homepage.html?categories=e_bis)

Canadian Statistics A business resource of online statistics for, and publications about, various business sectors, plus other information. (commerce.statcan.ca/english/commerce)

Canadian Economic Statistics A statistical overview of current Canadian economic conditions and a number of industry- and trade-related statistics. (strategis.ic.gc.ca/sc_ecnmy/engdoc/homepage.html?categories=e_eco)

Corporate Information Canada Information on world securities markets, including company profiles from 53 countries worldwide. (www.corporateinformation.com)

Canada in the Twenty-First Century A series of 11 "vision" papers that explore the broad trends reshaping the global economic order and examine the medium-term consequences of these developments for the Canadian economy. (strategis.ic.gc.ca/epic/internet/ineas-aes.nsf/vwGeneratedInterE/h_ra01883e.html)

Home-Based Business Tips and ideas for starting a home-based business. (www.cbsc.org/english/search/display.cfm?CODE=4078&Coll=FE_FEDSBIS_E)

Your Own Business The information and inspiration you can use to start and run a profitable small and home-based business. (www.life.ca/hb/index.html)

ExportSource Everything you need to know to take advantage of international trade and compete in a global marketplace with your goods and services. (exportsource.ca)

Take A World View: Export Your Services The necessary information to assist small- and medium-sized service firms that are interested in exporting to do so successfully. (strategis.ic.gc.ca/epic/internet/intawv-uamo.nsf/vwGeneratedInterE/Home)

Customized Market Research Reports for International Trade Detailed industry sector analysis reports for countries all over the world. (strategis.ic.gc.ca/epic/internet/inibi-iai.nsf/vwGeneratedInterE/bi18355e.html)

As you can see, there are a number of strong advantages to subcontracting certain aspects of your operations, but that does not necessarily mean this strategy should be employed in all situations. There are a number of disadvantages that should be considered as well:

- The cost of having a job done by a subcontractor may not be as low as if you did the work yourself. Subcontractors may have antiquated equipment; high-cost, unionized labour; or other problems to deal with that make their operations very expensive. Subcontractors also factor in some margin of profit for themselves into a job. The end result may be a total production cost that would make it very difficult for you to successfully compete.

- Your business may be jeopardized if the subcontractor should fail to meet commitments to you or divulge critical trade secrets about your product or process.

In any case, sometimes a suitable subcontractor is just not available. If you want your product produced, you may have no alternative but to do it yourself.

Regardless of the approach you decide to take, to cover your supply situation there are a number of key factors that have to be considered. These include:

- Delivered cost (total cost including transportation, etc.)
- Quality
- Delivery schedules
- Service level

All have to be at an acceptable level for you to have confidence that your supply situation is under reasonable control.

Video Case #6

·············· **Montreal Meat** ··············

Summary

Frederick Anuse has a business school background but no real business or restaurant experience. He found a business concept in Paris called la Linas — a restaurant that offers music, good food, and $10 luxury sandwiches. Anuse hadn't lived in Canada for a while, but he felt the concept could be transferred to the Canadian market so he purchased a franchise.

Questions for Discussion

1. Should Anuse have completed a formal market assessment before jumping into this venture? Why or why not?

2. Why was Anuse having such a hard time finding suppliers?

3. What was Anuse's marketing program?

4. Where did Anuse find start-up capital? What are some other places to find start-up capital?

TABLE 6.6   OTHER PUBLISHED SOURCES OF MARKET INFORMATION

GENERAL

Gale Directory of Publications and Broadcast Media
Gale Research, Inc.
27500 Drake Road
Farmington Hills, MI 48331
(www.gale.com)

Ulrich's Periodicals Directory
R.R. Bowker Company
630 Central Avenue
New Providence, NJ 07974
(www.bowker.com) or
(www.ulrichsweb.com for the online version)

The Standard Periodical Directory
Oxbridge Communications Inc.
186 Fifth Avenue
New York, NY 10010
(www.mediafinder.com)

Indexes to books and magazine articles on a wide variety of business, industrial, and economic topics:

Bibliographic Index: A Cumulative Bibliography of Bibliographies
H.W. Wilson Co.
950 University Avenue
New York, NY 10452
(www.hwwilson.com)

Business Periodicals Index
H.W. Wilson Co.
950 University Avenue
New York, NY 10452
(www.hwwilson.com)

Canadian Business and Current Affairs
Micromedia Limited
20 Victoria Street
Toronto, Ontario M5C 2N8
(www.mmltd.com)

A detailed listing of source books, periodicals, directories, handbooks, and other sources of information on a variety of business topics:

Encyclopedia of Business Information Sources
Gale Research Company
27500 Drake Road
Farmington Hills, MI 48331
(www.gale.com)

A general guide to business publications:

Business Information: How to Find It, How to Use It (by Michael R. Lavin)
Greenwood Publishing Group
88 Post Road W.
Westport, CT 06881
(www.greenwood.com)

Directories of business-oriented databases:

Gale Directory of Databases
Gale Research Inc.
27500 Drake Road
Farmington Hills, MI 48331
(www.gale.com)

LEXIS/NEXIS
Reed Elsevier
P.O. Box 933
Dayton, OH 45401
(www.lexis-nexis.com)

INDUSTRY AND MARKET INFORMATION

Data on income, population, expenditures, etc., by major market area:

Survey of Buying Power (annual special issue of *Sales and Marketing Management*)
VNU Business Publications USA
770 Broadway
New York, NY 10003
(www.billcom.com)

Information on population size and growth, income, expenditures, prices, and similar data by market area:

Market Research Handbook
Statistics Canada
Ottawa, Ontario K1A 0T6
(www.fedpubs.com/subject/business/mkthdbk.htm)

COMPANY INFORMATION

Detailed information on most major corporations:

Dun & Bradstreet Million Dollar Directory
Dun & Bradstreet Inc.
The D&B Corporation
103 JFK Parkway
Short Hills, NJ 07078
(www.dnb.com)

Globeinvestor.com
Bell Globemedia Publishing Inc.
9 Channel Nine Court
Scarborough, ON M1S 4B5
(www.globeinvestor.com)

Moody's Manuals and Investors Services
99 Church Street
New York, NY 10007
(www.moodys.com)

FP Infomart
CanWest Interactive Inc.
333 King Street East
Toronto, ON M5A 4R7
(www.fpinfomart.ca)

Listings of Canadian manufacturers by location and product category:

Fraser's Canadian Trade Directory
777 Bay Street
Toronto, Ontario M5W 1A7
(www.frasers.com)

Scott's Directories
Scottsinfo.com
1450 Don Mills Road
Don Mills Ontario M3B 2X7
(www.scottsinfo.com)

Scott's Directories:
- *Ontario Manufacturers Directory*
- *Quebec Industrial Directory*
- *Greater Toronto Business Directory*
- *Greater Montreal and Laval Business Directory*
- *Atlantic Industrial Directory*
- *Western Industrial Directory*

continued

Other Published Sources of Market Information — continued

MARKETING INFORMATION

Listings of rates and other information on radio, television, consumer magazines, trade magazines, direct mail, and newspapers:

Canadian Advertising Rates & Data
    Rogers Media Publishing
    777 Bay Street, 5th Floor
    Toronto, ON M5W 1A7
    (www.cardmedia.com)

SRDS Media Solutions
    1700 Higgins Road
    Des Plaines, IL 60018-5605
    (www.srds.com)
    SRDS Publications:
- *Canadian Advertising Rates & Data*
- *Business Publication Advertising Source*
- *Consumer Magazine Advertising Source*
- *Newspaper Advertising Source*
- *Community Publication Advertising Source*
- *Out-of-Home Advertising Source*
- *Direct Marketing List Source*
- *Technology Media Source*
- *TV & Cable Source*
- *Radio Advertising Source*
- *Interactive Advertising Source*
- *International Media Guides*

A listing of agents and firms representing manufacturers of all types:

Manufacturer's Agents National Association Directory of Members
    Manufacturer's Agents National Association
    One Spectrum Point, Suite 150
    Lake Forest, CA 92630
    (www.manaonline.org or www.manaonline.org/html/this_week/canada.html)

Comprehensive listings of U.S. and Canadian meetings, conventions, trade shows, and expositions:

Conventions and Meetings Canada
    Rogers Media Inc.
    777 Bay Street
    Toronto, Ontario M5W 1A7
    (www.bizlink.com/cmc.htm)

Trade Shows Worldwide
    Gale Research Inc.
    27500 Drake Road
    Farmington Hills, MI 48331
    (www.gale.com)

A comprehensive listing of mail order firms:

Mail Order Business Directory
    B. Klein Publications
    P.O. Box 8503
    Coral Springs, FL 33065

Catalogue of Canadian Catalogues
    Alpel Publishing
    P.O. Box 203
    Chambly, QC J3L 4B3
    (www.mailordercanada.com)

Directory of Mail Order Catalogues
    Grey House Publishing
    185 Millerton Road
    PO Box 850
    Millerton, NY, 12546
    (www.greyhouse.com)

A comprehensive listing of all trade and professional associations in Canada:

Directory of Associations in Canada
   Micromedia Ltd.
   20 Victoria Street
   Toronto, Ontario M5C 2N8
   (www.mmltd.com)

FIGURE 6.2	DEVELOPING A MARKET OR CUSTOMER PROFILE

1. Define your target customers in terms of geography, demographic characteristics, or other factors.

_____
_____
_____
_____
_____

2. How many of these target customers are in your trading or relevant market area?

_____
_____
_____
_____
_____

3. What are the principal features and benefits that these customers consider in the purchase of a product/service like yours?

_____
_____
_____
_____
_____

4. What psychographic or sociological factors are likely to distinguish your target customers and be important in the purchase of a product/service like yours?

_____
_____
_____
_____
_____

5. Why will they buy your product rather than your competitors'?

_____
_____
_____
_____
_____

FIGURE 6.3   OUTLINE FOR A CUSTOMER SURVEY

Name of Customer _____

1. NATURE OF THE CUSTOMER'S BUSINESS OR ROLE

_____
_____
_____

2. CUSTOMER'S REACTION TO YOUR PRODUCT OR SERVICE
a.   What advantages/benefits does the customer see?

_____
_____
_____

b.   What disadvantages does the customer see?

_____
_____
_____

c.   What questions does the customer raise?

_____
_____
_____

3. SPECIFIC NEEDS AND USES
What needs and uses does the customer have for a product/service such as yours?

_____
_____
_____

4. SELLING PRICE, SERVICE, AND SUPPORT
a.   What do you believe would be an acceptable selling price?

_____

b.   What level of service and support would the customer expect?

_____
_____
_____

c.   What other terms would the customer expect?

_____
_____
_____

5. CURRENT PURCHASING PRACTICES
Where does the customer currently buy this type of product or service (retailer, wholesaler, direct mail, broker, etc.)?

_____
_____
_____

6. NAME OF COMPETITIVE FIRMS

What competing firms' products and services is the customer currently using?

_____

_____

_____

_____

FIGURE 6.4   **FORM FOR ESTIMATING MARKET SIZE**

ESTIMATED TOTAL MARKET SIZE

1. DESCRIPTION OF PRINCIPAL MARKET

_____

_____

	Per Cent Change			
	200A–200B	200B–200C	200C–200D	200D–200E
Estimated total sales in units ____	_____	_____	_____	_____
Estimated total sales in $000 ____	_____	_____	_____	_____

2. OVERVIEW OF MAJOR SEGMENTS

a. Description of segment: _____

_____

	Per Cent Change			
	200A–200B	200B–200C	200C–200D	200D–200E
Estimated sales in units _____	_____	_____	_____	_____
Estimated sales in $000 _____	_____	_____	_____	_____

b. Description of segment: _____

_____

	Per Cent Change			
	200A–200B	200B–200C	200C–200D	200D–200E
Estimated sales in units _____	_____	_____	_____	_____
Estimated sales in $000 _____	_____	_____	_____	_____

FIGURE 6.5   **FORM FOR ANALYZING YOUR COMPETITORS**

Name of Competitor _____**Estimated Market Share** _____%

1. PRODUCT OR SERVICE

a. How does the company's product or service differ from others available in the marketplace?

_____

_____

_____

_____

continued

Form for Analyzing Your Competitors — continued

b. Does it offer a broad or narrow product line? _____
_____

c. Does it emphasize quality? _____

2. PRICE

a. What is its average selling price? _____
b. What is its estimated gross margin? _____
c. What type of discounts does it offer? _____
d. Does it emphasize a low selling price? _____

3. PROMOTION

a. How much does it spend on advertising and trade promotion? _____
b. How well known is it (brand recognition)? _____
c. In what media does it advertise? _____
_____

d. What other types of promotion does it use? _____
_____

e. How many salespeople does it have? _____

4. DISTRIBUTION/LOCATION

a. What type of distribution intermediaries does it use (brokers, own sales force, manufacturer's agents, etc.)?   _____
_____
_____

b. Where is it located? _____
c. Is location an important factor in this industry? _____

5. MARKETING STRATEGY

a. Does the company cater to any particular segment of the market? _____
_____

b. Does the company offer any unique product or service that makes it different from other competitors? _____
_____
_____

c. Does it offer a particularly low price? _____
d. What is the principal factor that accounts for the success of this firm? _____

6. MARKET POSITION

a. What is its market share? _____
b. Have its sales been growing? Stable? Declining? _____
_____

c. How successful is it overall? _____
_____

7. MAJOR STRENGTHS AND WEAKNESSES

a. What are its major strengths? _____
_____
_____

b. What are its major weaknesses? _____

_____

_____

_____

FIGURE 6.6	DEVELOPING A SALES FORECAST

1. Provide a summary overview of typical individuals, companies, and organizations that are likely prospects for your product/service offering as described in the market profile you prepared in Figure 6.2. Ask yourself such questions as: How old would these customers be? Where do they live? In what types of activities would they participate? What primary benefits are they looking for in my product or service? Think of as many relevant questions as possible.

_____

_____

_____

_____

_____

2. How many of the prospective customers you have described as good prospects are in your trading area?

_____

_____

_____

3. Describe how you feel these prospective customers would go about deciding whether to purchase your product/service rather than a competitor's offering. Would these potential customers be principally concerned with price, convenience, quality, or some other factor?

_____

_____

_____

_____

4. How often would prospective buyers purchase your product or service? Daily? Weekly? Monthly? Other? Where would they look for it or expect to buy it? What kind of seasonal or other patterns are likely to influence sales? How will holidays or other special events affect sales patterns within a month? A year?

_____

_____

_____

_____

5. How much (in dollars and/or units) would a typical customer purchase on each buying occasion?

_____

_____

continued

Developing a Sales Forecast — continued

6. How would your customers likely hear about your product/service offering? Through newspapers? TV or radio advertisements? Word of mouth? Salespeople? Intermediaries? Other?

_____

_____

_____

7. From the above information, estimate your expected annual sales in terms of *dollars* and/or *number of units by month* for the first three years of operation of your business.

	1st Year	2nd Year	3rd Year
January	_____	_____	_____
February	_____	_____	_____
March	_____	_____	_____
April	_____	_____	_____
May	_____	_____	_____
June	_____	_____	_____
July	_____	_____	_____
August	_____	_____	_____
September	_____	_____	_____
October	_____	_____	_____
November	_____	_____	_____
December	_____	_____	_____

FIGURE 6.7   RATING FORM FOR SELECTING A RETAIL LOCATION

FACTOR A: PRIMARY ACCEPTANCE OR REJECTION FACTORS
(RATE YES OR NO)

	Location No. 1	2	3	4
1. Will municipal zoning allow the proposed business?	___	___	___	___
2. Does this site meet the minimum operating needs of the proposed business?	___	___	___	___
3. Do existing buildings meet minimum initial needs?	___	___	___	___
4. Is the rent for this location within your proposed operating budget?	___	___	___	___
5. Is the rent for this location, with or without buildings, reasonable?	___	___	___	___

One "No" answer may be sufficient reason not to proceed with further investigation unless some modification can be achieved.

FACTOR B: SITE EVALUATION
(USE PERCENTAGE SCALE 0 TO 100)

	Location No. 1	2	3	4
6. How does this location compare with the best possible location available?	___	___	___	___
7. What rating would you give the present buildings on the site?	___	___	___	___
8. How would you rate the overall environment of this location with the best environment existing within your trading area?	___	___	___	___
9. How would you rate the availability of parking for vehicles?	___	___	___	___
10. How would you rate the nature and quantity of combined foot and vehicle traffic passing your location?	___	___	___	___

11. What is the improvement potential of this location?   — —— —— ——

  Total   — —— —— ——

FACTOR C: TREND ANALYSIS

(COMPARE THE ANSWER FOR EACH LOCATION AND RANK EACH BY
NUMBER FROM AMONG THOSE REVIEWED — i.e., 1st, 2nd, 3rd, or 4th)

Location No.

	1	2	3	4
12. Has the location shown improvement through the years?	—	—	—	—
13. Is the owner and/or landlord progressive and cooperative?	—	—	—	—
14. What major patterns of change are affecting this location?	—	—	—	—
a. Streets: Speed limits, paving	—	—	—	—
b. Shopping centres	—	—	—	—
c. Zoning	—	—	—	—
d. Financial investment	—	—	—	—
e. Dynamic leadership and action	—	—	—	—
f. Type of shopper or other potential customer	—	—	—	—
15. What businesses have occupied this location over the past 10 years?	—	—	—	—
16. Have the businesses identified in question 15 (above) been successful?	—	—	—	—
17. Why is this location now available?	—	—	—	—
18. Are a number of other suitable locations available?	—	—	—	—

FACTOR D: PRICE–VALUE DETERMINATION

Location No.

	1	2	3	4
19. What is the asking rent for each location?	—	—	—	—
20. What is the estimated cost of required leasehold improvements?	—	—	—	—
21. What numerical total for each site is developed for questions 6 through 11?	—	—	—	—
22. Is there a "No" answer to any of questions 1 through 5?	—	—	—	—
23. Do the answers to questions 12 through 18 develop a pattern that is:				
a. Highly favourable?	—	—	—	—
b. Average?	—	—	—	—
c. Fair?	—	—	—	—
d. Questionable?	—	—	—	—
e. Not acceptable?	—	—	—	—

Rank each location according to numerical totals and preferences as
to subjective Factors C and D.   — —— —— ——

Adapted from M. Archer and J. White, *Starting and Managing Your Own Small Business* (Toronto: Macmillan Company of
Canada, 1978), 38–40. Reproduced by permission.

FIGURE 6.8   A FRAMEWORK FOR DEVELOPING A PRELIMINARY MARKETING PLAN

1. **DEFINE YOUR GOALS**

    You need to start this process by defining two sets of goals:

    -   Personal goals
    -   Business goals

    a. Your personal goals need to be defined first. You want to be certain that the business you are considering is compatible with the attainment of your personal goals.

    Your Personal Goals

    How much money do you want, or need, to earn? _____

    _____

    _____

    What sort of lifestyle is desirable for you and your family? _____

    _____

    _____

    How will your business reflect you and your values? _____

    _____

    _____

    What are your risk parameters? What is your tolerance for risk?_____

    _____

    _____

    What do you want to achieve in five years?_____

    _____

    _____

    b. Your business goals need to be defined next. These are general statements of business intentions that you are aiming to accomplish, results that your business is committed to achieving over time. You can define your business goals by using such terms as "becoming the leading firm in this industry within this market" or "being the lowest cost or most efficient or most widely recognized business of its type within this area." Goals may also be more modestly defined such as to build "a business large enough to provide an income stream that will enable me to quit my current job."

    Your Business Goals

    How big do you want your business to be? _____

    _____

    _____

    _____

    What general goals would you like your business to achieve? _____

    _____

    _____

    _____

2. **WHAT DO YOU PLAN TO SELL?**

    You have given some thought to the concept or idea you would like to investigate as a prospective business opportunity. Now you need to translate that notion into a clear definition of your business and a description of the broad range of products and services you plan to offer. If you are able to explain clearly and succinctly what products or services you plan to sell, to whom, and why you think they will buy from you, you are well on the way to developing an effective marketing plan. Generally describe your proposed product/service offerings and whom you see as being your principal target market for each offering or your whole line. If you have many products/services, try to bundle them together into no more than five categories. You can always expand the list later — but for now, keep it simple.

Product/Service Offering

	Product/Service	Primary Target Markets
1.	_____	_____
2.	_____	_____
3.	_____	_____
4.	_____	_____
5.	_____	_____

3. ESTABLISH PRELIMINARY SALES ESTIMATES

For each of the products/services in your line, estimate what you feel your sales could be if everything went perfectly after you started up your business. What would your sales be if everything went wrong? What figure in between these two estimates do you think represents the most likely case?

Preliminary Sales Estimates

Sales Goals for Each Product/Service

	Worst Case	Most Likely Case	Best Case
1.	$ _____	$ _____	$ _____
2.	$ _____	$ _____	$ _____
3.	$ _____	$ _____	$ _____
4.	$ _____	$ _____	$ _____
5.	$ _____	$ _____	$ _____

Comments:

_____

_____

_____

_____

_____

4. ESTIMATE TOTAL MARKET SIZE AND TRENDS

A major component of market opportunity analysis and developing a marketing plan is determining the overall volume of unit sales, or dollar revenue, that may flow from a market. When analyzing market potential and size, it is important to refer only to that portion of the market you will be serving. For example, if you are planning to deal only with customers in Edmonton, or part of Edmonton, it does not make sense to include Calgary, Regina, or Toronto in your assessment of market size. On the other hand, if you hope to sell your product regionally or nationally, then those are the relevant market areas to be considered.

In addition to this broad analysis, you might also investigate whether, within this major market area, there are groups of potential buyers with different preferences, requirements, or purchasing practices. This process of breaking down large heterogeneous markets into more homogeneous groups is known as *market segmentation*, as discussed in this Stage.

Most markets can be segmented on the basis of a number of variables:

- geographic location (such as a part of a city or town, county, province, region, or country)

continued

A Framework for Developing a Preliminary Marketing Plan — continued

- demographic characteristics (such as age, gender, income, occupation, marital status, race, religion, or education). Institutional, industrial, and government markets can be classified on the basis of their Standard Industrial Classification category, their total purchases or sales, number of employees, or the nature of their organizational activity.

- a variety of sociological factors (such as lifestyle, user status, usage rate, timing and means of purchasing, and/or reasons for buying products similar to yours).

You can use the following templates to estimate approximate total market size (past, present, and future) and expected trends in terms of sales for your product or service type. You should do this for both the principal market and the market segments that may pertain to your product/service offering.

To obtain the information needed to complete this worksheet, there are a number of sources you may wish to consult. These have been mentioned earlier in this Stage, but include:

- trade publications, trade shows, and the trade associations for the industry in which your business will compete
- your local Chamber of Commerce or municipal office
- any local or regional economic development corporations or school board offices
- business resource centres and other agencies of your provincial government
- your Canada Business Services Centre of Industry Canada
- downtown business associations
- advertising agencies, local newspapers, radio and television stations
- your future competitors and prospective customers
- similar businesses in other locations
- prospective suppliers and their sales representatives
- commercial suppliers of industry studies and market research reports
- the Internet

Estimated Market Size—Principal Market
Description of Principal Market

_____

_____

_____

_____

_____

	Two Years Ago	Last Year	This Year	Next Year	Two Years From Now
Sales in units	_____	_____	_____	_____	_____
Sales in $000	_____	_____	_____	_____	_____

Overview of Market Segments
Describe each major segment and the principal product or service to be offered. Then, complete market size estimates for each segment.

	Description of Segment	Principal Product/ Service Benefits
1.	_____	_____
2.	_____	_____
3.	_____	_____

4. _____   _____
5. _____   _____

	Two Years Ago	Last Year	This Year	Next Year	Two Years From Now
Sales in units	_____	_____	_____	_____	_____
Sales in $000	_____	_____	_____	_____	_____

Description of Segment	*Principal Product/ Service Benefits*
1. _____	_____
2. _____	_____
3. _____	_____
4. _____	_____
5. _____	_____

	Two Years Ago	Last Year	This Year	Next Year	Two Years From Now
Sales in units	_____	_____	_____	_____	_____
Sales in $000	_____	_____	_____	_____	_____

Description of Segment	*Principal Product/ Service Benefits*
1. _____	_____
2. _____	_____
3. _____	_____
4. _____	_____
5. _____	_____

	Two Years Ago	Last Year	This Year	Next Year	Two Years From Now
Sales in units	_____	_____	_____	_____	_____
Sales in $000	_____	_____	_____	_____	_____

Description of Segment	*Principal Product/ Service Benefits*
1. _____	_____
2. _____	_____
3. _____	_____
4. _____	_____
5. _____	_____

	Two Years Ago	Last Year	This Year	Next Year	Two Years From Now
Sales in units	_____	_____	_____	_____	_____
Sales in $000	_____	_____	_____	_____	_____

continued

A Framework for Developing a Preliminary Marketing Plan — continued

5. ANALYZE YOUR COMPETITION

Unless your product is a "new to the world" innovation, it will have to compete with other products and services that perform a similar function. You have probably identified a number of other firms that offer products and services designed to meet the same customer need as yours. It is important you have a thorough understanding of each of these firms and the way it conducts its business. To obtain this perspective fill in a copy of this worksheet for each major competitor you have identified. This will enable you to get a better understanding of the sales and market share you might achieve, and the nature of the marketing program you could employ, to obtain a comparative advantage.

These competitors will likely not cooperate in providing you with this information directly. You may have to rely on articles in newspapers and the trade press, corporate annual reports, trade association reports and publications, and your own personal investigation to get all the information you require.

Form for Analyzing Your Competitors

Competitor Name: _____

Estimated Market Share (%): _____

1. PRODUCT OR SERVICE

a. How does the company's product or service differ from other products and services in the marketplace? _____

b. Does it offer a broad or narrow product line? _____

c. Does it emphasize quality? _____

2. PRICE

a. What is its average selling price? _____

b. What is its profit margin? _____

c. What type of discounts does it offer? _____

d. Does it emphasize a low selling price? _____

3. PROMOTION

a. How much does it spend on advertising and trade promotion? _____

b. How well known is it (brand recognition)? _____

c. Through which media does it advertise? _____

d. What other types of promotion does it use? _____

e. How many salespeople does it have? _____

4. DISTRIBUTION LOCATION

a. What type of distribution intermediaries does it use (brokers, company sales force, direct to wholesaler, etc.)? _____

b. Where is it located? _____

c. Is location very important in this industry? _____

5. MARKETING STRATEGY

a. Does the company cater to any particular segment of the market? _____

b. Does the company offer some unique product or service that makes it different from other competitors? _____

c. Does it offer a particularly low price? _____

d. What is the principal factor that accounts for the success of this firm? _____

6. MARKET POSITION

a. What is its market share? _____

b. Have its sales been growing? Stable? Declining? _____

c. How successful is it? _____

7. MAJOR STRENGTHS AND WEAKNESSES

a. What are its major strengths? _____

b. What are its major weaknesses? _____

6. DEFINE A BUDGET

Before spelling out the details of your tentative marketing program, you need to have some idea of the resources needed to implement it. This entails developing some sort of budget indicating what you feel is required to achieve your sales and profit goals, and how these expenditures should be distributed across the range of marketing activities. This worksheet provides a starting point for you to estimate the marketing expenditures you will have to make during your first year to get your business successfully off the ground. This is not an exhaustive list. Use it as a starting point. Your company will use some of these categories plus others peculiar to your marketing needs.

Tentative Marketing Budget

1. Selling (direct costs)

   Sales salaries and commissions: $ _____

   Travel & entertainment $ _____

2. Selling (indirect costs) training

   Marketing research $ _____

   Subscriptions and dues $ _____

3. Advertising $ _____

4. Sales promotion other than advertising $ _____

5. Public relations $ _____

6. Marketing administration $ _____

7. Other items $ _____

7. FLESH OUT YOUR MARKETING PROGRAM

You are now in a position to bring together everything you have learned about the total market potential for your product or service, customer attitudes toward your offering, and the nature of the competitive environment you will be facing. The goal is to put down on paper a preliminary marketing strategy, or plan, for your new venture concept. This involves making decisions regarding what you feel is an appropriate marketing mix for your business. The principal ingredients that must be blended together to form your overall strategy can be grouped together under the headings of:

- Product or service offering
- Pricing program

continued

A Framework for Developing a Preliminary Marketing Plan — continued

- Promotional plans
- Distribution strategy

This worksheet provides an outline to help you to lay out your marketing plans and programs.

Outline for a Preliminary Marketing Plan
YOUR CONCEPT

Describe the principal concept underlying your product or service idea.

_____
_____
_____
_____
_____

What is unique or distinctive about your idea? How does it differ from similar concepts already being employed in the marketplace?

_____
_____
_____
_____
_____

Who will be the primary customers for your concept and what are the principal benefits your concept will deliver to them?

_____
_____
_____
_____
_____

How innovative is your concept? How would you categorize it along the continuum from "copycatting" to being an entirely new invention?

_____
_____
_____
_____
_____

Is your idea technically feasible? Have you built a working model or prototype? Will you have to obtain Canadian Standards Association (CSA) approval or other permissions before the concept can be marketed?

_____
_____
_____
_____
_____

PRODUCTS AND SERVICES

What products or services will you sell? Be specific.

_____
_____
_____
_____
_____

What additional customer services (delivery, repair, warranties, etc.) will you offer?

_____
_____
_____
_____
_____

What is unique about your total product or service offering?

_____
_____
_____
_____
_____

CUSTOMERS

Who are your target customers?

_____
_____
_____
_____
_____

How many target customers are in your trading area?

_____
_____
_____
_____
_____

Why will they buy your product?

_____
_____
_____
_____
_____

continued

A Framework for Developing a Preliminary Marketing Plan — continued

COMPETITION

Who are your principal competitors? What is their market position? Have their sales been growing? Stable? Declining?

_____
_____
_____
_____
_____

How does your concept differ from each of these other products or services?

_____
_____
_____
_____
_____

LOCATION

What location have you selected for your business?

_____
_____
_____
_____
_____

Why did you choose that location?

_____
_____
_____
_____
_____

PRICING

Describe your pricing strategy.

_____
_____
_____
_____
_____

Complete the following table of markups from manufacturer to final customer:

Cost to manufacture	(A)	_____
Manufacturer's markup	(B)	_____
Manufacturer's selling price	(C = A + B)	_____

Agent's commission (if applicable)   (D)   _____

Wholesaler's cost   (E = C + D)   _____

Wholesaler's markup   (F)   _____

Wholesaler's selling price   (G = E + F)   _____

Retailer's markup   (H)   _____

Retailer's selling price   (I = G + H)   _____

How do your planned price levels compare to your competitors'?

_____

_____

_____

_____

_____

PROMOTION

What will be your primary promotional message to potential customers?

_____

_____

_____

_____

_____

What will be your promotion budget?

_____

_____

_____

_____

_____

What media will you use for your advertising program?

_____

_____

_____

_____

_____

Will you have a cooperative advertising program? Describe it.

_____

_____

_____

_____

_____

Describe your trade promotion program.

_____

_____

continues

A Framework for Developing a Preliminary Marketing Plan — continued

_____

_____

_____

Describe any publicity, public relations, or sales promotion program you will have.

_____

_____

_____

_____

_____

DISTRIBUTION

How do you plan to distribute your product? Direct to the consumer? Through traditional distribution channels? Through specialty channels such as exhibitions, mail order, or trade shows?

_____

_____

_____

_____

_____

Will you employ your own sales force or rely on the services of agents or brokers? How many?

_____

_____

_____

_____

_____

Once you have completed this series of worksheets you will have a better understanding of the likely market opportunity for your concept or idea, and you will have thought through the process of determining how you feel it can be most effectively marketed. This is an essential step in deciding whether the concept really does represent a worthwhile opportunity that ought to be aggressively pursued or whether it should be abandoned. This is also a key part of your business plan. Most of this information represents the foundation on which the business plan is built and can be directly transferred to that document.

Conducting a Feasibility Study

Part 2:
Cost and Profitability Assessment

In addition to determining the size and nature of the market for your new venture idea, it is also important to consider the financial components of your business. The costs associated with operating your business may include labour, materials, rent, machinery, etc. Collecting potential sales and cost information should put you in a better position to make reasonably accurate financial forecasts that can be used not only as a check on the advisability of proceeding with the venture but also for raising capital, if required. As an example, Bill Buckwold wants to evaluate the financial feasibility of opening a Tough Guys Sporting Goods store, and sets out to do a comprehensive analysis of its expected viability.

DETERMINE YOUR START-UP FINANCIAL REQUIREMENTS

The process of financial analysis begins with an estimate of the funds required to set up the business. The start-up financial requirements can be broken down into two components:

1. **One-time expenditures** that must be made before the business can open its doors. These include both *capital expenditures* for the purchase or lease of furniture, fixtures, equipment, and the purchase of beginning inventory or supplies and *soft costs* relating to such items as utility deposits and fees, pre-opening advertising and promotion expenses, and other prepaid expenses. In the case of a retail or manufacturing business, these requirements can be considerable, while a service business may not require a very large initial expenditure to get started. Remember, what we are trying to determine here is the amount of *cash* that will be needed to get the business launched. For example, a piece of required equipment may cost $20,000, but if the seller is prepared to take a deposit of $5,000 and finance the rest or if the business will be leasing the equipment for $500 per month rather then buying it outright, only the out-of-pocket cash cost needs to be factored in and not the total cost of the item. The estimated one-time financial requirements for the start-up of Tough Guys Sporting Goods is illustrated in Figure 7.1 on page 204.

CATHY

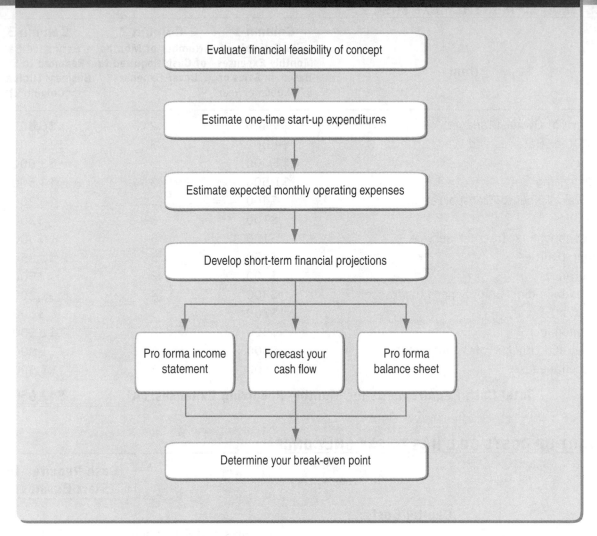

Evaluate financial feasibility of concept

↓

Estimate one-time start-up expenditures

↓

Estimate expected monthly operating expenses

↓

Develop short-term financial projections

↓

| Pro forma income statement | Forecast your cash flow | Pro forma balance sheet |

↓

Determine your break-even point

2. **Operating expenses** such as payments for Bill's and his employees' wages, rent, operating supplies, telephone, and postage, promotion, and other ongoing expenses that must be incurred until the business begins to show a profit. Many new businesses take several months or even years before they operate "in the black." Sufficient funds must be available to cover a minimum of two to three months' operations and provide a cash reserve for emergency situations. One way to determine just how much cash might be required is to review the cash flow statement to see how long it takes before business reaches a positive cash flow situation. If, for example, it is not until the sixth month after opening the doors, Bill will need enough cash to cover the expected losses up to that time plus some additional cash as a safety factor. The estimated funds required to cover these initial operating expenses for Tough Guys is also illustrated in Figure 7.1.

Note that a sporting goods store, like many retail businesses, is a relatively capital-intensive business to start. The bulk of the money is required to finance the initial inventory Bill will need to stock the store, while most of the remaining one-time funds go to decorating and providing the necessary fixtures for the store. In addition, he should have approximately $43,000 available to cover his estimated monthly expenses until the business starts generating a positive cash flow. He does not necessarily have to have the entire cash requirements available strictly from his own resources; $100,000 to $150,000 may be sufficient. Suppliers may be prepared to grant him credit terms so that he does not necessarily have to pay for some of the stock for 30 or 60 days. Or the bank may be prepared to extend him a term loan or line of credit that he can draw on to meet some of his working capital requirements as they arise.

FIGURE 7.1   ESTIMATED START-UP REQUIREMENTS FOR A SPORTING GOODS STORE

ESTIMATED MONTHLY EXPENSES

Item	Column 1 Bill's Estimate of Monthly Expenses Based on Sales of $700,000 per Year	Column 2 Number of Months of Cash Required to Cover Expenses*	Column 3 Estimated Cash Required to Start Business (Column 1 x Column 2)*
Salary of Owner-Manager	$3,400	2	$6,800
All Other Salaries and Wages	$4,000	3	$12,000
Rent	$1,000	3	$3,000
Advertising	$1,500	3	$4,500
Delivery Expense/Transportation	$400	3	$1,200
Supplies	$100	3	$300
Telephone, Fax, Internet Service	$100	3	$300
Other Utilities	$350	3	$1,050
Insurance	$300	3	$900
Taxes Including Employment Insurance	$300	4	$1,200
Interest	$200	3	$600
Maintenance	$500	3	$1,500
Legal and Other Professional Fees	$600	3	$1,800
Miscellaneous	$2,500	3	$7,500
Total Cash Requirements for Monthly Recurring Expenses: (A)			**$42,650**

START-UP COSTS BILL HAS TO PAY ONLY ONCE

	Cash Required to Start Business
Capital Costs	
Fixtures and Equipment	$40,000
Decorating and Remodelling	$10,000
Installation of Fixtures and Equipment	$5,600
Starting Inventory	$195,000
Soft Costs	
Deposits for Utilities	$2,000
Legal and Other Professional Fees	$1,500
Licences and Permits	$1,000
Advertising and Promotion for Opening	$1,000
Accounts Payable	$8,000
Cash	$5,000
Other	$5,000
Total One-Time Cash Requirements: (B)	**$274,100**
TOTAL ESTIMATED CASH REQUIRED TO START BUSINESS: (A) + (B)	**$316,750**

*These figures may be typical for one kind of business. You will have to decide how many months to allow for your business to offset expected shortages of cash flow.

Insufficient financing is a major cause of new business failure, so Bill should be certain he has sufficient financing to cover both his estimated one-time and his initial operating expenses.

DEVELOP SHORT-TERM FINANCIAL PROJECTIONS

PRO FORMA INCOME STATEMENT

Bill's next step is to develop a projected operating statement, or *pro forma income statement*. This involves estimating the initial profit or loss expected by the business. Simply put, the basic formula to calculate profit and loss is:

Revenue – Expenses = Net Profit before Taxes

This means he will have to estimate the total expected revenue and expenses for at least the first year of operation of his business.

An income statement then measures the company's sales and expenses during a specified period of time — usually a month or a year. Its function is to total all sources of revenue for the business and subtract all expenses related to generating that revenue. It shows a company's financial performance over a period of time, and the heading of the income statement should always indicate the time period that is being examined (i.e., for the month ending, for the year ending, etc.).

The information Bill must be able to provide to construct a pro forma income statement includes:

1. The predicted sales volume for the period for which he is making the forecast or his projected *Net Sales*

2. How much it is expected to cost to produce or purchase the products he will sell or his projected *Cost of Goods Sold*

3. His *Fixed Operating Expenses* such as rent, utilities, insurance premiums, and interest costs

4. His controllable or *Variable Operating Expenses* such as advertising and promotion expenses, wages and salaries, and delivery expenses

5. His expected *Net Operating Profit or Loss*

Net Sales is the total sales plus any transportation costs he expects to make during the month or year being examined *minus* any cash discounts, trade discounts, or expected returns.

Cost of Goods Sold is often called *Cost of Sales*. For retail and wholesale businesses it is the total price paid for the products Bill expects to sell during the period for which he is developing the forecast. It is just the price of the goods. It does not include selling and other expenses. These are shown elsewhere on the income statement.

For most service and professional businesses, there will be no cost of goods sold. These businesses receive their income from fees, commissions, and royalties, so they do not typically have inventories of physical products. Their costs to provide these services are included in the fixed and variable operating expense sections of the statement.

Most small retail and wholesale businesses determine their cost of goods sold by:

- Determining the value of their inventory at the beginning of the period being projected
- Adding the value of any products purchased during the period, and then
- Subtracting the value of any inventory left at the end of the period

This calculation will provide a value for the amount of inventory actually sold during the period for which the projection is being developed. Net sales minus cost of goods sold yields Bill's expected *Gross Margin* or *Gross Profit*.

Fixed Expenses are operating expenses or overhead that he must pay regardless of his expected level of sales. These include expenses such as rent, telephone, insurance premiums, business taxes and licences, and interest, as well as some provision for depreciation on any capital assets used in the business.

Variable Expenses are those that are expected to rise and fall in proportion to Bill's sales. These include most of his selling expenses such as sales salaries and commissions, travel costs, advertising and promotion, delivery and vehicle expenses, and similar costs.

Net Operating Profit or Loss is the difference between his gross margin and his fixed and variable operating expenses. This is his expected net profit or loss before any consideration of federal or provincial income taxes.

The creation of a pro forma income statement is an important event for a small business. It provides a summary of many of the important activities of the company and provides valuable information to both the prospective owner and to others who may be looking to lend money or potentially invest in a business.

One means Bill might use to develop a pro forma income statement for his business is to follow the *desired income approach* suggested by Szonyi and Steinhoff.[1] This approach enables him to develop financial projections on the basis of the actual operating performance of firms similar to the business he is contemplating. It also suggests that his business should provide him with not only a return for the time he will spend running the business but also a return on the personal funds he has to invest to launch the business. For example, instead of starting a business, he could keep his present job or obtain another one and earn a salary working for someone else. He could also invest his money in common stocks, bonds, guaranteed income certificates, or other investments, where it would yield some kind of return. Both possibilities should be kept in mind for comparison purposes when determining the expected minimum level of acceptable profit performance of your new venture.

To illustrate this approach, assume Bill has determined that he would like to have a salary of $40,000 per year from the business, plus $15,000 as a reasonable return on the investment he will have to make in the business. These represent his desired income and return levels. By referring to Dun & Bradstreet Canada key business ratio information, Robert Morris Associates industry statement studies, or the Industry Canada Performance Plus small business profiles he can obtain comprehensive financial data on sporting goods stores as well as dozens of other different lines of business.

Combining the information about his desired income and return goals with some of this published data will enable him to develop a pro forma income statement highlighting the level of operations he will have to reach to achieve his goals. The additional information he requires is:

- **The average inventory turnover for this type of business** is the number of times a typical firm's inventory is sold each year. If the business carries an inventory of $25,000 and its overall net revenue is $150,000, inventory turnover is six times per year.

- **The average gross margin** is the difference between the firm's net sales and cost of goods sold, expressed as a percentage. For example, if the business's net sales are $200,000 while cost of goods sold totals $140,000, its gross margin is $60,000 or 30 per cent.

- **Net profit** as a percentage of sales is relatively self-explanatory. It can be determined either before or after the application of any federal or provincial taxes. In the case of Industry Canada's Performance Plus small business profiles, it is shown before the application of any taxes.

DEVELOPING THE STATEMENT

With this data and an estimate of his desired salary and return levels, Bill can construct a pro forma income statement for a sporting goods store. Checking the 1997 Industry Canada Performance Plus small business profiles for Standard Industrial Classification code J6541 – Sporting Goods Stores[2] provides us with the following information:

Inventory turnover	3.4 times per year
Gross margin	34.4% of sales
Net profit as a percentage of sales	2.1%

Figure 7.2 illustrates how this data, along with the information about Bill's desired salary and return, can be used to develop a pro forma income statement. This statement indicates the minimum level of sales his business will have to generate to provide him with his desired salary and level of profitability. Sales above this level will probably provide a higher level of profits, while lower sales will likely mean he will not make as much money as he had hoped. It is assumed in this evaluation that his business will be operated as efficiently as, and in a similar manner to, other sporting goods stores across the country.

All the figures in this statement have been computed from our ratio data and our stated desired salary and return on investment. For example:

1. Our $15,000 desired profit is inserted on line (E).

1. A. J. Szonyi and D. Steinhoff, *Small Business Management Fundamentals*, 3rd Canadian ed. (Toronto: McGraw-Hill Ryerson, 1988), pp. 58–65.
2. Industry Canada (strategis.ic.gc.ca/cgi-bin/sc_mangb/contact/sbp/sbp_e.cgi?func=industry_selection&user_id=373896884&year=1997&area =0&business_type=inc&units=percent&customize_report=no&sic_code=J6541), accessed March 27, 2004.

2. Profits for a typical retail sporting goods store are very slim, at only 2.1 per cent of sales. To determine the sales level required to provide our desired level of profitability, we divide $15,000 by 0.021 to obtain our estimate of the required level of $714,000 for net sales on line (A).

3. Our statistics indicate that sporting goods stores typically have an average gross margin of 34.4 per cent of net sales. In our situation this would provide a gross margin estimate of $246,000 on line (C).

4. The difference between our estimated net sales and gross margin has to provide for our cost of goods sold. In this example our cost of goods sold will be $714,000 – $246,000 = $468,000 on line (B).

5. Sporting goods stores have a relatively low level of inventory turnover in comparison with other types of retail business. A typical retail firm will turn over its inventory from six to seven times per year, while our statistics indicate a turnover ratio of only 3.4 times for a sporting goods store. This means we need to have more money tied up in inventory to support our estimated level of net sales than most other retailers. Our projected average inventory level can be determined by dividing our net sales revenue by the inventory turnover rate or $714,000/3.4 = $210,000.

6. The difference between our expected gross margin and the net operating profit (before taxes) necessary to provide our desired income level represents our total operating expenses in line (D). In this case $246,000 – $15,000 = $231,000 should be available to cover such expenses as Bill's salary and those of his employees, rent, insurance, promotion, interest, and similar expenses. Note that his expected salary of $40,000 has to be included in this amount.

FIGURE 7.2   SAMPLE PRO FORMA INCOME STATEMENT

TOUGH GUYS SPORTING GOODS PRO FORMA INCOME STATEMENT
For the year ending (date)

Net Sales		$714,000 **(A)**
Less: Cost of goods sold		
Beginning Inventory	$195,000	
Plus: Net purchases	483,000	
Goods available for sale	$678,000	
Less: Ending Inventory	210,000	
Cost of goods sold		468,000 **(B)**
Gross margin		$246,000 **(C)**
Operating Expenses		231,000 **(D)**
Net Profit (Loss) before Income Tax		**$15,000 (E)**

This pro forma statement shows Bill the level of sales, investment in inventory, and similar information he needs to know to generate the level of income he feels he needs to obtain from the business.

The statement constructed in Figure 7.2 is based on the distinct financial characteristics of a small retail sporting goods business and relates only to that situation. A pro forma income statement for a store in another line of business could look very different due to variations in inventory turnover, gross margin percentage, and other factors reflecting the different character of that business.

This is even more true if we are considering the start-up of a service business or a manufacturing company. Service firms, like drycleaners and management consultants, typically do not carry an inventory of goods for resale and so do not have a "cost of goods sold" section on their income statement. Manufacturing companies, on the other hand, may have several types of inventory — raw materials, work in process, and finished goods. Appropriate levels for all three types of inventories should be determined and reflected in the projected income statement. The statement also tries to determine the value of raw materials and components, direct labour, factory overhead, and other inputs required to manufacture a product suitable for sale. This "cost of goods manufactured" replaces the cost of goods sold component on the pro forma statement.

DETERMINING REASONABLE OPERATING EXPENSES

So far, our pro forma income statement has lumped together together all Bill's business's projected operating expenses together under a single heading. For example, Figure 7.2 shows the overall, estimated operating expenses to be $231,000. This means that all operating expenses must be covered by this amount if he is to achieve his desired level of profitability.

The same statistical sources used to obtain the data for the overall pro forma statement can be used to obtain a breakdown of the typical operating expenses for his type of business. For example, the Performance Plus small business profiles provide data on the operating results of sporting goods stores. It indicates the following breakdown of operating expenses as a percentage of sales for the average incorporated firm:

Advertising	2.9%
Delivery expenses	0.8%
Depreciation	1.0%
Wages, salaries, and benefits	15.6%
Insurance	0.5%
Interest and bank charges	1.2%
Professional fees	0.6%
Rent	1.6%
Repairs and maintenance	0.5%
Fuel	0.1%
Utilities	1.0%
Other expenses	6.6%

These expenses total approximately 32.4 per cent of sales. If we translate these percentages to our pro forma income statement, Bill can obtain an approximation of the detailed breakdown of his operating expenses in dollar terms. His finalized pro forma income statement would look like Figure 7.3.

This complete pro forma statement can now serve as part of your plan for outlining the requirements of your proposed new business venture or as a guide or schedule to monitor the ongoing performance of your new business during its early stages.

A typical pro forma statement that you can use for projecting the first-year operating performance of your new business is illustrated in Figure 7.7, Outline for a Feasibility Study, on page 222.

FORECAST YOUR CASH FLOW

Your next step is to bring closer to reality the operating profit or loss Bill has projected by developing a cash flow forecast. It traces the expected flow of funds into and out of his business over some period of time. Cash flow is the lifeblood of any business. Therefore, this cash flow analysis is the most important document you will compile in assessing the financial feasibility of your business idea and also enables you to control the financial affairs of your business. It is quite a complex financial statement, so you will need to have some basic understanding of general accounting concepts to prepare it properly. As illustrated in Entrepreneurs in Action #22, failure to plan adequately for their future cash requirements is one of the principal reasons small businesses don't survive. Greg and Kate Williams's failure to estimate accurately the incoming revenue for the one-hour photo shop they purchased caused them not only to lose the business and the money they had invested in it but to have to declare personal bankruptcy as well. An accurate cash flow forecast can be your best means of ensuring continued financial solvency and the survival of your business.

Cash flow statements are similar to but differ from income statements in a number of ways. Cash flow is exactly as the name implies. The statement measures only the flow of cash into and out of the business. Non-cash accounting entries that may show up on an income statement such as depreciation, amortization, and asset transfers are ignored in forecasting the cash flow statement. Similarly, expenses that have been incurred but not yet paid and income that has been earned but not yet received are not included in the cash flow statement either.

The need for a cash flow analysis originates from the reality that in most businesses there is a time discrepancy between when your expenditures are incurred and when the cash is actually realized from the sale of the products or services you provide. This analysis is particularly important at the start-up stage, when businesses typically have lower revenues and higher expenditures. In fact, it is not uncommon for a new start-up to incur expenses requiring the outlay of cash several months prior to actually opening its doors. This outflow of cash should be taken into account in preparing the initial pro forma cash flow forecast.

FIGURE 7.3	SAMPLE COMPLETED PRO FORMA INCOME STATEMENT WITH BREAKDOWN OF OPERATING EXPENSES

TOUGH GUYS SPORTING GOODS PRO FORMA INCOME STATEMENT
For the Year (date)

1.	Gross Sales		$714,000
2.	Less: Cash Discounts		0
A.	**NET SALES**		**$714,000**
	Cost of Goods Sold:		
3.	Beginning Inventory	$195,000	
4.	Plus: Net Purchases	483,000	
5.	Total Available for Sale	$678,000	
6.	Less: Ending Inventory	210,000	
B.	**COST OF GOODS SOLD**		**$468,000**
C.	**GROSS MARGIN**		**$246,000**
	Less: Variable Expenses		
7.	Owner's Salary		40,000
8.	Employees' Wages and Salaries		71,384
9.	Supplies and Postage		0
10.	Advertising and Promotion		20,706
11.	Delivery Expense		5,712
12.	Bad Debt Expense		0
13.	Travel		0
14.	Legal and Accounting Fees		4,284
15.	Vehicle Expense		0
16.	Miscellaneous Expenses		46,124
D.	**TOTAL VARIABLE EXPENSES**		**$188,210**
	Less: Fixed Expenses		
17.	Rent		11,424
18.	Repairs and Maintenance		3,570
19.	Utilities (Heat, Light, Power)		7,140
20.	Telephone		1,000
21.	Taxes and Licences		1,000
22.	Depreciation		7,140
23.	Interest		8,568
24.	Insurance		3,570
25.	Other Fixed Expenses		0
E.	**TOTAL FIXED EXPENSES**		**$ 43,412**
F.	**TOTAL OPERATING EXPENSES**		**$231,000***
G.	**NET OPERATING PROFIT (LOSS)**		**$ 15,000**

* Numbers may not match operating expense percentages exactly due to rounding.

In a typical small business, sales revenue and expenses vary throughout the year. Your cash flow forecast tries to predict all the funds that you will receive and disburse within a certain period of time — e.g., a month, quarter, or year — and the resulting surplus or deficit. It allows you to estimate the total amount of cash you actually expect to receive each period and the actual bills that have to be paid. At times your cash inflows will exceed your outflows; at other times your cash outflows will exceed your inflows. Knowing your expected position and cash balance will enable you to plan your cash requirements and negotiate a line of credit with your bank or arrange other external financing.

22   Entrepreneurs in action

Over the Edge

Greg and Kate Williams (not their names) were only in their early fifties when Greg took early retirement. Still youthful and vigorous, the Williams had a mortgage to repay, car payments to make and three children in their twenties who still relied on their parents for the occasional handout between jobs. The Williams weren't rich, but they weren't worried either. They'd arrived in Canada from Scotland in 1966 with just $132 between them. Within days of their arrival, they were hard at work. A draughtsman by training, Kate found a job with the provincial government. Greg worked in a beer store, laid floor tile, maintained an apartment building and worked for Sears. Then, in 1969, he joined the city police force. "I was 26 and fit as a fiddle," he recalls.

As the years passed, the Williams saved their money, bought a new house for $19,000, sold it for $30,000 and moved to a larger house farther out of the city. By the late 1970s, their family included two daughters and a son. To earn more money, they opened a video store in the mid-1980s. "It went very well," Kate says, "but with three kids at home, we had to choose finally between running the business and raising our children. The kids were getting neglected."

By then, Greg was within sight of early retirement. He'd served the police force well, as an officer on the beat, a detective and an undercover officer. In 1988, Greg and Kate moved to a resort community about two hours from the city. They paid $119,000 for their one-year-old house, just as real-estate prices in the province began to soar. For the next seven years, until June 1995, Greg drove back and forth to work.

Before he left the police force "with exemplary service," Greg and Kate found a retail venture that would keep them busy and make some money to augment their savings and pension income. They met the owner of a one-hour photo shop in a nearby town, who wanted to sell out. For $60,000—less than half the price of new equipment alone—the Williams bought the business lock, stock and barrel. The former owner taught them how to operate the developing unit, and the Williams took over in May 1995. In June, Greg retired. And in November, when the lease expired, the Williams moved the shop from its original location to a newly built shopping mall in their home town.

The move was part of the Williams' plan. Before they invested in the business, they'd learned from their town planners that a photo shop was one of about a dozen businesses the town would need as it expanded over the next few years. Based on the current population of the town — about 11,000 — the Williams calculated the shop could break even if only one in four people in town used their shop to develop photographs, buy film and purchase the occasional picture frame, battery, camera strap or lens. Based on their business plan, the Williams had arranged financing through a local economic-development corporation, which provided a loan of $40,000, and through a local finance company, which provided another $10,000 to cover leasehold improvements. They raised $10,000 privately and scraped together the same amount from their own money. By the time they opened the new store, it had cost the Williams almost $75,000. "The store was beautiful," Kate says. "It was a treat for people to come into."

Unfortunately, not many people came. A couple of local real-estate agents used it to prepare photos and brochures for advertising. But with the resort closed down for the winter, there just weren't enough people walking through the door.

As 1996 began, the Williams realized they were in trouble. Rent alone cost them $1,400 a month. On top of that, they paid taxes and utilities. The Williams also realized they weren't competing on a level field with other one-hour photo services in the area. Department, grocery and drug-store chains have a steady demand for their services; they also pay far less for their equipment and supplies than the Williams since they buy in volume. A roll of developing paper, for example, for which the Williams paid $142 costs the chains about $60. And because of the volume of photographs the big chains develop, they receive the same equipment as the Williams $60,000 unit free of charge. No wonder they could develop a roll of film for $2 to $3 less than the Williams charged.

The fewer people who patronized the shop, the more expensive it became to run the place. The chemicals in the developing unit, which sat unused for days at a time, went bad and had to be replaced almost monthly, at a cost of $600. The rent had to be paid, whether there were customers or not. Greg began siphoning money from a retirement account he'd set up with the contributory surplus from his police pension, then had to find more money to cover the income tax on the withdrawals. By November 1996, Greg and Kate knew they were in trouble. "Everything that was coming in was going out again," says Greg, "but it still wasn't enough."

A financial consultant suggested they close the store and enjoy their Christmas, but the Williams hung on until February 1997, when they finally closed the store for good. Even then, they owed only $71,000, excluding their house and equipment. But as Diane Hessel of A. Farber & Partners Inc., observes, "It might as well have been $71 million for the Williams."

Besides, they didn't distinguish between their personal and business debts. No matter how you described it to them, a debt was a debt, and they had a lot of them. In addition to their loan from the local economic-development corporation, they owed another $17,000 to the credit union that had advanced them funds for a previous debt and lease-hold improvements, more than $9,500 to their equipment supplier and another $11,000 to Revenue Canada for tax on their previous video business. Along with their own personal debts on their van and house, the Williams owed a total of $229,000; their assets amounted to about $158,000.

On February 27, 1997, the Williams filed for bankruptcy. They expected their bankruptcy to proceed smoothly through the courts, but in October, two of their creditors opposed the Williams' application for discharge—which meant that, unlike the other creditors, they insisted on a court hearing, when they would seek some form of compensation from the estate. Under the stress of their financial predicament and after 25 years of police work, Greg Williams suffered an angina attack. In January 1998, he underwent triple bypass surgery.

The following month, the Williams appeared in bankruptcy court to explain why they could not repay every dollar they owed to their creditors.

After hearing their case, the judge ordered each of the Williams to repay $50 a month for distribution to their unpaid creditors, for a total payment of $2,500, as a condition of the terms for discharge from bankruptcy. They also had to come up with about $4,000 for Revenue Canada, which they arranged to pay off in installments. They can incur further debt, but they have to wait for seven years to have the bankruptcy removed from their credit record. "Pensions are exempt from seizure under the Pension Benefits Act," Hessel points out. "So they're much better off than most bankrupts. And remember, bankruptcy is not a punitive act. It's intended to get people back on their feet."

Slowly but surely, the Williams are doing just that. After closing their shop, Greg found part-time work as a security guard. A couple of months after their appearance in court, he received an invitation to work part-time for the provincial police force. Kate worked long hours in a donut shop for several months until the franchise was sold to a new owner. Now she collects Employment Insurance, which will run out shortly, "the first time in 30 years I've ever claimed it."

"I'm only 56," Greg says optimistically, "but retirement is out the window, at least for another few years. In any case," he adds, "sitting back playing golf and going fishing really wasn't for me."

Source: Bruce McDougall, "Over the Edge," *Financial Post Magazine*, November 1998, pp. 51–53. Reprinted with permission.

Your completed cash flow forecast will clearly show to the bank loans officer what additional working capital, if any, your business may need and demonstrate that there will be sufficient cash on hand to make the interest payments on a line of credit or a term loan for purchasing additional machinery or equipment or expanding the business.

There are three sections to a typical cash flow statement:

1. Operating activities
2. Investment activities
3. Financing activities

These three sections work together to show the expected net change in cash that will occur in the business over a particular period of time. Cash inflows into the business are *added* on the statement while outflows are *subtracted* to determine total net cash flow.

CASH FLOW FROM OPERATING ACTIVITIES

Cash flow from operating activities is probably the most complicated section to develop. It is important to distinguish between sales revenue and cash receipts in most businesses. They are typically not the same unless all the business's sales are for cash. Revenues are determined at the time a sale is made. Cash receipts, on the other hand are not recorded until the money actually flows into the business. This may not be for a month or two in the case of sales made on credit, which would be reflected in your *accounts receivable*. Similarly expenses are incurred when materials, labour, and other items are purchased and used, but payments for these items may not be made until sometime later when the cheques are actually issued. These deferred payments would be reflected in your *accounts payable*.

In addition, your net cash flow will typically be different from your net profit. Net cash flow is the difference between your cash inflows and cash outflows. Net profit is the difference between your expected sales revenue and expenses. One reason for this difference is the uneven timing of cash receipts and disbursements mentioned above. Another is that some items on the income statement such as depreciation are non-cash expenses. They represent a charge against the business's income for the use of fixed assets owned by the firm but don't involve a direct outlay of cash.

Cash flow from operating activities can be determined from the following formula:

> (+) **Cash received from customers**
> (+) **Any other operating cash receipts**
>   (=) **Total Cash Receipts from Operations (A)**
> (–) **Cash paid to suppliers**
> (–) **Cash paid to employees**
> (–) **Interest paid**
> (–) **Taxes paid**
> (–) **Other cash payments for expenses**
>   (=) **Total Cash Payments from Operations (B)**
>   **Total Net Cash Provided by Operations = (A) – (B)**

CASH FLOW FROM INVESTMENT ACTIVITIES

Cash flow from investment activities includes changes to your expected cash position owing to the purchase or sale of any assets owned by the business. This might include land and buildings, vehicles, equipment, securities, or anything else the business may have sold or acquired that resulted in the receipt or outlay of cash.

Cash flow from investment activities can be determined from the following formula:

> (+) **Cash proceeds from the sale of assets**
> (–) **Cash disbursements for the purchase of property or equipment**
>   (=) **Total Net Cash Provided by Investment**

CASH FLOW FROM FINANCING ACTIVITIES

Financing activities on a cash flow statement reflect cash received from borrowing money, issuing stock, or other cash contributions to the business as well as any payments made on loans, dividends paid to shareholders, or other similar payments.

Cash flow from financing activities can be determined from the following formula:

> (+) **Cash received from bank and other loans**
> (+) **Proceeds from issuing stock**
> (+) **Capital contributions by owners**
>   (=) **Total Cash Received from Financing (A)**
> (–) **Repayment of principal on loans**
> (–) **Dividends paid to shareholders**
> (–) **Cash withdrawals by owners**
> (–) **Other funds removed from the business**
>   (=) **Total Cash Payments for Financing (B)**
>   **Total Net Cash Provided by Financing (A) – (B)**

DEVELOPING YOUR CASH FLOW STATEMENT
ESTIMATE YOUR REVENUES

In most small businesses, not all sales are for cash. It is normal practice to accept credit cards or to extend terms to many customers. As a result, the revenue from a sale may not be realized until 30 days, 60 days, or even longer after the actual sale is made. In developing your cash flow forecast you must take into account such factors as:

- Your ratio of cash to credit card or credit sales
- Your normal terms of trade for credit customers
- The paying habits of your customers
- Proceeds from the sale of any auxiliary items or other assets of the business

Sales should be entered on the cash flow forecast only when the money has actually been received in payment.

DETERMINE YOUR EXPENDITURES

To estimate your cash outflow you must consider:

- How promptly you will be required to pay for your material and supplies. It is not uncommon that a new business will have to pay for its inventory and supplies up front on a cash on delivery (COD) basis until it establishes a reputation for meeting its financial commitments. Then it may be able to obtain more favourable credit terms from its trade suppliers. These terms of trade should be reflected in the cash flow forecast. For example, if you have to pay your suppliers' invoices right away, the cash pay-outs would be reflected in the cash flow forecast during the same month in which the purchases were made. However, if you have to pay your suppliers' invoices within 30 days, the cash payouts for July's purchases will not be shown until August. In some cases, even longer-term trade credit can be negotiated, and then cash outlays may not be shown for two or even three months after the purchase has been received and invoiced.

- How you will pay your employees' wages and salaries (weekly, biweekly, or monthly)

- When you must pay your rent, utility bills, and other expenses. For example, your rent, telephone, utilities, and other occupancy costs are normally paid every month. Other expenses like insurance and licence fees may be estimated as monthly expenses but not treated that way for cash flow purposes. Your insurance premium of $1,200 annually may have to be paid in three instalments: $400 in April, August, and December. That is how it must be entered on the cash flow worksheet. Your licence fees might be an annual expense incurred in January of each year and would be reflected as part of your estimated disbursements for that month.

- The interest and principal payments that you must make each month on any outstanding loans

- Your plans for increasing your inventory requirements or acquiring additional assets

RECONCILING YOUR CASH REVENUES AND CASH EXPENDITURES

To illustrate, let us continue to consider the situation of Tough Guys Sporting Goods. Tough Guys plans to open its doors at the beginning of the new year. Its owner wants to develop a monthly cash flow forecast for the expected first year of operation of the business and has made the following forecasts (see Figure 7.4):

- Total sales for the year are projected to be $714,000 with a strong seasonal pattern peaking in June and July.

- Of the store's monthly sales, 60 per cent are cash sales and 40 per cent are credit card sales for which the cash is received in the following month.

- Inventory is purchased one month in advance of when it is likely to be sold. It is paid for in the month it is sold. Purchases equal 66 per cent of projected sales for the next month.

- Cash expenses have been estimated for such items as the owner's salary and employees' wages and salaries, advertising and promotion expenses, delivery expense, rent, utilities, taxes and licences, insurance, and other expenses.

- The store's beginning cash balance is $10,000 and $5,000 is the minimum cash balance that should be available at the beginning of every month.

FIGURE 7.4   PRO FORMA CASH FLOW FORECAST FOR TOUGH GUYS SPORTING GOODS

12-MONTH CASH FLOW PROJECTIONS
Minimum Cash Balance Required = $5,000

	January	February	March	April	May	June	July	August	September	October	November	December	YEAR 1 TOTAL
Cash Flow from Operations (during month)													
1. Cash Sales	17,136	21,848	28,703	37,271	41,555	47,981	53,550	47,552	37,271	33,844	31,273	37,271	435254
2. Payments for Credit Sales	0	14,566	19,135	24,847	27,703	31,987	35,700	31,702	24,847	22,562	20,849	24,847	278746
3. Investment Income	0	0	0	0	0	0	0	0	0	0	0	0	0
4. Other Cash Income	0	0	0	0	0	0	0	0	0	0	0	0	0
A. TOTAL CASH ON HAND	$17,136	$36,414	$47,838	$62,118	$69,258	$79,968	$89,250	$79,254	$62,118	$56,406	$52,122	$62,118	$714,000
Less Expenses Paid (during month)													
5. Inventory or New Material	-27,049	-35,343	-42,883	-48,538	-55,229	-56,266	-47,784	-39,490	-36,097	-37,039	-24,599	-33,000	-483,317
6. Owner's Salary	-3,400	-3,400	-3,400	-3,400	-3,400	-3,400	-3,400	-3,400	-3,400	-3,400	-3,400	-3,700	-40,800
7. Employees' Wages and Salaries	-3,138	-4,057	-5,301	-6,432	-7,281	-8,284	-8,440	-7,168	-5,923	-5,415	-5,556	-3,700	-70,696
8. Supplies and Postage	0	0	0	0	0	0	0	0	0	0	0	0	0
9. Advertising and Promotion	-919	-1,189	-1,553	-1,884	-2,133	-2,427	-2,472	-2,100	-1,735	-1,586	-1,627	-1,081	-20,706
10. Delivery Expense	254	-328	-428	-520	-588	-669	-682	-579	-479	-438	-449	-300	-5,714
11. Travel	0	0	0	0	0	0	0	0	0	0	0	0	0
12. Legal and Accounting Fees	-1,000	-300	-300	-300	-300	-300	-300	-300	-300	-300	-300	-300	-4,300
13. Vehicle Expense	-32	-41	-54	-65	-74	-84	-85	-72	-60	-55	-56	-37	-714
14. Maintenance Expense	0	-1,000	0	0	-500	0	-800	0	-300	0	-900	0	-3,500
15. Rent	-950	-950	-950	-950	-950	-950	-950	-950	-950	-950	-950	-950	-11,400
16. Utilities	-350	-350	-350	-350	-350	-350	-350	-350	-350	-350	-350	-350	-4,200
17. Telephone	-80	-80	-80	-80	-80	-80	-80	-80	-80	-80	-80	-80	-960
18. Taxes and Licences	-1,000	0	0	0	0	0	0	0	0	0	0	0	-1,000
19. Interest Payments		160	260	348	392	436	420	284	124	52	28	0	2,504
20. Insurance	-1,000	0	0	-1,000	0	0	-1,000	0	0	-500	0	0	-3,500
21. Other Cash Expenses	-2,092	-2,705	-3,534	-4,288	-4,854	-5,523	-5,627	-4,778	-3,949	-3,610	-3,704	-2,460	-47,124
B. TOTAL EXPENDITURES	($41,265)	($49,583)	($58,573)	($67,459)	($75,346)	($77,897)	($71,550)	($58,983)	($53,499)	($53,670)	($41,943)	($45,658)	-695,427
Cash Flow from Investments													
Purchase of Fixed Assets	0	0	0	0	0	0	0	0	0	0	0	0	0
Sale of Fixed Assets	0	0	0	0	0	0	0	0	0	0	0	0	0
C. CHANGE IN CASH FROM PURCHASE OR SALE OF ASSETS	$0	$0	$0	$0	$0	$0	$0	$0	$0	$0	$0	$0	$0
Cash Flow from Financing													
Payment of Principal of Loan	0	0	0	0	0	-2,000	-17,000	-20,000	-9,000	-3,000	-3,500	0	-54,500
Inflow of Cash from Bank Loan	20,000	12,500	11,000	5,500	5,500	0	0	0	0	0	0	0	54,500
Issuance of Equity Positions	0	0	0	0	0	0	0	0	0	0	0	0	0
Repurchase of Outstanding Equity	0	0	0	0	0	0	0	0	0	0	0	0	0
D. CHANGE IN CASH FROM FINANCING	$20,000	$12,500	$11,000	$5,500	$5,500	($2,000)	($17,000)	($20,000)	($9,000)	($3,000)	($3,500)	$0	$0
E. INCREASE (DECREASE) IN CASH	($4,129)	($669)	$265	$159	($588)	$71	$700	$271	($381)	($264)	$6,679	$16,460	18,573
F. CASH AT BEGINNING OF PERIOD	$10,000	$5,871	$5,203	$5,467	$5,626	$5,037	$5,108	$5,808	$6,079	$5,698	$5,434	$12,113	10,000
G. CASH AT END OF PERIOD	$5,871	$5,203	$5,467	$5,626	$5,037	$5,108	$5,808	$6,079	$5,698	$5,434	$12,113	$28,573	28,573
MEET MINIMUM CASH BALANCE	ACCEPTABLE	ACCEPTABLE	ACCEPTABLE	ACCEPTABLE	ACCEPTABLE	ACCEPTABLE	ACCEPTABLE	ACCEPTABLE	ACCEPTABLE	ACCEPTABLE	ACCEPTABLE	ACCEPTABLE	ACCEPTABLE

- The store has negotiated a line of credit with the bank at an interest rate of 10 per cent annually but the interest due has to be paid monthly. This line of credit can be drawn on in order to ensure the business has its $5,000 minimum cash balance available each month up to a limit of $60,000, and will be paid down as surplus cash becomes available.

At the end of each month it shows the cash balance that is available to be carried over to the next month's operations. To this it adds the total of the next month's cash receipts and subtracts the total of the next month's cash expenditures to determine the adjusted balance to be carried forward to the following month. In summary form this relationship can be demonstrated by the following formula:

Forecasted Cash Flow in Month (x) = Cash Balance Carried Over from Month (x − 1) + Expected Cash Inflow in Month (x) − Estimated Cash Expenditures in Month (x)

As you can see, cumulative cash surpluses or shortfalls are clearly evident well in advance of their actual occurrence. Knowing this information in advance can assist you in scheduling your initial capital expenditures, monitoring your accounts receivable, and avoiding temporary cash shortages, and can enable you to plan your short-term cash requirements well in advance. Tough Guys, for example, does not achieve a positive cash flow until June. The business will be forced to draw on its line of credit in January, February, March, April, and May to make certain it will have the necessary minimum cash balance available to continue to run the business. Preparing a pro forma cash flow forecast enabled Bill to anticipate these needs and avoid the possibility of any nasty surprises.

A typical cash flow forecast that you can use to project your anticipated cash surplus or shortfall at the end of each month of the first year of operation of your business is illustrated in Figure 7.7, Outline for a Feasibility Study, on page 222.

PRO FORMA BALANCE SHEET

One more financial statement should also be developed — *a pro forma balance sheet*. A balance sheet provides a snapshot of your business's health at a point in time. It tells you the value of your business at any point by forecasting what your business will own (*assets*) and what it will owe to other people, companies, and financial institutions (*liabilities*) to determine its *equity* or *net worth*. The basic formula of the balance sheet is:

Assets = Liabilities + Net Worth

The first section of the balance sheet deals with assets. *Current assets* would include an estimate of your expected average accounts receivable, start-up inventory requirements, available cash, and similar items. *Fixed assets* are typically items like buildings, furniture, fixtures, machinery and equipment, automobiles, and other capital items that you will need to operate your business. Except for land, fixed assets typically are used up over a period of years, and therefore must be gradually *depreciated* in value.

The second part of a balance sheet lists liabilities. *Current liabilities* are debts you expect to incur that will fall due in less than 12 months. These usually include bills from your suppliers for the supplies and raw materials you will need for your initial inventory, short-term loans from banks and other financial institutions, any portion of your long-term debt that must be repaid during your initial year of operation, and so on. *Long-term liabilities* include any outstanding mortgages on land and buildings, notes on machinery and equipment, personal loans that you, your partners, and other stockholders may have made to the business, and any other outstanding loans of a long-term nature.

Net worth represents the value of your investment and equity in the business. Net worth can be composed of the total capital invested in the business by you and any other inside or outside investors plus any profits that have been generated by the business that have been retained within the company rather than being paid out in dividends or other means or minus any losses that may have accumulated in the business.

A typical pro forma balance sheet is illustrated in Figure 7.5.

HOW TO ANALYZE YOUR PRO FORMA STATEMENTS

Once you have created a pro forma income statement, cash flow statement, and balance sheet for your business there are some easy calculations you can perform that will give you a better understanding of your company. You can calculate a number of *financial ratios* that can help you manage your business and make knowledgeable decisions related to some key questions such as:

- Does the business have the capacity to meet its short-term financial obligations?

FIGURE 7.5   SAMPLE PRO FORMA BALANCE SHEET

TOUGH GUYS SPORTING GOODS BALANCE SHEET
End of Year 1

ASSETS

Current Assets:

1. Cash		28,500	
2. Accounts Receivable		32,500	
3. Inventory		210,000	
4. Other Current Assets		30,000	
A. Total Current Assets			**$301,000**

Fixed Assets:

5. Land and Buildings	0		
less depreciation	0	0	
6. Furniture and Fixtures	46,000		
less depreciation	2,300	43,700	
7. Equipment	0		
less depreciation		0	
8. Trucks and Automobiles	0		
less depreciation		0	
9. Other Fixed Assets	34,000		
less depreciation	3,000	31,000	
B. Total Fixed Assets			**$74,700**
C. Total Assets (C = A + B)			**$375,700**

LIABILITIES

Current Liabilities (due within 12 months)

10. Accounts Payable		123,000	
11. Bank Loans/Other Loans		39,000	
12. Taxes Owed		0	
D.Total Current Liabilities			**$162,000**

Long-Term Liabilities

13. Notes Payable (due after one year)		150,000	
14. Other Long-Term Liabilities		47,700	
E. Total Long-Term Liabilities			**$197,700**
F. Total Liabilities (F = D + E)			**$359,700**

NET WORTH (CAPITAL)

Share Capital

Common Shares			1,000
Preferred Shares			0
Retained Earnings			15,000
G. Total Net Worth (G = C − F)			**$ 16,000**
H. Total Liabilities and Net Worth (H = F + G)			**$375,700**

- Is the business producing adequate operating profits based on the level of assets it employs?
- Are the owners receiving an acceptable return on their investment?

A ratio shows the relationship between two numbers. It describes the relative size of the two numbers as they relate to one another, and so eliminates the problem of trying to compare things on different scales.

Financial ratios can be used to compare the financial performance of two businesses of different size or to compare the performance of a company with others in the same business or the industry average. This application was previously discussed in Stage 4 relative to analyzing the financial position of a business you might be looking to buy. Financial ratios can also be used to compare your business's performance from one time period to another, and that is the application we will look at here.

Financial ratios can be categorized into three common groups to analyze different aspects of your business:

1. **Liquidity ratios** help you understand your business's ability to meet its short-term obligations and continue to maintain its normal operations. The more liquid assets you have the better, because they can be readily converted into cash.

2. **Profitability ratios** tell you how well you measure up in creating financial value in your business. The money you have invested in the venture could just as easily have been invested in other things, such as real estate, bonds, and other securities, so you need to know whether your business can generate the kind of returns that justify the risks involved.

3. **Leverage ratios** measure the level of debt the business has and its ability to pay back this debt over a long period of time.

Examples of some of the more commonly used ratios of each type are illustrated in the Key Points box below.

Key points ········ EXAMPLES OF KEY FINANCIAL RATIOS ·········

Liquidity Ratios
1. Current Ratio = Current Assets/Current Liabilities
2. Quick Ratio = (Current Assets − Inventories)/Current Liabilities

Profitability Ratios
1. Gross Margin Ratio = Gross Profit Margin/Net Sales
2. Net Profit Ratio = Net Profit before Taxes/Net Sales
3. Return on Assets = Net Profit before Taxes/Total Assets
4. Return on Owner Investment = Net Profit before Taxes/Net Worth

Leverage Ratios
1. Times Interest Earned Ratio = Net Income before Interest and Taxes/Interest Expense
2. Debt-to-Equity Ratio = Long-Term Liabilities/Net Worth

DETERMINE YOUR BREAK-EVEN POINT

As your preliminary financial forecasts begin to clarify the size of the potential opportunity you are investigating, there is one other key question to explore: What sales volume will be required for your business to break even? This *break-even* point indicates the level of operation of the business at which your total costs equal your total revenue. The break-even point is important because it indicates when your business begins to make a profit. If your sales level is less than the break-even point, your business will suffer a loss.

The break-even point is affected by several factors, including your fixed and variable costs and your selling price. *Fixed costs* are those that remain constant regardless of your level of sales or production. *Variable costs* vary directly with the amount of business you do. For example, your rent is a fixed cost, because it remains the same regardless of your level of sales. Your cost of goods sold, however, is variable, because the amount you spend is directly related to how much you sell. Fixed costs typically include insurance, licences and permits, property taxes, rent, and similar expenses. Variable costs include supplies, salaries and wages, raw material, utilities, and delivery expenses. Variable costs are usually determined on a per-unit or per-dollar of sales basis.

The break-even point can be determined algebraically. The basic formula is:

$$\text{Break-Even Point (Units)} = \frac{\text{Total Fixed Costs}}{\text{Contribution Margin per Unit}}$$

where:

Contribution Margin per Unit = Selling Price per Unit − Variable Cost per Unit

and the *contribution margin* ratio can be determined by:

Contribution Margin Ratio = Contribution Margin per Unit Divided by the Selling Price per Unit

Algebraically that relationship can be expressed as:

$$\text{Contribution Margin Ratio} = \frac{1 - \text{Average Variable Cost per Unit}}{\text{Selling Price per Unit}}$$

Understanding this relationship enables us to also calculate the break-even point in dollars. The basic formula for this determination is:

$$\text{Break-Even Point (Dollars)} = \frac{\text{Total Fixed Costs}}{1 - \dfrac{\text{Average Variable Cost}}{\text{Selling Price per Unit}}}$$

$$= \frac{\text{Total Fixed Costs}}{\text{Contribution Margin per Unit}}$$

Or alternatively if we are looking at the global situation for a business:

$$\text{Break-Even Point (Dollars)} = \frac{\text{Total Fixed Costs}}{1 - \dfrac{\text{Total Variable Cost}}{\text{Total Net Sales}}}$$

The following example may help illustrate the break-even concept. Suppose that the financial statements for Gino's Pizzeria, a pizza delivery outlet, indicate that the business's fixed costs every month for rent, utilities, interest expense, insurance, and similar items are roughly $3,600 per month. In addition, Gino has determined that his variable costs for making a typical large pizza are as follows:

Dough	$1.40
Tomato sauce	0.35
Cheese	0.75
Toppings	0.75
Delivery box	0.25
Delivery cost	0.50
Total Cost	$4.00

Rather than take a regular salary, Gino has decided to take any net income the business might generate as his income. In addition, Gino's sells a typical large pizza for $10.00.

From this information you can see that after the $4.00 in variable costs have been covered, each pizza sold can contribute $6.00 toward covering the fixed costs of Gino's business. This is called his *contribution margin*. His contribution margin per unit can then be expressed as follows:

$$\text{Contribution Margin per Unit} = \text{Selling Price} - \text{Total Variable Cost}$$
$$= \$10.00 - \$4.00$$
$$= \$6.00 \text{ per pizza}$$

But how many pizzas will Gino have to sell every month in order to break even? This can be determined as follows:

$$\frac{\text{Total Fixed Costs}}{\text{Contribution Margin per Unit}} = \text{Break-Even Volume (Units)}$$

Or, in this case:

$$\frac{\$3,600}{\$6.00} = 600 \text{ pizzas per month}$$

Therefore, Gino must sell a minimum of 600 pizzas every month to cover his fixed costs of doing business. Even at that level of operation, he does not earn any income for himself. It is only after his sales exceed this level that the business starts to generate sufficient revenue to provide him with some compensation for his time and effort and give him a return on the money he has invested in the business. For example, if Gino should sell 800 pizzas one month, that would generate an income of $1,200 for him as a return on his time and money. On the other hand, if he sells only 500 pizzas his business would incur a loss of $600.

To determine the volume of sales that Gino will have to achieve each month to reach his break-even point we can use the formula:

$$\frac{\text{Total Fixed Costs}}{\text{Contribution Margin Ratio}} = \text{Break-Even Point (Dollars)}$$

Or, in this case:

$$\frac{\$3,600}{.6} = \$6,000 \text{ in sales per month}$$

Therefore, Gino must sell a minimum of 600 pizzas or generate at least $6,000 in sales every month to cover his fixed costs of doing business.

Relating this notion to Tough Guys Sporting Goods store, we can also determine the volume of sales Bill would require to break even. If we assume all the operating expenses indicated in Figure 7.3 are fixed at least in the short term, including such items as salaries and wages, as well as advertising and promotion expenditures, the financial statement can be summarized as follows:

Projected sales $714,000
Projected fixed expenses $231,000
Projected variable expenses $468,000
(basically the cost of goods sold)

$$\text{Total sales needed to break even} \; = \; \text{Fixed Expenses} \div 1 - \frac{\text{Variable Expenses}}{\text{Sales}}$$

$$= \; \$231{,}000 \div 1 - \frac{\$468{,}000}{\$714{,}000}$$

$$= \; \$231{,}000 \div (1 - 0.655)$$

$$= \; \$231{,}000 \div 0.345$$

$$= \; \mathbf{\$670{,}000}$$

Therefore the store needs to sell at least $670,000 worth of merchandise its first year to break even based on our estimate of its projected fixed costs and its average gross margin percentage and other variable costs. This concept is illustrated graphically in Figure 7.6.

FIGURE 7.6   GRAPHICAL REPRESENTATION OF THE BREAK-EVEN POINT FOR TOUGH GUYS SPORTING GOODS

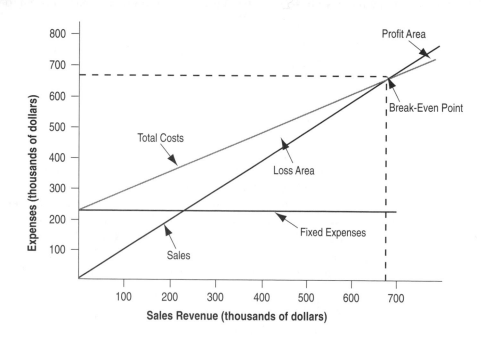

The value of break-even analysis is that it can be used to determine whether some planned course of action — for example, starting a new business, opening a new store, or adding a new item to your product line — has a chance of being profitable. Once you have estimated the break-even point for the action, you are in a better position to assess whether such a sales volume can be achieved and how long it will take to reach it.

It is essential that you determine the break-even level of operation for your business before you proceed very far with its implementation. Bankers and other financial people will expect to see this information as part of the financial documentation for your venture. In addition, if it appears that the break-even volume is not achievable, the business idea is probably destined to fail and should be abandoned before any money is invested.

CONDUCT A COMPREHENSIVE FEASIBILITY STUDY

Figure 7.7 provides a detailed framework that you can use to conduct a comprehensive feasibility assessment of your own new venture idea. Much of the information you have compiled in completing the worksheets in Stage 6 can be incorporated into Figure 7.7 to facilitate your feasibility assessment. When you have completed this evaluation, you need to give some thought to where you go from here. Does the business look sufficiently viable to proceed with the development of a comprehensive business plan? Have you identified all the potential flaws and pitfalls that might negatively impact your business? What role do you expect to play in the growth of the venture? Do you plan to produce and market the concept yourself, or do you hope to sell or license the idea to someone else? How much external money do you need and where do you think you can obtain it? These are the kinds of issues that need to be carefully considered and resolved before you will be in a position to move forward.

In most cases, the next stage is to write a complete *business plan*. This, however, requires a major commitment of time, effort, and money. Make sure your feasibility study indicates that your concept is clearly viable and that a reasonable profit can be expected.

And don't be too disappointed if your feasibility assessment indicates that your concept is not likely to be profitable. Think of all the time and money you have saved by not going forward with the implementation of a business that has a low probability of succeeding. That's why a preliminary assessment is so essential.

Video Case #7

A Fetish for Fashion

Summary

Fetish wear — a passing phase or a here-to-stay trend? Wayne Bernet and Simon Macintosh were betting on the latter with their fetish leatherwear store, Leatherwerx. But they lacked a couple of key ingredients for launching a business: They were short of cash and had little background knowledge on how to run a business. After six months, sales were creeping in but expenses were mounting, and the partners were spending far more on additional staff and new equipment than they were taking in. Eventually, this caught up with them and they were forced to lay off staff. Finally, the bailiff seized the store, and everything inside was sold to pay off their outstanding debts.

Questions for Discussion

1. As an entrepreneur, what is the danger of venturing into a business that is not mainstream, such as fetish wear?
2. Where can an entrepreneur go for information on how to run the financial aspects of a business?
3. Why is it so tempting for new entrepreneurs to want to expand a business quickly after generating some initial sales?
4. Why is communication so important in a partnership like Leatherwerx?

Video Case #8

·················· **Litebook with Update** ··················

Summary

Larry Peterson of Medicine Hat, Alberta, suffers from seasonal affect disorder (SAD) and requires ultraviolet light during short winter days. Like a true entrepreneur, he took his disorder and turned it into an opportunity. He developed a light that people like; now he has to develop his market before he runs out of money.

Questions for Discussion

1. What types of expenses should Peterson include in his start-up costs? What were some of the unique measures Peterson took to keep his costs low? Were these planned?

2. What impact can international events have on a product as small as a Litebook? Can you plan for these types of events?

3. What were the results of Peterson's feasibility study?

4. Where did Peterson find financing?

FIGURE 7.7   OUTLINE FOR A FEASIBILITY STUDY

YOUR CONCEPT

1. Describe the principal concept underlying your product or service idea.

_____
_____
_____
_____
_____

2. What is unique or distinctive about your idea? How does it differ from similar concepts already in the marketplace?

_____
_____
_____
_____

3. Who will be the primary customers of your concept and what are the principal benefits your concept will deliver to them?

_____
_____
_____
_____

4. How innovative is your concept? How would you categorize it along the continuum from "copycatting" to being an entirely new invention?

_____

_____

_____

5. Is your idea technically feasible? Have you built a working model or prototype? Will you have to obtain Canadian Standards Association (CSA) approval or other permissions before the concept can be marketed?

_____

_____

_____

_____

PRELIMINARY MARKETING PLAN

Products and Services

1. What products or services will you sell? (Be specific.)

_____

_____

_____

_____

_____

2. What additional customer services (delivery, repair, warranties, etc.) will you offer?

_____

_____

_____

_____

_____

3. What is unique about your total product or service offering?

_____

_____

_____

_____

Customers

1. Who are your target customers?

_____

_____

_____

_____

_____

continued

Outline for a Feasibility Study — continued

2. How many target customers are in your trading area?

_____

_____

_____

_____

3. Why will they buy your product?

_____

_____

_____

_____

Competition

1. Who are your principal competitors? What is their market position? Have their sales been growing? Stable? Declining?

a. _____

_____

b. _____

_____

c. _____

_____

d. _____

_____

2. How does your concept differ from each of these other products or services?

_____

_____

_____

_____

Location

1. What location have you selected for your business?

_____

_____

_____

_____

2. Why did you choose that location?

_____

_____

_____

_____

Pricing

1. Describe your pricing strategy.

_____
_____
_____
_____

2. Complete the following chain of markups from manufacturer to final customer:

Cost to manufacture	_____	(A)
Manufacturer's markup	_____	(B)
Manufacturer's selling price (C = A + B)	_____	(C)
Agent's commission (if applicable)	_____	(D)
Wholesaler's cost (E = C + D)	_____	(E)
Wholesaler's markup	_____	(F)
Wholesaler's selling price (G = E + F)	_____	(G)
Retailer's markup	_____	(H)
Retailer's selling price (I = G + H)	_____	(I)

3. How do your planned price levels compare to your competitors'?

_____
_____
_____
_____
_____

Promotion

1. What will be your primary promotional message to potential customers?

_____
_____
_____
_____

2. What will be your promotion budget?

_____
_____
_____
_____

3. What media will you use for your advertising program?

_____
_____
_____
_____

continued

Outline for a Feasibility Study — continued

4. Will you have a cooperative advertising program? Describe it.

_____
_____
_____
_____
_____

5. Describe your trade promotion program.

_____
_____
_____
_____
_____

6. Describe any publicity, public relations, or sales promotion programs you will have.

_____
_____
_____
_____
_____

Distribution

1. How do you plan to distribute your product? Direct to the consumer? Through traditional distribution channels? Through specialty channels such as exhibitions, mail order, or trade shows?

_____
_____
_____
_____

2. Will you employ your own sales force or rely on the services of agents or brokers? How many?

_____
_____
_____
_____
_____

THE SUPPLY SITUATION

1. What raw materials or component parts will you require to produce your product or service? What volume of these materials will you require? Who will be your major source of supply? Do you have alternative supply arrangements or other sources that can meet your requirements?

_____
_____
_____

2. What will be the cost of these materials and components? Are prices guaranteed for any length of time? Are volume or quantity discounts available? What credit terms will your suppliers make available to you?

_____

_____

_____

3. Describe your manufacturing requirements. Will you manufacture the product yourself or use subcontractors? What will it cost to establish your own manufacturing facility?

_____

_____

_____

4. If you are planning to use subcontractors, what alternatives are available? What are their capabilities and comparative costs? Will you have to incur any other costs — e.g., for moulds, etc.? Do any of these contractors provide additional services?

_____

_____

_____

COST/PROFITABILITY ANALYSIS

1. What do you estimate your costs would be and the funds required to successfully launch your business?

   a. Complete the following chart to determine your estimated start-up costs.

ESTIMATED MONTHLY EXPENSES

Item	Column 1 Your Estimate of Monthly Expenses Based on Sales of $ _____ Per Year	Column 2 Number of Months of Cash Required to Cover Expenses	Column 3 Estimated Cash Required to Start Business (Column 1 x 2)*
Salary of Owner-Manager	$0	2	$0
All Other Salaries and Wages	$0	3	$0
Rent	$0	3	$0
Advertising	$0	3	$0
Delivery Expense/Transportation	$0	3	$0
Supplies	$0	3	$0
Telephone, Fax, Internet Service	$0	3	$0
Other Utilities	$0	3	$0
Insurance	$0	3	$0
Taxes Including Employment Insurance	$0	4	$0
Interest	$0	3	$0
Maintenance	$0	3	$0
Legal and Other Professional Fees	$0	3	$0
Miscellaneous	$0	3	$0
Total Cash Requirements for Monthly Recurring Expenses: (A)			**$0**

*These figures may be typical for one kind of business. You will have to decide how many months to allow for your business to offset expected shortages of cash flow. This may be determined from your pro forma cash flow statement.

continued

Outline for a Feasibility Study — continued

START-UP COSTS YOU HAVE TO PAY ONLY ONCE

		Cash Required to Start Business
Capital Costs		
	Fixtures and Equipment	$0
	Decorating and Remodelling	$0
	Installation of Fixtures and Equipment	$0
	Starting Inventory	$0
Soft Costs		
	Deposits with Utilities	$0
	Legal and Other Professional Fees	$0
	Licences and Permits	$0
	Advertising and Promotion for Opening	$0
	Accounts Payable	$0
	Cash	$0
	Miscellaneous	$0
	Total One-Time Cash Requirements: (B)	**$0**

TOTAL ESTIMATED CASH REQUIRED TO START BUSINESS: (A) + (B)   **$0**

b. Do you have this much money available or have some ideas as to where you might be able to obtain it?

2. What do you estimate your sales will be, by product or service category, for your first 12 months? What will it cost you to produce those products or provide that service? What do you estimate your gross margin will be for each product or service? How does this compare with the norm for your industry? What operating expenses for such items as rent, travel, advertising, insurance, and utilities do you expect to incur? What profit do you estimate your business will show for its first 12 months?

Complete the pro forma income statement on page 230 for your first year of operation.

3. How are your sales and expenses expected to vary throughout the year? What proportion of your sales will be for cash? On credit? What credit terms, if any, will you provide to your customers? What credit terms do you expect to receive from your suppliers? What other expenses will you have to pay on a regular, ongoing basis?

a. Complete the table on page 231 to estimate your cash flow surplus or deficit for each month of your first year in business.

b. Can you arrange for more favourable terms from your suppliers, accelerate the collection of your outstanding accounts receivable, negotiate a line of credit with your bank, or take other action to enable your business to continue to operate if cash flow is insufficient?

4. What do you estimate your total fixed costs will be for your first year of operation? What did you estimate your average gross margin to be as a percentage of your total sales in preparing your pro forma income statement in question 2? (This amount is also known as your contribution margin per dollar of sales.)

Compute your break-even level of sales using the following formula:

$$\text{Break-Even Point (\$ sales)} = \frac{\text{Total Fixed Costs}}{\text{Contribution Margin per \$ of Sales}}$$

When do you expect to attain this level of sales? During your first year of business? Your second year? Your third year?

PLANS FOR FUTURE ACTION

1. According to your feasibility study, what were the strong points and weak points of your new venture idea? Can the weak points and potential problems be successfully overcome?

_____

_____

_____

_____

2. Does the feasibility assessment indicate that the business is likely to be profitable? Does it look sufficiently attractive that you should write a comprehensive business plan? What other information do you have to obtain, or what additional research do you have to do to develop this plan?

_____

_____

_____

_____

3. If you decide not to proceed with the development of a business plan, indicate the reasons why.

_____

_____

_____

_____

PRO FORMA INCOME STATEMENT

FOR THE PERIOD ENDING (DATE) _____

MONTH

	1	2	3	4	5	6	7	8	9	10	11	12	TOTAL
1. Gross Sales													
2. Less: Cash Discounts	$	$	$	$	$	$	$	$	$	$	$	$	$
A. NET SALES	$	$	$	$	$	$	$	$	$	$	$	$	$
Cost of Goods Sold:													
3. Beginning Inventory													
4. Plus: Net Purchases													
5. Total Available for Sale													
6. Less: Ending Inventory													
B. COST OF GOODS SOLD	$	$	$	$	$	$	$	$	$	$	$	$	$
C. GROSS MARGIN (C = A – B)	$	$	$	$	$	$	$	$	$	$	$	$	$
Less: Variable Expenses*													
7. Owner's Salary													
8. Employees' Wages and Salaries													
9. Supplies and Postage													
10. Advertising and Promotion													
11. Delivery Expense													
12. Bad Debt Expense													
13. Travel													
14. Legal and Accounting Fees													
15. Vehicle Expense													
16. Maintenance Expense													
17. Miscellaneous Expenses													
D. TOTAL VARIABLE EXPENSES	$	$	$	$	$	$	$	$	$	$	$	$	$
Less: Fixed Expenses*													
18. Rent													
19. Utilities (Heat, Light, Power)													
20. Telephone													
21. Taxes and Licences													
22. Depreciation													
23. Interest													
24. Insurance													
25. Other Fixed Expenses													
E. TOTAL FIXED EXPENSES	$	$	$	$	$	$	$	$	$	$	$	$	$
F. TOTAL OPERATING EXPENSES (F = D + E)	$	$	$	$	$	$	$	$	$	$	$	$	$
G. NET OPERATING PROFIT (LOSS) (G = C – F)	$	$	$	$	$	$	$	$	$	$	$	$	$
H. INCOME TAXES (estimated)													
I. NET PROFIT (LOSS) AFTER INCOME TAX (I=G–H)	$	$	$	$	$	$	$	$	$	$	$	$	$

* Expenses and other payments should be entered as negative (–) numbers.

TWELVE-MONTH CASH FLOW PROJECTIONS

	Month 1	Month 2	Month 3	Month 4	Month 5	Month 6	Month 7	Month 8	Month 9	Month 10	Month 11	Month 12	TOTAL
Cash Flow from Operations (during month)													
1. Cash Sales													
2. Payments for Credit Sales													
3. Investment Income													
4. Other Cash Income													
A. TOTAL CASH ON HAND	$	$	$	$	$	$	$	$	$	$	$	$	$
Less Expenses Paid (during month)[1]													
5. Inventory or New Material													
6. Owners' Salaries													
7. Employees' Wages and Salaries													
8. Supplies and Postage													
9. Advertising and Promotion													
10. Delivery Expense													
11. Travel													
12. Legal and Accounting Fees													
13. Vehicle Expense													
14. Maintenance Expense													
15. Rent													
16. Utilities													
17. Telephone													
18. Taxes and Licences													
19. Interest Payments													
20. Insurance													
21. Other Cash Expenses													
B. TOTAL EXPENDITURES	$	$	$	$	$	$	$	$	$	$	$	$	$
Capital													
Purchase of Fixed Assets													
Sale of Fixed Assets													
C. CHANGE IN CASH FROM PURCHASE OR SALE OF ASSETS	$	$	$	$	$	$	$	$	$	$	$	$	$
Financing													
Payment of Principal of Loan													
Inflow of Cash from Bank Loan													
Issuance of Equity Positions													
Repurchase of Outstanding Equity													
D. CHANGE IN CASH FROM FINANCING	$	$	$	$	$	$	$	$	$	$	$	$	$
E. INCREASE (DECREASE) IN CASH	$	$	$	$	$	$	$	$	$	$	$	$	$
F. CASH AT BEGINNING OF PERIOD	$	$	$	$	$	$	$	$	$	$	$	$	$[2]
G. CASH AT END OF PERIOD	$	$	$	$	$	$	$	$	$	$	$	$	$
MEET MINIMUM CASH BALANCE	ACCEPTABLE	ACCEPTABLE	ACCEPTABLE	ACCEPTABLE	ACCEPTABLE	ACCEPTABLE	ACCEPTABLE	ACCEPTABLE	ACCEPTABLE	ACCEPTABLE	ACCEPTABLE	ACCEPTABLE	ACCEPTABLE

1. Expenses and other payments should be entered as negative (−) numbers.
2. This entry should be the same amount as for the beginning of the year. All other rows will be the total for the entire year.

Organizing Your Business

One of the key issues you must resolve when starting your new venture is the legal form of organization the business should adopt. Making that decision means you should consider such factors as:

1. The complexity and expense associated with organizing and operating your business in one way or another

2. The extent of your personal liability

3. Your need to obtain start-up capital and operating funds from other sources

4. The extent to which you want ownership, control, and management of your business to be shared with others (if at all)

5. The distribution of your business's profits and losses

6. The extent of government regulation you are willing to accept

7. Tax considerations and implications

8. The need to involve other principals in your venture

The most prevalent forms your business might take are:

- An individual or sole proprietorship

- A partnership (general partnership or limited partnership)

- A corporation

INDIVIDUAL OR SOLE PROPRIETORSHIP

The *individual* or *sole proprietorship* is the oldest and simplest form of business organization. As owner or proprietor you have complete control over the conduct and management of your business. You alone are accountable for all business activities and their consequences. You control the business's profits and are liable for its debts. You and the business are one and the same. The sole proprietorship is the most common form of organization for small businesses, particularly in the early stages of their development.

ADVANTAGES OF SOLE PROPRIETORSHIP

- **Simple and inexpensive to start** A sole proprietorship is simple and inexpensive both to create and dissolve. It can be brought into existence with a minimum of legal formalities and terminated just as readily. Start-up costs are minimal — usually they are confined to registering your business name with the appropriate authorities and obtaining the necessary licences.

- **Individual control over operations** The operation of the business is coordinated by the mind and actions of a single individual. You are literally your own boss. If the business is not successful, you are free to dissolve it. And if the business does well, you can have a strong personal sense of accomplishment.

- **All profits to the owner** If the business does well you will reap the benefits of your efforts; no one will share in the profits of the business. You work for yourself and determine your own destiny. In addition, if your business incurs a loss during its early stages, that loss is deductible from any other income you may have.

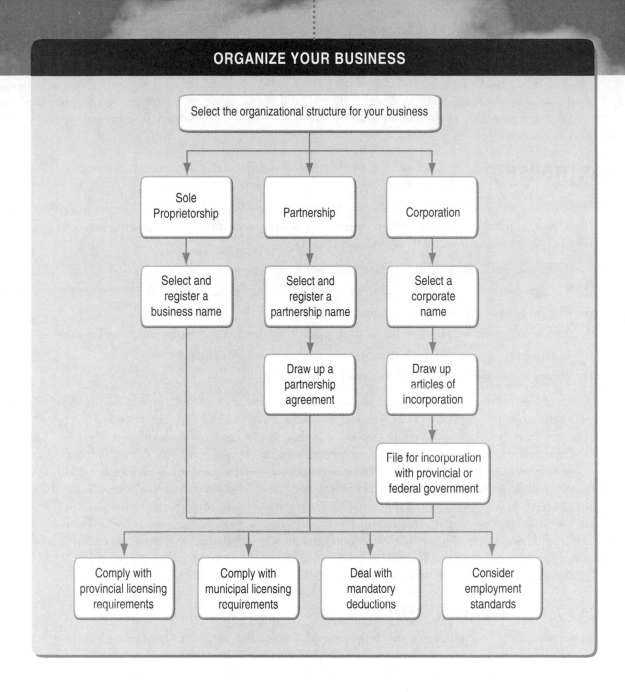

ORGANIZE YOUR BUSINESS

Select the organizational structure for your business

- Sole Proprietorship
- Partnership
- Corporation

Sole Proprietorship → Select and register a business name

Partnership → Select and register a partnership name → Draw up a partnership agreement

Corporation → Select a corporate name → Draw up articles of incorporation → File for incorporation with provincial or federal government

- Comply with provincial licensing requirements
- Comply with municipal licensing requirements
- Deal with mandatory deductions
- Consider employment standards

DISADVANTAGES OF SOLE PROPRIETORSHIP

- **Unlimited liability** Since the business and the proprietor are not recognized as being separate by law, you can be held personally liable for all the debts of your business. That means you may have to satisfy business debts with personal assets such as your house and car if the business is unable to meet its obligations. You may be able to protect some personal assets by putting them in your spouse's name before starting your venture but there is no real guarantee against domestic breakdown.

- **Higher tax rate** Any profits generated by a sole proprietorship are taxed at your higher personal tax rate, rather than at the more favourable small-business tax rate.

- **More difficult to obtain equity financing** Unlimited liability obviously limits the capital base of the business unless substantial security is available. It is not uncommon for sole proprietors to obtain the bulk of their initial funding by "maxing out" personal credit cards or by pledging their homes, cottages, or other personal assets as collateral for a loan.

- **Limited resources and opportunity** A sole proprietorship usually holds limited opportunity and incentive for employees, as it is not a form of ownership conducive to growth. One person can only do so much and may not have all the skills and knowledge necessary to run all phases of the business. Employees may have to be hired to perform these tasks. The life of the business in a proprietorship is limited to the life of the proprietor. If you should die, become ill, or encounter serious personal problems, your business is immediately affected, and unless other provisions are made, your business will die with you. This could lead to a forced sale of the business's assets by your beneficiaries, perhaps at a substantial loss.

PARTNERSHIP

A *partnership* is an association of two or more individuals carrying on a business for profit. The *principals* (partners) should jointly prepare a written partnership agreement outlining the following issues in terms that are clearly understood and mutually acceptable to all of them:

1. The rights and responsibilities of each partner
2. The amount and nature of the partners' respective capital contributions to the business
3. The division of the business's profits and losses
4. The management responsibilities of each partner involved in the operation of the business
5. Provision for termination, retirement, disability, or death of a partner
6. Means for dissolving or liquidating the partnership

Some of the potential problems that can occur in a partnership are illustrated by the case of Albert Sanges (Entrepreneurs in Action #23). He and his partner had worked together for seven years to build a thriving transportation company. After that time, however, a disagreement developed over their differing views of one of the key members of their management team that threatened to stifle the company and caused employee morale to plummet. To resolve the issue Sanges offered to buy out his partner but it still took over six months and an incredible amount of uncertainty and stress before the deal was completed and the issue finally resolved. In hindsight Sanges noted that one major issue in dealing with the situation was that he and his partner did not have any mechanism in place to resolve serious disagreements between them. Such a process would have made things much easier on everyone concerned and have enabled them to resolve their differences without jeopardizing the entire business.

Partnerships fall into two categories: general partnership and limited partnership.

GENERAL PARTNERSHIP

A *general partnership* is similar to a sole proprietorship except that responsibility for the business rests with two or more people, the partners. In a general partnership all the partners are liable for the obligations of the partnership and share in both profits and losses according to the terms of their partnership agreement.

SHERMAN'S LAGOON

©Jim Toomey. Reprinted with special permission of King Features Syndicate.

23 *Entrepreneurs in* action

Division of Labour

For a time, everything seemed to be going smoothly. My business partner and I worked side by side each day to develop and grow Link Logistics, the company we so dearly loved. And the company was indeed growing — by over 50 per cent each year. We were making very healthy profits, we were always on the leading edge of technology and we dominated the marketplace for our service. But after seven years of relative harmony, a management disagreement began to sour our relationship. I had a tough decision to make: Should I give in and side with a partner I had worked so well with over the years, or should I do what I felt was best for the company and risk damaging the friendship?

In the beginning, we each had our areas of responsibility, and we established our teams so the company could grow and prosper. My partner was in charge of IT development and the internal system required to run our service. I was responsible for everything else. Together, we made significant advances in all facets of the business, from IT development to sales and marketing. We built a strong company. In fact, after the first two years, our growth began to put us on lists of the fastest growing companies in Canada.

But my partner began to express serious concerns about the way our sales and marketing team was being handled. Clearly, there was a personality clash between him and our VP of sales and marketing. Eventually, my partner decided he could no longer work with this man and insisted on firing him. I, on the other hand, was pleased with the progress being made by our sales and marketing department, and wanted him to stay. With each of us holding equal say in running the business, we were at an impasse. My partner handled the situation by refusing to allow anyone to make normal management decisions without his express agreement. Our business began to suffer and staff morale plummeted.

For six months we struggled as a management team to get things done. I needed to make my choice, and in my heart, I knew that siding with my partner over company interests would affect many more people, including employees, customers and key suppliers, than just the two of us. Link Logistics had become an integral part of the daily trucking industry, and it seemed immoral to just walk away. We had worked way too hard to see the company fail now.

I finally decided to resolve the deadlock by offering to buy my partner's shares. After another six months and an incredibly stressful effort (that remains another story for another time), I completed the buy-out. In the process, we lost 12 employees out of a staff of 25, including our whole development team. Amazingly, we were able to stay focused enough to experience the company's largest growth rate ever — we even set records for the number of customers we signed to our service each month.

Since the buy-out, our new head of IT has put together a fresh, talented team of developers and systems people. The VP involved in the original conflict has formed strategic alliances with several different companies that complement and expand our service offerings. And we continue to expand at a rate that will keep us on the "fastest growth" lists for many years.

In retrospect, I see that my former partner and I did not have in place any mechanism to resolve serious disagreements that might arise between us. As a result, I have restructured the company holdings, and have adjusted the balance of voting rights in our shareholders' agreement to avoid deadlocks that block "business as usual." As unfair as it may seem, I've learned that one partner must have the final say. The deciding vote.

And I've learned the hard way that any partnership agreement should also contain provisions for breaking up the company or shareholders. Under a "shotgun agreement," for example, one shareholder may offer a fair price to buy out another shareholder.

But what do you do if all else fails and a partnership goes sour? If you are determined to keep the business going, as I was, you must stay focused on your objectives. Continue to work within the framework of any agreements that are in place. Do everything in your power to keep your staff loyal and their morale high. And make the success of the company your ultimate priority — even at the expense of a seemingly unshakeable friendship.

Source: Albert Sanges, "Division of Labour," *PROFIT* (www.profitguide.com/firstperson/F1_sanges.html), July 12, 2001. Used with permission.

ADVANTAGES OF A GENERAL PARTNERSHIP

- **Pooling of financial resources and talents**   The partnership is useful for bringing together two or more people who can combine their skills, abilities, and resources effectively. Management of the business is shared among the principals.

- **Simplicity and ease of organization**   A partnership, like a sole proprietorship, is easy and inexpensive to establish and is subject to a minimum amount of regulation.

- **Increased ability to obtain capital**   The combined financial resources of all the partners can be used to raise additional capital for the business. Income from the partnership is taxed as part of the personal income of each of the partners.

- **Potential for growth**   A partnership has a higher potential for growth than a proprietorship, since a valuable employee may be offered a partnership to dissuade him or her from leaving the firm. Growth, however, is still quite restricted compared to that possible with a limited company.

DISADVANTAGES OF A GENERAL PARTNERSHIP

- **Unlimited liability**   Partners are personally liable for all the debts and obligations of their business and for any negligence on the part of any of them occurring in the conduct of the business. This is similar to the situation with a sole proprietorship, except that the partners are liable both as a group and individually — not only for their own actions (severally) but also for the actions of all others in the partnership (jointly).

- **Divided authority**   There is less control for an individual entrepreneur in a partnership with divided authority. There may be possible conflicts among partners that can be difficult to resolve and could affect the conduct of the business.

LIMITED PARTNERSHIP

In a *limited partnership*, the partners' share in the liability of the business *is limited to the extent of their contribution to the capital of the business*. In such a partnership, however, there must also be one or more general partners, that is, partners with *unlimited liability*.

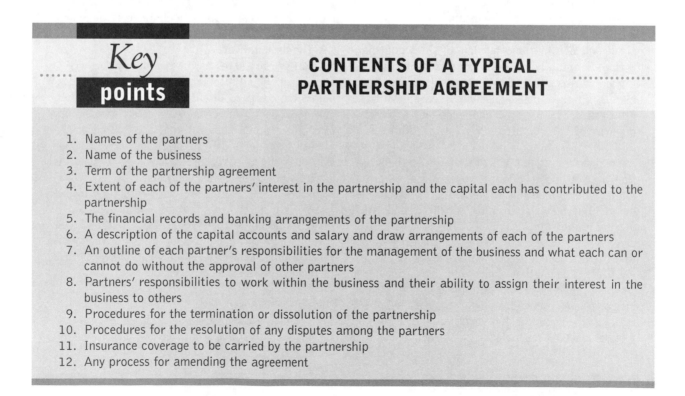

Key points

CONTENTS OF A TYPICAL PARTNERSHIP AGREEMENT

1. Names of the partners
2. Name of the business
3. Term of the partnership agreement
4. Extent of each of the partners' interest in the partnership and the capital each has contributed to the partnership
5. The financial records and banking arrangements of the partnership
6. A description of the capital accounts and salary and draw arrangements of each of the partners
7. An outline of each partner's responsibilities for the management of the business and what each can or cannot do without the approval of other partners
8. Partners' responsibilities to work within the business and their ability to assign their interest in the business to others
9. Procedures for the termination or dissolution of the partnership
10. Procedures for the resolution of any disputes among the partners
11. Insurance coverage to be carried by the partnership
12. Any process for amending the agreement

The limited partners may not participate in the day-to-day management of the business of the partnership or they risk losing their limited-liability status. Also, a limited partner is entitled to interest on his or her capital of no more than 5 per cent per year and some agreed-on share of the profits. Limited partners have one major power — the ability to remove the general partner(s).

ADVANTAGES OF A LIMITED PARTNERSHIP

- **Limited liability** If properly established and registered, the liability of the limited partners is restricted to the extent of their investment. Thus, you may find it easier to recruit investors.

DISADVANTAGES OF A LIMITED PARTNERSHIP

- **Centralized management** In a limited partnership only a small subgroup of the owners — the general partners — have decision-making authority and can participate in the management of the business.

- **Difficulty in changing ownership** It is generally difficult to change ownership in a partnership, since the partnership must be dissolved and reconstituted every time a partner dies or wants to retire. So it is important that the procedure for dealing with this issue be laid out in a partnership agreement.

CORPORATION

The *corporation* is the most formal and complex of the various forms of business organization. A firm that is *incorporated* is a separate legal entity from its owners — that is, legally, it is regarded as a "person" with a separate, continuous life. As a legal person, a corporation has rights and duties of its own: It can own property and other assets, it can sue or be sued, and it files its own tax return. Ownership of a corporation is recognized through the purchase of *shares*, or *stock*, which can be held by as few as one or as many as thousands of *shareholders*.

As in the case of a partnership, it is a good idea for the shareholders of a corporation to have a shareholders' agreement to protect their interests in case of friction or other conflicts that might arise among the principals. This agreement should be developed prior to the incorporation of the business and should deal with many of the same issues typically included in a partnership agreement. An overview of such an agreement is included in the Key Points feature below.

CONTENTS OF A TYPICAL SHAREHOLDER AGREEMENT

1. The structure of the company and how equity is divided among shareholders
2. Parties to the agreement
3. Officers and directors of the company and their responsibilities
4. Right of first refusal and pre-emptive rights to acquire new shares or those of another shareholder
5. Buy-out provisions for voluntary or involuntary withdrawal of shareholders
6. Option to purchase on death or disability of a shareholder
7. Restrictions on the transfer of shares
8. Any management contracts or key person agreements
9. Any ongoing shareholder financial obligations
10. Provisions for termination of the agreement
11. A mechanism for ongoing valuation of the business and the shares

A business need not be large to be incorporated. A sole proprietorship regularly earning in excess of $40,000 to $50,000 of taxable income annually probably should be incorporated.

Recent legislative changes in Ontario, Alberta, British Columbia, and other provinces now permit many groups of regulated professionals to enjoy the benefits of incorporation. These groups include lawyers, doctors, chartered accountants, dental hygienists, engineers, and management consultants. These professionals can now incorporate their practices in professional corporations. Some of the benefits of doing so are discussed in the FYI feature, "Filings Seen Rising as Awareness of Rules Spreads."

ADVANTAGES OF A CORPORATION

- **Limited liability** The owner or shareholder of a corporation is liable only for the amount he or she paid or owes for the shares, except where statutory provisions may create personal liability for the directors or officers of the company for outstanding wages, taxes, or similar obligations. In case of bankruptcy, creditors are not able to sue shareholders for outstanding debts of the business.

- **Continuity of the business even if the owner dies** Since it is an entity under the law, a corporation is not affected by the death or withdrawal of any shareholder. The shares of its stock can be sold or transferred to other individuals without difficulty. This ease of transfer allows for perpetual succession of the corporation, which is not the case with a sole proprietorship or partnership.

- **Easier to raise capital** Incorporation makes it easier to raise capital, which is done by selling stock. In addition, corporations with some history and a track record can negotiate more effectively with outside sources of financing than either a proprietorship or a partnership.

- **Employee benefits** A corporation has a better opportunity to provide benefits to employees and stockholders in a variety of ways such as salaries, dividends, and profit-sharing plans.

- **Tax advantages** Being an independent entity in the eyes of the law, a corporation receives different tax treatment than either a proprietorship or a partnership, and is taxed separately on its business profits. This may provide you with some opportunity for tax deferral, income-splitting, or the reduction of your actual tax costs through the deductibility of certain personal fringe benefits.

DISADVANTAGES OF A CORPORATION

- **Cost** Corporations are more expensive to start and operate. Initially, incorporation can cost in excess of $1,000 in legal and regulatory fees. In addition, a lawyer may charge upward of $300 per year to maintain the registered office and keep the *corporate book*, i.e., the record of annual meetings, directors' meetings, etc.

- **Legal formalities** A corporation is subject to more numerous and complicated regulatory requirements than a proprietorship or partnership. Corporations must typically file annual reports, hold annual meetings, and file federal and provincial tax returns. This can be expensive and time-consuming for a small-business person, and may require the ongoing services of an accountant and a lawyer.

- **Inability to flow losses through** It is not uncommon for a new business to incur substantial start-up costs and operating losses during its first few years. These losses are "locked in" — a corporation must accumulate them for its own use in future years, and cannot use them to offset income a shareholder may have from other sources. If your business never becomes very profitable, it is conceivable that its losses could never be used to reduce your tax liability.

  This is in contrast to a proprietorship or partnership, whose early losses would "flow through" to the owners of the business, to be deducted on their personal income tax returns in the year the losses were incurred. Therefore, it may be more beneficial financially not to incorporate, so you can offset other income for tax purposes. This can improve your overall cash flow when your business is just getting started, and cash flow is most critical. You can always decide to incorporate later without any tax consequences.

- **Guarantee** Lenders often require a personal guarantee. This largely negates the advantage of limited liability.

FYI FOR YOUR INFORMATION

FILINGS SEEN RISING AS AWARENESS OF RULES SPREADS

Ottawa lawyer Ted Mann jumped at the chance to incorporate his practice.

"I incorporated in June 2002, for two reasons: It allowed me to take advantage of the small-business deduction, which means I pay less tax on the money used to run the business — filing cabinets, letterhead — and incorporation affords some protection against supplier liability," Mr. Mann says.

Lawyers are just one of the many groups of regulated professionals now able to take advantage of amendments to the Ontario Business Corporations Act that allow them to incorporate their practices into professional corporations. The legislation is similar to that previously enacted in Alberta and British Columbia.

The list of other professions also benefiting from the Ontario amendments includes chartered accountants, dental hygienists and real estate agents. They join the ranks of such professions as software engineers and management consultants who had earlier won the ability to incorporate.

"Many professionals — lawyers, accountants, for example — found it unfair when they were doing work for small businesses and saw the advantages they were not able to access," Mr. Mann says. "It's a great relief."

Although the Ontario legislation was passed in January 2002, many of the associations governing regulated professionals have only recently put in place the programs needed to incorporate, explaining each governing body's exact rules and regulations.

Since the Ontario College of Physicians and Surgeons put its program in place in November of last year, for example, it has fielded about 750 inquiries about the process and issued close to 100 of the certificates needed to incorporate, a college spokeswoman says. The college currently has 20,000 practising members.

While some professional associations have not yet been promoting the concept, it's bound to take off in a changing workplace, where the number of "Me, Inc." small businesses is growing, predicts Toronto accountant George Wall. He is president of Wall & Associates and founder of CA4IP, a national association of independent accounting firms focused on independent professionals.

"Response has been slow," Mr. Wall says. "I don't believe people are aware of the changes and many professionals are slow to change." However, he expects many more individuals to go through the process, which takes about two days and costs about $800 in Ontario, because it can result in significant benefits to the independent professional.

Perhaps the most significant impact is that of lower taxes, because earnings can be retained within the corporation, Mr. Wall explains. Whereas the top tax rate in Ontario is about 46 per cent, the corporate tax rate on what is now the first $225,000 of income (raised from $200,000 in the last federal budget) earned by a small Canadian-controlled corporation in Ontario is about 20 per cent.

To demonstrate, he compares an employee earning $150,000 to someone who has incorporated. After a $14,000 RRSP contribution, the employee would pay $50,200 in taxes. The scenario would be radically different, however, should that person own a corporation earning $150,000 with expenses of $40,000. If he paid himself and his wife $35,000 each, and they each made RRSP contributions of $5,000, their total personal tax would be $13,200. The remaining $40,000 in the corporation would be taxed at 19.2 per cent, resulting in about another $7,600. All told, the tax savings in the second scenario would come close to $30,000, Mr. Wall notes.

"Incorporating offers the flexibility to get family involved," and the resulting income-splitting can reduce taxable income, he adds. And since a corporation can exist after death or retirement, it can provide pension and/or survivor benefits.

Another plus is the ability to borrow money from the corporation for a house or a car, either paid out as dividends or reinvested in the corporation, he adds.

A corporation can also act as a long-term investment or pension fund; the first $500,000 increase in the value of a private corporation is exempted from capital gains at the time of sale, Mr. Wall says.

Incorporation also limits the owner's liability, protecting personal assets from being seized should there be a problem with the business, Mr. Wall says, adding that incorporation does not protect against professional misconduct, such as malpractice charges.

If independent professionals are slow off the mark to take advantage of the opportunity to incorporate, it goes with the territory, he adds. "Ninety per cent of them work *in* their business versus *on* their business," Mr. Wall says.

Source: Catherine Mulroney, "Filings seen rising as awareness of rules spreads," *The Globe and Mail* (globeandmail.com, *Small Business Guide*), April 14, 2003.

GETTING INTO BUSINESS

REGISTRATION AND INCORPORATION — MAKING IT LEGAL

For a sole proprietorship, no formal, legal *registration* is required as long as the business is operated under your own name. However, if a specific business name like "Regal Dry Cleaners" or "Excel Construction" is used, or if more than one owner is implied by the use of "and Associates" or "and Sons" in conjunction with your name, your business must be logged with the Registrar of Companies or the Corporations Branch of the province in which the business is located. Registration is a relatively simple and inexpensive process that you can probably take care of yourself. Partnerships must be registered in a similar fashion.

Incorporation is a more complicated and considerably more expensive process that usually requires the services of a lawyer. If your business activities will initially be confined to a single province, you need incorporate only as a provincial company. Should your business plans include expansion to other provinces, however, you will be required to register in each province in which you wish to do business as an extra-provincial company, or register as a federally incorporated company.

Companies can be classified as either private or public. *Public companies* are those like Alcan and Great-West Life, which trade their shares on one of the country's public stock exchanges. They typically employ professional managers, external directors, and a number of shareholders who are the owners of the business.

Private companies, on the other hand, tend to have only one shareholder, or at most a small number of shareholders. There is some restriction on the transfer of their shares in their *articles of incorporation*, and their shares cannot be offered for sale to the public. A private corporation is sometimes called an *incorporated partnership*, because it usually consists of one, two, or three people who are personal friends, business associates, or family members, each of whom may play two or three roles, serving, for example, as an officer, director, and a shareholder of the company all at the same time.

PairoWoodies Publishing, highlighted in Entrepreneurs in Action #24, is a good example of an incorporated partnership. Ian Scott first met Wendy Woudstra through the Internet. He was an experienced entrepreneur who knew something about marketing but had almost no computer skills, while she had a technical background and experience at building Web sites. Both work in the business and have quite different roles and responsibilities but have had to learn to be flexible and willing to cover for each other when required. Oh, and how did they happen to acquire the unusual name? It turns out that Ian and Wendy both had the same nickname when they were kids — Woody. Ian came up with the name when they were discussing possible business names. While at first they were hesitant to use the name, it has paid off for them. No one ever forgets it.

If you choose to incorporate, a private corporation is probably the type you will establish.

CHOOSING A NAME

Like people, all businesses must have a name. The simplest procedure is to name the business after yourself — Harry Brown's Printing, for example. This type of name does not require formal registration for a sole proprietorship, but it does have disadvantages. For example, you might have people phoning you at home at all hours if you and your business's name are the same. In addition, your personal reputation may be tarnished if you experience some financial problems and are forced into receivership or bankruptcy. And if you ever sell your business, your name would go with it, and the new owner's actions could reflect negatively on your reputation.

For businesses to be registered or incorporated, the most important consideration in selecting a name is that it be acceptable to the Registrar of Companies in your province. All provinces require that a search be conducted of proposed names. Any name that is similar to a name already registered will be rejected to avoid public confusion. It is not uncommon to have to submit several names before one is finally approved. To avoid this problem, some individuals use a series of numbers rather than letters for the name of their corporation. On acceptance, the name is typically reserved for your exclusive use for 90 days, so that you can proceed with your registration or the filing of your articles of incorporation.

The best approach is usually to choose a distinctive name for the firm that *accurately describes* the type of business you plan to carry on. That is, a name like "Speedy Courier Service" or "Super-Clean Automobile Washing" is probably much better than one like "Universal Enterprises" or "General Distributing." A good way to check out names is to go through the Yellow Pages or local business directories and get some idea of the range of names currently in use in your business area and perhaps some inspiration for a brilliant new possibility.

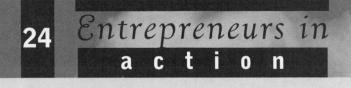

The Evolution of PairoWoodies

"Do what you can, with what you have, right where you are."

Ian Scott took these words of Theodore Roosevelt to heart and decided to start his fourth business, PairoWoodies Publishing, which began as a Web site design business, and has evolved into a full-service provider of Internet solutions for small- and medium-sized businesses and organizations.

It was definitely not the best of times for Ian to be starting a Web-based business. When the idea for PairoWoodies came to him, he had almost no computer skills and was deeply in debt due to the recent breakdown of his marriage.

So why would Ian decide to start an Internet-related business?

Ian was already an experienced entrepreneur. He had started his first business while he was in college, although he says that at that time "running a business was all a mystery to me." However, he persevered, and eventually started a part-time fishing tackle business. What Ian really wanted to do was build custom fishing rods and sell them, and selling tackle and saving the profits let him raise enough funds to make an initial wholesale order of custom fishing rod components.

It was while operating Wishbone Custom Rods that Ian first become involved with the Internet. He hired Steve Henry to create a Web site for his business, and was impressed by the new business and inquiries the site generated. "I quickly learned how to use newsgroups to market Wishbone, and began to learn more about the whole Internet 'thing.'"

When Ian's marriage ended and his house had to be sold, he no longer had the space to build custom rods. He shut down Wishbone and started surfing the Internet, looking for business ideas.

Ian found lots of business ideas on the Internet — but he realized that he needed more skills. He made a deal with Wendy Woudstra, whom he met through the Internet. He would get her more clients to build Web sites for if she would teach him HTML.

Ian started calling on his acquaintances, and "almost immediately, we had enough interest that I had to learn HTML pretty swiftly in order to assist Wendy in getting the work done!" Ian and Wendy decided to form a partnership, even though they lived 2000 miles away from each other at that time.

While many partnerships fail, Ian and Wendy's has flourished. If you're a partner, as Ian points out, you have to learn to be flexible, learn how to clearly explain your vision to your partner, and be able to define your own roles. At the same time, you need to be willing to cover for each other when need be.

On the other hand, establishing a partnership with someone who has the skills you don't can be extremely helpful in getting to where you want to be, faster. Ian says that his and Wendy's different strengths really complement each other's well. "I simply could not have developed the business without her, and I think there are many things I offer to the partnership that Wendy needed to get her business going."

As PairoWoodies Publishing grew, Ian and Wendy decided that it would be in the best interests of the business if they lived closer to one another. They moved to Toronto. Ian, however, envisioned being able to move back to the Orangeville area and seeing the business become more than a Web site design company. He wanted to be able to provide more services to clients, without being dependent on another company. He also wanted to be able to leave his full-time job.

When Ian and Wendy first started PairoWoodies Publishing, they realized that the key to independence was owning their own servers. Ian had kept in touch with Steve Henry. Last year Ian and Wendy purchased an interest in Steve's ISP, providing them with the speedy, high bandwidth Internet connection they needed to grow faster without depending on some other company's services, and the ability to provide services tailored for individual businesses. It also gave them the chance to move back to the Orangeville area.

Now PairoWoodies Publishing is located in "downtown" Orangeville. They have three full-time employees and one part-time employee, and will be adding at least one more part-time employee during the summer. They also contract out parts of projects when they need to. It took about three years for the business to grow to a point where Ian could leave his job and work full-time in the business, but that goal, too, has been realized.

Ian says, "When you really want something, and believe that it can be achieved, it is amazing the serendipitous events that take place!" (www.pairowoodies.com)

Source: *About* (sbinfocanada.about.com/library/weekly/ aa043001b.htm), accessed December 9, 2003.

Names that are likely to be rejected and should be avoided are those that:

1. Imply any connection with or approval of the Royal Family, such as names that include the word "Imperial" or "Royal"

2. Imply approval or sponsorship of the business by some unit of government, such as names containing "Parliamentary," "Premier's," or "Legislative"

3. Might be interpreted as obscene or not really descriptive of the nature of the firm's business

4. Are similar to or contractions of the names of companies already in business, even though they may be in a different field, such as "IBM Tailors" or "Chrysler Electronics"

The firm's name can become one of your most valuable assets if your business is successful, as has happened in the case of companies like McDonald's and Holiday Inn. Don't go for the first name that comes to mind. Think it over very carefully.

SHERMAN'S LAGOON

©Jim Toomey. Reprinted with special permission of King Features Syndicate.

OBTAINING A BUSINESS LICENCE

You may require a municipal as well as a provincial licence to operate your business. Your need for the former depends on the location and nature of your business; requirements for the latter depend solely on the nature of your business.

MUNICIPAL

Not all types of businesses require a municipal licence. Every municipality regulates businesses established within its boundaries and sets its own licensing requirements and fees. In Winnipeg, for example, 114 types of businesses and occupations require a licence. In general, these are amusement operations or ones that may affect public health and safety. The licensing fees can be as high as several thousand dollars, but in most cases the fees are quite nominal — a few dollars.

In addition, all businesses — whether or not they require a licence — must conform to local zoning regulations and bylaw requirements. In fact, zoning approval is usually a prerequisite to licence approval. Companies operating in their own facilities in most cities must also pay a business tax, assessed as a percentage of the rental value of their business facilities.

PROVINCIAL

Various provincial authorities also require a licence or permit. In Ontario, for example, all establishments providing accommodation to the public, such as hotels, motels, lodges, tourist resorts, and campgrounds, must be licensed by the province. Businesses planning to serve liquor, operate long-haul cartage and transport operations, process food products, produce optical lenses, or manufacture upholstered furniture or stuffed toys may also require licensing. You should check with the local authorities to determine the types of licences and permits your business might require.

SO WHAT'S IN A NAME ANYWAY?

So what's in a name anyway? According to naming experts—everything. Granted, as Shakespeare's Juliet noted, a rose by any other name would smell as sweet. . .but name it a thugwhistle and see if it sells half as much. There is power in a name. Look at the recall value and daring in a name like Rent-a-Wreck, a Canadian car rental business that's been around for years. Or the name Yahoo! We've all Yahooed even if we didn't know it was a verb. We get it. And we remember.

Some say if you're playing in the big leagues, it's wise to seek a consultant to help come up with a powerful business name. Naseem Javed, a Toronto-based naming consultant and president of ABC Namebank International, emphasizes that "the name of a product, service or company can often make the difference between survival and bankruptcy; between great success and crashing failure."

If there's nothing in the budget for a consultant, check out Industry Canada's Strategis Web site or books on small-business start-up to give you pointers on devising a winner on your own. Many young entrepreneurs across Canada, like Halifax pottery shop owner Laura MacKay, are coming up with their own business names.

To get ideas, MacKay, 24, searched the Internet for names of businesses like hers and hit on a few inventive ones, like You're Fired and Once Upon a Dish. That got her creative juices flowing and she started brainstorming. Since her business invites people to make and paint their own pottery, she wanted to convey something of the process. And then, "It clicked," she says. "Earth, Paint and Fire." The name indicated the elements involved, created vivid images, and had a catchy ring—a play on the name of the '70s band Earth, Wind & Fire. She ran the name by plenty of people "to see if it was cool and if they thought it would stick in their heads," she says. "Everyone was really positive."

Do-it-yourselfers should keep a few points in mind, says naming consultant Henri Charmasson. Through market research, clearly define the message you want to deliver. Then reduce it to a single theme or image and devise a name that conveys that theme. He says distinctiveness is the critical ingredient in a winning name. Distinctiveness will give the name its marketing value, effectiveness and legal power. Take, for example, the name Discount Mufflers. It's not an identifier, he says, but merely a definition. "Since there are hundreds of competitors also selling mufflers at a discount, the phrase is not distinctive. It's neither memorable, nor protectable." But look at the name Midas. It's a distinctive, memorable name, one that can't be copied or easily mimicked by competitors.

The name of a company should also motivate the customer to buy its product or services, and should position these above the competition. Compare the name Cover Girl to Revlon. "Cover Girl," Charmasson notes, "is motivating, conveying what most women want to look like; whereas Revlon is an empty name that requires advertising to communicate what it is."

Arpeggio, for example, targets a different audience than names like Chuck Wagon or Mr. Bubble. As does the name, The Urban Garage. That's the name of a luxury car boutique in West Vancouver that Duncan Pearce, 29, has just opened in what was a garage. The funky name is meant to target high-income baby boomers, Gen-Xers and car enthusiasts. "I sell performance cars, and I'm targeting enthusiasts who I think will relate to the name," Pearce says. "I was looking for a name that would differentiate my business from the typical car dealership, and one that would lend a feeling that this is a fun, funky place for car enthusiasts."

A memorable name is "catchy, loaded with pleasant evocation, or responsive to some inner desire or need of the customer," Charmasson notes. In Thunder Bay, Ontario, Tanya Wheeler, 34, and Laura McLennan, 27, founders of Blue Loon Adventures, used an evocative symbol in their eco-tour company name, and created a logo to match. "We thought if people couldn't remember the company name, they'd remember the image," says Wheeler. "We wanted a name that was Canadian, as we'd be appealing to international birders and outdoor enthusiasts. The name is memorable because of its association with the song ["Blue Moon"] and because the loon is identified as a Canadian symbol."

Since many family names are uninspiring and can lead to potential problems if the business is sold, many consultants advise against naming your business after yourself. Also remember, business names that are initials carry no message.

If your business is unincorporated, name registration isn't necessary. However, Vancouver business/intellectual property lawyer and federal trademark agent Paul Schwartz, advises: "If the new business is to be unincorporated, such as a sole proprietorship or a general partnership, it's still advisable to file the business name with the Registrar of Companies." For

continued

So What's in a Name Anyway? — continued

businesses to be registered or incorporated, the name must be acceptable to the Registrar of Companies in your province. Getting your corporate name approved at the federal level by the Corporations Directorate offers you added protection of your rights to that name, as this allows your business to operate using its corporate name across Canada. To be approved, the name must be distinctive, must not cause confusion with any existing name or trademark, must include a legal element (usually Ltd., Inc., or Corp.) and must not include unacceptable terms.

For more information, check Industry Canada's Web site at http://www.strategis.ic.gc.ca.

Source: Excerpted with permission from *Realm: Creating Work You Want*™, Fall 2000, published by YES Canada–BC. Available online at http://realm.net and in print by calling 1-877-REALM-99. For more information, Phone: (604) 412-4141; fax: (604) 412-4144; e-mail: info@realm.net.

LAND USE AND ZONING

You should check with the local municipal authorities to ensure that your business conforms to zoning and building regulations.

MANDATORY DEDUCTIONS AND TAXES

If your business has a payroll you will be required to make regular deductions from employees' paycheques for income tax, employment insurance (EI), and the Canada Pension Plan (CPP). These deductions must be remitted to the Canada Revenue Agency every month.

In addition, you may also be required to pay an assessment to your provincial Workers' Compensation Board. The size of your payment will be based on the nature of your business and its risk classification as well as the estimated size of your annual payroll. These funds are used to meet medical, salary, and rehabilitation costs of any of your employees who may be injured on the job.

Depending on the size of your venture, you may also be responsible for remitting taxes of various kinds to either the provincial or the federal government. All provinces, except Alberta, apply a retail sales tax to almost all products and services sold to the ultimate consumer. Exceptions in some provinces include food, books, children's clothing, and medicine. The size and the application of these taxes varies from province to province, but if your business sells to final consumers you must obtain a permit and are responsible for collecting this tax and remitting it to the government on a regular basis.

Federal taxes largely fall into the categories of the Goods and Services Tax and income tax. Several provinces have integrated their provincial sales tax with the federal government's Goods and Services Tax (GST) to create a Harmonized Sales Tax (HST). The GST/HST is levied on virtually all products and services sold in Canada. There are some minor exceptions for certain types of products. If your taxable revenues do not exceed $30,000 you do not have to register for the GST or HST, but you can still choose to register voluntarily even if your revenues are below this level. You should check and see whether these taxes apply in your business. If so, you will be required to obtain a Business Number (BN) and remit any taxes collected on a regular basis.

How income tax is collected depends on the form of organization of your business. Sole proprietorships and partnerships file income tax returns as individuals and the same regulations apply. Federal and provincial taxes are paid together and only one personal income tax form is required annually for both, although payments may have to be remitted quarterly on the basis of your estimated annual earnings.

A corporation is treated as a separate entity for income tax purposes and taxed individually. The rules, tax rates, and regulations that apply to corporations are very complex and quite different from those that apply to individuals. You should obtain professional advice or contact the local tax authorities to determine your obligations under the Income Tax Act and to keep the amount of tax you have to pay to a minimum.

EMPLOYMENT STANDARDS

All provinces have standards for employment and occupational health and safety that must be adhered to by all businesses within their jurisdiction. These requirements deal with such matters as:

1. Hours of work
2. Minimum wages

3. Statutory holidays

4. Overtime pay

5. Equal pay for equal work

6. Termination of employment

7. Severance pay

8. Working conditions

9. Health and safety concerns

You should contact the office of your provincial Ministry of Labour or its equivalent and request a copy of the Employment Standards Act in effect in your province as well as a copy of the Guide to the Act. This will provide you with specific information on all of these topics, or you can use the services of an accountant or lawyer.

FYI FOR YOUR INFORMATION

A Guide to Legally Setting Up Your Business in Canada Canada Business Service Centres provides a Web site that will help you navigate around some of the government requirements involved is setting up a business in each of the provinces and territories of Canada (bsa.cbsc.org). This site is intended to show you only a basic list of some of the most frequent requirements. You should be aware that these requirements will vary from province to province and differ for specific kinds of businesses. For each province or territory this Web site will provide you with information on the following (and other) topics:

- Basic Steps for Starting a Business
- Being an Entrepreneur
- Market Research
- Preparing a Business Plan
- Choosing a Business Type
- Selecting Your Business Name
- Registering Your Business
- Financing
- Taxation and Business Number

- Hiring Employees or Contractors
- Regulations
- Importing or Exporting
- Copyright, Patents, Trademarks
- * Doing Business on the Internet
- Managing Your Business
- Starting a Specific Business
- Municipalities

CanadaOne This Web site provides links for each province and territory to the forms, information, and phone numbers you may need to get things up and running. Just click on your province or territory and you are on your way. (www.canadaone.com/tools/provincial_links.html)

INSURANCE

Your business may include a number of valuable assets such as computers, product inventory, machinery and equipment, vehicles, documents, and even yourself, among other things. Therefore, unexpected events like fire, flood, or the death of your partner are some of the hazards you have to protect yourself against. For example, you need to ask yourself:

- What would happen if the contents of your business premises were destroyed by fire?
- What if there was a break-in and your equipment was stolen?
- What if an employee or a client was badly hurt on your premises?
- What if you or your partner passed away unexpectedly?

Would your business be able to absorb the costs associated with these events and still be able to continue? After weighing the risks against the costs, you may decide that you need some protection if your business is likely to survive. This can be done through the use of insurance.

There are a number of different types of insurance you should consider obtaining for your business. You should discuss your situation with your insurance agent to arrange an appropriate program.

1. **General liability insurance** covers your liability to customers injured on your premises, or injured off your premises by a product you have sold to them.

2. **Business premises insurance** will protect your business premises and equipment from loss due to fire, theft, and other perils.

3. **Business-use vehicle insurance** must be obtained for cars and other vehicles used in the conduct of your business.

4. **Business interruption or loss-of-income insurance** will enable you to continue to pay the bills if your business should be closed down by damage due to fire, flood, or other catastrophe.

5. **Disability or accident and sickness insurance** can continue to provide you with a source of income if you should become seriously sick or disabled and unable to continue to run your business for a period of time.

6. **Key-person insurance** can protect your business against the death of its key personnel. It is life insurance purchased by the business with the business being the sole beneficiary.

7. **Credit insurance** protects you from extraordinary bad debt losses due to a customer going out of business.

8. **Surety and fidelity bonds** protect you from the failure of another firm or individual to fulfil its contractual obligations.

9. **Partnership insurance** can protect you against suits arising from actions taken by other partners in your business.

10. **Workers' Compensation** provides compensation for your employees in case of illness or injuries related to their employment.

An insurance program won't protect you from *all* the risks associated with running your business, but it will provide you with some financial protection against unpredictable occurrence in several areas that could threaten the survival of your venture.

Key points — STARTING A NEW BUSINESS

1. **Plan for success** A business plan will help you think through a number of important aspects of your new business.
2. **Select the form of business** that is right for you.
3. **Register your business** The process and requirements vary from province to province.
4. **Do you need a business licence?** Check with your municipality to find out.
5. **Do you meet zoning and local bylaw requirements?** You'll need to check your local bylaws to find out.
6. **Register for provincial taxes and local permits, if they apply.** Depending on the type of business you are in, you may need to collect provincial sales tax and apply for a vendor licence or other permits.
7. **GST, PST, HST basics** The two main taxes that businesses collect are the Goods and Services Tax (GST) and retail or provincial sales tax (PST). Several provinces combine the two taxes into a single tax known as the harmonized sales tax (HST). Check out the situation in your province or territory.
8. **Research and purchase business insurance** Running a business carries some risks. There are many types of insurance that offer protection.
9. **Understand HR issues and responsibilities** If you will be hiring staff, you'll need to understand your obligations in three principal areas:
   • Payroll obligations re the remission of taxes
   • Local labour laws
   • Workers' Compensation Board (WCB) requirements
10. **Keep Necessary Records** When you run a business, you are required to keep permanent books and records for a specified period of time.

Source: CanadaOne (www.canadaone.com/ezine/oct03/checklist.html), accessed August 18, 2004.

CONCLUSION

There is no pat answer to the question of the legal form of organization you should adopt. A lot will depend on such issues as the expected size and growth rate of your new venture, your desire to limit your personal liability, whether you plan to start the business on a part-time or a full-time basis, whether you expect to lose or make money from a tax point of view during your first one or two years of operation, your need for other skills or additional capital, and so forth. Take a look at Figure 8.1, which summarizes many of the important differences between the various forms of organization available to you and may help you make your decision.

One word of caution: If you are considering any type of *partnership* arrangement, be extremely careful. In hard reality, partners should fulfil at least one of two major needs for you: They should provide either needed *money* or needed *skills*. If you allow any other factors to overshadow these two essential criteria, you may be taking an unnecessary risk.

One of the primary reasons new venture teams often fail is ill-advised partnerships. Partnerships entered into principally for reasons of friendship, shared ideas, or similar factors can create considerable stress for both the partnership and the individuals involved. It has often been said that a partner should be chosen with as much care as you would choose a spouse. However, in contemporary society, perhaps even greater care should be exercised, since a partnership may be even more difficult to dissolve than a marriage. An unhappy partnership can dissolve your business much faster than you can dissolve the partnership.

FIGURE 8.1   WHICH FORM OF BUSINESS ORGANIZATION IS BEST FOR YOU?

This figure summarizes many of the important differences between the various forms of business available to you. Review each of the alternatives on the dimensions indicated and select which one best fits with your particular circumstances. This may vary from characteristic to characteristic since there are pros and cons of each form. Once you have reviewed all dimensions, you should be able to select the organizational form that appears to be the best overall for your particular situation.

Form of Organization	(a) Initial Requirements and Costs	(b) Liability of Owners	(c) Control	(d) Taxes	(e) Transfer of Ownership	(f) Continuity	(g) Ability to Raise Money
(1) Sole Proprietorship	Minimum requirements; perhaps only registration of your business name	Unlimited liability	Absolute control over operations	Income from business taxed as personal income	May transfer ownership of assets	Business ceases to exist when owner quits or dies	Limited to what the owner can personally secure
(2) General Partnership	Easy and inexpensive to establish	Each partner is personally liable for all debts of the partnership	Requires majority vote of all general partners	Income from business is taxed as personal income of the partners	Requires agreement of all partners	Dissolved on with-drawal or death of partner unless specified in partnership agreement	Combined resources of all the partners can be used to raise capital
(3) Limited Partnership	Moderate requirements; should be registered provincially	Liability limited to the extent of their individual investment	May not participate in the day-to-day management of the business	Same as for general partners	May sell interest in the company	Same as general partnership	Limited liability may make it easier to raise capital but can be complicated

continued

Which Form of Business Organization Is Best for You? — continued

Form of Organization	(a) Initial Requirements and Costs	(b) Liability of Owners	(c) Control	(d) Taxes	(e) Transfer of Ownership	(f) Continuity	(g) Ability to Raise Money
(4) Corporation	Most expensive; usually requires a lawyer to file Articles of Incorporation	Liability limited to investment in company	Control rests with shareholders	Corporation taxed on its income and shareholders taxed on dividends received	Easily transferred by selling shares of stock	Not affected by the death or withdrawal of any shareholder	The most attractive form for raising capital

Which form best meets your needs on each dimension (select one)?

(a) _____ (b) _____ (c) _____ (d) _____ (e) _____ (f) _____ (f) _____

Which form of organization do you feel best meets your overall needs? _____

Video Case #9

Caribbean Beer

Summary

Alesha Harrison's father used to import Caribbean beer. She and her sister Paula decided to become partners and seize an opportunity to brew the beer under licence in Canada when her father moved to Ghana. Harrison's father bankrolled the company with $1 million and they purchased a bankrupt brewery. With Paula pregnant, a brewmaster who quit, an investor who wants to see a profit, and a very competitive brewing industry, the pressure on Harrison is increasing.

Questions for Discussion

1. In what way should this business (or any other business for that matter) be better organized?

2. What are some issues that people in a family business must be aware of?

3. Would you recommend incorporation, partnership, limited partnership, or sole proprietorship for this business?

4. Harrison and her sister hired a salesperson because he had good vibes. Is there some way they could improve their hiring process?

Protecting Your Idea

Many entrepreneurs are also inventors. One of the primary problems faced by these inventor/ entrepreneurs is how to protect the idea, invention, concept, system, design, name, or symbol that they feel may be the key to their business success. Legislators have long recognized that society should provide some protection for the creators of this "intellectual property." The laws they have developed provide a form of limited monopoly to the creators of intellectual property in return for their disclosure of the details of the property to the public.

Intellectual property is broken down into five components under the law:

1. Patents
2. Trademarks
3. Copyrights
4. Industrial designs
5. Integrated circuit topographies

Protection of your intellectual property can be expensive. While government costs may range from only a small fee for registration of a copyright to several hundred dollars for registration of a patent, many of the procedures can be quite complex and require you to obtain the services of a registered patent agent. This can increase the total cost of obtaining a patent by several thousand dollars, the cost depending on the complexity of the application. Therefore, it is important that you understand the advantages and disadvantages provided by this protection, and its likely impact on the success and financial viability of your business.

APPLYING FOR A PATENT

A *patent* is a government grant that gives you the right to take legal action, if necessary, against other individuals who without your consent make, use, or sell the invention covered by your patent during the time the patent is in force. Patents are granted for 20 years from the date on which the application was first filed and are not renewable. On expiration of its patent, a patented device falls into the *public domain* — anyone may make, use, or sell the invention.

To be patentable your device must meet three basic criteria:

1. Have "absolute novelty." The invention must be new (first in the world).
2. Be useful. A patent cannot be obtained for something that doesn't work or has no useful function.
3. It must show inventive ingenuity and not be obvious to someone skilled in that area.

A patent may be granted for a product, a chemical composition, an apparatus or machine, or a process. You *cannot* patent a scientific principle, an abstract theorem, an idea, a method of doing business, a computer program, or a medical treatment.

A patent may be applied for only by the legal owner(s) of an invention. You cannot apply for a patent for an invention you may have seen in another country even though that invention may never have been patented, described, or offered for sale in Canada.

Patents are now awarded to the *first inventor to file an application* with the Patent Office of the Canadian Intellectual Property Office (CIPO). This means you should file as soon as possible after completing your invention (though not prematurely if certain key elements or features of your idea would be

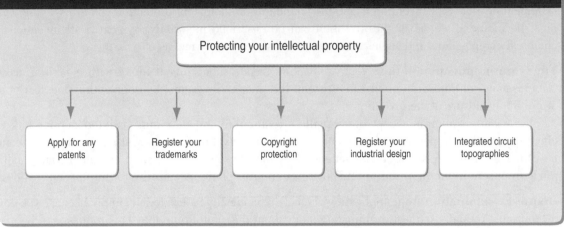

PROTECT YOUR IDEA

Protecting your intellectual property

- Apply for any patents
- Register your trademarks
- Copyright protection
- Register your industrial design
- Integrated circuit topographies

missing from your application). It is also important that you not advertise or display or publish information on your invention too soon, as this may jeopardize your ability to obtain a valid patent later on. There is a one-year grace period for disclosure by an applicant but it is suggested that the following rule of thumb be adopted: *Your application for a patent should be filed before your product is offered for public sale, shown at a trade show, or otherwise made public.*

HOW TO APPLY

If your idea is patentable and you wish to obtain patent protection, you should take the following steps:

1. **Find a patent agent** The preparation and prosecution (assessment) of patent applications is quite complex. You should consult a patent agent trained in this specialized practice and registered to represent inventors before the Patent Office of the CIPO. Though hiring such an agent is not mandatory, it is highly recommended. The Patent Office can provide you with a list of registered agents but will not recommend any particular one to you. Several may also be listed in your local telephone directory, but make certain they are registered with the Patent Office. The address of the office is:

   Patent Office
   Canadian Intellectual Property Office
   Industry Canada
   Place du Portage, Phase I
   50 Victoria Street, Room C-229
   Gatineau, Quebec K1A 0C9

   (cipo.gc.ca)

   General Inquiries: (819) 997-1936
   1-900-565-2476 ($3 flat rate per call)

2. **Conduct a preliminary search** The first step your agent will recommend is a preliminary search of existing patents to see if anything similar to your idea has already been patented, in which case you may conclude the process immediately. This can save you a lot of time and money that might otherwise be spent pursuing a futile application. The database search can be conducted in person by visiting the CIPO Patent Office in Gatineau or on the CIPO Web site. The online database has descriptions and drawings of patents issued in Canada since 1920.

3. **Prepare a patent application** A patent application consists of an abstract, a specification, and drawings.

   An *abstract* is a brief summary of the material in the specification. The *specification* is a document that contains (1) a complete description of the invention and its purpose and (2) *claims*, which are an explicit statement of what your invention is and the boundaries of the patent protection you are seeking. *Drawings* must be included whenever the invention can be described pictorially. Typically, all inventions except chemical compositions and some processes can be described by means of drawings.

4. **File your application** Filing your application means submitting it along with a petition asking the Commissioner of Patents to grant you a patent. In Canada, filing must be done within one year of any use or public disclosure of the invention.

   If your application is accepted, you will be required to pay an annual maintenance fee to keep it in effect for the 20-year period. Independent inventors and small businesses whose gross annual revenues are less than $2 million pay lower maintenance fees than businesses classified as "other than small." Fees range from zero in the first year to $225 in years 15 to 19 of the patent's life for these small entities.

5. **Request examination** Your application will not automatically be examined simply because you have filed it. You must formally request examination and submit the appropriate fee. This request can be made any time within five years of your filing date.

   Filing an application and not requesting examination can be a cheap and effective way of obtaining some protection for your invention without necessarily incurring all the costs of obtaining a patent. For example, let's assume you want to protect your idea but don't wish to spend all the money required to obtain a patent until you have assessed the financial feasibility of your invention. Filing an application establishes your rights to the invention and publication of the application by the Patent Office informs other people of your claim to the product or process. If someone infringes on your invention after your application is published, you have five years to decide whether to pursue the grant of a patent and seek retroactive compensation.

   Requesting an examination, however, is no guarantee that a patent will be granted. And if it is not, you will have no grounds to claim damages for infringement on your idea.

   The CIPO Patent Office receives over 35,000 applications a year, mostly from U.S. inventors and companies. As a result, the examination process can be very slow, commonly taking two to three years to complete.

6. **If necessary, file amendment letters** When you request an examination, the patent examiner will assess your claims and either approve or reject your application. If your application is rejected, you can respond by filing an *amendment letter* with the Commissioner of Patents. The letter will be studied by the examiner. If the patent is not then granted, there may be a request for further amendments. This process will continue until either the patent is granted, your application is withdrawn, or your application is rejected.

PROTECTION PROVIDED BY YOUR PATENT

As you can see, the patenting process is complex, costly, and time-consuming. If you have a patent application in process and are concerned that someone else may attempt to patent your invention, you may use the label "Patent Pending" or "Patent Applied For" to inform the public that your application for a patent has been filed. This, however, has no legal significance and does not mean that a patent will necessarily be granted. Of course, it is illegal to use this term if in fact no application is on file.

If your patent application is granted, the onus will be entirely on you to protect your rights under the patent, because the Patent Office has no authority to prosecute for patent infringement. If infringement occurs, you may (1) bring legal action to compel the offender to account for any profits made, (2) seek an injunction to prevent further use of your patent, or (3) obtain a court order for the destruction of any materials produced that infringe on your rights. This, however, can be a very expensive and time-consuming process, which may prohibit a small business from enforcing its rights.

A patent granted in Canada or the United States provides you with no protection outside the country in which it was originally granted. To obtain protection in other countries, you must register your patent in each country within the time limit permitted by law (typically one year from your initial application). You can apply for a foreign patent either from within Canada via the Canadian Patent Office, or directly through the patent office of the country or countries concerned. Under the terms of the Patent Cooperation Treaty, it is possible to file for a patent in as many as 43 countries, including the United States, Japan, and most of Europe, by completing a single, standardized application that can be filed in Canada. Ask your patent agent about these procedures before you decide to file in another country.

You should realize that holding a patent on a worthy idea does not necessarily mean commercial success. For example, Mich Delaquis and Fred Coakes (Entrepreneurs in Action #25) developed a set of state-of-the-art, self-draining cookware. They have secured patents in the United States and Canada for the locking mechanism on the lid of their pots and have invested virtually all of their savings and a good portion of their families' and friends' savings in developing the concept. Even though they have managed to interest a number of people in demonstrating their product, they still need to raise another $100,000 to get the cookware sets produced in Hong Kong, and are still a long way from making a profit. In fact, the odds are that they will never turn the corner.

An invention succeeds by acceptance in the marketplace. Your patent may be perfectly valid and properly related to your invention but commercially worthless. Thousands of patents are issued each year that fall into this category. A patent does not necessarily contribute to the economic success of an invention. In some high-technology fields, for example, innovations can become obsolete long before a patent is issued, effectively making the patent worthless.

Holding a patent may improve your profitability by keeping similar products off the market, giving you an edge. But there is no guarantee you will be able to prevent all competition. In fact, disclosing your idea in a patent might open the way for a competitor to steal your concept and introduce an imitation or "knock-off" of your product. Litigation, if it becomes necessary, can require considerable financial resources, and the outcome is by no means assured. A high percentage of patent infringements challenged in court result in decisions unfavourable to the patent holder.

However, there are many instances where patenting a product concept or idea has led to commercial success. Hermann Fruhm (Entrepreneurs in Action #26) has watched sales of his Megapro multi-bit screwdriver soar to over $40 million over the last 10 years and he has yet to take his invention to the retail consumer market. Not bad for a guy who started as a keyboard player in a rock band.

Even more impressive has been the market performance of Ron Foxcroft's pea-less whistle, the Fox 40, illustrated in Entrepreneurs in Action #27. Foxcroft developed the whistle after his regular whistle failed to blow while he was refereeing a key basketball game during a pre-Olympic tournament in Brazil. To date his company has sold almost 100 million whistles in 126 countries around the world. However, it has also spent $750,000 registering dozens of patents and trademarks in an effort to protect Foxcraft's

Key points ·········· BENEFITS OF A PATENT SEARCH ···········

If you are a small businessperson a patent search can help you:
- Identify trends and developments in a particular field of technology
- Discover new products that you may be able to license from the patentee or use without needing a licence
- Find information that keeps you from duplicating the research
- Identify unproductive areas of inquiry by reading about the current state of the art
- Keep track of the work of a particular individual or company by seeing what patents they have been granted
- Find a solution to a technical problem you may have
- Gain new ideas for further research in a particular field

Source: "Summary of benefits of a patent search" — adapted and reproduced as "Key Points: Benefits of a Patent Search." Reproduced with the permission of the Minister of Public Works and Government Services Canada, 2002.

25 Entrepreneurs in action

Feeling the Strain

POT INVENTORS REFUSE TO GIVE UP ON A DREAM

Take two [Winnipeg] east-end boys who made their living in a city snowmobile plant, lock them in a basement for three years and what do you get?

For Mich Delaquis and Fred Coakes, the answer is a state-of-the-art, self-draining cookware set.

Along the way, the two men exhausted their life savings and a sizable portion of their family's and friends', were knee-deep in flawed designs, fruitlessly wore out welcome mats at city banks, and were turned away by every cookware manufacturer in North America. . . .

What Delaquis and Coakes have produced is a set of pots and pans that are self-draining and with lids that lock on tight.

The design is simple. When cooking, the straining holes are covered. When it's time to strain, you line up the arrows on the lid with a matching arrow on the handle and turn clockwise; this locks the lid and exposes the holes.

The products are heavy-duty stainless steel with a thick bottom. The larger pots and pans come with an extra handle, making straining easier. . . .

Delaquis and Coakes are your typical entrepreneurs. Delaquis is the tinkerer; Coakes, the hustler and deal-maker. They saw a need and went about their way to find a product to fill that need.

Delaquis remembers the day three years ago when, still single and living on his own, he scalded his hand while straining a pot of pasta.

"I didn't have a strainer and I had to do it with just lifting the lid a little bit," Delaquis said. "The idea popped into my head that it would be a lot easier to do this if there was a strainer already inside the pot."

It was an idea that wouldn't go away. He went to Coakes, who was then head of the receiving department at Polaris, and told him of his plan.

They went into Coakes' basement and they tinkered. First, using snips and sheet metal, they tried to make their own pots and lids.

Then they concentrated on just designing the lid.

Their first design incorporated a spinning disc and a spring mechanism under the lid.

"The first five manufacturers we showed it to said it couldn't be made," said Coakes, 28. "We had to start all over again."

Along the way, the pair took a 10-week small-business course from the Canada Business Service Centre. Then they found a helpful lawyer and an accountant.

Even when they came up with what they believed was a sure thing, they couldn't find anyone in North America to make it.

They secured patents in the United States and Canada for their locking mechanism and got the name trademarked, but 14 manufacturers turned them away.

"They either said it wouldn't work or they were too busy," Coakes said. . . .

It cost them $30,000 just to get the moulds designed.

"A year ago, I told Mich we've got to start selling some of these and stop writing all these cheques," said Coakes, who now sells Yellow Pages advertising for MTS Advanced.

© MARC GALLANT/WINNIPEG FREE PRESS. REPRINTED WITH PERMISSION

But don't ask the pair to do a commercial for the Canadian banking industry. They've put $77,000 into the project to date and they need another $100,000 to make the minimum 1,250 sets the Hong Kong manufacturer will produce on a first order. All of that has been money from their own savings and that of family and friends.

"We'd be nowhere if it wasn't for the support and help from our family and friends," Delaquis said.

"One banker had the nerve to tell me that he so admired my tenacity he was certain I'd be a millionaire one day," Coakes said. "I told him I didn't need any lip service." . . . .

It's not over for Coakes and Delaquis. They're confident they'll find the investors necessary to bring the first 500 sets to market in February. Once the sales take off, they're planning on larger pots and smaller pans.

After that, they will concentrate on direct marketing, with infomercials in the United States and trade shows. Then they'll go retail.

And Delaquis is not finished.
"I've got an idea or two for some other products."

Source: Aldo Santin, "Pot Inventors Refuse to Give Up on a Dream," © *Winnipeg Free Press*, November 20, 1998, pp. B3–B4. Reprinted with permission.

invention, and in 2001 was involved in 11 infringement cases against other firms who are either making a cheaper version of the Fox 40, selling an identical product under another name, or are just passing a cheaper imitation off as a genuine Fox 40 whistle.

Bob Dickie of Spark Innovations Inc. has built his whole business around patentable products. He holds 80 patents for his inventions and thinks patent protection is crucial to business success these days. Dickie's first product was the FlatPlug, billed as the first innovation in electrical plug design in 75 years. The FlatPlug lies flat against the wall, unlike a conventional electrical plug that sticks out perpendicular to the wall. As a result, it doesn't waste space behind furniture and is more difficult for children to pry out. Dickie got the idea when he saw his daughter reach through her crib bars for a conventional plug. FlatPlug is protected by eight U.S. and worldwide patents. Even the package — a cardboard sleeve that keeps the extension cord and the plug in place — is patented.

Dickie has a number of strict criteria that he feels a product idea should have to meet commercial potential:

- **It must be 10 times better** Rather than evolutionary improvements in product design, he looks for concepts with enough of a "story" to make distribution channels take serious notice.

- **It must be patentable** "If we can't get a patent, the business is absolutely dead," says Dickie.

- **It must be a mass-production item** High-volume products have a higher turnover, reducing much of the risk of holding inventory.

- **It should be smaller than a bread box** Small items are easier to make and less costly to design, package, and transport.

- **It must lend itself to distribution through existing channels** Going through established market lines speeds the acceptance of a new product.

- **It should have no government involvement** Spark Innovations stays away from products that are motivated by or are dependent on government support at any level.

- **It must be useful** Dickie works only with products that have long-term, practical usefulness. No novelties, fads, or games.[1]

COMMERCIALIZING YOUR PATENT

Once you have taken steps to protect your idea, you will have to give some thought to the best way to market it and hopefully turn a profit. There are a number of possible options.

- Setting up your own business like the individuals profiled in the Entrepreneurs in Action examples is the option that usually comes to mind. It allows you to retain full control of your idea but also means you assume all the risk.

- Another possibility is to license the invention. With a licence you grant one or more individuals the right to manufacture and sell your innovation in exchange for royalties. The licence can apply generally or only to a specific market or geographic region, as long as you have obtained patent protection for that area.

---

1. Adapted from Ellen Roseman, "Spark of Genius," *The Globe and Mail*, September 26, 1994.

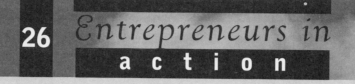

26 Entrepreneurs in action

Invention Sweet Music for Ex-City Rocker

When Hermann Fruhm played keyboards with local rock band Mood Jga Jga, its biggest hit was "Gimme My Money."

Now Fruhm is singing that song for real as gross sales of his Megapro "world's greatest multi-bit screwdriver" soar to $40 million.

"We're not rich yet, but we're on our way," said Fruhm, with nearly two million Megapro screwdrivers already sold worldwide and patent protection in 16 countries.

That's with sales mostly to the tradesman and industrial market. Fruhm is getting set to take his invention to the retail market, which is at least 10 times larger. . . .

"My goal, my dream — and this is no joke — is to put a Megapro into every kitchen drawer, every weekend warrior toolbox, in North America and Europe," said the ex-Winnipegger from his office in New Westminster, B.C.

"I had dropped my screw bits once too often," said Fruhm, explaining how he came to build a better multi-bit screwdriver. "You know. You had to dump the screw bits into your hand, find the one you wanted, then funnel them into the hollow handle."

In fact, that prototype of the multi-bit screwdriver, originally called the Uni-driver, was patented by another Canadian, George Cluthe of Waterloo, Ontario. "For some reason, Canada is the land of multi-bit screwdrivers. Don't ask me why," said Fruhm.

The Cluthe design, patented in 1967, is the screwdriver with the orange handle and the spring-loaded cap that lifts up and swings away to the side. Screw bits rattle around inside the hollow handle.

Fruhm had moved to Vancouver in 1980 because his then-band, Crowcuss, wanted to reunite there for a shot at the larger West Coast market. Four band members did relocate, but the band never reunited.

Fruhm spent the next couple of years playing piano with West Coast bands, then realized his wife, Marilyn . . . and their two young sons needed a more stable home. So he got a day job at Acklands-Granger, the tool and building material supplier for the industrial market.

In his spare time, Fruhm tinkered with Cluthe's screwdriver design.

"I started thinking about this, started making some sketches," he said. "I just had this epiphany one day."

So he got parts like Plexiglas tubing from a hobby shop, and started building the "retractable cartridge" for a multi-bit screwdriver. "After I built the prototype, I became absolutely passionate in believing this was a viable, commercial product."

He patented his 15-in-one screwdriver in 1993. At the public library, he scanned the Thomas Registry, which lists every manufacturer in the United States, and looked up screwdriver makers and found someone to build Megapro.

The retractable cartridge, located inside the screwdriver handle, is the main feature. A carousel of screw bits lifts out of the handle almost as if on a hydraulic cushion of air.

Then, when pushing the carousel back inside the handle, the cartridge makes "this wonderful clicking sound," as Fruhm puts it, as it snaps shut. That clicking sound is also patented.

MELVYN KSIONZEK/WINNIPEG FREE PRESS

Fruhm has a lot less hair today but a lot more money than when he played keyboards with the '70s band Mood Jga Jga.

Another Megapro feature that handymen will appreciate is the rotating red cap when the cap is closed. That allows the handler to push down on the screwdriver "for two-fisted power drive when you have to bear down to torque a screw," Fruhm explained.

It also has a rotating front bushing, or collar, that allows a user to line up the screwdriver and hold it in place and not have to constantly regrip the screwdriver handle.

There are seven double-ended bits in the 15-in-one screwdriver. The 15th bit is the socket head itself, which is a quarter-inch hex chuck, and industry standard for such things as sheet metal screws. There is also a magnetized version of Megapro.

"There is no shortage of bad multi-bit screwdrivers out there," said Fruhm. One design on the market has screw bits in slots covered by a rotating cap, but the bit falls out when turned upside down. Another design has the bits slotted into the handle. . . .

Fruhm feels lucky. Many kids from bar bands have trouble finding an occupation if music doesn't pan out.

"I was so smitten with music when I was 16. It was all-consuming. The downside is you don't go to college or university, and have nothing to fall back on," he said. . . .

"When I was 23 years old, I wanted to be a rock 'n' roll musician. I never dreamed I would be in the hand tool business," said Fruhm, 54. "Sometimes I still pinch myself. This is crazy." . . . .
(www.megaproscrewdrivers.com)

Source: Bill Redekop, "Invention sweet music for ex-city rocker," *Winnipeg Free Press*, April 17, 2003, p. A-1.

- A third option is to sell your patent. By selling your patent you give up all rights to the idea in return for a lump sum of money. However, then you don't have to worry about whether the product becomes a commercial success.

WATCH OUT FOR INVENTION SCAMS

Many people with a new idea immediately start looking for a company that they think will buy or license their idea. Any number of companies advertise on radio, TV, or in magazines, offering to help you patent your idea and market it for you. They offer their assistance as a "one-stop" do-it-all-for-you ticket to success for your great new idea. Most of these offers are outright scams. These firms generally follow a three-step process:

1. They send you a free kit with a pre-signed *confidentiality* or *non-disclosure* agreement and some general information about the services they provide.

2. Next, they offer to do a marketing evaluation of the potential for your idea. This may cost several hundred dollars.

3. They then present a package offering to patent your invention and promote your idea by submitting it to manufacturers, potential licensees, and industry in general. This time the fee can be anywhere from $3,000 to $10,000 or higher.

Only after a year of two of unfulfilled promises and zero activity do you begin to realize that you might have been scammed, but by then it is too late. It's best to avoid these kinds of operators in the first place. The truth is that commercializing a new idea is a long, complicated process that takes time, energy, knowledge, and persistence. No one can guarantee you success.

REGISTERING YOUR TRADEMARK

A *trademark* is a word, symbol, picture, design, or combination of these that distinguishes your goods and services from those of others in the marketplace. A trademark might also be thought of as a "brand name" or "identifier" that can be used to distinguish the products of your firm. For example, both the name "McDonald's" and the symbol of the golden arches are (among others) registered trademarks of the McDonald's Corporation.

To *register* a trademark means to file it with a government agency for the purpose of securing the following rights and benefits:

1. Exclusive permission to use the brand name or identifier in Canada

2. The right to sue anyone you suspect of infringing on your trademark to recover lost profits on sales made under your trade name, and for other damages and costs

3. The basis for filing an application in another country should you wish to export your product

27 Entrepreneurs in action

Defensive Strategy

Summer in Indianapolis can be extremely hot, but it wasn't the temperature that had me on edge as I walked across the floor of the gymnasium to referee a Pan-American basketball game. I was clutching one of the only two operating prototypes of my new Fox 40 pea-less whistle. We had spent three-and-a-half years and $150,000 in production, and the whistle had never been heard by anyone other than our small development group. Would the new whistle work when it counted most?

The idea for a pea-less whistle came to me in 1984 after I needed a police escort out of a gymnasium in Brazil when my regular whistle failed to blow at a crucial point in a pre-Olympic basketball game. Now, as I crossed the floor for the start of the Pan-Am game, I made a mental note of where the exits, security staff and police were located—in case my new invention failed to utter a sound.

The whistle not only worked, it was so loud and clear that it startled everyone in the gym. When the games were over, I came home with orders for 20,000 Fox 40 pea-less whistles, and the funds to put my invention into full production.

Today, we have sold close to 100 million whistles in 126 countries. The Fox 40 whistle is used in almost every professional and amateur league and sports association worldwide, and we have developed variations for dog trainers, hunters, hikers, campers, rescue workers and police departments. We know the whistle works, it's accepted and it sells. Now we're fighting another battle—one that has cost us legal fees in the hundreds of thousands of dollars—with no end in sight. Fox 40, like many companies with useful new products, faces the scourge of imitators supplying cheap rip-offs. But I've learned that with some foresight and planning, any inventor can nip this problem in the bud with proper patent and trademark protection.

When you look for money for a new invention, your bank manager and potential investors always ask those same two questions: 1) Do you have a business plan, and 2) Do you have a patent? Although you need both to raise money to bring your product to market, most businesspeople never read the full business plan; even fewer understand how patents and trademarks work, or how they protect your product. For the record, patents describe exactly what your products are. Trademarks describe who you are and what your company is all about.

Thousands of patents are filed every year. Few commercial patents ever reach the marketplace and those that do are successful only if the patent is written properly and the product marketed aggressively. Patent searches must be conducted worldwide to protect your invention from infringement by others, and also to protect you from infringing on other patents. The process is incredibly detailed and far too complicated for novices to attempt on their own. Some companies advertise that they can raise money for your invention or help get your invention to market. Get references and check them out thoroughly. Many inventors have learned very expensive lessons trying to get to market using the services of these companies.

I knew we needed help navigating the patent process. The late Chuck Shepherd, from Oakville, Ontario, was a guru in the field of developing and patenting new products and ideas. But when I first showed him my concept, he immediately declined to take on the project. He soon changed his mind, not because of the whistle itself, but because he found out I was the guy who owned Fluke Transport Group, the trucking company with the slogan, "If it's on time, it's a Fluke." He said if I could be successful with that slogan, I could probably sell a pea-less whistle.

We protected our whistle with dozens of patents. Chuck made sure that the technical description of the Fox 40 pea-less whistle was comprehensive and all encompassing. When the whistle design was complete, he took me to meet Stan Rogers of Rogers & Scott, Patent Attorneys, in Oakville. Chris Scott soon joined the team and together we filed world patents for the Fox 40 whistle.

This team prepared me to take my invention to market. They told me that having a patent wouldn't make a product successful. Success would only come from making a better whistle and marketing it more aggressively than the competition. It was simple yet sound advice.

Patents — valuable assets that can be sold or licensed if necessary — are important and are absolutely necessary if you have a product with a world market or a product that can be copied easily. But I soon learned that I also needed trademark protection. Patents have an expiry date and others can patent or introduce similar patents.

Trademarks, however, are yours and provide greater protection against new products. Products are recognized by their name, and as the product becomes more popular so does the value of the trademark. I have never had a customer call me and order two dozen of a specific patent number. They ask for two dozen black Fox 40 pea-less whistles. I needed to protect the name.

My team had prepared me for this phase of our development and had filed trademarks in all the markets where we would be doing business. I often say that there is a great deal of Chuck Shepherd in the Fox 40 whistle and there was a great deal of Fox 40 in Chuck Shepherd. I owe a great deal to him and to Stan Rogers and Chris Scott.

We have now spent over $750,000 on patent and trademark registrations to protect our product and our name. We are currently involved with 11 infringement cases against the Fox 40 patents or trademarks. These patent and trademark infringements usually originate from one of three sources:

1. Competition who have the capability of making a similar product

2. Companies who see that a large profit can be made by selling a similar product and have the resources to fight us in court

3. Companies who get in and out of the market fast, passing their cheap imitation off as our product

These imitators find it tougher to beat a charge of trademark infringement than one of patent infringement. Companies can argue that their pea-less whistle is different than our pea-less whistle or that their patent does not infringe on ours. But no one can say that they own the Fox 40 pea-less whistle.

Imitation may be the highest form of flattery, but fighting it without the proper protection can also be extremely costly. When all is said and done, our trademarks provide the best long-term protection for our products. My best advice is to patent for design protection and trademark for revenue protection. (www.fox40whistle.com)

Source: Ron Foxcroft, "Defensive Strategy," *PROFIT* (www.profitguide.com/firstperson/F1_foxcroft.html), July 12, 2001. Reprinted with permission.

To be registerable, a trademark must be distinctive and not so similar in appearance, sound, or concept to a trademark already registered, or pending registration, as to be confused with it. For example, the following trademarks would not be registerable: "Cleanly Canadian" for a soft drink (too close to Clearly Canadian, a fruit-flavoured mineral water); "Extendo" for a utility knife (too close to Exacto).

The value of a trademark lies in the goodwill the market attaches to it and the fact that consumers will ask for your brand with the expectation of receiving the same quality product or service as previously. Therefore, unlike a patent, a trademark should be registered only if you have some long-term plans for it that will result in an accumulation of goodwill.

It is possible for you to use a trademark without registering it. Registration is not mandatory and unregistered marks have legal status. But registration is advised for most commonly used identifiers, since it does establish immediate, obvious proof of ownership, particularly if the business is looking to expand geographically.

Failing to properly register your trademarks can sometimes lead to future problems. Robert Arthurs of the True North Clothing Company in Entrepreneurs in Action #28 learned this lesson the hard way. Despite consulting with a lawyer and a government agency, his company's failure to do appropriate due diligence and search out previous registrations of the "True North" trade name ended up costing it a lot of money in legal and other fees. In the end the company had to buy the rights to use the name from the registered owner despite assurances that the term was part of the "public domain" and available for use by anyone.

HOW TO REGISTER YOUR TRADEMARK

In Canada it is possible for you to register your trademark before you actually use it, but the mark will not be validated until it is actually put into service. Registration of a trademark involves the following steps:

1. **A search of previous and pending registrations** As with a patent, a search should be conducted to determine that your trademark does not conflict with others already in use. The search can be conducted at the CIPO Trade-marks Branch in Gatineau, Quebec, where a public inventory of all registered trademarks and pending applications is maintained. You can also conduct a search electronically the CIPO Web site.

28 *Entrepreneurs in* action

The Name Game

We began like so many other young companies, merrily building our company and brand name. Many years and hundreds of thousands of dollars went into laying the groundwork for our name "True North Clothing Company." And like many other young companies, we assumed we were protected against infringing on someone else's trademark. I have since learned that you should never assume.

When we began our company in February 1992, my business partner spoke with a government agency in Hull, Quebec, regarding the use of trademarks. We were informed that because the phrase "True North" is part of Canada's national anthem, it is public domain and available for anyone's use. Beyond that, without the money for extensive legal advice, we could only briefly consult a lawyer. We were assured that by doing a "poor man's trademark"—sending the designs to ourselves by registered mail and not opening them unless there was a dispute—we were effectively protecting our interest in the name.

In 1996, believing our trademark secure, we started an aggressive advertising campaign in *The Globe & Mail* mail-order section, featuring our new shirt "True North Strong & Free."

After only two days of advertising, we received by registered mail a cease-and-desist letter from lawyers representing a company in Ontario. The company claimed to own the name, and ordered us to stop using their trademark. We spent the next three years involved in faxes, phone calls and face-to-face meetings (with and without lawyers present) in an attempt to come to a peaceful resolution between the Ontario company and ourselves. But it seemed that no matter what solution was proposed, we could not reach an agreement. Our costs were rising. We even made a [five-figure] purchase of a competitor's

company and trademark as a safeguard, in case we were forced to stop using "True North" and needed another name. Our legal costs were also into five figures. It reached the point where our lawyer said, "I can't keep taking your money anymore . . . you guys just can't take these legal bills."

It was clear our competitor had much deeper pockets than we did, and we could no longer afford to fight a strict enforcement of the cease and desist order. We decided to end the dispute by purchasing the trademark from the Ontario company.

So what happened to "public domain"? To this day, nobody has been able to provide us with an answer. Even representatives of the federal government, which is responsible for trademark legislation, have been at a loss for a clear explanation. And over the years, we have received so much mixed and conflicting information from lawyers that we have yet to see one firm support advice another firm has given.

If there is a lesson here, it is that trademarks and copyright should be taken more seriously. We live in an age of corporate branding, and companies have become more vigilant than ever in protecting their trademarks. But more information regarding trademark and copyright laws is available to entrepreneurs today than was available to us, both on the Internet and in libraries across Canada. Many of these resources are absolutely free. My advice to up-and-coming companies is to check out as much material as you can locate. Because even when you think you're right, you can't always win.

Source: Robert Arthurs, "The Name Game," *PROFIT* (www.profitguide.com/firstperson/F1_arthurs.html), December 7, 2001. Reprinted with permission.

---

2. **An application to register your trademark** This involves filing an application for registration of your trademark.

Once your application is received, it is published in the *Trade-marks Journal* to see if anyone opposes your registration.

Even though registering a trademark is relatively simple compared with applying for a patent, it is recommended that you consult a trademark agent who is registered with the CIPO Trade-marks Branch.

MAINTAINING AND POLICING YOUR TRADEMARK

It normally takes about a year from the date of application for a trademark to be registered. Registration is effective for 15 years, and may be renewed for a series of 15-year terms as long as the mark is still in use.

As with a patent, it is up to the owner of the trademark to police its use, since the government provides no assistance in the enforcement of trademark rights. Some firms have gone to considerable lengths in an effort to enforce what they feel are their legal rights. For example, The Brick Warehouse, an Edmonton-based national chain of furniture stores, sued Ted and Cynthia Brick of the family-owned Brick's Fine Furniture in Winnipeg to get them to stop using the name "Brick" for their store. This was despite the fact that the Brick family began operating their provincially registered Winnipeg outlet in 1969, while The Brick began operating under that name in Edmonton only in 1977 and was incorporated federally in 1987. After four years of legal battles and hundreds of thousands of dollars in legal fees, the sides finally agreed to an out-of-court settlement. Part of the agreement is that both stores will display a sign at their entrances stating that there is no association between The Brick or The Brick Warehouse and Brick's Fine Furniture.[2]

More recently, in another David vs Goliath situation, Starbucks Corp., the Seattle-based multinational coffee retailer, threatened legal action for trademark infringement against a small cafe/restaurant called HaidaBucks Cafe in Masset on the Queen Charlotte Islands, off the coast of British Columbia. Starbucks demanded that the owners of the small local cafe change its name and logo because these were creating confusion in the marketplace by being too similar to their own, even though there are no Starbucks coffee shops in Masset. The owners refused to comply and with the assistance of a high-powered Victoria law firm, the exchange of correspondence and a considerable outpouring of public support appear to have won the battle. HaidaBucks eventually received a letter from Starbucks that concluded, "Starbucks considers this matter closed."[3]

Similarly, Lululemon Athletica, a Vancouver-based clothing chain, has accused Madmax Worldwide Resources Inc. of selling a copycat version of its popular line of "yoga-inspired" clothing in Vancouver-area Costco stores and at a number of smaller retailers. While this situation has not yet been resolved, Chip Wilson, the founder of Lululemon, said he is not "hung up" on the trademark infringement but is acting only because his lawyer said that failing to protect the trademark could mean losing his rights.[4]

Registration of a trademark in Canada provides no protection of your trademark in other countries. If you are involved with or contemplating exporting to any other country, you should consider registering your trademark in that country as well.

MARKING REQUIREMENTS

The Trade-marks Act does not contain any marking requirements. However, trademark owners can indicate their registration through the use of certain symbols, namely ® (registered), ™ (trademark), SM (service mark), MD (marque déposée), or MC (marque de commerce). Although the act does not require the use of these symbols, it is advisable to use them.

OBTAINING COPYRIGHT

A *copyright* gives you the right to preclude others from reproducing or copying your original published work. Materials protected by copyright include books, leaflets, periodicals and contributions to periodicals, lectures, sermons, musical or dramatic compositions, maps, works of art, photographs, drawings of a scientific or technical nature, motion pictures, sound recordings, databases, and computer programs. A copyright exists for the duration of your life plus 50 years following your death.

HOW TO OBTAIN A COPYRIGHT

In Canada, there is no legal requirement that your work be registered in order to obtain copyright; it is automatically acquired on creation of an original work. Nevertheless, you may wish to apply for voluntary registration. When your work has been registered, a certificate is issued that can, if necessary, be used in court to establish your ownership of the work.

2. R. Pederson, "Legal Battle of the Bricks Finally Ends; Sides Agree to Coexist," *Edmonton Journal*, June 20, 1992, p. F1.
3. HaidaBucks Cafe (www.haidabuckscafe.com/news.htm), accessed March 7, 2004.
4. P. Brieger, "When Mediation Fails, Call Your Lawyer: Yoga Clothier Files Trademark Lawsuit," *National Post*, September 25, 2003, p. FP.01.F.

You can register a copyright by completing the required application form and sending it to CIPO's Copyright Office along with the appropriate fee. You do not need to send a copy of your work with the application but you may need to send copies to the National Library of Canada. The registration process typically takes around four weeks but may be longer if amendments are required.

INDICATING COPYRIGHT

There is no requirement to mark your work under the Copyright Act. However, you may choose to mark it with the symbol ©, your name and the year of first publication of the work, for example, © John Doe, 2001. You may use this mark even if you have not formally registered your work with the Copyright Office.

PROTECTION PROVIDED BY COPYRIGHT

Your copyright enables you to control the copying and dissemination of your own works. This includes publishing, producing, reproducing, and performing your material. As with patents and trademarks, the responsibility for policing your copyright rests with you.

It is important to understand some of the limitations of copyright protection as well. For example, for purposes of copyright protection, the term "computer program" refers to "a set of instructions or statements, expressed, fixed, embodied or stored in any manner, that is to be used directly or indirectly in a computer in order to bring about a specific result." This means that a specific computer program such as Microsoft Excel can be protected as a literary work but not the idea of spreadsheet programs in general. In addition, any accompanying documentation for a program, such as a user's guide, is considered a separate work and must be registered separately.

Unlike patents and trademarks, a copyright in Canada provides simultaneous protection in most other countries of the world.

REGISTERING YOUR INDUSTRIAL DESIGN

An industrial design comprises the features of shape, configuration, pattern, or ornament applied to a finished article made by hand, tool, or machine. This may be, for example, the shape of a table or chair, or the shape of the ornamentation of a knife or a spoon. The design must have features that appeal to the eye and be substantially original. Registering your design gives you exclusive rights to the design and enables you to prevent others from making, importing, renting, or selling any article on which the design has been registered and to which the design or a design not substantially different has been applied. However, no prior disclosure of the design is allowed, including publication in a college or university thesis. Unlike trademark and copyright protection, you can make no legal claim of ownership and have *no legal protection against imitation unless your design has been registered.*

HOW TO REGISTER YOUR INDUSTRIAL DESIGN

You can file your own application for industrial design registration; however, it is generally recommended to hire a patent agent to prepare and follow through on your application. An application for an industrial design must contain:

- a completed application form
- at least one photograph or drawing of the design

Your application will be examined to ensure that it is original and registerable. It cannot be the same or similar to a design already applied to a similar article of manufacture. Following this assessment the examiner will either approve the application or issue a report indicating what further information or amendments may be required. You have four months to reply to the report. This process can take up to a year, but once registered, designs are valid for 10 years from that date.

MARKING YOUR PRODUCT

You do not have to mark your design to indicate that it has been registered but marking does give you some extra protection. The proper mark is a capital "D" inside a circle along with your name or an abbreviation of it on the article itself, its label, or its packaging. If your product is marked in this way, a court may award a remedy of some kind such as financial compensation if someone is found to be infringing on or violating your design. Otherwise the court can merely issue an injunction to forbid the other party from using your design.

PROTECTION PROVIDED BY INDUSTRIAL DESIGN REGISTRATION

As with other forms of intellectual property, you may take legal action against anyone who infringes on your design in Canada. As the proprietor of the registered design, however, you have exclusive right to use it and may sell all or some of these rights to other people or authorize them to use the design, subject to certain conditions. These rights, however, relate only to Canada. To obtain similar rights in other countries you must apply for them in each country separately.

PROTECTING INTEGRATED CIRCUIT TOPOGRAPHIES

The circuits incorporated into an integrated circuit (IC) are embodied in a three-dimensional hill-and-valley configuration called a topography. These designs are protected by the Integrated Circuit Topography Act. IC products, commonly called "microchips" or "semiconductor chips" are incorporated into a variety of consumer and industrial products. The protection associated with the design of a topography is entirely distinct from that of any computer program embodied in the chip. Computer programs are subject to protection under the Copyright Act.

WHAT PROTECTION DOES THE ACT PROVIDE?

The legislation provides exclusive rights in regard to:

- Reproduction of a protected topography or any substantial part of it
- Manufacture of an IC product incorporating the topography or any substantial part of it
- Importation or commercial exploitation of a topography, or of an IC product that embodies a protected topography or any substantial part of it
- Importation or commercial exploitation of an industrial article that incorporates an IC product that embodies a protected topography

The Act provides for a full range of civil remedies, including injunctions and exemplary damages. Protection for registered integrated circuit topographies is provided for approximately 10 years.

HOW TO PROTECT AN IC TOPOGRAPHY

To protect an IC topography you must apply to CIPO's Registrar of Topographies. Applications for "commercially exploited" topographies must be filed within two years of the date of first commercial exploitation anywhere. The application may be rejected if the topography was first exploited outside Canada. Owners must be Canadian or nationals of countries having reciprocal protection agreements with Canada.

FOR MORE INFORMATION ON INTELLECTUAL PROPERTY

Further information on the protection of intellectual property can be obtained from:

Canadian Intellectual Property Office
Industry Canada
50 Victoria St., Room C-229
Place du Portage, Phase 1
Gatineau, Quebec K1A 0C9
(cipo.gc.ca)
Tel: (819) 997-1936 or 1-900-565-2476 ($3 flat rate per call)
or contact your local Canada Business Service Centre.

The deadlines for filing, the length of time for which protection is provided, and the current registration fees for several types of intellectual property are summarized in Table 9.1.

TABLE 9.1	INFORMATION ABOUT PROTECTION OF INTELLECTUAL PROPERTY IN CANADA

Type	Application Deadline	Period of Coverage	Government Fees for Small Entities	
Patents	File within 1 year of publication (file before publication for most other countries)	20 years from filing of application	Filing fee	$200
			Examination fee	$400
			Allowance fee (Grant)	$150
			Maintenance fee	
			Years 2, 3 & 4	$ 50
			Years 5 to 9	$100
			Years 10 to 14	$125
			Years 15 to 19	$225
Trademarks	(None)	15 years; renewable indefinitely	Filing fee	$250–300
			Registration fee	$200
Copyright	(None)	50 years plus life of author	Registration fee	$50–65
Industrial Designs	File within 12 months of publication	10 years from date of registration	Examination fee	$400 plus $10 for each page over 10 pages
			Maintenance of registration fee	$350

CONCLUSION

As we have discussed, in addition to various *tangible* assets such as land, buildings, and equipment, your business may also own certain *intangible* assets, such as patents, trademarks, and copyrights. These can be just as important as, or even more important than, your tangible assets. And like tangible assets, with the permission of their owner they can be bought, sold, licensed, or used by someone else.

Ideas that are not patentable and are not otherwise protected may be protected by contract law either by means of a written *non-disclosure* agreement or by treating them as *trade secrets*. This can be done by taking every precaution to keep valuable knowledge a secret and/or by placing specific provisions in any agreement you may have with your employees that they will neither disclose to anyone else nor use for their own purposes any trade secrets they may acquire while in your employ. The advantages of this type of protection may be even greater than those of patent protection. The success of this approach depends on your ability to control the access of outsiders to the information, as there are no *legal rights* in a trade secret. Typically, once confidential information has been publicly disclosed, it becomes very difficult to enforce any rights to it.

Video Case #10

···················· **Protecting Your Product** ····················

Summary

Entrepreneurs and inventors dream of the fortunes they may make from their unique products, but how can they ensure that they protect their products from copycats? Patents are a guarantee that your product cannot be cheaply duplicated — right? Wrong, according to one of the oldest law firms specializing in patents in Canada. Trevor Downey of Pro-Lab Product Development, Ron Foxcroft of Fox 40 International Inc., and Roy Mayer of Roy Mayer Public Relations share the stories of the hard lessons learned in obtaining and protecting their patent rights.

Questions for Discussion

1. Were you aware that having a patent did not necessarily protect a product from cheaper duplication by competitors?

2. Does the likelihood of patent infringement make it impossible for small entrepreneurs to start a business on the basis of a new invention or idea, when they may not have the resources to protect their legal interests?

3. What can you do to protect yourself from copycats?

Video Case #11

························· **Hockey Lites** ·························

Summary

Jim Boone had a great new idea — or so he thought. He wanted to light up the goal net instead of the goal light when the puck went into the net in a hockey game. When Boone went to patent his idea, he found that someone else had the same idea and had patented it already — just four months earlier.

Boone immediately called the patent holder and they created a partnership. Duncan Craig would own the patent and Boone would market the idea for a commission on sales. The two men had differing ideas as to what the end product should look like, but they worked past the differences and developed a prototype that they were able to use in a demonstration to the National Hockey League.

Questions for Discussion

1. Entrepreneurs tend to have a passion for their ideas. Boone and Craig had the same type of idea but there were some strong differences of opinion and a long-distance partnership that they had to deal with. How did they work through these issues?

2. Did Boone apply for a patent, trademark, or copyright? When should each be used?

3. Does the likelihood of patent infringement make it impossible for small entrepreneurs to start a business on the basis of a new invention or idea, when they may not have the resources to protect their legal interests?

4. What can you do to protect yourself from copycats?

Arranging Financing

Quite a number of sources of financing are available to established businesses. However, there are relatively few sources of *seed capital* for ventures that are just getting off the ground and have no track record. Obtaining such capital can require persistence and determination. Usually you must submit a formal proposal to a prospective source of funding in which you outline your needs, plans for the money, the investors' expected return, and a loan repayment schedule. Many financing proposals have to be revised several times before receiving a positive response. In addition, you may have to be prepared to combine financing from several sources to raise all the funds you require.

Two kinds of funds are potentially available to you: *debt* and *equity*.

DEBT FINANCING

Debt financing is borrowing money that must be repaid in full, usually in periodic payments with interest. Three important parameters associated with debt financing are:

1. Amount of principal to be borrowed
2. Interest rate on the loan
3. Maturity date of the loan

Together these three factors determine the extent of your obligation to the creditor. Until the debt has been repaid, the provider of the loan has a legal claim against the assets and cash flows of your business. In many cases the creditor can demand payment at any time and possibly force your business into bankruptcy because of overdue payments.

The *principal* of the loan is the total amount of money you hope to borrow. This could be the difference between the amount shown on your estimate of your required start-up funding (as illustrated back in Figure 7.1) and the sum you are personally able to provide to get your business started.

The *interest rate* is the "price" you will have to pay for the borrowed funds. In most cases it will be tied to the current *prime rate*. This is generally considered to be the rate of interest that banks charge their best customers — those with the lowest risk. For example, a bank might be prepared to offer loans to a small business for prime plus some fixed percentage, perhaps 3 or 4 per cent. The prime rate may fluctuate somewhat due to periodic decisions by the Bank of Canada, so the effective interest rate on your loan may vary somewhat as well.

The *maturity* of the loan refers to the length of time for which you will obtain the use of the funds. This should coincide with your intended use of the money. Short-term needs require short-term financing. For example, you might use a short-term loan to purchase inventory that you intend to sell within a month or two or to finance some outstanding accounts receivables. A short-term loan such as a *line of credit* typically has to be repaid within a year.

Purchasing a building or a major piece of equipment may require a long-term loan or a *term* loan. This is a loan that will be repaid over an extended period of time, typically several years. The purpose of the loan will determine the maturity period.

The primary sources of debt financing are shareholder loans provided by the owners of the business and operating loans and term loans provided by banks and other financial institutions such as trust companies, Alberta Treasury Branches, and credit unions. Providing some funds as a loan rather than as an equity investment can have some advantages for you as the owner of a small business. The interest payments made to you are income tax deductible by the business and it may be easier to withdraw the money if necessary than if it was tied up in equity.

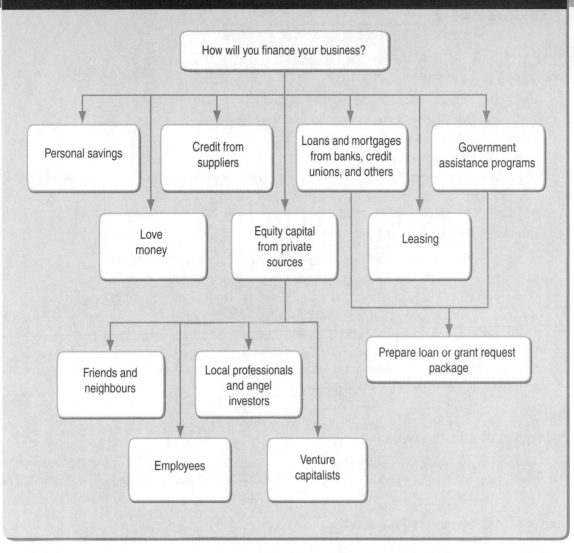

FINANCING

How will you finance your business?

- Personal savings
- Credit from suppliers
- Loans and mortgages from banks, credit unions, and others
- Government assistance programs

- Love money
- Equity capital from private sources
- Leasing

- Friends and neighbours
- Local professionals and angel investors

- Employees
- Venture capitalists

- Prepare loan or grant request package

EQUITY FINANCING

Equity funding is money supplied by yourself or investors in exchange for an ownership position in your business. Unlike debt, equity funding does not need to be repaid. Providers of equity capital forego the opportunity to receive interest and periodic repayment of the funds they have extended to your business; rather, they share in the profits their investment is expected to generate. Other than making your own personal investment, it is not easy to attract other investors to a new business. No matter how sure you are that your business will be successful, others will not necessarily share your confidence and will need to be persuaded to invest in your idea by your enthusiasm and your business plan.

In addition to providing the funds, equity investors will usually demand a voice in how your business is run. This can substantially reduce your ability to run your business as you would like. They expect to receive their return from any dividends that may be paid out periodically from the net profits of the business or, more significantly, from the increased value of the business as it grows and prospers. They expect to be able to sell all or part of their investment for a considerable profit, although the shares of a small private company may have a very limited market.

The most common sources of equity financing for start-up businesses are your own personal savings and your family and friends.

The advantages of debt versus external equity financing from your perspective as owner of the business are summarized in the following Key Points box.

Key points .... DEBT vs EQUITY

Debt

ADVANTAGES OF DEBT FINANCING

- It's useful for meeting a short-term deficit in cash flow.
- You do not have to give up or share control of your business.
- The term of the debt (loan) is generally limited.
- It may be acquired from a variety of lenders. You can shop around.
- The information needed to obtain a loan is generally straightforward and normally incorporated into a business plan.
- Interest paid is tax-deductible.

DISADVANTAGES OF DEBT FINANCING

- It can be difficult to obtain when the project is risky and its success uncertain.
- Taking on more debt than the business needs can be a burden on your cash flows.
- If the funds aren't used properly, it may be difficult for the business to repay the loan.
- If it is a "demand" loan, it can be called by the lender at any time.
- The lender may require you to provide a personal guarantee for the loan.
- Lenders will often insist on certain restrictions being put in to place. For instance, there may be a limit on how much you can draw out of the business in the form of a salary or dividends or the amount you can spend on equipment or other acquisitions without their approval.

Equity

ADVANTAGES OF EQUITY FINANCING

- An appropriate investor can contribute expertise, contacts, and new business as well as money.
- Equity may be the only way to fund high-risk ventures, where the cost of debt could be prohibitive.
- It can be used to fund larger projects with longer time frames.

DISADVANTAGES OF EQUITY FINANCING

- Owner has to give up some ownership and control of the business.
- There is always the danger of incompatibility and disagreement among the investors.
- It is much more difficult to terminate the relationship if disagreements occur.

MAJOR SOURCES OF FUNDS

The major sources of funds for small-business start-ups are personal funds, "love money," banks, government agencies and programs, and venture capital. You may be able to "piece together" the combination of debt and equity funding that you require from a mix of these sources.

PERSONAL FUNDS

The first place to look for money to start your business is your own pocket. This may mean cleaning out your savings account and other investments, selling your second car, postponing your holiday for this year, cashing in your RRSPs, extending your credit cards to the limit, mortgaging the cottage, taking out a second mortgage on the family home, or any other means you may have of raising cash.

"LOVE MONEY"

Once you have scraped together everything you can from your resources and personal savings, the next step is to talk to other people. Additional funds may come from your friends, family, and close personal relations. This is known as "love money."

Recent estimates indicate that, in fact, love money makes up more than 90 per cent of the new business start-up capital in Canada. This personal funding is necessary because banks and other conventional sources usually will not lend money without extensive security. For example, Amanda Harburn, whose case is described in Entrepreneurs in Action #29, was able to launch her Prestige Dance Academy in Calgary only with the help of her parents, largely due to her relative lack of experience and other tangible assets.

29 Entrepreneurs in action

Youth an Obstacle to Being an Entrepreneur

Amanda Harburn is a dancer, a performer, and an artist. She is also a bookkeeper, receptionist, market analyst, manager, master negotiator, teacher, typist and an extremely experienced buffer of floors.

Just 21, Harburn is an entrepreneur — and a very successful one.

Harburn's two-year-old Prestige Dance Academy Inc. in Calgary now provides instruction to more than 200 students.

Giving her business some legs, however, required some fancy footwork.

"Everyone says, 'Yeah, yeah, yeah, we love young entrepreneurs,' but they really don't take you seriously, and they certainly don't want to give you any money," says Harburn. "It's frustrating and discouraging." . . . .

The problem is that in most cases, young entrepreneurs are inexperienced and underestimated — not to mention broke. Harburn got past that particular obstacle with some help from home.

"I ended up taking my business proposal to my parents," says Harburn. "I had looked into banks and different funding programs, but the processes were very long and complex. I probably could have eventually gotten a line of credit, but to be honest, I didn't have the patience. My most significant expenses were my lease and my renovation costs. Since I don't have any inventory, I really didn't require as much capital as some other businesses."

Unfortunately there are fewer options available for young entrepreneurs now than there were just a few years ago, says Margaret Brown, an instructor at the Bissett School of Business at Mount Royal College in Calgary.

"One of the best options for students used to be the Business Development Bank of Canada's interest-free loans for youth, but last year they pulled it," says Brown. "Now most students who need only a few thousand dollars are using lines of credit instead. The best source of financing for young people though is still family and friends.

Groups like the Canadian Youth Business Foundation [CYBF] are picking up the slack in Canada, offering entrepreneurs both financial and intellectual support.

WIL ANDRUSCHAK

continued

Youth an Obstacle to Being an Entrepreneur — continued

The CYBF is a non-profit charitable group that was founded by the CIBC, the Royal Bank, and the Canadian Youth Foundation in 1996.

The foundation has financed almost 1,000 new businesses and assisted more than 2,000 youth through the CYBF loan program. It has created more than 3,000 jobs, and has provided mentoring for about 2,000 entrepreneurs.

"The problem is that usually the young entrepreneur doesn't have experience and they don't have any collateral," says Chris Ransom, a program manager for CYBF. "In my experience, there are so few grants available that they might as well not exist, and the ones they do have are extremely niche-oriented. Approaching financial institutions can be extremely intimidating and discouraging, because often they won't even look at your business plan. Banks are conservative, and they don't like risk."

That is very unfortunate considering the potential impact that these small businesses could have on the economy.

Small- and medium-sized enterprises employ six out of ten Canadians, and they created the bulk of 500,000 new jobs in 2002, according to the Canadian Federation of Independent Business.

"We do a great job of recycling money and creating business to contribute to the economy," says Vivian Woytiuk, chief executive officer of the CYBF. "Whenever you're involved in micro-lending, you're taking a chance and there will be failures, but we've seen some unbelievable successes, too."

Being an entrepreneur is also about a strong work ethic, says Harburn. While she may soon be able to hire on some more help to lighten her workload, she's not there quite yet.

"There are days when I just don't feel like cleaning the floors. But I know if I don't do it, it won't get done, and I take pride in my studio," she says. "When I drive into the parking lot and see my sign, I just say, 'Wow, its really mine,' and then I know it's worth all the long hours and movies missed with my friends. There's no better feeling in the world."

Source: Shannon Sutherland, "Youth an obstacle to being an entrepreneur," *Winnipeg Free Press,* October 20, 2003, p. F4.

The biggest risk with this source of capital is that if your new business fails and the investors lose money, it can create considerable hard feelings among family and friends. This possibility can be reduced if you lay out all the terms and conditions of the investment in advance, just as you would for any other investors. You should explain the nature of your business, your detailed implementation plans, the risks associated with the venture, and other relevant factors. In fact, it is best if you give both yourself and your investors some measure of comfort by translating your understanding into a formal, legal shareholders' agreement. If the money is provided to you as a loan, another important reason for putting it into writing is that if, for some reason, you are unable to repay the money and your investor must write it off, the amount of a properly documented loan becomes a capital loss for income tax purposes and can be offset against any capital gains, thereby providing the investor with the potential for some tax relief from the loss.

This most basic kind of financing is often not enough to get the business started, but it is important for external funding sources to see that you and your family are prepared to invest most of your personal resources in the venture. Without a strong indication of this type of individual commitment, it will be extremely difficult to raise any other money. Why should someone not directly involved in the business risk money in your business if you are not prepared to put your own assets on the line?

BANKS, TRUST COMPANIES, CREDIT UNIONS, AND SIMILAR INSTITUTIONS

Banks and similar institutions are the most popular and widely used external source of funds for new businesses. A visit to the local banker becomes almost a mandatory part of any new venture start-up situation. Banks historically have provided debt financing in the form of self-liquidating, short-term loans to cover small businesses' peak working capital requirements, usually in the form of an *operating loan* or *line of credit.*

An operating loan extends credit to you up to a prearranged limit *on an ongoing basis*, to cover your day-to-day expenses such as accounts receivable, payroll, inventory carrying costs, office supplies, and utility bills. If you happen to be in a highly seasonal or cyclical business, for example, such a line of credit can be used to purchase additional inventory in anticipation of your peak selling period. An operating loan is intended to *supplement your basic working capital*. An operating loan can also be used to bridge unexpected cash flow interruptions and/or shortfalls. It may also give you the ability to take advantage of supplier discounts for prompt payment.

Operating loans, however, can have some restrictions. For example, your banker may prohibit you from taking retained earnings out of your company during the early stages of your business. In addition, he or she may even veto the purchase of machinery, equipment, and other fixed assets above a certain amount. These operating loans are subject to annual review and renewal by mutual agreement but can often be terminated by the lender at its option unless specific conditions have been incorporated into the loan agreement. Interest on operating loans is usually *tied to the prime rate*. That means the interest rate can change either up or down as the prime rate changes. This can be an advantage when interest rates are declining but a major issue if rates are increasing rapidly.

Banks also provide *term loans* to small businesses — loans for the purchase of an existing business or to acquire fixed assets such as machinery, vehicles, and commercial buildings, which typically must be repaid in three to ten years. The term of the loan is usually linked to the expected lifespan of the asset. Three to four years is common for a truck or computer, while the term of a loan to acquire a building could be considerably longer. Term loans typically have a fixed interest rate for the full term. Therefore your interest cost is predetermined in advance and your budgeting process is simplified. However, the loan amount tends to be limited to a percentage of the value of the asset being financed. In addition, term loans often command a one-time processing fee of half a per cent of the value of the loan.

You should realize that business bank loans, both operating and term loans, are *demand* loans so that regardless of the term, the bank can and will demand they be paid back if it feels the company is getting into trouble. While this usually occurs only when the business has real problems, there is the potential for difficulties; what the banker may perceive as a serious situation may be perceived as only a temporary difficulty by the owner of the business.

Janine DeFreitas, whose situation is described in Entrepreneurs in Action #30, is a typical new business owner. She was initially unable to obtain a bank loan despite the fact that she had a business plan, love money provided by her father, and a commitment from her principal supplier to provide the necessary inventory for her store. When her request was finally approved on the third try, it was only because it was government-guaranteed and co-signed by her father. She was very frustrated in her initial efforts to obtain this bank financing but recognized she would need bank support to develop and grow her business beyond its current stage now that it is more firmly established.

The bank may ask for your personal guarantee of business loans as well as a pledge of collateral security for the full value of the loan or more. This means that even though your business might be incorporated, your personal liability is not necessarily limited to your investment in the business; you could lose your house, car, cottage, and other personal assets if the business fails and you are unable to repay your loans to the bank.

To qualify for a loan you must have sufficient equity in your business and a strong personal credit rating. Banks do not take large risks. Their principal considerations in assessing a loan application are the safety of their depositors' money and the return they will earn on the loan. It is critical that you take these factors into account in preparing your loan proposal and try to look at your situation from the banker's point of view.

FEDERAL GOVERNMENT FINANCIAL ASSISTANCE PROGRAMS

Governments at all levels in Canada have developed a proliferation of financial assistance programs for small business. It is estimated that more than 600 programs are available from both the federal and provincial governments to help people begin a business or assist those that have already started. Many of these programs are aimed at companies in more advanced stages of their development who are looking to grow and expand, but quite a number can be utilized by firms in the start-up stage. Many of these programs offer financial assistance in the form of low-interest loans, loan guarantees, interest-free loans, or even forgivable (non-repayable) loans. Others offer incentives like wage subsidies, whereby the government will pay an employee's wage for a certain period of time. These programs are too numerous to describe in any detail, but let us briefly look at several of the more important ones.

30 *Entrepreneurs in* action

Controlling Interest

Government guarantees, proven products, a 100-page business plan and cold hard cash sounds like a perfect recipe to lure bank financing. Janine DeFreitas knows otherwise.

After the former Rubbermaid Canada sales and merchandising manager watched the company's first full-line retail display sell out in just four weeks, DeFreitas got the urge to open a Rubbermaid-only store [The Rubbery Inc. in Mississauga, Ontario]. Equipped with her business plan, $50,000 from her father and the promise of product from her supplier, DeFreitas was rebuffed by two banks — and two male loans officers — before a female lender at Toronto-Dominion issued a $110,000 loan. Still, the loan was government-guaranteed and co-signed by DeFreitas' father. "They said I didn't put enough personal equity into it," she says.

The bank should have few worries now: at $3 million a year, sales have doubled projections. DeFreitas is now planning to go national within five years. She's considering franchising to finance out-of-province openings, but is looking at bank debt to fund up to five corporate stores in Ontario. "I wanted to open my own business so I wouldn't have to answer to anybody," DeFreitas explains. "If I go through an investor, I lose a certain amount of control." (www.therubbery.com)

Source: Excerpted from Charise Clark "How I Raised Funds," *PROFIT,* November 1998, pp. 35–36. © Charise Clark.

CANADA SMALL BUSINESS FINANCING PROGRAM

New and existing businesses with gross revenues of less than $5 million may be eligible to obtain term loans from chartered banks, caisses populaires, credit unions, or other lenders and have the loan partially guaranteed by the federal government under the Canada Small Business Financing Act (CSBFA: previously known as the Small Business Loans Act, SBLA). These loans are provided at a reasonable rate of interest (prime plus no more than 3 per cent for floating rate loans, or the lender's residential mortgage rate plus 3 per cent for a fixed-rate loan). In addition, lenders are required to pay a one-time loan registration fee to the government equal to 2 per cent of the amount loaned. This fee is recoverable from the borrower. These loans may be used for any number of purposes, such as the purchase or renovation of machinery and equipment and the purchase and improvement of land and buildings for business purposes. Loan proceeds may be used to finance up to 90 per cent of the cost of the asset, while the maximum value of loans a borrower may have outstanding under the CSBFA cannot exceed $250,000. For more information, contact any private sector lender or:

Canada Small Business Financing Program
Industry Canada
235 Queen Street
8th Floor, East Tower
Ottawa, Ontario K1A 0H5

(strategis.ic.gc.ca/csbfa)

Telephone: (613) 954-5540 Fax: (613) 952-0290

Key points

ADVICE WORTH BANKING ON

One of the biggest adventures an entrepreneur can undertake is obtaining or renewing business financing — a trail that often determines the survival of many new and small businesses. Unfortunately, the application and approval process for obtaining and renewing commercial credit can be more of a nightmare than an adventure.

In my previous career, I was a branch manager with one of Canada's largest financial institutions. Since I have sat on both sides of the desk, let me share some of my thoughts and advice about seeking bank financing.

As a branch manager supervising the application and investigation process, I believed that assessing the information provided and getting to know my customers were both crucial in making lending decisions. When evaluating potential customers, I made sure not only to review personal credit histories, but I also tried to understand individuals and their personalities. I could usually determine whether I was dealing with a client who would make every effort to repay his or her debt, and I took this factor into account when making the lending decision. Many times applicants did not meet the existing lending criteria or have sufficient collateral for a loan. But if during the interview process they appeared genuine, honest, and hard working, and if they were open about their credit history and how they planned to repay the loan, I would more then likely have approved the loan.

So far, however, as a client applying for commercial credit I have experienced this same flexibility and understanding only twice in seven years. Banks often give the impression that they support and help small business In Canada, but each year our company faces a major challenge to renew credit or obtain new financing. For the approval of commercial loans, it appears that equity, the net worth of borrowers and how much they are risking are more important to banks than the strength of the business plan, the product or the individual.

From my experience as a client, I have learned the importance of being prepared when approaching a bank for commercial financing. Here is my advice:

Provide a solid business plan with financial details of the company and its principals. Include a complete outline of the company's current and projected financial status. But remember, no matter how strong your business plan is or how good your credit history is, if you don't maintain the bulk of the risk, the bank will probably not look at your request seriously. The reality is you must not only sell yourself and your business plan, but you must also be willing to sign everything you own over to the bank.

After jumping through hoops and loops to obtain financing, it is important to establish a good working relationship with your lenders. Provide them with timely and accurate reporting as they request. Share information. And keep the lines of communication open — they need to know you are on top of your operation and that you will present bad news as well as good news to them for discussion. Build the trust factor.

Remember that no matter how strong you feel your relationship with the bank is, there are no guarantees that the staff you deal with now will be involved in future decisions. One year, during our credit renewal process, our file was handed off to a new account manager and branch manager who didn't know anything about our business or the principals. The staff changes resulted in a review of our file, the decision not to deal with our company any more, and a sudden need to seek alternative financing — even after a year of excellent growth and profit.

Prepare for unforeseen financing obstacles by periodically reviewing and updating your business plan, and have strategies ready if you need to seek out new financing. Alternative financing options could include approaching smaller financial institutions such as credit unions or regional banks (which may suit smaller businesses), using the services of companies that trade accounts receivables for cash, or seeking out privately held capital companies. You might also consider finding investment funding, obtained through private placement by selling an equity position in your company, usually to friends, family, or someone willing to take an active role in the business.

Source: Ryan Magnussen (president, WDC Mackenzie Distributors Ltd., Calgary), "Advice Worth Banking On," *PROFIT* (www.profitguide.com/magazine/article.jsp?content=1027). Used with permission. Accessed August 19, 2004.

INDUSTRIAL RESEARCH ASSISTANCE PROGRAM

The National Research Council's Industrial Research Assistance Program (IRAP) provides scientific and technical advice and limited financial assistance for projects designed to enhance a company's technical capability under three program elements:

1. IRAP provides non-repayable contributions on a cost-shared basis to small and medium-sized companies (up to 500 employees) for research and pre-competitive development technical projects.

2. The IRAP Technology Partnerships Canada (TPC) program provides repayable financial assistance for projects at the pre-commercialization stage. Firms use these funds to develop technology for new or significantly improved products, processes, or services, as well as to support initial demonstration and pilot projects. Contributions do not normally exceed 33 per cent of total eligible project costs. The contributions are conditionally repayable based on royalties on company gross revenues. Repayments are calculated to return the initial contribution plus an amount appropriate to the program's principle of sharing in the risks and rewards of the project. Repayments are not limited to the face amount of the contribution.

3. IRAP's Internship Program provides financial assistance for the hiring of post-secondary graduates to work on innovation projects in small and medium-sized firms. Internships last between six to twelve months and are available anywhere in Canada. Maximum support provided is $12,000 to help cover a part of the graduate's salary.

National Research Council
Industrial Research Assistance Program
1200 Montreal Road, Building M55
Ottawa, Ontario K1A 0R6
(www.nrc.ca/irap)
Telephone: (613) 993-5326 or 1-877-994-4727
Fax: (613) 952-1086

PROGRAM FOR EXPORT MARKET DEVELOPMENT

The Program for Export Market Development (PEMD) is designed to increase export sales of Canadian goods and services by encouraging Canadian companies to become exporters and helping existing Canadian exporters to develop new markets. PEMD shares the cost of export market development activity that these companies would not normally undertake on their own. Market Development Strategies supports a combination of visits, trade fair participation, and market support activities with a repayable contribution ranging from $5,000 to $50,000. New exporters may be eligible to receive a maximum of $7,500 for either a market identification visit or for participation in an international trade fair. The contribution is repayable based on four per cent of incremental export sales in the target market over a four-year period.

For more information contact:
International Trade Canada
125 Sussex Drive
Ottawa, Ontario K1A 0G2
(www.itcan-cican.gc.ca)
Telephone: (613) 944-4000 or 1-800-267-8376

COMMUNITY FUTURES DEVELOPMENT CORPORATIONS

Industry Canada's Community Futures Development Corporations (CFDCs) provide their communities with a variety of business development services including the following.

Business Development Loans

- CFDCs each offer specific loan programs that target its community's needs, assisting entrepreneurs who may have had trouble accessing capital from traditional lenders. In some cases, these include special loans to youth entrepreneurs and entrepreneurs with disabilities.

- They can lend a maximum of $125,000 to new or existing businesses.

- CFDC loans are fully repayable and are negotiated at competitive interest rates.

Contact your nearest CFDC for further information or go to www.communityfutures.ca for information on the entire cross-Canada Community Futures network.

Technical Support

CFDCs provide services that include:

- Business advice, counselling, information, and referrals
- Help with business plans
- Advice on export readiness and supplier development

Training

Training is available in, among other areas:

- Self-employment skills
- Marketing
- Bookkeeping
- Computer literacy

Information

CFDCs can provide information on relevant federal and provincial programs and services, as well as access to business libraries and business databases.

WOMEN'S ENTERPRISE INITIATIVE LOAN PROGRAM

Western Economic Diversification, through the local Women's Enterprise Initiative in each western province, provides access to a loan fund for women entrepreneurs seeking financing for start-up or expansion of a business. To qualify, the business must have a fully completed business plan and be 51 per cent owned or controlled by a woman or women. Loans up to $100,000 are available.

For more information contact the Women's Enterprise Initiative in your province or go to www.wd.gc.ca/finance/programs/weilp_e.asp.

ABORIGINAL BUSINESS CANADA

Canadian status and non-status Indians, Inuit, and Métis individuals between the ages of 18 and 35 are eligible for support with the preparation of business plans, marketing, and financing the start-up, expansion, modernization, or acquisition of a commercially viable business under Industry Canada's Aboriginal Business Canada program. The business opportunity can be in any sector. The minimum cash equity required by the applicant is equivalent to 10 per cent of eligible project costs and the contribution level can range from 30 to 75 per cent, depending on the nature of the project. These contributions are non-repayable.

For more information, contact one of the Aboriginal Business Canada offices located in each of the provinces and territories, or the program's head office at:

Aboriginal Business Canada
Industry Canada
235 Queen Street
Ottawa, Ontario K1A 0H5
(strategis.ic.gc.ca/epic/internet/inabc-eac.nsf/en/home)
Telephone: (613) 964-4064 Fax: (613) 957-7010

BUSINESS DEVELOPMENT BANK OF CANADA

The Business Development Bank of Canada (BDC) is a federal Crown corporation that provides a wide range of financial, management counselling, and information services to small business through its broad network of over 80 branches across the country. Its financial services complement those of the private sector by providing funds for business projects that are not available from the commercial banks and other sources on reasonable terms. The BDC will provide term loans for the acquisition of fixed assets, working capital or operating loans, venture loans, and venture capital. Its primary focus is on small- and medium-sized businesses operating in knowledge-based, growth-oriented industries and export markets.

The BDC offers an extensive variety of management and financial services including:

CO-VISION Start-up financing program that provides customized term financing up to $100,000 for new businesses demonstrating long-term viability. The BDC can also provide personalized management support for such businesses. These loans cannot be used for financing changes in ownership or self-employed, home-based businesses.

Brian Titus, profiled in Entrepreneurs in Action #31, was able to obtain a BDC loan under what is now the Co-Vision program to help launch his successful micro-brewery in Halifax. To do so, he had to prepare a comprehensive business plan and overcome some other obstacles, but his determination and perseverance paid off as he was able to attract the capital necessary to get the business off the ground.

TERM FINANCING Flexible term financing for a variety of commercially viable projects, including business expansion, plant improvements and upgrades, the purchase of existing businesses, the acquisition of fixed assets, or the replenishment of working capital.

GROWTH CAPITAL FOR ABORIGINAL BUSINESS Specialized financing for aboriginal entrepreneurs wanting to buy an existing business or start a new one on or off a reserve in Canada. The program will provide up to $100,000 for existing businesses or up to $25,000 for a start-up. Ongoing mentoring and business management counselling are also available for the first two years, on approval.

BDC VENTURE CAPITAL Venture capital for every stage of the business development cycle, from start-up through expansion. Its focus is on technology-based businesses with high-growth potential that are positioned to become dominant players in their markets. Typical investments range from $500,000 to $3 million, usually as part of a larger round of financing. Investments are almost exclusively in such areas as life sciences, telecommunications, information technologies, and other advanced technology businesses.

For further information on these and other programs contact one of the BDC offices located in each of the provinces and territories, or the BDC head office at:

Business Development Bank of Canada
5 Place Ville Marie, Suite 400
Montreal, Quebec H3B 5E7
(www.bdc.ca)
Telephone: Toll-free 1-877-232-2269 Fax: 1-877-329-9232

PROVINCIAL GOVERNMENT FINANCIAL ASSISTANCE PROGRAMS

Most of the provincial governments provide a range of grants, loans, and other forms of assistance to small business. For example, Manitoba offers the Business Start Program that provides a loan guarantee for loans up to $10,000 along with an educational component to assist new entrepreneurs launching their new business. Similarly, Ontario provides the My Company program, a financing and business training program for people 18 to 29 who are interested in starting and operating a new business in the province 12 months a year. On completion of the My Company training workshop or the online training program, successful applicants can receive loans of up to $15,000 at an interest rate of prime plus 1 per cent.

The list of these programs is much too extensive to provide here, but you can obtain specific information on the programs offered in your province by contacting the appropriate government department listed in the For Further Information section of this book, or you can contact your local Canada Business Service Centre (www.cbsc.org).

VENTURE CAPITAL

Venture capital involves equity participation in a start-up or growing business situation. Conventional venture capital companies, however, really don't offer much opportunity for firms still in the concept or idea stage. These investors are generally looking for investment situations in proven firms requiring in excess of $1 million and on which they can earn a 40 to 50 per cent annual return. While these companies will often accept high-risk situations, most new venture start-ups don't meet their primary investment criteria.

There are some exceptions to this general rule, however. During the dot-com frenzy of the late 1990s the business press was full of stories of young, Canadian entrepreneurs barely out of school who had received millions of dollars in venture capital financing to launch their latest Internet idea. This situation

31 Entrepreneurs in action

Tapping into Success

Before Brian Titus got his business off the ground, he made sure he did his homework.

"I spent months doing research and just learning about what was out there," says the president and general manager of Halifax-based Garrison Brewing Company Ltd., a highly successful microbrewery that he founded in 1997.

At that time, beer was a whole new business for the naval diving officer, so he first visited other microbreweries in Newfoundland and British Columbia to learn the ropes. "People felt comfortable sharing their knowledge with me, and it was time well spent. There's a lot of camaraderie in this industry, and I was able to gain invaluable insight," he says.

Looking back, Titus takes pride in having put together a comprehensive business plan to attract financing, including a BDC loan under the Young Entrepreneur Financing Program (now replaced by Co-Vision.) "It took about five months to put the plan together. It was a real dream for me to start this business and I wasn't going to let it fall through," he says. His sheer determination paid off when the company immediately attracted investors and was able to purchase costly equipment to brew his darker ales using traditional brewing methods.

Titus emphasizes that the company had to overcome a few obstacles along the way. "People in Nova Scotia are traditionally domestic-beer drinkers so we first had to get our product out there and prove ourselves," he says. To get his beer selling in the same hot spots as larger breweries, the company innovated by offering its product in smaller twenty-litre kegs, which are ideal for fitting into tight places in bars. "We eliminated the need for expensive cooler systems, and once we got our beer in the hands of consumers, I knew the company was going to take off," he adds.

Titus' instinct was right because after one year in business, Garrison Brewing saw 50% growth. Five years later, the company now produces 600,000 bottles of beer a year with a minimal staff of four full-time people, and still maintains five to six percent annual growth. "We've had to stay on our toes to keep our market share nonetheless," he says. For instance, rather than go the traditional advertising route, the company markets its products by sponsoring a local jazz festival and film festival. "Those events fit our profile very well. We sponsor sports too, but in our case, we work with squash tournaments rather than hockey or football," he says.

Now that his company is maturing, Titus has some words of wisdom to share with entrepreneurs starting up today. "In the beginning, be prepared to really focus on your goals, and don't let go of them, no matter what," he concludes.

Source: Business Development Bank of Canada, *PROFIT$*, Spring 2003, p. 1.

has cooled considerably. Corporate funds, pension funds, private independent venture funds, and labour-sponsored venture capital funds still have billions of dollars looking for investment opportunities, principally in the high-technology sector, but investors are being much more careful in determining where it goes.

Christopher Frey, Kisha Ferguson, and Matt Robinson are among the lucky few who have been successful in raising a significant amount of money for a somewhat more traditional business situation. (Entrepreneurs in Action #32). They were looking for a $300,000 equity infusion to help develop their adventure travel magazine, *Outpost*. Sometimes, however, the price can be too high. The initial offer they received to provide the funds demanded a majority stake in the business in return. Though they desperately needed the money to grow their business, they still had sufficient funds to limp along while searching out other options, so turned the offer down. In the end they connected with a Toronto venture capitalist who provided

FYI FOR YOUR INFORMATION

For detailed information on specific federal or provincial programs, you can check the Industry Canada Strategis Web site at strategis.ic.gc.ca/sc_mangb/sources/Language_selection_page.html, contact your local Canada Business Service Centre, or check out one of the following publications at your local library:

Your Guide to Government Financial Assistance for Business in: (separate publication available for each province and territory)

Productive Publications
1930 Yonge St., Suite 1210
Toronto, Ontario M4S 1Z4
Telephone: (416) 483-0634
(www.productivepublications.ca)

Government Assistance Manual Canadian Small Business Financing and Tax Planning Guide

CCH Canadian Limited
6 Garamond Court
Don Mills, Ontario M3C 1Z5
(www.cch.ca)

The Business Guide to Government Programs

The Business Guide Incorporated
Box 29077
Torbay Road
St. John's, NF A1A 5B8
Telephone: (877) 754-8433
(www.businessguide.net)

them with some bridge financing and told them how to beef up their business to make it more attractive to other investors. After 18 months they finally hooked up with another firm in the communications business that provided them with the money they needed to solidify their operations, and they learned a number of valuable lessons along the way.

There are a number of venture capital firms that may be prepared to consider smaller investments, some of which listed in the For Further Information section at the back of this book. However, keep in mind that of 100 proposals considered by a typical venture capital firm, only four or five are selected for investment purposes. Therefore, the probability of receiving any financial assistance from this source is very slim. For more information, however, you can contact:

Canadian Venture Capital Association
234 Eglinton Avenue East, Suite 200
Toronto, Ontario M4P 1K5
(www.cvca.ca)
Telephone: (416) 487-0519

A new business start-up probably has a better chance of obtaining equity capital from small, private venture capitalists — often called "angels" — or provincially supported venture capital programs. There may be doctors, dentists, lawyers, accountants, and other individuals in your community who could be approached for investment funds. Many of these people may be looking for situations where they can invest small sums (less than $50,000) with the possibility of earning a larger return than that offered by more-conventional investments, and they are often prepared to invest in start-up situations.

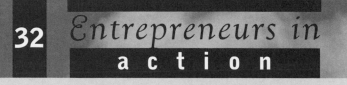

32   Entrepreneurs in action

In Search of Adventure Capital

It was the kind of tough call that confronts many entrepreneurs searching for capital. Christopher Frey, Kisha Ferguson and Matt Robinson, partners in adventure travel magazine *Outpost*, badly needed the $300,000 equity infusion being dangled in front of them. The Toronto-based firm was limping along with limited money and had debts to repay. But the investor was demanding a majority stake. Would the trio have to give up control to keep their dream alive?

Frey and Ferguson had launched their quarterly magazine in the spring of 1996 to chronicle Canadians' adventures in exotic locales. But their own 18-month search for capital, as they struggled to secure funding before their cash ran out, was as exciting as any trip from the pages of *Outpost* itself. And, as with any worthwhile quest, what the partners learned along the way — including the power of relationships and the need to think big — was as valuable as the pot of gold that they hoped to discover.

1. YOU NEED A MAP AND A COMPASS

The adventurers started with meagre rations: Frey's experience working on his university newspaper, Ferguson's editorial vision, and $60,000 from savings, family and friends. Frey and Ferguson believed the adventure travel market — growing at an estimated 25% a year — offered a fertile source of readers and advertisers. But that wouldn't be enough. "We knew enough to start, but not enough to have a long-range plan," says Frey. "But we were quick learners, and from the very first day we started, we went about filling in the gaps in our knowledge."

One gap was filled when Matt Robinson joined *Outpost* in June 1997 as a third partner and advertising director. Robinson brought badly needed marketing savvy from a stint with Toronto publishing giant Maclean Hunter Ltd. Until then, Frey and Ferguson had been traveling without a map. "When I came aboard," recalls Robinson, "Chris was in the process of developing a business plan. It was a living document we developed through the summer and fall." To secure its future, *Outpost* needed ad revenue. To sell ads, it needed to find more readers — an expensive venture. So the trio set out to raise $300,000.

From August until October, the *Outpost* team cold-called more than 200 potential investors culled from a variety of sources, including business and publishing trade magazines. The phone calls yielded a list of some 50 interested people and companies, and the partners mailed promotional packages to them all.

2. BUILD THE VALUE IN YOUR BUSINESS

Meantime, the trio took steps to increase ad revenue, which would make *Outpost* more attractive to investors. "The advertisers are the canaries in our investment world," says Robinson. "Advertisers want value. If they come on board and are singing the praises of the publication, you can translate that to investors as an expression of confidence in the product." The partners relaunched the magazine, doubling the print run to 25,000 copies, adding new editorial sections and more color to the magazine, and producing a media kit to sell

© NADIA MOLINARI

Outpost to advertisers. With finances tight, they funded the improvements in part by an extended overdraft of $12,000 — guaranteed against a GIC owned by Frey's parents. The improved magazine debuted in October with $16,000 of advertising — up from $4,000 in the previous issue. Even better, for the first time several brand-name advertisers bought space. "It improved our story [to investors]," says Robinson.

On the financing front, one magazine publisher in Toronto (whom the partners decline to identify) was

continued

In Search of Adventure Capital — continued

particularly responsive. The partners met with him six times starting in late summer, 1997. "The first few meetings were a reality check, coming to grips with how difficult the publishing business is," says Frey. The lessons covered both the magazine business and the gruelling requirements of venture capitalists. "It became evident that we had to evaluate every aspect of the company to reach an adequate return to investors," says Robinson. "We learned that the standard return on venture capital is 30% to 40% a year. We did our best to get our projected returns close to that amount."

Outpost was willing to give up a 30% interest for $300,000, but the publisher demanded control. The partners agonized. "We were in an onerous financial situation," says Robinson. "We weren't about to go bankrupt — we could limp along with the three of us putting the magazine out — but the money would have allowed us to repay people who had supported us. And we were sitting on this fabulous market, and we had to get the resources to take advantage of it." But, he says, "We got involved in this project because we wanted to control our destiny. You end up working for someone else and it takes some of that wonderful energy out of your sails." No deal, the trio decided.

Though Frey, Ferguson and Robinson walked away from the money, they had grown as entrepreneurs. "The fact that [the publisher] was willing to talk with us at such length gave us a great deal of confidence in our direction and our ideas," says Robinson. "And he really helped us massage our presentation."

Still, losses for 1997 were $61,000. Robinson gave up his salary for a month and reduced it for the rest of the year. *Outpost* stayed afloat through low overheads, such as renting space for only $450 a month, and by doing what Robinson calls "the 30-60-90 day shuffle," stretching out payments to creditors.

3. LEARN FROM REJECTION

By now the partners had a 25-page business plan which, says Robinson, "was tweaked and morphed many times, not from a lack of focus on our part, but based on an educational process that was going on each time we got feedback from venture capitalists and publishers."

But fishing for investors could be discouraging. "Nothing happens 90% of the time," says Robinson. "You've got to keep your spirits up." Where they couldn't find money, the partners looked for information. "A fair number of people will sit down and listen to you, but often they're doing that just to see what ideas are out there," says Frey. "They may not have any interest at all [in investing]. Then it becomes a smart move to try to turn the meeting to your advantage by getting as much information out of them as possible."

4. ASK FOR MORE THAN YOU NEED

In the spring and summer of 1998, the partners held another important round of meetings, this time with Bob Shoniker, a Toronto venture capitalist. Shoniker asked some tough questions, including, "Do you guys really think $300,000 is enough?" Shoniker noted that it takes as much work to evaluate a $300,000 investment as a $1-million investment. "Up to that point, we had gotten by with the notion of doing as much as possible with as little as possible," says Frey. "But any investor will only invest if they think they're giving you an adequate amount of money." Before their second of three meetings with Shoniker, *Outpost* got the hint and upped the ante — to $1 million.

Shoniker didn't give *Outpost* the $1 million, but he did provide $50,000 in bridge financing. It was a life-saver. "If the bridge capital wasn't there, we would have gone back and negotiated an agreement with the independent publisher and lost control," says Robinson.

Shoniker also challenged *Outpost* to elaborate on its idea for multimedia spin-offs. "The person who just wants to sell a print page of advertising in their publication is going to have a hard time these days," says Robinson. "We really wanted ultimately to develop a brand, with the magazine at the core." *Outpost* had been producing a 10-minute segment for a Toronto community radio station, CJRT, since early 1998. Now, convinced they shouldn't hold off until the magazine was on a sound footing, the partners added plans for a syndicated radio show, website and TV program. *Outpost* was now presented to investors as "an integrated adventure travel communications company that publishes Canada's only adventure travel magazine."

With their new, more aggressive plan and higher revenues — up from $30,000 in 1997 to $150,000 in 1998 — the three partners had turned *Outpost* into a promising investment prospect. Still, the company lost $92,500 in 1998, and was rapidly using up its bridge financing. Frey, Ferguson and Robinson slogged on. When the breakthrough finally came at the end of 1998, everything they had learned along the way helped them succeed.

One of the companies they had approached in mid-1997 was BHVR Communications, a Montreal media and entertainment company founded by digital video software entrepreneur Richard Szalwinski. Their approach had gone unanswered. But now *Outpost* was a substantial property with a vision— and the unreceptive executive who had run BHVR's publishing division was no longer there. Plus, BHVR was looking for new properties after selling its interest in software maker Discreet Logic.

To approach BHVR again, the *Outpost* partners called on their friend Andrew Heintzman, publisher of *Shift* magazine, which had been bought by BHVR in 1996. Heintzman helped arrange a conference call between *Outpost* and BHVR in December 1998. Out of that came a seven-hour meeting in Montreal.

Claude Thibault, vice-president of BHVR subsidiary Normal Net, was impressed. He says BHVR went through "the usual checklist: How much money are they seeking? Where will that take them? Will they need more? What is the valuation? Is it fair? What's their business plan? Does it fit with ours? We were satisfied on all those points rapidly."

Sounds simple, but the partners needed to draw on all they had learned on their journey. They had a sound business plan and were asking for an appropriate investment. They had shown the confidence and the management skills to improve their magazine issue by issue, working on their own. And the multimedia plan urged on them by Shoniker was a perfect fit with BHVR's own vision. BHVR, says Robinson, wanted to leverage content across print and the Net — right up *Outpost*'s alley. *Outpost*'s audience also matched BHVR's target, which Thibault defines as "the edgier half of the 18 to 30 crowd."

There was a discrepancy when it came to valuation. "It's impossible to value a company by any of the standard practices at that stage in its development," says Robinson. He and his two partners valued the company at $1 million; BHVR's number was $700,000. But, with everything else looking positive, BHVR agreed to pay a premium — $1 million for 47% of the company, plus the rights to use *Outpost*'s content on its website.

5. LEVERAGE YOUR RELATIONSHIPS

Robinson believes that Heintzman's recommendation carried weight. "I don't know if we would have had this opportunity if that relationship hadn't been there," he says. He adds this advice: "Adopt an attitude that invites relationships. Don't take any relationships for granted. Any one of them could help."

On December 24, Thibault called to say they had a deal. "We gave a whoop and a holler in the office," says Robinson, "then went home and had a nice Christmas with our families."

The agreement was signed five months later. *Outpost* earmarked the money for investment in circulation, marketing and additional staff. Starting this February, the magazine will come out six times a year. The partners have run a successful direct-mail subscription campaign—with a 3% response rate, according to Robinson—and run a series of TV ads on the Outdoor Network. On the multimedia front, they have obtained an initial commitment from a Canadian broadcaster to partially fund a pilot for a TV series. And they're looking at expanding into Australia, Europe and the United States. *Outpost* has launched a website (www.outpostmagazine.com), and when Normal Net's website launches shortly, *Outpost*'s content will be there too. Robinson forecasts a loss of $130,000 for 2000, but expects to break even for the first time on the November issue. To fund its new initiatives, *Outpost* will need more equity, either from BHVR or outside investors. The quest for financing never ends, but at least Frey, Ferguson and Robinson are now experienced travelers. (www.outpostmagazine.com)

Source: Sheldon Gordon, "Adventure Capital," *PROFIT*, February–March 2000, pp. 45–48. Used with permission.

A number of communities and organizations have programs to bring entrepreneurs together with private investors. York University and the MIT Alumni Club of Toronto as well as other organizations sponsor "enterprise forums" in which small companies get an opportunity to tell their stories before a group of prospective investors and other experts. The Manitoba Department of Industry, Economic Development and Mines periodically sponsors the Invest Manitoba Venture Showcase, where local firms who need capital and have a preliminary business plan get the opportunity to make a 10-minute presentation to an audience of prospective investors and others in the community who provide business financing (www.gov.mb.ca/itm).

In 1996 the federal government started the Canadian Community Investment Plan (CCIP) as a means to improve access to risk capital for small and medium-sized firms located in smaller communities across the country. One of the more successful of these demonstration projects is Capital Connexion (www.capital-connexion.com) located in Quebec. It is a continuously updated database of proposals from entrepreneurs looking for financing, along with a list of angel investors searching for business projects in which to invest. The database is heavily oriented toward most regions of Quebec but has been expanded to include parts of other provinces such as Newfoundland, Alberta, New Brunswick, Nova Scotia, and Ontario as well. Registration of both investors and entrepreneurs on the database is free but they must be validated by a local economic development organization.

Canada's chartered banks are often criticized for not providing this kind of risk capital to small business. Banks, however, are principally low-risk lenders of their depositor's money and traditionally provide debt financing. Venture capitalists and other private investors provide financing in exchange for shares or other interest in the company. Banks have neither the mandate nor the expertise to participate in this specialized market.

Leon Rudanycz, who is profiled in Entrepreneurs in Action #33 is a typical "angel." He had a very successful business of his own, sold it, and used some of the proceeds to invest in other people's ideas. These investments gave him a way to keep involved, to continue to participate in the growth and development of these businesses, to contribute to major company decisions, and an opportunity to make a good financial return on his investments.

WHAT'S ON THE TABLE?

Negotiations with private venture capital sources can be lengthy and complex. It's important to keep in mind the main issues that may be under discussion in the process. These will likely include:

- **Price** What are the business and the opportunity worth? How much will the investor pay in exchange for a position in your business? You have to have a realistic idea of the range of values you might be prepared to accept and the values an investor might be prepared to consider.

- **Control** How much of your business will the investor get for his or her investment and how much control will the investor be able to exercise over its affairs? Most private investors aren't trying to gain control of your business but they are looking to manage their risk by putting some controls in place to protect their investment. These may include:
  - Requiring prior consultation or imposing some restrictions on your ability to make financial decisions
  - Requiring representation on your board of directors
  - Determining the amount of equity you may have to give up based on pre-determined performance-based targets
  - Requiring a provision giving the investors the first opportunity to participate in the future sale of equity in the business or asking for a ban on the sale of future shares without investor agreement.

- **Establishment of Performance Expectations** The investment may be laid out in stages and tied to specific achievement milestones and objectives. You and the investor need to agree on the performance measures that will be used to determine if the business is succeeding as expected in order to trigger these additional contributions or somehow change the terms of the initial deal.

- **Exit Strategy** Some of the available options by which investors might cash in their investment in your business include:
  - **Acquisition by a third party** An outright sale of the company in which the investor's shares would be sold as part of the sale of the company to a third-party acquirer. This is often viewed as the ideal route to go, especially if the buyout is for cash instead of stock.
  - **Sale of the investor's interest to a third-party investor** This can be an option, but minority interests in private companies can be very difficult to sell due to the lack of control and liquidity. Significant costs can be associated with finding new investors, and the process can consume a great deal of time and effort.
  - **Buy-back agreement** The investor's shares may be repurchased by the company. This could be in the form of a *put option* or a *retraction clause* in which the investor maintains the legal right to force you to repurchase his or her shares at an agreed and prespecified price at particular points in time.[1]
  - **Management or employee buyout** The founders and early investors can often realize a gain from the business by selling it to other partners or some of the key managers in the business in a management buyout or to a number of the employees through an employee stock ownership plan (ESOP).

---

1. G.H. Haines Jr, J.J. Madill, and A.L. Riding, "Financing Small Business Growth: Informal Investing in Canada," *Journal of Small Business and Entrepreneurship*, Spring 2003, pp. 13–40.

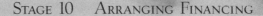

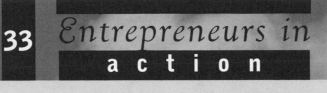

33   Entrepreneurs in action

Looks Like an Angel

How do you find an angel? You might hear about him or her from your lawyer, from an investment company or from somebody at a cocktail party.

"You'd hear that Leon had a business and sold it, and invested in a couple of other ones successfully and has some money to invest," says Leon Rudanycz, a typical contributor to the largely unmeasured pool of informal investment capital that nurtures budding young companies.

Rudanycz, who has degrees in law and engineering, started up a computer distributing company in the mid-'80s. Now called Tech Data Canada Inc., it's one of the country's largest high-tech distributors. Rudanycz sold out, then became an angel by investing some of the proceeds in two other fledgling computer companies.

"Both were started out of people's homes, very lean and mean. I ended up selling my interest in both companies — one within four years, the other three. But they were both profitable from day one."

That's not always the case, and most venture capitalists make their money back when they take the company public, usually seeking an annual return of 30%–40%. In the crapshoot of angel investing, only a few ventures hit the big time, so the winners have to make up spectacularly for the many losers.

"Angel investing, by its nature, is less formal, involves smaller sums of money and usually does not involve a full-time position in the company," says Rudanycz. "It's generally more in the $100,000 range."

Carleton University has carried out the most extensive research into Canada's informal investment market, conducting a survey of 279 angels. "The investors were found to be significantly more wealthy than most Canadians ... and occupy the top one percentile of wealth among Canadian households," says the Carleton report.

In plumbing the angel psychology, the research found that "investors tend to be men with an internal locus of control, very high needs for achievement and dominance."

Almost 90% expected to serve on a board of directors or advisers when investing. A third of them participate directly as an operating principal. And nearly two-thirds also stipulate some sort of operating covenants in the form of periodic reports, authorization of cash disbursements over a certain amount, and control of salaries and dividends.

Rudanycz fits the mould perfectly. "I demand a seat on the board, cheque-signing authority along with the owner, a good handle on the accounting and a hand in major decisions," he says.

His two subsequent high-tech investments were made in the form of a secured loan, and the shares were simply "the kicker, the bonus. I don't always do that, though." For example, Rudanycz says he's considering a straight equity investment in a clothing manufacture and design business. He'd get a piece of the action for a relatively measly $10,000.

"Projected sales in the first year are $100,000 and probably a million in the third, and for them this $10,000 is pivotal," says Rudanycz, describing a deal that's well beneath the threshold of the mainstream venture capital industry. (www.cornermarkcapital.com)

Source: Excerpted from Gord MacLaughlin, "Divine Intervention," *Financial Post*, May 6, 1995, p. 7. Reprinted with permission.

- **Debt repayment** The financing structure used could include some form of subordinated debt with specific repayment terms on exit. The debt agreement may carry conversion privileges that allow the investor to convert the debt into common shares under certain circumstances.

- **An initial public offering (IPO)** The investor's shares would be sold when the business decides to raise additional capital through the sale of shares to the public. This exit mechanism is commonly viewed as the "holy grail" for both the company and the investor, and can be the most satisfying and financially rewarding. However, very few private firms ever actually achieve this level of success and it does come with a number of potential negative considerations. For example, going public can mean the loss of a significant portion of your ownership and leave you in a minority position. In a addition, a portion of your and the investors' shares may be held in escrow, possibly for years, forcing you to remain invested in the business. It also means that by becoming "public," a lot of previously private and sensitive information must now be shared with the public.

ANGEL INVESTORS: THE DEFINITION

Angel investors are individuals who invest in businesses looking for a higher return than they would see from more traditional investments. Many are successful entrepreneurs who want to help other entrepreneurs get their business off the ground. Usually they are the bridge from the self-funded stage of the business to the point that the business needs the level of funding that a venture capitalist would offer. Funding estimates vary, but usually range from $150,000 to $1.5 million.

The term "angel" comes from the practice in the early 1900s of wealthy businessmen investing in Broadway productions. Today "angels" typically offer expertise, experience and contacts in addition to money. Less is known about angel investing than venture capital because of the individuality and privacy of the investments. The Center for Venture Research at the University of New Hampshire, which does research on angel investments, has developed the following profile of angel investors:

- The "average" private investor is 47 years old with an annual income of $90,000, a net worth of $750,000, is college educated, has been self-employed and invests $37,000 per venture.
- Most angels invest close to home and rarely put in more than a few hundred thousand dollars.
- Informal investment appears to be the largest source of external equity capital for small businesses. Nine out of ten investments are devoted to small, mostly start-up firms with fewer than 20 employees.
- Nine out of ten investors provide personal loans or loan guarantees to the firms they invest in. On average, this increases the available capital by 57%.
- Informal investors are older, have higher incomes, and are better educated than the average citizen, yet they are not often millionaires. They are a diverse group, displaying a wide range of personal characteristics and investment behavior.
- Seven out of ten investments are made within 50 miles of the investor's home or office.
- Investors expect an average 26% annual return at the time they invest, and they believe that about one-third of their investments are likely to result in a substantial capital loss.
- Investors accept an average of 3 deals for every 10 considered. The most common reasons given for rejecting a deal are insufficient growth potential, overpriced equity, lack of sufficient talent of the management, or lack of information about the entrepreneur or key personnel.
- There appears to be no shortage of informal capital funds. Investors included in the study would have invested almost 35% more than they did if acceptable opportunities had been available.

For the business seeking funding, the right angel investor can be the perfect first step in formal funding. It usually takes less time to meet with an angel and to receive funds, due diligence is less involved and angels usually expect a lower rate of return than a venture capitalist. The downside is finding the right balance of expert help without the angel totally taking charge of the business. Structuring the relationship carefully is an important step in the process.

What Does an Angel Investor Expect?

There are almost as many answers to what angels expect as there are angels. Each has his or her own criteria and foibles because they are individuals. Almost all want a board position and possibly a consulting role. All want good communication although for some that means quarterly reports, while for others that means weekly updates. Return objectives range from a projected internal rate of return of 30% over five years to sales projections of $20 million in the first five years to the potential return of five times their investment in the first five years. Most are looking for anything from a five to 25 per cent stake in the business. Some want securities — either common stock or preferred stock with certain rights and liquidation preferences over common stock. Some even ask for convertible debt, or redeemable preferred stock, which provides a clearer exit strategy for the investor, but also places the company at the risk of repaying the investment plus interest. Additionally, the repayment may imperil future financing since those sources will not likely want to use their investment to bail out prior investors.

Some angels ask for the right of first refusal to participate in the next round of financing. While this sounds eminently reasonable, some venture capitalists will want their own players only or certain investment minimums so this strategy may limit who future participants might be.

Future representation of the board of directors also needs to be clarified. When a new round of financing occurs, do they lose their board rights? Or should that be based on a percentage ownership — when their ownership level drops below a certain level, they no longer have board representation.

In order to protect their investment, angels often ask the business to agree to not take certain actions without the angel investor's approval. These include selling all or substantially all of the company's assets, issuing additional stock to existing management, selling stock below prices paid by the investors or creating classes of stock with liquidation preferences or other rights senior to the angel's class of security. Angels also ask for price protection, that is anti-dilution provisions that will result in their receiving more stock should the business issue stock at a lower price than that paid by the angels.

To prepare to solicit an angel, several critical factors will aid in making the approach successful. First, assemble an advisory board that includes a securities accountant and an attorney. Two important functions of the board are to recommend angels to contact and to work with the management team to develop a business plan to present to the angel. The business plan itself should define the reason for financing, how the capital will be spent and the timetable for going public or seeking venture capital funding.

Most of all, take your time in forming a relationship with an angel. You are going to be spending a number of years together at a critical time in your business's life. Take the time to assure yourself that this is a person with whom you are comfortable through both the ups and downs the future will bring.

As you can see, obtaining money from private venture capital sources might pose a number of interesting problems for you. You will probably have to give up at least partial ownership and control of your business. In addition, angel investors usually have limited resources, so additional funds may not be available if required later. Finally, as amateur investors, these people may not have the patience to wait out the situation if things don't work out as quickly as you originally planned.

The decisions you make regarding any of these issues are very important, extremely complex, and often critical to the success of your prospective deal. You should consult with a professional financial advisor before preparing any proposal for presentation in a search for private capital.

ADDITIONAL SOURCES OF FINANCING

PERSONAL CREDIT CARDS

The credit limit extended by financial institutions on personal credit cards can provide you with ready access to a short-term loan, but usually at interest rates that are considerably higher than more conventional financing (upward of 18 to 22 per cent or more). There may be occasions, however, where other sources of working capital are not available and drawing on the personal line of credit associated with your cards may be the only source of funds available to sustain your business. This can be risky since you are personally liable for the expenditures on the card even though they may have been made for business purposes, but it may be useful if you are expecting a major payment or other injection of cash into the business within a few days.

CANADIAN YOUTH BUSINESS FOUNDATION

The Canadian Youth Business Foundation (CYBF) is a national not-for-profit organization that enables young entrepreneurs (18 to 34 years old) to pursue their aspirations of building successful businesses by providing them with several forms of business assistance. These include:

- a loan program that will provide up to $15,000 to cover the start-up costs of a business

- mentorship programs like Entre Nous for CYBF loan clients and Odyssey for other young people who do not require a business loan but might like a mentor

- an interactive online resource called YouthBusiness.com that provides young entrepreneurs with information, feedback, and other support.

For further information contact one of the CYBF regional offices or the CYBF national office at:
Canadian Youth Business Foundation
123 Edward Street, Suite 1404
Toronto, ON M5G 1E2
(www.cybf.ca)
Telephone: 1-800-464-2923/(416) 408-2923 Fax: (416) 408-3234

SUPPLIERS' INVENTORY BUYING PLANS

In some industries one way of obtaining working capital may be through supplier financing. Suppliers may be prepared to extend payment terms to 60, 90, or even 120 days for some customers. Other suppliers may offer floor plan financing or factoring options to help their dealers finance inventory purchases, usually in advance of the peak selling season. In addition, many suppliers offer discounts off the face value of their invoice (typically 2 per cent for payment within 10 days) or penalize slow-paying customers with interest charges (often 1.5 per cent a month). These programs can impact your financing requirements.

LEASING vs BUYING

In competitive equipment markets, specialized leasing and finance companies will arrange for the lease of such items as expensive pieces of equipment, vehicles, copiers, and computers. Leasing, often with an option to buy rather than purchasing, can free up your scarce capital for investment in other areas of your business. While the interest rates charged on the lease contract may be somewhat higher than you might pay through the bank, the lease expenses are usually fully deductible from your taxable income. A lease contract will fix your cost of having the equipment for a specific term and may provide the flexibility to purchase the equipment at a later date at a predetermined price.

LEASEHOLD IMPROVEMENTS

When locating your business in rented premises, it is usually necessary to undertake a number of leasehold improvements to make the premises appropriate to your needs. Installing new electrical outlets, adding additional partitions and walls, laying carpet, painting, installing fixtures, and similar modifications can add considerably to the cost of launching your business. Sometimes it may be possible to get the landlord of your location to assist in making these improvements, particularly if there is a lot of other space available to rent. The landlord or property manager may agree to provide a portion (an allowance of a dollar amount per square foot of space) or cover all of your leasehold improvement in return for a longer-term lease (typically three to five years). Reducing your initial expenditures in this way can reduce the start-up cash and equity you require to launch your business, even though you will be paying for these improvements in your monthly rent over the course of the lease.

ADVANCE PAYMENT FROM CUSTOMERS

It may be possible to negotiate a full or partial payment from some customers in advance to help finance the costs of taking on their business. In some industries, construction for example, it is customary to receive a partial payment at certain defined stages during the course of the project rather than waiting until completion. These payments can reduce the cash needs of running your business. Any work that involves special orders or custom designs for products specifically tailored to the requirements of one customer should require a significant deposit or full payment in advance.

With this extensive number of alternatives available to you as potential sources of financing, it may be useful for you to give some thought to the range of possibilities you might tap into in putting together the start-up requirements for your new venture. Figure 10.1 provides a framework for you to identify how much money you think you will need to launch your business and where you think that financing might possibly come from: your personal resources; friends, relations, and other personal contacts; lending agencies; grant programs; and other sources that may be available to you.

FIGURE 10.1	WHERE WILL YOU GET THE MONEY?

Starting a business usually requires some money. As we have pointed out in this Stage, there are any number of sources from which this financing can be obtained. You may need to give some thought to approximately how much money you think you will need to launch your business and just where you feel you will be able to obtain it. Completing a form like the one below will give you a good estimate of roughly what your start-up financial requirements are likely to be.

How much money do you think you will need to launch your business? $ _____

Where can you get the funds?

SOURCE	POSSIBLE AMOUNT
Personal Sources	
Cash	$ _____
Stocks/Bonds	_____
Mutual Funds	_____
Term Certificates	_____
RRSPs	_____
Cash Value of Life Insurance	_____
Other Investments _____	_____
Real Estate	_____
Vehicles	_____
Other Assets _____	_____
Credit Card Limits	_____
Other Personal Sources	_____
Total Available from Personal Sources	$ _____
Personal Contacts	
Family Members	$ _____
Friends	_____
Colleagues and Acquaintances	_____
Partners	_____
Other Private Investors _____	_____
Total Available from Personal Contacts	$ _____
Lending Agencies	
Chartered Banks	$ _____
Business Development Bank	_____
Caisse Populaires and Credit Unions	_____
Finance Companies	_____
Government Agencies	_____
Other Lending Agencies _____	_____
Total Available from Lending Agencies	$ _____
Grant Programs	
Federal Government Programs	$ _____
Provincial Government Programs	_____
Municipal Programs	_____
Other _____	
Total Available from Grants	$ _____
Other Sources	
Supplier Credit	$ _____
Customers	_____
Others _____	_____
Total Available from Other Sources	$ _____
TOTAL AVAILABLE FROM ALL SOURCES	$ _____

EVALUATING YOUR ABILITY TO SECURE FINANCING

Financing is not a business's right. Johanne Dion, the CEO of TRANS-HERB e Inc. and one of Canada's top women entrepreneurs, says, "Banks are not there to lend you dollars. They're there to make a profit. If you don't have a good plan, if you don't do your (financial) statements every year, they'll say 'Sorry we need our money.'"[2]

When seeking a loan, it is wise to shop around for the best available terms. This includes comparing obvious features of the loan such as the interest rate but also evaluating:

- Size of transaction fees
- Prepayment policies
- Flexibility of payment terms
- Fixed or floating interest rate
- Security and personal guarantees required
- Quality of overall service provided by the institution
- Expected processing time

An important aspect of your financial condition is your ability to obtain financing. In preparing to approach a banker regarding a loan, the following are several suggestions you should keep in mind to increase your probability of getting the funds:

- Don't just drop in on your bank manager; make an appointment.
- Start your presentation by briefly describing your business and the exact reason you require a loan.
- Be prepared to answer any questions your banker may have. He or she wants to determine how well you really understand your business. If you can't answer certain questions, explain why and say when you will be able to provide the information.
- Be prepared to discuss collateral and other security you may be required to provide.
- If your business is currently operating, invite the banker to stop by to see it first-hand.
- Ask when you can expect a reply to your request. If there is a delay, inquire whether there is additional information you need to provide.

PROFIT magazine asked entrepreneurs, bankers, and financial consultants their most successful time-tested secrets for getting the best from their banker. Here are their suggestions:

- **Know what your banker is looking for** Before you set foot inside a bank, you should understand the ground rules of credit. Banks are not in the business of financing risk. Before they sign on the dotted line they need evidence you have a comprehensive plan and the management skills to successfully implement it. Ask yourself the question, "If I were a banker, would I lend money to me?" The bank needs to be reassured that you can repay your loan. The bank will also look for an existing strong base of equity investment in the company. Don't expect the bank to invest in something you wouldn't invest in yourself. To reduce its risk the bank will want some form of collateral security. In many cases, the bank will require collateral worth two or three times the amount of the loan.

- **Don't "tell" your banker, "show him"** Don't just tell your banker about the great new product you have devised. Bring it or a prototype of it along to your banker and demonstrate what makes it so great. Bring in a sample of whatever it is you plan to sell and let your banker see it, taste it, or try it firsthand.

- **Interview your banker** There are no good banks, only good bankers. Be prepared to shop around. Make certain you are dealing with the right person and the right branch for you. Visit at least three different banks before making a decision. Ask your accountant, lawyer, customers, or suppliers for a referral.

- **Passion makes perfect** The most persuasive thing entrepreneurs can do when negotiating a loan is to show how much passion they have for what they are doing. You should try to present the attitude that you are prepared to do everything possible to make the business succeed.

---

2. Kara Kuryllowicz, "Learning the Ropes," *PROFIT*, October 2001, p. 42.

- **Ask for more money than you need** One of the worst mistakes you can make is to not consider your future requirements when calculating the size of the loan or the line of credit you think you will need. If you have to go back to the bank in five or six months to ask for an increase, the bank is going to be very concerned. It reflects badly on your ability to plan and you are also making extra work for the bank that could be reflected in extra charges for your loan.

- **Get your banker involved in your business** Invite your banker over, at least every six months, even if it's just for coffee. Make time to get to know your banker, to get him or her involved, and ask them for advice. Take advantage of opportunities to network with bankers and their colleagues. If the bank holds a reception, or open house, make an effort to attend.

- **Increase your credit when you don't need it** Many entrepreneurs begin looking for outside financing only when their own resources are tapped out. You should start to begin sourcing funds at least a year before you need it. Advanced planning will give you time to adequately explore all your options, meet with several banks, and ultimately work out the best deal for your business.

- **Make professional introductions** Introduce your lawyer and your accountant to your banker. Make sure your accountant reviews the bank's proposal outlining the terms and conditions of your loan or line of credit.

- **If all else fails, keep looking** Finding the money to start or expand a business is hard work. Most entrepreneurs have been turned down many times for financing. The key is continuing to pursue every available means of securing the capital you need.[3]

A financial institution may turn down your loan application for any of a number of reasons, and it is important that you ask what they are. This knowledge may help you in future attempts to secure funding. Some of the most frequent reasons why a loan application can be rejected are as follows:

1. The business idea might be considered ill-advised or just too risky.

2. You may not have offered sufficient collateral. Lenders want some assurance that they will be able to recover most or all of their money should you default on the payments.

3. The lender may feel there is insufficient financial commitment on your part.

4. You have not prepared a comprehensive and detailed business plan.

5. Your reason for requesting the loan is unclear or not acceptable to the lender. It is important that you specify the intended application of the requested funds and that this application be outlined in detail. This outline should also show your planned schedule for the repayment of the loan.

6. You do not appear confident, enthusiastic, well-informed, or realistic enough in your objectives. The lender's assessment of your character, personality, and stability are important considerations in his or her evaluation of your loan application.

The worksheet shown in Figure 10.2 will allow you to assess some of the critical factors that may affect your ability to secure external funding. It will also give you some indication of what aspects of your personal character, development of your business plan, or quality of the basic idea underlying your new venture could be improved. On the worksheet, indicate your assessment of your personal situation for each of the indicated factors as honestly as you can. How do you rate? Could some factors be improved upon? What can you do to strengthen these areas, or how might you overcome these negative factors?

One question you should consider is "How much can I possibly lose on my venture should it fail?" The losses in some types of businesses can wipe out virtually all of the funds you have invested or personally guaranteed. This tends to be true in situations like a financial planning and counselling business, travel agency, or hair salon, in which very little property or equipment is owned by the business. In other situations, such as manufacturing, construction, or real estate, there is usually an opportunity to sell the assets solely or partially owned by the business to recover at least part of your initial investment.

The way to explore this question is to consider alternative scenarios for different ways in which the business might fail and estimate the liquidation value of any residual assets. To the extent that this value falls short of the initial cost of those assets less any outstanding claims, you could lose that amount of money plus the opportunity cost of the time and effort you spent in trying to develop the business.

---

3. Adapted from David Menzies, "Getting the Best From Your Bank," *PROFIT*, November, 1998, pp. 26–32. Reprinted with permission.

FIGURE 10.2   LOAN APPLICATION ASSESSMENT WORKSHEET

Assessment Factor	Poor 1	2	Good 3	Excellent 4	5
Personal credit rating	____	____	____	____	____
Capacity to pay back loan from personal assets if business fails	____	____	____	____	____
Collateral to pay back loan from personal assets if business fails	____	____	____	____	____
Character (as perceived in the community)	____	____	____	____	____
Commitment (your personal investment of time, energy, and money)	____	____	____	____	____
Clarity and completeness of your business plan	____	____	____	____	____
Viability of business concept (e.g., moderate risk)	____	____	____	____	____
Personal experience in the proposed business	____	____	____	____	____
Successful experience in your own business	____	____	____	____	____
Balanced management team available	____	____	____	____	____
Suitability of your personality to the pressures and responsibilities of the business	____	____	____	____	____

What can you do to improve the weak areas (where you have rated yourself 1 or 2)?

_____

_____

_____

_____

Adapted from D. A. Gray, *The Entrepreneur's Complete Self-Assessment Guide* (Vancouver: International Self-Counsel Press Ltd., 1986), p. 123.

FYI   FOR YOUR INFORMATION

For more information on obtaining financing for your new business, you could consult the following Web sites:

Industry Canada This site contains an extensive directory of Canadian financial providers, a powerful search engine of financial providers, information on different types of financing and financial providers, and tips to help you secure financing. (strategis.ic.gc.ca/epic/internet/insof-sdf.nsf/vwGeneratedInterE/Home)

Canadian Youth Business Foundation This organization is a non-profit, private-sector initiative designed to provide mentoring, business support, and loans to young Canadian entrepreneurs who are starting new businesses. (www.cybf.ca)

Canadian Bankers Association, Small Business Financing This site provides information on sources and types of small business financing. (www.cba.ca/en/viewPub.asp?fl=6&sl=23&docid=33&pg=1)

Business Development Bank of Canada This site provides an overview of Business Development Bank financial products aimed at young entrepreneurs, Aboriginal people, and small business in general. (www.bdc.ca)

Atlantic Canada Opportunity Agency (ACOA) Programs This site provides an overview of a number of programs provided by ACOA to help Atlantic Canada entrepreneurs start new businesses or upgrade existing ones. (www.acoa.ca/e/financial)

About Canada — Small Business, Canada Places to find the money and financial information you need to start and grow your Canadian small business, including types of financing, sources of funds, attracting investors, and financial advice from experts. (sbinfocanada.about.com/cs/financing)

Doing Business In Canada, Canadian Business Guide, Money Matters An overview of financial matters as they relate to small business in Canada including financing and insurance. (www.dbic.com/guide/m5-1.html)

Idea Cafe, Idea Cafe's Feast of Financing This is a U.S. site but has lots of interesting information. (www.businessownersideacafe.com/financing/index.html)

America's Business Funding Directory A guide to over 4,000 business loan and venture capital sources of funding (principally in the United States). (www.businessfinance.com)

Banks You might also check the Web sites of Canada's major chartered banks.

Video Case #12

Sugar High

Summary

Two young entrepreneurs have a sweet plan to corner the candy market in Canada. Chris Emery and Larry Finson have sunk everything they have into Clodhoppers candy, a confectionery based on Chris's grandma's secret recipe, produced by their company, Krave's Candy Co. While the two have been successful in nailing down some big orders with Wal-Mart, Zellers, and other chains, getting the candy from the factory to the store shelves and then into people's mouths has been a difficult and expensive process. Emery and Finson are on the brink of success, but need to find a million dollars fast. How will they raise the money and still try to keep control of their long-term dream?

Questions for Discussion

1. What do young entrepreneurs like Emery and Finson risk when they put everything they have and can raise into a business that always seems to be on the verge of a meltdown?

2. How did Emery and Finson manage to solve their financial woes, even though the solution was only temporary?

3. What are the risks of giving up control of your company, even though it may be only partial control?

4. What are the advantages and disadvantages of a small company like Kraves going international in a large market like the United States, with many strong, established competitors?

Preparing Your Business Plan

The final stage in building a dream for a new venture of your own is developing your business plan. A business plan is a written document that describes all aspects of your business venture — your basic product or service, your prospective customers, the competition, your production and marketing methods, your management team, how the business will be financed, and all the other things necessary to implement your idea. It might be called the "game plan" of your business.

BUSINESS PLANNING — THE "BIG PICTURE"

WHY CONSIDER THE "BIG PICTURE"?

When you start your business you will find that there are many things that happen that you didn't expect, or didn't work out the way you expected. Don't worry. Your experience in this regard won't be unique. This happens to almost everyone. What is important is for you to be prepared for this to happen and ready to make adjustments. In making these changes it is important that you don't lose sight of what it is that you are really trying to do. This means that you need to keep in mind the "big picture," which is brought together in the business planning process.

THE STEPS IN THE BUSINESS PLANNING PROCESS

The business planning process focuses on the future. It enables you to relate what you wish to achieve to what your business concept or idea can deliver. It entails working your way through each of the following steps in a logical and sequential way.

1. DEVELOP A VISION STATEMENT

A *vision statement* focuses on the "what" of your business and should describe your idealized perception of what your business will look like under perfect conditions, if all your goals and objectives have been met. It lays out the "super goal" that you would like your business to achieve. The key components of your vision statement will be:

- Name of your planned business venture
- Product/service offering you plan to provide
- Target market(s) you intend to serve

Your vision statement should be short (a sentence or two). It should also be easy to understand and easy to remember.

For example, a typical vision statement for a new sporting goods retailer might be:

The Hockey House plans to provide a wide range of hockey-related products and services to casual skaters, minor league hockey players, community clubs and organizations, and competitive hockey teams and players.

2. FORMULATE A MISSION STATEMENT

A *mission statement* focuses on the "how" of your business. It defines the purpose of your venture, outlines the reason for the existence of your business, and provides some understanding of how your business will be operated. It is, in fact, the "super strategy" of your business. The key components of your mission statement will describe:

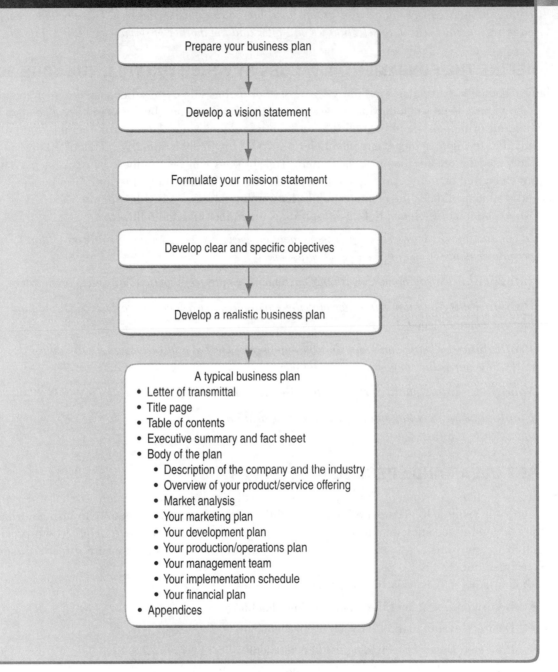

BUSINESS PLAN

Prepare your business plan

↓

Develop a vision statement

↓

Formulate your mission statement

↓

Develop clear and specific objectives

↓

Develop a realistic business plan

↓

A typical business plan
- Letter of transmittal
- Title page
- Table of contents
- Executive summary and fact sheet
- Body of the plan
    - Description of the company and the industry
    - Overview of your product/service offering
    - Market analysis
    - Your marketing plan
    - Your development plan
    - Your production/operations plan
    - Your management team
    - Your implementation schedule
    - Your financial plan
- Appendices

- What your business will do
- Its market focus, niche, or particular image
- Your planned location and the geographic market served
- How you plan to grow the business
- Your sustainable uniqueness, or what will distinguish your business from others and will continue to do so on a long-term basis

Your mission statement should be a series of short phrases that addresses each of these elements. For example, a mission statement for The Hockey House might state:

The Hockey House will provide a broad range of skates, sticks, pads, sweaters, and other related hockey equipment and services intended to meet the requirements of ice and in-line hockey players at all levels of ability, from beginners to semi-professional and professionals. It will also sell related supplies and equipment such as goal nets and timers, with a view to being the one-stop shop for hockey in Manitoba and northwestern Ontario. It will sell to individuals, teams, and community clubs through a retail outlet located adjacent to a major hockey complex in Winnipeg but will also produce a four-colour catalogue and call personally on groups in communities outside the city. Our principal competitive edge will be the breadth of selection we can offer and the quality of service we plan to provide.

3. DEFINE THE FUNDAMENTAL VALUES BY WHICH YOU WILL RUN YOUR BUSINESS

Many arguments, particularly in family businesses or partnerships, occur because the members do not share common values, even when they often assume that they do. For a new business to have a good chance of succeeding, all principals should agree on a basic set of values by which they will operate. The process of discussing and trying to achieve agreement on these values is likely to identify points of difference that should be addressed before the business is started. This process can be conducted in two steps. The first step requires you and any other principals associated with the business to define their own personal values. The second step consolidates the common values by which the business will be operated.

An example of a statement of business values might look like the following:

In conducting our business, we will implement our vision by conducting our affairs so that our actions provide evidence of the high value we place on:

Integrity *by dealing honestly with our customers, employees, suppliers, and the community*

Responsibility *by taking into account the environment in which we do business, community views, and the common good*

Profitability *by being conscious that an appropriate level of profit is necessary to sustain the business and allow our values to continue to be observed*

Value *by providing quality products that are recognized as delivering value for money*

Employees *by providing quality, equitable opportunities for development in a healthy workplace, with appropriate rewards*

4. SET CLEAR AND SPECIFIC OBJECTIVES

Setting objectives for your business provides you with yardsticks with which to measure your ability to achieve your vision. Objectives define measurable targets whose achievement can also contribute directly to the successful accomplishment of the mission of your business. Unlike "goals," which provide a broad direction for your business, "objectives" provide you with the means to measure directly the performance of your business.

Business objectives usually relate to such issues as:

- Return on investment the business should achieve
- Desired level of market position or market share
- Projected stages of technological development
- Specific levels of financial performance

To be effective an objective should:

- Refer to a specific outcome, not an activity
- Be measurable
- Be realistic and achievable based on the actual capabilities of the business
- Contain a specific time deadline

For example, a reasonable set of objectives for The Hockey House might be:

1. *To generate $xxxx in sales by the end of year one*
2. *To achieve $yyy in after-tax profits in year one*
3. *To increase inventory turnover from x times to y times during year one*

Figure 11.3 on page 313 near the end of this Stage outlines a framework that will enable you to develop the "big picture" for your business.

5. MAKE IT HAPPEN! DEVELOP A REALISTIC BUSINESS PLAN

Your business plan is the most important business document you will ever prepare and it is also probably the most difficult. It takes a lot of time, research, self-discipline, and commitment to complete properly and is not a lot of fun. However, regardless of whether you intend to start a small, part-time business in the basement of your home or launch a sophisticated, high-growth venture, you still need a business plan.

Your business plan is the culmination of all your self-evaluation, ideas, research, analysis, assessment, round-table discussions, bull sessions, schemes, and daydreams. It lays out the details so that everyone can see precisely where you are now, where you are going, and how you plan to get there. It presents everything about you and what you intend to do — your goals and objectives, opportunities and threats facing you, your business strengths and weaknesses, and so on. It is a comprehensive but concise disclosure of all aspects of your business venture.

How you define your business plan, however, affects your approach to writing it. If you view it as a very complex and boring task, your plan will come across that way to any reader. As a result, many business plans are dry, rambling, and highly technical because the entrepreneurs behind them see them largely as some sort of formal academic exercise.

Your business plan should be viewed as a selling document, not unlike a piece of sales literature you would distribute about your company. Except that with your business plan, rather than just promoting a particular product or service, you are selling the whole company as a package. If you are really excited about your company and the idea on which it is based, it should come through in your business plan. Your plan should convey to readers the excitement and promise that you feel about your venture.

Notice in Entrepreneurs in Action #34 the time and effort Kent Groves dedicated to the development of his business plan. He spent over a year researching the mail-order industry, studying the competition, and asking questions of people who were experts in the business. Then, with the assistance of an accountant, he wrote his "road map" to guide him through every aspect of the implementation of his business. With the plan, he was also able to win the confidence of a banker who provided him with the necessary line of credit to carry his seasonal business over its slow periods. His business plan has become a combined operations manual/corporate bible that can be continually referred to so that he knows if, in fact, the business is evolving as he had originally anticipated.

WHY DEVELOP A BUSINESS PLAN?

Your business plan can accomplish many things for you and your proposed venture. These can largely be categorized into two basic areas:

1. **For the internal evaluation of your business,** both as a checklist to see that you have covered all the important bases and as a timetable for accomplishing your stated objectives
2. **For external use** in attracting resources and obtaining support for your venture

From an internal perspective, developing a plan forces you to seriously consider the important elements of your venture and the steps you feel are necessary to get it off the ground. Your plan can be used to inform employees about the goals and direction of your business. It lets everyone know how they fit into the organization and what you expect of them. Your plan can also help you develop as a manager. It requires you to deal with problems relating to competitive conditions, promotional opportunities, and other situations that your business will encounter.

Externally, your business plan can serve as an effective sales document and is considered by many experts to be the heart of the capital-raising process. Any knowledgeable banker or prospective investor will expect you to be professional in your approach, fully prepared, and armed with a thoroughly researched, well-written business plan when seeking their support. Very little money has been raised for business ideas scribbled on the back of envelopes or on restaurant placemats, despite considerable folklore to the contrary.

In the course of attracting external support for your venture, a number of people may have occasion to read your plan. These include bankers, suppliers, prospective customers, and potential investors. Each of

34 Entrepreneurs in action

Business Plans: The Lies We Tell Our Bankers?

Some business people call them "the lies we tell our bankers." In this economy, however, a company looking for credit must put a lot more than creative writing in its business plan.

Kent Groves, president of catalogue retailer Maritime Trading Co. [MTC] of Falmouth, N.S., and a former Nutrilawn International manager who spent a lot of time approving franchises, knows the importance of business plans. "Some of the best plans I saw were put together by people who totally ignored them once the loan was approved. And their franchises were in trouble."

Groves took a year to research the mail-order industry, studying catalogues, trade magazines and reports, and asking questions of industry experts. Then, with an accountant, he spent six weeks writing what he calls a "road map to guide you through every aspect of your operations."

The result: a 68-page plan with 16 appendices. Groves' Rand-McNally approach to mapping business highways offers an executive summary, mission statement ("we are the leader in the direct marketing of the highest quality Maritime products in the world"), profile, industry overview, and bibliography. And he provided details on sales and marketing, operations, and financing. "It helped to have an accountant who would say, 'Those figures don't make sense,'" says Groves. "She asked the hard questions."

Most of Groves' efforts were geared to winning a line of credit — essential for a firm that makes all its money at Christmas. But the effort proved frustrating: MTC's application was rejected by Scotiabank, CIBC, and Hongkong Bank. The setback soured Groves: "The banks advertise 'We support small business.' Yeah, until you need money. What a crock!"

After moving to Nova Scotia full-time in June, Groves approached the Royal Bank in Halifax. There he met account manager Earl Covin, who got excited by his plan. "It was a breath of fresh air," says Covin. "I didn't have to do a lot of background work. It had more detail than most bankers ever expect, and it was very realistic." Once past the collateral hurdle — Groves' father helped out — the bank approved a $75,000 credit line in a day.

Beyond winning financial support, MTC's business plan has become a combined operations manual/corporate bible. Says Groves, "We continually check our expenses and they're right on track. We know where we stand." So when he saw catalogue costs coming in 25% below projections, he knew he could boost marketing spending 20%.

More importantly, revenue projections are also on budget. Another catalogue company, using one of the same mailing lists as Groves, received a 1.5% response rate — "dead on" for MTC's projections. MTC forecast an operating deficit of $49,200 at the end of September; the actual amount was $45,000. With his catalogues just hitting the market in October, Groves still expects sales to reach $100,000 by Dec. 31.

Like most road maps, MTC's business plan allows for dirt roads and detours. "When we stray," says Groves, "we know it and at what capacity we're varying. What's important is flexibility that allows you to make changes." (www.maritimetrading.com)

Source: Allan Lynch, *PROFIT*. Lynch is also author of *Sweat Equity: Atlantic Canada's New Entrepreneurs* (Halifax, NS: Nimbris Publishing 1996).

them will be viewing your business from a slightly different perspective. Bankers, for example, are primarily interested in the business's fixed assets and other available collateral. They want to know if you can pay back their loan at prevailing interest rates. Venture capitalists and other private investors, on the other hand, are more interested in their expected return on investment. They tend to like innovative products and services in growth industries that promise significant returns. These differing viewpoints should be taken into account in developing your plan.

Heidi Lang of the Transatlantic Marketing Group definitely learned the value of having a well-formulated business plan when she went looking for financing to fund the expansion of her business producing and selling photo frames (Entrepreneurs in Action #35). The business was started largely on the basis of what she felt was a market opportunity and her family's economic need at the time. There was no real plan. However, when it came

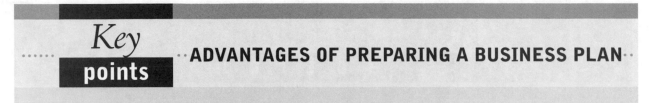

ADVANTAGES OF PREPARING A BUSINESS PLAN

A business plan:

- Helps you to face reality and the facts
- Forces you to think ahead and consider the future
- Assists you in summarizing your skills and points out the strengths of others involved in your venture
- Helps you identify and define your product/service, pricing strategy, distribution strategy, and marketing and promotional strategy
- Establishes the amount of financing or outside investment you require
- Outlines the financial future of your business through projected statements such as cash flow, income and expenses, and balance sheets
- Provides you with an effective sales tool
- Inspires confidence in yourself and projects that confidence to others

Source: Dawn Braddock, "How to Write a Business Plan that Makes Good Business Sense," *Business Sense*, November 2000, pp. 16–17.

time to look for financing for the business beyond what she could personally provide, Lang discovered that no one would talk to her because she didn't have a clear vision of where she was going with the business and what she planned to do with the money she was seeking. Somewhat frustrated, she got some expert advice and put together a five-year plan. This plan, combined with the strong market performance the company had achieved up to then, enabled her to obtain the financing she was looking for. Now business planning has become an integral part of her ongoing activities. It gives her business a clear focus and enables her to look beyond the day-to-day activities and keep on track in relation to the changing environment she sees occurring around the business.

HOW LONG SHOULD YOUR BUSINESS PLAN BE?

Business plans can be broadly categorized into three types: the summary business plan, the full business plan, and the operational business plan.

THE SUMMARY BUSINESS PLAN

Summary business plans commonly run about 10 pages or so, considerably shorter than the 40 or so pages traditional for business plans. Summary business plans have become increasingly popular and accepted for use by early-stage businesses in applying for a bank loan, or they may be all that is required for a small, lifestyle business such as a convenience store, home-based business, graphic design company, or consulting firm. A summary business plan may also be sufficient to whet the appetite of friends, relatives, and other private investors who might subsequently receive a copy of the full plan if they are sufficiently interested.

THE FULL BUSINESS PLAN

A full business plan similar to the one you would develop by following the samples at the end of this Stage will likely run from 10 to 40 pages. This is the traditional plan. It covers all the key subjects in enough depth to permit a full exploration of the principal issues. The full business plan is most appropriate when you are trying to raise a substantial amount of external financing or if you are looking for a partner or other major private investors.

THE OPERATIONAL BUSINESS PLAN

The operational business plan will usually exceed 40 pages in length but is used only infrequently, such as when a business is planning to grow very rapidly and must try to anticipate a wide variety of issues. Or it might be part of an annual process where it is necessary to get into great detail about distribution, production,

35 Entrepreneurs in action

The Road Ahead

I must make a confession: I did not set out to create a multimillion-dollar business. I mean, like everyone else, I was looking for an opportunity. But I did not have a road map.

And so I find a certain paradox around the subject of planning. I still have grave doubts about the efficacy of making big plans in a world that is shifting gears at G-force speeds. Having said this, I can tell you that the ability at Transatlantic Marketing Group (TMG) to forge cohesive business plans and anticipate shifting market growth has been critical to the success we are currently experiencing.

Our story began in 1993. My husband had just lost his job, and though I was managing a successful independent sales agency, I was certainly not earning enough money to support our household without a second income. We were eating through our savings just to live.

And so necessity became the mother of invention. At work, I had identified a small niche in the marketplace for interesting lines of photo frames, and I decided to try filling it. But after no luck sourcing the product, I thought, "Hey, how tough can this be? I am going to find someone who can make these up for me." So I took the last $10,000 of our savings and waded in. And that's how my company started — there was no grand plan.

Working from home, I found someone who would make up custom frames for me and I began showing them to my retail clients. The product was greeted enthusiastically right from the beginning, particularly in the United States. My background is in sales, and I'm pretty good at it, so I knew how to open the right doors.

I initially capitalized the venture with personal savings and a small grant from the government. The banks were unavailable to us (as they are to many new businesses) so we financed inventory with my Visa card. We also factored our receivables, which was expensive, but it meant we were able to manage our cash flow.

My respect for a well-formulated business plan really grew out of the company's requirements in our second phase of growth. Right from the start, the major retail chains embraced our products. But just over five years into the business, TMG experienced an explosion in sales of over 4,000 per cent. With individual orders in the $50,000 to $80,000 range, it was difficult to find suppliers who would provide TMG with the quality and quantity of materials to meet that kind of demand. Part of the solution lay in finding a reliable source of financing.

My epiphany came when I went out to meet with banks about securing additional financing. No one would talk to me because I didn't have a clearly laid out vision of where I was going and what I wanted to do with the new money I was seeking.

I am nothing if not honest about my own strengths and weaknesses. I have good instincts about the market and I have a ferocious work ethic. But I had no previous experience with systematic marketing analysis. I didn't know anything about long-range business planning and cash flow projections. So I found some expert advice to help put together a five-year projection. We assembled a complete analysis of our competitors to find the windows of opportunity in our category. This plan, combined with our strong track record, helped us win support from a venture capital company that has proven to be a strong financial ally. Even though our business is unusual in their portfolio, our professional approach to management and planning gave them the confidence to go forward with us and our aggressive growth strategy. Our new financing allowed us to move into our own plant and bring production under our direct control.

Of course, all the planning in the world cannot anticipate the unforeseen. There are no rules that lead safely to a predictable outcome. Things change by the day — sales, people and cash flow. But a solid plan can help avoid many of the pitfalls that confront every small business, and can help stabilize problems when they do occur. Exigency plans give us the ability to turn on a dime, quickly and sure-footedly if (and when) our circumstances change. I don't believe in waiting till I have a major problem on my hands; I seek help from experts early. I apply my energies where my skills really count. I stay on the road close to my customers and rely on my advisors to provide professional advice.

Planning is a part of everything I do now. It offers us vision, the ability to clamber over the day-to-day grind and see into the distance for changes and alterations in the terrain ahead. Our map is based on all we know about our existing business and everything we can extrapolate about the future. It reflects the economy and a business environment that is not static but dynamic. You have to be ready to accommodate change and absorb shifts in the marketplace. Planning is the name of the game in a world that is roiling with the forces of economic upheaval. As I see it, there really isn't any other way.

Source: Heidi Lang, "The Road Ahead," *PROFIT* (www.profitguide.com/firstperson/Fl_lang.html), July 12, 2001. Reprinted with permission.

Key points ······ TIPS FOR DEVELOPING YOUR BUSINESS PLAN ···

Here are some pointers to consider in developing your business plan:

- **Business planning involves a great deal of work** Be prepared to spend weeks—or months—completing your plan.
- **Work on sections at a time** While this undertaking may appear overwhelming at first, don't get discouraged. Break the project down into manageable chunks and work on each chunk separately.
- **Be brief but complete** Although you may have volumes of important material, aim for a plan that is brief and succinct but includes everything important to the business.
- **Focus on your intended reader** Use your plan to organize your efforts around your objectives to ensure you have all the bases covered.
- **Use layman's terms** Avoid highly technical descriptions of your products, processes, and operations.
- **A business plan is a "living" document** Update it as your knowledge grows and whenever your plans become more concrete.
- **Be realistic** Base your projections on the results gathered from your analysis. Be honest about both positive and negative findings.
- **Discuss your firm's business risks** Your credibility can be seriously undermined if existing risks and problems are discovered by readers on their own.
- **Don't make vague or unsubstantiated statements** Back up your statements with background data and market information.

Source: Adapted from *Entrepreneurial Edge*, Edward Lowe Foundation, "How to Develop and Use a Business Plan" (edwardlowe.org).

---

advertising, and other areas where it is essential for everyone involved with the organization to understand clearly everything that is going on. Traditional business plans that grow to this length should be avoided as they reflect a lack of discipline and focus.

WHO SHOULD WRITE YOUR BUSINESS PLAN?

You should write your business plan. If someone else develops the business plan for you, it becomes their plan, not yours. If you are part of a management team, each individual should contribute his or her part to the overall project.

Do not under any circumstances hire someone else to write the plan for you. This doesn't mean that you shouldn't get help from others in compiling information, obtaining licences, permits, patents, and other legal considerations, or preparing your pro forma financial statements — only that the final plan should be written by you and your team.

The people who may be assessing your plan want to know that you see the big picture as it relates to your business and understand all the functional requirements of your company, not that you can hire a good consultant. It is very difficult to defend someone else's work. If you put your business plan together yourself, you have a better understanding and feel for the business. Your business plan should be a personal expression written in your own unique style, though of course it should look professional and businesslike.

HOW LONG DOES IT TAKE?

Putting together a business plan does not happen overnight; the process can stretch over several months. Table 11.1 outlines the steps that should be taken to prepare a business plan, and the amount of time it may take to complete each step.

The flow chart in Figure 11.1 indicates how all these steps in developing a business plan interrelate. It shows how certain key steps cannot be undertaken until others have been completed. For example, you cannot effectively research the market (step 4) until you have selected a particular product or service idea (step 3). Similarly, until the market has been researched (step 4), a site chosen (step 6), and a revenue forecast prepared (step 5), you can't develop your detailed marketing plan (step 8).

The 16-week time span shown here is only for illustrative purposes — the actual time required to prepare your business plan will vary with the nature of your venture. A plan for a relatively simple, straightforward business might be completed within a few weeks, while a plan for a complex, high-growth new venture could take many months.

WHAT SHOULD YOUR PLAN CONTAIN?

Your business plan is the nuts and bolts of your proposed business venture put down on paper. You will have to decide exactly what information to include, how your plan can be best organized for maximum effectiveness, and what information should be given particular emphasis. All plans, however, require a formal, structured presentation so that they are easy to read and follow and tend to avoid confusion. A number of forms and sample outlines for a business plan are available, but virtually all suggest that business plans contain the following components: (1) letter of transmittal, (2) title page, (3) table of contents, (4) executive summary and fact sheet, (5) body, and (6) appendices. The contents of a typical business plan are outlined in Figure 11.2. on page 303. You can use this framework as a guideline to assist you in the development of the plan for your business.

TABLE 11.1   SUGGESTED STEPS IN DEVELOPING YOUR BUSINESS PLAN

Step	Description	Completion Date
1	Decide to go into business for yourself.	
2	Analyze your strengths and weaknesses, paying special attention to your business experience, business education, and desires.	Third week
3	Choose the product or service that best fits your strengths and desires.	Fourth week
4	Research the market for your product or service.	Seventh week
5	Forecast your share of market if possible.	Eighth week
6	Choose a site for your business.	Eighth week
7	Develop your supplier/production plan.	Tenth week
8	Develop your marketing plan.	Tenth week
9	Develop your personnel plan.	Twelfth week
10	Decide whether to form a sole proprietorship, a partnership, or a corporation.	Twelfth week
11	Explain the kinds of records and reports you plan to have.	Twelfth week
12	Develop your insurance plan.	Twelfth week
13	Develop your financial plan.	Fifteenth week
14	Write a summary overview of your business plan, stressing its purpose and promise.	Sixteenth week

SHERMAN'S LAGOON

©Jim Toomey. Reprinted with special permission of King Features Syndicate.

1. LETTER OF TRANSMITTAL

The letter of transmittal officially introduces your business plan to the reader. It explains your reason for writing the plan, gives the title of the plan or the name of your business, and outlines the major features of your plan that may be of interest.

FIGURE 11.1 **FLOW CHART OF THE STEPS IN DEVELOPING A BUSINESS PLAN**

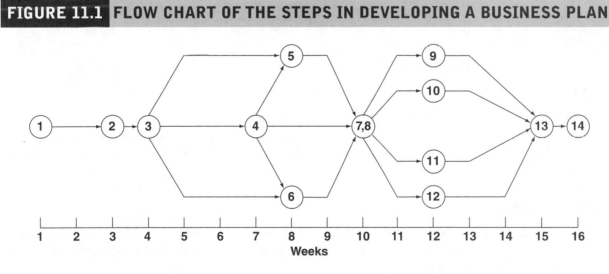

KEY

1. Decide to go into business.
2. Analyze yourself.
3. Pick product or service.
4. Research market.
5. Forecast sales revenues.
6. Pick site.
7. Develop supplier/production plan.

8. Develop marketing plan.
9. Develop personnel plan.
10. Decide whether to incorporate.
11. Explain need for records.
12. Develop insurance plan.
13. Develop financial plan.
14. Write summary overview.

Adapted from Nicholas C. Siropolis, *Small Business Management: A Guide to Entrepreneurship*, 2nd ed. (Boston: Houghton Mifflin Co., 1982), pp. 138–141.

FYI FOR YOUR INFORMATION

BUSINESS PLAN OUTLINES AND TEMPLATES

Here are some examples of Web sites that have detailed instructions, outlines, or templates for developing a comprehensive business plan.

Interactive Business Planner The IBP is a business planning software product designed specifically to operate on the World Wide Web. It uses the capabilities of the Internet to assist entrepreneurs in preparing a three-year business plan for a new or existing business. (www.cbsc.org/ibp)

The Entrepreneurship Centre Business Plan Outline A downloadable Business Plan Workbook. (www.entrepreneurship.com/tools/businessplanworkbook.asp)

Online Small Business Workshop A well-developed business plan outline plus a number of sample business plans for fictitious small companies. Presented by the Canada/British Columbia Business Services Centre. (www.smallbusinessbc.ca/workshop/busplan.php)

Deloitte & Touche, Writing an Effective Business Plan A guide to help you write an effective business plan. (www.deloitte.com/dtt/article/0,2297,sid%253D2000%2526cid%253D9021,00.html)

BizPlanIt's Virtual Business Plan This unique and free online resource mirrors the major sections of a business plan, and enables you to learn the fundamentals of writing a business plan. (www.bizplanit.com/vplan.htm)

Money Hunt Business Plan Template A U.S. site claiming to have the best business plan outline on the Web. (www.moneyhunter.com)

2. TITLE PAGE

The title page, or cover page, of your plan provides identifying information about you and your proposed business. It should include the name, address, and telephone number of the business as well as similar information about yourself. The date the plan was finalized or submitted to the recipient should also be included on the title page.

3. TABLE OF CONTENTS

The table of contents is a list of the major headings and subheadings contained in your plan. It provides readers with a quick overview of the contents of your plan and allows them to quickly access the particular sections that may be of primary interest to them.

4. EXECUTIVE SUMMARY AND FACT SHEET

The executive summary may be the most important part of your business plan. It must capture the attention of the reader, stimulate interest, and get the reader to keep on reading the rest of your plan. In two or three pages this summary should concisely explain your business's current status; describe its products or services and their benefits to your customers; provide an overview of your venture's objectives, market prospects, and financial forecasts; and, if you are using the plan to raise external financing, indicate the amount of financing needed, how the money is to be used, and the benefits to the prospective lender or investor.

This summary should give the essence of your plan and highlight its really significant points. In many instances the summary will either sell the reader on continuing to read the rest of the document or convince him or her to forget the whole thing; the game may be won or lost on the basis of the executive summary.

FIGURE 11.2 A TYPICAL BUSINESS PLAN

Business Plan Contents

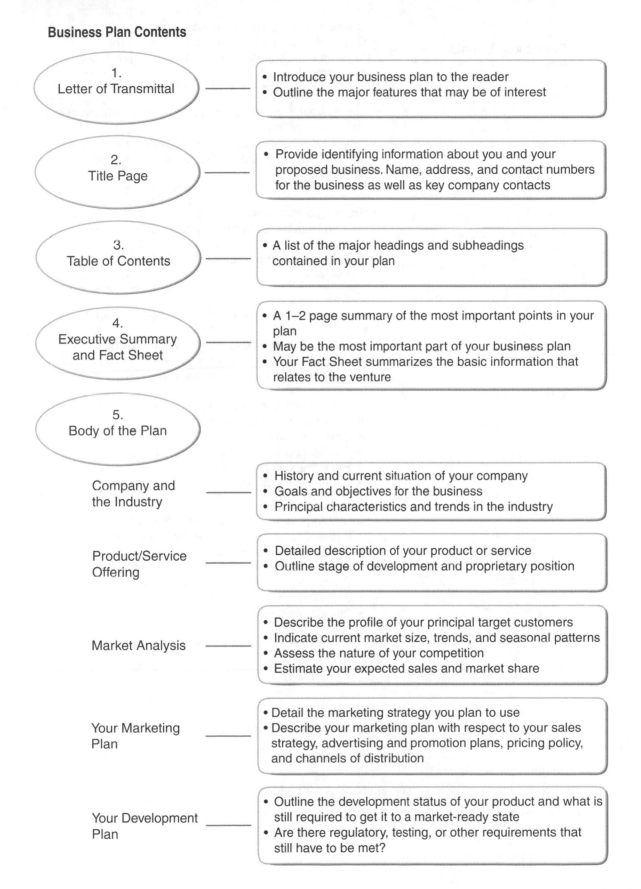

1. Letter of Transmittal
- Introduce your business plan to the reader
- Outline the major features that may be of interest

2. Title Page
- Provide identifying information about you and your proposed business. Name, address, and contact numbers for the business as well as key company contacts

3. Table of Contents
- A list of the major headings and subheadings contained in your plan

4. Executive Summary and Fact Sheet
- A 1–2 page summary of the most important points in your plan
- May be the most important part of your business plan
- Your Fact Sheet summarizes the basic information that relates to the venture

5. Body of the Plan

Company and the Industry
- History and current situation of your company
- Goals and objectives for the business
- Principal characteristics and trends in the industry

Product/Service Offering
- Detailed description of your product or service
- Outline stage of development and proprietary position

Market Analysis
- Describe the profile of your principal target customers
- Indicate current market size, trends, and seasonal patterns
- Assess the nature of your competition
- Estimate your expected sales and market share

Your Marketing Plan
- Detail the marketing strategy you plan to use
- Describe your marketing plan with respect to your sales strategy, advertising and promotion plans, pricing policy, and channels of distribution

Your Development Plan
- Outline the development status of your product and what is still required to get it to a market-ready state
- Are there regulatory, testing, or other requirements that still have to be met?

continued

A Typical Business Plan — continued

Your Production/Operations Plan
- Outline the operating side of your business
- Describe your location, kind of facilities, space requirements, capital equipment needs, and labour requirements

Your Management Team
- Identify your key management people, their responsibilities, and their qualifications
- Indicate the principal shareholders of the business, your principal advisors, and the members of your board of directors

Your Implementation Schedule
- Present an overall schedule indicating what needs to be done to launch your business and the timing required to bring it about
- Discuss the major problems and risks that you will have to deal with

Your Financial Plan
- Indicate the type and amount of financing you are looking for and how the funds will be used
- Outline your proposed terms of investment, the potential return to the investor, and what benefit is being provided
- Provide an overview of the current financial structure of your business
- Prepare realistic financial projections that reflect the effect of the financing; include:
  - Cash flow forecasts
  - Pro forma profit and loss statements
  - Pro forma balance sheet
  - Break-even analysis

6. Appendices
- Supporting material for your plan including:
  - Detailed résumés of the management team
  - Product literature and photographs
  - Names of possible customers and suppliers
  - Consulting reports and market surveys
  - Copies of legal documents
  - Publicity material
  - Letters of reference

The fact sheet should appear as a separate page at the back of the executive summary. It summarizes the basic information that relates to your venture:

1. Company name
2. Company address, telephone/fax numbers, e-mail address
3. Type of business and industry
4. Form of business organization (proprietorship, partnership, or corporation)
5. Principal product or service line
6. Registered patents or trademarks
7. Number and name of founders/partners/shareholders

8. Length of time in business

9. Current and/or projected market share

10. Funds invested in the business to date and their source

11. Additional financing required

12. Proposed terms and payback period

13. Total value or net worth of the business

14. Name of business advisors (legal counsel, accountant, others)

5. BODY OF THE PLAN

The body of your business plan is by far the longest component, because it presents the detailed story of your business proposition. It should be broken down into major divisions using headings, and each major division divided into sections using subheadings. It is probably better to have too many rather than not enough headings and subheadings.

What follows is a typical overview of the kind of material that should be included in the body of your plan.

YOUR COMPANY AND THE INDUSTRY

Describe the start-up and background of your business and provide the reader with some context within which to fit all the information you will be providing later in your plan.

Familiarize the reader with your company; the industry within which you will be competing, your understanding of it, and where it is headed; and what opportunities you see for your business.

YOUR COMPANY

BACKGROUND Give the date your business was started, its present form of organization, its location, and pertinent historical information on the firm. Name the founders and other key people, how your key products or services were chosen and developed, and what success the business has achieved to date.

CURRENT SITUATION Discuss such issues as how you have identified your market opportunity, assessed the competition, and developed some unique factor or distinctive competence that will make your business stand out from the rest.

FUTURE PLANS Discuss your goals and ambitions for the business and your strategy for achieving them.

THE INDUSTRY

PRINCIPAL CHARACTERISTICS Describe the current status and prospects for the industry in which your business will operate. How big is the industry? What are its total sales in dollars? In units? What are typical industry standards, gross margins, seasonal patterns, and similar factors?

MAJOR PARTICIPANTS Identify the major industry participants and describe their role, market share, and other performance measures. What are their principal strengths and weaknesses and how do you feel you will be able to successfully compete in this situation?

INDUSTRY TRENDS Discuss how you feel the industry will evolve in the future. Is it growing or stable? What do you feel industry sales will be five and ten years from now? What general trends are evident and how is the industry likely to be affected by economic, social, technological, environmental, and regulatory trends?

YOUR PRODUCT/SERVICE OFFERING

DESCRIPTION Describe in detail the product or service you plan to sell, explaining any unique characteristics or particular advantages. How will features of your product or service give you some advantage over competitors?

Indicate the stage of development your product is at and whether prototypes, working models, or finished production units are available. Include photographs if possible.

PROPRIETARY POSITION Describe any patents or trademarks you may hold or have applied for, or any licensing agreements or other legal contracts that may provide some protection for your product or service.

Are there any regulatory or government-approved standards or requirements your product must meet? How and when do you plan to obtain this certification?

POTENTIAL Outline your market opportunity as you see it and explain how you plan to take advantage of it. What are the key success factors in this business and how do you plan to exploit them to your advantage?

MARKET ANALYSIS

This section of your plan should convince the reader that you thoroughly understand the market for your product or service, that you can deal with the competition and achieve sufficient sales to develop a viable and growing business. You should describe the total market and how you feel it can be broken down into segments. You can then indicate the segment or niche you plan to concentrate on and what share of this business you will be able to obtain.

Your analysis of the market may be based on:

1. Market studies available from private research firms and government departments and agencies
2. Statistics Canada or U.S. Census Bureau data
3. Information from trade associations and trade publications
4. Surveys or informal discussions with dealers, distributors, sales representatives, customers, or competitors

This is often one of the most difficult parts of the business plan to prepare, but it is also one of the most important. Almost all other sections of your business plan depend on the sales estimates developed from your market analysis. The outline provided in Stage 6 can help you in this process.

TARGET MARKET AND CUSTOMERS Identify who constitute your primary target markets — individual consumers, companies, health care or educational institutions, government departments, or other groups.

Examine beforehand if these target markets can be segmented or broken down into relatively homogeneous groups having common, identifiable characteristics such as geographic location, age, size, type of industry, or some other factor. Present these facts in the most logical or appropriate format.

Describe the profile of your principal target customers. Who and where are they? What are the principal bases for their purchase decisions? What are their major applications for your product? What principal benefit will they obtain from using your product rather than one of your competitors'?

Identify, if possible, some major buyers who may be prepared to make purchase commitments. If possible, get a purchase order.

MARKET SIZE AND TRENDS Estimate the size of the current total market for your product or service in both units and dollars. How are sales distributed among the various segments you identified? Are there any strong weekly, monthly, or seasonal patterns? Ensure you include answers to these questions.

Describe how the market size for each of these segments has changed over the past three to four years in units and dollars. Outline how it is expected to change over the next three to four years.

Include the major factors that have affected past market growth (e.g., socioeconomic trends, industry trends, regulatory changes, government policy, population shifts). What is likely to happen in these areas in the future?

COMPETITION Identify each of your principal competitors. Make a realistic assessment of each of these firms and its product or service offering. Compare these competing products or services on the basis of price, quality, performance, service support, warranties, and other important features.

Present your evaluation of the market share of each segment by each competitor, its relative profitability, and its sales, marketing, distribution, and production capabilities. How do you see these factors changing in the future?

ESTIMATED SALES AND MARKET SHARE Estimate the share of each segment of the market and the sales in units and dollars that you feel you will acquire for each of the next three to five years. This should be developed by month for the next year and annually for each year thereafter. This information can best be presented in tabular form. Indicate on what assumptions you have based these projections.

YOUR MARKETING PLAN

Your marketing plan outlines how your sales projections will be achieved. It details the marketing strategy you plan to use to establish your product or service in the marketplace and obtain a profitable share of the overall market. Your marketing plan should describe *what* is to be done, *when* it is to be done, *how* it is to be done, and *who* will do it insofar as your sales strategy, advertising and promotion plans, pricing policy, and channels of distribution are concerned.

PRICING Summarize the general financial characteristics of your business and the industry at large. What will be typical gross and net margins for each of the products or services you plan to sell? How do these compare with those of other firms in the industry? Provide a detailed breakdown of your estimated fixed, variable, and semivariable costs for each of your various products or services.

Discuss the prices you plan to charge for your product. How do they compare with your major competitors'? Is your gross margin sufficient to cover your transportation costs, selling costs, advertising and promotion costs, rent, depreciation, and similar expenses — and still provide some margin of profit?

Detail the markups your product will provide to the various members of your channel of distribution. How do these compare with those they receive on comparable products? Does your markup provide them with sufficient incentive to handle your product?

Indicate your normal terms of sale. Do these conform to industry norms? Do you plan to offer cash, quantity, or other discounts?

Indicate how long it will take you to break even, basing your opinion on your anticipated cost structure and planned price.

SALES AND DISTRIBUTION Indicate the methods you will use to sell and distribute your product or service. Do you plan to use your own salaried or commissioned salespeople, rely on manufacturers' agents or other wholesalers and distributors, or utilize a more non-traditional means of distributing your product such as export trading companies, direct-mail selling, mail-order houses, party plan selling, or other means of selling directly to the final consumer?

If you plan to use your own sales force, describe how large it will be and how it will be structured. Indicate how salespeople will be distributed, whom they will call on, how many calls you estimate it will take to get an order, the size of a typical order, how much you estimate a typical salesperson will sell each year, how he or she will be paid, how much he or she is likely to make in a year, and how this compares with the average for the industry.

If you plan to use distributors or wholesalers, indicate how they have been or will be selected, who they are if possible, what areas or territory they will cover, how they will be compensated, credit and collection policies, and any special policies such as exclusive rights, discounts, and cooperative advertising programs.

Indicate any plans for export sales or international marketing arrangements.

ADVERTISING AND PROMOTION Describe the program you plan to use to make consumers aware of your product or service. What consumers are you trying to reach? Do you plan to use the services of an advertising agency? What media do you plan to use — radio, television, newspapers, magazines, billboards, direct mail, coupons, brochures, trade shows? How much do you plan to spend on each medium? When? Which specific vehicles?

Outline any plans to obtain free publicity for your product or company.

SERVICE AND WARRANTY PROGRAM Indicate your service arrangements, warranty terms, and method of handling service problems. Describe how you will handle customer complaints and other problems. Will service be handled by the company, dealers and distributors, or independent service centres? How do these arrangements compare with those of your competitors?

YOUR DEVELOPMENT PLAN

If your product or service involves some further technical development, the planned extent of this work should be discussed in your business plan. Prospective investors, bankers, and others will want to know the nature and extent of any additional development required, how much it will cost, and how long it will take before your business has a finished, marketable product.

DEVELOPMENT STATUS Describe the current status of your product and outline what still remains to be done to make it marketable. Do you presently have only a concept, detailed drawings, a laboratory prototype, a production prototype, or a finished product? Is further engineering work required? Has the necessary tooling to produce the product been adequately developed? Are the services of an industrial designer or other specialist required to refine the product into marketable form?

COSTS Indicate how much money has been spent on product development to date and where it has been spent. Present a development budget indicating the additional funds required, how they will be spent, and the timing involved in completing the project.

PROPRIETARY ISSUES Indicate any patents or trademarks that you own, have, or for which you plan to apply. Are there any regulatory requirements to produce or market the product? Has the product undergone standardized testing through the Underwriters' Laboratory, the Canadian Standards Association, or some other agency? If not, what are your plans? Have you tested the product at all in the marketplace? What was the result?

YOUR PRODUCTION/OPERATIONS PLAN

Your production/operations plan outlines the operating side of your business. It should describe your plant location, the kind of facilities needed, space requirements, capital equipment needed, and your labour requirements.

If your plan is for a manufacturing business, you should also discuss such areas as your purchasing policy, quality control program, inventory control system, production cost breakdown, and whether you plan to manufacture all subcomponents of the product yourself or have some of them produced for you by someone else.

LOCATION Describe the planned location of your business and discuss any advantages or disadvantages of this location in terms of the cost and availability of labour; proximity to customers; access to transportation, energy supplies, or other natural resources; and zoning and other legal requirements.

Discuss the characteristics of your location in relation to market size, traffic flows, local and regional growth rates, income levels, and similar market-related factors.

FACILITIES AND EQUIPMENT Describe the property and facilities currently used or that will be required to operate your business. This should include factory and office space, selling space, storage space, property size and location, etc. Will these facilities be leased or purchased? What is the cost and timing of their acquisition?

Detail the machinery and equipment that is required for your manufacturing process. Is this highly specialized or general-purpose equipment? Is it leased or purchased? New or used? What is the cost? What will it cost for equipment set-up and facility layout? What is its expected life? Will it have any residual or scrap value?

If possible, provide a drawing of the physical layout of the plant and other facilities.

MANUFACTURING PLANS AND COSTS Develop a manufacturing cost outline that shows standard production costs at various levels of operation. Break down total costs into raw material, component parts, labour, and overhead. Indicate your raw material, work-in-process, and finished goods inventory requirements at various sales levels. How will seasonal variations in demand be handled?

Indicate your key suppliers or subcontractors for various raw materials and components. What are the lead times for these materials? Are back-up suppliers or other alternatives available?

Outline the quality control procedures you will use to minimize service problems. Do you need any other production control measures?

On the basis of this configuration of facilities and equipment, indicate your production capacity. Where can this be expanded? Do you have any plans to modify existing plant space? What is the timing and cost?

LABOUR Describe the number of employees you have or need and their qualifications. Will they be full-time or part-time? Have you developed a job description for each position? What in-house training will be required? How much will each employee be paid? What kinds of pension plan, health insurance plan, profit-sharing plan, and other fringe benefits will be required? Have you registered with the necessary government departments?

Indicate whether your employees will be union or non-union. If employees will be members of a union, describe the principal terms of their contract and when it expires.

ENVIRONMENTAL AND OTHER ISSUES Indicate any approvals that it may be necessary for you to obtain related to zoning requirements, permits, licences, health and safety requirements, environmental approvals, etc. Are there any laws or regulatory requirements unique to your business? Are there any other legal or contractual matters that should be considered?

YOUR MANAGEMENT TEAM

Your management team and your directors are the key to success. You should identify who your key people are; their qualifications; what they are being paid; who has overall authority; who is responsible for the various functional areas of the business such as sales, marketing, production, research and development, and financial management; and so forth.

In most small businesses there are no more than two or three really key players — including yourself. Concentrate on these individuals, indicating their education, qualifications, and past business achievements. Indicate how they will contribute to the success of the present venture. Don't hire friends, relatives, or other people for key positions who do not have the proper qualifications.

Many external investors are more concerned about the management of the business than the business itself. They invest in the people rather than the project. They will conduct a thorough and exhaustive investigation of each of your key players to determine whether they are the kind of people in which they wish to invest. This portion of your plan should instill confidence in the management of your business in the mind of the reader.

DESCRIPTION OF MANAGEMENT TEAM   Outline the exact duties and responsibilities of each key member of your management team. Prepare a brief résumé of each individual indicating age, marital status, education, professional qualifications, employment experience, and other personal achievements. (You will include a complete, more detailed résumé for each of these individuals in an appendix to your plan.)

DIRECTORS   Indicate the size and composition of your board of directors. Identify any individuals you are planning to invite to sit on your board. Include a brief statement about each member's background indicating what he or she will bring to the company.

MANAGEMENT AND DIRECTORS' COMPENSATION   List the names of all members of your management team and board of directors and the compensation they will receive in fees or salary. Initially, at least, you and your management team should be prepared to accept modest salaries, perhaps well below what you received in your previous job, if you hope to attract external investors to your business.

SHAREHOLDERS   Indicate the name of each of the individual shareholders (or partners) in your business, the number of shares each owns, the percentage of ownership, and the price paid.

Describe any investors in your business other than your management team and members of your board. How many shares do they have? When were these shares acquired? What price did the investors pay?

Summarize any incentive stock option or bonus plans that you have in effect or plan to institute. Also indicate any employment contracts or agreements you may have made with members of your management team.

PROFESSIONAL ADVISORS   Indicate the name and complete address of each of your professional advisors, for example your lawyer, accountant, banker, insurance broker, and management or technical consultants. Disclose any fees or retainers that may have been paid to any of these people.

IMPLEMENTATION SCHEDULE AND RISKS ASSOCIATED WITH THE VENTURE

It is necessary to present an overall schedule indicating the interrelationship among the various events necessary to launch your business and the timing required to bring it about. This is similar to the type of framework in Figure 11.1. A well-prepared schedule demonstrates to external investors that you have given proper thought to where you are going and have the ability to plan ahead. This schedule can be a very effective sales tool.

Your plan should also discuss the major problems and risks you feel you will have to deal with in developing your business.

MILESTONES   Summarize the significant goals that you and your business have already reached and still hope to accomplish in the future. What still needs to be done for the business to succeed? Who is going to do these things? When will they be completed?

SCHEDULE   Develop a schedule of significant events and their priority for completion. What kind of strategic planning has been done to see that things occur as necessary? Have you developed a fallback or contingency position in case things don't come off as you have planned?

RISKS AND PROBLEMS   You might start by summarizing the major problems you have already had to deal with and how they were resolved. Were any particularly innovative or creative approaches used in addressing these issues?

Identify the risks your business may be faced with in the future. What are you attempting to do to avoid these? How will you deal with them if they arise? How can their impact on your business be minimized?

Summarize the downside risk. What would happen in the "worst case" scenario? What, if anything, could be salvaged from the business for your investors? Have you developed any contingency plans in case any of these risks should occur?

YOUR FINANCIAL PLAN

Your financial plan is essential to enable a prospective investor or banker to evaluate the investment opportunity you are presenting. The plan should illustrate the current financial status of your business and represent your best estimate of its future operations. The results presented should be both realistic and attainable.

Your financial plan should also describe the type of financing you are seeking, the amount of money you are looking for, how you plan to use these funds in the business, the terms of repayment and desired interest rate, or the dividends, voting rights, and redemption considerations related to the offering of any common or preferred stock.

FUNDING REQUESTED Indicate the amount and type (debt or equity) of funding you are looking for. For what do you intend to use the money? How will it be applied in your business — to acquire property, fixtures, equipment, or inventory, or to provide working capital?

Give an overview of the current financial structure of your business. Indicate the level of investment already made in the business and where the funds came from. What effect will the additional capital have on your business in terms of ownership structure, future growth, and profitability?

Outline your proposed terms of investment. What is the payback period and potential return on investment for the lender or investor? What collateral, tax benefit, or other security is being offered?

CURRENT FINANCIAL STATEMENTS If your venture is already in operation, you should provide copies of financial statements (profit and loss statement and a balance sheet) for the current year and the previous two years.

FINANCIAL PROJECTIONS In developing your financial plan, a number of basic projections must be prepared. These should be based on realistic expectations and reflect the effect of the proposed financing. The projections should be developed on a monthly basis for the first year of operation and on a quarterly or annual basis for another two to four years. These projections should include the following statements:

1. **Profit and loss forecasts** These pro forma income statements indicate your profit expectations for the next few years of operation of your business. They should be based on realistic estimates of sales and operating costs and represent your best estimate of actual operating results.

2. **Pro forma balance sheet** Your pro forma balance sheet indicates the assets you feel will be required to support your projected level of operations and how you plan to finance these assets.

3. **Projected cash flow statements** Your cash flow forecasts are probably your most important statements, because they indicate the amount and timing of your expected cash inflows and outflows. Typically, the operating profits during the start-up of a new venture are not sufficient to finance the business's operating needs. This often means that the inflow of cash will not meet your business's cash requirements, at least on a short-term basis. These conditions must be anticipated so that you can predict cash needs and avoid insolvency.

4. **Break-even analysis** A break-even analysis indicates the level of sales and production you will require to cover all your fixed and variable costs. It is useful for you and prospective lenders and investors to know what your break-even point is and how easy or difficult it will likely be to attain.

An example of each of these statements and a discussion on how to determine the break-even point for your venture is presented in Stage 7 of this book.

6. APPENDICES

The appendixes are intended to explain, support, and supplement the material in the body of your business plan. In most cases this material is attached to the back of your plan. Examples of the kind of material that might be included in an appendix are:

1. Product specifications and photographs
2. Detailed résumés of the management team

3. Lists of prospective customers

4. Names of possible suppliers

5. Job descriptions for the management team

6. Consulting reports and market surveys

7. Copies of legal documents such as leases, franchise and licensing agreements, contracts, licences, patent or trademark registrations, and articles of incorporation

8. Letters of reference

9. Relevant magazine, trade journal, and newspaper articles

Key points

THE MOST COMMON BUSINESS PLAN MISTAKES

1. **Putting it off** Don't wait to write your plan until you think you will have enough time. Too many businesses develop a business plan only when they have no choice in the matter. Unless the bank or investors want a plan, there isn't one.

2. **Cash flow casualness** Cash flow is more important than sales, profits or anything else in your business plan. Understanding cash flow is critical. If you only have one table in your business plan, make it the cash flow forecast.

3. **Idea inflation** Don't overestimate the importance of your idea. Very few successful businesses are based entirely on new ideas. Investors invest in people, not ideas. You don't need a great idea to start a business; you need time, money, perseverance and common sense.

4. **Fear and dread** Doing a business plan isn't as hard as you think. There are books like this, advisors, software and other materials available to help you.

5. **Spongy and vague goals** Remember that the objective of a plan is to indicate expected results. For results you need specific dates, management responsibilities, budgets and performance milestones that can be tracked and followed up.

6. **One size fits all** Business plans can be different things used for different purposes. Tailor your plan to its particular purpose.

7. **Diluted priorities** A clear strategy is focused. A priority list with 3–4 items is focused. A priority list with 20 items is something else.

8. **Hockey stick-shaped growth projections (flat to straight-up)** Have cash flow, sales and profit projections that are conservative so that you can readily defend them. When in doubt be less optimistic.

Source: Business Book Press (businessbookpress.com/articles/article150.htm), accessed August 19, 2004.

CONCLUSION

It is important that your plan make a good first impression. It should demonstrate that you have done a significant amount of thinking and work on your venture. You should ensure your material is presented to prospective investors, lenders, and others in an attractive, readable, and understandable fashion.

Figure 11.4 on page 316 provides a checklist that you can use to assess your finished plan for completeness, clarity, and persuasiveness.

The length of your business plan should not exceed 40 double-spaced, typewritten pages, not including appendices. Each section should be broken down into appropriate and clearly identifiable headings and subheadings. Make sure your plan contains no errors in spelling, punctuation, or grammar.

Prepare a number of copies of your plan and number each one individually. Make sure each copy is appropriately bound with a good-quality cover on which the name of your business has been printed or embossed.

FYI FOR YOUR INFORMATION

SAMPLE BUSINESS PLANS

Before starting on your business plan, it may be a good idea to see what a typical plan actually looks like. There are a couple of examples included with this book, but here are some Web sites that have some sample plans as well.

CCH Business Owner's Toolkit This site provides the component elements of sample business plans for three fictitious companies to illustrate the type of information that is essential to the creation of a high-quality business plan. (www.toolkit.cch.com/tools/buspln_m.asp)

Palo Alto Software This site contains sample business plans for 60 different businesses including a flower importer, software publisher, tennis pro shop, buffet restaurant, Internet cafe, medical equipment company, and many others. (www.bplans.com)

Business Plan Archive An educational Web site created by the University of Maryland to archive business plans and other information about companies; covers a broad range of industries, principally from the dot-com era. You must register first and can then access the plans in the archive. (www.businessplanarchive.org)

Moot Corp Competition—The Super Bowl of Business Plan Competitions A library of different business plans, each of which was a finalist in the Moot Corp competition for MBA students from all over the world. (www.businessplans.org/mootcorp.html)

SmallBusinessPoint.com, Inc. A sample of business plans from existing successful profitable companies and start-ups. The business plans are available for a nominal fee. (www.smallbusinesspoint.com/businesspoint/sampleplans.htm)

Junior Achievement Student Entrepreneur Center A full business plan library that contains over 400 real business plans for very simple business concepts and ideas. Click on Business Plan and then on Sample Plans. (www.ja.org/studentcenter/entrp/default.shtml#)

Video Case #13

YoonTown

Summary

Sebastian Yoon is the successful owner of Sebastian Yoon Fine Arts, but he has an idea for a new venture. With $500,000 borrowed from a relative, he wants to build a restaurant where patrons can watch people blow glass while they eat. Yoon's task is to find investors to support his idea. He tried banks, but they weren't interested. How can he get a bank interested in his venture when it encompasses the high-risk business areas of retail and restaurants?

Questions for Discussion

1. Are all business plans the same? What are some reasons for preparing a business plan? Why did Yoon create a business plan?
2. Who should write your business plan?
3. How can a business plan be used to attract investors?
4. When you bring a business plan to investors, what are they going to be looking for?

FIGURE 11.3   DEVELOPING THE "BIG PICTURE"

1. DEVELOP YOUR VISION STATEMENT

a. Write short phrases to describe each of the three elements in your vision statement:

  – the name of your planned venture

  – your product/service offering

  – the target market(s) you plan to serve

b. Combine these phrases into a single sentence

_____

_____

_____

_____

_____

2. FORMULATE YOUR MISSION STATEMENT

a. Write short phrases to describe each of the following elements of your business:

  – what your business will do

  – its market focus, niche, or particular image

  – its planned location and geographic market served

  – how growth of the business will be achieved

  – your sustainable uniqueness or distinguishing characteristics

b. Combine these phrases into short, linked sentences.

_____

_____

_____

_____

_____

3. DEFINE THE FUNDAMENTAL VALUES BY WHICH YOUR BUSINESS WILL BE RUN
Step 1 Personal Values

Have each principal involved in the business complete the following framework for five values that they hold to be personally important.

a. *Value:* Express as a single word _____

  What: A brief explanation of what the word means to you. _____

_____

_____

  Why? Outline why it is important to you that the business operate this way.

_____

_____

b. *Value:* Express as a single word _____

  What: A brief explanation of what the word means to you. _____

_____

_____

continued

Developing the "Big Picture" — continued

Why? Outline why it is important to you that the business operate this way. _____

_____

_____

c. *Value:* Express as a single word _____

    What: A brief explanation of what the word means to you. _____

_____

_____

Why? Outline why it is important to you that the business operate this way. _____

_____

_____

d. *Value:* Express as a single word _____

    What: A brief explanation of what the word means to you. _____

_____

_____

Why? Outline why it is important to you that the business operate this way. _____

_____

_____

e. *Value:* Express as a single word _____

    What: A brief explanation of what the word means to you. _____

_____

_____

Why? Outline why it is important to you that the business operate this way. _____

_____

_____

Step 2 Values by Which the Business Will Be Managed

Complete Step 2 from the information provided by each of the principals in Step 1. Include only values that were *common to all principals*. Others should be included only after discussion, negotiation, and consensus among all individuals. Since some values will differ, it is necessary for all parties to agree which will be the common values used to guide the operations of the business. This list should contain five or six values at a maximum and it is important that they be compatible with each other. Each principal will then have to decide whether he or she will be able to work in a business where, perhaps, only some or none of his or her personal values will be given expression.

a. *Value:* _____

_____

    What: _____

_____

_____

_____

    Why? _____

_____

_____

b. *Value:* _____

_____

What: _____

_____

_____

_____

Why? _____

_____

_____

_____

c. *Value:* _____

_____

What: _____

_____

_____

_____

Why? _____

_____

_____

_____

d. *Value:* _____

_____

What: _____

_____

_____

_____

Why? _____

_____

_____

_____

e. *Value:* _____

_____

What: _____

_____

_____

_____

Why? _____

_____

_____

_____

continued

Developing the "Big Picture" — continued

4. DEFINE YOUR OBJECTIVES

The business's vision will be achieved when the following objectives have been attained:

a. Objective _____

b. Objective _____

c. Objective _____

d. Objective _____

e. Objective _____

FIGURE 11.4   CHECKLIST FOR ASSESSING YOUR BUSINESS PLAN

After completing your business plan you should thoroughly review it. This checklist will help you to do so. Decide whether or not you think the answers you have provided are clear and complete. Evaluate the information from the standpoint of a prospective investor or lending agency and ask yourself whether you are satisfied with your responses.

	Answer Is Included (X)	Answer Is Clear (Yes/No)	Answer Is Complete (Yes/No)
1. YOUR COMPANY AND THE INDUSTRY			
a. Type of business you are planning	_____	_____	_____
b. Products or services you will sell	_____	_____	_____
c. History of the company	_____	_____	_____
d. Why does the business promise to be successful?	_____	_____	_____
e. Your future goals and objectives	_____	_____	_____
f. Description of the industry	_____	_____	_____
g. Major participants and significant trends	_____	_____	_____

General Comments

_____

_____

_____

_____

_____

2. PRODUCT/SERVICE OFFERING			
a. Description of your product/service	_____	_____	_____
b. Present stage of development	_____	_____	_____
c. Patent/trademark position	_____	_____	_____
d. Other formal requirements	_____	_____	_____
e. Growth opportunities and key factors for success	_____	_____	_____

General Comments

_____

_____

_____

	Answer Is Included (X)	Answer Is Clear (Yes/No)	Answer Is Complete (Yes/No)

3. MARKETING ANALYSIS AND PLAN

a. Who are your target customers?

b. What are their characteristics?

c. How do they buy?

d. How large is the market and its various segments?

e. Factors affecting the market

f. Who are your competitors? How are they doing?

g. How much of the market will you be able to attract?

h. What will be your principal marketing strategy?

i. Have you detailed all aspects of your marketing plan?

   (i) Pricing

   (ii) Sales and distribution

   (iii) Advertising and promotion

General Comments

_____

_____

_____

_____

_____

4. PRODUCTION/OPERATIONS PLAN

a. Where will your business be located?

b. What are the characteristics of your location?

c. Description of machinery and equipment you will require

d. What are your costs to produce your product?

e. What are your inventory requirements?

f. Who will be your principal suppliers or subcontractors?

g. Description of your quality control procedures

h. How many employees will you require?

   (i) What type?

   (ii) How will they be paid?

i. Will you require any licences, permits, or other authorizations?

continued

Checklist for Assessing Your Business Plan — continued

General Comments

_____

_____

_____

_____

_____

	Answer Is Included (X)	Answer Is Clear (Yes/No)	Answer Is Complete (Yes/No)
5. MANAGEMENT TEAM			
a. Who will manage your business?	_____	_____	_____
b. What are their qualifications?	_____	_____	_____
c. What is the size and composition of your board of directors?	_____	_____	_____
d. What are your managers and directors being paid?	_____	_____	_____
e. What is the ownership structure of the business?	_____	_____	_____
f. Who are your advisors and consultants?	_____	_____	_____

General Comments

_____

_____

_____

_____

_____

	Answer Is Included (X)	Answer Is Clear (Yes/No)	Answer Is Complete (Yes/No)
6. FINANCIAL PLAN			
a. How much money will you need to start the business and sustain it for the first few months?	_____	_____	_____
b. How much money do you have now?	_____	_____	_____
c. How much more do you need?	_____	_____	_____
d. How will this additional money be used?	_____	_____	_____
e. What kind of collateral or security will be provided?	_____	_____	_____
f. How will this money be repaid?	_____	_____	_____
g. Provided financial statements:			
For the current year	_____	_____	_____
For the past two years	_____	_____	_____
h. Total estimated net income:			
Monthly for the first year	_____	_____	_____
Quarterly or annually for the next two to four years	_____	_____	_____
i. Estimated cash flow situation:			

      Monthly for the first year   _____   _____   _____

      Annually for the next two years   _____   _____   _____

j.   What is your estimated financial position at
      the end of each of the next three to five years?   _____   _____   _____

k.   What sales volume will you need to break even?   _____   _____   _____

General Comments

_____

_____

_____

_____

_____

7. APPENDICES

Do you need to include the following appendixes?	Yes	No
a. Product photographs and specifications	_____	_____
b. Résumés of your management team	_____	_____
c. List of prospective customers	_____	_____
d. List of possible suppliers	_____	_____
e. Job descriptions for management team	_____	_____
f. Consulting reports	_____	_____
g. Market surveys	_____	_____
h. Legal agreements and contracts	_____	_____
i. Publicity articles and promotional pieces	_____	_____
j. Other supporting material	_____	_____

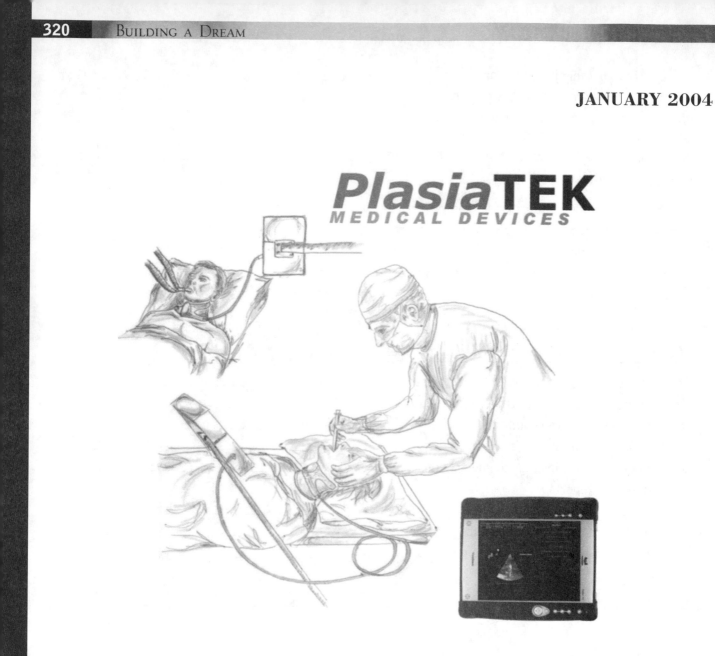

Company Name: **PlasiaTEK, Inc.**

Lead Product: **PlasiaTEK Endvantage™**

Description: ***Superior system for placement, confirmation, and monitoring of endotracheal tube in airway during intubation using patent-pending ET tube and application-specific portable ultrasound.***

Capital Required: **$ 2,500,000**

TABLE OF CONTENTS

EXECUTIVE SUMMARY

Failed endotracheal intubations comprise the biggest problem facing the 26,000 anesthesiologists and 35,000 nurse anesthetists in America today. Hundreds of malpractice lawsuits are filed each year for mishaps during intubation resulting in death, brain damage, vocal cord damage, and esophageal injury. PlasiaTEK, Inc. is an early stage medical device company that has been formed to solve this problem and change the world of anesthesia and emergency medicine with the introduction of Ultrasound Assisted Intubation. With the development of PlasiaTEK's patent-pending technology, the use and benefits of electronic imaging during intubation have only now become possible. This technology has the potential to be required in every operating room, emergency room, intensive care unit, and ambulance across the United States and around the world.

Intubation is a medical procedure in which an endotracheal tube is positioned into the trachea, effectively bypassing the mouth, nose, and throat and providing direct access to the lungs. Once intubated, the patient relies on ventilation through an endotracheal tube in order to breathe. An intubation is performed on any person who cannot manage his/her own airway. In the hospital setting, this normally occurs when a patient receives general anaesthetic, or in the emergency medicine environment where injury or trauma impairs one's own airway management.

Forty million intubations are performed per year in the United States by anesthesiologists and nurse anesthetists in the operating room setting alone. Despite the frequency with which this procedure is performed, complications during intubations are common. Statistics show that in the operating room, 8% of intubations are difficult, leading to an increased risk of esophageal intubation. A recent study published in the *Annals of Emergency Medicine* confirmed 37% of intubations performed in the EMS setting resulted in the improper placement of the endotracheal tube in the patient. Difficult intubation as a cause of death has increased from 5% in 1970 to 12% in the 1990s.

Injuries involving endotracheal intubations constitute the single largest source of liability in anesthesiology practice, accounting for 25% of total anesthesiology malpractice claims in the United States. The difficulties and risks associated with intubation are well known and no one has yet solved the intubation problem. Ultrasound Assisted Intubation, developed by Michal Miller, MD, uses an unprecedented approach to intubation. Current devices all fail in the same respect – they attempt to visualize a patient's anatomy by looking directly through the mouth, which is inconsistent and never addresses the core problems inherent to intubation. PlasiaTEK's patent is for "Ultrasonic Placement and Monitoring of a Tube Within the Body" and specifically addresses using ultrasound to place and monitor an endotracheal tube during intubation. The intellectual property is strong. Utilizing PlasiaTEK's patent-pending endotracheal tube technology and a specialized ultrasound device, the Endvantage™ System of Intubation images the endotracheal tube and anatomy externally, providing unparalleled placement, confirmation, and monitoring of the endotracheal tube in the airway. PlasiaTEK's technology will virtually eliminate the risks, trauma, and unnecessary costs associated with current practices.

PlasiaTEK's Endvantage™ System and pipeline of products present a rewarding investment opportunity. Having already completed proof of concept research, prototype development, and cadaver studies, equity financing will provide a means for completing the production-ready product, conducting further clinical testing, meeting regulatory requirements, and financing business operations. Financial projections show sales in 2007 and 2008 of $27 million and $36 million, respectively. However, if a larger company with existing medical marketing and distribution capabilities purchased PlasiaTEK, it could realize sales of $200 million relatively quickly because of the large worldwide market potential in excess of $3 billion a year. This, combined with PlasiaTEK's intellectual property position, makes PlasiaTEK a very desirable acquisition, enhancing the exit strategy for current investors.

1. COMPANY INFORMATION

1.1 HISTORY

PlasiaTEK, Inc. is an early stage medical device company that seeks to improve the world of anesthesia and emergency medicine with the introduction of Ultrasound Assisted Intubation. The concept for Ultrasound Assisted Intubation was conceived by Michal Miller, MD, a resident anesthesiologist having completed four years of specialized training at the University of Manitoba, in Canada. Upon proving the concept with the completion of his initial prototype, Miller was encouraged by his peers and professors to pursue the full development and commercialization of the Endvantage™ System. In September 2002, Miller partnered with Kevin Michaluk, a business student in his final year of studies at the University of Manitoba, to develop a business plan while Miller continued improving the technology.

Michaluk and Miller, eager to move forward with the company, quickly realized that in order to be successful, business operations would need to be more formalized. Paul Pesek and Peter Leslie, two individuals with extensive business experience in the medical field, were approached and they formed PlasiaTEK, Inc. in May 2003.

1.2 EXECUTIVE MANAGEMENT TEAM

President – C. Paul Pesek: Possessing an Engineering degree from Yale University and an MBA from Harvard, Pesek has been involved in the start up, operation, and profitable exit of several high-tech, medical-related companies. After founding and selling two companies in the printed circuit board industry in 1978, Pesek began Moniterm Corporation, a manufacturer of high-resolution monitors and display systems. A pioneer in the high-volume manufacturing of high-resolution monitors, he quickly built Moniterm up to sales of $35 million before exiting. In the last 10 years, Pesek has been involved with the start-up and sell-out of two more companies in the medical imaging industry, including Monitor Technology and Aurora Technology. Nortech Industries, a NASDAQ publicly traded company, acquired Monitor Technology in 1997. Aurora Technology manufactured radiological diagnostic stations used in Picture Archiving Communication Systems (PACS). Merge Technologies, a publicly traded NASDAQ company, acquired Aurora Technology in 1998.

Executive Vice President, Interim CFO – Kevin Michaluk: Kevin Michaluk was responsible for PlasiaTEK's initial business development and the formation of PlasiaTEK's current management team. Michaluk recently graduated with a Bachelor of Commerce Degree, majoring in Finance and Entrepreneurship, from the I.H. Asper School of Business at the University of Manitoba. During his time in university, Michaluk won numerous national and international awards for his outstanding achievements in both finance and entrepreneurship. Michaluk, in addition to being PlasiaTEK's interim CFO, will work in cooperation with management to foster business and investor relations, plan corporate strategy, and aid in sales and marketing efforts.

Vice President, Sales – Peter Leslie: Peter Leslie has over 20 years of sales and marketing experience in the medical industry, with expertise in the field of medical imaging. He has worked as Director of International Sales and Director of North American Sales for several companies in recent years, and has been instrumental in the negotiation of strategic partnerships among suppliers to medical OEMs. Companies he has worked for include: Moniterm, E for M, Clinton Electronics, Image Systems, and Monitor Technology. His knowledge and experience in European and Asian markets will aid PlasiaTEK's overseas sales efforts.

Vice President, Technology – Michal Miller, MD: Michal Miller is responsible for inventing and developing PlasiaTEK's lead technology. Miller is eager to see the commercialization process of the Endvantage™ System through. To accomplish this in a timely and cost-effective manner, Miller has enrolled in a Special Masters Program (combining radiology and anesthesia) at the University of Minnesota. Miller holds a medical degree from the University of Manitoba. He has completed four years of anesthesia residency focusing on medical airway management. Miller will oversee PlasiaTEK's research and development and clinical testing. He will also aid in sales efforts and be involved in the design and implementation of PlasiaTEK's orientation and training programs.

1.3 BOARD OF DIRECTORS

Officers on the Board of Directors will include Mr. Pesek, Mr. Michaluk, Mr. Leslie, and Dr. Miller.

Mark Michel: Mark Michel has over 40 years of management experience and consulting over a wide range of healthcare, manufacturing, service, financial, and distribution businesses. He is currently Chairman of Healthcare Practice Management Associates. Consulting assignments in healthcare and elsewhere include strategic issues and operations, interim management, executive counselling, and the forming of Boards of Directors and Advisory Boards. He is currently a director of a number of other companies including Computer Systems Products and iMillennium. He has a Bachelor of Arts Degree from Lafayette College and an MBA from the Wharton School at the University of Pennsylvania.

Duane Carlson: Duane Carlson is currently a business consultant and sits on several company and advisory boards, including the boards of two publicly held companies. He founded Netstar Inc., a computer networking company where he served as Executive Vice President and Chief Financial Officer. Prior to Netstar's acquisition by Lucent Technologies, Carlson was responsible for raising start-up funds from venture capitalists and for subsequent financial offerings. He also founded Lee Data, which is now part of Oracle. Carlson has significant experience in start-up funding, finance, and mergers and acquisitions.

Claire Hovland: Claire Hovland has founded several medical technology companies including Applied Biometrics, Inc. that developed and marketed a trans-tracheal Doppler ultrasound device for monitoring cardiac output, and Sonometrics, Inc. that developed low-cost ultrasound imaging technology. He earned an MS in electrical engineering from the University of Minnesota and a BS in Physics from Northern Arizona University. He worked for Perkin Elmer in product management and sales for 15 years prior to founding Applied Biometrics.

Dr. Kenneth Holmen: Dr. Holmen is a noted anesthesiologist and is the President/CEO of Associated Anesthesiologists, the largest anesthesiology practice in the upper Midwest. In addition, he is also the President of Associated Health Services and serves on numerous Boards of Directors, including United Hospital, NyGun, Inc., Sonometrics, Inc., and Waldorf College. He has written several articles for *Anesthesiology, The Journal of the American Society of Anesthesiologists*, including, "Continuous cardiac output determination using trans-tracheal Doppler: Initial results in humans."

1.4 MEDICAL ADVISORY BOARD

PlasiaTEK is assembling a medical advisory board comprised of specialists from anesthesiology, radiology, emergency medicine, and industry. The medical advisory board will further complement the expertise and industry knowledge possessed by the company, aiding in PlasiaTEK's commercialization and marketing processes. The advisory board will also be involved in evaluating clinical testing and subsequent technologies. Glen Nelson, Vice-Chairman of Medtronic from 1986 to 2003, and many other experts are members of PlasiaTEK's growing advisory board. Please contact PlasiaTEK for full advisory board membership.

1.5 STRATEGIC ALLIANCES

PlasiaTEK will enter into relationships with other organizations that will aid in the timely and effective commercialization of the Endvantage™ System.

University of Minnesota – PlasiaTEK has partnered with the University of Minnesota (U of M) to work on the final development and clinical testing of PlasiaTEK's patent-pending technology. Partnering with the University of Minnesota provides Dr. Miller with a facility for testing and refining the Endvantage™ System; it provides resources for performing clinical testing on cadavers and humans; it provides a knowledge pool of expertise; and it is more cost-effective, timely, and convenient than performing these tasks privately.

Kumar Belani, MD, Immediate Past President of the Minnesota Society of Anesthesiologists and current Head of Anesthesiology at the U of M, is chief investigator in PlasiaTEK's clinical testing. Cadaver studies, which have been very successful, will be complete by mid-January 2004, and human testing will begin in

March 2004. Though clinical studies are not required for regulatory approval of the Endvantage™ System, partnering with the University of Minnesota will aid in the future marketing and adoption of Ultrasound Assisted Intubation. While clinical studies will demonstrate the efficacy of PlasiaTEK's technology, credible endorsement from the University of Minnesota, via published medical and scientific journal articles, will aid in the market adoption and selling processes.

2. INTUBATION AND AIRWAY MONITORING

2.1 WHAT IS IT?

Endotracheal intubation is a medical procedure in which an endotracheal tube (ET tube) is positioned into the trachea, effectively bypassing the mouth, nose, and throat, providing direct access to the lungs. Once intubated, the patient relies on ventilation through the tube in order to breathe. Airway monitoring is the ability to reliably determine the location and depth of an endotracheal tube throughout the duration a patient is intubated. An intubation is performed on any person who cannot manage his/her own airway. In the hospital setting, this occurs when a patient receives general anaesthetic for surgery, or in the emergency medicine environment when the airway cannot be managed due to injury or trauma.

2.2 CURRENT METHODOLOGY

Within the hospital setting, an anesthesiologist or nurse anesthetist normally performs the intubation procedure (anesthesiologist hereafter refers to both anesthesiologists and nurse anesthetists unless otherwise specified). Prior to surgery, the patient is visually inspected to assess the degree of difficulty of the impending intubation. In intubations assessed as simple, the anesthesiologist typically administers a general anaesthetic, rendering the patient unconscious and unaware of the intubation. During this state the patient is not breathing, thus requiring the anesthesiologist to insert the endotracheal tube and begin ventilation of the lungs within a short time frame. In intubations assessed as difficult, the anesthesiologist may opt to perform the intubation while the patient is awake and breathing, thus reducing the time constraint (at much greater discomfort to the patient). In these situations, the anesthesiologist will normally have an assistant present to aid in the intubation.

The greatest risk to patients occurs when the intubation is assessed as simple, but proves to be difficult. The visual inspection method of assessment is unreliable, as 48% of difficult intubations are initially assessed as simple. These cases become a medical emergency, where the unprepared anesthesiologist requires more time and help to complete the now-difficult intubation, putting the patient at tremendous risk, as the patient is not breathing on his/her own. If the intubation is not completed within a few minutes, a tracheotomy must be performed. If the patient is not ventilated within 5 minutes, permanent anoxic brain damage will occur.

In situations outside the hospital, paramedics are often required to perform intubations. Paramedics frequently work in less than ideal conditions compared with an operating room. As well, paramedics are not granted the luxury of an assessment prior to intubation. Under these circumstances, the risk of positioning the endotracheal tube in the stomach, known as esophageal intubation, as well as other detrimental outcomes is further increased.

Once the endotracheal tube is inserted, prior to ventilation of the lungs, the anesthesiologist or paramedic must try and confirm the correct location of the tube to minimize the chance of an esophageal intubation, which is life-threatening. There currently exists no device on the market capable of directly confirming the location of the placed endotracheal tube. The indirect methods currently used include visualizing the chest expanding with ventilation, listening to air movement in the lungs, and evaluation of the capnograph from an end-tidal carbon dioxide ($ETCO_2$) analyzer. These methods, in addition to being time-consuming during a procedure, are prone to error and misinterpretation, especially when performed in adverse conditions, such as on a helicopter.

Once the endotracheal tube has been inserted and its location confirmed, the last phase of the intubation process is the ongoing monitoring of the established airway. Airway monitoring is an absolute necessity for any patient being transported in a vehicle such as an ambulance or aircraft, as the unstable environment greatly increases the likelihood of an extubation (the ET tube dislodges) occurring. Once the endotracheal tube has been inserted and confirmed to be in the trachea, ET tubes are most often secured only with a piece of tape, predisposing to unanticipated and unrecognized extubations, which in addition to being extremely life-threatening, damage the sensitive laryngeal structures such as the vocal cords. There is currently no device on the market that directly monitors the physical position of the tube. The $ETCO_2$ analyzer is often used to monitor the established airway by measuring the carbon dioxide level normally emitted from the lungs. As this is an indirect indicator of tube position, if the $ETCO_2$ alarms, it is not easily known whether it is a tube problem (the ET tube has physically moved/slipped out of place) or if the person is not breathing for another reason.

2.3 THE STATISTICS, THE OPPORTUNITY

Endotracheal intubation is one of the most commonly performed procedures in the field of medicine, occurring in virtually every operation or surgery utilizing general anaesthetic. In the United States, 40 million intubations will be performed on medical patients this year by anesthesiologists and nurse anesthetists alone. Worldwide, 200 million intubations are performed annually. Trauma patients add to this number as paramedics perform intubations in the Emergency Medical Services (EMS) setting. The number of endotracheal intubations performed is estimated to be increasing at over 3% per year based on three current trends: the aging population, the increased number of people undergoing aesthetic operations, and the growing obesity epidemic. Despite the frequency with which this procedure is performed, complications during intubations are common. Endotracheal tubes are often misplaced in the esophagus or main-stem bronchus, which can lead to adverse outcomes including: death, permanent brain damage, cardiopulmonary arrest, unnecessary tracheotomy, airway trauma and damage to teeth. A recent study published in the *Annals of Emergency Medicine* proved that complications in endotracheal intubations are more common than previously believed. In the emergency room setting, 14% of intubation procedures resulted in misplaced endotracheal tubes because the airway professional performing the procedure could not visualize the patient's anatomy during the intubation nor confirm the location of the inserted endotracheal tube. In EMS, an alarming 37% of patients were intubated incorrectly upon arrival to the emergency room. The frequency and severity of errors and mishaps associated with endotracheal intubation are well known. Even the popular television show *ER*, this season alone, has had two story lines focusing specifically on endotracheal intubation mishaps. In fact, *ER* cited the rate of misplaced endotracheal tubes in the EMS setting to be 50%.

Injuries involving endotracheal intubations constitute the single largest source of liability in anesthesiology practice, accounting for 25% of total anesthesiology malpractice claims in the United States. Litigations arising from the malpractice of endotracheal intubations produce an average payout of $196,000 and have ranged as high as $6 million. However, the legal and insurance costs of malpractice are dwarfed by the enormous additional healthcare costs manifested by added procedures and prolonged hospital stay. The worst and most incalculable costs are to the patients and their families, especially since most deaths and injuries would be preventable through the utilization of improved technology.

2.4 CURRENT DEVICES AND DRAWBACKS

Many devices currently exist to aid doctors and paramedics in correctly positioning the endotracheal tube during intubation. The ongoing development and presence of these devices on the market reinforces the fact there is still a need to improve the intubation procedure and that no device has solved the intubation problem yet. Michal Miller, MD, after many years of research and interest in the area, concluded that all of the current devices fail in the same respect. The inadequacy of the current devices used in endotracheal intubation occurs from the common problem of attempting to visualize the anatomy by looking through the open mouth itself. Abnormalities in the airway and unfavorable conditions (blood and vomit) impair the view when looking through the mouth, making reliable placement and confirmation of the endotracheal tube extremely difficult. To solve these problems, Dr. Miller concluded a new approach would be needed.

The current market for devices for use in intubations is divided into two segments: products that establish the airway and products that monitor the airway.

AIRWAY ESTABLISHING DEVICES:

Fiberoptic Bronchoscope (FOB):

Consisting of a long maneuverable cable with a preloaded endotracheal tube and a camera attached to the end, the fiberoptic bronchoscope is currently the primary device for use in difficult intubations according to the American Society of Anesthesiologists (ASA) guidelines. Despite its ASA recommendation, several disadvantages plague the FOB. Firstly, extensive training is required to become adept with the FOB, so many anesthesiologists and nurse anesthetists do not use it. The FOB requires the presence of secretion-free conditions as blood and/or saliva can block the camera lens. Likewise, the lens of the fiberoptic bronchoscope is prone to fogging. The FOB also requires a prolonged set-up time requiring an assistant and is not typically on hand in the operating room, which does not provide any benefit when a difficult intubation was initially assessed as simple since the FOB will not have been readied for use. Furthermore, it is difficult to clean; thus, reports of life-threatening infections have resulted. Lastly, the passage of the endotracheal tube through the vocal cords is still blind and it cannot easily confirm correct placement of the endotracheal tube in the trachea, nor monitor the airway once the endotracheal tube is placed correctly.

Trachlight:
The Trachlight utilizes a trans-illuminated light to help place the endotracheal tube. The Trachlight's usefulness in large necks is limited and it cannot be used when there are abnormalities in the upper airway. The Trachlight uses an indirect method of confirmation to determine placement in the airway; however, it is subject to interpretation as it is based on the brightness of the light illuminating from the neck, which varies from patient to patient based on their anatomy. The possibility of a "confirmed" endotracheal intubation actually being an esophageal intubation greatly exists. As well, the Trachlight cannot monitor the endotracheal tube in the airway once positioned.

"Classic" Laryngoscopic Intubation:
Though it is the most popular method for routine intubations, the use of the laryngoscope depends on direct visualization of the airway to be effective. (Appendix 2) In difficult intubations where direct visualization is not possible, the laryngoscope's use is limited. Also, it cannot confirm the correct placement of the endotracheal tube and it cannot monitor the airway once the tube has been positioned.

Laryngeal Mask:
This is a sealed mask that sits above the vocal cords. It is not an endotracheal tube; thus, it does not protect the lungs from the stomach's contents and therefore can only be used in limited, specific circumstances.

AIRWAY MONITORING DEVICE:

End-Tidal Carbon Dioxide (ETCO$_2$) Analyzer:
This device monitors the established airway by measuring the carbon dioxide level normally emitted from the lungs. If measurements are abnormal, an alarm will sound. Despite being a gold standard for confirming endotracheal tube placement and monitoring the established airway, the carbon dioxide/gas analyzer is prone to error, and is ineffective in cardiac arrests. Given the device relies on carbon dioxide emitted from the lungs as a method of air monitoring, any number of changes in the body can cause carbon dioxide levels to fluctuate, creating false alarms. When an alarm sounds, the anesthesiologist is unable to reliably determine if a dislodged endotracheal tube caused it or if the patient is incurring a different crisis.

2.5 THE FUTURE OF INTUBATIONS

The ideal device for use during both simple and difficult intubations would allow the anesthesiologist or paramedic to clearly visualize the larynx and trachea at all times, regardless of the patient's anatomy or mouth's contents. This device would also allow for immediate direct confirmation of the inserted endotracheal tube within the trachea, and directly monitor its location in real time for the duration of time the patient is ventilated. The only plausible manner that satisfies these criteria is to image the anatomy externally.

The majority of non-surgical invasive procedures in use today employ diagnostic imaging for their accuracy and reliability. Three major diagnostic-imaging technologies currently used are Magnetic Resonance Image (MRI), X-Ray, and ultrasound. MRI machines are large, expensive, and not mobile. Repeated exposure to X-Rays is harmful. Due to the frequency with which intubations are performed and the part of the body being imaged, ultrasound is the only practical, viable and safe method in assisting intubations. Ultrasound devices in recent years have also become portable, very small in size, and have declined in price significantly. Since its inception, however, it has been documented that an image of the larynx and trachea cannot be generated using ultrasound, as the presence of air interferes with the image. PlasiaTEK, with the development of its patent-pending technology has proven otherwise, now allowing external electronic imaging of the larynx and trachea during intubations to become a reality, via reliable ultrasound.

3. THE PLASIATEK ENDVANTAGE™

3.1 OVERVIEW

The PlasiaTEK Endvantage™ System of Intubation (ESI) will *revolutionize* the method by which endotracheal intubations are performed. The PlasiaTEK Endvantage™ System of Intubation is comprised of two main components that work together to provide an all-in-one solution to intubation that offers unparalleled guidance, confirmation, and monitoring of the endotracheal tube. An intubation-specific, portable ultrasound device works seamlessly with a modified endotracheal tube to make external electronic imaging during intubation possible, thus providing a multitude of benefits. Combining off-the-shelf components and merging existing technologies has allowed PlasiaTEK to develop a breakthrough product that is demonstrably superior to existing methods and devices and still meets the requirements for FDA (510[k]) approval.

3.2 WHY THE ENDVANTAGE™?

There are four reasons why PlasiaTEK has chosen the Endvantage™ name:

1. **END** for endotracheal.
2. **VANTAGE** because a new vantage point is used to visualize the procedure.
3. It cites several *advantages* over the devices and methods currently in use.
4. It is the *end* to the intubation problem.

3.3 ENDVANTAGE™ SYSTEM OF INTUBATION

The market-ready Endvantage™ portable ultrasound device will be built specifically for intubation use. The ultrasound device will be portable and small to address the lack of space within operating rooms and to meet the demands for patient mobility in intra-hospital and inter-hospital transport. No experience with ultrasound is necessary to use the Endvantage™ System of Intubation. The design of the ultrasound probe allows it to be fitted and remain stable on the patient's neck, providing for a quick and easy set-up. The software will be easy to use and settings will be specifically pre-programmed for use in intubations, deeming previous experience and knowledge of ultrasound totally unnecessary.

To use the device during intubation, it simply has to be turned on, with the ultrasound probe properly placed on the patient's neck. The anesthesiologist or paramedic, utilizing an Endvantage™ endotracheal tube, then begins the insertion of the endotracheal tube as normal. The ultrasound device's display screen *brightly shows* the endotracheal tube as it is correctly inserted into the trachea. It is an all-or-nothing phenomenon – insertion of the tube into the esophagus results in no image. Correct placement of the endotracheal tube can instantly be confirmed on screen, and the ultrasound will continuously monitor the endotracheal tube's location as long as the ultrasound probe is left on the patient's neck. If the tube moves outside allowable parameters, the ultrasound device will sound an alarm, immediately bringing attention to the problem. This feature of the Endvantage™ is highly beneficial in unstable environments (the patient is being transported via ambulance, airplane, or helicopter) where there is a greater chance of an unanticipated and unrecognized extubation occurring.

3.4 ADVANTAGES OF THE ENDVANTAGE™

Electronic imaging during intubation yields many benefits over the current methods and devices used. The table above compares the PlasiaTEK Endvantage™ System of Intubation to the fiberoptic bronchoscope, the current gold standard for difficult intubations, and the laryngoscope, the device most commonly used in the majority of less difficult intubations.

COMPARISON OF INTUBATION DEVICES

	PlasiaTEK Endvantage™	Fiberoptic Bronchoscope	"Classic" Laryngoscope
1 = Most Desirable 5 = Least Desirable			
Set-Up Time	1	4	1
Performance Time	1	4	2
Skill Required (Ease of Use)	1	4	3
Rate of Failed Intubations	1	1	4
Confirmation of Correct Intubation	1	3	5
Teaching Device	1	3	5
Use in EMS	1	5	1
Price	2	3	1
Ability to Record Procedure	1	na	na
Direct Monitoring of ET Tube	1	na	na
$ETCO_2$ Analyzer	1	na	na
Pulse Oximeter	1	na	na
Compatibility w/Other Devices	1	na	na

Set-Up Time: Set-up time for the Endvantage™ is extremely fast. The ultrasound needs only to be turned on and the probe placed on the patient's neck.

Performance Time: The time actually required to perform a successful intubation is substantially reduced with the Endvantage™ system. As confirmation of the tube is seen instantly on screen, the tube can be guided in correctly on the first attempt. With both the FOB and the laryngoscope, much time may be spent confirming and realizing a failed intubation attempt, which must be performed again.

Skill Required: The time required to become comfortable in performing intubations with the Endvantage™ System is much less than the FOB, which can be extremely difficult to master, and the laryngoscope, which requires a considerable amount of developed "feel."

Rate of Failed Intubations: The all-or-nothing confirmation capability of the Endvantage™ should eliminate failed intubations.

Confirmation of Correct Intubation: The Endvantage™ can confirm the result of an intubation attempt more quickly and accurately than all other existing devices.

Teaching Device: Training anesthesiologists, nurse anesthetists, and paramedics to perform intubations is difficult, as it is virtually impossible for the instructor to see what the student is doing with the tube inside the person. It may takes thousands of intubations for a student to develop the "feel" that many airway experts have for performing intubations. Due to the direct feedback of the intubation procedure provided on screen, the Endvantage™ is a powerful training tool for teaching and learning how to perform intubations.

Use in EMS: The FOB, due to its size and complexity, is not feasible for use in EMS. The Endvantage™ is small, portable, and quick to use, making it ideal for use in EMS. The ability of the Endvantage™ to instantly confirm the location of the endotracheal tube makes it ideally suited for this environment, where the rate of failed intubations is the highest.

Price: While ultrasound has gone through substantial price reductions in recent years, it is PlasiaTEK's goal to drive the cost and price of the Endvantage™ portable ultrasound as low as possible (possibly giving the ultrasound unit away for free), making it feasible for use in intubations. This can be achieved by eliminating unneeded diagnostic tools and other components not required for the Endvantage's intubation-specific ultrasound. Endvantage™ ET tubes will be priced on par with existing tubes. Exhibit 2 depicts PlasiaTEK's projected product prices and costs.

Ability to Record Procedure: Due to the fact the Endvantage™ ultrasound device provides imaging electronically, the entire intubation procedure can be recorded as an ultrasound movie. Several anesthesiologists have expressed the view that recording the intubation would be beneficial in potential litigation issues, as there would be recorded evidence.

Direct Monitoring of the ET Tube: The Endvantage™ is the only device in existence that can directly monitor the location of the placed endotracheal tube during intubation.

ETCO$_2$ Analyzer, Pulse Oximeter: As the Endvantage™ is an electronic-based platform, models of the Endvantage™ ultrasound will be released that include a built-in ETCO$_2$ and pulse oximeter, both of which are required standard monitors for anesthesia. This would provide an even more effective solution to total anesthesia patient management.

Compatibility With Other Devices: All existing devices used in intubation follow the "open-mouth" approach. As the Endvantage™ ultrasound probe is external to the body, the ability to combine devices exists. For example, if an Endvantage™ ET tube is used on a classic laryngoscope, the laryngoscope can aid in the placement of the endotracheal tube, while the Endvantage™ ultrasound provides additional guidance and confirms and monitors the intubation.

3.5 BUSINESS MODEL

The business model for the development and sale of the patent-pending Endvantage™ ultrasound system and endotracheal tubes is a proven one in the medical industry. The revenue streams from PlasiaTEK's sales are flexible and diversified as they are realized from the sale of a non-disposable device requiring disposable products for use (Razor/Razor Blade Model). The production of Endvantage™ components will be outsourced to existing manufacturers.

3.6 COMPONENTS AND SOURCING

PlasiaTEK will source its ultrasound device and endotracheal tube manufacturing to reputable, established companies. Partnering with these industry-leading firms will grant PlasiaTEK access to the most current technology available. All of the suppliers being considered utilize the necessary manufacturing practices (GMP, ISO 9001, CE Marking Approval, and EN 46001) and have experience in dealing with and meet the standards required by regulatory bodies such as the FCC, UL, FDA and Conformité Européene.

Endotracheal Tubes: The Endvantage™ ET tube is a unique patent-pending tube that Michal Miller, MD has developed that allows ultrasound imaging of objects within air containing structures. In view of this new technology, PlasiaTEK has redesigned the endotracheal tube and modified the ultrasound to allow unprecedented levels of imaging detail of the tube within the previously inaccessible airway structures. PlasiaTEK is currently speaking with Hudson Respiratory Care Inc. to manufacture PlasiaTEK's line of ET tubes. Hudson RCI is an established manufacturer with existing distribution channels. Partnering with Hudson RCI would be very valuable to PlasiaTEK, as it would create a substantial barrier to entry for future competitors. As well, a company such as Hudson RCI would be in the position to acquire PlasiaTEK upon proof of sufficient market adoption. Final Endvantage™ ET tube development is expected to be complete by April 2004.

Portable Ultrasound Device: PlasiaTEK is currently working with Terason to complete final product development of the Endvantage™ portable ultrasound device. Terason is a leader in ultrasound development and technology, and has the technical know-how and resources to produce PlasiaTEK's Endvantage™ portable ultrasound device. The market-ready device is expected to be complete by June 2004.

3.7 INTELLECTUAL PROPERTY

PlasiaTEK has filed patent protection for "Ultrasonic Placement and Monitoring of a Tube Within the Body." Standard endotracheal tubes do not image when conventional ultrasound is performed on the neck; however, PlasiaTEK has redesigned the endotracheal tube, which now provides a clear image during intubation when used with the Endvantage™ portable ultrasound. PlasiaTEK's patent covers the method of using ultrasound (including Doppler imaging) to place and monitor any tube in the body. The patent itself specifically describes ultrasound imaging of endotracheal tubes for intubation purposes. The law firm of Crompton/Seager/Tufte are overseeing PlasiaTEK's intellectual property portfolio. The firm specializes in medical device patents, and has found no competing claims. The broad nature of this patent provides PlasiaTEK with a *strong* intellectual property position. PlasiaTEK expects to file several more patents when applicable on intellectual property developments arising during final product development.

3.8 REGULATORY APPROVAL

The manufacture and sale of medical devices are subject to extensive regulation by numerous governmental authorities, principally the U.S. Food and Drug Administration, as well as several other state and foreign agencies. FDA approval is the most stringent and difficult to acquire, and possessing FDA clearance typically means the requirements necessary to sell anywhere in the world have been surpassed.

All of PlasiaTEK's Endvantage™ components are substantially equivalent to medical devices that have previously received FDA clearance. As such, PlasiaTEK qualifies for an exemption and will file for FDA approval through an abbreviated 510(k). PlasiaTEK's FDA consultants and all other investigation thus far into regulatory approval of the Endvantage™ suggest 510(k) application will suffice. PlasiaTEK plans to file for FDA approval by June 2004, and expects approval within four months.

3.9 ADOPTION AND REIMBURSEMENT

PlasiaTEK's team has extensively analyzed the products and technology employed in the fields of endotracheal intubations and airway monitoring, and strongly feels that PlasiaTEK's technology is demonstrably better, and is deliverable at a lower price. The Endvantage™ system truly offers an all-in-one solution to intubation, in that it can be used for the placement, confirmation, and monitoring of the endotracheal tube. The Endvantage™, in one device, accomplishes the tasks where currently several devices and techniques are needed, and it performs tasks that no other device can match (direct confirmation and direct monitoring of the endotracheal tube). In addition, improved technology provides long-term healthcare savings through the reduction of injuries and by preventing needless ICU stays. PlasiaTEK is currently working with the Princeton Reimbursement Group to determine the issues surrounding the reimbursement of PlasiaTEK's portable ultrasound device and endotracheal tubes and develop a strategy to capitalize upon the existing reimbursement environment. From preliminary research, management believes reimbursement received for using the Endvantage™ will be at least as favorable as current situations.

4. MARKET ANALYSIS

4.1 MARKET POTENTIAL

In the United States, 40 million intubations will be performed this year by anesthesiologists and nurse anesthetists alone. The market potential in terms of how many Endvantage™ ultrasound devices can be sold is well in excess of 250,000 units in the United States. With 6,634 hospitals in the United States, representing over 105,000 operating rooms and intensive care suites, the potential to place an Endvantage™ portable ultrasound device in every room where intubations are performed exists. 16,681 ambulance services, 329 air ambulance services, 3,166 urgent care centers, and 1,559 trauma centers further increase the market potential. Outpatient surgical centers and military use further inflates the potential market size. Europe and Asia typically represent medical device buying markets equivalent to that of the United States.

200 million intubations are performed annually worldwide. The market for consumable endotracheal tubes alone is valued at $1 billion annually. Including devices and monitors directly related to intubation, the potential market is over $3 billion annually.

4.2 TARGET MARKETS

Individuals performing intubations fit into one of three distinct categories based on the frequency with which they perform intubations, thus providing at least three different market segments for PlasiaTEK to target.

Anesthesiologists and Nurse Anesthetists: Performing intubations on a frequent basis, anesthesiologists and nurse anesthetists are responsible for 35 of the 40 million intubations performed in the United States yearly, with nurse anesthetists actually accounting for 65% of this number. As anesthesiologists are recognized as the experts in airway management, they may be hesitant to adopt new methods and technology. Despite this, they will certainly be among the first to purchase a limited number of units to test the device and put the product through its paces. On the other hand, nurse anesthetists should readily adopt PlasiaTEK's technology for the advantages provided by external imaging during intubation. Even the most experienced performers of intubation will benefit from the direct confirmation and monitoring aspects of the Endvantage™ System of Intubation.

Paramedics: Paramedics perform intubations on an infrequent basis in challenging conditions. The Endvantage™ System's ability to quickly guide, confirm, and monitor the location of the endotracheal tube will be greatly welcomed by this market segment, where statistics for failed intubations are highest. The Endvantage™ System's ability to perform these functions in unstable and noisy environments, such as in a helicopter or an ambulance, will make the Endvantage™ a must-have device. Demand from LifeFlight, an air ambulance provider, has already been expressed.

Infrequent Performers of Intubations: Doctors (who are not anesthesiologists or nurse anesthetists) and some emergency responders are often required to perform intubations. However, the lack of training in comparison to anesthesiologists and paramedics and the infrequency with which they perform the procedure makes this segment most likely to encounter difficulty during the intubation process. This market will readily adopt the Endvantage™ for use during intubations, due to its ease of use and multiple advantages over existing devices and methods.

4.3 MARKET STRATEGY

Upon successful clinical testing and regulatory approval of the Endvantage™ System, PlasiaTEK will approach the American Society of Anesthesiologists. The ASA is an educational, research and scientific association of physicians organized to raise and maintain the standards of the medical practice of anesthesiology and improve the care of the patient. Currently, the ASA has cited the fiberoptic bronchoscope as the gold standard device for use in difficult intubations. PlasiaTEK's long-term marketing strategy is to prove the efficacy and vast improvements of the Endvantage™ System of Intubation over the fiberoptic bronchoscope and all other devices to the ASA. If the ASA recognizes the vast improvements offered by the Endvantage™ System of Intubation, the ASA will add Ultrasound Assisted Intubation or Externally Imaged Intubation to their clinical guideline recommendations. This means that every operating room in the United States will be required to use (or at least have on hand) an Endvantage™ portable ultrasound device and required Endvantage™ endotracheal tubes. PlasiaTEK's Medical Advisory Board will play an important role in carrying out this strategy.

As the ASA adoption process may take several months to a few years to complete, an extensive sales, marketing, and promotion campaign will be undertaken. This initiative will focus on developing strong hospital and EMS demand for the Endvantage™ through aggressive niche market advertising, strategic communications, and public relations. Specifically, PlasiaTEK aims to build demand through a "push" strategy of direct marketing and promotions to potential device users and buyers (GPOs) at medical device trade shows, academic conferences, and through trade-specific publications. PlasiaTEK's partnership with the University of Minnesota will greatly add to the impact of this effort. Working in association with a reputable and distinguished organization such as the University of Minnesota adds additional credibility to PlasiaTEK, and especially to the literary publications (research papers, medical journal articles, etc.) that are being written by Dr. Belani and Dr. Miller.

4.4 PRICING STRATEGY

PlasiaTEK is currently investigating several pricing strategies for the Endvantage™ System of Intubation. PlasiaTEK's goal is to drive the cost of the Endvantage™ portable ultrasound as low as possible, or even undertake a strategy in which the ultrasound devices are given away for free. PlasiaTEK's intellectual property position may allow the company to provide ultrasound devices to hospitals for free, and charge an annual license fee or per-use license fee for each intubation performed. Current portable ultrasounds range in retail price from $20,000 to $60,000 or more. PlasiaTEK expects to begin selling the portable ultrasound in 2005 for $12,000, but will quickly bring the price to under $10,000. (Exhibit 2) At this price, it is comparable and even less expensive than current devices used during intubations (the FOB and $ETCO_2$). PlasiaTEK expects to sell Endvantage™ ET tubes in 2005 for $12 per tube, and will pass the savings on to the customer as increases in the volume of tubes sold reduce unit costs. (Exhibit 2) The Endvantage™ ET tubes will sell at a cost above that of basic endotracheal tubes, but much less than various specialty tubes on the market.

5. FINANCIAL SUMMARY

5.1 FINANCIAL STATEMENTS SUMMARY

PlasiaTEK lost $51,000 in 2003 and expects losses of $927,000 in 2004. Revenues from the sale of the Endvantage™ System occur beginning January of 2005, yielding subsequent annual sales revenues of $4.9 million in 2005, $11.4 million in 2006, $26.1 million in 2007, and $36.4 million in 2008, respectively. After-tax earnings in years 2006, 2007, and 2008 are projected to be $1.6 million, $4.6 million, and $6.6 million. Exhibits 1 through 7 depict PlasiaTEK's most likely sales and financial scenario.

PlasiaTEK's management feels the market potential for external imaging in intubation is vast, and that a larger company with established medical distribution and marketing capabilities could penetrate the United States market faster and more fully exploit the worldwide market potential. Exhibit 8 depicts this scenario. With market penetration beginning the third quarter of 2006, sales revenues for 2006, 2007, and 2008 are $27.6 million, $91.8 million, and $225.5 million.

5.2 FINANCING ACTIVITIES

PlasiaTEK's equity structure will be determined by financial contribution of investors and from equity positions offered to founders and executives. In addition to the founders' contributions over the past year, Paul Pesek personally invested $50,000 seed money into PlasiaTEK. In addition to financing business operations and intellectual property expenses, this seed money allowed the company to facilitate Dr. Miller's relocation and entrance into the University of Minnesota, where he has furthered product development and proven the capabilities of PlasiaTEK's patent-pending technology on cadavers.

PlasiaTEK is currently engaged in an early stage equity financing round seeking to raise an investment of $300,000 from angel investors. The minimum investment required is $30,000, which is deliverable to PlasiaTEK in whole or with the option of investing over three months at $10,000 per month. $90,000 has been secured from three angel investors thus far, with $50,000 received and $20,000 to be collected in January and February 2004. The remaining $210,000 is expected to be secured and received by March 2004. These funds will provide a means of beginning commercial product development, conducting human studies, and financing business operations.

PlasiaTEK is now seeking a second round of equity financing that will allow the company to finish the commercial development of its Endvantage™ System of Intubation, receive regulatory body approval, finance business operations, and allow PlasiaTEK to begin sales in 2005. $2.5 million will be required, receivable in two tranches. $750,000 will be required in April 2004, and the remaining $1,250,000 will be required in October 2005, upon receiving FDA approval. Both tranches may, but are not required to come from the same investor.

5.3 HARVEST/EXIT STRATEGIES

Acquisition by an Existing Company: Upon PlasiaTEK's successful launch of the Endvantage™ to market, sale of PlasiaTEK to an existing company or competitor is probable. The acquisition of PlasiaTEK would allow current investors to sell their equity share for a profit.

IPO: PlasiaTEK may seek to sell company equity on a publicly traded stock exchange. The proceeds obtained from the IPO would be used to finance further market expansion of the Endvantage™ and develop new technologies.

PlasiaTEK, Inc.
Business Plan
Exhibits

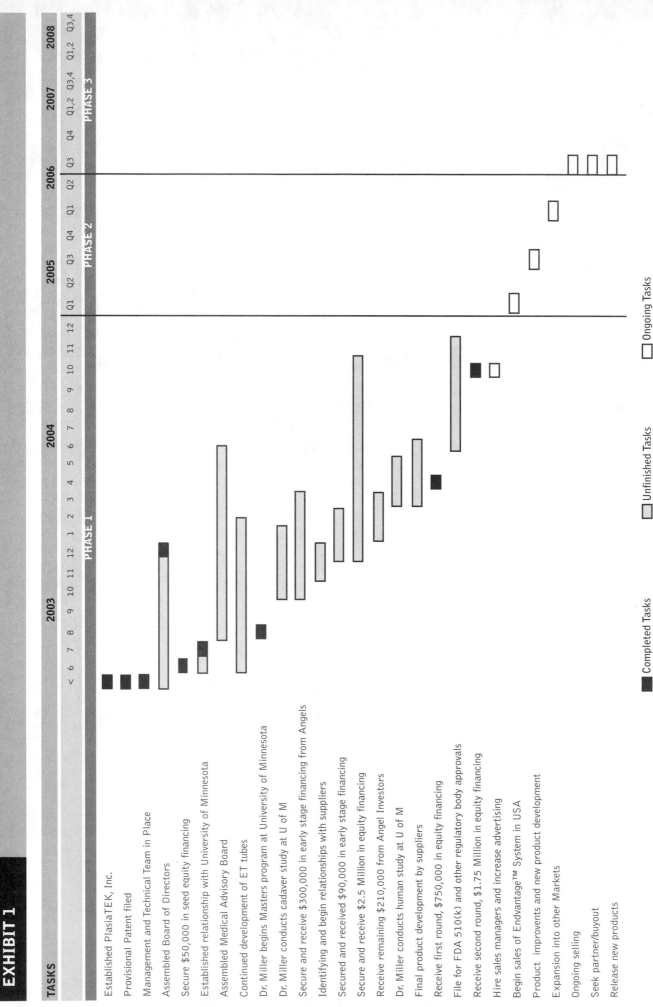

PlasiaTEK
EXHIBIT 2

PROJECTED UNIT SALES
January 1, 2005 to December 31, 2008

COMPONENT PRICE BREAKDOWN (per unit)

		2005	2006	2007	2008
Endvantage™ Device	PRICE	$12,000.00	$8,500.00	$7,000.00	$5,000.00
Endvantage™ Device	COST	$7,500.00	$5,500.00	$4,000.00	$3,000.00
Endvantage™ Device	MARGIN	37.50%	35.29%	42.86%	40.00%
Endvantage™ ET Tubes	PRICE	$12.00	$12.00	$6.00	$5.00
Endvantage™ ET Tubes	COST	$5.00	$5.00	$3.00	$2.50
Endvantage™ ET Tubes	MARGIN	58.33%	58.33%	50.00%	50.00%

USAGE OF ENDVANTAGE™ ENDOTRACHEAL TUBES

	2005	2006	2007	2008
# used per year per sold Endvantage™ Device	365	365	730	913
# used per quarter per sold Endvantage™ Device	120	120	240	300
# used per month per sold Endvantage™ Device	30	30	60	75
# used per day per sold Endvantage™ Device	1.0	1.0	2.0	2.5

MARKET POTENTIAL & ESTIMATED CAPTURE

	2005	2006	2007	2008
Intubations/year (North America)*	40,000,000	41,200,000	42,436,000	43,709,080
Market Capture (intubations)	49,410	372,480	2,212,630	4,923,850
Market Capture (intubations)	0.12%	0.90%	5.21%	11.27%
Endvantage™ Device Potential (units)**	255,000	258,825	262,707	266,648
Endvantage™ Devices in Use	365	1186	3031	5396
Market Capture (devices)	0.14%	0.46%	1.15%	2.02%

PROJECTED UNIT SALES

2005	January	February	March	April	May	June	July	August	September	October	November	December	Total
Endvantage™ Device	8	11	12	12	16	23	28	35	58	64	48	50	365
Endvantage™ ET Tubes	240	570	930	1,290	1,770	2,460	3,300	4,350	6,090	8,010	9,450	10,950	49,410

2006	Quarter 1	Quarter 2	Quarter 3	Quarter 4	Total
Endvantage™ Device	86	170	225	340	821
Endvantage™ ET Tubes	54,120	74,520	101,520	142,320	372,480

2007		Total
Endvantage™ Device		1,845
Endvantage™ ET Tubes		2,212,630

2008		Total
Endvantage™ Device		2,365
Endvantage™ ET Tubes		4,923,850

Notes to Financials:

* Number of intubations performed annually in the United States, in both the Hospital and EMS setting. Expected to grow at 3% annually for next 4-6 years.

** Potential market size of 255,000 units in U.S. based on 73,000 operating rooms, 16,681 ambulance services (containing 2 – 25+ ambulances each), 329 air ambulance services, 3,166 urgent care centers, and 1,559 trauma centers. ERs and ICUs further increase the potential market. Expected to grow at 1.5% annually for next 4 years.

	January	February	March	April	May
CASH INFLOWS					
Investment Income	188	177	274	343	2,846
Revenues from Endvantage™ Ultrasound Device	-	-	-	-	-
Revenues from Endvantage™ Consumables	-	-	-	-	-
Royalties	-	-	-	-	-
TOTAL CASH INFLOWS	$188	$177	$274	$343	$2,846
CASH OUTFLOWS					
Product Expense					
Inventory Purchases Endvantage™ Ultrasound Device					
Inventory Purchases Endvantage™ Consumables	-	-	-	-	-
Total Product Expense	$-	$-	$-	$-	$-
Sales, Marketing, & Training					
VP Sales & Marketing - Peter Leslie	-	-	-	4,000	4,000
Regional Sales Managers	-	-	-	-	-
Office Assistants - Sales	-	-	-	-	-
Total Payroll	-	-	-	4,000	4,000
Payroll Taxes & Benefits	-	-	-	640	640
Travel & Travel Expenses - Sales	-	-	-	-	1,800
Advertising & Literature	-	-	-	-	2,500
Trade Shows & Seminars					
Total Sales, Marketing, & Training Expense	$-	$-	$-	$4,640	$8,940
# of Sales & Marketing Employees	1	1	1	1	1
Administration					
President - Paul Pesek	-	-	-	-	-
CFO/Executive Vice President - Kevin Michaluk	-	-	-	4,000	4,000
Office Assistants - Admin/Accounting	-	-	-		
Total Payroll	-	-	-	4,000	4,000
Payroll Taxes & Benefits	-	-	-	640	640
Travel & Travel Expenses - Admin	1,000	1,000	2,000	4,000	4,000
Accounting/Legal Fees	-	-	4,500	4,500	3,500
Rent, Utilities, Building Insurance	1,000	1,000	1,000	1,000	1,000
Postage, Supplies, Phone, Internet	1,000	1,000	1,000	1,000	1,000
Insurance	-	-	1,500	1,500	1,500
Membership & Subscriptions					
Total Administration Expense	$3,000	$3,000	$10,000	$16,640	$15,640
# of Administration Employees	2	2	2	2	2
Research & Development					
VP Technology - Michal Miller, MD	4,000	4,000	4,000	4,000	4,000
Technicians	-	-	-	-	-
Total Payroll	4,000	4,000	4,000	4,000	4,000
Payroll Taxes & Benefits	640	640	640	640	640
Product Development (contract expense)	-	5,000	15,000	45,000	75,000
Equipment	1,000	1,000	1,000	1,000	1,000
Travel & Travel Expenses - R&D	-	-	-	1,500	1,500
University of Minnesota Tuition, Misc. Fees	1,000	1,000	1,000	1,000	-
Apartment	1,200	1,200	1,200	1,200	1,200
Clinical Testing Expenses (including insurance)	2,000	2,000	2,000	2,000	-
Agency Fees - Patents, FDA, FCC, UL	7,000	3,000	3,000	3,000	3,000
Total Research & Development	$16,840	$17,840	$27,840	$59,340	$86,340
# of R&D Employees	1	1	1	1	1
Other					
Miscellaneous Expenses	250	250	250	250	250
Directors and Advisors Expense	-	-	-	-	-
Consultants	-	3,000	4,000	2,000	2,000
Interest Payments	-	-	-	-	-
Income Taxes	-	-	-	-	-
Total Other	$250	$3,250	$4,250	$2,250	$2,250
TOTAL CASH OUTFLOWS	$20,090	$24,090	$42,090	$82,870	$113,170
FINANCING					
Government Grants	-	-	-	-	-
Bank Line of Credit	-	-	-	-	-
Issuance of Common Shares	20,000	50,000	60,000	750,000	
Issuance of Preferred Shares	-	-	-	-	-
CHANGE FROM FINANCING	$20,000	$50,000	$60,000	$750,000	$-
CASH AT BEGINNING OF PERIOD	$47,000	$47,098	$73,184	$91,369	$758,841
CASH AT END OF PERIOD	$47,098	$73,184	$91,369	$758,841	$648,517

June	July	August	September	October	November	December	Year
2,432	1,915	1,572	1,170	632	6,953	6,407	24,907
-	-	-	-	-	-	-	-
-	-	-	-	-	-	-	-
$2,432	$1,915	$1,572	$1,170	$632	$6,953	$6,407	24,907
							-
					75,000	45,000	120,000
-	-	-	-	-	12,500	13,750	26,250
$-	$-	$-	$-	$-	$87,500	$58,750	146,250
							-
4,000	4,000	4,000	4,000	4,000	4,000	4,000	36,000
-	-	-	6,000	6,000	6,000	6,000	24,000
3,000	3,000	3,000	3,000	3,000	3,000	3,000	21,000
7,000	7,000	7,000	13,000	13,000	13,000	13,000	81,000
1,120	1,120	1,120	3,000	2,080	2,080	2,080	13,880
1,800	1,800	1,800	3,600	3,600	3,600	3,600	21,600
2,500	-	2,500	2,500	2,500	2,500	2,500	17,500
7,500	3,000	3,000	3,000	3,000	3,000	3,000	25,500
$19,920	$12,920	$15,420	$25,100	$24,180	$24,180	$24,180	159,480
2	2	2	3	3	3	3	
							-
-	5,000	5,000	5,000	5,000	5,000	5,000	30,000
4,000	4,000	4,000	4,000	4,000	4,000	4,000	36,000
3,000	3,000	3,000	3,000	3,000	3,000	3,000	21,000
7,000	12,000	12,000	12,000	12,000	12,000	12,000	87,000
1,120	1,920	1,920	1,920	1,920	1,920	1,920	13,920
4,000	4,000	4,000	4,000	4,000	4,000	4,000	40,000
3,500	3,500	3,500	3,500	-	-	-	26,500
1,500	1,500	1,500	1,500	1,500	1,500	1,500	15,500
1,250	1,250	1,250	1,250	1,250	1,250	1,250	13,750
1,500	1,500	1,500	1,500	1,500	1,500	1,500	15,000
5,000	-	-	-	-	-	-	5,000
$24,870	$25,670	$25,670	$25,670	$22,170	$22,170	$22,170	216,670
3	3	3	3	3	3	3	
							-
4,000	4,000	4,000	4,000	4,000	4,000	4,000	48,000
-	2,500	2,500	2,500	2,500	2,500	2,500	15,000
4,000	6,500	6,500	6,500	6,500	6,500	6,500	63,000
640	1,040	1,040	1,040	1,040	1,040	1,040	10,080
65,000	-	-	75,000	-	-	-	280,000
5,000	1,000	1,000	1,000	1,000	1,000	1,000	16,000
1,500	1,500	1,500	1,500	1,500	1,500	1,500	13,500
-	-	-	1,000	1,000	1,000	1,000	8,000
1,200	1,200	1,200	1,200	1,200	1,200	1,200	14,400
-	15,000	50,000	-	-	-	-	73,000
3,000	3,000	3,000	3,000	3,000	3,000	3,000	40,000
$80,340	$29,240	$64,240	$90,240	$15,240	$15,240	$15,240	517,980
1	2	2	2	2	2	2	
							-
250	500	500	500	500	500	500	4,500
-	-	-	-	-	-	-	-
15,000	25,000	3,000	3,000	3,000	3,000	3,000	66,000
-	-	-	-	-	-	-	-
-	-	-	-	-	-	-	-
$15,250	$25,500	$3,500	$3,500	$3,500	$3,500	$3,500	70,500
$140,380	$93,330	$108,830	$144,510	$65,090	$152,590	$123,840	1,110,880
-	-	-	-	-	-	-	-
-	-	-	-	-	-	-	-
-	-	-	-	1,750,000	-	-	2,630,000
-	-	-	-	-	-	-	-
$-	$-	$-	$-	$1,750,000	$-	$-	2,630,000
$648,517	$510,569	$419,153	$311,895	$168,555	$1,854,097	$1,708,460	$47,000
$510,569	$419,153	$311,895	$168,555	$1,854,097	$1,708,460	$1,591,027	$1,591,027

PRO FORMA MONTHLY CASH FLOW STATEMENTS
FOR START UP PHASE
January 1, 2005 to December 31, 2005

	January	February	March	April	May	June
CASH INFLOWS						
Investment Income	5,966	5,498	5,033	4,474	3,730	3,276
Revenues from Endvantage™ Ultrasound Device	-	48,000	114,000	138,000	144,000	168,000
Revenues from Endvantage™ Consumables	-	1,440	4,860	9,000	13,320	18,360
Royalties	-	-	-	-	-	-
TOTAL CASH INFLOWS	**$5,966**	**$54,938**	**$123,893**	**$151,474**	**$161,050**	**$189,636**
CASH OUTFLOWS						
Product Expense						
Payments to Supplier - Endvantage™ Ultrasound Device	-	60,000	82,500	90,000	90,000	120,000
Payments to Supplier - Endvantage™ Consumables	-	1,200	2,850	4,650	6,450	8,850
Postage/Shipping Expense - Materials	400	550	600	600	800	1,150
Sales Commissions	-	890	1,250	1,396	1,435	1,919
Rep Commissions	-	5,795	8,002	8,774	8,826	11,775
Total Product Expense	**$400**	**$68,434**	**$95,202**	**$105,420**	**$107,511**	**$143,694**
Sales, Marketing, & Training						
VP Sales & Marketing - Peter Leslie	6,250	6,250	6,250	6,250	6,250	6,250
Regional Sales Managers	6,000	12,000	12,000	12,000	12,000	18,000
Office Assistants - Sales	3,500	3,500	3,500	3,500	3,500	3,500
Total Payroll	15,750	21,750	21,750	21,750	21,750	27,750
Payroll Taxes & Benefits	2,520	3,480	3,480	3,480	3,480	4,440
Travel & Travel Expenses - Sales	6,000	9,000	9,000	9,000	9,000	12,000
Advertising & Literature	10,000	10,000	10,000	10,000	10,000	10,000
Trade Shows & Seminars	25,000	-	12,500	-	-	12,500
Total Sales, Marketing, & Training Expense	**$59,270**	**$44,230**	**$56,730**	**$44,230**	**$44,230**	**$66,690**
# of Sales & Marketing Employees	3	4	4	4	4	5
Administration						
President - Paul Pesek	6,250	6,250	6,250	6,250	6,250	6,250
CFO/Executive Vice President - Kevin Michaluk	5,000	5,000	5,000	5,000	5,000	5,000
Office Assistants - Admin/Accounting	7,000	7,000	7,000	7,000	7,000	7,000
Total Payroll	18,250	18,250	18,250	18,250	18,250	18,250
Payroll Taxes & Benefits	2,920	2,920	2,920	2,920	2,920	2,920
Travel & Travel Expenses - Admin	5,000	5,000	5,000	5,000	5,000	5,000
Accounting/Legal Fees	3,000	3,000	3,000	3,000	3,000	3,000
Rent, Utilities, Building Insurance	2,000	2,000	2,000	2,000	2,000	2,000
Postage, Supplies, Phone, Internet	1,500	1,500	1,500	1,500	1,500	1,500
Insurance	3,300	3,300	3,300	3,300	3,300	3,300
Membership & Subscriptions	5,000	-	-	-	-	-
Total Administration Expense	**$40,970**	**$35,970**	**$35,970**	**$35,970**	**$35,970**	**$35,970**
# of Administration Employees	4	4	4	4	4	4
Research & Development						
VP Technology - Michal Miller, MD	6,250	6,250	6,250	6,250	6,250	6,250
Technicians	8,000	8,000	8,000	8,000	8,000	8,000
Total Payroll	14,250	14,250	14,250	14,250	14,250	14,250
Payroll Taxes & Benefits	2,280	2,280	2,280	2,280	2,280	2,280
Product Development (contract expense)	-	-	15,000	85,000	65,000	15,000
Equipment	1,500	1,500	1,500	1,500	1,500	1,500
Travel & Travel Expenses - R&D	3,000	3,000	3,000	3,000	3,000	3,000
University of Minnesota Tuition, Misc. Fees	1,000	1,000	1,000	-	-	-
Apartment	1,200	1,200	1,200	1,200	1,200	1,200
Clinical Testing Expenses (including insurance)	-	-	30,000	50,000	-	-
Agency Fees - Patents, FDA, FCC, UL	3,000	3,000	3,000	3,000	3,000	3,000
Total Research & Development	**$26,230**	**$26,230**	**$71,230**	**$160,230**	**$90,230**	**$40,230**
# of R&D Employees	3	3	3	3	3	3
Other						
Miscellaneous Expenses	1,000	1,000	1,000	1,000	1,000	1,000
Directors and Advisors Expense	-	-	10,000	-	-	-
Consultants	3,000	3,000	3,000	3,000	3,000	3,000
Interest Payments	-	-	-	-	-	-
Income Taxes	-	-	-	-	-	-
Total Other	**$4,000**	**$4,000**	**$14,000**	**$4,000**	**$4,000**	**$4,000**
TOTAL CASH OUTFLOWS	**$130,870**	**$178,864**	**$273,132**	**$349,850**	**$281,941**	**$290,584**
FINANCING						
Government Grants	-	-	-	-	-	-
Bank Line of Credit	-	-	-	-	-	-
Issuance of Common Shares	-	-	-	-	-	-
Issuance of Preferred Shares	-	-	-	-	-	-
CHANGE FROM FINANCING	**$-**	**$-**	**$-**	**$-**	**$-**	**$-**
CASH AT BEGINNING OF PERIOD	**$1,591,027**	**$1,466,123**	**$1,342,196**	**$1,192,958**	**$994,581**	**$873,690**
CASH AT END OF PERIOD	**$1,466,123**	**$1,342,196**	**$1,192,958**	**$994,581**	**$873,690**	**$772,742**

	July	August	September	October	November	December	Total
	2,898	2,568	2,255	2,019	1,855	2,156	41,728
	234,000	306,000	378,000	558,000	732,000	672,000	3,492,000
	25,380	34,560	45,900	62,640	84,600	104,760	404,820
	-	-	-	-	-	-	-
	$262,278	**$343,128**	**$426,155**	**$622,659**	**$818,455**	**$778,916**	**3,938,548**
							-
							-
	172,500	210,000	282,500	455,000	500,000	380,000	2,442,500
	12,300	16,500	21,750	30,450	40,050	47,250	192,300
	1,400	1,750	2,900	3,200	2,400	2,500	18,250
	2,750	3,380	4,250	6,922	7,777	6,205	38,174
	16,914	20,635	25,826	42,637	47,233	35,921	232,338
	$205,864	**$252,266**	**$337,226**	**$538,209**	**$597,461**	**$471,875**	**2,923,562**
							-
	6,250	6,250	6,250	6,250	6,250	6,250	75,000
	18,000	24,000	24,000	24,000	24,000	24,000	210,000
	3,500	3,500	3,500	3,500	3,500	3,500	42,000
	27,750	33,750	33,750	33,750	33,750	33,750	327,000
	4,440	5,400	5,400	5,400	5,400	5,400	52,320
	12,000	15,000	15,000	15,000	15,000	15,000	141,000
	10,000	10,000	10,000	10,000	10,000	10,000	120,000
	-	-	12,500	-	12,500	12,500	87,500
	$54,190	**$64,150**	**$76,650**	**$64,150**	**$76,650**	**$76,650**	**727,820**
	5	6	6	6	6	6	
							-
	6,250	6,250	6,250	6,250	6,250	6,250	75,000
	5,000	5,000	5,000	5,000	5,000	5,000	60,000
	7,000	7,000	7,000	7,000	7,000	7,000	84,000
	18,250	18,250	18,250	18,250	18,250	18,250	219,000
	2,920	2,920	2,920	2,920	2,920	2,920	35,040
	5,000	5,000	5,000	5,000	5,000	5,000	60,000
	3,000	3,000	3,000	3,000	3,000	3,000	36,000
	2,000	2,000	2,000	2,000	2,000	2,000	24,000
	1,500	1,500	1,500	1,500	1,500	1,500	18,000
	3,300	3,300	3,300	3,300	3,300	3,300	39,600
	-	-	-	-	-	-	5,000
	$35,970	**$35,970**	**$35,970**	**$35,970**	**$35,970**	**$35,970**	**436,640**
	4	4	4	4	4	4	
							-
	6,250	6,250	6,250	6,250	6,250	6,250	75,000
	8,000	8,000	8,000	8,000	8,000	8,000	96,000
	14,250	14,250	14,250	14,250	14,250	14,250	171,000
	2,280	2,280	2,280	2,280	2,280	2,280	27,360
	25,000	45,000	-	-	-	-	250,000
	1,500	1,500	1,500	1,500	1,500	1,500	18,000
	3,000	3,000	3,000	3,000	3,000	3,000	36,000
	-	-	-	-	-	-	3,000
	1,200	1,200	1,200	-	-	-	10,800
	-	-	-	-	-	-	80,000
	3,000	3,000	3,000	3,000	3,000	3,000	36,000
	$50,230	**$70,230**	**$25,230**	**$24,030**	**$24,030**	**$24,030**	**632,160**
	3	3	3	3	3	3	
	1,000	1,000	1,000	1,000	1,000	1,000	12,000
	-	-	10,000	-	-	-	20,000
	3,000	3,000	3,000	3,000	3,000	3,000	36,000
	-	-	-	-	-	-	-
	-	-	-	-	-	-	-
	$4,000	**$4,000**	**$14,000**	**$4,000**	**$4,000**	**$4,000**	**68,000**
	$350,254	**$426,616**	**$489,076**	**$666,359**	**$738,111**	**$612,525**	**4,788,182**
	-	-	-	-	-	-	-
	-	-	-	-	-	-	-
	-	-	-	-	-	-	-
	$-	**$-**	**$-**	**$-**	**$-**	**$-**	
	$772,742	**$684,767**	**$601,279**	**$538,358**	**$494,658**	**$575,002**	**$1,591,027**
	$684,767	**$601,279**	**$538,358**	**$494,658**	**$575,002**	**$741,392**	**$741,392**

PlasiaTEK EXHIBIT 5

PRO FORMA ANNUAL CASH FLOW STATEMENTS
January 1, 2004 to December 31, 2008

	2004	2005	2006	2007	2008
CASH INFLOWS					
Investment Income	24,907	41,728	33,404	82,965	332,813
Revenues from Endvantage™ Ultrasound Device	-	3,492,000	6,819,725	12,024,525	12,579,750
Revenues from Endvantage™ Consumables	-	404,820	3,987,396	11,954,877	24,148,692
Royalties/Licensing Fees	-	-	-	-	-
TOTAL CASH INFLOWS	**$24,907**	**$3,938,548**	**$10,840,525**	**$24,062,367**	**$37,061,255**
CASH OUTFLOWS					
Product Expense					
Payments to Supplier - Endvantage™ Ultrasound Device	120,000	2,442,500	4,474,950	7,093,550	7,141,088
Payments to Supplier - Endvantage™ Consumables	26,250	192,300	1,818,410	6,206,019	11,742,452
Postage/Shipping Expense - Materials	-	18,250	41,050	92,250	118,250
Sales Commissions	-	38,174	114,769	277,202	398,463
Rep Commissions	-	232,338	533,541	1,106,093	1,247,324
Total Product Expense	**$146,250**	**$2,923,562**	**$6,982,720**	**$14,775,114**	**$20,647,576**
Sales, Marketing, & Training					
VP Sales & Marketing - Peter Leslie	36,000	75,000	84,000	108,000	120,000
Salesmen/Trainer	24,000	210,000	375,000	450,000	600,000
Office Assistants - Sales	21,000	42,000	65,000	90,000	100,000
Total Payroll	**81,000**	**327,000**	**524,000**	**648,000**	**820,000**
Payroll Taxes & Benefits	12,960	52,320	83,840	103,680	131,200
Travel & Travel Expenses - Sales	21,600	141,000	210,000	300,000	315,000
Advertising & Literature	17,500	120,000	150,000	325,000	450,000
Trade Shows & Seminars	25,500	87,500	125,000	200,000	250,000
Total Sales, Marketing, & Training Expense	**$158,560**	**$727,820**	**$1,092,840**	**$1,576,680**	**$1,966,200**
# of Sales & Marketing Employees	3	6	8	9	10
Administration					
President - Paul Pesek	30,000	75,000	100,000	120,000	144,000
CFO/Executive Vice President - Kevin Michaluk	36,000	60,000	84,000	108,000	120,000
CFO	-	-	72,000	84,000	108,000
Office Assistants - Admin/Accounting	21,000	84,000	120,000	160,000	210,000
Total Payroll	87,000	219,000	376,000	472,000	582,000
Payroll Taxes & Benefits	13,920	35,040	60,160	75,520	93,120
Travel & Travel Expenses - Admin	40,000	60,000	70,000	80,000	90,000
Accounting/Legal Fees	26,500	36,000	42,000	50,000	60,000
Rent, Utilities, Building Insurance	15,500	24,000	40,000	60,000	75,000
Postage, Supplies, Phone, Internet	13,750	18,000	22,000	30,000	45,000
Insurance	15,000	39,600	50,000	60,000	75,000
Membership & Subscriptions	5,000	5,000	10,000	10,000	10,000
Total Administration Expense	**$216,670**	**$436,640**	**$670,160**	**$837,520**	**$1,030,120**
# of Administration Employees	3	4	6	7	8
Research & Development					
VP Technology - Michal Miller, MD	48,000	75,000	84,000	108,000	120,000
Technicians	15,000	96,000	200,000	260,000	315,000
Total Payroll	63,000	171,000	284,000	368,000	435,000
Payroll Taxes & Benefits	10,080	27,360	45,440	58,880	69,600
Product Development (contract expense)	280,000	250,000	350,000	450,000	550,000
Equipment	16,000	18,000	25,000	35,000	50,000
Travel & Travel Expenses - R&D	13,500	36,000	40,000	50,000	60,000
University of Minnesota Tuition, Misc. Fees	8,000	3,000	-	-	-
Apartment	14,400	10,800	-	-	-
Clinical Testing Expenses (including insurance)	73,000	80,000	60,000	75,000	100,000
Agency Fees - Patents, FDA, FCC, UL	40,000	36,000	75,000	125,000	150,000
Total Research & Development	**$517,980**	**$632,160**	**$879,440**	**$1,161,880**	**$1,414,600**
# of R&D Employees	2	3	5	6	7
Other					
Miscellaneous Expenses	4,500	12,000	24,000	24,000	24,000
Directors and Advisors Expense	-	20,000	40,000	60,000	60,000
Consultants	66,000	36,000	50,000	75,000	75,000
Interest Payments	-	-	-	-	-
Income Taxes	-	-	-	-	2,363,078
Total Other	**$70,500**	**$68,000**	**$114,000**	**$159,000**	**$2,522,078**

continued

TOTAL CASH OUTFLOWS	$1,109,960	$4,788,182	$9,739,160	$18,510,194	$27,580,574
FINANCING					
Government Grants	-	-	-	-	-
Bank Line of Credit	-	-	-	-	-
Issuance of Common Shares	2,630,000	-	-	-	-
Issuance of Preferred Shares	-	-	-	-	-
CHANGE FROM FINANCING	$2,630,000	$-	$-	$-	$-
CASH AT BEGINNING OF PERIOD	$47,000	$1,591,947	$742,312	$1,843,677	$7,395,851
CASH AT END OF PERIOD	$1,591,947	$742,312	$1,843,677	$7,395,851	$16,876,532

PlasiaTEK EXHIBIT 6

PRO FORMA ANNUAL INCOME STATEMENTS
January 1, 2004 to December 31, 2008

	2004	2005	2006	2007	2008
SALES					
Revenues from Endvantage™ Ultrasound Device		4,380,000	6,978,500	12,915,000	11,825,000
Revenues from Endvantage™ Consumables		592,920	4,469,760	13,275,780	24,619,250
TOTAL SALES	$-	$4,972,920	$11,448,260	$26,190,780	$36,444,250
COST OF GOODS SOLD					
Payments to Supplier - Endvantage™ Ultrasound Device		2,737,500	4,515,500	7,380,000	7,095,000
Payments to Supplier - Endvantage™ Consumables		247,050	1,862,400	6,637,890	12,309,625
TOTAL COST OF GOODS SOLD	$-	$2,984,550	$6,377,900	$14,017,890	$19,404,625
VARIABLE EXPENSES					
Sales Commissions	-	44,756	120,207	294,646	409,998
Rep Commissions	-	269,915	551,072	1,167,762	1,256,164
Postage/Shipping Expense - Materials	-	18,250	41,050	92,250	118,250
TOTAL VARIABLE EXPENSES	$-	$332,921	$712,328	$1,554,658	$1,784,412
GROSS PROFIT	$-	$1,655,449	$4,358,032	$10,618,232	$15,255,213
Gross Profit Margin Ratio	-	33.29%	38.07%	40.54%	41.86%
FIXED EXPENSES					
Wages, Payroll Taxes and Benefits	267,960	831,720	1,373,440	1,726,080	2,130,920
Travel & Travel Expenses	75,100	237,000	320,000	430,000	465,000
Advertising and Promotion	43,000	207,500	275,000	525,000	700,000
Rent, Utilities, Building Insurance	15,500	24,000	40,000	60,000	75,000
Postage, Supplies, Phone, Internet	13,750	18,000	22,000	30,000	45,000
Research & Development	375,400	343,800	410,000	525,000	650,000
Accounting/Legal Fees	26,500	36,000	42,000	50,000	60,000
Insurance	15,000	39,600	50,000	60,000	75,000
Membership & Subscriptions	5,000	5,000	10,000	10,000	10,000
Agency Fees - Patents, FDA, FCC, UL	40,000	36,000	75,000	125,000	150,000
Directors and Advisors Expense	-	20,000	40,000	60,000	60,000
Consultants	66,000	36,000	50,000	75,000	75,000
Interest Payments	-	-	-	-	-
Depreciation	4,550	9,050	15,300	23,500	32,000
Miscellaneous Expenses	4,500	12,000	24,000	24,000	24,000
TOTAL FIXED EXPENSES	$952,260	$1,855,670	$2,746,740	$3,723,580	$4,551,920
NET OPERATING PROFIT (LOSS)	$(952,260)	$(200,221)	$1,611,292	$6,894,652	$10,703,293
OTHER INCOME					
Investment Income	24,907	41,728	33,404	82,965	332,813
Royalties	-	-	-	-	-
Government Grants	-	-	-	-	-
TOTAL OTHER INCOME	$24,907	$41,728	$33,404	$82,965	$332,813
TOTAL TAXABLE INCOME	$(927,353)	$(158,494)	$1,644,696	$6,977,618	$11,036,107
Income Taxes	-	-	657,878	2,791,047	4,414,443
Research Tax Credit	-	-	-	-	-
Benefit of Loss Carryforward	-	-	657,878	427,969	-
NET INCOME	$(927,353)	$(158,494)	$1,644,696	$4,614,539	$6,621,664
Net Profit Margin Ratio	-	-3.19%	14.37%	17.62%	18.17%

PlasiaTEK EXHIBIT 7	PRO FORMA ANNUAL BALANCE SHEET January 1, 2004 to December 31, 2008					

	January, 2004	End 2004	2005	2006	2007	2008
CURRENT ASSETS						
Cash	47,000	1,591,947	742,312	1,843,677	7,395,851	16,876,532
Accounts Receivable	-	-	1,076,100	1,717,239	3,928,617	3,644,425
Inventory	-	146,250	226,250	349,750	395,428	413,016
TOTAL CURRENT ASSETS	**47,000**	**1,738,197**	**2,044,662**	**3,910,666**	**11,719,896**	**20,933,973**
FIXED ASSETS						
Equipment	2,200	18,200	36,200	61,200	96,200	146,200
less depreciation	550	5,100	14,150	29,450	52,950	84,950
TOTAL FIXED ASSETS	**1,650**	**13,100**	**22,050**	**31,750**	**43,250**	**61,250**
TOTAL ASSETS	**$48,650**	**$1,751,297**	**$2,066,712**	**$3,942,416**	**$11,763,146**	**$20,995,223**
CURRENT LIABILITIES						
Accounts Payable	-	-	429,750	637,790	1,401,789	1,940,463
Sales Commissions Payable	-	-	6,583	12,021	29,465	41,000
Rep Commissions Payable	-	-	37,577	55,107	116,776	125,616
Taxes Payable					2,363,078	4,414,443
Bank Loans	-	-	-	-	-	-
TOTAL CURRENT LIABILITIES	**-**	**-**	**473,909**	**704,918**	**3,911,108**	**6,521,521**
LONG TERM DEBT						
Long Term Debt	-	-	-	-	-	-
Other Long Term Liabilities	-	-	-	-	-	-
TOTAL LONG TERM DEBT	**-**	**-**	**-**	**-**	**-**	**-**
TOTAL LIABILITIES	**-**	**-**	**473,909**	**704,918**	**3,911,108**	**6,521,521**
SHAREHOLDERS' EQUITY						
Common Shares Issued	100,000	2,730,000	2,730,000	2,730,000	2,730,000	2,730,000
Preferred Shares Issued	-	-	-	-	-	-
Retained Earnings	(-51,350)	(978,703)	(1,137,197)	507,499	5,122,038	11,743,702
TOTAL SHAREHOLDERS' EQUITY	**48,650**	**1,751,297**	**1,592,803**	**3,237,499**	**7,852,038**	**14,473,702**
TOTAL LIABILITIES & SHAREHOLDERS' EQUITY	**$48,650**	**$1,751,297**	**$2,066,712**	**$3,942,416**	**$11,763,146**	**$20,995,223**

PlasiaTEK
EXHIBIT 8

POTENTIAL MARKET PENETRATION SCENARIO
January 1, 2005 to December 31, 2008

COMPONENT PRICE BREAKDOWN (per unit)

		2005	2006	2007	2008
Endvantage™ Device	PRICE	$12,000.00	$8,500.00	$7,000.00	$5,000.00
Endvantage™ Device	COST	$7,500.00	$5,500.00	$3,250.00	$2,500.00
Endvantage™ Device	MARGIN	37.50%	35.29%	53.57%	50.00%
Endvantage™ ET Tubes	PRICE	$12.00	$12.00	$6.00	$5.00
Endvantage™ ET Tubes	COST	$5.00	$5.00	$1.50	$1.25
Endvantage™ ET Tubes	MARGIN	58.33%	58.33%	75.00%	75.00%

USAGE OF ENDVANTAGE™ ENDOTRACHEAL TUBES

	2005	2006	2007	2008
# used per year per sold Endvantage™ Device	365	730	1,278	1,643
# used per quarter per sold Endvantage™ Device	120	240	420	540
# used per month per sold Endvantage™ Device	30	60	105	135
# used per day per sold Endvantage™ Device	1.0	2.0	3.5	4.5

MARKET POTENTIAL & ESTIMATED CAPTURE

	2005	2006	2007	2008
Intubations/year (Worldwide)	200,000,000	206,000,000	212,180,000	218,545,400
Market Capture (intubations)	49,410	1,097,760	9,263,153	32,551,065
Market Capture (intubations)	0.02%	0.53%	4.37%	14.89%
Endvantage™ Devices in Use	365	2,071	7,251	19,818

PROJECTED UNIT SALES

2005	January	February	March	April	May	June	July	August	September	October	November	December	Total
Endvantage™ Device	8	11	12	12	16	23	28	35	58	64	48	50	365
Endvantage™ ET Tubes	240	570	930	1,290	1,770	2,460	3,300	4,350	6,090	8,010	9,450	10,950	49,410

2006	Quarter 1	Quarter 2	Quarter 3	Quarter 4	Total
Endvantage™ Device	86	250	650	720	1,706
Endvantage™ ET Tubes	108,240	168,240	324,240	497,040	1,097,760

2007		Total
Endvantage™ Device		5,180
Endvantage™ ET Tubes		9,263,153

2008		Total
Endvantage™ Device		12,567
Endvantage™ ET Tubes		32,551,065

EXPLANATION FOR EXHIBIT:

This exhibit shows the potential unit sales, market share, revenues, and profitability attainable to a firm with established distribution and greater financial resources.

Notes to Financials:

Projections for 2005 and the first six months of 2006 are the same as Exhibit 3. Projections beginning 3rd Quarter 2006 assume either PlasiaTEK has been sold to another company or partnered with an existing company. Increased sales and adoption are a result of increased marketing and distribution. Direct sales force in Europe and Asia are implemented, complemented by 3rd party distributors.

APPENDIX 1

FINANCIAL NOTES AND ASSUMPTIONS

1. All funds are expressed in US dollars.

2. Beginning cash balance (January 1, 2004) is $47,000.

3. Equity invested into company as of January 1, 2004, is $100,000 with additional $40,000 pledged ($20,000 to be received in both January and February, respectively).

4. Taxes are based on an effective rate of 40%. Losses in previous years can be carried forward to offset profits in current years.

5. Investment income is calculated by multiplying the beginning monthly cash balance by a monthly investment rate of 0.375% (4.5% annually).

6. Sales revenues are based on base case scenario projected unit sales (Exhibit 2).

7. Sales and consumption of Endvantage™ ET tubes will vary with use. Consumption per day per machine may be six to ten tubes within the hospital setting (OR), or only one every few days in the EMS setting. An average tube use per placed machine is used in the calculation of sales revenues and expenses. ET tube consumption per machine increases early to reflect increased adoption and increased intra-hospital use. (Exhibit 2).

8. To reflect future competition and cost savings from increased unit sales, the selling price of the device and consumables is budgeted to reduce yearly. (Exhibit 2)

9. Sales rep commissions are calculated at 10% of Endvantage™ device sales and 2% of Endvantage™ ET tube sales. Sales rep sales as a percentage of total sales are 60% in 2005, 70% in 2006, and 75% in 2007 and 2008.

10. Sales commissions for regional managers calculated at 1.5% of sales attributed to the sales reps they are responsible for.

11. Commissions paid within 30 days of product delivery.

12. 50% of payment from customers collected within 30 days, remainder collected within 60 days.

13. 100% of payments owing to suppliers made within 45 days.

14. Payroll taxes and benefits expense is calculated at 16% of total payroll.

15. Sales begin January 2005.

16. Directors' Fees include honorarium, travel expenses, and liability insurance.

APPENDIX 2

"CLASSIC" LARYNGOSCOPIC INTUBATION

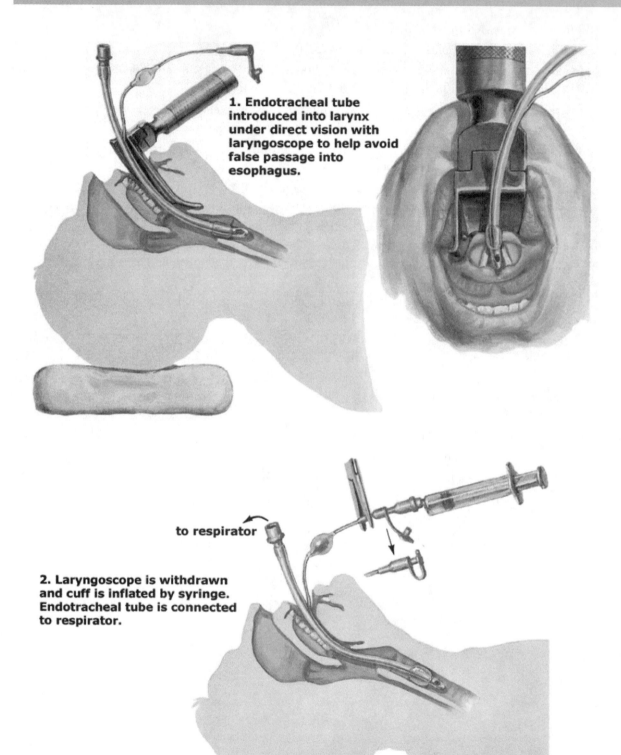

1. Endotracheal tube introduced into larynx under direct vision with laryngoscope to help avoid false passage into esophagus.

to respirator

2. Laryngoscope is withdrawn and cuff is inflated by syringe. Endotracheal tube is connected to respirator.

APPENDIX 3

REFERENCES

The following references have been used in the writing of this document.

1. Benjamin B: Laryngeal trauma from intubation: Endoscopic evaluation and classification, Otolaryngology Head & Neck Surgery, 3rd edition. Edited by Cummings CW, Fredrickson JM, Harker LA, Krause CJ, Schuller DE, Richardson MA: St. Louis, Mosby, p 2013-35, 1998.

2. Owings MF, Kozak LJ: Ambulatory and inpatient procedures in the United States, 1996. National Center for Health Statistics. Vital Health Stat 13(139). 1998.

3. Fasting S, Gisvold SE: Serious intraoperative problems: a five-year review of 83844 anesthetics. Can J Anesth 49:6, 2002.

4. Tiret L, Desmonts JM, Hatton F et al.: Complications associated with anesthesia: a prospective study in France, Can Anesth Soc J 33:336, 1986.

5. Kottke TE, Wu LA, Hoffman RS: Economic and psychological implications of the obesity epidemic, Mayo Clin Proc. Jan;78(1):92-4, 2003.

6. Kimm SY, Obarzanek E: Childhood obesity: a new pandemic of the new millennium. Pediatrics Nov;110(5):1003-7, 2002.

7. Domino KB, Posner KL, Caplan RA, Cheney FW: Airway injury during anesthesia: a closed claims analysis. Anesthesiology; 91:1703-11, 1999.

8. Gamlin F, Caldicott LD, Shah MV: Mediastinitis and sepsis syndrome following intubation. Anesthesia; 49:883-5, 1994.

9. Newland MC, Ellis JC, Lydiatt CA, Peters R, Tinker JH, Romberger DJ, Ullrich BS, Anderson JR: Anesthetic related cardiac arrest and its mortality. Anesthesiology; 97:108-15, 2002.

10. Irish JC, Gullane PJ: Complications of intubation and other airway management procedures. Anest Clin North Am; 13: 709-723, 1995.

11. Katz SH, Falk JL: Misplaced endotracheal tubes by paramedics in an urban emergency medical services system. Ann Emerg Med Jan;37(1):32-7, 2001.

12. Caplan RA, Posner KL, Ward RJ, Cheney FW: Adverse respiratory events in anesthesia: A closed claims analysis. Anesthesiology; 72:828-833, 1990.

13. Brennan TA, et al.: Incidence of adverse events and negligence in hospitalized patients: Results of the Harvard Medical Practice Study, N Engl J Med 324:370, 1991.

14. Hiatt HH, et al.: A study of medical injury and medical malpractice: an overview, N Engl J Med 321:480, 1989.

15. Bainton CR: Complications of managing the airway. In, Airway Management Principles and Practice. Edited by Jonathan L. Benumof: St. Louis, Mosby, p886-930,1996.

16. Mallampati SR: Recognition of the difficult airway. In, Airway Management Principles and Practice. Edited by Jonathan L. Benumof: St. Louis, Mosby, p126-142, 1996.

17. Ovassapian A, Wheeler M: Fiberoptic endoscopy aided techniques. In, Airway Management Principles and Practice. Edited by Jonathan L. Benumof: St. Louis, Mosby, p282-318, 1996.

18. Michele TM, Cronin WA, Graham NM, Dwyer DM, Pope DS, Harrington S, Chaisson RE, Bishai WR: Transmission of Mycobacterium tuberculosis by a fiberoptic bronchoscope. Identification by DNA fingerprinting. JAMA Oct 1;278(13):1093-5, 1997.

19. Kolmos HJ, Lerche A, Kristoffersen K, Rosdahl VT: Pseudo-outbreak of pseudomonas aeruginosa in HIV-infected patients undergoing fiberoptic bronchoscopy. Scand J Infect Dis 1994;26(6):653-7.

20. Salem MR, Baraka A: Confirmation of tracheal intubation. In, Airway Management Principles and Practice. Edited by Jonathan L. Benumof: St. Louis, Mosby, p531-560, 1996.

21. Standard and Poor's Industry Surveys: Healthcare: Products & Supplies. 1-32. 2002. McGraw Hill.

Lite Bites Grill

A BUSINESS PLAN BY:

Bill Fenton

February 2003

TABLE OF CONTENTS

LITE BITES GRILL
(LBG Enterprises Inc.)

#7 – 1045 St. James Street	Phone: 204-555-1349
Winnipeg, Manitoba R3Y 2B6	Fax: 204-555-9345

(www.litebites.com)

MISSION

"To be the leading alternative to traditional fast-food restaurants, offering healthy and flavorful meals in a quick-service format."

COMPANY MANAGEMENT

Name	Position	Experience	Share
Bill Fenton	President & GM	Operations Management Finance & Accounting	100%
Leonard Bogucki	Restaurant Manager	Restaurant Management	

ADVISORY TEAM

Name	Position	Experience
Bonnie Van Steelandt	Banker	Finance
Gordon Hudek	Accountant	Certified Management Accountant
Lorena Prakash	Dir. Of Marketing	Marketing
Ian A. Restall	Lawyer	Commercial Law

EXECUTIVE SUMMARY

LITE BITES GRILL is an exciting new restaurant concept geared to busy professionals who don't have the time to cook due to today's increasingly hectic lifestyle. The fast-food industry is experiencing explosive growth of 20% per year, yet industry giants offer a very limited variety of healthful and nutritious meals. Research shows that lighter meal options are the fastest-growing menu items, and the majority of consumers take these options into consideration when determining where to eat. Furthermore, 2.5% of the population can be considered vegetarian — another market segment that has been traditionally under-serviced. The LITE BITES GRILL concept is intended to fill these niche markets with a wide variety of tasty and healthful meals, including several attractive vegetarian offerings.

The typical customer is expected to be a homeowner, educated, mid- to upper income, 25 to 54 years old, and health-conscious. Based upon this profile and factoring in the vegetarian population, the Winnipeg, Manitoba, test market is estimated to consist of 70,850 individuals, 16,942 of whom live within the vicinity of the original test restaurant location. The restaurants will be richly appointed and will possess a relaxing color scheme consisting of muted earth tones. With an average meal price in the $6 to $9 range, first-year sales are anticipated to be $300,000, reaching $600,000 for each location within three years.

The business is led by Bill Fenton, a seasoned operations manager and professional engineer, who is also nearing completion of an MBA. Bill is the sole owner of LBG, based upon his $47,000 equity investment. Day-to-day management will be handled by Leonard Bogucki, who has over 20 years of industry experience, primarily with the Denny's chain. The management team is supported by an exceptional advisory group that will provide guidance in their areas of expertise.

A capital investment in equipment and leasehold improvements of $126,500 is required to launch the business. Financing has been arranged with the CIBC through the Canada Small Business Financing Act (CSBFA) program for $113,985 of this amount. The balance of the funding will come via an initial equity investment by the owner. This will provide for the necessary operating expenses as well as the portion of the capital investment not covered by the CSBFA loan. The owner estimates that up to $100,000 could be made available by refinancing his home and cashing in investments. This should provide for any contingencies as well as adequate reserve funds.

The first restaurant will open July 1, 2003, and is expected to post a healthy profit in the second year of operation. After three years, profitability is forecast to be more than double the industry average of 2.4% net profit. By the end of the fifth year, the business will have three locations in operation and net profits (after tax) are forecast to be a healthy $63,200, with retained earnings reaching $100,000. A strong cash position will allow the flexibility to aggressively reduce debt to facilitate developing additional Winnipeg locations in years 3 and 5. Long term, the goal of the business is to have 20 company-owned locations across Western Canada.

LITE BITES GRILL

LITE BITES GRILL (LBG) is an incorporated business that plans the development of a chain of corporate-owned restaurants catering to busy, health-conscious professionals and vegetarians. Presently, the large fast-food outlets are under-servicing these rapidly growing market segments, with very limited product offerings. The LBG vision is to exploit this opportunity by developing a premium quick-service menu offering a wide variety of healthful and nutritious meals.

BUSINESS GOALS

The mission of the LITE BITES GRILL concept is "To be the leading alternative to traditional fast-food restaurants, offering healthy and flavorful meals in a quick-service format." Long term, the goal of the business is to have 20 company-owned locations across Western Canada.

THE INDUSTRY

North Americans spent over $120 billion on fast food in 2000 and fast-food sales are growing at a rate of more than 20% per year (1). This can at least partly be attributed to today's increasingly hectic lifestyle. In 1999,

41% of Canadians claimed to be short of time — a 19% increase in just two years (2). A contributing factor is the return of women to the workforce, leaving them little time to shop, plan, or prepare meals that they once did. Not surprisingly, attitudinal studies reveal that Canadian consumers would like to simplify their lives — in the food realm, they do this by delegating some of the responsibility to foodservice.

It's estimated that 61% of Canadian adults are either overweight or obese (3). Consequently, in choosing where to eat, consumers are taking their health into greater consideration. As evidence of this trend, a recent study by the Canadian Restaurant and Foodservices Association (CRFA) indicated that 60% of fast-food customers rate the availability of healthful or nutritious foods as important in their decision of where to eat. In a further study by the CRFA, newer menu items such as veggie burgers and wrap sandwiches were "among the fastest-growing menu items in 2001." Furthermore, Canadians are eating more salads, while the popularity of French fries and hamburgers is slipping (4).

THE CONCEPT

A quick-service restaurant offering busy health-conscious consumers, including vegetarians, a healthy and flavorful alternative to traditional fast food.

The LITE BITES GRILL menu will include soups, veggie burgers, grilled chicken breast sandwiches, salmon burgers, tuna steak sandwiches, veggie pastas, Asian noodles, vegetarian chili, veggie wraps, and an assortment of fresh salads with low-fat dressings. Low-fat, multi-grain breads will be baked fresh on the premises. Several beverage options will be offered, including a juice bar. A small kids' menu will offer items like baked chicken nuggets and baked fries. Only lunch and dinner items will be offered, with hours of operation from 10:30 a.m. to 9:00 p.m.

The initial restaurant model is intended for a strip mall location, requiring approximately 2,000 square feet, with a seating capacity of 40 people. Bold signage will be employed to intrigue people from a distance. Both carry-out and dine-in options will be available and, based upon similar concepts, it's estimated that 40% of sales will be taken out (5). Customers will be given a number once they've ordered and paid for their meals. Numbers will be called out as the orders are ready. For the benefit of take-out customers awaiting their orders, a small lounge area will be located next to the juice/coffee bar. The day's top news stories will be displayed in Plexiglas cases to help make the brief wait enjoyable.

In terms of physical amenities, the restaurant will be more richly appointed than typical fast-food outlets, with padded booths and chairs and wood trim throughout. Flooring will consist of low-maintenance ceramic tile. The color scheme will consist of muted earth tones, while the décor will include baskets of fresh vegetables and fruit to convey a healthy image. High ceilings will help create an inviting open-air atmosphere within the confines of a small setting. Nutritional information (including fat grams, calories, cholesterol, etc.) will be posted so that customers can match their orders to their specific dietary needs. An open-kitchen concept will be used to allow the customers to see their food being prepared and to permit direct selection of various ingredients like spices, sauces, and dressings.

Winnipeg is an ideal test location as it's a demanding market. Evidence of the city's suitability as a test market is the fact that McDonald's uses Winnipeg to test the viability of new products. After two years of testing this model restaurant at the Polo Park location, LITE BITES GRILL will add a second and third location in years 3 and 5, respectively. Subsequently, the concept will gradually be rolled out across Western Canada with additional outlets that will remain company-owned.

MARKET ANALYSIS

TARGET MARKET

In considering the aforementioned trends, the target market for this concept is the on-the-go, health-conscious business professional. This concept will primarily appeal to adults within the range of 25 to 54 years of age, seeking tasty and healthful food on the run that's more appealing than what traditional fast food has to offer. Women are expected to comprise 60% of the target market, based on prototypes of similar ventures in the United States.

A secondary, but not insignificant, market is the growing number of vegetarians who are typically poorly serviced, with limited offerings from the major fast-food chains — particularly for true vegan offerings.

Vegans are strict vegetarians who refrain from eating any animal products, including all meats (beef, pork, seafood, fish, and poultry), dairy products, eggs, and honey. The number of Canadians who rarely or never eat meat is on the rise — approximately 2.5% of the population can be considered vegetarian (6). This does not include people who occasionally or rarely eat meat or animal products.

Consumers want to eat healthy, but do not want to sacrifice taste. D'Lites, a vegetarian chain that grew to 86 locations throughout the United States before closing its doors, cut calories at the expense of flavor, and this led to its demise. Furthermore, consumers are finding a limited variety of healthy options available at the traditional fast-food chains. Most chains have little to offer beyond veggie burgers and salads. LITE BITES GRILL will offer a comprehensive menu of tasty and nutritious quick-service meals. All menu items will be health-oriented, so that consumers will not have to resist the temptations offered by calorie-laden menu items.

MARKET SIZE

A variety of detailed information for the target market is available in the 2001 Census data released by Statistics Canada (7). The typical customer profile for this concept is expected to be a homeowner, educated, mid- to upper income, aged 25 to 54, and health-conscious. Using the relevant education and age demographics for the City of Winnipeg, we learn that 19.1% of the individuals in our target age bracket have a university education. Assuming that the university-educated individuals within the age bracket of 25 to 54 are representative of the target market, it is estimated that this market in Winnipeg consists of 57,250 individuals. Furthermore, using this same methodology, the market in Canada for this concept is estimated to be 2,580,000.

These figures do not reflect the vegetarian component of the potential market. Using the 2.5% approximation, vegetarians comprise an additional 13,600 Winnipeg customers and 607,000 Canadians. Only individuals over the age of 14 were considered in making these calculations. It was assumed that vegetarians under the age of 15 would not have much say in making decisions of where to dine, and consequently this segment of the market is not expected to comprise a significant portion of our clientele.

Thus, our total potential market size is expected to be 70,850 (57,250 + 13,600) Winnipeggers and 3,187,000 (2,580,000 + 607,000) Canadians.

ESTIMATED SALES AND MARKET SHARE

Based upon Census data (8), the typical household in the Winnipeg test market is spending $1,367.08 per year, on average, for foods purchased from restaurants. It is assumed that this *household* data will apply to *individuals* in the target market, due to the higher income levels and hectic schedules that will make restaurant visits more common than at lower income levels. Based on this assumption, the 16,942 individuals in the Winnipeg target market spend a total of $23,161,069 in restaurants. This figure represents the total market potential for this concept in the market area of the test restaurant. This is expected to be a conservative estimate, as it does not include that spent by visitors to the city or commuters from surrounding areas.

O'Naturals (see "Competition" section below) appears to have achieved the highest sales success of similar concepts, with sales of $2,000 to $3,000 per day, roughly on par with a typical Burger King (9). However, based upon surveys of other restaurants, typical annual sales for a mature restaurant in this market are expected to be approximately $600,000. Using a start-up year factor of about 50%, as recommended by the Canada Business Service Centre (10), the forecasted sales for the first year are $300,000. Using a "top down" approach to estimate sales (11) would yield our first-year sales forecast at an estimated market share of 1.3%, which appears highly achievable.

Preliminary sales estimates are outlined in Appendix 1. Sales are expected to be relatively strong the first month due to grand opening sales promotions. The forecast tapers off for the next few months, followed by gradual growth as the business begins to establish itself.

COMPETITION

The fast-food industry is intensely competitive and the large traditional chains, with their considerable brand equity, are evolving product lines to address changes in consumer preferences. Among the primary competition:

MCDONALD'S (www.mcdonalds.com): The world's largest restaurant operator, McDonald's had a 43% share of the quick-service hamburger market in 2001 — down slightly from the previous two years as McDonald's struggled to expand its product line. Recent additions to the menu include salads, chicken burgers, veggie burgers, and a low-fat yogurt/granola snack. In 2001 McDonald's purchased a minority stake in the London, England, Pret a Manger, a 16-year-old chain specializing in fresh, handmade wraps, salads, and sandwiches that are free of additives and preservatives. The company plans to develop 20 Manhattan units by the end of the year and an additional 40 New York City shops before expanding into other markets.

BURGER KING (www.burgerking.com): Considered to have the burgers with the highest fat content in the industry, Burger King is revamping its product offerings to include a vegan-friendly veggie burger, a Chicken Whopper, and better-tasting coffee. It's not so much the vegetarian or health-conscious consumer that the chain is targeting, but rather the veto power this market segment may have over a minivan full of hungry, burger-eating family members. Market share at the number-two hamburger chain has eroded to 18.4% in 2001, down from 19.6% in 1999.

WENDY'S (www.wendys.com): The number-three hamburger chain, with a 13.2% market share in 2001, has been boosting its market share for five consecutive years. Unlike its two larger rivals, who compete on price, Wendy's has been boosting market share without discounting core menu items. Recent additions to the menu include a popular line of salads.

SUBWAY (www.subway.com): With more than 17,000 locations in 75 countries, SUBWAY has now overtaken McDonald's as the largest restaurant chain by number of stores in the United States. SUBWAY is heavily promoting its low-fat line of subs (7 subs with 6 grams of fat or less) through its "Jared" campaign. Jared Fogle, SUBWAY's weight-loss hero, lost 245 pounds through his own diet and exercise regime, incorporating SUBWAY's "7 under 6" menu of low-fat sandwiches.

In addition to the large chains, there are many small concepts emerging, primarily in the United States, with plans to franchise out to regions that include the Canadian market. These are considered a distant threat, as the concepts are still being tested and developed in regional areas and do not have plans to aggressively pursue the Canadian market for the foreseeable future. These include:

TOPZ (www.topz.com): A Southern California concept with healthier versions of traditional fast-food fare — soy, turkey, and lean-beef burgers are on the menu, as well as baked "fries." Topz has six locations in the greater Los Angeles market. Franchising will add 10 to 12 stores in the next year, and in the longer term it plans 100 to 200 more.

O'NATURALS (www.onaturals.com): An emerging concept in the New England area of the United States that represents "family-friendly, tasty, natural, and organic fast food." Not specifically a low-fat or vegetarian concept, the company is targeting consumers with an ethical and environmental consciousness — offering meat from free-range livestock that has been raised without unnecessary chemicals and hormones. There is presently only one prototype location, in Falmouth, Maine. Plans included two new units in 2002 and three additional restaurants in 2003. From there, O'Naturals plan to roll out the concept throughout the Northeast and nationally, with the potential for several hundred locations.

HEALTHY BITES GRILL (www.hexs.com): Claims to be the United States' "first fast-food restaurant franchise to feature gourmet health food." The concept is presently being rolled out in the Fort Lauderdale, Florida, region.

MARKETING PLAN

PRICING

The pricing strategy employed will be that of a premium quick-service restaurant. Based upon similar concepts in the United States, the average meal will cost between $6 and $9. LBG will not be competing based on price, but rather will be focusing on value. The higher quality and more nutritious meals will command a higher price in the market. In support of this strategy, the focus group established for the purpose of defining this market indicated that many senior businesspeople are very conscious of their image. Consequently, there is a perception that executives would not come back to the office with a take-out bag from the typical fast-food chain because it would give the image that they have low standards. LBG's concept will appeal to a mid-to upscale market and will be priced accordingly.

A detailed breakdown of fixed and variable costs can be found in Schedule 2 (the financial statements follow the body of this business plan). Typical gross margins in this industry are approximately 70%, while net margins are a slim 2.4%. LBG margins are expected to be on par with the industry norm. However, after the second year of operation, net income is forecast to be more than double the industry average. Although the break-even sales volume of $318,900 is not expected to be achieved in the first year, it is anticipated the restaurant will be profitable in its second year of operation. As restaurants are a cash business, they have the significant advantage of having no potential credit issues that can negatively impact operations.

ADVERTISING AND PROMOTION

A multi-faceted promotional campaign is planned for the official launch of the concept and grand opening of the first restaurant. A complete summary of the first-year marketing budget is shown in Appendix 2. The Industry Canada Performance Plus Small Business Profiles (12) indicate that the typical company in this industry spends, on average, 3% of gross sales on advertising. Based on first-year forecast sales of $300,000, this would put $9,000 into the advertising budget. However, due to the fact that this is a start-up, a 100% premium will be used to bring the first-year advertising budget to $18,000. Factoring in expenses for sales promotions, personal selling, and the development of a website, brings the total first-year marketing budget to $25,125.

To help build brand awareness and to support general inquiries, a website will be developed and will go "live" approximately one month prior to the grand opening. The website will be established to ensure that information on the concept is readily available to the computer-savvy consumers that make up a large percentage of the target market. The site will include pictures of the restaurant, as well as a menu, complete with information on the applicable nutritional content. This nutritional information will compare and contrast with that of typical menu items at the large fast-food chains. In addition, general health and dietary facts will be provided in an interactive menu format. Patrick Doerksen, a freelance computer programmer, will develop the site for a quoted $2,500 fee plus $50 per month for updating. Other costs include $35 annually for a domain name and $20 per month for hosting services.

The promotions program will officially begin approximately one week prior to the grand opening of the restaurant. Two university marketing students will be hired to visit local businesses within the target market to conduct personal selling. Menus will be dropped off, in addition to sales promotions consisting of coupons for a free menu item. Eighty hours has been budgeted for this activity at $10 per hour. In addition, a promotional billboard will be developed and displayed approximately one week prior to the grand opening. It will be in place for a four-week period.

The marketing program will also include a comprehensive newspaper advertising campaign. This will include sponsoring a sampling campaign in conjunction with *The Winnipeg Sun*. For a nominal $1,500, the *Sun* offers a full-page wrap that is delivered with a free paper to approximately 3,000 to 4,000 homes and businesses within the target area. The wrap is issued the day of the grand opening. The front page announces the opening with the specials for that day. The second and third pages provide special coupons for the second and third days of the grand opening period. The back page of the wrap will have a ballot that can be dropped off to enter a draw for a DVD player. Thus, the wrap generates at least three days of traffic.

After the grand opening, an ongoing newspaper advertising program will be established. The campaign will stress the availability of a new alternative to traditional fast food — an alternative that offers more variety than the few bland options available from the big chains. Both *The Winnipeg Sun* and the *Winnipeg Free Press* will be utilized, as each paper targets different market segments. *The Winnipeg Sun* is number one in readership among adults 25–34, based on NADbank 2002 (13), an independent survey measuring 72 daily newspapers in 46 urban markets. The overall reach of the *Sun* is 266,400 weekly readers. Meanwhile, the *Winnipeg Free Press*, with a reach of 404,700 weekly readers, has higher readership in the 35+ category, and is more skewed to females than the *Sun*. Thus, the *Free Press* advertising will reach the mature female component of the target market. The budgeted $9,650 will include one more wrap-style campaign in the *Sun*, as well as four inserts in the *Free Press* at $2,000 each. These advertisements will be spread evenly throughout the remainder of the year.

A small radio budget of $2,500 will be established for the grand opening. Radio station BOB FM was chosen for the campaign due to its listener base being well represented by members of the target market. Radio advertising will begin on the day of the grand opening and the campaign will last for a period of three days. During the actual day of the grand opening, BOB FM will have on-air giveaways and live broadcasts on location.

MANAGEMENT TEAM

Bill Fenton is the President and General Manager of the LITE BITES GRILL and will be responsible for overall operation of the business. Bill received a Bachelor of Science degree in Industrial Engineering from the University of Manitoba in 1990. He received his Professional Engineer designation in 1992 from the Association of Professional Engineers of Manitoba. Bill has held a variety of senior-level operations positions and is presently Operations Manager for Melet Plastics Inc. This position has overall P & L responsibility for the company's three divisions and includes direct and indirect supervision of 75 employees. To complement his diverse work experience, Bill has been working toward receiving a Masters of Business Administration in the part-time program at the University of Manitoba. He will graduate from the program in April 2003, at which time he plans to focus his efforts on developing and growing the LITE BITES GRILL restaurant concept. Bill has previous entrepreneurial experience, having founded and successfully run a private automobile wholesaling business for three years.

Leonard Bogucki is the Restaurant Manager and will be in charge of running day-to-day operations. Leonard has 20 years' experience in the restaurant industry, working in a variety of capacities. His experience ranges from cooking and waiting tables through to managerial positions. One of his most recent achievements involved managing a Denny's restaurant for eight years in Calgary, Alberta. Leonard will assume a "hands-on" role at LITE BITES GRILL, supervising his staff as well as helping out as needed during peak demand. As Manager, he will be responsible for the hiring and training of all restaurant personnel. In addition, he will perform all purchasing of food supplies and management of the supply base. Basic accounting software will be utilized to maintain a system of bookkeeping. In this capacity, Leonard will report directly to the General Manager. A detailed resume for Leonard, outlining his vast work experience in the food-services industry, can be found in Appendix 7.

MANAGEMENT COMPENSATION

Bill Fenton will remain with his present employer for the first two years of operations. During this time, he will not draw a salary from the business, although he plans to work evenings and weekends furthering the development of the chain. As Restaurant Manager, Leonard Bogucki will receive a salary of $30,000 per annum

SHAREHOLDERS

Bill Fenton will be the sole shareholder in the business, with 100% ownership as a result of the $47,000 initial personal capital investment.

ADVISORY TEAM

To successfully launch and develop a new venture like this, a team of advisers has been assembled to support the management team. The team has been selected based on their relevant expertise and proven abilities.

Bonnie Van Steelandt is a Financial Adviser with CIBC. LBG has consulted Bonnie regarding CIBC commercial banking for securing start-up capital. Bonnie, in conjunction with Al French — CIBC's General Manager, Small Business — has helped LBG management determine the appropriate financing for the business. The CIBC will also provide financial guidance during periods of expansion. Bonnie is a Certified Financial Planner and has a Masters of Business Administration from the University of Manitoba.

Gord Hudek is the Controller of Melet Plastics Inc. and has held a variety of senior-level accounting positions over the past 20 years. Gord has several years' experience as a consultant specializing in setting up accounting systems for small businesses. He has a Bachelor of Commerce (Honors) and is a Certified Management Accountant (CMA). Gord will advise LBG in the set-up and implementation of its accounting system.

Lorena Prakash is Director of Marketing with *The Winnipeg Sun*. Lorena recently graduated with an MBA from the University of Manitoba and has extensive experience in the field of marketing. She will provide guidance to LBG in areas of marketing, advertising, and promotions.

Ian A. Restall practises commercial law and is a partner in the firm Restall & Restall. The practice has emphases in the following areas of law: business organizations, corporate and commercial transactions, real estate, general contractual matters, and employment law. Ian's extensive academic accomplishments include a Masters degree in Law from Oxford University. He teaches the Commercial Law course at the University of Manitoba in the Asper School of Business. Ian has been retained by LBG to provide all legal advice.

OPERATIONS PLAN

LOCATION

The site chosen for the initial restaurant is at 1045 St. James Street in The Brick Plaza commercial complex. A detailed facility location and site plan are provided in Appendix 3. The site is ideally located at Ellice Avenue and St. James Street, an intersection with one of the busiest traffic counts in Winnipeg. The site offers additional benefits of superior access and egress, signage offering maximum exposure, and an excellent, well-lit parking lot with an ample supply of parking spaces.

The location is just north of the Polo Park Shopping Centre, Winnipeg's premier shopping complex. This site has all of the desirable features for this concept: (1) it is close to the downtown area, home to the employers of many business professionals, (2) it is within reasonable proximity of the mid- to upscale neighborhoods of St. James, River Heights, Linden Woods, Tuxedo, and Whyte Ridge, and (3) the area is home to a number of large retail outlets and a major shopping center, which is expected to ensure adequate traffic volume around the restaurant throughout all hours of the day and into the early evening. Census data for the relevant areas for the City of Winnipeg can be found in Appendix 4 (8). As indicated in the exhibit, it is estimated that 16,942 individuals who fit our target market profile reside within the vicinity of the original restaurant location.

FACILITIES

The total space available of 1,913 square feet will provide ample room for the dining area, kitchen, storage, and a small office. At present, the facility is serving as warehouse space for an adjacent business. Drywall is in place but the area is otherwise unfinished, with the exception of separate male and female handicap-accessible washrooms. The premises are zoned C-2, which is suitable for a restaurant.

The premises are available for lease at an asking rate of $12 per square foot, net. However, the listing agent felt that if the lessee developed the space, the lessor would reduce this amount to around $10 per square foot. Additional fees for common area management (CAM) amount to $4.06 per square foot. The CAM includes exterior building maintenance, real estate taxes, landscaping, and snow removal. Furthermore, a management fee of 5% of net rent would be applicable. This would bring the total annual rent to $27,853, which equates to $2,321 per month. The lessor is requesting a lease of between a three- to five-year term. With the substantial investment in leasehold improvements, LBG will seek a five-year lease and will likely gain further concessions for doing so. The lessee will be expected to give a personal guarantee together with the first and last months' rent as a security deposit. All utilities and business taxes are separate.

In terms of general leasehold improvements, decorating and remodeling is estimated to be $55,000. This amount was based upon the average leasehold improvement cost for opening a SUBWAY restaurant in Canada (14).

Signex Manufacturing Inc. will provide and install a 5-foot × 8-foot internally illuminated sign for the front entrance of the restaurant. The sign will have a white acrylic face with high-performance translucent graphics applied to the surface. Cost for the sign is $1,800. An additional fee of $155 is required for a standard City of Winnipeg permit.

EQUIPMENT

A wide variety of equipment is required to ensure the restaurant is capable of preparing the breadth of menu items to be offered. Due to the specific nature of some of the equipment and the lack of availability of good used equipment on the market, all items will be purchased new from Russell Food Equipment. All kitchen equipment will be of commercial quality, with National Sanitation Foundation (NSF) or equivalent approval. A detailed equipment listing can be found in Appendix 5. The optional dishwasher will be purchased to allow the staff to focus on cooking and service activities and to keep staffing levels to a minimum. The prices listed include delivery and setting in place. Also included is the mounting of the menu sign, the set-up of the storage shelves, and the set-up and testing of the walk-in cooler/freezer. Total cost of the equipment amounts to $63,000. Due to the magnitude of the purchase, it is expected that a 5% discount will be negotiated, reducing the total cost to $59,850. Lead time for delivery of the equipment is four to six weeks. The expected life of the equipment is approximately 10 years.

Electrical hook-up and plumbing costs are extra. Industrial Electrical Services has estimated $3,000 for electrical hook-up of the equipment, including the permit, labor, and all materials. The 200-amp service presently available on the premises was deemed sufficient to meet the electrical requirements of the installed equipment. Elmwood Plumbing and Heating has estimated $2,000 for all plumbing connections, including all materials.

Russell Food Equipment provides consultant services on a no-charge basis to its clients during new start-ups. In addition, the owner of LBG is a Registered Professional Engineer. Thus, design of the layout and the development of drawings and specifications for tendering the leasehold improvements will be performed at a minimal out-of-pocket expense.

SUPPLY CHAIN

SYSCO Food Services has been chosen to be the primary supplier for food and general supplies. SYSCO is a broadline food distributor, offering a complete line of products including produce, meats, poultry, seafood, frozen foods, paper, cleaning supplies, chemicals, dairy, and full beverage programs featuring Citavo fresh ground coffee and Sunkist premium juices. Over 9,000 items are carried at the local branch and 40,000 items are stocked by SYSCO's parent company. These are standard items and availability is not a problem. Nutritional information is available so that fat content, cholesterol, and calorie information can be passed on to LBG customers. Meats are cryogenically frozen and vacuum-packed in single-serving portions so that the entire case need not be thawed. Most menu items are available in a heat-and-serve format, minimizing the need to develop recipes from scratch.

Deliveries are offered free of charge on orders above $500 and will take place once per week. Orders can be made through a convenient Web-based system or via direct contact with a marketing associate. Specialists are on staff to assist with a wide range of matters, from nutritional information and cooking tips to kitchen design assistance.

Due to unpredictable market elements, the longest pricing contract that can be arranged is for a period of six months. Products like poultry are heavily dependent on weather conditions. Poultry is sourced locally and a hot dry stretch, for example, could lead to high death rates and significant upward price pressure. However, with SYSCO's nationwide network, items can be sourced in other regions, minimizing the impact of regional conditions. Until a credit history can be established, orders will remain C.O.D. for the first several months. However, a direct electronic funds transfer (EFT) service is offered at no charge to SYSCO customers. This system essentially provides up to one week of working capital by delaying electronic transfer of funds until the following Tuesday morning, allowing time for deposit of funds from the busy weekend period.

Additional benefits will be achieved by selecting specific brands to be utilized in the restaurant. For example, Campbell's Soups has a soup kettle program that provides some equipment, as well as slide cards and menu displays, when Campbell's Soup products are used exclusively. Similarly, a paper program is available whereby towel and paper dispensers are offered free of charge when paper products are purchased through SYSCO. Likewise, beverage equipment is provided at no charge when Citavo coffee and Sunkist juices are purchased exclusively.

Due to the size and stability of the SYSCO organization, backup suppliers are not deemed necessary. However, alternative suppliers are available if the need ever did arise. For example, To-Le-Do Foodservice distributes a full line of top-quality chilled and frozen products including beef, veal, pork, smoked meats, chicken, turkey, seafood, and fresh-cut produce.

HUMAN RESOURCES

Each LBG location will employ two full-time serving personnel and an additional four casual workers in a non-unionized environment. Serving personnel perform a range of duties, including taking customer orders, preparing meals, operating the cash register, and performing general clean-up activities. A staffing schedule can be found in Appendix 6. During peak periods, one full-time employee will be supported by two casual workers. It is also expected that the restaurant manager will assist staff during peak hours.

Employees hired must be personable and well organized. Previous restaurant experience is desired but not mandatory, as all employees will receive extensive training. To entice employees to work for LBG in this environment of low unemployment, a starting wage of $7 per hour will be paid to all casual labor. This represents a $0.50 per hour premium over the $6.50 per hour minimum wage that is typically paid in the industry. The two full-time employees will be paid a more attractive $8 per hour to help retain these key personnel.

Initial start-up training will consist of one week of "hands-on" training conducted by representatives of the foodservices supply industry and the equipment manufacturers. Likewise, ongoing training will be performed on an as-needed basis by various suppliers. New hires will receive a brief indoctrination to the company by the Manager. After indoctrination, the "buddy" system will be used for the following week by pairing up the new hire with an experienced employee.

Every effort will be made to create a fun, stimulating, and rewarding environment whereby employees feel appreciated and respected. Incentives will be provided to achieve targets in areas like customer satisfaction, workplace cleanliness, and safety. These promotions may include tickets for sporting events, T-shirts, gift certificates, and company-sponsored recreational activities. Additional benefits include vacation pay ranging from 4% for new hires up to 8% for employees with 10 years of tenure.

REGULATORY REQUIREMENTS

The foodservices industry is heavily regulated. Consequently, there are several permits and licences that will be obtained prior to the opening of the first restaurant:

- A Food Handling Establishment Licence (By-Law 6551/95) must be obtained from the City of Winnipeg Licence Branch. Licences are valid for one year and must be renewed annually. There is a $311 fee for each licence. To be approved, the premises must comply with applicable zoning regulations and must be examined by a Medical Health Officer and deemed to be in a fit, clean, and suitable condition.

- An Occupancy Permit must be obtained from the City of Winnipeg Zoning and Permits Branch. Five sets of detailed plans and specifications must be submitted to a Zoning Officer at the Plan Approval Office. The one-time fee of $585.85 includes the occupancy permit itself, the building permit for renovations (a variable fee, based on development costs), the fire department review fee, and the health department review fee.

- A Food Health Permit must be obtained from an Environmental Health Officer at Manitoba Conservation in order to operate a foodservice establishment. The Food Health Permit is issued upon completion of an inspection by an Environmental Health Officer and satisfactory compliance with the Food Service Establishment By-Law 5160/89. In addition, the applicant must register for the Certified Food Health Training Program. The Food Health Permit must be posted and displayed in a clearly visible location in the establishment. There is no cost for the permit itself. The premises are, however, subject to ongoing monitoring to ensure compliance.

INSURANCE PLAN

MILNCO Insurance has developed a comprehensive insurance program for LBG, with protection from a range of perils. A detailed outline of the insurance coverage can be found in Appendix 8. There are several key elements to the insurance plan. Firstly, the business premises insurance will provide coverage for loss of physical assets, including equipment, inventory, and improvements/betterments. Coverage is based on replacement cost of equipment and fixtures and actual cash value on inventory. Secondly, the $2,000,000 comprehensive general liability coverage will cover liability to customers injured on the premises or off the premises when attributed to products sold by LBG. Lastly, business interruption insurance will enable LBG to continue to pay the bills if the business were to be closed down by fire or any other insured peril. The annual premium for this package would be $1,798, with a $500 deductible applying to each loss.

IMPLEMENTATION SCHEDULE

A comprehensive implementation schedule has been developed to ensure that all phases of the venture have been adequately planned. The development of the concept has been broken down into four distinct components: preliminary phase, development phase, pre-opening phase, and growth phase.

The preliminary phase took approximately seven months to complete — the bulk of which was involved with the development of the formal business plan. The development phase will commence shortly. The first steps of this phase will be to register the business name at the Companies Office ($30 fee) and to contact the Tax Services Office to arrange for a business number, a Provincial Sales Tax (PST) number and a Goods and Services Tax (GST) number. Subsequently, the business will be incorporated and the financing will be formally secured, as previously arranged in the business plan. The development phase is expected to take three months, with the majority of the time consumed by leasehold improvements and installation of equipment. This work is expected to be completed by May 30, 2003.

The pre-opening phase is primarily involved with two elements. The first element consists of the hiring of the restaurant manager, after which the menu will be finalized. Cooking and serving personnel will be hired shortly thereafter. These employees will receive a comprehensive one-week training program to primarily become familiarized with the menu and equipment. The second element of the pre-opening phase involves the extensive grand opening advertising and promotion campaign, as outlined under the marketing plan. Lastly, the long-term growth of the restaurant is outlined in the growth phase. This involves the development of a comprehensive operations manual in addition to planned openings of the second and third locations.

FINANCIAL PLAN

FUNDING REQUESTED

The major capital costs involved in launching this concept are the fixtures and equipment, installation of the fixtures and equipment, and decorating and remodeling (leasehold improvements). These costs are $61,650, $10,000, and $55,000, respectively, for a total of $126,650. LBG will be financed through a combination of debt and an equity investment. The Canadian Imperial Bank of Commerce (CIBC) has agreed to finance a large portion of this major expenditure.

For fixtures, equipment, and installation, the CIBC will use the government-guaranteed Canada Small Business Financing Act (CSBFA) program, which allows financing up to 90% of the cost. The interest rate is prime plus 2.25%, which includes a 1.25% administration fee paid to the federal government. Payments would be monthly for a period of seven years. Security would be via a general security agreement with a specific charge over the various pieces of equipment, the assignment of fire insurance, and a personal guarantee from the owner for 25% of the loan amount. Likewise, renovation expenses also qualify for the CSBFA loan. Thus, CIBC has agreed to a loan for $113,985.

The balance of the funding will come via a $47,000 equity investment by the owner, giving him 100% of the common shares in the corporation. Proceeds will fund operating expenses as well as the portion of the capital investment not covered by the CSBFA loan. The owner estimates up to $100,000 in total, including the initial investment, could be made available by refinancing his home and cashing in investments. This should provide for any contingencies as well as adequate reserve funds.

The second and third locations will be added in years 3 and 5, respectively. Growth will again be financed through the CIBC, under the same terms and conditions. For planning purposes, it is assumed that equipment and renovation costs will remain approximately the same. No further equity investment will be required on the part of the owner to finance the expansion.

FINANCIAL PROJECTIONS

Detailed financial projections have been provided in several schedules with this business plan. As indicated, LBG is expected to lose $13,264 in its first year of operations, primarily due to an aggressive promotions campaign. The $300,000 estimated first-year sales figure falls short of the break-even point of $318,900. However, operations are expected to be profitable in the second year. By year 4, profitability is forecast to be more than double the industry norm of 2.4% net profit (as a percentage of sales). After five years, the business will have three locations in operation and net profits (after tax) are forecast to be a healthy $63,200, with retained earnings reaching $100,000.

As indicated in the cash flow projections in Schedule 4, the initial CIBC loan and $47,000 equity investment give the operation more than adequate cash flow. This will give the business the advantage of paying down debt more aggressively and/or possibly reducing the start-up capital required for the launch of the additional locations. Dividends will not be paid to the owner initially in order to maximize funds available for growth. The current and quick ratios provide further evidence that there should be no problem meeting financial obligations going forward. If cash is drawn down to reduce debt, it will be done under the condition that the current ratio be maintained at a minimum of 2:1.

RISK FACTORS

In undertaking any new business venture, there are many risks that must be identified and contended with. LBG has identified the key risks present in the foodservices industry as well as risks associated with this particular concept:

1. **Fire or other damage forcing closure:** LBG will limit the impact of a fire by ensuring the business has comprehensive insurance protection, including adequate business premises insurance as well as business interruption insurance.

2. **Liability for illness related to foods served:** The $2,000,000 comprehensive general liability insurance coverage will ensure the business has adequate liability coverage in the event a customer becomes injured on the premises or where an illness is attributed to products sold by LBG.

3. **Delays in construction from leasehold improvements and equipment installation:** Penalty clauses will be written into the contracts to ensure that LBG is compensated for damages resulting from delays to opening.

4. **Stagnant or inadequate sales:** If sales growth proves unacceptable and/or the concept is not well received in the marketplace, the theme will be modified accordingly, based upon further assessment of the market.

5. **Difficulties with suppliers:** This is considered to be a minor risk as there are several general suppliers to the foodservice industry so that a switch could be made if warranted.

6. **Limited experience of the owner in the foodservices industry:** This is not a major concern as LBG has an experienced advisory team, a seasoned restaurant manager, and reputable suppliers. In addition, were the situation severe enough, a consultant could be hired to guide the operation through short-term difficulties. The owner will seek out training opportunities to minimize the impact of any shortcomings.

DIVESTITURE/HARVEST STRATEGY

In the event that the LBG owner desires to exit the business, every attempt will be made to sell the business as a going concern. If a sale cannot be made, however, the assets of the business will be sold off individually. There is a market for used commercial cooking equipment and if satisfactory arrangements cannot be made locally, the equipment will be sold over the Internet. The proceeds of any such sale shall be used to pay off the debt obligations of the business and any remaining funds will be paid to the owner. Furthermore, due to the prime location(s) of the restaurant(s), subletting the premises is not expected to be difficult.

The owner does feel, however, that the concept has significant upside potential. As LBG adds locations and builds market share, it is expected to attract the attention of large national chains. LBG may become a takeover target as chains look to consolidation as a means to achieve growth targets while the market for traditional fast-food menu items stagnates. The owner would give serious consideration to selling the business if it could be sold for a substantial profit.

SCHEDULE 1

LBG REQUIRED START-UP FUNDS

ESTIMATED MONTHLY EXPENSES

ITEM	COLUMN 1 ESTIMATE OF MONTHLY EXPENSES BASED ON SALES OF $300,000 PER YEAR	COLUMN 2 NUMBER OF MONTHS OF CASH REQUIRED TO COVER EXPENSES*	COLUMN 3 CASH REQUIRED TO START BUSINESS (COLUMN 1 X COLUMN 2)*
Salary of Manager	$2,500	2	$5,000
All Other Salaries and Wages	$4,700	3	$14,100
Rent	$2,321	3	$6,963
Advertising	$1,500	3	$4,500
Delivery Expense/Transportation	$300	3	$900
Supplies	$100	3	$300
Telephone, Fax, Internet Service	$200	3	$600
Other Utilities	$700	3	$2,100
Insurance	$150	3	$450
Taxes Including Employment Insurance	$300	4	$1,200
Principal & Interest (Loan)	$1,734	3	$5,202
Maintenance	$450	3	$1,350
Legal and Other Professional Fees	$175	3	$525
Miscellaneous	$3,650	3	$10,950
Total Cash Requirements for Monthly Recurring Expenses: (A)			**$54,140**

START-UP COSTS THAT HAVE TO BE PAID ONLY ONCE

	CASH REQUIRED TO START BUSINESS
Capital Costs	
Fixtures and Equipment	$61,650
Decorating and Remodelling	$55,000
Installation of Fixtures and Equipment	$10,000
Starting Inventory	$7,500
Soft Costs	
Deposits with Public Utilities	$2,000
Legal and Other Professional Fees	$1,200
Licences and Permits	$1,052
Advertising and Promotion for Opening	$14,705
Accounts Receivable	$0
Cash	$5,000
Miscellaneous	$5,000
Total One-Time Cash Requirements: (B)	**$163,107**
TOTAL ESTIMATED CASH REQUIRED TO START BUSINESS: (A) + (B)	**$217,247**

SCHEDULE 2

PRO FORMA INCOME STATEMENT FOR LITE BITES GRILL
for the Year Ending June 31, 2004

	July	August	September	October	November	December	January	February	March	April	May	June	TOTAL
1. Gross Sales	30,000	28,000	24,000	20,000	20,000	22,000	24,000	24,000	24,000	26,000	28,000	30,000	300,000
2. Less: Cash Discounts	0	0	0	0	0	0	0	0	0	0	0	0	0
A. NET SALES	**$30,000**	**$28,000**	**$24,000**	**$20,000**	**$20,000**	**$22,000**	**$24,000**	**$24,000**	**$24,000**	**$26,000**	**$28,000**	**$30,000**	**$300,000**
Cost of Goods Sold:													
3. Beginning Inventory	7,500	7,500	7,500	7,500	7,500	7,500	7,500	7,500	7,500	7,500	7,500	7,500	7,500
4. Plus: Net Purchases	8,940	8,344	7,152	5,960	5,960	6,556	7,152	7,152	7,152	7,748	8,344	8,940	89,400
5. Total Available for Sale	16,440	15,844	14,652	13,460	13,460	14,056	14,652	14,652	14,652	15,248	15,844	16,440	96,900
6. Less: Ending Inventory	7,500	7,500	7,500	7,500	7,500	7,500	7,500	7,500	7,500	7,500	7,500	7,500	7,500
B. COST OF GOODS SOLD	**$8,940**	**$8,344**	**$7,152**	**$5,960**	**$5,960**	**$6,556**	**$7,152**	**$7,152**	**$7,152**	**$7,748**	**$8,344**	**$8,940**	**$89,400**
C. GROSS MARGIN	**$21,060**	**$19,656**	**$16,848**	**$14,040**	**$14,040**	**$15,444**	**$16,848**	**$16,848**	**$16,848**	**$18,252**	**$19,656**	**$21,060**	**$210,600**
Less: Variable Expenses													
7. Owner's Salary	0	0	0	0	0	0	0	0	0	0	0	0	0
8. Employee's Wages and Salaries	7,200	7,200	7,200	7,200	7,200	7,200	7,200	7,200	7,200	7,200	7,200	7,200	86,400
9. Supplies and Postage	100	100	100	100	100	100	100	100	100	100	100	100	1,200
10. Advertising and Promotion	14,705	70	2,070	70	70	3,720	70	2,070	2,070	70	70	2,070	25,125
11. Delivery Expense	360	336	288	240	240	264	288	288	288	312	336	360	3,600
12. Bad Debt Expense	0	0	0	0	0	0	0	0	0	0	0	0	0
13. Travel	0	0	0	0	0	0	0	0	0	0	0	0	0
14. Legal and Accounting Fees	1,200	0	0	0	0	0	0	0	0	0	0	2,100	3,300
15. Vehicle Expense	0	0	0	0	0	0	0	0	0	0	0	0	0
16. Maintenance Expense	540	504	432	360	360	396	432	432	432	468	504	540	5,400
17. Miscellaneous Expenses	3,960	3,696	3,168	2,640	2,640	2,904	3,168	3,168	3,168	3,432	3,696	3,960	39,600
D. TOTAL VARIABLE EXPENSES	**$28,065**	**$11,906**	**$13,258**	**$10,610**	**$10,610**	**$14,584**	**$11,258**	**$11,258**	**$13,258**	**$11,582**	**$11,906**	**$16,330**	**$164,625**
Less: Fixed Expenses													
18. Rent	2,321	2,321	2,321	2,321	2,321	2,321	2,321	2,321	2,321	2,321	2,321	2,321	27,852
19. Utilities (Heat, Light, Power)	700	700	700	700	700	700	700	700	700	700	700	700	8,400
20. Telephone	200	200	200	200	200	200	200	200	200	200	200	200	2,400
21. Taxes and Licenses	1,052	0	0	0	0	0	0	0	0	0	0	0	1,052
22. Depreciation	825	825	825	825	825	825	825	825	825	825	825	825	9,900
23. Interest	702	628	689	660	676	648	662	656	628	642	615	629	7,835
24. Insurance	150	150	150	150	150	150	150	150	150	150	150	150	1,800
25. Other Fixed Expenses	0	0	0	0	0	0	0	0	0	0	0	0	0
E. TOTAL FIXED EXPENSES	**$5,950**	**$4,824**	**$4,885**	**$4,856**	**$4,872**	**$4,844**	**$4,858**	**$4,852**	**$4,824**	**$4,838**	**$4,811**	**$4,825**	**$59,239**
F. TOTAL OPERATING EXPENSES	**$34,015**	**$16,730**	**$18,143**	**$15,466**	**$15,482**	**$19,428**	**$16,116**	**$16,110**	**$18,082**	**$16,420**	**$16,717**	**$21,155**	**$223,864**
G. NET OPERATING PROFIT (LOSS)	**($12,955)**	**$2,926**	**($1,295)**	**($1,426)**	**($1,442)**	**($3,984)**	**$732**	**$738**	**($1,234)**	**$1,832**	**$2,939**	**($95)**	**($13,264)**
H. INCOME TAXES (estimated)													$0
I. NET PROFIT (LOSS) AFTER INCOME TAX													($13,264)

SCHEDULE 3

PRO FORMA INCOME STATEMENT FOR LITE BITES GRILL
for the Year Ending June 31

	2004	2005	2006	2007	2008
1. Gross Sales	300,000	400,000	900,000	1,000,000	1,300,000
2. Less: Cash Discounts	0	0	0	0	0
A. NET SALES	**$300,000**	**$400,000**	**$900,000**	**$1,000,000**	**$1,300,000**
COST OF GOODS SOLD:					
3. Beginning Inventory	7,500	7,500	7,500	15,000	15,000
4. Plus: Net Purchases	89,400	119,200	268,200	298,000	374,400
5. Total Available for Sale	96,900	126,700	275,700	313,000	389,400
6. Less: Ending Inventory	7,500	7,500	15,000	15,000	22,500
B. COST OF GOODS SOLD	**$89,400**	**$119,200**	**$260,700**	**$298,000**	**$366,900**
C. GROSS MARGIN	**$210,600**	**$280,800**	**$639,300**	**$702,000**	**$933,100**
Less: Variable Expenses					
7. Owner's Salary	0	0	30,000	40,000	60,000
8. Employee's Wages and Salaries	86,400	115,200	229,200	248,000	314,400
9. Supplies and Postage	1,200	1,200	2,400	2,400	3,600
10. Advertising and Promotion	25,125	12,000	43,125	30,000	55,125
11. Delivery Expense	3,600	4,800	10,800	12,000	15,600
12. Bad Debt Expense	0	0	0	0	0
13. Travel	0	0	0	0	0
14. Legal and Accounting Fees	3,300	2,800	6,300	7,000	9,100
15. Vehicle Expense	0	0	0	0	0
16. Maintenance Expense	5,400	7,200	16,200	18,000	23,400
17. Miscellaneous Expenses	39,600	52,800	118,800	132,000	171,600
D. TOTAL VARIABLE EXPENSES	**$164,625**	**$196,000**	**$456,825**	**$489,400**	**$652,825**
Less: Fixed Expenses					
18. Rent	27,852	27,852	55,704	55,704	83,556
19. Utilities (Heat, Light, Power)	8,400	12,000	27,600	31,200	39,600
20. Telephone	2,400	2,400	4,800	4,800	7,200
21. Taxes and Licenses	1,052	0	1,052	0	1,052
22. Depreciation	9,900	13,200	29,700	33,000	42,900
23. Interest	7,835	6,885	13,654	11,579	17,139
24. Insurance	1,800	2,400	5,400	6,000	7,800
25. Other Fixed Expeses	0	0	0	0	0
E. TOTAL FIXED EXPENSES	**$59,239**	**$64,737**	**$137,910**	**$142,283**	**$199,247**
F. TOTAL OPERATING EXPENSES	**$223,864**	**$260,737**	**$594,735**	**$631,683**	**$852,072**
G. NET OPERATING PROFIT (LOSS) (G = C - F)	**($13,264)**	**$20,063**	**$44,565**	**$70,317**	**$81,028**
H. LOSS CARRIED FORWARD	N/A	($13,264)	N/A	N/A	N/A
I. INCOME TAXES (estimated)	$0	$4,414	$9,804	$15,470	$17,826
J. NET PROFIT (LOSS) AFTER INCOME TAX	**($13,264)**	**$15,649**	**$34,761**	**$54,847**	**$63,202**

SCHEDULE 4

PRO FORMA CASH FLOW FORECAST FOR LITE BITES GRILL
12-Month Cash Flow Projections

Minimum Cash Required = 5000	July	August	September	October	November	December	January	February	March	April	May	June	2003/04 TOTAL	2004/05 TOTAL	2005/06 TOTAL
Cash Flow From Operations (during month)															
1. Cash Sales	30,000	28,000	24,000	20,000	20,000	22,000	24,000	24,000	24,000	26,000	28,000	30,000	300,000	400,000	900,000
2. Payments for Credit Sales	0	0	0	0	0	0	0	0	0	0	0	0	0	0	0
3. Investment Income	0	0	0	0	0	0	0	0	0	0	0	0	0	0	0
4. Other Cash Income	0	0	0	0	0	0	0	0	0	0	0	0	0	0	0
A. TOTAL CASH FLOW ON HAND	$30,000	$28,000	$24,000	$20,000	$20,000	$22,000	$24,000	$24,000	$24,000	$26,000	$28,000	$30,000	$300,000	$400,000	$900,000
Less Expenses Paid (during month)															
5. Inventory or New Material	-16,440	-8,344	-7,152	-5,960	-5,960	-6,556	-7,152	-7,152	-7,152	-7,748	-8,344	-8,940	-96,900	-119,200	-268,200
6. Owner's Salary	0	0	0	0	0	0	0	0	0	0	0	0	0	-30,000	-30,000
7. Employee's Wages and Salaries	-7,200	-7,200	-7,200	-7,200	-7,200	-7,200	-7,200	-7,200	-7,200	-7,200	-7,200	-7,200	-86,400	-115,200	-229,200
8. Supplies and Postage	-100	-100	-100	-100	-100	-100	-100	-100	-100	-100	-100	-100	-1,200	-1,200	-2,400
9. Advertising and Promotion	-14,705	-2,070	-2,070	-70	-70	-3,720	-70	-70	-2,070	-70	-70	-2,070	-25,125	-12,000	-43,125
10. Delivery Expense	-360	-336	-288	-240	-240	-264	-288	-288	-288	-312	-336	-360	-3,600	-4,800	-10,800
11. Travel	0	0	0	0	0	0	0	0	0	0	0	0	0	0	0
12. Legal and Accounting Fees	-1,200	0	0	0	0	0	0	0	0	0	0	-2,100	-3,300	-2,800	-6,300
13. Vehicle Expense	0	0	0	0	0	0	0	0	0	0	0	0	0	0	0
14. Maintenance Expense	-540	-504	-432	-360	-360	-396	-432	-432	-432	-468	-504	-540	-5,400	-7,200	-16,200
15. Rent	-2,321	-2,321	-2,321	-2,321	-2,321	-2,321	-2,321	-2,321	-2,321	-2,321	-2,321	-2,321	-27,852	-27,852	-55,704
16. Utilities	-2,700	-700	-700	-700	-700	-700	-700	-700	-700	-700	-700	-700	-10,400	-12,000	-27,600
17. Telephone	-200	-200	-200	-200	-200	-200	-200	-200	-200	-200	-200	-200	-2,400	-2,400	-4,800
18. Taxes and Licenses	-1,052	0	0	0	0	0	0	0	0	0	0	0	-1,052	-1,052	-1,052
19. Interest Payments (CIBC Loan)	-702	-628	-689	-660	-676	-648	-662	-656	-628	-642	-615	-629	-7,835	-6,884	-13,654
20. Insurance	-150	-150	-150	-150	-150	-150	-150	-150	-150	-150	-150	-150	-1,800	-2,400	-5,400
21. Other Cash Expenses	-3,960	-3,696	-3,168	-2,640	-2,640	-2,904	-3,168	-3,168	-3,168	-3,432	-3,696	-3,960	-39,600	-52,800	-118,800
B. TOTAL EXPENDITURES	($51,630)	($24,249)	($24,470)	($20,601)	($20,617)	($25,159)	($22,443)	($22,437)	($24,409)	($23,343)	($24,236)	($29,270)	($312,864)	($366,736)	($833,235)
Capital															
Purchase of Fixed Assets	-126,650	0	0	0	0	0	0	0	0	0	0	0	-126,650	-126,650	0
Sale of Fixed Assets	0	0	0	0	0	0	0	0	0	0	0	0	0	0	0
C. CHANGE IN CASH FROM PURCHASE OR SALE OF ASSETS	($126,650)	$0	$0	$0	$0	$0	$0	$0	$0	$0	$0	$0	($126,650)	($126,650)	$0
Financing															
Payment of Principal of Loan	-1,032	-1,106	-1,046	-1,074	-1,059	-1,087	-1,072	-1,078	-1,106	-1,092	-1,119	-1,106	-12,977	-13,928	-27,970
Inflow of Cash From Bank Loan	113,985	0	0	0	0	0	0	0	0	0	0	0	113,985	113,985	0
Issuance of Equity Positions	47,000	0	0	0	0	0	0	0	0	0	0	0	47,000	0	0
Repurchase of Outstanding Equity	0	0	0	0	0	0	0	0	0	0	0	0	0	0	0
D. CHANGE IN CASH FROM FINANCING	$159,953	($1,106)	($1,046)	($1,074)	($1,059)	($1,087)	($1,072)	($1,078)	($1,106)	($1,092)	($1,119)	($1,106)	$148,008	$100,057	($27,970)
E. INCREASE (DECREASE) IN CASH	$11,673	$2,645	($1,516)	($1,675)	($1,676)	($4,246)	$485	$485	($1,515)	$1,565	$2,645	($376)	$8,494	$6,671	$38,795
F. CASH AT BEGINNING OF PERIOD	$0	$11,673	$14,318	$12,802	$11,127	$9,451	$5,205	$5,690	$6,175	$4,660	$6,225	$8,870	$0	$8,494	$15,165
G. CASH AT END OF PERIOD	$11,673	$14,318	$12,802	$11,127	$9,451	$5,205	$5,690	$6,175	$4,660	$6,225	$8,870	$8,494	$8,494	$15,165	$53,960
MEET MINIMUM CASH BALANCE	Acceptable	Acceptable	Acceptable	Acceptable	Acceptable	Acceptable	Acceptable	Acceptable	Acceptable	Acceptable	Acceptable	Acceptable	Acceptable	Acceptable	Acceptable

SCHEDULE 5

PROF FORMA BALANCE SHEET FOR LITE BITES GRILL

ASSETS	OPENING		JUNE 31/04		JUNE 31/05		JUNE 31/06	
Current Assets:								
1. Cash	26,835		8,494		15,165		53,960	
2. Accounts Receivable	0		0		0		0	
3. Inventory	7,500		7,500		7,500		15,000	
4. Other Current Assets	0		2,000		2,000		2,000	
A. TOTAL CURRENT ASSETS		$34,335		$17,994		$24,665		$70,960
Fixed Assets:								
5. Land and Buildings	0		0		0		0	
less depreciation	0	0	0	0	0	0	0	0
6. Furniture and Fixtures	65,000		65,000		130,000		130,000	
less depreciation	0	65,000	0	65,000	0	130,000	29,700	-29,700
7. Equipment	61,650		61,650		123,300		123,300	
less depreciation	0	61,650	0	61,650	0	123,300	0	123,300
8. Trucks and Automobiles	0		0		13,200		13,200	
less depreciation	0	0	0	0	13,200	-13,200	13,200	-13,200
9. Other Fixed Assets	0		0		0		0	
less depreciation	0	0	9,900	-9,900	9,900	-9,900	9,900	-9,900
B. TOTAL FIXED ASSETS		$126,650		$116,750		$230,200		$200,500
C. TOTAL ASSETS		$160,985		$134,744		$254,865		$271,460
LIABILITIES								
Current Liabilities: (due within 12 months)								
10. Accounts Payable	0		0		0		0	
11. Bank Loans / Other Loans	12,977		13,928		27,970		30,045	
12. Taxes Owed	0		0		0		0	
D. TOTAL CURRENT LIABILITIES		$12,977		$13,928		$27,970		$30,045
Long-term Liabilities:								
13. Notes Payable (due after one year)	101,008		87,080		173,095		143,050	
14. Other Long-term Liabilities	0		0		0		0	
E. TOTAL LONG-TERM LIABILITIES		$101,008		$87,080		$173,095		$143,050
F. TOTAL LIABILITIES		$113,985		$101,008		$201,065		$173,095
NET WORTH (Capital)								
SHARE CAPITAL								
Common Shares	47,000		47,000		33,736		53,800	
Preferred Shares	0		0		0		0	
RETAINED EARNINGS		0		-13,264		20,064		44,565
G. TOTAL NET WORTH		$47,000		$33,736		$53,800		$98,365
H. TOTAL LIABILITIES AND NET WORTH		$160,985		$134,744		$254,865		$271,460
		BALANCED		BALANCED		BALANCED		BALANCED

SCHEDULE 6

FINANCIAL RATIOS FOR LITE BITES GRILL

			End of Year 1		End of Year 2		End of Year 3	
1. Gross Margin/Sales	=	Gross Profit / Net Sales	$210,600 / $300,000	0.70	$280,800 / $400,000	0.70	$639,300 / $900,000	0.71
2. Current Ratio	=	Current Assets / Current Liabilities	$17,994 / $13,928	1.29	$24,665 / $27,970	0.88	$70,960 / $30,045	2.36
3. Quick Ratio	=	Current Assets – Inventories / Current Liabilities	$10,494 / $13,928	0.75	$17,165 / $27,970	0.61	$55,960 / $30,045	1.86
4. Net Profit/Sales	=	Net Income (After Tax) / Net Sales	($13,264) / $300,000	-0.04	$15,649 / $400,000	0.04	$34,761 / $900,000	0.04
5. Net Profit/Net Worth	=	Net Profit / Net worth	($13,264) / $33,736	-0.39	$15,649 / $53,800	0.29	$34,761 / $98,365	0.35
6. Sales/Net worth	=	Net Sales / Net Worth	$300,000 / $33,736	8.89	$400,000 / $53,800	7.43	$900,000 / $98,365	9.15
7. Fixed Assets/Net Worth	=	Fixed Assets / Net Worth	$116,750 / $33,736	3.46	$230,200 / $53,800	4.28	$200,500 / $98,365	2.04
8. Current Liabilities/ Net Worth	=	Current Liabilities / Net Worth	$13,928 / $33,736	0.41	$27,970 / $53,800	0.52	$30,045 / $98,365	0.31
9. Total Liabilities/Net Worth	=	Total Liabilities / Net Worth	$101,008 / $33,736	2.99	$201,065 / $53,800	3.74	$173,095 / $98,365	1.76
10. Debt/Net Worth	=	Total Outstanding Debt / Net Worth	$87,080 / $33,736	2.58	$201,065 / $53,800	3.74	$173,095 / $98,365	1.76
11. Return On Assets	=	Net Income (After Tax) / Total Assets	($13,264) / $134,744	-0.10	$15,649 / $254,865	0.06	$34,761 / $271,460	0.13

SCHEDULE 7

BREAK-EVEN POINT FOR FIRST YEAR

OPERATING EXPENSES

Owner's Salary	0
Employee's Wages	86,400
Supplies and Postage	1,200
Advert. and Promotion	25,125
Delivery Expense	3,600
Bad Debt Allowance	0
Travel	0
Professional Fees	3,300
Vehicle Expense	0
Maintenance Expense	5,400
Other Variable Expenses	39,600
Rent	27,852
Utilities	8,400
Telephone	2,400
Taxes & Licenses	1,052
Depreciation	9,900
Interest	7,835
Insurance	1,800
Other Fixed Expenses	0

TOTAL OPERATING EXPENSES   **$223,864**

CONTRIBUTION MARGIN = $\dfrac{\text{Gross Margin}}{\text{Net Sales}}$ **70.20%**

BREAK-EVEN POINT ($Sales) = $\dfrac{\text{Total Operating Expenses}}{\text{Contribution Margin}}$

$318,894.59

BIBLIOGRAPHY

1. **Welcome to Health Express USA, Inc.**
    www.hexs.com/info/about.html

2. **Canadian Restaurant and Foodservices Association**
    www.crfa.ca/research/foodservicetrends/research_foodservicetrends_evolutionofmealtime.htm

3. **Fast Food Gets Healthy Too**
    www.cnn.com/2002/HEALTH/diet.fitness/09/23/healthy.fast.food.ap/

4. **Canadian Restaurant and Foodservices Association**
    www.crfa.ca/research/research_dinersoptforlighterfare.htm

5. **Burgers Go Green**
    www.chainleader.com/archive/1101/1101segments.html

6. **The Vegetarian Resource Group, Baltimore, Md.**
    www.vrg.org/nutshell/poll2000.htm

7. **Statistics Canada**
    www.statcan.ca/english/Pgdb/famil27g.htm

8. **City of Winnipeg Census Data**
    www.city.winnipeg.mb.ca/census1996/data/05-00.pdf

9. **Fast Food for Fitness Fans**
    www.inc.com/magazine/20011101/23597.html

10. **Canada Business Service Centre, Sales Forecasting for a New Business**
    www.cbsc.org/osbw/salefore.html#new

11. **Good, Walter S. *Building a Dream: A Canadian Guide to Starting Your Own Business*,**
    5th edition, Toronto: McGraw-Hill Ryerson Ltd., 2002, p. 151.

12. **Industry Canada Performance Plus Small Business Profiles**
    strategis.gc.ca

13. **Newspaper Audience Databank**
    www.nadbank.com

14. **SUBWAY Restaurants**
    www.subway.com

APPENDICES

Appendix 1 Preliminary Sales Forecast

Appendix 2 Marketing Budget for First Year

Appendix 3 Facility Location and Site Plan

Appendix 4 Market Size of First Restaurant Location

Appendix 5 Detailed Equipment Listing

Appendix 6 Staffing Schedule

Appendix 7 Resume: Leonard Bogucki

Appendix 8 Insurance Proposal

APPENDIX 1

PRELIMINARY SALES FORECAST

	YEAR ONE	YEAR TWO	YEAR THREE
January	$30,000		
February	$28,000		
March	$24,000	$90,000 (Q1)	$120,000 (Q1)
April	$20,000		
May	$20,000		
June	$22,000	$90,000 (Q2)	$140,000 (Q2)
July	$24,000		
August	$24,000		
September	$24,000	$110,000 (Q3)	$160,000 (Q3)
October	$26,000		
November	$28,000		
December	$30,000	$110,000 (Q4)	$180,000 (Q4)
TOTAL	**$300,000**	**$400,000**	**$600,000**

APPENDIX 2

MARKETING BUDGET FOR FIRST YEAR

Selling (direct costs)

- Sales salaries for personal selling	$800	(80 hrs @ $10/hr)
- Printing menus/brochures/coupons	$250	

Advertising

- Newspaper sampling campaign	$1,500	
- Ongoing newspaper advertising	$9,650	
- Radio promotion (Grand opening)	$2,500	
- Billboard (one month)	$4,350	

Sales promotions (coupons)

	$2,500	(Coupons)
	$200	(DVD player — draw)

Website

	$2,500	(Development)
	$600	(Maintenance)
	$35	(Domain name)
	$240	(Hosting)

TOTAL MARKETING BUDGET (YEAR 1)	**$25,125**

APPENDIX 3

FACILITY LOCATION AND SITE PLAN

THE BRICK PLAZA

1045 ST. JAMES STREET
IN WINNIPEG'S MOST POWERFUL SHOPPING AREA

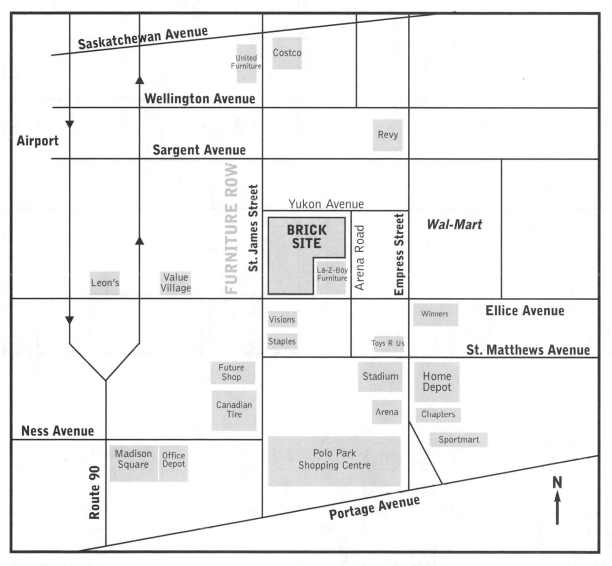

HIGH TRAFFIC:

- Ellice Avenue & St. James Street has one of the busiest traffic counts in Winnipeg
- superior access and egress

RENT: $12 sq. ft., net
ADDITIONAL RENT: $4.06 sq. ft. (2002) + Management Fees

HIGH VISIBILITY:

- signage offering maximum exposure
- excellent, well-lit parking lot

SPACE AVAILABLE:

- 1,913 sq. ft.

(Site plan on next page)

Areas and sizes are approximate. Reasonable efforts have been made to ensure that the information contained herein is accurate. All details are subject to final confirmations by all interested parties.

continued

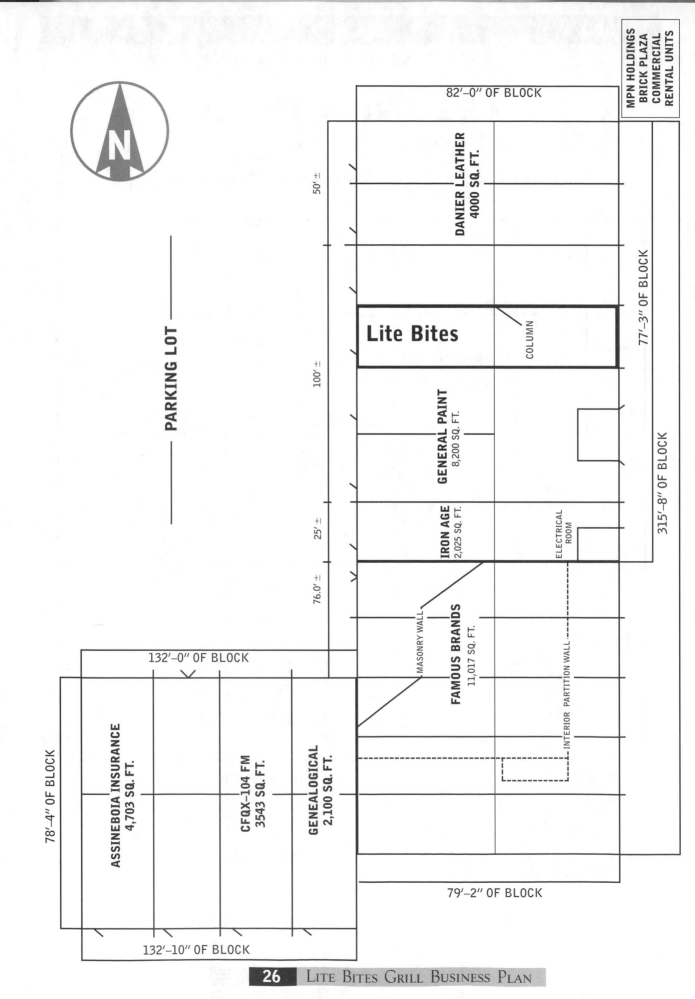

MPN HOLDINGS
BRICK PLAZA
COMMERCIAL
RENTAL UNITS

82'–0" OF BLOCK

DANIER LEATHER
4000 SQ. FT.

50' ±

PARKING LOT

Lite Bites

COLUMN

77'–3" OF BLOCK

100' ±

GENERAL PAINT
8,200 SQ. FT.

315'–8" OF BLOCK

IRON AGE
2,025 SQ. FT.

ELECTRICAL
ROOM

25' ±

76.0' ±

MASONRY WALL

FAMOUS BRANDS
11,017 SQ. FT.

INTERIOR PARTITION WALL

132'–0" OF BLOCK

78'–4" OF BLOCK

ASSINEBOIA INSURANCE
4,703 SQ. FT.

CFQX–104 FM
3543 SQ. FT.

GENEALOGICAL
2,100 SQ. FT.

79'–2" OF BLOCK

132'–10" OF BLOCK

APPENDIX 4

MARKET SIZE OF FIRST RESTAURANT LOCATION

	POPULATION
St. James (Age 25–54)	15,295
River Heights (Age 25–54)	17,855
Fort Garry (Age 25–54)	20,995
Fort Rouge (Age 25–54)	19,885
Total (Age 25–54)	74,030
19.1% University Educated	*14,139*
Total Population over 15 (in above areas)	112,100
Vegetarian market (2.5%)	*2,803*
TOTAL MARKET	**16,942**

APPENDIX 5

DETAILED EQUIPMENT LISTING

951 Erin Street
Winnipeg, MB R3G 2W8

RUSSELL
FOOD EQUIPMENT LTD.

To: Bill Fenton   Fax: 1 page
From: Russell Food Equipment Ltd.   Date: December 18, 2002

( ) Urgent   (X) For Review   ( ) Please Comment   ( ) Please Reply   ( ) Please Recycle

Hi Bill:

I have updated your budget quote for your business plan. Please note changes made.

1)   12" Electric Slicer added.

2)   Delivery and set in place includes:
     - Set up and testing of Walk-in Cooler/Freezer
     - Set up of all storage shelving
     - Mounting menu signs

3)   Electrical and plumbing connections by others
     - This part of your costing will vary by building depending on what plumbing and electrical is existing.
     - When you have selected a building location we take into consideration existing electrical and
       plumbing supply in our overall design.

I will mail out an original quote for your presentation.

Best wishes with your proposal and have a good holiday season.

RUSSELL FOOD EQUIPMENT LTD.

951 Erin Street
Winnipeg, MB R3G 2W8

RUSSELL
FOOD EQUIPMENT LTD.

To: **Bill Fenton**   Fax: 1 page

From: **Russell Food Equipment Ltd.**   Date: December 16, 2002

( ) Urgent   (X) For Review   ( ) Please Comment   ( ) Please Reply   ( ) Please Recycle

Hi Bill:

Further to your request for quotation we are pleased to submit the following.

1 only	3 Compartment Sink	2000.00
1 only	Undercounter Dishwasher	5000.00 optional
1 only	2 Door Reach-In Cooler	2400.00
1 only	Walk-in Cooler/Freezer Combo c/w Shelving	15,000.00
2 only	Soup Warmers	600.00
2 only	Pannini Grills	2000.00
1 only	Electric Convection Oven	7000.00
1 only	Microwave Oven	600.00
1 only	Electric Range	4400.00
1 only	Refrigerated Prep Table	4000.00
1 only	4 Slice Toaster	1000.00
1 only	Refrigerated Display Case	3500.00
1 lot	Tables and Chairs	150.00/person
1 only	12" Electric Slicer	1000.00
1 lot	Menu Signage	2000.00
1 lot	Smallwares	2000.00
1 lot	Millwork	3000.00
1 lot	Dry Storage Shelving	1000.00
1 only	Delivery and Set in Place	2000.00

Electrical and Plumbing Connections by others.

Please allow 4–6 weeks for delivery.

The above pricing is for budget purposes only, f.o.b. Winnipeg and all taxes are extra. Trusting this information will be helpful in developing your business plan. Overall equipment specified will depend on building layout, budget, and specific menu items.

Our consultant services are provided on a no-charge basis to our clients when we are handling the project. Where tendering is desirable or mandatory, we can provide drawings and specifications for equitable tendering at modest fees and have many advantages to offer over the independent consultant that we would be glad to review with you.

Food services require considerable investment. Professional planning can avoid pitfalls and give you a well-planned food facility that will go a long way toward ensuring an efficient and profitable operation.

RUSSELL FOOD EQUIPMENT LTD.

APPENDIX 6

STAFFING SCHEDULE

Shift Time	# Employees Mon. – Fri.	# Employees Sat./Sun.	Hrs./Shift	Total hrs./week
10:30 a.m.–11:30 a.m.	1	2	1	9
11:30 a.m.–1:00 a.m.	3	3	1.5	31.5
1:00 p.m.–4:00 p.m.	1	2	3	27
4:00 p.m.–5:00 p.m.	2	2	1	14
5:00 p.m.–6:30 p.m.	3	3	1.5	31.5
6:30 p.m.–8:00 p.m.	1	2	1.5	13.5

TOTAL: 126.5 HRS./WEEK
(506 hrs./month)

LEONARD T. BOGUCKI   RESUME

Calgary, AB T2Z 1M3
Telephone: 555-2971

EDUCATION

1980–1983   High School Diploma: John Taylor H.S., Winnipeg, MB
1983–1985   Business Administration
            Red River Community College, Winnipeg, MB

WORK EXPERIENCE

2001–2002   **General Manager**, *ABC Restaurant*, Calgary, AB
            Responsibilities included: food & labour cost control, purchasing, maintenance,
            repairs, payroll, supervision, observation of sanitation standards, customer service,
            staff selection, computerized POS system management

1993–2001   **Restaurant Manager**, *Denny's Restaurant*, Calgary, AB
            Responsibilities included: food & labour cost control, purchasing, maintenance,
            repairs, payroll, supervision, observation of sanitation standards, customer service,
            staff selection

1988–1993   **Head Cook**, *Boyd's Seafood Kitchen*, Calgary, AB
            Responsibilities included: portion control, preparation of homemade chowders,
            general operation of kitchen

1987–1988   **Installation Supervisor**, *Pacific Warehouse Ltd.* Calgary, AB
            Responsibilities Included: supervising job sites and crew, ensuring timely
            completion of installation of industrial shelving units

1983–1987   **Evening Supervisor**, *Jim's Fish & Chips Restaurant*, Winnipeg, MB
            Responsibilities included: purchasing, customer service, balance cash out,
            supervision, cooking as necessary

1983–1987   **Owner/Manager**, *Jim's Seafood Shop* (Retail Fish Market), Winnipeg, MB
            Responsibilities included: purchasing, customer service, payroll, supervision, staff
            selection, marketing, cost control.

INTERESTS

            Fishing, big game hunting, cross-country skiing, hockey, model building

References available upon request.

BILL FENTON

O/A

FENTON'S HEALTH FOOD BAR

INSURANCE PROPOSAL

MILNCO INSURANCE
200 – 207 Donald Street
Winnipeg, MB R3C 1M5

MILNCO INSURANCE
Ste. 200 – 207 Donald St., Winnipeg, MB R3C 1M5

Mr. Bill Fenton
o/a Fenton's Health Food Bar

PROPERTY INSURANCE

Coverage on all real and personal property of the Insured or for which they may be held responsible against the perils as set out below and in the amounts specified. Property is insured to 100% of value in recognition of the possibility of a total loss.

Equipment (including improvements and betterments)		$ 125,000
Stock		$ 7,500
Business Interruption – Profits Form		$ 165,000
Auditors' Fees		$ 5,000
Sign		$ 2,000
Crime – Broad Form Money & Securities	Inside	$ 2,000
	Outside	$ 2,000
Comprehensive General Liability		
Limit of Insurance	Inclusive	$2,000,000

Basis of coverage – will pay those sums that the insured becomes legally obligated to pay as compensatory damages because of bodily injury or property damage to which this insurance applies.

Includes the following:

Products/Completed Operations
Premises/Operations
Personal Injury – includes illegal trespass and wrongful eviction, libel and slander
Employees as additional insureds
Blanket Contractual (all written contracts)
Contingent Employers
Non-Owned Automobile
Medical Payments - $2,500 per person/$25,000 per accident (to cover all reasonable medical expenses for bodily injury to any persons arising out of your operation or condition on your premises subject to the terms, conditions and exclusions of the policy wording.)

Tenants Legal Liability – *Comprehension General Liability* will not pay for damage to the portion of the building leased to you. Coverage against this contingency is provided by means of a *Tenants Fire Legal Liability* insurance. Limit - $150,000.

continued

Terms & Conditions:

PERILS INSURED: Coverage is against "All Risks of Direct Physical Damage or Loss" subject to the terms, conditions and exclusions of the policy wording.

Deductible of $500 applies to each loss

Basis of Loss Settlement – Replacement Cost on Equipment and Fixtures and Actual Cash Value on Stock. Co-Insurance Condition – 90% (equipment and fixtures must be insured for at least 90% of the replacement cost values).

Business Interruption – Limit is based on projected sales of $300,000 plus cost of sales of approximately 33% and ordinary payroll of approximately $35,000.

Boiler & Machinery coverage covers an accident or loss to property resulting from the explosion of pressure vessels or from accidental breakdown including miscellaneous electrical apparatus, switch panels and transformers.

Limit	**$135,000**
Deductible	**$500**

Includes consequential loss to stock for an amount of $5,000 (this would cover spoilage of food due to a mechanical or electrical breakdown of the refrigerator units).

PREMIUM SCHEDULE

Equipment		$ 325
Stock		$ 20
Business Income – Profits		$ 396
Sign		$ 5
Broad Form Money & Securities		$ 100
Commercial General Liability -	**$1,000,000** Limit	$ 500
	$2,000,000 Limit	$ 650
Tenants Legal Liability		$ 52
Boiler & Machinery		$ 250

For Further Information

BANKS

HSBC BANK CANADA
(www.hsbc.ca)
ONLINE BUSINESS ASSISTANCE:
www.hsbc.ca/hsbc/business_en

- Click on Small Business, then:
  - Choosing the Right Business
  - Self-Assessment
  - Researching Your Business
  - Business Planning
  - Getting Started

ROYAL BANK OF CANADA
(www.royalbank.com)
ONLINE BUSINESS ASSISTANCE:
www.royalbank.com/sme/index.html

- Small Business & Entrepreneurs
  - Starting a Business
  - Products & Services
  - Managing Your Business
  - Women Entrepreneurs
  - Young Entrepreneurs

BANK OF MONTREAL
(www.bankofmontreal.com or www.bmo.com)
ONLINE BUSINESS ASSISTANCE:
www4.bmo.com/business/
0,4344,35490_35899,00.html

- Business Coach Series (pdf downloads)
  - Creating a Financial Proposal
  - Finding Sources of Capital
  - Planning Your Cash Flow
  - Cash Flow Worksheet
  - Developing Your Business Plan
- Business Planning Resources
  - I Have an Idea
  - I'm Expanding Into New Markets
  - I'm Starting a Business
  - My Business Could Use Some Help
  - My Business is Growing

TORONTO DOMINION BANK
(www.tdbank.ca or www.td.com
or www.tdcanadatrust.com)

ONLINE BUSINESS ASSISTANCE:
www.tdcanadatrust.com/smallbusiness/
resources.jsp

- Economic Trends for Small Business
- A Good Plan Is Necessary Ingredient to Reach Success: Business Planner

SCOTIABANK
(www.scotiabank.com)
ONLINE BUSINESS ASSISTANCE:
www.scotiabank.com

- Small Business & Professionals
  - Planning and Starting Your Business
  - Building and Growing Your Professional Career
  - Expanding Your Business
  - Managing Business Challenges
  - Your Business & Personal Rewards
  - Scotiabusiness Plan Writer

BUSINESS DEVELOPMENT BANK OF CANADA
(www.bdc.ca)
ONLINE BUSINESS ASSISTANCE:
www.bdc.ca

- Starting a Business
- Acquisition
- Growth
- Exporting
- E-business

ACCOUNTING FIRMS

ERNST & YOUNG
(www.ey.com)
ONLINE BUSINESS ASSISTANCE:
www.ey.com/global/content.nsf/Canada/Home

- Entrepreneurial Survey: Reputation at Risk

KPMG (www.kpmg.com)

- Industry summaries and overviews

Deloitte (www.dc.com)

- Articles, books, and newsletters on industry trends and facts

FEDERAL GOVERNMENT

INDUSTRY CANADA
(www.ic.gc.ca)

PUBLICATIONS (ONLINE BOOKS, PAMPHLETS, AND PDF FILES)

- Assessing Changing Needs (booklet)
- Become Investor Ready — Build Investor Relationships: Steps to Growth Capital (book)
- Canada Small Business Financing Act: Assessing New Opportunities (booklet)
- Canada Small Business Financing Program: Buy or Lease — Now the Choice is Yours (pamphlet)
- Interactive Business Planner (pamphlet)
- Small Business Guide to Federal Incorporation
- Small Business Quarterly Newsletter
- Your Guide to Government of Canada Services and Support for Small Business (pamphlet)
- The Canadian Entrepreneurs' Guide to Securing Risk Capital — Steps to Growth Capital (pamphlet)

ONLINE BUSINESS ASSISTANCE:
www.ic.gc.ca/cmb/welcomeic.nsf/icPages/IndustryCanadaOnLine#online14

- Aboriginal Business
- Bankruptcy
- Company Directories
- Competition
- Corporations
- Electronic Commerce
- Environment
- Innovation
- Small Business
- Telecommunications
- Trade
- Industry Portfolio

INTERNATIONAL TRADE CANADA/TRADE COMMISSIONER SERVICE
(www.infoexport.gc.ca)

ONLINE BUSINESS ASSISTANCE:
www.infoexport.gc.ca

- Virtual Trade Commissioner
- Offices Abroad
- Market Reports by Industry Sector
- Businesswomen in Trade
- Science and Technology
- Canada Export Awards

- Team Canada Missions
- International Business Opportunities Centre
- CanadExport Trade Newsletter
- ExportSource (exportsou rce.ca/gol/exportsource/interface.nsf/engdocBasic/0.html)
  - Getting Started
  - Developing Your Export Plan
  - Identifying Your Target Market
  - Entering Your Market
  - Planning Your Export Financing
  - E-Business for Exporters
  - Industry Sector Resources
  - Exporting Your Services

CANADA BORDER SERVICE AGENCY
(www.cbsa-asfc.gc.ca)

- Importing (www.cbsa-asfc.gc.ca/import)
  - Free and Secure Trade (FAST) Program (www.cbsa-asfc.gc.ca/import/fast/menu-e.html)
- Exporting (www.cbsa-asfc.gc.ca/export)
  - Handy Customs Guide for Exporters

CANADA REVENUE AGENCY
(www.cra-arc.gc.ca)

- Guide for Canadian Small Business (www.cra-arc.gc.ca/E/pub/tg/rc4070/rc4070eq.html)

GOVERNMENT ON-LINE

- Business Gateway (www.businessgateway.ca)
  - Business Start-up
  - Tax
  - Regulations
  - Business Statistics and Analysis
  - Financing
  - Human Resources Management
  - Exporting/Importing

PUBLIC WORKS AND GOVERNMENT SERVICES CANADA
(www.pwgsc.gc.ca)

- Serving Business (www.pwgsc.gc.ca/text/business/index-e.html)
  - Opportunities
  - Doing Business
  - Money Matters
  - Publications

PROVINCIAL GOVERNMENTS

PRINCE EDWARD ISLAND ECONOMIC DEVELOPMENT AND TOURISM
(www.peibusinessdevelopment.com)

- Invest in PEI
- Sectors of Excellence
- Starting or Expanding Your Business
- Trade & Export Development
- Media Centre
- Business Parks

NEW BRUNSWICK DEPARTMENT OF ECONOMIC DEVELOPMENT AND TOURISM
(www.gnb.ca)

- Doing Business
  - Investment Opportunities
  - Business Start-up
    - Accurate Market Research
    - Naming and Registering Your Business
    - Planning Your Financing
    - Prepare a Business Plan

GOVERNMENT OF QUEBEC
(www.entreprises.gouv.qc.ca/wps/portal)

AVAILABLE ONLY IN FRENCH; CLICK ON BUSINESS SERVICES, THEN ON DÉMARRAGE:

- Préciser votre projet
- Établir votre profil
- Préparer votre plan d'affaires
- Remplir vos obligations
- Obtenir du financement
- Installer votre entreprise
- Faire la promotion de votre entreprise
- Cheminement de démarrage

ONTARIO MINISTRY OF ECONOMIC DEVELOPMENT AND TRADE
(www.gov.on.ca)

- Starting Your Business
  - Starting a Small Business in Ontario
  - Canada Business Service Centre (Ontario)
- Relocating Your Business to Ontario
  - Ontario Investment Service
- Doing Business
  - Business Development
  - Small Business Central
  - Ontario Business Connects
  - Agricultural Business Development

- Doing Business with the Ontario Government
- Licensing and Registration
  - Business Information
- Laws and Taxes
  - Business Tax
  - Small Business Tax Help
  - E-Laws
- Trade
  - Ontario Exports

MANITOBA DEPARTMENT OF INDUSTRY, ECONOMIC DEVELOPMENT AND MINES
(www.gov.mb.ca/itt/index.html)

SERVICES FOR SMALL BUSINESS
(www.gov.mb.ca/itm/sbcd/index.html)

PUBLICATIONS (PDF)

- Bookkeeping
- Construction Business Plan
- How to Be a Consultant
- Manufacturing Business Plan
- Marketing
- Retail Business Plan
- Service Business Plan
- Small Business Finance Plan

MANITOBA BUSINESS
(www.gov.mb.ca/business.html)

- AgriBusiness Development
- Business Development Assistance
- Business Events Calendar
- Business Resources
- Business Services for Canada
- Export Services
- Highlights of Manitoba's Recent Economic Performance
- Manitoba Business Information Service
- Manitoba Markets
- Public Sector Buying/Selling
- Small Business Information

SASKATCHEWAN DEPARTMENT OF ECONOMIC AND CO-OPERATIVE DEVELOPMENT
(www.ir.gov.sk.ca)

- Business and Cooperative Development
  - Entrepreneurship and Small Business
  - Business Services
  - Co-ops
  - Saskbiz.ca

- Small Business Loans Association Program
- Aboriginal Service Network
- Business Gateway
- Saskatchewan Facts

ALBERTA CANADA
(www.alberta-canada.com/index.html)
- Investing in Alberta
- Locating Your Business in Alberta
- Exporting Your Products
- Alberta Products and Services
- Starting Your Business
- The Alberta Economy
- Statistics and Publications

BRITISH COLUMBIA BUSINESS
(www.gov.bc.ca)
- Planning Your Business
- Interactive Business Planner
- Small Business: Entrepreneur
- BC Bid
- BC OnLine
- OneStop Business Services

ASSOCIATIONS AND OTHER ORGANIZATIONS

CANADIAN FRANCHISE ASSOCIATION
(www.cfa.ca)
- Franchise Listings
- Franchise Support and Services
- Investigate and Evaluate
- Shop CFA's Book Store
- CFA Franchise Canada — Magazine
  - CFA Franchise Canada — The Official Directory
  - How to Franchise Your Business
  - CFA Information Kit
  - Canadian Franchise Legislation

DUN & BRADSTREET

(www.dnb.ca)
- Reduce Credit Risks
- Find Profitable New Customers
- Optimize Your Supplier Base
- Enhance Your Knowledge

SOME USEFUL CONTACTS

FEDERAL GOVERNMENT

INDUSTRY CANADA (www.ic.gc.ca)
Enquiry Services
Communications & Marketing Branch
Industry Canada
Second Floor, West Tower
C.D. Howe Building
235 Queen St.
Ottawa, ON K1A 0H5
Phone: 613-947-7466
Fax: 613-954-6436
E-mail: Online form on Web site

FOREIGN AFFAIRS CANADA
(www.fac-aec.gc.ca)

INTERNATIONAL TRADE CANADA
(www.itcan-cican.gc.ca)
Enquiries Service (SXCI)
125 Sussex Dr.
Ottawa, ON K1A 0G2
1-800-267-8376
Phone: 613-944-4000
TTY: 613-944-9136
Fax: 613-996-9709
E-mail: Online form on Web site

STATISTICS CANADA (www.statcan.ca)
Statistical Reference Centre
Room 1500, Main Building
Holland Ave.
Ottawa, ON K1A 0T6
1-800-263-1136
Phone: 613-951-8116
E-mail: infostats@statcan.ca

CANADIAN INTELLECTUAL PROPERTY OFFICE
(www.cipo.gc.ca)
Industry Canada
Place du Portage I
50 Victoria St., Room C-229
Gatineau, QC K1A 0C9
Phone: 819-997-1936
Fax: 819-953-7620
E-mail: cipo.contact@ic.gc.ca

CANADA BUSINESS SERVICE CENTRES
(www.cbsc.org)

CANADA/BRITISH COLUMBIA BUSINESS SERVICES SOCIETY (www.smallbusinessbc.ca)

601 West Cordova St.
Vancouver, BC V6B 1G1
Phone: 604-775-5525 or 800-667-2272 (within BC)
Fax: 604-775-5520
InfoFax: 604-775-5515 or 800-667-2272
E-mail: askus@smallbusinessbc.ca

THE BUSINESS LINK BUSINESS SERVICE CENTRE (www.cbsc.org/alberta)

100 – 10237 104th St. NW
Edmonton, AB T5J 1B1
Phone: 780-422-7722 or 800-272-9675
Fax: 780-422-0055
E-mail: buslink@cbsc.ic.gc.ca

CANADA/SASKATCHEWAN BUSINESS SERVICE CENTRE (www.cbsc.org/sask)

345 - 3rd Ave. South
Saskatoon, SK S7K 2H6
Phone: 306-956-2323 or 800-667-4374
Fax: 306-956-2328
E-mail: saskatchewan@cbsc.ic.gc.ca

CANADA/MANITOBA BUSINESS SERVICE CENTRE (www.cbsc.org/manitoba)

PO Box 2609
250 – 240 Graham Ave.
Winnipeg, MB R3C 4B3
Phone: 204-984-2272 or 800-665-2019
Fax: 204-983-3852
TTY: 800-457-8466
E-mail: manitoba@cbsc.ic.gc.ca

CANADA/NOVA SCOTIA BUSINESS SERVICE CENTRE (www.cbsc.org/ns/index.html)

1575 Brunswick St.
Halifax, NS B3J 2G1
Phone: 902-426-8604 or 800-668-1010
Fax: 902-426-6530
TTY: 902-426-4188 or 800-797-4188
E-mail: halifax@cbsc.ic.gc.ca

CANADA/NEWFOUNDLAND AND LABRADOR BUSINESS SERVICE CENTRE (www.cbsc.org/nf)

PO Box 8687, Station A
90 O'Leary Ave.
St. John's, NF A1B 3T1
Phone: 709-772-6022 or 800-668-1010
Fax: 709-772-6090
TTY: 800-457-8466
E-mail: info@cbsc.ic.gc.ca

CANADA/ONTARIO BUSINESS SERVICE CENTRE (www.cbsc.org/ontario)

Toronto, ON M5C 2W7
Phone: 416-775-3456 or 800-567-2345
Fax: 416-954-8597
E-mail: ontario@cbsc.ic.gc.ca

INFO ENTREPRISES (www.ccmm.qc.ca/Infoentreprises)

380 St. Antoine West
Local 6000
Montreal, QC H2Y 3X7
Phone: 514-496-4636 or 800-322-4636
TTY: 800-457-8466
Fax: 514-496-5934
E-mail: infoentrepreneurs@cbsc.ic.gc.ca

CANADA/NEW BRUNSWICK BUSINES SERVICE CENTRE (www.cbsc.org/nb)

570 Queen St.
Fredericton, NB E3B 6Z6
Phone: 506-444-6140 or 800-668-1010
TTY: 506-444-6166 or 800-887-6550
Fax: 506-444-6172
E-mail: cbscnb@cbsc.ic.gc.ca

CANADA/PRINCE EDWARD ISLAND BUSINESS SERVICE CENTRE (www.cbsc.org/pe)

PO Box 40
75 Fitzroy St.
Charlottetown, PE C1A 7K2
Phone: 902-368-0771 or 800-668-1010
Fax: 902-566-7377
TTY: 800-457-8466
E-mail: pei@cbsc.ic.gc.ca

CANADA/YUKON BUSINESS SERVICE CENTRE (www.cbsc.org/yukon)

101 – 307 Jarvis St.
Whitehorse, YT Y1A 2H3
Phone: 867-633-6257 or 800-661-0543
TTY: 800-457-8466
Fax: 867-667-2001
E-mail: yukon@cbsc.ic.gc.ca

CANADA/NWT BUSINESS SERVICE CENTRE
(www.cbsc.org/nwt/index.html)

PO Box 1320
8th Floor Scotia Centre
Yellowknife, NT X1A 2L9
Phone: 867-873-7958 or 800-661-0599
TTY: 800-457-8466
Fax: 867-873-0101
E-mail: yel@cbsc.ic.gc.ca

CANADA/NUNAVUT BUSINESS SERVICE CENTRE
(www.cbsc.org/nunavut)

PO Box 1000, STN 1198
Parnaivik Building
Iqaluit, NU X0A 0H0
Phone: 877-979-6813 or 877-499-5199
TTY: 800-457-8466
Fax: 867-979-6823
E-mail: cnbsc@gov.nu.ca

SINIKTARVIK BUILDING

Bag 002
Rankin Inlet, NU X0C 0G0
Phone: 867-645-5067 or 877-499-5199
TTY: 800-457-8466
Fax: 867-645-2346 or 877-499-5299
E-mail: cnbsc@gov.nu.ca

ENOKHOK CENTRE

PO Box 316
Kugluktuk, NU X0E 0H0
Phone: 867-982-3701 or 877-499-5199
TTY: 800-457-8466
Fax: 867-982-3701 or 877-499-5299
E-mail: cnbsc@gov.nu.ca

PROVINCIAL GOVERNMENTS

BRITISH COLUMBIA

Ministry of Competition, Science
and Enterprise
PO Box 9046, STN PROV GOVT
Room 109 – Parliament Buildings
Victoria, BC V8W 9E2
Phone: 250-356-7411
Fax: 250-356-6376
E-mail: enquiryBC@gems3.gov.bc.ca
Web: www.gov.bc.ca/cse/Default.htm

ALBERTA

Alberta Economic Development
Economic Development Authority
6th Floor, Commerce Place

10155 102nd St.
Edmonton, AB T5J 4L6
Phone: 780-415-1319
Web: www.alberta-canada.com/aed/index.cfm

SASKATCHEWAN

Saskatchewan Industry and Resources
Head Office
2103 11th Ave.
Regina, SK S4P 3V7
Phone: 306-787-2232
Fax: 306-787-2159
E-mail:
jmcdowell@ir.gov.sk.ca,webmaster@ir.gov.sk.ca
Web: www.gov.sk.ca/topic-picklists/?13

MANITOBA

Manitoba Industry, Economic Development and Mines
Small Business Branch
P.O. Box 2609
250 – 240 Graham Ave.
Winnipeg, MB R3C 4B3
Phone: 204-984-2272 or 800-665-2019
E-mail: manitoba@cbsc.ic.gc.ca
Web: www.gov.mb.ca/itm/index.html

ONTARIO

Economic Development and Trade
8th Floor, Hearst Block
900 Bay St.
Toronto, ON M7A 2E1
Phone: 416-325-6666 or 866-6684249
Fax: 416-325-6688
E-mail: info@edt.gov.on.ca
Web: www.ontario-canada.com

QUEBEC

Developement economique et regional Quebec
710, Place d'Youville
Québec, QC G1R 4Y4
téléphone: 418-691-5950
télécopieur: 418-644-0118
E-mail: info@mic.gouv.qc.ca
Web: www.mic.gouv.qc.ca/index.html
or
380, rue St-Antoine Ouest
Montréal, QC H2Y 3X7
téléphone: 514-499-2550
télécopieur: 514-873-9913

NEW BRUNSWICK

Business New Brunswick
P.O. Box 6000

Centennial Building
670 King St.
Fredericton, NB E3B 5H1
Phone: 506-453-3984
Fax: 506-453-5428
E-mail: www.gnb.ca/0398/sendmail-e.asp
(online form)
Web: www.gnb.ca/0398//Index.htm

NOVA SCOTIA

Nova Scotia Business
P.O. Box 2374
520 - 1800 Argyle St.
Halifax, NS B3J 2R7
Phone: 903-424-6650 or 800-260-6682
E-mail: nsbi@gov.ns.ca
Web: www.novascotiabusiness.com

PRINCE EDWARD ISLAND

Prince Edward Island Business Development
P.O. Box 910
94 Easton St.
Charlottetown, PE C1A 7L9
Telephone: 902-368-6300 or 800-563-3734
Facsimile: 902-368-6301
E-mail: business@gov.pe.ca
Web: www.peibusinessdevelopment.com/

NEWFOUNDLAND AND LABRADOR

Information
Department of Industry, Trade, and Rural Development
P.O. Box 8700
4th Floor, Confederation Building
St. John's, NF A1B 4J6
Phone: 709-729-7000
Fax: 709-729-7444
E-mail: ITRDinfo@gov.nl.ca
Web: www.gov.nl.ca/itrd/default.htm

NORTHWEST TERRITORIES

Department of Resources, Wildlife, and Economic Development
P.O. Box 1320
Yellowknife, NT X1A 2L9
Phone: 867-669-2388
Fax: 867-873-0563
E-mail: brendan_bell@gov.nt.ca
Web: www.gov.nt.ca/RWED/index.html

YUKON TERRITORY

Economic Development
P.O. Box 2703
Whitehorse, YT Y1A 2C6
Phone: 867-393-7191 or 800-661-0408
Fax: 867-393-6944
E-mail : Sandra.Harder@gov.yk.ca
Web: www.economicdevelopment.gov.yk.ca

NUNAVUT

Communications
P.O. Box 1000, STN 204
Iqaluit, NU X0A 0H0
Phone: 867-975-6000 or 888-252-9869
Web: www.gov.nu.ca
E-mail: www.gov.nu.ca/Nunavut/English/contacts
(online form)

OTHERS:

CANADIAN FRANCHISE ASSOCIATION

300 – 2585 Skymark Ave.
Mississauga, ON L4W 4L5
Phone: 905-625-2896 or 800-665-4232
Fax: 905-625-9076
E-mail: info@cfa.ca
Web: www.cfa.ca

INTERNATIONAL FRANCHISE ASSOCIATION

900 - 1350 New York Ave. NW
Washington, DC 20005-4709
U.S.A.
Phone: 202-628-8000
Fax: 202-628-0812
Web: www.franchise.org
E-mail: ifa@franchise.org

CANADIAN VENTURE CAPITAL ASSOCIATION

200 - 234 Eglinton Avenue East
Toronto, ON M4P 1K5
Phone: 416-487-0519
Fax: 416-487-5899
E-mail: cvca@cvca.ca
Web: www.cvca.ca

Glossary of Financial Terms

Accounts payable Money owed by a firm to its suppliers for goods and services purchased for the operation of the business. A current liability.

Accounts receivable Money owed to a firm by its customers for goods or services they have purchased from it. A current asset.

Amortization To pay off a debt over a stated time period, setting aside fixed sums for interest and principal at regular intervals, like a mortgage.

Angels Private individuals with capital to invest in business ventures.

Assets The resources or property rights owned by an individual or business enterprise. Tangible assets include cash, inventory, land and buildings, and intangible assets including patents and goodwill.

Bad debts Money owed to you that you no longer expect to collect.

Balance sheet An itemized statement that lists the total assets and total liabilities of a given business, to portray its net worth at a given moment in time.

Bankruptcy The financial and legal position of a person or corporation unable to pay its debts.

Break-even point The level of sales in either units or dollars at which sales revenue and costs are equal so that a business is neither making nor losing money.

Capital asset A possession, such as a machine, that can be used to make money and has a reasonably long life, usually more than a year.

Capital costs The cost involved in the acquisition of capital assets. They are "capitalized," showing up on the balance sheet and depreciated (expensed) over their useful life.

Capital gain The difference between the net cost of an asset and the net sales price, if the asset is sold at a gain.

Capital loss The difference between the net cost of an asset and the net sales price, if the asset is sold at a loss.

Capital requirement The amount of money needed to establish a business.

Capital stock The money invested in a business through founders' equity and shares bought by stockholders.

Cash discount An incentive provided by vendors of merchandise and services to speed up the collection of accounts receivable.

Cash flow The movement of cash in and out of a company. Its timing is usually projected month by month to show the net cash requirement during each period.

Cash flow forecast A schedule of expected cash receipts and disbursements (payments) highlighting expected shortages and surpluses.

Collateral Assets placed by a borrower as security for a loan.

Contribution margin The difference between variable revenue and variable cost.

Conversion In the context of securities, refers to the exchange of a convertible security such as a bond for shares in a company.

Cost of goods sold The direct costs of acquiring and/or producing an item for sale. Usually excludes any overhead or other indirect expenses.

Current assets Cash or other items that will normally be turned into cash within one year (accounts receivable, inventory, and short-term notes) and assets that will be used up in the operation of a firm within one year.

Current liabilities Amounts owed that will ordinarily be paid by a firm within one year. Such items include accounts payable, wages payable, taxes payable, the current portion of a long-term debt and interest, and dividends payable.

Current ratio Current assets divided by current liabilities. Used as an indication of liquidity to show how easily a business can meet its current debts.

Debt Money that must be paid back to someone else, usually with interest.

Debt capital Capital invested in a company that does not belong to the company's owners. Usually consists of long-term loans and preferred shares.

Debt-to-equity ratio The ratio of long-term debt to owners' equity. Measures overall profitability.

Demand loan A loan that must be repaid in full, on demand.

Depreciation A method of writing off the costs to a firm of using a fixed asset, such as machinery, buildings, trucks, and equipment, over time.

Employee stock ownership plan (ESOP) A company contributes to a trust fund that buys stock on behalf of employees.

Equity The difference between the assets and liabilities of a company, often referred to as *net worth*.

Equity capital The capital invested in a firm by its owners. The owners of the equity capital in the firm are entitled to all the assets and income of the firm after all the claims of creditors have been paid.

Escrow Property or money held by a third party until the agreed-on obligations of a contract are met.

Factor A financial institution that buys a firm's accounts receivable and collects the accounts.

Financial statements Documents that show your financial situation.

Fiscal year An accounting cycle of 12 months that could start at any point during a calendar year.

Fixed assets Those things that a firm owns and uses in its business and that it keeps for more than one year (including machinery, land, buildings, vehicles, etc.).

Fixed costs or expenses Those costs that don't vary from one period to the next and usually are not affected by the volume of business (e.g., rent, salaries, telephone, etc.).

Floor plan financing An arrangement used to finance inventory. A finance company buys the inventory, which is then held in trust for the user.

Franchise The right to sell products or services under a corporate name or trademark, usually purchased for a fee plus a royalty on sales.

Goodwill The value of customer lists, trade reputation, etc., which is assumed to go with a company and its name, particularly when trying to arrive at the sale price for the company. In accounting terms it is the amount a purchaser pays over the book value.

Gross margin or gross profit margin The difference between the volume of sales your business generates and the costs you pay out for the goods that are sold.

Income statement The financial statement that looks at a business's revenue, less expenses, to determine net income for a certain period of time. Also called *profit-and-loss statement*.

Industry ratios Financial ratios established by many companies in an industry, in an attempt to establish a norm against which to measure and compare the effectiveness of a company's management.

Initial public offering (IPO) A company's first sale of stock to the public. Securities offered in an IPO are often, but not always, those of young, small companies seeking outside equity capital and a public market for their stock. Investors purchasing stock in IPOs generally must be prepared to accept considerable risks for the possibility of large gains.

Intangible assets Assets such as trade names or patent rights that are not physical objects or sums of money.

Interest A charge for the use of money supplied by a lender.

Inventory The supply of goods, whether raw materials, parts, or finished products, owned by a firm at any one time, and its total value.

Inventory turnover The number of times the value of inventory at cost divides into the cost of goods sold in a year.

Investment capital The money set aside for starting a business. Usually this would cover such costs as inventory, equipment, pre-opening expenses, and leasehold improvements.

Lease An agreement to rent for a period of time at an agreed price.

Leverage ratios Measures of the relative value of stockholders' capitalization and creditors' obligations, and of the firm's ability to pay financing charges.

Liabilities All the debts of a business. Liabilities include short-term or current liabilities such as accounts payable, income taxes due, and the amount of long-term debt that must be paid within 12 months; long-term liabilities include long-term debts and deferred income taxes. On a balance sheet, liabilities are subtracted from assets; what remains is the shareholders' equity.

Line of credit An agreement negotiated between a borrower and a lender establishing the maximum amount of money against which the borrower may draw.

Liquid assets Cash on hand and anything that can easily and quickly be turned into cash.

Liquidation value The estimated value of a business after its operations are stopped and the assets sold and the liabilities paid off.

Liquidity A term that describes how readily a firm's assets can be converted into cash.

Liquidity ratios Ratios that measure a firm's ability to meet its short-term financial obligations on time, such as the ratio of current assets to current liabilities.

Loan guarantee The assumption of responsibility for payment of a debt or performance of some obligation if the liable party fails to perform to expectations.

Long-term liabilities Debts that will not be paid off within one year.

Management buyout (MBO) A leveraged buyout in which the acquiring group is led by the firm's management.

Markup The amount vendors add to the purchase price of a product to take into account their expenses plus profit.

Maturity For a loan, the date on which the principal is required to be repaid.

Net worth The value of a business represented by the excess of the total assets over the total amounts owing to outside creditors (total liabilities) at a given moment in time. Also referred to as *book value*.

Operating costs Expenditures arising out of current business activities; what it costs to do business — the salaries, electricity, rental, deliveries, etc., that are involved in performing the operations of a business.

Operating loan A loan intended for short-term financing, supplying cash flow support, or to cover day-to-day operating expenses.

Overhead Expenses such as rent, heat, property tax, etc., incurred to keep a business open.

Principal The face amount of debt; the amount borrowed or loaned.

Pro forma A projection or estimate. A pro forma financial statement is one that shows how the actual operations of the business will turn out if certain assumptions are realized.

Profit The excess of the selling price over all costs and expenses incurred in making the sale. Gross profit is the profit before corporate income taxes. Net profit is the final profit of the firm after all deductions have been made.

Profitability ratios Ratios that focus on how well a firm is performing. Profit margins measure performance with relation to sales. Rate-of-return ratios measure performance relative to some measure of size of the investment.

Profit-and-loss statement A financial statement listing revenue and expenses and showing the profit (or loss) for a certain period of time. Also called an *income statement*.

Profit margin The ratio of profits (generally pre-tax) to sales.

Put option The right to sell (or put) a fixed number of shares at a fixed price within a given period of time.

Quick ratio Current cash and "near" cash assets (e.g., government bonds, current receivables, but excluding inventory) compared to current liabilities (bank loans, accounts payable). The quick ratio shows how much and how quickly cash can be found if a company gets into trouble. Sometimes called the *acid test ratio*.

Retained earnings The profits that are not spent or divided among the owners but kept in the business.

Return on investment (ROI) The determination of the profit to be accrued from a capital investment.

Royalty Payment for the right to use intellectual property or natural resources.

Seed capital The first contribution by an investor toward the financing of a new business.

Stock buyback A corporation's purchase of its own outstanding stock.

Subordinated debt Debt over which other senior debt takes priority. In the event of bankruptcy, subordinated debt holders receive payment only after senior debt claims are paid in full.

Term loan A loan intended for medium-term or long-term financing to supply cash to purchase fixed assets such as land or buildings, machinery and equipment, or to renovate business premises.

Terms of sale The conditions concerning payment for a purchase.

Trade credit The credit terms offered by a manufacturer or supplier to other businesses.

Transactions fees Fees charged to cover the time and effort involved in arranging a loan or other financial package.

Turnover The number of times a year that a product is sold and reordered.

Variable expenses Costs of doing business that vary with the volume of business, such as manufacturing cost and delivery expenses.

Venture capital Funds that are invested in a business by a third party either as equity or some form of subordinated debt.

Working capital The funds available for carrying on the day-to-day operation of a business. Working capital is the excess after deduction of the current liabilities from the current assets of a firm, and indicates a company's ability to pay its short-term debts.

Index